FILLED WITH THE SPIRIT

FILLED WITH THE SPIRIT

John R. Levison

WILLIAM B. EERDMANS PUBLISHING COMPANY
GRAND RAPIDS, MICHIGAN / CAMBRIDGE, U.K.

Published 2009 by
Wm. B. Eerdmans Publishing Co.
2140 Oak Industrial Drive N.E., Grand Rapids, Michigan 49505 /
P.O. Box 163, Cambridge CB3 9PU U.K.
www.eerdmans.com

Printed in the United States of America

14 13 12 11 10 09   7 6 5 4 3 2 1

Library of Congress Cataloging-in-Publication Data

Levison, John R.
Filled with the Spirit / John R. Levison.
p.   cm.
ISBN 978-0-8028-6372-0 (cloth: alk. paper)
1. Holy Spirit — Biblical teaching.
2. Gunkel, Hermann, 1862-1932. Wirkungen des heiligen Geistes.
I. Title.

BS680.H56L48   2009
231'.3 — dc22

2009023801

For Priscilla
my inspiration

Contents

vii

Acknowledgments

Several sources of funding have made it possible to spend stretches of time occupied with this book. The first presented itself when Louis Feldman selected me for participation in his National Endowment for the Humanities Summer Seminar at Yeshiva University. Louis has been a lifelong mentor, and under his tutelage and among the keen coterie of young scholars that he gathered during that splendid summer, I wrote my first article on the spirit.

A few months later, Larry Hurtado sent my name to Martin Hengel, who became my sponsor for an Alexander von Humboldt fellowship. Priscilla and I, with our fifteen-month-old daughter in tow, headed to Tübingen, where I wrote much of what became my first book on this topic, *The Spirit in First Century Judaism.*

A decade later, Professors A. J. M. (Sandy) Wedderburn and Jörg Frey invited me to spend my next research leave at Ludwig-Maximilians-Universität München. After I received a six-month renewal of my Alexander von Humboldt fellowship, which I paired with a quarter of sabbatical granted by Seattle Pacific University, Priscilla and I again headed to Germany, this time with Chloe and her brother, Jeremy. Thanks to Professor Frey, my family and I stayed at the Internationales Begegnungszentrum, a wonderful apartment complex in Schwabing, just a fifteen-minute walk from the fabled Marienplatz, a ten-minute stroll from the English Garden, and a ninety-second dash to my office. While in Munich, I unearthed nearly inaccessible articles on Hermann Gunkel, who figures in this book. Jörg and I also codirected an Oberseminar on early Christian pneumatology, and we planned, over strong coffee and Bavarian torts, to apply for grants from the International Catacomb Society and the TransCoop Program of the Alexander von Humboldt Foundation — both of which we received. These grants will allow us, in the near future, to gather interdisciplinary research teams to study the historical roots of the holy spirit.

Between our two visits to Germany, I enjoyed a year at the National Humanities Center in North Carolina, which I began by writing an article on the spirit in a Festschrift for Jerry Hawthorne, who had encouraged me to pursue an academic career while I was a sophomore in college. In the sustained quiet of my study at the NHC, I became enamored of the history of religions school, of which Hermann Gunkel was a founder.

Last year, the Louisville Institute granted me a summer stipend for the research project, "For Snake-handlers and Sacramentalists: An Essential Guide to the Holy Spirit." This stipend gave me the opportunity to devote a summer to completing this book and to writing the final chapters of another book on the holy spirit.

In the final stages of my work, Seattle Pacific University offered me a faculty research grant to hire Shannon Smythe, a doctoral student at Princeton Theological Seminary who had, at one time, been Priscilla's and my student at Seattle Pacific University. Shannon is responsible for the thorough indexes in this book. Seattle Pacific University has also provided a community of earnest teachers and capable scholars. I have enjoyed meaningful conversations about the spirit here, particularly with my colleagues in the field of New Testament, Rob Wall and Gene Lemcio.

None of this funding would have been available to me were it not for the support of distinguished scholars along the way. In particular, David Aune, John Collins, and Louis Feldman have written timely and persuasive letters on my behalf whenever I have requested them.

When it came time to publish this book, I had protracted conversations with several publishers. My decision to publish with Eerdmans was due, in large measure, to Michael Thomson. I could attribute my decision to the hilarious dinners we shared together, but that would be to sell Michael short. Michael's enthusiasm for this book was matched by regular communication and a commitment to putting this book into the hands of the right people. One such person is Allen Myers, whose team edited this volume; the five pages of attentive editorial questions and comments that Allen supplied were exactly what I had hoped for when I signed on with Eerdmans.

Writing this book has been an immense pleasure. I have enjoyed exquisite hours alone, working at my desk, looking out at the lovely Seattle garden that Priscilla, my wife, tends. And beyond its pages I savor the company of friends and family. One friend in particular, David Laskin, read vast segments of the manuscript and responded with a careful combination of criticism and appreciation. David is the author of an award-winning book, *The Children's Blizzard*, but I know him simply as the dearest of friends.

I am also sustained — and constantly delighted — by my two teenage children. Chloe infuses my life with her laughter, her wanderlust, and her love of books. Jeremy would be any father's buddy; he is a transparent, genial kid who could make friends with a trash can. There is a magnificent symbiosis, as far as I can tell, between my research on the spirit and their spirited lives.

Finally, I am grateful to my wife, Priscilla, who has been by my side in prayer and in service, in scholarship and at play, for twenty-seven years. When I am at my desk, I listen for the click-clacking of her keyboard in the room next door. When I am elsewhere, it is always with the desire to be at her side. And, in ways that only she knows, I owe this book to her. She was the one, a few years back, who said, "Just start writing." So I did. And never once has she told me to stop, though she needn't, since I do stop, hungry for her company. I am dedicating this book to her because she leaves me breathless and inspired all at once.

Abbreviations

AB	Anchor Bible
ABD	*Anchor Bible Dictionary*, ed. D. N. Freedman. 6 vols. (1992)
AGJU	Arbeiten zur Geschichte des antiken Judentums und des Urchristentums
AGSU	Arbeiten zur Geschichte des Spätjudentums und Urchristentums
ATD	Das Alte Testament Deutsch
BRS	Biblical Resource Series
BZNW	Beihefte zur Zeitschrift für die neutestamentliche Wissenschaft
CBC	Cambridge Bible Commentary
CBET	Contributions to Biblical Exegesis and Theology
CBQ	*Catholic Biblical Quarterly*
CBQMS	Catholic Biblical Quarterly Monograph Series
EKK	Evangelisch-katholischer Kommentar zum Neuen Testament
EvT	*Evangelische Theologie*
FRLANT	Forschungen zur Religion und Literatur des Alten und Neuen Testaments
Hen	*Henoch*
HTR	*Harvard Theological Review*
IDB	*The Interpreter's Dictionary of the Bible*, ed. G. A. Buttrick. 4 vols. (1962)
Int	*Interpretation*
JBL	*Journal of Biblical Literature*
JPTSup	Journal of Pentecostal Theology Supplement Series
JSHRZ	Jüdischer Schriften aus hellenistich-römischer Zeit
JSJ	*Journal for the Study of Judaism in the Persian, Hellenistic, and Roman Periods*
JSJSup	Supplements to the Journal for the Study of Judaism

Abbreviations

JSNT	*Journal for the Study of the New Testament*
JSNTSup	Journal for the Study of the New Testament: Supplement Series
JSPSup	Journal for the Study of the Pseudepigrapha: Supplement Series
JTS	*Journal of Theological Studies*
KJV	King James Version
MT	Masoretic Text
NIB	*The New Interpreter's Bible*, ed. L. Keck. 13 vols. (1994-2004)
NIGTC	The New International Greek Testament Commentary
NovTSup	Supplements to *Novum Testamentum*
NRSV	New Revised Standard Version
NTS	*New Testament Studies*
OCD	*The Oxford Classical Dictionary*, ed. S. Hornblower and A. Spawforth. (3rd ed., 1996)
OTP	*Old Testament Pseudepigrapha*, ed. J. H. Charlesworth. 2 vols. (1983-1985)
RGG	*Die Religion in Geschichte und Gegenwart*, 1st ed. (1909-1913); 2nd ed. (1927-1931); 3rd ed. (1957-1965)
SBLDS	Society of Biblical Literature Dissertation Series
SBT	Studies in Biblical Theology
SC	Sources chrétiennes
SNTSMS	Society for New Testament Studies Monograph Series
SPhilo	*Studia philonica Annual*
STDJ	Studies on the Texts of the Desert of Judah
SUNT	Studien zur Umwelt des Neuen Testaments
TBl	*Theologische Blätter*
TDNT	*Theological Dictionary of the New Testament*, ed. G. Kittel and G. Friedrich. 10 vols. (1964-1976)
THAT	*Theologisches Handwörterbuch zum Alten Testament*, ed. E. Jenni and C. Westermann. 2 vols. (1971-1976)
TNIV	Today's New International Version
VTSup	Supplements to Vetus Testamentum
WBC	Word Biblical Commentary
WUNT	Wissenschaftliche Untersuchungen zum Neuen Testament
ZTK	*Zeitschrift für Theologie und Kirche*

Introduction

When Hans Schmidt stood on a late winter day in the Bartholomäus-Kirche in Halle, Germany, he reflected upon the stunning spell that Hermann Gunkel, who had died four days earlier on March 11, 1932, had cast over Old Testament scholars. Schmidt traced for this auspicious and sober gathering the impact of Gunkel's scholarship: the lasting value of his commentary on Genesis; the enduring qualities of his form-critical analysis of the Psalms; and the variety of his contributions to a modern understanding of the private and public dimensions of Israelite prophecy.[1]

What Schmidt barely mentioned was Gunkel's earnest and early work in the field of New Testament. Gunkel had wanted, like his friends Wilhelm Bousset, William Wrede, and Johannes Weiss, to become a New Testament scholar. He chose, therefore, to write a Habilitation at the Univer-

---

1. Schmidt's eulogy was published in *TBl* 11/4 (1932) 97-98. I have reconstructed Gunkel's biography from several reliable — and fascinating — sources: W. Klatt, *Hermann Gunkel: Zu seiner Theologie der Religionsgeschichte und zur Entstehung der formgeschichtlichen Methode.* FRLANT 100 (Göttingen: Vandenhoeck & Ruprecht, 1969); W. Baumgartner, "Zum 100. Geburtstag von Hermann Gunkel," *Congress Volume: Bonn 1962,* ed. G. W. Anderson et al. VTSup 9 (Leiden: Brill, 1962) 1-18; K. von Rabenau, "Hermann Gunkel auf rauhen Pfaden nach Halle," *EvT* 30 (1970) 433-44; H. Rollmann, "Zwei Briefe Hermann Gunkels an Adolf Jülicher zur religionsgeschichtlichen und formgeschichtlichen Methode," *ZTK* 78 (1981) 276-88; R. Smend, "Wellhausen in Greifswald," *ZTK* 78 (1981) 141-76. Klatt's essay is the most thorough and informative. Baumgartner's essay is the most profound and humorous. Rollmann's is the most puzzling to me, as Gunkel's deferential tone toward Adolf Jülicher, whom he never met, is very much that of a junior colleague to a senior one — despite Gunkel's enormous scholarly stature.

sity of Göttingen on the teaching of the holy spirit in the New Testament — a study that did not, in the years that lay ahead, serve him well.

After the Habilitation had been completed, on November 23, 1887, Gunkel's father requested, on behalf of his twenty-five-year-old son, a stipend to become a Privatdozent from the Prussian Cultural Minister, a certain von Gossler. The letter that came from the Göttingen theological faculty was disheartening: "Those in the circles of the theological faculty . . . agree that his scholarly ability, despite every acknowledgement of his effort, is not outstanding, that his personality, despite every acknowledgement of his personal qualities, is not congenial, and that accordingly his Habilitation is not wanted."[2] The faculty encouraged him not to pursue the academic track and thus to forgo the second theological exam. How events changed, it may not be possible to know, but on October 19, 1888, Hermann Gunkel was awarded his degree, and he received as well an annual stipend of twelve hundred marks, beginning on April 1, 1889. It lasted two years, and its extension was contingent upon further accomplishments.

Although he was awarded a degree and stipend, fate was against him, or so it would seem. After he wrote his Habilitation and became a Privatdozent at the university in Göttingen, the ministerial director of culture in Prussia, Friedrich Althoff, ordered Gunkel to move to Halle, where, at the time, there was no room for a Privatdozent in New Testament.[3] The faculty at Halle would have none of Gunkel. When he was considered for a position in Old Testament at the university in Halle in 1889, following the publication of his book on the holy spirit[4] in 1888, he was fourth on the list. Further, his inaugural lecture on eschatological expectation in Judaism was judged to be immature. Gunkel was compelled by this unfortunate state of affairs to take advantage of an opportunity at a local Hochschule. There he became Privatdozent for the study of the Old Testament, though he was unprepared for the task, for Old Testament scholars were expected to be grounded in Semitic languages and cultures in a way that Gunkel simply was not. He also had few students at Halle, although he was appar-

2. Where translations are unavailable, translations of the German into English are my own.

3. Klatt (40-41) ventures several explanations, none of them, by his own admission, firm.

4. Although I have generally accepted translations of ancient texts, including the *New Revised Standard Version* of the Bible, I have consistently written "holy spirit" without capitalization in order to prevent a misunderstanding that is based on the unnecessary distinction between an allegedly divine Holy Spirit and a human spirit.

ently a gifted teacher, at least if the word of his colleague Emil Kautzsch
and later students Otto Dibelius, Walter Baumgartner, and Karl Barth be
taken seriously, and if the undeniable impact of his form-critical approach
upon Martin Dibelius and Rudolf Bultmann, who later attended his Berlin
lectures, be taken into consideration.[5]

With respect to this formidable setback, only years later would Gunkel
talk of "certain fates" that forced him to move "to another if also related
field."[6] Schmidt, in the Bartholomäus-Kirche, more than forty years later,
would note the resilience that developed in Gunkel: "But even out of this
difficulty he grew wings."[7] That resolve is evident in Gunkel's ability during those unheralded years to write his first magisterial, independent
book, *Schöpfung und Chaos in Urzeit und Endzeit, eine religionsgeschichtliche Untersuchung.*[8] With characteristic foresight and independence, and
with unspeakable tenacity, Gunkel succeeded in extending his competence
from the New to the Old Testament by comparing two widely disparate
texts, Genesis 1 and Revelation 12. As a further sign of his tenacity, this
book drew from the soil of his earlier lecture on Jewish eschatology, which
had been deemed immature.[9] In his eulogy, Schmidt rendered a verdict
with which his congregation would have agreed: "Also in this book is everything new, is everything surprising."[10]

New and surprising. Whether it comes to his provocative juxtaposition
of Genesis 1 and Revelation 12, his pioneering study of oral forms rather
than literary strands, or his role in forging the parameters of the history of
religions school, Gunkel's work is nothing if not new and surprising.[11] Yet

5. Note esp. Smend, 166, and much of Baumgartner's encomium.

6. Klatt, 164.

7. *TBl* 11.4 (1932) 99.

8. This book, the full title of which is *Schöpfung und Chaos in Urzeit und Endzeit: Eine
religionsgeschichtliche Untersuchung über Gen 1 und Ap Joh 12* (Göttingen: Vandenhoeck &
Ruprecht, 1895), has now been translated, more than a century after its publication, by K. W.
Whitney Jr., under the title, *Creation and Chaos in the Primeval Era and the Eschaton: A
Religio-historical Study of Genesis 1 and Revelation 12.* BRS (Grand Rapids: Wm. B. Eerdmans,
2006).

9. This book reflects not only tenacity but a certain malleability. Gunkel pored over
Richard Lepsius's volumes on Egyptian monuments, and for an acquaintance with Babylonian culture he turned to his new friend, the Assyriologist Heinrich Zimmern, who translated relevant cuneiform texts for him. See Klatt, 42.

10. *TBl* 11.4 (1932) 99.

11. In his commentaries on Genesis and the Psalms Gunkel demonstrates the forceful-
ness and fruitfulness of the form-critical method.

there is, from the perspective of our study, a further trace of significance in Schmidt's choice of the word "also," for it suggests that Gunkel's earlier work on the holy spirit was *also* something completely new, something altogether surprising. Though at the time Gunkel's colleagues in Göttingen considered it unwelcome, and though it landed him no higher than fourth on a list for a position at Halle, Gunkel would be asked to revise this work — a task he resolutely refused — as late as twenty-one years after it was first published. In his preface to the third, unrevised edition, published in 1909, Gunkel would take note of an "unexpected favorable reception. . . . The esteemed publisher tells me that a new edition of the book, which for some time has been out of print, continues to be requested, so he has decided to publish it anew."[12]

There is good reason, we shall see, for the ongoing demand for this book. This small study, which Gunkel himself would refer to merely as a *Werkchen* or *Büchlein* — "little work" or "little book" — was published in 1888, when Gunkel was still a twenty-six-year-old Privatdozent.[13] In it Gunkel argued a spectacularly fresh thesis that inaugurated the modern era in the study of early Christian pneumatology. This scant study, as Schmidt remarked forty-four years after its initial publication, "speaks in truth a new word. . . . It is no conclusion but a beginning."[14]

Because this study was so fresh, a beginning rather than a conclusion, in truth a new word, Gunkel naturally parted company with prior scholars. He did so especially by opening three doors.

Gunkel first opened a new door into the study of early Christian pneumatology by focusing upon the extraordinary *Wirkungen*, the inspired effects, of the spirit. This new direction — what his distant senior colleagues clearly considered a misdirection — rejected the notion of spirit, in the German idealist sense, as the substance of human potential, as the force of ordinary human life.

Gunkel opened another door by contending that early Christian pneumatology needed to be understood in light of early Judaism. He re-

---

12. *Die Wirkungen des heiligen Geistes nach der populären Anschauung der apostolischen Zeit und der Lehre des Apostels Paulus* (Göttingen: Vandenhoeck & Ruprecht, 1888) iii. English translation: *The Influence of the Holy Spirit: The Popular View of the Apostolic Age and the Teaching of the Apostle Paul*, trans. R. A. Harrisville and P. A. Quanbeck II (Philadelphia: Fortress, 1979). For a brief summary of Gunkel's *Wirkungen*, see Klatt, 29-36.

13. In his preface to *Wirkungen*, 3rd ed., iii, viii; *The Influence of the Holy Spirit*, 2, 8.

14. *TBl* 11.4 (1932) 98. By "kein Abschluss" Schmidt means that this is a fresh start, free of Albrecht Ritschl's conception of the spirit.

jected the tack of his predecessors, who had leapt readily, according to the model of biblical theology in his day, from the Old Testament to the New. This approach, of course, raised a variety of objections: Judaism could be seen to supplant the Hebrew scriptures; the canon would dissolve with the incorporation of other texts, such as 4 Ezra; Christianity would be said to lose its distinctiveness. Gunkel's contention, of course, was that a knowledge of Judaism would function to illuminate early Christianity and to underscore what was distinctive about it.

The third door had already been cracked by Gunkel's predecessors, Bernhard Weiss and Otto Pfleiderer, though not to the extent that Gunkel's study would fling it open. Pfleiderer and Weiss had already distinguished Pauline theology from that of the early church.[15] Gunkel followed lockstep by launching, on the very first page of his study, into a critique of the biblical-theological scholarship that was occupied with Paul's teaching on the holy spirit without setting it into the context of the apostolic church. Gunkel espoused instead an exposé of the teaching of Paul and the apostolic church that contains elements of both continuity and discontinuity. While Paul had much in common with the apostolic church, in Gunkel's opinion he also stood on his own, marking early Christian pneumatology with his own particular Pauline stamp.

It is difficult to imagine that a slender book of just over one hundred pages written by a budding scholar in his mid-twenties who would never again return to the subject could have wielded such influence. Yet the freshness of these three emphases simply rendered prior approaches to pneumatology passé; their combination, in such short supply, goes a long way to explain why Gunkel gained the intellectual high ground while forfeiting the political low ground of German university life, for this *Büchlein* became nothing less than midwife to the birth of more than a century of research into early Christian pneumatology.[16] Though his publications

---

15. B. Weiss, *Lehrbuch der Biblischen Theologie des Neuen Testaments*, 2nd ed. (Berlin: Hertz, 1873); O. Pfleiderer, *Paulinism: A Contribution to the History of Primitive Christian Theology* (London: Williams and Norgate, 1877; German original: Leipzig: Fues, 1873).

16. Gunkel also wrote *Zum religionsgeschichtlichen Verständnis des Neuen Testaments*. FRLANT 1 (Göttingen: Vandenhoeck & Ruprecht, 1903; 2nd ed. 1908) and *Der erste Brief des Petrus*, ed. J. Weiss. Die Schriften des Neuen Testament (Göttingen: Vandenhoeck & Ruprecht, 1906; 2nd ed. 1908; 3rd ed. 1917). Further, while he left behind New Testament studies almost entirely when he left Göttingen, the seeds of his later research into Hebrew literature lay embedded in this *Werkchen*. The privileged place that Judaism would occupy in the development of Christian pneumatology anticipated Gunkel's adherence to the tenets

Introduction

would never lead him to full acceptance in the academic community — as late as 1920, when he was fifty-seven years of age, he was offered an ordinary professorial chair at Halle[17] — the impact of his little book was extensive, particularly in the further studies of the spirit that it catalyzed. Within eight years, Martien Beversluis, from the Netherlands, adopted the word *Wirkungen* in the title of his massive *De heilige Geest en zijne werkingen*

---

of the history of religions school, which he would incorporate, not only in his study of eschatology in *Schöpfung und Chaos,* but in the entire course of his research. The emphasis upon experience in his *Wirkungen* anticipated Gunkel's pioneering conceptualization of form criticism.

17. Gunkel himself, on September 8, 1925, when he was sixty-three years old, penned a letter to Adolf Jülicher, in which he admitted that he might have been responsible for a sense of isolation in his earliest years as a scholar — presumably the years that encompassed his research on *Wirkungen:*

> Long, long years have I waited in vain for understanding and collegiality. . . . What a prize I would have had at that time if I had found an older friend to whom I could pose my 1000 questions and who might have advised me! So I have had to take the difficult way for such a long time thoroughly alone. Perhaps I myself bear the guilt for this loneliness because I, in youthful exuberance, was probably too blunt in opposition to older opinions, although I always took care not to drag the dispute into the personal realm.

Gunkel hoped that his meeting with Jülicher might be a sign "that my life, which began with such a storm, will end in peace and calm" (Rollmann, "Zwei Briefe," 281-82). Within four years of his meeting with Jülicher, Gunkel would be ill with gastrointestinal pain and arteriosclerosis, and within seven he would be memorialized in the Bartholomäus-Kirche in Halle. Whether he achieved the peace and freedom for which he yearned one cannot know, but there were certainly other signs in his lifetime that pointed to his success. These signs were unfortunately not institutional. He was first offered an *ordentlich* professorship at the age of forty-five, in 1907, and this only in place of his teacher, Stade, and in Giessen rather than in his native Prussia. Even as late as 1919, when Carl Heinrich Cornill retired at Halle, the name of Gunkel, who was now fifty-seven years of age, did not appear on the list of candidates. Even a letter from the cultural minister, written on March 9, 1920, demanding that a representative of the history of religions perspective *(religionsgeschichtliche Richtung)* be appointed, had little effect upon the faculty, who responded on March 27 with a list that did not include Gunkel. The cultural minister rejected this list because none of these was a true representative of the history of religions school, and so finally, on June 29, 1920, Gunkel was appointed to an ordinary professorship in Prussia. That this decision met with the displeasure of the faculty is apparent in the dean's description, penned on August 7, according to which Gunkel was offered the professorship because of the cultural minister's nomination — but in the face of public anger *(aufgeregten Öffentlichkeit).* For further biographical information, see Rabenau, 438-41. On Gunkel's appointment to a post in Halle, see Hugo Gressmann's interesting letter cited in Klatt.

volgens de Schriften des Nieuwen Verbonds.[18] Other prescient studies followed, taking Gunkel's study in disparate directions. The nineteenth century ended with Heinrich Weinel's *Die Wirkungen des Geistes und der Geister im nachapostolischen Zeitalter bis auf Irenäus,* which extended Gunkel's approach to the second century c.e.[19] A decade after that, and one year after the publication of Gunkel's third edition, Paul Volz published the first substantive contribution to ancient pneumatology of the twenty-first century, *Der Geist Gottes und die verwandten Erscheinungen im Alten Testament und im anschliessenden Judentum.*[20] Hans Leisegang devoted two volumes to the topic of the spirit, the first of which he gave to a publisher as early as 1916, though it lay on the publisher's desk and failed to appear until after the First World War. Leisegang addressed precisely the history of religions question that Gunkel had raised, though he swung the pendulum in the other direction by identifying Hellenism rather than Ju-

---

18. (Utrecht: Breijer, 1896). 508 pp.

19. (Tübingen: Mohr, 1899). One paragraph in Weinel's foreword (vii) provides both a superb précis and a tribute to the ongoing significance of Gunkel's little book:

> Whoever intends to describe the pneumatology of earliest Christianity must in the first place depict the experiences themselves upon which the teaching of the Spirit was based. It is the enduring service of Gunkel. . . [who] understood this way to be the right way from the start and who followed with determination the treatment of a particular question. A single question — Gunkel depicts, that is to say, not the effects of the Spirit, but he wants to answer the question, 'From which symptoms could people in early Christianity say that a phenomenon should be seen as an effect of the Holy Spirit?' . . . He answered this question so correctly and completely that his explanations are foundational for all further research.

If Weinel intended this book as a tribute to Gunkel, this was not lost upon his teacher, who commended it in the first and last paragraphs of his preface to the second and third editions of his own *Wirkungen.* He explained at the start that he would not revise his first book; he suggested instead (*The Influence of the Holy Spirit,* 2) that Weinel's study was precisely what he had in mind: "The model for such teaching is Weinel's work mentioned above, which has as its theme the period from Paul to Irenaeus. I hope that the other epochs of history will soon claim the attention of scholars; that the early apostolic period and Paul, to the extent not yet covered by Weinel, will not on that account be forgotten; and that the present little book will soon be totally outdated by an abundance of new discoveries." Ironically, the discovery of the Dead Sea Scrolls would corroborate rather than undermine Gunkel's position and render his study more, not less, prescient and relevant.

20. (Tübingen: Mohr, 1910). Volz's notes are few. He refers to Gunkel on pp. 94-95 n. 1; 110 n. 2 contains a reference to Gunkel's study of the Psalms — not of the spirit. Nonetheless, Volz (78-145) too explored the effects of the spirit, such as inspired speech and poetry, prophetic and predictive speech, inspired writing and translation, and inspired wisdom.

daism as the matrix of Christianity.[21] The last in this relative flurry of studies was penned by Friedrich Büchsel, in the 1920s; Büchsel took his cue from Gunkel and Volz, against Leisegang, by dealing expansively with Judaism and by introducing, nearly from the start, the effects and conceptions of the spirit in tandem in a section entitled "Effects and Representation of the Spirit in Ancient Israel (Geistwirkungen und Geistvorstellung im alten Israel)."[22]

Gunkel's *Die Wirkungen des heiligen Geistes*, therefore, was a benchmark in the study of the spirit, and it provides a salient point of departure for the present study, though they are separated from one another by more than a century. The questions Gunkel raised about the spirit provide indispensable directions for this study: the question of whether the spirit is invariably an extraordinary impulse; the role of early Judaism in reconstructing early Christian pneumatology; and the diversity of pneumatologies within the New Testament. Its limitations too will prove of value, as they offer signposts of what ought to be avoided in a study of the spirit. His little book set the course for subsequent studies, which both his detractors and his admirers undertook, and the present study stays that course in many respects. Yet in a book of this size — this is no *Büchlein* — I will also demur and attempt to forge new, perhaps occasionally surprising, paths in the study of the spirit.

The possibility of writing a diminutive study on the spirit fell to Gunkel in some measure because so little had been written by his academic predecessors and peers. More significant, I think, is that he chose his focus well. He devoted nearly two-thirds to the apostolic church, about one-third to Paul's writings, and a single line on the last page to the Fourth Gospel.[23]

---

21. It is perhaps a misrepresentation of Leisegang to suggest that he sought the roots of Christianity in Hellenism rather than Judaism. In fact he saw Philo as a representative of the matrix that combined both cultures and provided the soil of Christianity. In an indirect way, Leisegang followed Gunkel by identifying the spirit's primary effect as supernatural in origin, though Leisegang located that sort of extraordinary experience in the popular Hellenistic-Jewish mysticism which he believed Philo's writings embodied. See further on Leisegang, J. R. Levison, "The Spirit in the Gospels: Breaking the Impasse of Early Twentieth-Century German Scholarship," in *New Testament Greek and Exegesis*, ed. A. M. Donaldson and T. B. Sailors (Grand Rapids: Wm. B. Eerdmans, 2003) 55-76.

22. *Der Geist Gottes im Neuen Testament* (Gütersloh: Bertelsmann, 1926) 5-14.

23. *The Influence of the Holy Spirit*, 127: "The theology of the Gospel of John clearly indicates its dependence on Paul on this subject."

Among these studies, he interspersed brief analyses on various topics, such as the symptoms of the spirit in the Old Testament and Judaism.

I intend to develop Gunkel's work by offering far more in-depth analyses of Israelite, early Jewish, and early Christian literature and by pressing the case for farther-reaching implications in the study of ancient pneumatology. Consequently, it falls to me to make certain choices, for which ultimately I will take responsibility.

I will not, for example, limit my focus to a single author, individual corpus, or isolated topic, such as speaking in tongues. The contribution of such studies is undeniable, so that it would be ill-advised to study the spirit without perusing Gordon Fee's massive *God's Empowering Presence*,[24] Friedrich Wilhelm Horn's painstakingly thorough *Das Angeld des Geistes*,[25] both of which focus upon Paul's letters, Max Turner's superb analysis of Luke-Acts, *Power From on High*,[26] or even Christopher Forbes's *Prophecy and Inspired Speech*.[27] Ultimately, however, the agenda I intend to set compels me to incorporate a more breathtaking array of diverse texts. More than half a century has passed since someone has gathered together as many texts as readers will find in this book; not since the end of the Second World War, when Gérard Verbeke published his monumental *L'Évolution de la Doctrine du Pneuma du Stoicisme a S. Augustin*,[28] has a study of the spirit incorporated such a diverse selection of ancient Israelite, Jewish, Greco-Roman, and early Christian literature. Naturally, readers will quibble on countless occasions, no doubt justifiably, with my reading of ancient texts; I trust, nonetheless, that my fundamental theses will provoke new discussions and renewed reflection upon this most significant of topics.

Rather than limiting the number of literary texts, I plan to adopt the approach that is characteristic of a small handful of studies which have, since 1926, ventured beyond the confines of a single author or literary cor-

---

24. *God's Empowering Presence: The Holy Spirit in the Letters of Paul* (Peabody: Hendrickson, 1994).

25. *Das Angeld des Geistes: Studien zur paulinischen Pneumatologie.* FRLANT 154 (Göttingen: Vandenhoeck & Ruprecht, 1992).

26. *Power From on High: The Spirit in Israel's Restoration and Witness in Acts.* JPTSup 9 (Sheffield: Sheffield Academic, 1996).

27. *Prophecy and Inspired Speech in Early Christianity and Its Hellenistic Environment* (Peabody: Hendrickson, 1997). This is a somewhat confusing book, though the texts he surveys in his effort to demonstrate the uniqueness of early Christian glossolalia are extensive.

28. (Paris: Desclée de Brouwer; Louvain: L'Institut Superior de Philosophie, 1945).

pus.[29] Among these can be counted Friedrich Büchsel's *Der Geist Gottes im Neuen Testament*, James D. G. Dunn's *Baptism in the Holy Spirit*,[30] and Michael Welker's *God the Spirit*.[31] Because they chose not to occupy the world of a single author or corpus, these authors were compelled to invent other ways to approach the vast subject of the spirit in antiquity. What is startling is how well, how convincingly, they were able to do so by adopting a single prism as a point of entry to their study.

Büchsel's singular lens was the figure of the Spirit-bearer *(Pneumatiker)*. Early Christianity was unified in its recognition that everyone, from Jesus to early believers to Paul himself, were Spirit-bearers — those who exist in a peculiar relationship with the Father.[32] Dunn adopted the prism

---

29. Introductions have, of course, been published, though even these are few and far between. Introductory does not mean elementary in any of these; all are insightful and extremely well-informed by scholarship, much of it their own. Nonetheless, although each of these occupies an important niche in the study of pneumatology, none is written as a first-line scholarly contribution intended to reshape the study of the spirit in antiquity. Christopher J. H. Wright, *Knowing the Father through the Old Testament* (Downers Grove: InterVarsity, 2006); see also Wilf Hildebrandt, *An Old Testament Theology of the Spirit of God* (Peabody: Hendrickson, 1996). Eduard Schweizer's *The Holy Spirit* (Philadelphia: Fortress, 1980) is an insightful introduction to teachings about the holy spirit in the New Testament. George Montague's *The Holy Spirit: Growth of a Biblical Tradition* (New York: Paulist, 1976) offers insightful commentaries on all relevant texts from the Jewish Bible, the New Testament, the Apocrypha, and the Dead Sea Scrolls, though he does not attempt to connect the dots of these disparate commentaries. C. F. D. Moule's *The Holy Spirit* (Grand Rapids: Wm. B. Eerdmans, 1978), while it contains a chapter devoted to the New Testament, includes principally Moule's reflections, which are always worth reading, on topics such as "Spirit, Church, and Liturgy" and "Inspiration and Incarnation." Max Turner's *The Holy Spirit and Spiritual Gifts in the New Testament Church and Today* (Peabody: Hendrickson, 1998) is an excellent in-depth introduction to the spirit in the New Testament, including as well theological reflection upon spiritual gifts aimed particularly at the modern church.

30. *Baptism in the Holy Spirit: A Re-examination of the New Testament Teaching on the Gift of the Spirit in Relation to Pentecostalism Today* (Philadelphia: Westminster, 1970).

31. (Minneapolis: Fortress, 1994), translated from *Gottes Geist: Theologie des Heiligen Geistes* (Neukirchen-Vluyn: Neukirchener, 1992).

32. Büchsel's prism was two-pronged. Against Leisegang, who had rooted Christian pneumatology in Hellenism, Büchsel contended that early Christian pneumatology had its origins in Israelite and early Jewish belief. He devoted 147 pages to the *Vorgeschichte* of early Christianity, covering the Hebrew Bible, Greco-Roman authors such as Plutarch, the Apocrypha and Pseudepigrapha, Hellenistic-Jewish authors such as Philo and Josephus, the Greek mystery cults, rabbinic literature, and John the Baptist. Against Gunkel, however, who had argued that Paul's pneumatology could be distinguished from that of the apostolic church, Büchsel discerned a common ground, the figure of the *Pneumatiker*. Büchsel was provided with this perspective by his able predecessor, Paul Volz, who had devoted

of baptism in the holy spirit in order to unravel rival claims to this baptism by two constituencies in the church: the Sacramentalists, for whom the gift of the spirit is tied inextricably to the sacraments, particularly water-baptism; and Pentecostals, for whom baptism in the holy spirit is identified with a discrete and demonstrable second and subsequent experience. Dunn proceeded unrelentingly, book by New Testament book, to demonstrate that the holy spirit was associated, neither with water-baptism nor with a postconversion spirit-baptism, but with conversion-initiation into the new covenant, with "the beginning of a new stage in salvation history."[33] Welker's chosen prism lay in the application of feminist and liberation perspectives to pneumatology in both testaments in order to challenge the burgeoning "Worldwide Charismatic Renewal" to root their experiences of the spirit in the social and political realism that feminist and liberation theologies offer.[34]

Each of these studies exhibits enduring qualities precisely because each author selected a particular prism through which to interpret the presence of the spirit in antiquity. Büchsel was able to track through a monumental amount of literary texts the commanding figure of the Spirit-bearer. Dunn's single-minded offensive, coupled with the acuity of

---

over sixty pages of *Der Geist Gottes* to pneumatic figures in Israelite and early Jewish literature (78-145).

33. *Baptism*, 28; see 4. An example of Dunn's eloquence occurs in his description of Jesus' baptism (36): "it was in response to and as a result of this [Jesus'] repentance, submission and commitment that the Spirit was given and the new era was begun with the apocalyptic roll of drums and the heavenly proclamation." Dunn refers to Israelite and Jewish literature in notes.

34. Welker's interpretation of the story of Samson evinces the tenacity with which he champions this hermeneutical lens. It is not difficult for readers of the book of Judges to suppose that the spirit prompts the violent responses of Gideon, Samson, and, later still, in 1 Samuel, Saul. Not so, argues Welker. The earliest stirrings of the spirit in the book of Judges evoke "an unexpected, unforeseeable renewal of the people's unanimity and capacity for action, a renewal of the people's power of resistance in the midst of universal despair, and a resulting change of fate"; *God the Spirit*, 53. This is nothing if not the ideology of liberation theology, the language of what Paulo Freire understood as conscientization of the oppressed; *Pedagogy of the Oppressed* (New York: Herder & Herder, 1970). The spirit did not bring immediate deliverance, prompt military action, or offer miraculous intervention. There is rather a clear liberative lesson to be learned from *"experiences of how a new beginning is made toward restoring the community of God's people. They are experiences of the forgiveness of sins, of the raising up of the 'crushed and oppressed,' and of the renewal of the forces of life"* (65). Welker deals exclusively with the canonical New and Old Testament, with a few references to the Apocrypha.

his exegetical skills, launched a re-examination of the Pentecostal under-standing of baptism in the spirit as a subsequent endowment.[35] Through an unswerving application of the ideology of liberation theology to scripture, Welker offered an exceptionally timely corrective to a global movement that has exhibited a tendency to confine the influence of the spirit to individual and church rather than to political and social realities.

My engagement with antiquity has guided me, through the years, to adopt the principal lens of *filling with the spirit*. This may, at first blush, seem rather pedestrian. Why not other ancient claims to the spirit's pres-ence: it rushed upon, came upon, rested upon, was poured out over, leapt upon, accompanied, and stood among those who believed, those who would come to believe, even forlorn nature itself?

I can offer, of course, dispassionate rationales for this choice. The lan-guage of filling with the spirit extends farther than these others, all the way from creation to new creation. It applies more universally than most of these, encompassing individuals and communities. It spans a wider array of cultures, including Israelite, Greco-Roman, early Jewish, and early Christian literature. The language of filling with the spirit would become the most popular way of expressing the spirit's presence for first-century Christians, more so than the others.

All of this is true, but that is not why I have made this choice. I suspect what ultimately, through years of reflection, led me in this direction is the expansiveness, the open-endedness of this claim. Images of inbreathing prompted wrenching reflections upon the tensions of creation and the promise of new creation. Individuals, such as Joseph, Bezalel, Daniel, and the recipients of the Paraclete in the Fourth Gospel, were believed to ex-hibit exceptional skill and knowledge because the spirit resided within them. Claims to the spirit within buttressed claims to the inspired inter-pretation of scripture. The lens of filling with the spirit, then, is exhilarat-ing in its expansiveness, and so I have installed it as my rudder for navigat-ing the deep and occasionally stormy waters that circulated around conceptions of the spirit in antiquity.

Each of the three main sections of this study opens with a prescript that is framed by the relevant experiences and research initiatives of Hermann

---

35. The title of H. M. Ervin's book, *Conversion-Initiation and the Baptism in the Holy Spirit: An Engaging Critique of James D. G. Dunn, "Baptism in the Holy Spirit"* (Peabody: Hendrickson, 1984), is hardly oblique.

Gunkel. Israelite literature is the focus of Part I of this book. Jewish literature of the Greco-Roman era provides the focus of Part II. Early Christian literature is the focus of Part III. No sooner have I adopted what seems to be a straightforward outline, however, than do all sorts of caveats arise. The book of Daniel, for example, is included in Part I although, from the standpoint of chronology, it belongs to Part II; Sirach, which is included in Part II, was probably composed prior to the book of Daniel. Again, the apocalypse known as 4 Ezra is included in Part II, though it was composed decades after Paul's letters, which are treated in Part III. Readers familiar with Judaism and Christianity during the Greco-Roman era are painfully aware of these issues, and I appeal to them for leniency.

What ought to be said in the strongest of terms, in conclusion, is that this book is not intended exclusively to provide a background to early Christian pneumatology. What I have to say about the spirit in the shadow of death in Psalm 104 or about Daniel's holy spirit in the book of Susanna is possessed of a significance that is on a par with what I have written about Luke's depiction of Pentecost or the portrait of the Paraclete in the Fourth Gospel. It would be a grave mistake to read cursorily through my reflections upon Israelite and early Jewish literature and to brake only at my interpretations of the literature of the early church. There may be long moments in my analysis of Paul's letters, the Fourth Gospel, and the book of Acts when I refer in detail to Jewish and other Greco-Roman texts. It is my hope that these provide fresh insight into the beliefs of the early churches, yet I have tried not simply to cite Jewish texts as a means to understanding the churches' beliefs as background sources. I have rather interpreted them at length and set them alongside early Christian texts, on an equal footing, for the purpose of mutual illumination.

I have offered in this book, therefore, many points at which to pause and to reflect. What Elihu may get wrong in the book of Job, for example, is as valuable for understanding the spirit in antiquity as what Paul may get right in his passionate portrayal of the second Adam. Much can be culled from the errors to which Elihu is liable; it would be a mistake to rush past him en route to Paul or the Fourth Gospel or Acts. Again, the lopsided declarations of the author of the letter called 1 John are of no less value than Ezekiel's extraordinary vision of the unimaginable new life that pulses in a resurrected community in a valley of very many, very dry bones. Much is to be garnered from the misguided advice the author of this little letter gives; it would be a mistake to allow the grandiose and familiar to eclipse this little corner of early Christian spirituality. Once more, there is a rich symbiosis between the Qumran conviction that there is a communal spirit which transcends individual experience and Paul's metaphor of the new temple; it would be a mistake to rush through the Dead Sea Scrolls because they do not belong to the Christian canon. Both deserve a protracted pause. If there is counsel I would give a reader of this book, therefore, it is to pause for what is striking, to ponder what is fresh, and not to rush to the more familiar territory of Pentecost or Paraclete or Pauline pneumatology.

PART I

Israelite Literature

Hermann Gunkel, the Spirit, and the Spectacular

The simple word "effects," or "influence" (German *Wirkungen*), in the title of Gunkel's little book, his *Büchlein*, set the grounds for a confrontation that would only rarely take place visibly on the high ground of academic publications but which may have been fought instead on the political plain by means of hindrances that plagued Gunkel's professional career. Gunkel discerned in early Christianity an early Christian conception of spirit that represented "the mysterious and overwhelming in human life."[1] He would contend that "it is clear what the apostolic age had in mind by the term *Spirit*. It is the supernatural power of God which works miracles in and through the person."[2] By emphasizing the extraordinary and inexplicable effects of the spirit, Gunkel confronted — and perhaps alienated — one of the most influential professors at Halle, the famed Albrecht Ritschl, who associated *Geist*, in accordance with the long-standing tradition of German Idealism that shaped his thought, with the moral sphere of human attainment.

The momentous import of Gunkel's stance becomes glaring when his view is compared with the pneumatology of the nineteenth-century New Testament luminary F. C. Baur, who discussed the spirit under the rubric

1. Gunkel, *Die Wirkungen des heiligen Geistes nach der populären Anschauung der apostolischen Zeit und der Lehre des Apostels Paulus* (Göttingen: Vandenhoeck & Ruprecht, 1888) 3; English translation: *The Influence of the Holy Spirit: The Popular View of the Apostolic Age and the Teaching of the Apostle Paul*, trans. R. A. Harrisville and P. A. Quanbeck II (Philadelphia: Fortress, 1979) 32. I think that "effects" is a better translation of *Wirkungen* than "influence" because it communicates the plurality and palpability of the effects of the spirit more than the more abstract word, "influence."

2. *The Influence of the Holy Spirit*, 35.

3

"Principle of the Christian Consciousness."[3] According to Baur, the Apostle Paul adopts "the term, 'spirit' . . . to denote the Christian consciousness." This consciousness is an "essentially spiritual principle, which forbids him [a Christian] to regard anything merely outward, sensuous, material as in any way a condition of his salvation."[4] Baur's effort to identify the spirit that comes from God with the Christian consciousness is especially evident in his interpretation of the spirit of adoption, which causes believers to cry, "Abba," according to Rom 8:14-16. Here Baur attempted, somewhat fitfully, to demonstrate that subjective Christian consciousness, according to Paul, is identical with the absolute and objective reality of the spirit of God.[5] Christian consciousness "is a truly spiritual consciousness, a relation of spirit to spirit, where the absolute spirit of God, in becoming the principle of the Christian consciousness, opens itself up to the consciousness of man."[6] This interpretation of spirit comes again to the fore in Baur's interpretation of the two covenants in 2 Corinthians 3, about which he wrote at length: "The essence and principle of Christianity is thus defined here as simply spirit, and in what sense it is such is very clearly apparent from all those contrasts between the old . . . and the new [covenants]. It is spirit, because in the consciousness of the man who stands upon this platform there is no barrier, no veil, nothing disturbing or obstructing, nothing finite or transitory; it is a consciousness clear and free within, and one with itself."[7] Even justification takes place only when a human being "has received the spirit into himself as the principle of his Christian consciousness and life."[8] The "law of the spirit" (Romans 8) "designates the principle of the Christian consciousness."[9] Baur continued along the same vein: "Thus the spirit is the element in which God and man are related to each other as spirit to spirit, and where they are one with each other in the unity of the spirit."[10]

Gunkel's vision of early Christian pneumatology could hardly lie farther from Baur's conception. Although the book is not peppered with

3. In his *Paul the Apostle of Jesus Christ, His Life and Work, His Epistles and His Doctrine* (London: Williams and Norgate, 1875).
4. Baur, *Paul the Apostle*, 126.
5. Baur, *Paul the Apostle*, 127.
6. Baur, *Paul the Apostle*, 128.
7. Baur, *Paul the Apostle*, 132.
8. Baur, *Paul the Apostle*, 140.
9. Baur, *Paul the Apostle*, 160.
10. Baur, *Paul the Apostle*, 163.

footnotes that dispute Baur's — or Ritschl's — reconstruction of early Christianity, the line in the sand that Gunkel drew between the association of spirit with Christian consciousness and the presence of spirit in the supernatural is inescapable. Gunkel drove with a resounding thud a wedge between his own perception of early Christianity and that of his predecessors: "The relationship between divine and human activity is that of mutually exclusive opposition. The activity of the Spirit is thus not an intensifying of what is native to all. It is rather the absolutely supernatural and hence divine."[11]

Gunkel would contend that this effect is apparent in both the book of Acts and Paul's letters. In Acts, the spirit is associated not with what is humanly comprehensible, with a discernible purpose, but with the inexplicable and overpowering effects it exercises over its witnesses. Peter, for example, responds to his midday vision of clean foods obediently, although he has no clue at the time that this will function as part of God's plan to incorporate the Gentiles into the people of God.[12] Such stories as these are an indication that "an activity of the Spirit is ascertained not within the scheme of means and ends but rather within the scheme of cause and ef-

---

11. *The Influence of the Holy Spirit*, 34. Gunkel also took Johannes Gloël (*Der heilige Geist in der Heilverkündigung des Paulus*. Halle: Niemeyer, 1888) to task for supposing that in the book of Acts the moral and religious life of the early Christians was an effect of the spirit. Even faith, he argued, is not attributed to the spirit in Acts. Believers do not receive faith through a work of the spirit; they receive the spirit because they already have faith — though there are exceptions, including Acts 6:5 and 11:24, in which faith and spirit are intimately aligned, and Acts 9:31 and 13:52, where persistence in faith is an act of the spirit. If the spirit were associated with the ordinary, with the moral and religious sphere, Gunkel asked, then why would Simon, the magician of Acts 8:18, have imagined that he could purchase the power to transmit the spirit (*The Influence of the Holy Spirit*, 18)? Gunkel also argued that there is little in the Hebrew scriptures or Judaism to support the claim that the spirit inspires the moral-religious sphere, though he cites (*The Influence of the Holy Spirit*, 19) as exceptions Isa 11:1, 2; 28:6; 32:15ff.; Ezek 36:27; perhaps Zech 12:10; Ps 51:13(Eng. 11); and 143:10. On the Hebrew scriptures and Judaism, see *The Influence of the Holy Spirit*, 16-21. With respect to Judaism, Gunkel failed to take into consideration Philo Judaeus, for whom the spirit, when it is inbreathed, imparts the capacity for virtue. For brief but useful summaries in English of Gunkel's contributions, see Robert P. Menzies, *The Development of Early Christian Pneumatology: with special reference to Luke-Acts*. JSNTSup 54 (Sheffield: Sheffield Academic, 1991); Max Turner, *Power from on High: The Spirit in Israel's Restoration and Witness in Luke-Acts*. JPTSup 9 (Sheffield: Sheffield Academic, 1996).

12. Acts 10–11. Later, Paul is prevented by the holy spirit from entering Bithynia in Asia. Paul has no idea of why this is so but obeys anyway. See *The Influence of the Holy Spirit*, 21-26.

fect. Belief in the Spirit is not for the purpose of grasping God's plan for the world but for the purpose of explaining the presence of certain, above all inexplicable, phenomena by means of the transcendent."[13]

What then is the quintessential symptom of the spirit's presence?[14] Glossolalia. Speaking in tongues was, in the apostolic age, the "most striking and characteristic" effect of the spirit.[15] In what would appear to irreverent spectators as madness and drunkenness, believers in the apostolic age would pinpoint the indisputable effect of God's spirit.[16]

It took quite enough courage — or arrogance — for Gunkel to challenge so many of his professors and peers. Yet the most poignant dimension of this scenario is perhaps not that a young scholar had the academic courage to launch such an unflinching critique of renowned — and influential — German professors who possessed the power to manipulate his destiny. More profound still is the chasm that separated his reconstruction of early Christian pneumatology, according to which the effects of the spirit lay exclusively in powerful and inexplicable mystery, from his own understanding of the spirit, which echoed the beliefs of his own teachers, who aligned the spirit with Christian consciousness. Notwithstanding his reconstruction of early Christian pneumatology, Gunkel himself was more a man of his own century than an adherent of first-century Christian religiosity, as a codicil to his stunning little study of the miraculous and mysterious effects of the holy spirit reveals: "The gifts of the Spirit in the apostolic age have vanished, though in isolated Christian circles something similar may perhaps be observed to this day. But we can also do without these miraculous gifts. For even now we daily perceive other activities of the Spirit in our life. Even for us, the Christian is a miracle of God."[17] Gunkel would express in poetry as well his personal conviction that there is no breach between the divine and human spirits, no chasmic divide separating the supernatural realm of the spirit from the human realm:

13. *The Influence of the Holy Spirit*, 32-33.

14. *The Influence of the Holy Spirit*, 33-34.

15. *The Influence of the Holy Spirit*, 30.

16. 1 Cor 14:23 and Acts 2:13, respectively. Other gifts of the spirit, too, were attributed to the spirit, and none was seen as an ordinary act that any Christian at any time could perform. Even such gifts as giving and mercy were recognized as acts that were especially sacrificial, spontaneous, and magnificent acts effected by the spirit. The believers at Macedonia, who provide more than amply despite their poverty, illustrate this sort of spirit-inspired giving. See *The Influence of the Holy Spirit*, 37-38.

17. *The Influence of the Holy Spirit*, 96.

From all the commerce of earthly spirits
    [*Aus allem Handeln irdischer Geister*]
Is woven a gown of the eternal Lord
    [*Webt sich ein Kleid der ewige Meister*].[18]

Small wonder that more than four decades later, Hans Schmidt described Gunkel's *Wirkungen des heiligen Geistes,* which grated so harshly against the beliefs of his own era, even his own convictions, not as "a conclusion but a beginning" and "a new word."[19]

This uncanny ability, at such a young age, to lay aside his own nineteenth-century assumptions in order to unearth first-century points of view — the transference of the spirit from the realm of the known to the mysterious, from the arena of human potential to that of an overwhelming force — had so much intellectual purchase that it effected an overhaul of pneumatology during the twentieth century. No more than a year after the third edition of Gunkel's *Wirkungen* was published, for example, Alfred Bertholet's article on "Geist und Geistesgaben im AT," in the first edition of *Die Religion in Geschichte und Gegenwart,* described "the effects of rûach" as "originally completely spontaneous . . ."[20] and its "powerful effects" as "unknowable in the main or at least full of mystery" — words that might have been lifted from the pages of Gunkel's *Wirkungen.*[21]

The monumental shift in perspective that Gunkel's book precipitated brought with it a new problem for pneumatology: If the spirit is to be associated exclusively with the supernatural and mysterious, what then is to be made of the spirit of life, the spirit that gives breath? Gunkel seems to have stumbled over this nagging distinction between the spirit as creative power and the spirit as *superadditum* in his attempt to understand the inspiration of Jesus. Unlike other inspired people, Jesus was originally, through his conception by the holy spirit, inspired: ". . . for Jesus, and not as for ordinary persons chosen by God to be prophets, the Holy Spirit was not something added to nature, a *donum superadditum,* but rather the agent who continually and totally filled his life, just as it was the Spirit who began it. This thought is conveyed by the idea of the Spirit of God as

---

18. W. Klatt, *Hermann Gunkel: Zu seiner Theologie der Religionsgeschichte und zur Entstehung der formgeschichtlichen Methode.* FRLANT 100 (Göttingen: Vandenhoeck & Ruprecht, 1969) 33.

19. *TBl* 11/4 (1932) 98.

20. *RGG,* 1st ed., 2:1199. The second edition (1928) is largely unchanged.

21. *RGG,* 1st ed., 2:1197.

a creative spirit of life, an idea usually separated from that of the Spirit as a principle of divine activities in and through the person."[22] This is a tricky move that Gunkel felt compelled to make. Here in the life of Jesus lies an anomalous confluence of the spirit as creative life-giver and the spirit as the cause of divine effects in human beings. There is here a perplexing — and untypical — ambiguity in Gunkel's typically coherent façade. Here as well lies a distinction that would plague subsequent analyses of pneumatology.

The divide between the creative life-spirit and the spirit as the principle of divine effects in human beings — which Gunkel entered as little more than an aside, the threads of which he left dangling — would come to full flower in twentieth-century studies of pneumatology. It would, in fact, become one of the most unfortunate and least examined legacies of those studies: scholars would absorb Gunkel's interpretation of the spirit as wonder-worker and distinguish it from the allegedly less spectacular spirit that remains within from birth. Perhaps the least taxing way of demonstrating this is to survey a few influential dictionary entries in order to till some very compact soil in preparation for the seeds I hope to plant in this, the first part of our study.

In the third edition of *RGG*, published in 1958, Gillis Gerlemann introduces an unnecessary amount of ambiguity in the relationship between the "anthropological and psychological" *Geist* and the "charismatic" *Geist:* "As an anthropological or psychological term, *rûah* denotes something dynamic much more than concrete. The life-spirit of the creation is not understood to be a substance but a powerful action of God (Ez 37,5.6.9; Gen 6,17; 7,15.22). As a power or inspiration that goes out from God, the Spirit makes itself known in appearances that signify the elevation of natural human ability. People are overcome by the Spirit and equipped for extraordinary achievements. This charismatic Spirit is a fundamental factor of Yahwistic religion."[23]

---

22. *The Influence of the Holy Spirit,* 16.

23. *RGG,* 3rd ed. (1958) 2:1270. Compare this with Bertholet who, in the first edition of *RGG* (2:1198), still derived both the spirit within human beings and the spirit that exercises powerful effects from the notion of wind, thereby avoiding the possibility of this bifurcation. "Should one wish to develop a conception of *rûach* on the basis of its essence, one will best proceed from this, that, in contrast to *nephesh,* which originally is breath (Job 41:13), *rûach* is . . . not only life-breath (Genesis 6:17; 7:15; Isaiah 11:4; 42:5) but also the air-breath, that is, wind. To this it corresponds that the *rûach,* in a large number of cases, stands opposed to human beings. . . ."

The unifying point of this definition is that the spirit is not so much material as power. Yet Gerlemann also introduces, inadvertently or otherwise, a distinction between the anthropological and psychological life-spirit *(Lebens-Geist),* under the category of "Terminus," and the charismatic spirit, a constitutive factor of Yahweh-religion.²⁴ What are we to make of a shift from the anthropological and psychological spirit to the charismatic spirit, which is accentuated by a shift from the language of *Terminus* to *constitutive factor?* It is difficult to answer this question because Gerlemann's analysis plunges us into a region rich with anachronism: anthropological and psychological and charismatic are conceptions that cannot be said to arise genetically from Israelite literature.

Notwithstanding the distinction Gerlemann creates, he appears nonetheless to understand the anthropological and psychological *terminus,* "spirit," as the same power that raises human capacity, enabling people to accomplish extraordinary feats. Nothing could be farther from the case with respect to G. W. H. Lampe's entry in what was arguably the most influential English-language reference work of the twentieth-century, *The Interpreter's Dictionary of the Bible,* which was published four years later.

Lampe began his entry on the holy spirit with a lopsided description of the spirit as "the mysterious power of God, conceived in the first place as the mode of God's activity, manifested especially in supernatural revelation to selected individuals and in their being possessed by a force which gave them marvelous strength, courage, wisdom, and the knowledge of God's will and his dealings with men; later identified with the personal presence of God, and regarded as the distinctive endowment of his people."²⁵ The point of departure for "OT conceptions of the Spirit" is the drama of Israel's heroes, the judges, in which the spirit "is a supernatural and unpredictable power, which takes possession of a man, and controls his actions like a tremendous inner force."²⁶ Lampe's description of the holy spirit, like Bertholet's in the first edition of *RGG,* is reminiscent of Gunkel's *Wirkungen des heiligen Geistes.*

Unlike Bertholet, Lampe introduces into the discussion a superfluous dichotomy between the human spirit and the divine Spirit that serves further to muddy the waters of pneumatology. In one of nine sections devoted to "OT conceptions of the Spirit," subtitled "in creation," Lampe dis-

---

24. This includes such phenomena as prophecy and military power.
25. *IDB* 2:626.
26. *IDB* 2:626-27.

cusses briefly the spirit as breath, wind, and life-breath.[27] "In these last instances, the thought is primarily of the 'inbreathing' by God of the life principle or 'soul' of living creatures, but although this life principle is not to be identified with the actual Spirit of God, it is represented by the Hebrew writers as an effect of its operations."[28] This statement is surprisingly convoluted. What rationale can Lampe offer to explain why the spirit which God inbreathed is not the "actual Spirit of God?" None that I can see. Are we to assume that, because the spirit of God must be a powerful and mysterious superadditum, an endowment that is "manifested especially in supernatural revelation . . . ," then, as a consequence, the inbreathed spirit cannot be the "actual Spirit of God?"

The egregiously errant character of this distinction is exacerbated by the distinction between the actual spirit of God and the human soul, for the notion of a "soul" is an anachronism better suited to the later Alexandrian Wisdom of Solomon and the writings of Philo than to Israel prior to the Greco-Roman era. Yet it is with this anachronistic dichotomy that Lampe, although (or perhaps *because*) he is such an astute scholar of patristic literature, characterizes the life-principle as a soul, as something that cannot finally be identified with the spirit of God — though this soul is somehow the product of the actual Spirit's operations.

Lampe's influential entry illustrates the difficulties that emerge with the introduction of a dichotomy between the spirit of God as life-principle and the powerful spirit of God, with its many amazing effects. Ultimately, the life-principle becomes the human soul, whose existence is dependent, in some inchoate way, upon the actual spirit of God.

A generation later, the opening definition of the holy spirit in Friedrich Wilhelm Horn's entry in the *Anchor Bible Dictionary* would prove as constrictive as Lampe's: "The manifestation of divine presence and power perceptible especially in prophetic inspiration."[29] His analysis of the Hebrew Bible begins in earnest with a discussion of the "Meaning of the Term." Here one finds *ruach* as wind, demon, and, in what Horn calls "this essentially physical meaning," the spirit as breath. Only after dispensing with these apparently lexical issues does he address the "History of the

---

27. These sections include: possessing Israel's heroes; inspiring rulers; transferred from ruler to ruler (Deut 34:9; Num 27:18-23); inspiring the prophets; effecting sanctification and judgment; presence of God with Israel; eschatological expectation; creation; in relation to the being of God (e.g., Isa 34:16; 63:10-14).

28. *IDB* 2:629.

29. *ABD* 3:260.

Concept," a section that begins with a very different tenor: "References to the power of the spirit of God in the OT period occur first with the charismatic judges and ecstatic prophets." The bifurcation is clear: the meaning of the *term* includes the life-breath, while the history of the *concept* concerns the power of the spirit. The life-breath is "essentially physical," while the spirit of God has to do with charisma and ecstasy.[30]

This entry persists in propagating an unfortunate two-tiered evaluation of inspiration not unlike Lampe's — and with no fewer questions in its wake. Why begin the analysis of the *concept* of the holy spirit with charismatic judges and ecstatic prophets while reducing the divine inbreathing to an essentially physical meaning? What, in fact, does this distinction imply? Did Israelites believe that the spirit which inspired Samson to slay enemies with the jawbone of an ass or ecstatic prophets to writhe upon the ground was *not* as physical as the breath within? I suspect we are discovering yet again the presence of anachronism: the breath is an essentially physical term, while the spirit is a powerful nonphysical concept. Moreover, the implication of this bifurcation is that they are not one and the same spirit.

This run-through of influential articles leads to this fundamental question: *What is the relationship between the spirit that human beings possess by dint of birth — the life principle or breath within — and the spirit that exhibits awesome effects?* These entries move away from a relationship of identity, or even continuum, to one of distinction, which is then framed in a variety of ways: an anthropological and psychological life-spirit *(Lebens-Geist)*, as opposed to the charismatic Spirit (Gerlemann); a life principle or "soul" that "is not to be identified with the actual Spirit of God" (Lampe); an "essentially physical meaning" of spirit as breath versus the power of the Spirit of God in charismatic judges and ecstatic prophets (Horn); and a lexical *term* that lies in contrast to a power (Gerlemann) or a *concept* (Horn) that has its own history.

In the first part of this volume, I will offer an unapologetically alternative point of view, a fresh point of departure into this dimension of ancient pneumatology. It is undoubtedly evident from the tone of my survey that I regard these entries to have espoused an artificial, anachronistic, and decidedly unnecessary division that serves only to obscure the relationship

---

30. *ABD* 3:262. The history of the concept undergoes specific phases: charismatic judges and ecstatic prophets, followed by kingship, the promise of the spirit for the messiah and the whole people.

that exists in Israelite literature between God's initial gift of the spirit and a subsequent endowment of the spirit. There is need for reparation here, for a redefining of the assumptions that underlie our modern approaches to ancient pneumatology.

First, I hope to redraw the relationship between the initial endowment of the spirit and what Gunkel would refer to as the mysterious effects of the spirit. It is time to supplant Gerlemann's distinction between the anthropological-psychological spirit and the charismatic spirit, between Lampe's soul and the actual spirit of God, and between Horn's essentially physical breath and the charismatic spirit that inspires judges and prophets. The two, the so-called life principle and the spirit of God, I am convinced, were understood to be one and the same. The initial endowment of God's spirit at birth must not, therefore, be understood as an inferior presence, a merely physical reality, in comparison with charismatic endowments, but rather in its own right as a vital and powerful presence with its own supernatural effects.

Second, I hope to reframe Israelite conceptions of the spirit without recourse to anachronism. Gunkel was absolutely justified in identifying early Christian conceptions of the holy spirit with miraculous and mysterious effects. Early Christians did believe that filling with the spirit was a special endowment, a superadditum, which brought extraordinary abilities in the swells of its powerful wake. Yet twentieth-century scholars interpreted Israel's scriptures all too quickly in light of this early Christian conception of the spirit. Accordingly, anyone said to be filled with God's spirit or to have God's spirit within must have received a charismatic endowment or a superadditum. On this point I demur. Many texts are to be read differently from this, in light of a long-held Israelite belief that the spirit of God — not merely the soul or an essentially physical breath — was given at birth. While early Christians put their stock, even their self-definition, on the line in a subsequent experience of the spirit, Israelites did not. In their narratives, the spirit which effected extraordinary insight was not necessarily the product of a charismatic endowment.

Part I is undoubtedly the most ambitious portion of this study precisely because it presses in so many ways against the pressure of what I have identified as false assumptions. Its most conspicuous contribution, should I succeed, will be the redefinition of inspiration in such a way that it will no longer be possible to define the presence of the holy spirit exclusively as a subsequent endowment, as supernatural revelation that arrives wholly in a charismatic endowment, as the onslaught of the inexplicable and the advent of the mysterious. Nor will it be possible to caricature the initial instance of inspiration as a purely physical reality, a poor step-sister to the actual spirit. In other words, what may be true of early Christian belief cannot be said to characterize all Israelite claims to inspiration, particularly those claims in which the spirit is said to reside within or to fill an individual.

Notwithstanding the significance of this thesis and the reframing it demands, this is not the whole of what follows. There are dimensions of filling with the spirit that may lie at a distance from this thesis but offer, nonetheless, profound insight into perceptions of the presence of God. These, too, are worth pondering, and they will offer focus and intensity to this study although they provide no fodder for the underlying thesis of Part I.

CHAPTER 1

Spirit in the Shadow of Death

Spirit, Earth, and Water

In the opening scene of Israel's scripture, death enters only thinly disguised in the specter of "dust from the earth." The first human, *adam* in Hebrew, emerges not merely from the earth, nor simply from dust, but as dust from the earth.[1] This repetition — dust and earth in tandem — is an adumbration of human mortality, set as the curtain rises, to alert us to the inevitability of death, in order that the first births of man and woman which follow should not bewitch us into the belief that breath will last unendingly.

Adam rises not "from" dust but *as* dust from the ground: "the Lord God formed *adam* (as) dust from the ground." The first human does not merely come *from* dust; the first human *is* dust from the ground. Dust is, in brief, a human's substance, not merely a human's source. Not even the animals are depicted in this story with such mortal hues; though God creates them, as God created *adam* from the ground, they are not depicted as dust: "So out of the ground the Lord God formed every animal . . ." (Gen 2:19).[2]

Then, just a few narrative moments later, rings another jarring note: God decrees death to *adam,* recalling the confluence of dust and ground in

1. Hebrew lacks the word "from" before dust: *wayyiṣer yhwh 'ĕlōhîm 'et-hā'ādām 'āpār min-hā'ădāmâ.* NRSV adds the word "from": "then the Lord God formed man from the dust of the ground."

2. Biblical translations are typically taken from the New Revised Standard Version. From time to time, however, I will modify these translations without commentary to avoid clumsiness. On other occasions, I will offer my own translations, again without commentary.

which humans are rooted: "In the sweat of your face you shall eat bread until you return to the *ground,* for out of it you were taken; you are *dust,* and to *dust* you shall return" (Gen 3:19). Once again, *adam's* substance is dust and his source, the ground.

Once we learn that *adam* is dust from the earth, and before we learn that human beings will return to dust of which they are made and to the earth from which they were taken, we glimpse God's bending and breathing into the first human's nostrils the breath of life (Gen 2:7). As a result, the human being becomes more than dust from the earth; the human being becomes a living being, a person with a capacity to till the garden, to converse with God, to name the animals. Although there is as yet no mention of the spirit, of *ruach,* per se, there is nonetheless no dearth of vitality in this opening scene. This inbreathing is not merely a "life principle or 'soul'" which cannot "be identified with the actual Spirit of God," as G. W. H. Lampe would have it, or, in Friedrich Wilhelm Horn's terms, an "essentially physical meaning."[3] Much more is going on in this story — and all of this without even a mention of *ruach.* The intimacy with which God bestows life, the face-to-face bestowal of breath, the dramatic transformation of lifeless dust from earth into a progenitor — all of these together convey an emphatic affirmation of life, the quintessence of creation, and the core of human vitality.

Yet it would be a violation of this opening scene in scripture to underscore human vitality without giving death its due or, by the same token, giving death its due without underscoring the exclamation of human vitality. There occurs rather a juxtaposition of life and death in Genesis 2–3 that provides entrée to the spirit in Israelite scripture. The unfortunate clash between energy and emptiness, life and death, breath and dust is an essential ingredient in taking hold of the amorphous world of the spirit in the Hebrew Bible, where the giving of life is hemmed in by punctuations of death (like exclamation points in a Spanish sentence), where a single, shared intimate moment between God and *adam* is bordered by the inevitability of death: dust then life then dust. The opening scene of the human drama, though set amidst a garden of delight, echoes against the implacable cliffs of the valley of the shadow of death.

The rare privilege that the gift of being filled with divine breath brings, therefore, comes into focus particularly when that breath comes under threat, which it does in the perplexing story of the sons of the gods who

3. G. W H. Lampe, "Holy Spirit," *IDB* 2:629; F. W. Horn, "Holy Spirit," *ABD* 3:262.

mate with human daughters. What exactly the sons of the gods (or "of God") do wrong is obscure.[4] Still, the situation is dire enough to prompt God to become heartbroken and to break silence, with the words: "My spirit shall not abide in mortals forever, for they are flesh; their days shall be one hundred twenty years" (Gen 6:3). Set within a puzzling tale to begin with, this is an extremely thorny decree to interpret.[5] Yet it may contain the very first description of human beings as those who are kept alive by the spirit of God within, if only for three generations' worth.

In this story it is possible to detect reverberations of themes from the tale of Eden. There the breath which God infused lay implicitly at odds with the dust of which Adam was made. Here there is a similar yet starker contrast: the *spirit* within human beings cannot remain forever because they are *flesh*.[6] Not only have the terms shifted slightly since the story of creation — from dust versus breath to flesh versus spirit — but the level of their incompatibility has risen. The implicit contrast is now explicit.

What we encounter, furthermore, in the story of the flood which follows on the heels of this tale, is another mirror image of the creation story. The expression "breath of life" has now become "spirit of life": "everything on dry land in whose nostrils was the spirit *of life*."[7] The crescendo rises when we recognize that this spirit belongs, not to humankind alone, but to all flesh, all animals, clean and unclean, everything under heaven. This is an overture to life, all of life, living beings, human and animal, whose nostrils flare with the spirit of life.

Yet this story is equally a horrific denial of life. The affirmation of the presence of the spirit of *life* for *all* creatures crescendos only on the cusp of a universal fatality, at the point of catastrophic death, when God destines to a watery destruction "all flesh in which is the spirit of life; everything that is on the earth *shall die*" (Gen 6:17). This is the sort of poignant, ines-

4. The obscurity of this text lent itself to an expansive exercise of Jewish imagination during the Greco-Roman era. In a collection of literature called 1 Enoch, these sons of God, designated "the Watchers," are responsible for the entrance of sin into the world.

5. This is especially so in light of the ambiguity of the Hebrew verb, *yādôn*. It may be that God is saying, in this text, something to the effect of "My spirit shall not adjudicate among [judge or govern] humans forever, for they are flesh. . . ." The verb may suggest this, as does the Greek version of Symmachus, which reads *krineî*. Other versions, including the Septuagint *(katameinē)*, Targum Onkelos, and the Syriac, read "remain," and thus yield the English translation "abide in."

6. This contrast of spirit and flesh, of course, comes full-blown in the letters of the Apostle Paul (e.g., Romans 8; Galatians 3).

7. Gen 7:22; see 6:17; 7:15.

capable tension which lies, yet again, at the base of Israel's conviction that the spirit of life resides within.

A hint of the poignancy in this juxtaposition between the living spirit and suffocating death occurs in an expression in Gen 7:22, which does not simply read "everything on dry land in whose nostrils was the *breath* of life died," or even "in whose nostrils was the *spirit* of life." It reads instead, "everything in whose nostrils was (a) *breath* of the *spirit* of life."[8] The two words, taken together, underscore perhaps that this is the last gasp of the living as they slip beneath the floodwaters, a final gulp of life as they enter the realm of death. All who had any breath left of the spirit of life in them were lost in the indiscriminate flood that brought nearly universal death in its torrential wake.

Spirit on the Ash Heap

Death would echo whenever Israel's ancient thinkers pondered the parameters of existence, no more so than on that infamous ash heap, where a failing Job was destined to debate his detractors. At one point, Job contests that even the animals know that what has happened to him is at the hand of God:

> But ask the animals, and they will teach you;
> the birds of the air, and they will tell you;
> ask the plants of the earth, and they will teach you;
> and the fish of the sea will declare to you.
> Who among all these does not know
> that the hand of the Lord has done this?
> In his hand is the life [*nephesh*] of every living thing
> and the spirit [*ruach*] of every human being. (Job 12:7-10)

This is another instance of the association that is drawn between spirit and physical life. The parallel between the *life*, the *nephesh*, of every living being and the *spirit* of every human being, both of which are in the hand of God, is quite like the association of the breath God inbreathed at creation and the first human's becoming a living *nephesh*.

---

8. This is not the only interpretation, of course. See, e.g., *THAT* 7:399, in which this expression is said to be the result of a redactional mixture of breath of life (Gen 2:7) and spirit of life (6:17; 7:15). To what narrative or theological end, however, does such a redactional mixture function?

Later in the book, a beleaguered Job protests that he would never speak wrongly or deceitfully as long as he lives, "as long as my breath is in me and the spirit of God is in my nostrils" (Job 27:2-4).[9] Here again is the quintessential expression of the spirit in the shadow of death. Job reckons with the reality of pending, perhaps impending, death, when he knows that he will speak only "as long as" he has breath and spirit within him.

Job, however, is not alone with his thoughts; there is an unwelcome character at the ash heap, alongside Job, who understands the reality of the spirit as well. Like Job, this strong-headed and disagreeable companion, Elihu, plays on the creation story: "The spirit of God has made me, and the breath of the Almighty gives me life. . . . See, before God I am as you are; I too was formed from a piece of clay" (Job 33:4, 6). This affirmation cuts to the heart of Gen 2:7, where *adam* is nothing — nothing but dust — without the spirit of God. Human beings are unmade without the spirit, lifeless clay without God's breath.

There is, nonetheless, a deep divide that separates Job's and Elihu's perceptions of the spirit within: Elihu's perspective is forged on the anvil of youth and health, untainted by age and debilitation. Elihu has tired of listening to Job and his three older companions. He is angry at Job for Job's indefensible self-justification, and he is equally worn by his elders because they find fault with Job but fail to offer an acceptable alternative explanation of his horrifying plight. In a way that is so very uncharacteristic of Job, Elihu introduces the spirit of God in vibrant tones that skirt the shadow of death and evade the reality that all creatures, human and animal, are given God's spirit. The true compass guiding Elihu's grasp of the spirit is his own inflated self-image. Elihu acknowledges only *the spirit within himself*, and it is his experience alone that is the benchmark for all experiences: "The spirit of God has made me," he claims, "and the breath of the Almighty gives me life" (Job 33:4).[10] This is a patent reversal of Job's tendency to expand the scope of God's spirit in a way that encompasses the animal world. It is, further, a constriction that flies in the face of the psalmist's claim: "When you send forth your spirit, they [animals] are created, and you renew the face of the ground" (Ps 104:30). Set against the expansive claims of Job and the psalmist, Elihu's is shrivelled and self-absorbed: God has made *me*; the Almighty's breath gives *me* life.

This is hardly an instance of good therapeutic care — rambling on at

---

9. Hebrew: *kî-kol-'ôd nišmātî bî wĕrûaḥ 'ĕlôah bĕ'apî.*
10. Hebrew: *rûaḥ-'ēl 'āśātnî wĕnišmat šadday tĕḥayyēnî.*

such length about his vitality and wisdom in the presence of a man who sits defeated, disconsolate, and disconcerted on an ash heap. Yet there is something else no less disturbing about Elihu's perception of the spirit. When he introduces the spirit self-referentially, he characterizes it in exclusively triumphalistic terms. He fails even to offer a whisp of awareness that the spirit is bordered by dust, that life goes on in the shadow of death. The creation and flood narratives acknowledge this. Even Job knows this. Yet Elihu's grand effort to shore up his right to speak impels him to introduce only those positive dimensions of the spirit — its capacity to create and impart wisdom to him — without so much as a glance at the possibility that God may take that spirit away from him.

When he claims that "truly it is the spirit in a mortal, the breath of the Almighty, that makes for understanding," he is not so much drawing a general observation as bolstering his own point of view over against the elders, for he continues, "it is not the aged that understand what is right," and then he begins his monologue in earnest, "Therefore I say, 'Listen *to me* . . .'" (Job 32:8-10). In other words, it is his conviction that the spirit within rather than age has a concrete and constricted application: to offer a rationale for why Job and the elders should give him a hearing. Slightly later in this speech, Elihu claims that the length of his reply is the product, not of impatience or of anger, but of the spirit within which constrains him (32:18). Once again, Elihu claims that the source of his words lies ultimately in the divine spirit rather than in his flawed temperament. No wonder the simple claim that God's spirit and breath give life is expressed exclusively in terms of Elihu's own vitality: "The spirit of God has made me, and the breath of the Almighty gives me life" (33:4).

What is disturbing about Elihu's ability to co-opt God's creative act to provide a foundation for his own self-centered stance is that, later in his soliloquy, he acknowledges the reality of the shadow of death when he claims that if God:

> should take back his spirit *(rûḥô)* to himself,
>   and gather to himself his breath *(nišmātô)*,
> all flesh would perish together,
>   and *adam* would return to dust. (34:14-15)

This is familiar territory: Elihu recognizes that the withdrawal of God's spirit would, as in Gen 3:19, cause human beings to return to dust. Further, rich verbal associations connect Elihu's words with Psalm 146, in which princes are sons of *adam* who will return to the earth when their spirits depart. The *adam* which Elihu has in mind, like the sons of *adam* in Psalm 146, includes unjust rulers, kings and princes, nobles and the wealthy: "In a moment they die; at midnight the people are shaken and pass away, and the mighty are taken away by no human hand" (Job 34:20). This too, then, is characteristic of Elihu. When he does ultimately acknowledge the inevitability of death, as he speaks of the spirit, he does so to criticize the elite who live unjustly; he fails to offer the slightest self-referential hint.

There is nothing theologically errant in Elihu's conception of the spirit that would allow it to be dismissed out of hand. The spirit of God does give understanding. The spirit does provide edifying words. The spirit does give life and create — even Elihu's life. Yet while there may be nothing we can pinpoint that is calculably incorrect in Elihu's conception, there is a disturbing self-centeredness in his perception of the spirit. It is *Elihu's* understanding, *Elihu's* words, *Elihu's* creation that the spirit provides. Elihu is alive, full to the brim, overflowing with the vitality that God gives.

There is a telling disparity, moreover, between what Elihu says about his experience of the spirit and what he acknowledges about the spirit in the lives of others. Death comes to the elite, who die in a moment; God's heart and spirit are taken back, and they return to dust. Vitality in overfull measure, on the other hand, is Elihu's; the spirit gives him wisdom, energy, life. This is a naïve and unfortunate disparity, and it belies both Elihu's self-congratulatory perspective and his quick condemnation of others. What he fails to acknowledge, in the compass of his speech, is that he too will die when God takes back the spirit. In the bulldozing energy of his younger years, the breath within Elihu appears to remain in unending supply, in contrast to Job, who is taking what seems to Elihu to be his last breaths. He is as yet unable to understand the power of the spirit to sustain — "as long as" I have breath — life in the inevitable shadow of death. Nor does he seem able to ascend to the cusp of the cliff of his own experience: Elihu speaks repetitively of the spirit within *him* and the breath that gives *him* life. For all his claims to wisdom, therefore, his discernment is paltry, his insight shrivelled, while Job's vision of the spirit, in his shrivelled and deflated state, is more realistic, for Job has made his peace with the inevitability that the spirit survives until it is eclipsed by the shadow of death.

Another way to appreciate the divide that separates Job from Elihu is by comparing their points of view with Ecclesiastes, in which the spirit is swallowed up by defeatism. The Preacher recalls:

I said in my heart with regard to *the sons of adam* that God is testing them to show that they are but animals. For the fate of *the sons of adam* and the fate of the animal is the same fate; as one dies, so dies the other. They all have the same spirit, and the *adam* has no advantage over the animal; for all is vanity. All go to one place; all are from the dust, and all turn to dust again. (Eccl 3:18-20)

The Preacher's thoughts here seem tired; they contain stock elements that emerge as well in the book of Job, though they are left unearthed, undeveloped. There is, of course, a predictable allusion to Gen 3:19, with the return to dust, as well as references to *adam,* which may mean merely human beings, though they are more likely evocative of the creation story. There is even the conviction, expressed by Job, that the spirit of an animal is no less a gift of God than the spirit of a human being. Yet both characteristics of the spirit — its presence in the shadow of death and its universal power of life — fail to capture the imagination of the Preacher. No sooner does he make these assertions than he professes ignorance, throwing up his hands in light of the unsolvable mystery before him, as if to surrender his energies and move along in Eccl 4:1-3 to what seems to the Preacher, surprisingly, to be a less intractable and more palpable issue, such as the presence of oppression on the earth: "Who knows whether the spirit of the *sons of adam* goes upward and the spirit of the animal goes downward to the earth? So I saw that there is nothing better than that all should enjoy their work, for that is their lot; who can bring them to see what will be after them?" (3:21-22).

The shadow of death has grown so grey, so potent, that it has entirely obscured the spirit of life. The marvellous conception of the spirit *of life,* discernible in both the tragic tale of the flood and Job's own observation that even animals possess the spirit, is subsumed here entirely by death. The Preacher brings up the spirit, in fact, only to underscore the universality of death, the animal-fate of humans, the inevitability of lost life: all are dust, and to dust they will return. There is no real spirit here; its brief mention serves only to lock the gates of death firmly shut.

Even when the Preacher returns to the topic of death, he does so desultorily, in a list of experiences that will comprise the "days of trouble," when youth is spent, "before the silver cord is snapped, and the golden bowl is broken, and the pitcher is broken at the fountain, and the wheel broken at the cistern, and the dust returns to the earth as it was, and the spirit returns to God who gave it" (Eccl 12:6-7). This is no clear statement of mortality or immortality, but a fragmentary resignation, according to which the final phase of life is submerged under the early phase of death. What this text offers, therefore, is of decisive importance: the soulful loss of the playful vitality of Gen 2:7. This vitality is transformed to a whimper in the face of the divine decree, to dust you will return.

We can appreciate the triumphalistic and egocentric conviction of Elihu by comparing it with the seasoned but saddening perspective of the Preacher. Both self-proclaimed sages reckon with the reality that all flesh have the spirit, and both know that the loss of spirit brings the advent of death. Yet Elihu is not yet ready to admit this of himself. He is full of life, vitality, wisdom: "The spirit of God has made me, and the breath of the Almighty gives me life" (Job 33:4). He claims to know more than the elders, and he fails to acknowledge that he cannot escape the fate of the elite, who forfeit their spirits in the face of death. Elihu is, ultimately, immature, insensitive toward Job, and self-deceived about the quality of his insight. The Preacher, on the other hand, finds no vitality in the spirit whatsoever, no respite from disease, no escaping death. He mentions the spirit only when death has the upper hand. The spirit which humans have is no different from the spirit of animals, and all succumb to the same fate. The spirit which God gave returns to God when a human returns to dust. Life is swallowed up by death.

Elihu and the Preacher, then, are like equally balanced playmates on a teeter-totter — with one failing to acknowledge the shadow of death and the other seeing narrowly only the shadow of death. The tragic figure of Job, in contrast, falls prey to neither of these simplistic conceptions of the spirit within. His understanding is more profound, his convictions more nuanced by the closeness of death to his body, by life on the ash heap, by the awareness that there is still at least some of God's spirit creating life in his nostrils, as it had breathed life into the first *adam*.

> As God lives, who has taken away my right,
>   and the Almighty, who has made my soul [*napší*] bitter,
> as long as my breath [*nišmātî*] is in me
>   and the spirit of God [*rûaḥ 'ĕlôah*] is in my nostrils,
> my lips will not speak falsehood,
>   and my tongue will not utter deceit.
> Far be it from me to say that you are right;
>   until I die I will not put away my integrity from me. (Job 27:2-5)

There is a great deal that could be said about Job's gasping confession. Especially poignant is the way in which the bitterness of Job's life, his *nephesh*, lies in contrast to the pristine moments after the creation of *adam*. The first *adam* had become a "living soul," while Job has been turned into a "bitter soul." The breath within Job, the spirit in his nostrils, produces no fresh beginning, no life from inanimate clay; the duration of Job's breath is diminished, the spirit's scope constrained.

Yet even greater profundity lies in Job's ability to avoid the pitfalls in the route taken by Elihu and the Preacher. As long as his body maintains a foothold in life, vitalized by breath and spirit, he is embittered, and in this bitterness he arrives at an understanding of the spirit of life, not as a triumphant spirit that exists to bolster his youth and to validate his opinions, as Elihu would have it, but as a spirit that keeps death at arm's length — a death that breathes heavily upon Job's neck. Further, despite his bitterness, he does not resign himself, as the Preacher would have it, to the inescapability of death. Instead, he raises his fist to mortality with words such as "not speak falsehood," "not utter deceit," and "integrity." Compare this with the Preacher, who is so resigned to mortality that the spirit functions as the shadow of death's slave-child — given to all flesh to demonstrate that all alike die and return to God when the body returns to dust. Job is not resigned but pugnacious, weakened yes but willful as well, stubborn in his grasp upon life. As long as the spirit of God is in his nostrils he will be truthful; until he dies he will maintain his integrity.

What is staggering about this comparison is how very much Job has in common with Elihu and the Preacher. All three agree that animals and humans alike have the spirit, and each of them contrasts the spirit with death. Yet in what different directions these convictions concerning the spirit thrust these three ancient thinkers! Elihu, untainted by bitterness, is self-absorbed in his claim to the spirit. The Preacher is resigned altogether to the loss of the spirit. Only Job holds both convictions in tension: death may be near, but he will speak with integrity as long as the spirit is in him. For Job, this spirit is, as strange as it may sound, a spirit of life, yes, and also a spirit of not death, not yet anyway.

Spirit, Praise, and the Shadow of Death

It has not taken terribly long to encounter the tension between life and death that inheres in the capacity of human beings to be filled with God's spirit. References to dust and earth, the first apparently benign (Gen 2:7) but the second decidedly fatal (Gen 3:19), signal the confines of human life, the limits which circumscribe the vitality of divine inbreathing. Human beings breathe and thrive within the walls of mortality. If readers of the Hebrew scriptures fail to learn this lesson from the story of their first ancestors, they should not be able to avoid this reality in light of the story of the illicit union of sons of gods and human daughters and the flood that follows from their breach of the divine-human boundary. This contains an enthusiastic affirmation of life, of the spirit of life, of the breath of the spirit of life. Life positively pulses in these expressions, which characterize every animal on the face of the earth and not just the primeval pair. Yet it is of no small consequence that this affirmation of the spirit of life rises with the waters of the flood.

This harsh, though not entirely disheartening, reality of the spirit, which some authors would capture in narrative form, others express in poetic frame. Ancient Israelite worshipers occupied with praise of God express this tension between the bane of bereavement and the lavishness of life. This concern, for example, slips subtly into Israel's book of worship in two climactic expressions of individual praise:

I will sing to the Lord as long as I live;
I will sing praise to my God *while I yet live.* (Ps 104:33)

I will praise the Lord as long as I live;
I will sing praises to my God *while I yet live.* (Ps 146:2)[11]

Song and praise punctuate these refrains and suggest, it would appear, nothing other than an unabashedly positive affirmation of life. Yet the words "as long as" and "while," as in Job's protest, hint at the limits of life that circumscribe praise. In light of what we have discovered in Israel's formative narratives and wisdom literature, it comes as no surprise that both psalms express the awareness that life's end is concurrent with the loss of God's spirit.

Psalm 104 is one of several spellbinding poems which honor God's magnificence as creator. For several stanzas, there is not the slightest hint of anything gone awry.[12] All exists in rare harmony. The winds are God's messengers, the earth is firmly set on its foundations, springs and streams satisfy the earth, cattle eat grass, humans drink wine, trees are watered,

---

11. Though the Hebrew is the same, NRSV translates the final words of Ps 104:33 with "while I have being" and the final words of Ps 146:2 with "all my life long." Italics represent my translation.

12. With the possible exception of a reference to a boundary God set so that there would never again be a flood (Ps 104:9), although, in the context of this poem, this is praise for God's promise never to cover the earth again with water.

birds and goats and storks have suitable homes, the sun and moon mark time, people labor until evening, ships sail the seas, even Leviathan sports in the water! The poem comes to a lovely climax with a description of the openhandedness of God:

> These all look to you
> to give them their food in due season;
> when you give to them, they gather it up;
> when you open your hand, they are filled with good things.
>
> (Ps 104:27-28)

All is indeed right with the world, leading to this paean, "May the glory of the Lord endure forever. . . . I will sing to the Lord as long as I live; I will sing praise to my God while I yet live" (104:31a, 33). All is indeed well except for death; as in the same stubborn stanza uttered by Job, the psalmist plans to sing "as long as I live." This is but a hint, a sliver of the reality that death lies ahead — a hint that has crescendoed already in the prior lines, in which death disrupts and dismays the animals that have learned to expect good things from God's hand:

> When you hide your face, they are dismayed;
> when you take away their *spirit [rûḥām]*, they die
> and return to their dust.
> When you send forth your spirit *[rûḥăkā]*, they are created;
> and you renew the face of the ground. (104:29-30)

The psalmist has here delicately shaped this ambivalent conviction about the spirit, life, and death through poetic mirror-imaging:

> You hide *your face . . .*
> You take away *their spirit . . .*
> They die and return to their dust . . .
> You send forth *your spirit . . .*
> They are created . . .
> You renew the *face* of the ground.[13]

13. Hebrew:

> *tastîr pānêkā*
> *tōsēp rûḥām*
> *wĕ'el-'ăpārām yĕšûbûn*
> *tĕšallaḥ rûḥăkā*
> *yibbārē'ûn*
> *ûthaddēš pĕnê 'ădāmâ*

Along with a crystalline poetic ordering, there is in these few lines a concentrated cluster of allusions to the creation and curses of *adam*. This is not surprising, as the psalm in its entirety consists of praise of God as creator. What is remarkable is the creative reimagining that occurs in the brief compass of these few lines.

The psalmist knows that death is no neutral reality, no benign passing from one sphere of existence to another. Death is nothing less than the hiding of God's face, the extraction of God's spirit, and a return to dust. The hiding of God's face is a haunting reminiscence of Gen 3:8, the moment at which Adam and his wife first hid themselves from God's face. Death also portends spiritless or breathless existence; thus the creative inbreathing of Gen 2:7 is reversed in a negative image of the first creation, in which God's face pressed intimately against *adam*'s to breathe life into lifeless dust. Now, in reverse mirror image, God's face turns away and takes away the spirit. Death entails, finally, disintegration into dust, fulfilling the curse of Gen 3:19: "you are dust, and to dust you shall return."

If the pendulum of this refrain swings toward death and loss of spirit in its reimagining of Genesis, it also swings toward the creative impulse of God. As in the narrative of the flood and wisdom thinkers Job, Elihu, and the Preacher, what characterized *adam* in Gen 2:7 is expanded to encompass the entirety of the animal world. All animals — domestic cattle (Ps 104:14), birds in the trees (v. 17), mountain-dwelling goats (v. 18), nocturnal prowlers, such as young lions at night (vv. 20-21), fish of the sea (v. 25), and even Leviathan (v. 26) — look to God for food. Animals are not merely objects of human hunger but subjects who have a relationship with God akin to their human kin. They live in God's presence (God's face), possess God's spirit, and return to the dust. These are the dimensions of the entire animal creation which are not, as in the Genesis narratives of creation, the sole prerogatives of human beings.[14] Alongside the expansion of the spirit's presence so as to include the animal realm, the spirit is given within, the breath invigorates. The sending of God's spirit creates the animals and renews the face of the ground.

This is not an image of new creation in any simple sense, the end of one era and the beginning of another. This is rather a realistic image of hope intertwined with despair. The psalmist grasps with remarkable acu-

---

14. Further, animals are "created," as in the harmonious masterpiece of Gen 1:1–2:4a, instead of being "formed," as are *adam* and the first woman in 2:7 and the animals themselves in 2:19.

26

ity that a life abounding in praise and song is possible within the boundaries of disintegration and death. He will sing to the Lord *as long as* he lives; he will sing praise while he *yet* lives. Praise and song persevere despite the intractability of death. The psalmist, in other words, stands squarely in the tradition of Job. The psalmist refuses, in contrast to Elihu, to avoid death. The psalmist equally refuses, with the Preacher, to become resigned to death. The psalmist reckons frontally with the tension that exists between death and creation, between the face of God and the face of the earth.

Pivotal to this perception is God's spirit. Its absence brings a world of dismay, of God's hiddenness, of death and dust. Yet its presence brings life, creation, and renewal of the ground. The pendulum does indeed swing in this song, between death and life, life and death, but it swings more widely toward life than it does toward death. The dust of death is never final in the face of renewal by the spirit. The spirit may be taken away, but it will also always be given and, along with it, refreshment of the earth. Death — dearth of God's spirit — cannot have the final say; life — creation by God's spirit — comes along to renew the lifeless earth. The psalmist can sing in the brief compass of a lifetime, not because he ignores the harsher realities of existence, but because he knows precisely this, that the dust of one generation is renewed into another by the successive taking and sending of the spirit of God.

Another psalm, this one in praise of God's reign over prisoners and the oppressed, evokes a similar association of spirit and death. In this particular psalm, the familiar refrain, "I will praise the Lord as long as I live; I will sing praises to my God while I yet live" (Ps 146:2), leads to the command not to trust in princes. No mortal is reliable; to trust in a son of *adam* is futile because his thoughts or plans, prince though he may be, will die when his spirit goes out of him:

> Put not your trust in princes,
>   in a son of *adam* [*běben-'ādām*], in whom there is no help.
> When his *spirit* [*rûḥô*] departs he returns to his earth [*lĕ'admātô*];
>   on that very day his plans perish. (Ps 146:3-4)

As in Psalm 104, this portion of the psalm is a pastiche of allusions to the early chapters of Genesis, though with different creative twists. First, the psalmist puts rulers in their place by referring to them as nothing more

27

than "sons of *adam*." Like the first *adam*, their father, they come from the earth. It may be useful in this regard to recollect God's words to Baasha, king of Israel: "Since I exalted you out of the dust [*min-he'āpār*] and made you leader over my people Israel . . ." (1 Kgs 16:2). Second, the phrase "he returns to his earth" recalls Gen 3:19, though in the psalm death is personalized. It is not the earth generically that the prince returns to but his own earth, his own plot of ground. This is a fascinating detail, particularly in light of Psalm 104, in which animals are said to return to *their* dust as well. Might this be a further denigration of princes?[15] Third, the psalmist includes the spirit in his description of a prince's death: "When his spirit [*rûḥô*] departs he returns to his earth." With this description of death, the psalmist has replaced the original breath, of Gen 2:7, with spirit, although the meaning seems to be much the same. This characterization of death also draws the familiar association between the forfeit of spirit and the return to the earth.[16]

There is in this psalm no positive portrait of the spirit as a creative and life-inducing element of existence, as in Psalm 104. There is rather only the negative image of the spirit's withdrawal at the moment of death, of a return to earth, of an immediate destruction of plans. This is due no doubt to the effort of the psalmist to put princes in their places and to commend a life of trust in God, who reigns, unlike the sons of *adam*, "forever" (Ps 146:10).

Because the shadow of death draped itself heavily over the destinies of countless unnamed Israelite individuals, the literature they have left behind affords poignant glimpses of the power which the spirit was believed to hold, not exclusively in the world of miracles, in the immense power of a Samson or David, but perhaps even more profoundly in the wrestling match with death and the great effort of living a life of virtue in the shadow of death. In the world of the penitent, both struggles take on immense proportions, no more so than in Psalm 51:

> Have mercy on me, O God,
>   according to your steadfast love;

---

15. The words "on that day" (Ps 146:3) may recollect the divine prohibition not to eat from the tree of the knowledge of good and evil, "for in the day that you eat of it you shall die" (Gen 2:17) — in which case the psalmist suggests again that the fate of a prince is no better than the fate of the first *adam*.

16. This association, though widespread, does not occur in Gen 3:19.

according to your abundant mercy
  blot out my transgressions.
Wash me thoroughly from my iniquity,
  and cleanse me from my sin.
For I know my transgressions,
  and my sin is ever before me.
Against you, you alone, have I sinned,
  and done what is evil in your sight,
so that you are justified in your sentence
  and blameless when you pass judgment.
Indeed, I was born guilty,
  a sinner when my mother conceived me. (Ps 51:1-5[MT 3-7])

Such trenchant self-awareness can lead to self-denigrating hopelessness, or the psalmist can fetch for hope elsewhere than in his purloined psyche. The psalmist does find a solution elsewhere, in a series of pleas:

Create in me a clean heart, O God,
  and put a new and right spirit within me.
Do not cast me away from your presence,
  and do not take your holy spirit from me.
Restore to me the joy of your salvation,
  and sustain in me a generous spirit. (Ps 51:10-12[MT 12-14])[17]

This prayer for purification is atypical; the psalmist begins not with the language of public temple worship or private devotion but with the language of creation: "Create in me a clean heart, O God, and put a new and right spirit within me." The command, "create," recalls vividly the second word in the Hebrew Bible, "In the beginning *created* God . . ." (Gen 1:1). This command resembles as well Ezekiel's grand vision of re-creation, where a new spirit within a shattered Israel replaces the old, where a new *adam* emerges, inspired, from the dust and bones of death (Ezekiel 37). The next line in the psalm, where the psalmist prays for God to make a *new* spirit within, underscores this heartfelt reality. Despite this cousinlike resemblance to the creation of the cosmos and the re-creation of Israel, however, Psalm 51 is concerned with a different arena of existence: not the

---

17. Hebrew: *lēb ṭāhôr bĕrā'-lî 'ĕlōhîm wĕrûaḥ nākôn ḥaddēš bĕqirbî. 'al-tašlikēnî millĕpānêkā wĕrûaḥ qodšĕkā 'al-tiqqaḥ mimmennî. hāšîbâ lî śĕśôn yiš'ekā wĕrûaḥ nĕdîbâ tismĕkēnî.*

deepest waters of the abyss but the depths of the human heart; not the nation rising from the dust but the spirit within — which is beyond the reach of human reparation.

This psalm suggests that hope does not rest entirely upon a new and altogether different heart. The psalm's first plea is for washing and cleansing rather than an entirely new creation. Then, even following the assertion that the psalmist was born guilty and conceived in sin, a series of pleas points to the possibility of rehabilitation: the belief that God can teach the psalmist wisdom deep within (Ps 51:6[MT 8]); the conviction that cleansing and purging are still available (51:7[MT 9]); and the assumption that physical healing is still possible, that crushed bones can again rejoice (51:8[MT 10]). In light of these assumptions, the urgent plea which follows, "Create in me a clean heart . . . ," ought to be understood as a prayer for cleansing, for transformation, for instruction in wisdom rather than for a miraculous transformation that does away with the old heart altogether. This is the gist of what the psalmist says later:

> For you have no delight in sacrifice;
>   if I were to give a burnt offering, you would not be pleased.
> The sacrifice acceptable to God is a broken spirit;
>   a broken and contrite heart, O God, you will not despise.
>   (Ps 51:16-17[MT 18-19])[18]

There is still something that is acceptable to God: unadulterated contrition. There remains, then, a measure of hope for forgiveness, for education, and for healing. There remains the possibility of a clean heart, a steadfast and generous spirit.

What might a reference to "your holy spirit" (Ps 51:11[MT 13]) mean in this context?[19] Certainly not the holy spirit, or spirit of holiness, of early Judaism and Christianity; such an understanding would be drenched in anachronism. In this poem, rather, the adjective "holy" is set readily beside other adjectives that are not technical terms, such as "steadfast" and "generous." Further, the spirit lies, in these strophes, in an indispensable relationship with the "heart," which is also conceived as a permanent reality at the core of the psalmist's life. Together, heart and spirit represent the essence of the psalmist, or what must be cleansed, instructed, and redirected.

---

18. Hebrew: *kî lōʾ-taḥpōṣ zebaḥ wĕʾettēnâ ʿōlâ lōʾ tirṣeh. zibḥê ʾĕlōhîm rûaḥ nišbārâ lēb-nišbār wĕnidkeh ʾĕlōhîm lōʾ tibzeh.*

19. See Isa 63:10-11 for the only other references to "holy spirit" in the Hebrew Bible.

The relationship between these two core realities, heart and spirit, is evident in the taut parallels between a "clean heart" and "right spirit" (Ps 51:10[MT 12]), and particularly between a "broken spirit" and "broken . . . heart" (51:17[MT 19]), where the same word, "broken," describes in close succession both spirit and heart.[20]

The psalmist is not praying, therefore, in this unprecedented reference, about *the* holy spirit which he or she received in an act of faith or a moment of inspiration. The holy spirit is yoked to the steadfast heart; both must be broken, and both can be cleansed.

The spirit, understood as a core dimension of the psalmist, alongside the heart, brings clarity to the tandem request, "Do not cast me away from your presence, and do not take your holy spirit from me." At its most fundamental level, casting from God's presence entails death. Jeremiah, after all, denounces false prophets and the Israelites who support them with the threat of annihilation: "I will . . . cast you away from my presence, you and the city that I gave to you and your ancestors. And I will bring upon you everlasting disgrace and perpetual shame, which shall not be forgotten" (Jer 23:39-40).[21] We can draw even closer to the psalmist's frantic plea by returning full circle to Ps 104:29, where, as we noted, the spirit lies in the shadow of death: "When you hide your face [presence], they [the animals] are dismayed; when you take away their spirit, they die and return to their dust" (104:29). The uncomplicated interpretation serves to explain the plea, "Deliver me from bloodshed" (Ps 51:14[MT 16]).[22] Quite simply, it may be that the psalmist does not want to die, and the perennial presence of God's holy spirit, the psalmist believes, keeps him from doing so.[23]

---

20. This intimate association of heart and spirit is evident as well in the description of the spirit as "right" or "steadfast" and "generous" — words elsewhere associated with the heart: "My heart is steadfast [right], O God, my heart is steadfast. I will sing and make melody" (Ps 57:7[MT 8]); "Their heart was not steadfast [right] toward him; they were not true to his covenant" (Ps 78:37); "My heart is steadfast [right], O God, my heart is steadfast; I will sing and make melody. Awake, my soul!" (Ps 108:1[MT 2]); "They are not afraid of evil tidings; their hearts are firm [right], secure in the Lord" (Ps 112:7). The word "generous" repeatedly depicts the generous hearts of those who gave offerings voluntarily for the construction of the tent of presence (Exod 35:5, 22).

21. See 2 Kgs 13:23.

22. This is supported by the observation that, in nearly every request for deliverance of this sort, the one who prays is the victim or potential victim, not the perpetrator. This means that the potential victim is pleading to God to have his or her life spared (e.g., Gen 32:11; Ps 31:15[MT 16]; 69:14[MT 15]; see Isa 44:17).

23. The Septuagint translators of this psalm seem to follow the Hebrew original when

We have now returned to where we began this brief venture: to the shadow of death. By doing so, we can appreciate the fundamental life-giving force of the spirit in Israelite literature. Does this mean that the tentative, even inadvertent, distinction which Gerlemann made in 1958 between the spirit understood as an "anthropological and psychological term," as opposed to a charismatic experience,[24] was correct? Does this mean that Lampe was more judicious than I when he drew a clear line in the sand between "the life principle or 'soul' of living creatures" and "the actual Spirit of God?" Does this analysis support the way in which Horn structured his entry, when he distinguished between an "essentially physical meaning" and the "spirit of God" that inspired "the charismatic judges and ecstatic prophets"?

Much that we have mined supports these distinctions. The gift of breath at creation is bordered by adumbrations of death: dust from the earth and return to the earth. The duration of life, the spirit within, is shortened shortly later, when the sons of the gods mate with human daughters. With the onslaught of flood, moreover, the breath of the spirit is acknowledged only at the moment of their death, when the floodwaters roll. Sages and psalmists alike understand that all flesh, human and animal, will forfeit life when God takes away their spirit. Even the elite, rulers and princes, are in peril because they are merely sons of *adam* who return to their earth when the spirit leaves them.

The "essentially physical" vitality this spirit gives to those who live finds further expression in the widespread realization that animals too have this spirit within. All flesh in which is the breath of the spirit of life faces the floodwaters. Even Job (implicitly at least) and Elihu, who disagree on so much, together recognize that animals and human beings have God's spirit within. It is this reality that allows the Preacher another outlet

---

they interpret the holy spirit as the life-breath that sustains life. This is indicated by the selection of the Greek verb *antairein* to translate the Hebrew verb *tiqqaḥ,* "to take away." Though this verb occurs only ten times in the Septuagint, eight of them in the Psalms, two of these are situated in contexts in which life and death are at issue. In Psalm 104, which we analyzed earlier, it can be said of the animals that, when God takes away *their* spirit, they are cut off and return to the ground (LXX Ps 103:29). Further, in LXX Ps 140:8 the psalmist implores God not to take away his or her life or soul. In both instances, the verb *antairein* is associated with the loss of life, the taking away of the spirit. The choice of this verb in LXX Psalms 103 and 140 may indicate that the translators of LXX Ps 50:13 understand that the psalmist is begging God not to take away what sustains life and prevents a return to the earth. For a fuller discussion of both Hebrew and Greek versions, see J. R. Levison, *The Spirit in First Century Judaism.* AGJU 29 (Leiden: Brill, 1997) 65-66.

24. *RGG,* 3rd ed., 2:1270.

for his pessimism: because animals and humans have the same spirit, they all go to one place — to the dust from which they came. One of the psalmists puts this notion into the shape of lovely poetry by describing the respective taking away and sending of God's spirit. The spirit is indeed the fundamental force that keeps the entire world alive. In this regard prince and puma are alike; the spirit is eventually taken from both, and both return to their dust and the earth from which they were created.

Although it is vital to capture the essential power of the spirit to give life to animals and humans alike, to keep death at bay, the distinction that scholars such as Lampe and Horn draw between the physical or anthropological spirit given at birth and the spirit understood as a subsequent charismatic endowment leads to an unnecessary eclipse. Ancient Israelite literature fails to make such a distinction. Neither Job nor Elihu considers the possibility that the spirit *merely* gives life; they contend that the spirit which gives life is also the source of their respective truth-telling. Elihu, in particular, adopts the language of creation as he simultaneously lays claim to insight (Job 33:4). The psalmist too understands that life, should it not be taken away, will be guided by a steadfast and holy and generous spirit within, a spirit that will lead to a life of teaching (Ps 51:13[MT 15]) and singing (51:14[MT 16]). The spirit that gives life is simultaneously the spirit that is the locus of virtue. If the spirit that gives life in the shadow of death is the font of the psalmist's life of worship, it is also the source of the sage's insight, layers of which will emerge in the next chapter of this study.

Wisdom and Spirit Within

Elihu's Rage

Elihu is infuriated. His anger rises because Job justifies himself rather than bowing to God. It rises because Job's elderly companions "found no answer, though they had declared Job to be in the wrong" (Job 32:3). Consequently, Elihu jams his foot in the door of the elders' doggerel and stakes a claim for himself despite his youth: "it is the spirit in a mortal, the breath of the Almighty, that makes for understanding" (32:8).

Slightly later, the dam bursts, and Elihu floods the perplexed silence with the apoplexy of his impatience:

> And am I to wait, because they do not speak,
>> because they stand there, and answer no more?
> I also will give my answer;
>> I also will declare my opinion.
> For I am full of words;
>> the spirit within me lays siegeworks against me
>> [*kî mālētî millîm hĕṣîqatnî rûaḥ biṭnî*].
> My heart is indeed like wine that has no vent;
>> Like new wineskins, it is ready to burst.
> I must speak, so that I may find relief;
>> I must open my lips and answer. (Job 32:16-20)

Shaking with impatient rage — this is how Elihu depicts the impact of the spirit within him. The verb he chooses to describe the spirit's effect (Heb.

ṣwq) is used elsewhere of enemies' *bringing on a siege,* which results in such desperate straits that the Israelites will eat the flesh of their sons and daughters (Deut 28:53, 55, 57). Jeremiah describes such a siege, which will *afflict* Jerusalem (Jer 19:9), and Isaiah surprises with the image that God will *distress* — besiege — Jerusalem, as David had besieged it, and that "there shall be moaning and lamentation . . . siege works against you" (Isa 29:2-3). Yet, imagines Isaiah, the many nations who fight against Jerusalem, "who *distress* her," will evaporate (Isa 29:7). A later prophet in the line of Isaiah criticizes Israel for cowering before the fury of the *oppressor* who is bent on destruction (Isa 51:13). The verb is used more colloquially of the relentless *nagging* of Delilah that finally drives Samson to divulge the meaning of a riddle (Judg 14:17) and the mystery of his hair (16:16).

There is no mere constraint here, as one might be constrained by good manners to put a napkin on one's lap or as one is constrained by a compelling argument to admit to the truth of some idea. Something altogether more visceral occurs here. The spirit within Elihu besieges him, laying siege works against his patience and attacking his restraint in the presence of inept elders. His heart is about to burst like fermenting wine in new wineskins.

The verb *ṣwq,* "distress," suggests how palpably Elihu experiences the spirit within as a physical force that violently impels speech after a period of infuriating onlooking. The sheer physicality of the spirit is apparent, furthermore, in its intimate association with the contrition of the heart in the following line. Elihu's spirit lays siege works; his heart is ready to burst. There is, once again, no distinction between the spirit as a life-principle and the spirit as the source of extraordinary feats or insight. Not in the least. The way in which Elihu frames his compulsion to speak shatters any sort of contemporary effort to sequester the anthropological from the charismatic spirit (Gillis Gerlemann), the life-principle from the "actual Spirit of God" (G. W. H. Lampe), or the "essentially physical meaning" of spirit from the impact of the spirit upon judges and prophets (F. W. Horn).[1] If Elihu began his monologue with reference to the spirit given by virtue of creation, when he said, "it is the spirit [*rûaḥ*] in a mortal, the breath of the Almighty [*wĕnišmat šadday*], that makes for understanding" (Job 32:8), he now continues by reckoning with the power of that spirit-breath to besiege him so that he will speak. The spirit will invariably, claims Elihu, tumble out of his mouth, across his tongue, taking shape in the words that fill him — not just any words, but words that will be full of wisdom (32:18).

---

1. Gerlemann, *RGG,* 3rd ed., 2:1270; Lampe, *IDB* 2:626-27; Horn, *ABD* 3:260.

Elihu's raging hubris is fueled by the tales of ancient heroes who were full as well of God's spirit and, consequently, capable of extraordinary feats of clear and clairvoyant thinking. Pharaoh acknowledged that Joseph, who interpreted dreams correctly, was "one in whom is (the) spirit of God" (Gen 41:38). Bezalel, the architect of the tabernacle, was a leader whom God "filled with (the) spirit of God" (Exod 31:3). Joshua is described twice, once as "one in whom was (the) spirit" (Num 27:18), and again as one who was "full of (the) spirit of wisdom" (Deut 34:9). Micah, an eighth-century rural prophet in Judah, had claimed, "But as for me, I am filled with power, with (the) spirit of the Lord, and with justice and might . . ." (Mic 3:8). This perspective on the spirit continued well beyond the period that probably gave rise to the book of Job: a young but extremely faithful Daniel, more than any other Israelite individual, is said repeatedly to have had spirit in him (Dan 4:8, 9, 18[MT 5, 6, 15]; 5:11, 12, 14; 6:3).

The Dilemma of Translation

There is a tenacious interpretative tradition that discovers a charismatic gift in Israelite references to the spirit within individuals, that attributes the extraordinary qualities of these figures to the ephemeral presence of the spirit. Joseph allegedly received the spirit to interpret a dream. Bezalel, it is said, received the spirit to offer leadership in the construction of the tabernacle. Joshua putatively received the spirit to function as Moses' successor. Micah, it is assumed, received the spirit to prophesy courageously. Daniel, so the interpretative line goes, received the spirit to demonstrate extraordinary knowledge and to rescue Susanna. The intractability of this interpretation is rooted in what I suspect are misleading translations. In order to appreciate the ways in which translations fuel — or are fueled by — the reading of Israelite literature in this regard, I have selected three English translations of the texts by way of illustration: the Authorized Version (King James Version), the New Revised Standard Version, and Today's New International Version.

Mic 3:8: I am full of power by the spirit of the Lord (KJV)
I am filled with power, with the spirit of the Lord (NRSV)
I am filled with power, with the Spirit of the Lord (TNIV)
'ānōkî mālē'tî kōaḥ 'et-rûaḥ yhwh

Gen 41:38:   a man in whom the Spirit of God is (KJV)
one in whom is the spirit of God (NRSV)
one in whom is the spirit of God (TNIV)
'îš 'ăšer rûaḥ 'ĕlōhîm

Exod 28:3:   whom I have filled with the spirit of wisdom (KJV)
whom I have endowed with skill (NRSV)
to whom I have given wisdom in such matters (TNIV)
'ăšer millē'tîw rûaḥ ḥokmâ

Exod 35:31:[2]   And he hath filled him with the spirit of God, in
wisdom, in understanding, and in knowledge, and
in all manner of workmanship (KJV)
he has filled him with divine spirit, with skill,
intelligence, and knowledge in every kind of craft
(NRSV)
and he has filled him with the Spirit of God, with
wisdom, with understanding, with knowledge and
with all kinds of skills (TNIV)
*wayĕmallē' 'ōtô rûaḥ 'ĕlōhîm bĕḥokmâ bitĕbûnā
ûbĕdaʿat ûbĕkol-mĕlā'kâ*

Num 27:18:   a man in whom is the spirit (KJV)
a man in whom is the spirit (NRSV)
a man in whom is the spirit of leadership [or, Spirit]
(TNIV)
'îš 'ăšer-rûaḥ bô

Deut 34:9:   [Joshua] was full of the spirit of wisdom (KJV)
[Joshua] was full of the spirit of wisdom (NRSV)
[Joshua] was filled with the spirit [or, Spirit] (TNIV)
mālē' rûaḥ ḥokmâ

Dan 4:8(MT 5):[3]   in whom is the spirit of the holy gods (KJV)
who is endowed with a spirit of the holy gods (NRSV)
the spirit of the holy gods is in him (TNIV)
rûaḥ-'ĕlāhîn qaddîšîn bēh

---

2. See also Exod 31:3.
3. See also Dan 4:9(MT 6); see 4:18(MT 15) and 5:11.

Dan 5:14:   the spirit of the gods is in thee (KJV)
a spirit of the gods is in you [or, a holy, divine spirit]
(NRSV)
the spirit of the gods is in you (TNIV)
dî rûaḥ 'ĕlāhîn bāk

Dan 6:3(MT 4):   because an excellent spirit was in him (KJV)
because an excellent spirit was in him (NRSV)
by his exceptional qualities (TNIV)
dî rûaḥ yattîrā' bēh

The most significant observation to be made is that these translations typically include the definite article: *the* spirit of the Lord fills Micah; *the* spirit of God is in Joseph; Israel's artisans are filled with *the* spirit of wisdom (KJV); *the* spirit of God fills Bezalel; *the* spirit is in Joshua; and Joshua is full of *the* spirit of wisdom (or simply, in the TNIV, the Spirit). These translational choices play into the hands of the assumption that the spirit within, when it is associated with wisdom or knowledge, should be understood as an endowment. Yet invariably the underlying Hebrew phrases are anarthrous, and it is this consistent lack of the definite article that calls into question the thrust of these translations.

The translations themselves stumble occasionally over the challenges posed by rendering an anarthrous Hebrew noun in English. In Exod 35:31, for example, the NRSV opts for the ambiguous translation "divine spirit," which could signify either *the* divine spirit with which Bezalel was endowed at that moment or *a* lifelong divine spirit that was permeated by extraordinary skills and knowledge.[4] In other words, filling might have occurred initially or at some time subsequently — presumably at this moment. The TNIV prefers the unambiguous translation "the Spirit of God." Presumably the spirit is an endowment given to Bezalel at that moment. Again, in Dan 5:14, the NRSV prefers "a spirit of the gods" to "the spirit of the gods," a translation for which KJV and TNIV opt. There are also occasions when the TNIV translation responds to the ambiguity of the Hebrew by offering alternatives. Num 27:18, for instance, reads, "a man in whom is the spirit of leadership," though the note supplies "or, Spirit." The translators are evidently caught on the horns of a dilemma: does Num 27:18 suggest that the quality of spiritual leadership or the very Spirit of God itself lies within Joshua?[5]

---

4. LXX translates "divine spirit" (Greek *pneuma theion*).

5. Once again, in Deut 34:9, TNIV reads, "[Joshua] was filled with the spirit," while the

The ambiguity of the Hebrew demands a reappraisal of both how to translate and how to interpret these texts, in which the spirit within an individual is associated with wisdom and knowledge. More to the point, the ambiguity of the Hebrew calls for a fresh assessment of whether the Hebrew texts refer to a pattern of charismatic endowment of *the* spirit. Take, for example, the story of Joseph, in which a foreigner, an Egyptian pharaoh, discerns in Joseph "spirit of God" *(rûaḥ ʾĕlōhîm)*. The three translations we have cited certainly suggest the possibility of an endowment by introducing the definite article: one "in whom is *the* spirit [Spirit] of God."

This is not, however, how a recent commentator interprets Gen 41:38 and other texts cited above: "The Spirit of God rests on Joseph (v. 36) [*sic*]. . . . Generally Joseph's empowerment should be understood in terms of Exod 31:3; 35:31 (cf. Dan 5:14), which connect particular *gifts suitable for the task at hand* with the presence of the divine spirit. These texts recognize God-given talents rather than a pouring out of the Spirit for the occasion, a way in which the people of God might well speak of the work of the Spirit of God in every age."[6] The introduction of the definite article need not, then, necessarily provide the foundation for an interpretation of *the* spirit as an endowment. It is no less possible that the Egyptian ruler discerns a permanent wisdom within Joseph that he describes as "the spirit of God."

What would happen, then, if we were to tweak these translations so that Gen 41:38 were to read, with the Septuagint, "one who has spirit of God in him" or, more fluidly, "one who has a godly spirit in him" or even, "one who has a divine spirit in him?"[7] This would suggest spiritual vitality but no special endowment, giftedness without a definitive moment in which that gift was imparted. By blending the notions of spirit as life-principle and source of knowledge, these translations would not drive an unnecessary wedge between spirit as life-principle and spirit as charismatic power.[8]

---

note adds, "or, Spirit." This is baffling. To what would the Spirit, with capitalization, refer that the spirit, without capitalization, does not? *The* spirit — lower case — is still a reference to the spirit.

6. T. E. Fretheim, "Genesis," *NIB* 1:622-23. Two aspects of this quotation are inaccurate: the verse number, which should read 41:38; and the notion of resting, which is taken from texts such as Isaiah 11, where the gift of the spirit is an endowment; resting is not characteristic of Gen 41:38, where spirit is "in" Joseph.

7. As in LXX Exod 31:3, which reads, *kai eneplēsa auton theion sophias kai syneseōs kai epistēmēs en panti ergō*.

8. This translation would also overcome the rift that these translations create between Gen 41:38 and Dan 4:5, 5:14, and 6:3 — a rift that is especially evident in the NRSV. The sto-

Let me suggest a few other translational possibilities, without undue explanation — we will attend to this shortly — that might vitiate such bias. The NRSV and TNIV have already done so for Exod 28:3, in which "spirit of wisdom" *(rûaḥ ḥokmâ)* is translated by "skill" (NRSV) and "wisdom" (TNIV) rather than "spirit of wisdom" (KJV). Mic 3:8 might be translated, following the Septuagint, "with strength, by (a) spirit of the Lord and of justice and of power."[9] More accurately tied to the Hebrew, as we know it, would be "I am filled with power, a spirit of the Lord, justice, and might." This would express the tenacity of his commitment and the divine origin of his words. Exod 35:31, 34a might be translated, with a slight modification of the Septuagint, "Now God had filled him with a divine spirit of wisdom, understanding, and knowledge of all things. . . . And God put in his heart to teach."[10] Num 27:18 might be translated simply, "in whom is spirit" rather than "in whom is the spirit." It is vitality, a quality of life, that makes Joshua the evident successor to Moses — a decision that is affirmed by the priestly Urim. This translation of Num 27:18, like the translation I suggested for Gen 41:38, has the advantage of folding together the vitality of life and the charisma of leadership into one. Deuteronomy 34:9 can be accurately translated, "he [Joshua] was full of a spirit of wisdom" rather than "full of the spirit of wisdom." This translation expresses the effect of a long apprenticeship to Moses. Even if he received some sort of endowment, Joshua developed as well a spirit of wisdom through a lengthy process of observation and learning.

The purpose of this brief analysis of translations is not to suggest that

---

ries of Daniel are undoubtedly constructed out of materials from the Joseph narratives. There is a foreign ruler, a similar phrase ("spirit of gods/god/God"), a similar emphasis upon interpretation, similar success in administration, and a similar rise to power in foreign courts. Yet NRSV renders Gen 41:38, "the spirit of God," while Dan 4:5 and 5:14, which contain precisely the same phrase in Aramaic, it translates, "a spirit of the (holy) gods." Daniel 6:3 goes on to clarify that this was a lifelong spirit within Daniel that exhibits extraordinary qualities. (TNIV here even underscores this point by avoiding the word "spirit" altogether, and translating, "by his exceptional qualities.") Would it not have been more consistent for the NRSV translation to have taken its cue from an ancient interpreter of Genesis and to present the spirit in both instances as a lifelong, distinctive spirit within: Joseph and Daniel both were acknowledged by foreign rulers as having either "a spirit of God" or "a spirit of gods" in him — that is, the sort of distinctive spirit that is acknowledged in Dan 6:3.

9. LXX: *ean egō emplēsō ischyn en pneumati kyriou kai krimatos dynasteias tou apangeilai tō Iakōb asebeias autou kai tō Israēl hamartias autou.*

10. LXX: *kai eneplēsen autou pneuma theion sophias kai syneseōs kai epistēmēs pantōn. . . kai probibasai ge edōken autō en tē dianoia autō.*

other translations are inaccurate and my *ad hoc* ones reliable, since there is in every translation a note of betrayal of the original text. I have, nonetheless, tried to uncover a relatively stable translational tendency to introduce the definite article in references to spirit *(rûaḥ)* when it is understood as the inner source of wisdom and knowledge. This tendency allows for these texts to be co-opted by the view that some of Israel's greatest figures had the spirit within through a charismatic endowment — a view that is often further rooted in the presumption that there existed a rift between, as Lampe frames it, the spirit as life-principle and the spirit understood as the actual Spirit of God.

Elihu, for all his faults, offers a few lines that put the lie to this dichotomy when he regards the spirit within as the source of wisdom. In the following studies, I will suggest, nearly without exception, that his words encapsulate a long-standing Israelite tradition. We might even have been led to include him alongside Joseph, Bezalel, Joshua, Micah, and Daniel, were his claim to the wisdom of the spirit within not reeking with hubris. Unfortunately, he wields his alleged wisdom to bludgeon Job. While Elihu may be nearly right when he presumes that the cultivation of the spirit, and not an accumulation of years, yields a harvest of wisdom, he handles the truth with such clumsiness that it verges upon brutality. Other Israelites who are described as being full of (the) spirit wield their knowledge with a greater measure of finesse and to the advantage of their contemporaries. These are the heroes who are distinguished because they have a particularly salient spirit within them.

Spirit, Justice, and Power: Micah

We learn quickly that Elihu is a pedant but not a prophet, one who speaks arrogantly but not advisedly. The case is otherwise with the eighth-century Judean prophet Micah, who too lays claim to a powerful spirit within. Though he is a contemporary of Isaiah, Micah's attitude toward urban life and the mystique of Jerusalem is far more ambivalent, and he presages a more sustained judgment of Jerusalem than does Isaiah.

Although Micah indicts Judah's rulers for their inattention to justice, his particular bone of contention lies with other prophets, whom he lambastes for their readiness to utter platitudes in order to earn their keep. He implicates the people and leaders as well in the duplicity of the other prophets: "If someone were to go about uttering empty falsehoods, saying,

'I will preach to you of wine and strong drink,' such a one would be the preacher for this people!" (Mic 2:11). The prophets preach just what the people want, and for this the prophets are paid their handsome due.

Prophetic indictments appear to have travelled in both directions. Presumably other prophets have accused Micah of claiming that the "spirit of the Lord has been cut short" (Mic 2:7). The expression "to cut short one's spirit" is an idiom for the loss of patience or for exhaustion (NRSV). Job expresses his impatience before God by asking: "Should I not be impatient *(lō'-tiqṣar rûḥî)*" — literally, "Should my spirit not be cut short?" (Job 21:4). The parallel phrase, "to cut short the *nephesh*," typically signifies that someone has been worn out or lost patience: the Israelites *lost patience* — their *nephesh* was cut short — in the desert (Num 21:4); Samson *gave in* as the result of Delilah's pestering (Judg 16:16); God could *no longer bear* with Israel's suffering (Judg 10:16); and God *became impatient* with the shepherds of Israel (Zech 11:8). Therefore, the idiom in Mic 2:7 probably points to God's exhaustion and impatience toward Judah.

Although this phrase is an idiom meaning, "become impatient," it is, notably, the *Lord's* spirit that is cut short, and it is this claim that other prophets appear to have imputed to Micah. The give-and-take of their confrontation, though difficult at first to discern, is nonetheless apparent in Mic 2:6-7:

- Micah says that other prophets refuse to preach anything negative about Judah: "Do not preach" — they tell him — "one should not preach of such things; disgrace will not overtake us."
- Other prophets, in turn, accuse Micah, asking, "Should this be said [as Micah allegedly does], O house of Jacob? 'Is the Lord's spirit cut short?' Are these his doings?"
- Micah responds by urging that his words are not unqualified condemnations, for they comprise affirmations of those who embrace justice, "Do not my words do good to one who walks uprightly?"

According to Micah, the other prophets have misunderstood his message. The spirit of the Lord is *not* finally cut short, as long as there are those who embrace justice.

This rebuttal eventuates in a second, apparently unrelated but no less unfriendly tête-à-tête with rival prophets. Micah claims:

Thus says the Lord concerning the prophets
who lead my people astray,

42

who cry "Peace" when they have something to eat,
    but declare war against those who put nothing into their mouths.
Therefore it shall be night to you, without vision,
    and darkness to you, without revelation.
The sun shall go down upon the prophets,
    and the day shall be black over them;
the seers shall be disgraced,
    and the diviners put to shame;
they shall all cover their lips,
    for there is no answer from God.
But as for me,
    I am filled with power *('ānōkî mālē'tî kōaḥ),*
    with the spirit of the Lord *('et-rûaḥ yhwh),*
    and with justice and might *(ûmišpāṭ ûgĕbûrâ),*
to declare to Jacob his transgression and to Israel his sin. (Mic 3:5-8)

If earlier Micah was on the defensive (2:6-7), he has now taken the offensive against other prophets. He claims explicitly that other prophets will fail because they preach for pay, and he implies that their methods — revelations, visions, and divination — lack legitimacy. Between their preaching, visions, and divination and his prophetic experience lies a vast gulf, and he signals that disparity with the words "But as for me," followed by the emphatic first person pronoun, "I!" *('ānōkî):* "But as for me, I am filled with power, with spirit of the Lord, and with justice and might, to declare to Jacob his transgression and to Israel his sin." He, and he alone, is filled with strength, with spirit that is the Lord's, with justice and might.

    There is a tidy parallel between the first and second references to the spirit of the Lord, both of which occur in the context of Micah's confrontation with other prophets. In the first, Micah contends that the spirit of the Lord has *not* been cut short, for Micah's words do good to those who walk the right way. In the second, Micah claims that he, notwithstanding the accusations of his detractors, is filled with the spirit of the Lord, with power, justice, and might. The spirit, in both cases, Micah ties to those who do what is right; in the second, the circle of the righteous is drawn tightly around one — "But as for me, I . . ."

How ought we to construe Micah's claim to being "filled with power, with (the) spirit of the Lord, and with justice and might?" Since this claim may be the earliest in Israelite literature — it is undoubtedly the earliest autobiographical claim — it must be interpreted by clues and hues within the text of Micah's oracles itself and not in terms of a general theory or perception of prophetic inspiration.[11] None of the few instances that exist provides an adequate point of comparison. It is especially vital not to take too precipitous a leap through the centuries in order to read Micah's assertion anachronistically through later, widespread conceptions of prophetic inspiration as possession by an external spirit — like Plato's poets or Philo's prophets or Luke's Pentecost.[12] Any interpretation of the spirit in this rejoinder as a temporary prophetic endowment that enables Micah to undertake the daunting task of proclaiming justice must pass muster with the text of Micah itself. Clues in the literary context of Micah's claim, in fact, point in a different direction: toward an understanding of the spirit as a permanent endowment within Micah that inspires him to live justly and to speak powerfully.

The keystone of this interpretation is the reference to filling, not just with the spirit of the Lord, but with three permanent qualities alongside a reference to the spirit: strength, justice, and might. These contiguous qualities cannot be taken, in this context, to mean temporary charismatic endowments. Justice, for example, is not the product of prophetic revelation. It is so integral to Israelite life that Micah incredulously begins his cross-examination of the leaders with the rhetorical question, "Should you not know justice?" (3:1).[13] Though they should know the whole of what justice is, they live instead a life of inverse justice, hating the good and loving the evil, flaying the skin off God's people, breaking up their bones, and cook-

---

11. This is the first prophetic claim of that sort in Israelite literature. Hosea's excoriation of prophets as fools and people of the spirit as mad is too vague to be of help (Hos 9:7), and the stories of the seventy elders (Numbers 11) and of Micaiah ben Imlah (1 Kings 22) are too idiosyncratic to be of any use in the explanation of Micah's claim to inspiration. There is, therefore, no early precedent in Israelite literature that helps to interpret this text. Nor do other prophets make a similar claim for themselves. Even if the description of the spirit upon the servant in Isaiah 40–55 is meant to be taken autobiographically (42:1), the presence of the spirit is understood as an anointing rather than the presence of the spirit within. Ezekiel experiences the spirit in full measure, though he never attributes his oracles to it. It is principally later, postexilic authors who reflect upon the association of spirit and prophets. The author of Zechariah 1–8 indicts Israel for adamant hearts which heard neither Torah nor "the words that the Lord of hosts had sent by his spirit through the former prophets" (7:12). Nehemiah's indictment is similar: "Many years you were patient with them, and warned them by your spirit through your prophets; yet they would not listen" (Neh 9:30).

12. See Parts II and III below.

13. Hebrew: *hălô' lākem lāda'at 'et-hammišpāṭ.*

ing them in a caldron (3:2-3). Micah, in contrast, concludes this indictment with another reference to justice: "I am filled . . . with justice and might" (3:8). What the leaders fail to know, Micah has grasped, and this fundamental knowledge of justice is integral to his prophetic persona.

The axiomatic quality of justice rises in the very next line, which opens still another oracle: "Hear this, you rulers of the house of Jacob and chiefs of the house of Israel, who abhor justice [*mišpāṭ*] and pervert all equity, who build Zion with blood and Jerusalem with wrong! Its rulers give justice [*yišpōṭû*] for a bribe, its priests teach for a price, its prophets give oracles for money . . ." (Mic 3:9-11a). This provides a startling counterpoint to Micah's claim: while he is filled with power, (the) spirit of the Lord, justice, and might, Israel's leaders abhor justice and sell it for a bribe. Micah is astounded that Israel's leaders fail to know justice (3:1) and choose instead to substitute for it the flaying of their people, bribes, and bloodshed. He, however, is not cowed by them and claims, unlike them, to be filled with justice.

The quality of justice is so axiomatic, in fact, that, in the conclusion to his law court confrontation with Israel, Micah presupposes its meaning when he includes it as the overarching point in a blanket demand for God's requirements:

> God has told you, O mortal, what is good;
>   and what does the Lord require of you
> but to do justice, and to love kindness,
>   and to walk humbly with your God? (6:8)

Justice is a permanent quality that requires no temporary endowment. It is not the product of a peculiar prophetic revelation. People know justice already, or ought to: God has told you, O mortal, what is good. The justice with which Micah is filled, therefore, is a permanent part of his character, not a transitory endowment, like Samson's, that prompts him on occasion to preach or occasionally to perform an act of justice.

If this is so, if justice is a foundational quality that God has made known already to mortals, if it can be paired with kindness and humility, on the one hand, or sold to the highest bidder, on the other, then the other qualities to which it is melded — strength, spirit of the Lord, and might — should also be understood as permanent qualities. Certainly there is no problem understanding strength and might in this way: Micah is portrayed as nothing in this book if not consistently courageous. One might even say, to capture the essence of Micah's claim, that he is filled with an indomitable spirit from the Lord.

Another clue to the meaning of Micah's claim to be filled with the spirit of the Lord is implicit in Micah's comparison of other prophets' oracles with his own. The false prophets look for inspiration in visions, revelations, and divinations. All of these are temporary activities, short-lived modes of divine presence. Visions arrive and then dissipate. Divinations are also momentary, such as when a seer receives a message from the dead (Deut 18:9-14). Micah's declaration against Israel, by way of contrast, is rooted elsewhere. He is always filled with power, habitually committed to justice, inevitably full of spirit, grounded in might. Their tinny and temporary revelations and visions will end: "Therefore it shall be night to you, without vision, and darkness to you, without revelation. The sun shall go down upon the prophets, and the day shall be black over them . . ." (Mic 3:6).

Micah does not allow this contrast to evaporate. It is not enough that the other prophets will know only night, void of vision and revelation; rather, "the seers shall be disgraced, and the diviners put to shame; they shall all cover their lips, for there is no answer from God" (3:7). These so-called prophets will have nothing to say in the wake of God's unwillingness to answer them. In other words, no spirit will pass through their lips, no breath will cross their tongue. In contrast, Micah claims, in the very next lines, that he will be filled with (the) spirit of the Lord; he will declare to Israel its sins because he is full of strength and spirit, justice, and might. Words will pass through his lips and over his tongue.

It is difficult to absorb Micah's terse claim without at least a sideways glance at the impudent Elihu and the elders. Infuriated that the three elders "ceased to answer Job" (Job 32:1), Elihu was "full of words" because "the spirit within besieged" him (32:18). Elihu's more expansive claim may help to unfold Micah's more laconic one: while the other prophets will have nothing to say — they will cover their lips to signify this — Micah will speak because he is full of strength and (the) spirit of the Lord. Elihu's association of words, spirit and siege, certainly illuminate Micah's initial reference to being filled with strength. Although that word (Heb. *kōaḥ*) does not belong to the vocabulary of other eighth-century prophets, including Isaiah and Hosea, it ably communicates here a sense of vitality and vigor, the resources necessary to declare to Israel its sins.

These observations about Mic 3:8 provide every indication that the compiler of these oracles could scarcely have believed that justice, spirit, strength might come and go. The key word, "justice" *(mišpāṭ)*, which occurs in Mic 3:1, 9, and 8 (in Micah's claim), is hardly a quality that fills Micah occasionally. The juxtaposition of the spirit with strength, justice, and might indicates that Micah understands himself, in this book, to be permanently endowed with such qualities, ready ever to declare Israel's sins. In this vocation, further, his source of inspiration could hardly differ more from that of the other prophets. While they depend upon occasional visions, revelations, and forms of divination, all of which will dissipate, his oracles are at the ready because he is filled with (the) spirit of the Lord. Further still, while other prophets look to revelations for what to say, the content of Micah's oracles is grounded in what is foundational, what everyone ought to know. Micah does not indict Israel for what they fail to receive by various modes of divination but for how they abhor what ought to be patently obvious to every Israelite, such as doing justice, loving kindness, and walking humbly with God. Finally, the contrast between the other prophets' having to cover their mouths and Micah's being filled with (the) spirit "to declare to Jacob his transgression and to Israel his sin" suggests an understanding of spirit as the source within that fills a prophet, or a self-proclaimed sage, for that matter, with compelling words.

Micah has carved out very little common ground between himself and the other prophets: they support the status quo, while he declares transgressions; they hope for visions and revelations, while he is filled with strength, (the) spirit of the Lord, justice, and might; they preach peace, while he recognizes danger ahead. No less important, Micah's opponents have misconstrued his message of the spirit. The spirit of the Lord is not cut short; on the contrary, it exists at full strength within Micah and is discernible in Micah's words. These words contain harsh judgments against false prophets but will "do good to one who walks uprightly" (Mic 2:7).[14]

---

14. A brief note about the eclectic organization of this chapter is in order. The chapter is organized neither chronologically nor in canonical order. It begins with a text from Job because this text most aptly exposes some of the salient themes of this chapter. It continues with Micah because this is a saying with a relatively assured date in the eighth century B.C.E.; it is relatively assured at least in comparison with narratives, whose dates of origin are far less certain. The chapter then follows the canonical order, from Genesis to Exodus to Numbers and Deuteronomy. The book of Daniel is included last for two reasons. It offers, first, a resounding resumption of key dimensions of this chapter. It is, second, probably the latest text on the spirit in the Jewish Bible. Thus its resumptive quality is related to its late provenance during the Maccabean era. I should note as well that I have made very few judgments about the historicity of narratives. Frequently, for example, I open a section with a review of

Spirit and the Dreamer: Joseph

In Israel's collective memory, there were many grand figures who walked in the right, few more so than Joseph, who, it was believed, had the spirit of God in him. Joseph, once pitifully left for dead by his jealous brothers, later jailed on the trumped-up charge of Potiphar's wife, whose seductive on-slaughts Joseph had persistently spurned, rose to prominence by dint of his clairvoyant wisdom. Joseph knew enough to acknowledge that his wisdom, his ability to retell dreams, to interpret them, and to develop pragmatic solutions in response to them, lay with God. The realization that lean and fat cows represented seven years of plenty followed by seven of drought, the plan to store away tons of grain during the first period against the dire hunger of the second period — all of this, Joseph knew, belonged to God's province: "It is not I; God will give Pharaoh a favorable answer" (Gen 41:16).

Pharaoh would say much the same about this scheme in a slightly different way, by asking, "Can we find anyone else like this — one in whom is (the) spirit of God?" (41:38).[15] He then nimbly proceeds to answer his own question: "Since God is making known all of this to you, there is no one discerning and wise like you" (41:39). There is a clear connection between question and answer. Pharaoh asks if anyone can be found *"like this* one — one in whom is (the) spirit of God," and answers that "there is no one discerning and wise *like you."* Not only do both question and answer underscore Joseph's distinctiveness; they do so by drawing an association between spirit of God in him and discernment and wisdom.

How ought the presence of the spirit to be interpreted in such a context? The only other reference to the spirit of God in Genesis affords the most salient indication of its meaning: "My spirit shall not remain *in adam* forever, because he is flesh, but the days shall be a hundred and twenty years" (Gen 6:3). While we have already paused over this text, it gains renewed significance as a key to understanding Gen 41:38. At issue in Gen 6:3 is nothing other than the length of an entire life span. Though the language is different, the scenario is much the same in the ensuing narrative,

---

the story as it stands in the Jewish Bible. I trust my readers will recognize that to enter into a debate about historicity would be a distraction. I have not even raised historical questions vis-à-vis such figures as Bezalel and Daniel. Once again, I trust my readers will acknowledge the judiciousness of this move. How ever could we verify statements about "spirit" in the lives of ancient figures?

15. Hebrew: *hănimṣāʾ kāzeh ʾîš ʾăšer rûaḥ ʾĕlōhîm bô.*

in which God destroys nearly all of those who have "spirit of life" (6:17; 7:15) or "the breath of the spirit of life" (7:22).

If we set aside a false dichotomy between the spirit as physical life-force and the spirit as a temporary endowment, we are able to grasp the gist of Gen 41:38. Pharaoh attributes Joseph's ability to interpret dreams to the divine character of the spirit within him — not the divine spirit that has come upon him. This is not an endowment akin to early Christian belief in charismatic gifts, but to the spirit that resides within Joseph, the spirit which can be acknowledged even by a foreigner as divine in character.[16]

The reliability of this interpretation deepens when we note how the remarkable, even divine quality of Joseph's spirit is set in this story in distinctive contrast to Pharaoh's. Following his dream, Pharaoh awoke, and "his spirit was troubled" (41:8). His experience mirrors that of the distressed psalmist, whose spirit faints and who is "so troubled" as to be unable to speak.[17] Pharaoh's troubled spirit provides an apposite backdrop for Joseph's spirit. Because Pharaoh's spirit was troubled and his advisors impotent in the face of his dream, it fell to Joseph, whom Pharaoh would identify as "one in whom is (the) spirit of God," to interpret his dream and to hatch a plot to rescue Egypt from famine.

This contrast between the spirits of Pharaoh and Joseph is consistent

---

16. Montague, *The Holy Spirit*, 13, simply assumes that this refers to a special, secondary endowment. We might also add other references in Genesis, such as Isaac and Rebekah's bitterness of spirit, which is brought about by Esau and his wives (26:34-35), or the revival of Jacob's spirit when he recognizes the telltale signs of Joseph's hand in his family's survival of famine (45:27). While these are common enough idioms in the Hebrew Bible, neither is merely physical, purely life-breath; both texts reflect a belief that the spirit is the home of emotions and qualities.

17. "In the day of my trouble I seek the Lord;
   in the night my hand is stretched out without wearying;
   my soul refuses to be comforted.
   I think of God, and I moan;
   I meditate, and *my spirit faints*.
   You keep my eyelids from closing;
   I am so troubled that I cannot speak.
   I consider the days of old, and remember the years of long ago.
   I commune with my heart in the night;
   I meditate and search my spirit:
   'Will the Lord spurn forever,
   and never again be favorable?
   Has his steadfast love ceased forever?
   Are his promises at an end for all time?'" (Ps 77:2-8[MT 3-9])

with Gen 6:3, in which the spirit of God ("my spirit") is the source of life for a limited time. In the narrative of Joseph, this spirit of God in Joseph evinces those peculiar abilities that allow Pharaoh to identify Joseph's spirit as supremely divine. Understood as a transitory gift, however, this spirit would be an aberration that chafes both against the principal other text in this book, Gen 6:3, in which (the) spirit of God gives life for limited years, and the contrast that is drawn between Pharaoh's troubled spirit and Joseph's divine one. What Pharaoh recognized in Joseph was not a temporary infilling but a spirit of supremely divine character which evinced the sort of qualities that would equip Joseph for leadership on a permanent basis. The spirit of God within Joseph was the source of wisdom and discernment that would, from Pharaoh's perspective, qualify him in the long term to function as second-in-command.

Nothing in the unravelling narrative of Joseph undermines this interpretation of the spirit of God. No hint of an extraordinary, ephemeral experience accompanies his clairvoyant knowledge of dreams. Dream interpretations, on the contrary, are described in formulaic and pedestrian language: interpretations belong to God (40:8); God will give a favorable answer (41:16); Joseph remembered his dreams when his brothers approached him (42:9). Joseph's success, furthermore, is not attributed to extraordinary moments but to the fundamental reality that God accompanied and prospered him: Potiphar saw that God was with Joseph and that God prospered Joseph (39:3); God was with Joseph, loved him, gave him favor in the eyes of the chief jailer, and prospered him (39:21, 23); God sent Joseph ahead of his brothers (45:4-8). Most pointedly, his ability to interpret dreams is practiced. His own dream (Gen 37:5-11) is followed later by the dreams of the cupbearer and butler (40:1-23), which he correctly interprets, and only then by Pharaoh's dream about the seven fat and lean cows (41:1-36). In other words, Joseph has experience in the art of dream interpretation.

Nor is Joseph's ability to scheme for the salvation of Egypt or the manipulation of his brothers attributed to an influx of the spirit. He appends to Pharaoh's dream pointed instruction that goes well beyond dream interpretation: Pharaoh should set aside a fifth of the grain during the good years, etcetera. This sort of advice is also the product of experience. Joseph had served so well over both Potiphar's house and the prison that neither Potiphar nor the chief jailer was compelled to pay the least attention to what lay under Joseph's care (39:6; 39:23). Therefore, by the time Pharaoh identifies Joseph as one in whom is (the) spirit of God [the gods], Joseph has shown himself to have been, years earlier, practiced in both dream interpretation and administration. It is this combination of dream interpretation and sage advice that prompts Pharaoh to ask whether there is anyone else like him, one in whom is (the) spirit of God [the gods].

In other words, there is not the slightest indication in the narrative of Joseph to suggest that Joseph's ability to interpret dreams, his rise to power, or his capacity for plotting and planning is due to moments of inspiration. His is, rather, a life lived well, wisdom articulated well, discernment executed well. It is these characteristics, which re-emerge in the course of this narrative, that prompt Pharaoh to ask, "Can we find anyone else like this — one in whom is (the) spirit of God?" (41:38), and then to answer his own question, "Since God is making known all of this to you, there is no one discerning and wise like you" (41:39).

Spirit and Generosity: Bezalel

If the ascension of Joseph to the Egyptian circles of power represents the zenith of the life of Israel's ancestors, it was a short-lived one. A surge in Egyptian nationalism and consequent rejection of foreign influences would yield, according to Israel's corporate memory, centuries of slavery. The moment for liberation would occur when Jewish midwives courageously and creatively rescued the sons of Israel whose assassination Pharaoh had demanded. Moses' own mother would be no less creative in her maladjustment toward Egyptian oppression: she obeyed the Pharaoh scrupulously by throwing her baby into the Nile, though not until she had set him in a watertight basket. With no less cunning, Moses' sister Miriam offered her own mother as a wet-nurse to Pharaoh's daughter.

The subsequent decades, according to the baldly critical biblical narratives, were a period of far less imagination. Moses would lead the creative rabble into the wilderness, where they spurned his leadership and, in a crisis of epic proportions, melted symbols of their own gods from the jewelry they had taken with them from Egypt (Exodus 32). Worst yet, they would melt this jewelry into golden calves while waiting for Moses to descend with the fabled tablets, the ten words. Curiously bracketing, more or less, this horrendous tale of impatience and rebellion emerge meticulous instructions on how the tent of presence, the tabernacle, should be prepared (Exod 25:1–31:11 and 35:4-33). The tent of presence would offer unsurpassed stability in the midst of transition, a symbol of steadiness among an impatient people. The story of its construction, furthermore, would offer examples of unsurpassed munificence and extraordinary technical skill. This is no mandatory assignment, no required task. The tent of presence will not be the product of divine compulsion but of human desire: "The Lord said to Moses: Tell the Israelites to take for me an offering; from all whose hearts prompt them to give you shall receive the offering for me" (25:1-2). From the gold, silver, linens and leathers, woods, oils, gems, and yarns, Israel will make for God "a sanctuary, so that I may dwell among them" (25:8).

If this magisterial endeavor begins with God's request for an offering from those who are willing, whose hearts prompt them, it ends with an even more decisive divine decree, though an astonishing one. The freewill offerings which Moses and his artisans collect, under the able leadership of Bezalel and Oholiab, prove so beneficent as to overflow the boundaries of what is needed to complete the tent of presence. Moses is forced by this outpouring of generosity to offer this command: "No man or woman is to make anything else as an offering for the sanctuary" (36:6). There is no begging and pleading for more; there is, simply put, too much beneficence.

Although this characteristic of the story may be overshadowed by what seems to be a dreary inventory of provisions and physical dimensions, it is this degree of detail that drives home the level of Israelite generosity which rose at the foot of Mount Sinai. All of what was made, constructed, woven, sewn, and overlaid came from the freewill offering of those whose hearts prompted them. This was a moment when the coffers were full, a protracted instance of sumptuous giving, and it is no surprise that the lavish language of filling with spirit should occur here, for the first time in the Jewish canon.

Exodus 28:1-3

When it comes time to prepare the vestments for Aaron and the priesthood, Moses is told, "And you shall speak to all the *wise of heart* [*kol-ḥakmê-lēb*] whom *I have filled with spirit of wisdom* [*millē'tîw rûaḥ ḥokmâ*], and they will make Aaron's vestments . . ." (28:3; my translation).[18] Here the mass of generous Israelites whose contribution is to give an offer-

18. Because the translations in Exodus 28–36 are idiomatic, I will typically offer my own to reflect the Hebrew phrases.

ing is narrowed to artisans, skilled workers who are distinct from the whole.

What does such filling entail? Are we to imagine a temporary communal experience that equipped the people to create Aaron's vestments? This is improbable. First of all, Moses is instructed to speak only to some of the Israelites, to those who *already* have the ability to make the sacred vestments. These skilled laborers are not identified so that they may receive an influx of skill but because they have already developed and demonstrated their skill.

Throughout this story, in fact, the phrase "wise of heart" refers simply to skilled laborers in contrast to unskilled laborers, as in Exod 36:8: "All the 'wise of heart' [skilled laborers] among the workers [unskilled laborers] made the tabernacle. . . ."[19] This is a description of the sort of skill and leadership that distinguishes the few from the many, those with special skills from those who undertake manual labor.

What does it mean, then, that these artisans are depicted as those "whom God filled with spirit of wisdom"? Translators have certainly not been keen to discern in these words infilling by the spirit of God, and in avoiding such language they have probably understood the gist of this description correctly. TNIV translates: "Tell all the *skilled workers* to whom *I have given wisdom* in such matters that they are to make garments for Aaron, for his consecration, so he may serve me as priest." The NRSV reads similarly: "And you shall speak to *all who have ability,* whom *I have endowed with skill,* that they make Aaron's vestments to consecrate him for my priesthood." The gift of wisdom is rendered vaguely; neither translation even mentions the spirit.

By ignoring the language of filling, both translations fail to communicate the lavishness of this scene. The ingredients of priestly garments are listed profusely, as are, in extensive detail, the ephod, the breastplate, other priestly garments such as tunics and sashes, and even the ordination of the priests. The scene is splashed with hues of gold, blue, purple, and crimson — vivid colors woven together. In such a luxuriant scene, it is no less appropriate that the artisans who produce such splendid garments should be depicted in lavish terms as "the wise of heart whom I filled with spirit of wisdom." They are filled with (a) spirit of wisdom, wholehearted, full to the brim with wisdom.

19. Hebrew: *wayyaʿăśû kol-ḥăkam-lēb bĕʿōśî hammělāʾkâ ʾet-hammiškān.* See also Exod 35:10; 36:1; Job 9:4; Prov 10:8.

The interpretation of the spirit within as an abundant reservoir of skill and knowledge is supported as well by the taut correspondence — probably synonymy — between heart and spirit.[20] Both heart and spirit, taken in tandem, are core characteristics of human beings; to say that they are wise of heart is tantamount to saying that they are filled with spirit of wisdom.[21] We might, in fact, put it this way: they were characterized by "a

20. Along a slightly different vein runs the idea that the spirit within is the locus of human character. The spirit within is not merely a physical reality but, like the human heart, "das 'Innere' des Menschen, sein geistiges Zentrum, von dem aus die ganze 'Person' engagiert ist" ("the 'inner' part of a person, his spiritual center, from which the whole person takes part"; *THAT* 7:396). Therefore, "nicht wenige und nicht nur späte Stellen [in the Hebrew Bible] sind aber zu finden, in denen *rûaḥ*. mit 'Herz' gleichbedeutend steht . . . und der weit häufigere Gebrauch des Wortes par. zu *lēb* zur Bezeichnung von Fähigkeiten, moralischen Tugenden, willens- und gefühlsmässigen Dispositionen ist davon nicht wesentlich unterschieden" ("not a few and not only late references [in the Hebrew Bible] are to be found, in which *rûaḥ* is synonymous with 'heart' . . . and the far more frequent use of the word par. to *lēb* as a designation for capacities, moral virtues, temperate dispositions of will and emotion, is not to be distinguished from it"; *THAT* 7:398). The psalmist knows that God will accept a broken spirit, a broken and contrite heart (Ps 51:17[MT 19]). An exilic or postexilic prophet in the line of Isaiah knows that the God who inhabits eternity, who dwells in the high and holy place, dwells "also with those who are contrite and humble in spirit, to revive the spirit of the humble, and to revive the heart of the contrite" (Isa 57:15). The spirit is the locus of both error and instruction, according to Isaiah. God will look on God's children, "the work of my hands," knowing that these children will sanctify God, "and those who err in spirit will come to understanding, and those who grumble will accept instruction" (Isa 29:23-24).

21. The correlation between a spirit and heart of wisdom that characterizes those who make Aaron's garments rises frequently to the surface throughout the story of the construction of the tent of presence. Of particular significance is that all of the people are said to be *prompted* to give generously to the construction of the tent — their spinning, their growing of spices, and their crafting of clasps and coverings, linen and oils. Typically it is the *hearts* of the people that are prompted. Prior to the golden calf experience, the Israelites were asked to make an offering "from all whose hearts prompt them to give" (Exod 25:2). Following the debacle of the golden calf, "whoever is willing [prompted] of heart" (35:5), "all who were willing [prompted] of heart" (35:22), are requested to bring an offering. Women are especially responsive in this narrative; they bring their lovely blue and purple and crimson yarns and fine linens. These women are depicted in familiar terms as "wise of heart," as those "whose heart lifted them with wisdom" (35:25-26). It is in this context of generosity that the narrative contains as well a corresponding reference to the spirit of the people:

> And they came, everyone whose heart lifted them
>   [*wayyāb'û kol-'îš 'ăšer-nĕśā'ô libbô*],
>   everyone whose spirit prompted [*wĕkōl 'ăšer nādĕbâ rûḥô 'ōtô*],

54

heart of wisdom" and a "spirit of wisdom," or, to turn it around, they were "wise of heart" and "wise of spirit." Once again, we need to recall that the spirit within could be understood as that core reality, that vitality, that presence of God within which required no further impartation of spirit. Furthermore, this was not a human spirit, a mere physical reality or life-principle that could be contrasted with "the actual Spirit of God." That is a false dichotomy. Israelite authors were capable rather of grasping that the spirit within was very much like the heart: the locus of wisdom or holiness or exceptional knowledge.

As if this combination of heart and spirit were not enough, as if to re-inforce the measure of this wisdom, the verb "filled" appears: their wisdom was not theirs in short measure. Their lavish wisdom would match the generosity of the people, who would provide for them lavish gifts. The artisans were not partly prepared for the task ahead; they were not slightly skilled in weaving and stonework. They were *filled* with spirit of wisdom, unquestionably able to do what would be demanded of them. Israel's artisans were precisely this: artisans who in the past had developed their skills and who now, in this pivotal moment in Israel's history, were fully prepared to exercise these skills in the extraordinary task of making Aaron's priestly vestments and constructing the tent of presence.

The depth of this lavishness is resonant in the single verb, "to fill" *(ml')*, which recurs in this story of lavish giving to describe the spirit's presence within the artisans and leaders who devoted themselves to the design and construction of the tent of presence. At first blush, this verb, used with a direct object such as "spirit," appears to point to an initial filling: a skin is filled with water (Gen 21:19), a horn with oil (1 Sam 16:1), houses with corpses (Jer 33:5), a bag with grain (Gen 42:25), and a cistern with the slain (Jer 41:9).

Notwithstanding this impression, the verb *ml'* draws us away from the notion of an endowment with the spirit. Such a charismatic endowment could have been communicated by a variety of other verbs. Elsewhere the

---

and brought the Lord's offering to be used for the tent of meeting, and for all its service, and for the sacred vestments. (Exod 35:21)

Spirit and heart in this description are synonymous. Both represent that inner core which can be characterized by generosity and moved to action by being prompted or lifted. Both represent the learned skill and acquired knowledge that are voluntarily donated to the construction of the tent of presence — the "wise of heart" who have been filled with "spirit of wisdom" are among those whose hearts are lifted and whose spirits are prompted to contribute their skills to the making of the tent of meeting, its service, and the sacred vestments.

spirit is "put upon" people (Num 11:29), "comes upon" them (e.g., Num 24:2; Judg 3:10; 1 Sam 10:6; 16:13), "clothes" them (Judg 6:34), "rests upon" them (Isa 11:2), and is "put within" them (1 Kgs 19:7). All of these verbs vibrate with the pulse of charisma, with a gift that yields an extraordinary result.

The verb *ml'* takes the reader in another direction, away from initial filling, and toward fullness or completeness or topping up — that is, toward lavishness and richness, toward a reality that is more than enough, as in this remarkable story in the wilderness, when Israel gives too much to God rather than too little, when the artisans are wholly focused, wholeheartedly devoted to the task at hand, when Israel's leaders are capable of bringing the project to fruition, of fulfilling — filling full — their vocation. They are filled with all that it will take to design and to construct a tent for God's presence in a desert that otherwise is apparently empty, void of God.

This verb's sense of full-filling is especially apparent in temporal contexts, when periods of time must be completed or fulfilled. Jacob's wait for Rachel was over — "filled" (Gen 29:21). A period of purification could be completed — "filled" (Lev 12:4, 6). A pregnancy could come to term — "be filled" (Gen 25:24). A vow could be "fulfilled" (Num 6:5). Sieges could come to an end — "be filled" (Esth 1:5). Babylonian exile would eventually be over — *be filled* (Jer 25:12). All of these sorts of completion are depicted by the verb *ml'*, which functions synonymously with the verb *tmm*, to indicate completeness, fullness, or an end (Lev 25:29-30). The same sense of completion attends the verb *ml'* when the fulfillment of words, and not just periods of time, is at stake. God's own hand or power fills — brings to fruition — what has been promised by God's mouth (e.g., 1 Kgs 8:15; 2 Chr 6:4). People, too, are capable of filling promises (Jer 44:25).

This verb, which takes us to the experience of completion, of full-filling, also appears in spatial contexts. God is able to fill the tent of meeting (Exod 40:34), the earthly temple (1 Kgs 8:10), and the heavenly temple (Isa 6:1). These mysterious depictions of God's presence do not fixate upon the moment at which God filled these loci but upon the reality that God's presence is *fully* in them. When Jeremiah contends that the glory of God fills the earth (Jer 23:24), the prophet is underwriting the ubiquity of God, the inescapability of the divine everywhere in the creation, just as Habakkuk contends that the knowledge of the glory of the Lord fills the earth (Hab 2:14). This is very much the case with respect to the glory of God, or the cloud, which fills the temple (1 Kgs 8:11; Ezek 43:5). When

Ezekiel remembers, "I looked, and lo! the glory of the Lord filled the temple of the Lord; and I fell upon my face" (Ezek 44:4), he is not describing the initial endowment of the glory, the entry of God's glory into the temple, but the reality that not a corner of the temple was void of God's presence, empty of God's glory.[22]

The related noun, "fullness," points with no less clarity to the notion of just what it says — fullness — rather than to the initial point of filling. A very large number of nations is a "fullness of nations" (Gen 48:19). A whole band of shepherds is, literally, "fullness of shepherds" (Isa 31:4). It expresses most often the whole earth in its abundance (e.g., Deut 33:16; Ps 24:1). Though this may seem an obvious point, the word communicates the fullness with which something is filled, in distinction from the beginning of the process of filling or even a partial filling. It is used to refer to a handful (Eccl 4:6), an omerful (Exod 16:32), a houseful (Num 22:18), a bowlful (Judg 6:38), even a lapful (2 Kgs 4:49).

By the same token, the simple phrase "whom I have filled with spirit of wisdom" means something more than might be suggested by similar phrases which suggest initial endowment, such as "upon whom I have caused the spirit to come" or "into whom I have given my spirit." Filling suggests something more than entry, something other than endowment. Filling connotes completion, full-filling, fruition, wholeness, fullness. When it is predicted that Egyptian houses will be filled with swarms of flies, more than a few flies buzzing about can be expected (Exod 8:17 MT). When God's train fills the temple, in Isaiah's grand vision, this train does more than occupy a narrow slice of the inner sanctum (Isa 6:1). When Jeremiah protests that the land is filled with idols, it is not because he is troubled by the occasional idol that dots Judah's hillsides (Jer 16:18). When the Jordan is said to fill all its banks during the time of harvest, what is meant is that it overflows those banks, filling them — flooding them — beyond the brink (Josh 3:15).

One of the best examples apropos of the filling of the artisans and their leaders is Exod 40:35, which describes the filling of the tent of presence with God's glory: "Moses was not able to enter the tent of meeting because the cloud settled upon it, and the glory of the Lord filled the taber-

---

22. There is no appreciable difference, as far as I can tell, between the *qal, niphal,* and *piel* stems of this verb. The *piel,* which is the stem that occurs in the texts from Exodus with respect to the spirit, ranges in meaning from a simple filling, such as filling a cup with drink (Isa 65:11), to accomplishing or completing something (e.g., Gen 29:27-28; Exod 23:26; Isa 65:20; Job 39:2; 2 Chr 36:21).

nacle." The glory is here so palpable and dense — it has *filled* the tabernacle — that Moses cannot even enter the tent of presence. Even if the syntax were tweaked to bring it into conformity with the statements about the spirit, so that it read "the Lord filled the tabernacle with glory," the emphasis of this description would lie less upon an initial filling than upon the exquisite density of the glory's presence, which had so filled the tent that Moses could not even enter.

From the perspective of this simple verb *ml'*, then, the artisans responsible for the temple, and their leaders, Bezalel and Oholiab, are full to the brim with spirit of wisdom. When God says, "whom I have *filled* with spirit of wisdom," the emphasis lies upon the lavishness of this filling much more than upon the initial gift of this spirit. When, in fact, God filled these people is left entirely out of the picture. What lies at the center of this depiction in a hale and hearty way is the conviction that there is more than enough spirit within these gifted laborers to accomplish the task, to complete it perfectly. They are not partially prepared or moderately well-equipped. God calls them to work because they are *filled* with spirit of wisdom so that they can *ful-fill* the extraordinary task ahead of them.[23]

Exodus 31:1-6; 36:1-2; 35:30-35

If the ingredients that were offered by common Israelites are depicted lavishly, if the skills brought by the artisans are described even more profusely, then there can be little wonder that Bezalel and Oholiab, who are designated as leaders in this astonishing endeavor, are portrayed in the most lavish terms of all. Toward the end of the story, this is less so, when Bezalel and Oholiab are included as first among equals in the coterie of artisans, the wise of heart:

> Bezalel and Oholiab and everyone wise of heart to whom the Lord has given wisdom and understanding to know how to do every craft in the

---

23. In addition to my own concordance-based research and Gesenius's lexicon, two resources have provided useful thumbnail sketches in their entries on this verb and its cognates: *Theological Dictionary of the Old Testament,* ed. G. J. Botterweck, H. Ringgren, and H. J. Fabry (Grand Rapids: Wm. B. Eerdmans, 1990) 8:297-308; *New International Dictionary of Old Testament Theology and Ethics,* ed. W. A. VanGemeren (Grand Rapids: Zondervan, 1997) 2:939-41.

construction of the sanctuary shall work in accordance with all that the Lord has commanded. Moses then called Bezalel and Oholiab and every one wise of heart to whom the Lord had given wisdom in his heart, everyone whose heart was stirred to come to do the work. . . . (Exod 36:1-2)

Earlier in the story, however, their stature is unparalleled:

The Lord spoke to Moses: See, I have called by name Bezalel son of Uri son of Hur, of the tribe of Judah: and I have filled him with spirit of God, with wisdom, intelligence, and knowledge in every kind of craft, to devise artistic designs, to work in gold, silver, and bronze, in cutting stones for setting, and in carving wood, in every kind of craft. Moreover, I have appointed with him Oholiab son of Ahisamach, of the tribe of Dan; and I have given wisdom in the heart of all the wise of heart, so that they may make all that I have commanded you. . . . (Exod 31:1-6)

It is not difficult to understand why so many twentieth-century interpreters understand the filling of Bezalel in this second text as the product of an endowment given to Bezalel in order to accomplish an astonishing task. Charged with leading in the planning and construction of the tent of presence, Bezalel must be given a fresh infilling of the divine spirit to perform this significant and central task in Israel's fledgling life.[24]

---

24. So J. D. G. Dunn, *The Theology of Paul the Apostle* (Grand Rapids: Wm. B. Eerdmans, 1998) 648 n. 111, who includes it alongside later wisdom texts; G. Fee, *God's Empowering Presence* (Peabody: Hendrickson, 1994) 835; M. Turner, *The Holy Spirit and Spiritual Gifts in the New Testament Church and Today* (Peabody: Hendrickson, 1998) 4; M. Welker, *God the Spirit* (Minneapolis: Fortress, 1994) 102-4, who contrasts this, interestingly, with human spirits in Exod 35:21 (the prompting of spirits), though he acknowledges some of the difficulties inherent in such a dichotomy. Among the dictionary entries we have perused, Gerlemann (*RGG*, 3rd ed., 2:1271) writes, "Die Weisheit wird als eine charismatische Begnadigung verstanden" ("Wisdom is understood as a charismatic blessing"). Lampe (*IDB* 2:628) includes it in a discussion intended to demonstrate that the Spirit was also the source of intellectual and spiritual gifts, and not merely ecstatic phenomena. Horn does not discuss this passage. Although many twentieth-century interpreters have situated Bezalel and Oholiab in a long line of inspired figures endowed with the spirit, not all interpreters have done so. H. B. Swete, in his entry on the holy spirit in J. Hastings's *A Dictionary of the Bible,* published in 1899 (Edinburgh: T. & T. Clark) — no doubt before Gunkel's *Büchlein* exercised much influence in the English-speaking world — set this text in a subsection entitled "Bestowal of intellectual gifts," which begins with the inbreathing of Gen 2:7. This inbreathing, writes Swete (2:403) "represents the Breath of God as originating the personal life of man, together with the intellectual and spiritual powers which distinguish it from the life of the mere animal." He continues, "The Divine Spirit is said to be 'in' (Gn

Bezalel resurfaces, however, in a reprisal of this story that occurs in the context of Israel's extraordinary generosity, of the lifting of their hearts and prompting of their spirits:[25]

> Then Moses said to the Israelites: See, the Lord has called by name Bezalel son of Uri son of Hur, of the tribe of Judah; he has filled him with spirit of God, with wisdom, intelligence, and knowledge in every kind of craft, to devise artistic designs, to work in gold, silver, and bronze, in cutting stones for setting, and in carving wood, in every kind of craft. And he put into his heart to teach, both him and Oholiab son of Ahisamach, of the tribe of Dan. He has filled them with wisdom of heart to do every kind of work done by an artisan or by a designer or by an embroiderer in blue, purple, and crimson yarns, and in fine linen, or by a weaver — by any sort of artisan or skilled designer. (Exod 35:30-35)

In this continuation — virtually a recapitulation — of Exod 28:3 and 31:3, the correspondence between the spirit and heart is even more lucid.

28:3:   speak to all the *wise of heart* whom *I have filled with spirit of wisdom*

31:1:   and *I have filled him with spirit of God,* with wisdom, intelligence, and knowledge in every kind of craft

31:6:   and *I have given wisdom in the heart of all the wise of heart* so that they may make all that I have commanded you

35:31:   [*God*] *has filled him* [Bezalel] *with spirit of God, with wisdom . . . for every craft*

35:35:   [*God*] *filled them* [Bezalel and Oholiab] *with wisdom of heart . . . to do every craft*

41:38; Nu 27:18) or 'upon' (Nu 11:17f.; 24:2) the man who possesses exceptional powers of any kind; he is what he is, because he is filled with the spirit of wisdom of understanding." Swete cites in this regard Exod 28:3; 31:3; 35:31, and Deut 34:9. By connecting these texts to divine inbreathing, Swete has drawn a salient association. Rather than distinguishing the spirit that is resident in human beings by dint of inbreathing from the allegedly charismatic spirit of God, Swete places both on a single spectrum of inspiration. This, in my opinion, is an apt interpretation of the conception of the spirit in Exod 28:3; 31:3; and 35:35.

25. This is a literary doublet.

The correspondence between spirit and heart which characterized the description of artisans in Exod 28:3 recurs in both Exodus 31 and 35 with increasing precision and unavoidable clarity.[26] The narrative logic of the lucid parallel between heart and spirit in each of these passages is telling. In all three cases, there is a crescendo of wisdom in the heart.

28:3:   Artisans are *wise of heart*. This phrase identifies select skilled leaders in contrast to Israel en masse.

31:6:   God "has given wisdom in the heart of all the wise of heart." This picks up on the phrase "wise of heart" from 28:3. Only artisans are in view. To these God has *given* wisdom in the heart. It is not clear whether God has given wisdom in the past or now, on the cusp of constructing the tent of presence.

35:35:   The word *given* is replaced by *filled*, when Bezalel and Oholiab are in view. They, like the artisans, have wisdom of heart, though to an even fuller measure, so that they can lead construction in every craft.

In each of these instances, the narrator clearly understands that the locus of wisdom, or skill, is the heart. Artisans are the "wise of heart" to whom God gives "wisdom in the heart"; the hearts of the artisans' leaders God fills with wisdom in the heart. God's filling of Bezalel (and Oholiab) "with wisdom of heart" does not mean that he received a fresh influx of heart or a new heart altogether. These words do mean that his heart was richly imbued with wisdom, with skills that enabled him to lead in every craft.

---

26. In Exod 31:3, Bezalel's filling with spirit of God, with wisdom, intelligence, and knowledge, is similar to God's filling the artisans, the "wise of heart," with spirit of wisdom (28:3). He, like they, is chosen because he is filled with the requisite skills to lead Israel. In Exod 31:6, the phrase "wise of heart" recalls exactly the involvement of artisans, reminding us that this accomplishment will incorporate many leaders in many spheres of skill. What the third and fourth descriptions, in Exod 35:31 and 35:35, accomplish is to fold both images together: filling with the spirit and the phrase "wisdom of heart" recollect still again the artisans in Exod 28:3. To what end? To communicate that Bezalel (and Oholiab), while leaders of the whole enterprise, are still themselves artisans — which is precisely what they are in the ensuing narrative, where they are set alongside the others: "Bezalel and Oholiab and every one *wise of heart* to whom the Lord has given *wisdom and understanding* to know how to do *every craft* in the construction of the sanctuary shall work in accordance with all that the Lord has commanded" (36:1).

The narrative symbiosis of heart and spirit suggests that "spirit" ought to be understood similarly, in which case the emphasis would lie here less upon an irruption of the spirit than upon an enhancement of spirit, which is too closely aligned with heart to be understood as a fresh endowment. There is no new heart, no new spirit, in this narrative. There is indeed something new here: at this point in Israel's history, spirits are, in an unparalleled way, full to the brim with skill, overflowing with competence. Taken alongside the corresponding image of wisdom-of-heart, God's filling Bezalel with "spirit of God, wisdom," does not mean that he received an entirely fresh influx of spirit, a rush of the spirit, or a new spirit altogether, though the language of filling may at first blush suggest something akin to this. The parallel between giving wisdom in the heart of the wise-of-heart, filling of the wise-of-heart with a spirit of wisdom, and filling Bezalel with spirit of God and wisdom, suggests that the most suitable interpretation is this: the spirit of God with which God had filled Bezalel and the artisans from the start, the spirit in them that was already the source of skill, was ever more richly enhanced with wisdom, insight, and intelligence at this salutary moment in Israel's history. In short, Bezalel and the skilled workers did not first receive the spirit and wisdom at this particular point in time. Their skill, their wisdom, increased to an extraordinary extent. As to when or where this occurred, the text is entirely vague, though we may know this: since they were artisans, their hearts were already wise, their spirits already knowledgeable, in which case this gift of wisdom would come to hearts and spirits that were already wise through acquired learning.[27]

If we turn our attention away from the notion of some sort of charismatic endowment, we are able to discern the gist of this narrative, which lies yet again in the surfeit of the spirit. A single reference to a heart filled with wisdom would have sufficed to communicate more economically that Bezalel and Oholiab were sufficiently skilled to lead Israel in the construction of the tent of presence. So too would have a single reference to the spirit. In tandem, however, they provide a narrative exclamation point that underscores the lavishness of Israel's leadership. Fullness — twice-over filling — aptly fits the atmosphere of this wonderful story, in which Israel,

---

27. It is conceivable that the language of filling indicates an increase in the measure of spirit within to the point of overflow. I think this is unlikely because the heart, which is so tautly paralleled with spirit in these texts, is a stable entity that does not increase. Both, however, increase in wisdom and skill.

unimpeded by schisms, unhindered by complaints, undistracted by Moses' delays, joins in unique harmony and supplies a supersaturated offering for a tent in which God will now dwell.

In a scene so populated with laborers who are themselves lavishly skilled, since they are the "wise of heart whom God filled with spirit of wisdom," what distinguishes Bezalel (and Oholiab)? Bezalel's fullness has to do with the range of his expertise. It is this breadth of skills, this array of abilities, that calls forth the language of being filled with "spirit of God, with ability, intelligence, and knowledge *in every kind of craft*." While the other artisans have no less mastery over specific tasks — they too are wise of heart and filled with spirit of wisdom — he, with his co-leader Oholiab, is skilled in every craft. If this were not apparent in the tidy parallel between the divine claims, "I filled him with spirit of God . . . for every craft" (Exod 35:31) and "I filled them with wisdom of heart . . . to do every craft" (35:35), then the narrator, with what appears to be a delighted exclamation point, offers an inventory of select skills: "He [God] has filled them [Bezalel and Oholiab] with wisdom of heart to do every kind of work done by an artisan or by a designer or by an embroiderer — by any sort of artisan or skilled designer" (35:35).

Although Bezalel may appear as a footnote — or not appear at all, as in Horn's entry in the *Anchor Bible Dictionary* — in studies of the holy spirit, his few appearances are rather more like epiphanies in our effort to re-evaluate the ways in which Israel understood what it meant to be filled with the spirit. He was, first of all, considered to be one of Israel's artisans and, as such, was chosen because he was already wise of heart, or skilled. Like the artisans, who "were filled with spirit of wisdom," he "was filled with spirit of God, wisdom."

The language of filling, second, is not an indication of an irruption of the divine spirit. Rather, the taut parallel that exists between filling the heart with wisdom and filling with spirit of God indicates that there is no new reception of the spirit. Just as there is no gift of a new heart, there is no gift of the spirit here.

Third, the language of filling occurs twice to underscore that Bezalel and Oholiab had every skill that would be required to construct the tent of presence. While all artisans, including Bezalel, had acquired the skill, the "wisdom of heart" that would enable them to lead manual laborers in the grand endeavor that lay before them, he and Oholiab alone possessed abilities that were wider still, and so the language of filling is adopted twice over, set alongside the nouns "wisdom, insight, and understanding," to suggest a remarkable level of munificence and competence. This impression of fullness, of fulsomeness, is even expanded with an inventory of arenas in which he and Oholiab were capable of leadership.

Finally, the language of filling reflects the atmosphere of lavishness that permeates this magnificent drama. The hearts of the people at large are repeatedly prompted to unimaginable generosity. The artisans, for their part, exhibit tremendous skill; they are "the wise of heart whom God filled with spirit of wisdom." And their skilled leaders? They too were people of extraordinary skill, who could be identified as those with hearts filled with wisdom, as those who were filled with spirit of God, wisdom, intelligence, and knowledge. These were artisans to the nth degree, who were skilled in every craft. These were full to the brim with expertise, which now, in short measure, would overflow in a moment that provided Israel with one of its most magnificent memories of communal largesse.

Exodus 35:34

I have adopted the word "lavish" to characterize the narrative of the tent of presence. I might have said that it is "wholehearted." If in the debauchery of the golden calf Israel flings itself full-fledged into a massive failure of will, in this story Israel finds wholehearted success. If Israel tosses its trinkets into the tub while Moses lingers on the mountain, here they bring so much that Moses is compelled to make them stop: "So Moses gave command, and word was proclaimed throughout the camp: 'No man or woman is to make anything else as an offering for the sanctuary.' So the people were restrained from bringing" (Exod 36:6). If, therefore, the word "heart" occurs so many times in this story, it is not without reason. Israel shows no half-hearted devotion to God; theirs is wholehearted. If their leaders come to the task, they do so full of spirit, of skill, of wisdom, of understanding, of insight.

In the context of this communal splendor — a glorious blip in Israel's memory of a particularly unfaithful period in the wilderness — Moses delegates leadership to Bezalel and Oholiab. The question of course is, What uniquely do they accomplish with this leadership, with their acquired knowledge, with the spirit of God, wisdom, knowledge, and understanding that fill them? There is one inconspicuous line in this story that offers simple insight into their leadership: "And he gave in his heart to teach, both him and Oholiab son of Ahisamach, of the tribe of Dan" (Exod

35:34).[28] This is, frankly, a lovely image of their role. Here are two remarkably skilled craftspeople in Israel who have before them a task of monumental proportions: to build a mobile tent in the wilderness to absorb God's presence. Their role is not to take over and dominate the project. Nor is it to spend most of their time in the trenches. Their vocation is to impart to others the skills that they have mastered. For all of the vaunted language that coalesces around them in this story, what Bezalel and Oholiab are to do, quite simply, is to teach.

This inconspicuous line may also suggest a good deal about how the artisans were "filled with spirit of wisdom," how God could claim, "I have given wisdom in the heart of all the wise of heart" (Exod 31:6). While the language of filling with spirit and giving of wisdom may evoke images of the direct, divine impartation of knowledge, this line suggests otherwise. Whom did Bezalel and Oholiab teach? The artisans, of course. The artisans were filled with spirit of wisdom, given wisdom in the heart, because they had capable teachers, who had insight into every craft.

Is this prompting to teach a temporary endowment destined to dissipate once the tent of presence becomes a reality? The text does not say. What we know is that this ability to teach is put into their heart, that core of their being which is also the font of the artisans' wisdom of heart and the locus of the prompting of common Israelites to give unfathomably. The ability these two leaders supremely possess, the skill they exercise as they build the tent of meeting, according to a sliver of Israel's memory, includes the gift of teaching a remarkable cadre of willing and skilled craftspeople. If there is something of note, then, it is a simple prompting to teach extraordinary skills to extraordinary workers in a period of extraordinary generosity to provide a nascent nation with an extraordinary mobile sanctuary.

Conclusion

If we recognize that the language of filling with spirit is joined at the hip with the language of the heart, then we can see that the language of filling

---

28. The NRSV translation, with the verb "inspire," is too evocative of a special endowment: "And he has inspired him to teach, both him and Oholiab son of Ahisamach, of the tribe of Dan." It is better to translate the Hebrew verb *nātan* as "gave," following the lead of the LXX (Greek *edōken*). God gave into his heart to teach.

is not about a particular experience at a particular moment with an eye toward a particular task. This verb, *ml'*, belongs, rather, to the vocabulary of surfeit. In this light, filling is actually about fullness, about *the expansiveness of the spirit within*. This, of course, is precisely what Elihu attempts to communicate to Job. He recognizes, first, that wisdom belongs to the province of the spirit within, of the influx of life that all humans receive: "it is the spirit in a mortal, the breath of the Almighty that makes for understanding" (Job 32:8). He understands, second, that spirit and heart are, if not synonymous, at least associated expressions of the inner reality. And, third, Elihu is full to bursting with heart and spirit. The spirit within lays siegeworks; the heart within is ready to burst. In brief, he is *full* of words. Filled with the spirit, heart about to burst, Elihu must give release to his breath and let the words roll over his tongue:

> For I am full of words;
>> the *spirit* within me besieges me.
> My *heart* is indeed like wine that has no vent;
>> like new wineskins, it is ready to burst.
> I must speak, so that I may find relief;
>> I must open my lips and answer. (Job 32:18-20)

Elihu communicates through dialogue what the narrative of the tent of presence communicates more obliquely: some people have within them a distinctive spirit in fullest measure. Filling is, in other words, an expression both of quality and measure, and in the story of the tent of meeting, as in Elihu's soliloquy, the emphasis lies upon both. Some Israelites are selected to make Aaron's vestments because they are wise of heart or, simply put, skilled. They are filled, in other words, with spirit of wisdom. Yet the spirit with which God filled them is also ample, full to the brim with wisdom, so that they are *completely prepared* to make Aaron's vestments. The scenario with respect to Bezalel is not at all dissimilar; the wording differs only slightly. What distinguishes Bezalel is that the spirit, as in the cases of Joseph and the artisans before him, exhibits qualities — wisdom, intelligence, and discernment — that mark it as God's. This is the sort of spirit within him that is full to the brim, qualifying him to lead the entire enterprise of the tent of presence.

It may require a measure of historical self-discipline to resist reading the words "filled with (the) spirit of God" as an endowment aimed at equipping Bezalel to construct the tent of meeting. It requires putting aside the influence of misleading bifurcations that arose through the mis-application of Hermann Gunkel's fresh thesis, as well as later Jewish refer-ences to filling with the spirit and the language of Pentecost (Acts 2:4). Nonetheless, several pivotal observations suggest that the emphasis of this narrative lies elsewhere. (1) The intimate association of heart and spirit, even with respect to the language of filling, confirms that the spirit is un-derstood as a core human characteristic. They are both the locus of wis-dom in this narrative. (2) Artisans, including Bezalel, are selected because they are already skilled, already filled with spirit of wisdom. (3) The lan-guage of filling, in a narrative preoccupied with voluntary munificence, is an indication of fullness of skill, expertise at the ready. The verb itself con-veys completeness, a presence of wholeness, and fullness. (4) The language of filling is also, in the cases of Bezalel and Oholiab, an indication of the vast range of their skills. Theirs is spirit of God in association, not only with wisdom, as in the case of the artisans, but also with understanding and knowledge, and their hearts are also said to be filled with wisdom. They are competent, therefore, in every craft. (5) Albeit obliquely, the spirit of God within is undramatically associated with the task of teaching; this, ultimately, is how Bezalel and Oholiab are prompted to communicate their wisdom, knowledge, and insight. (6) This brief reference to teaching sug-gests as well that the artisans acquired wisdom from their leaders rather than unmediated from God, without human intervention. (7) Finally, this language is lavish and speaks of God's generosity linked harmoniously to human generosity. Such moments are preserved only infrequently in Is-rael's memory, and it is perhaps propitious that leadership at such a grand moment rests in the hands of those who are identified single-mindedly as wise of heart and filled with spirit *of God,* with wisdom, with insight, with knowledge.

Spirit within Joshua

Far more prominent than Bezalel and Oholiab in the annals of Israel's rec-ollections is Moses' successor, Joshua son of Nun. Moses himself had changed Joshua's name from the generic "Salvation" to "Salvation of Yah." Moses had commissioned him to battle the Amalekites and stood on the hill in fervent and persistent prayer on his behalf. Moses had mentored his protégé by taking him with him to Sinai and the tent of meeting, and Mo-ses had been rewarded when Joshua stood in the gap between Moses and the people in one of the many mini-uprisings that plagued Moses' leadership of the fledgling Israelites. When Moses was about to die, it was only natural that Joshua would take on Moses' role. The authors of the books of Numbers and Deuteronomy concur that the succession took place by the laying of Moses' hand upon Joshua, though they differ decidedly on the relationship between the presence of the spirit and the laying of Moses' hand. In Numbers, Moses is to lay his hands upon Joshua because Joshua already has (the) spirit within him; in Deuteronomy, Joshua first receives (the) spirit of wisdom because Moses lays his hand upon him.

Numbers 27:18-23

The longer of the two accounts reads:

> Moses spoke to the Lord, saying, "Let the Lord, the God of the spirits of all flesh, appoint someone over the congregation who shall go out before them and come in before them, who shall lead them out and bring them in, so that the congregation of the Lord may not be like sheep without a shepherd." So the Lord said to Moses, "Take Joshua son of Nun, a man in whom is (the) spirit, and lay your hand upon him; have him stand before Eleazar the priest and all the congregation, and commission him in their sight." (Num 27:15-19)

Earlier in the book of Numbers, Korah has just led an unsuccessful uprising against Moses. God intends to destroy — "consume them in a moment" (16:21) — the entire Israelite congregation that has gathered with Korah at the tent of meeting. Moses and Aaron enter the breach, asking God not to destroy the entire congregation when only one person sins. To edge God in this direction, they pray, "O God, the God of the spirits of all flesh, shall one person sin and you become angry with the whole congregation?" (16:22). The implication? God knows the inner core, the life-giving impulse of each being that imparts to it the sort of individuality which defies summary executions. A God who knows the spirits of each and every living being cannot — *must* not — consume in a moment an entire congregation.

When the time comes to appoint a successor, Moses addresses God similarly as "the God of the spirits of all flesh." This request puts God on the spot, edging God toward a positive response to the request Moses is about to make. By addressing God in this fashion, Moses is suggesting that God alone knows the inner life, the core, the heart of all Israelites, and God alone is capable of selecting a successor to Moses. The sense is not unlike the scene in which God tells Samuel to stop grieving over Saul, for mortals "look on the outward appearance, but the Lord looks on the heart" (1 Sam 16:7).

Although Moses favors Joshua, who has been his faithful protégé for years, Moses, in a moment of peculiar humility, pries the door of his life's work open to God's selection. And the God of the spirits of all flesh knows the spirit of one person in particular. Joshua possesses the sort of spirit that makes him capable of becoming Moses' successor. Joshua is, literally, a "person who (the) spirit is in him." Here is a person of adequate vitality and skill and wisdom, who is equipped to undertake the unprecedented task of following in Moses' steps.

Once again, perhaps, we ought to remind ourselves of Israel's ability to prize the spirit within as the locus of wisdom, insight, and intelligence. Because of Joshua's abilities — the spirit in him — Moses lays his hand upon him to appoint him to lead Israel. There is no need to introduce an artificial bifurcation between the so-called "actual spirit of God" and a physical life-principle. In this instance, rather, the spirit must be understood to encompass both simultaneously.

This understanding of the spirit is borne out by the way in which it evokes the portrayal of another who was identified by Pharaoh as a person "in whom was (the) spirit of God" (Gen 41:38). Joseph, with acuity and foresight, had led the ancestors of Israel through dire famine into a verdant land of promise. Joshua, who is similarly identified as one "in whom is (the) spirit," will lead the descendants of Joseph's family into another fertile land. The parallel between Joseph and Joshua is inescapable: both have "spirit [of God] in them." Both have within them spirit rife with knowledge, foresight, and wisdom acquired through experience.[29]

---

29. This description recalls, on the other hand, the fascinating story of Moses and the elders (Numbers 11), in which an overwhelmed Moses begs God for help, to which God responds, "Gather for me seventy of the elders of Israel, whom you know to be the elders of the people and officers over them; bring them to the tent of meeting, and have them take their place there with you. I will come down and talk with you there; and I will take some of the spirit that is on you and put it on them; and they shall bear the burden of the people along with you so that you will not bear it all by yourself" (Num 11:16-17). Once the seventy elders were gathered, "the Lord came down in the cloud and spoke to him, and took some of the spirit that was on him and put it on the seventy elders; and when the spirit rested upon them, they prophesied. But they did not do so again" (11:25). Although the story of Moses and the elders is fraught with puzzlement, one lesson is clear: there is a distinctive difference

While Joshua may not receive a fresh endowment of the spirit, he does receive, along with the laying on of Moses' hand, a portion of Moses' magnificence, the sort of majesty that the psalmist consistently attributes to God and which was, later in Israel's history, apportioned to kings.[30] God commands Moses, "You shall give him some of your *majesty,* so that all the congregation of the Israelites may obey" (Num 27:20). He also receives his final marching orders, a last command, a commission: ". . . and he [Moses] laid his hands on him and commanded him . . ." (27:23). Joshua receives a great deal from Moses, including some of Moses' majesty and a final public command. What he does *not* receive is a fresh infilling of the holy spirit.

This scenario offers a glimpse into the intimacy of the relationship between Moses and God. Moses acknowledges that God alone knows the spirits of all flesh, that God alone can discern who has the sort of spirit that can bear the weight of prodding a recalcitrant community over the Jordan River to the challenges of a new land. With this address, Moses also acknowledges that his choice of Joshua may not have been the best, the most suitable for Israel's future. Still, God does confirm Moses' successor and passes on to Joshua, through the laying on of Moses' hand, the majesty that has accompanied Moses from the Nile to Mount Nebo through decades of desert debacles. Moses receives in his final hours another stamp of divine approval, as his protégé, whom Moses selected, renamed, prayed for, and accompanied, is now identified by God as the one whose spirit is up to the formidable task of leading Israel into the promised land.

Deuteronomy 34:9

The briefer account of Joshua's commissioning creates its own troubles, for it disrupts the conclusion to Deuteronomy, which is otherwise preoccupied with praise for Moses:

---

between the longevity of the spirit that is believed to be upon Moses and the spirit that rests upon the elders. By every indication, the spirit upon Moses is permanent. Even its distribution is partial: "I will take *from* the spirit upon you. . . ." The presence of the spirit that rests upon the elders, in contrast, is ephemeral: "they prophesied. . . . But they did not do so again." This story ought not to be directly paired with the story of Joshua's succession; Moses does *not* impart the spirit to Joshua. What lies embedded in both, nonetheless, is the conviction that Moses and Joshua have a permanent share in the spirit. Consequently, Moses lays his hand upon Joshua and sets him before Eleazar for public affirmation.

30. E.g., Job 40:10; Ps 96:6; 104:1.

The Israelites wept for Moses in the plains of Moab thirty days; then the period of mourning for Moses was ended. *Joshua son of Nun was full of the spirit of wisdom, because Moses had laid his hands on him; and the Israelites obeyed him, doing as the Lord had commanded Moses.* Never since has there arisen a prophet in Israel like Moses, whom the Lord knew face to face. He was unequaled for all the signs and wonders that the Lord sent him to perform in the land of Egypt, against Pharaoh and all his servants and his entire land, and for all the mighty deeds and all the terrifying displays of power that Moses performed in the sight of all Israel. (Deut 34:8-12)

Absent a reference to Joshua, this paragraph segues smoothly from threnody (34:8) to praise of Moses (34:9). It looks as if an editor, at some later time, has introduced the reference to Joshua in Deut 34:9 in anticipation of the book of Joshua. Its intrusiveness here, coupled with its brevity, makes it difficult to answer a question that attends this text: Was Joshua full of the "*spirit* of wisdom" for the first time with the laying on of Moses' hands, or was he now full of a "spirit of *wisdom*" with the laying on of Moses' hands? In other words, does he receive an influx of spirit, or does his spirit receive a flush of wisdom with the laying on of Moses' hands? The difference between these alternatives is the difference between understanding this filling as a subsequent influx of spirit or as the influx of wisdom into the spirit that is already within Joshua.

An interpretation of these few words to mean that Joshua received wisdom in his spirit is rooted in its relationship to Numbers 27. In both, Joshua has spirit within him. In both, Moses imparts a quality to Joshua that brings about obedience among the Israelites. In both, the impartation of this quality is associated with the laying on of Moses' hand. In both, Joshua receives a quality from Moses that will equip him for leadership: majesty (Numbers) and wisdom (Deuteronomy). In Numbers, the presence of spirit in Joshua — a spirit with which the God of the spirits of all flesh is intimately acquainted — identifies him as the clear choice for succeeding Moses, with the result that he receives a portion of Moses' majesty when Moses lays his hands upon him, to the end that Israel will obey him. Deuteronomy 34:9, interpreted in light of Num 27:15-23, paints a similar picture: Joshua's spirit is particularly receptive to Moses' wisdom, which he receives in full when Moses lays his hands upon him, to the end that Israel obeys him.

According to the alternative interpretation, Joshua received a full and first-time infusion of spirit to prepare him for his future role as the leader of Israel. This irruption of the spirit would anticipate others in the drama of the Deuteronomistic History. Othniel judged Israel when the spirit came upon him (Judg 3:10). The spirit clothed Gideon (6:34). Then, of course, there was Samson, in whom the spirit stirred (13:25), upon whom the spirit of the Lord rushed before he tore a lion apart barehanded (14:6), upon whom it rushed again so that he killed thirty men (14:19), and upon whom it again rushed so that ropes which bound "his arms became like flax that has caught fire, and his bonds melted off his hands" (15:14). The spirit later rushed upon Saul, transforming him into another person and causing him to prophesy (1 Sam 10:10-12). At the nexus of his power as king, when he heard of the conflict with Nahash the Ammonite, which would lead to the gouging out of Israelite eyes, "the spirit of God rushed upon Saul in power when he heard these words, and his anger was greatly kindled. He took a yoke of oxen, and cut them in pieces and sent them throughout all the territory of Israel by messengers, saying, 'Whoever does not come out after Saul and Samuel, so shall it be done to his oxen!' Then the dread of the Lord fell upon the people, and they came out as one" (11:6-7). At Saul's demise, however, the spirit left Saul and came to David: "Then Samuel took the horn of oil, and anointed him in the presence of his brothers; and the spirit of the Lord came mightily upon David from that day forward. Samuel then set out and went to Ramah. Now the spirit of the Lord departed from Saul, and an evil spirit from the Lord tormented him" (16:13-14).[31]

Throughout the Deuteronomistic History, the spirit comes powerfully upon renowned heroes and kings, supplying them with extraordinary power to accomplish fantastic feats. An irruption of the spirit upon Joshua would not be unsuitable to such a powerful divinely drafted drama. However, even if there is an association between Joshua, judges, and kings, it is

---

31. The story featuring Micaiah ben Imlah in 1 Kings 22 is anomalous; here God puts lying spirits into the mouths of false prophets, and Micaiah's nemesis, Zedekiah son of Chenaanah, slaps Micaiah on the cheek and asks, "Which way did the spirit of the Lord pass from me to speak to you?" (22:24). The LXX translation differs: "What sort of spirit of the Lord has spoken in you (*Poion pneuma kyriou to lalēsan en soi*)? Later still in the Deuteronomistic History, Elisha's servants ask for permission to search for Elijah: "They said to him, 'See now, we have fifty strong men among your servants; please let them go and seek your master; it may be that the spirit of the Lord has caught him up and thrown him down on some mountain or into some valley.' He [Elisha] responded, 'No, do not send them'" (2 Kgs 2:16).

a tenuous one. Most obvious, of course, is that there is no rushing or falling or clothing of the spirit in the brief encounter with Joshua that Deut 34:9 offers. Joshua, rather, is depicted as "full of spirit." If there is an irruption of the spirit, it comes peaceably. In fact, there is no verb at all in Deut 34:9 that describes the spirit's presence.

Second, this influx of spirit, if that is how we are to read Deut 34:9, is directly tied to Moses' laying on of hands. In this respect, the inspiration of Joshua resembles the inspiration of David, over which Samuel exercises some measure of control, although the depiction of David's reception of the spirit — the spirit of the Lord *rushed upon* him — is more characteristic of the Deuteronomistic History than is the depiction of Joshua (1 Sam 16:13).

Third, the laying on of hands, even if it causes the influx of spirit, does not generate dramatic abilities in Joshua. Nowhere else in the entirety of the Bible does anything occur automatically for Joshua because he has a spirit of wisdom he received from the laying on of hands. He tears apart no lions, participates in no prophesying, slays no giants.

From here on out, the fullness of spirit of wisdom in Joshua offers no miraculous solutions, no charismatic insight to determine Israel's future. From this point on, Joshua's wisdom is the product of dogged effort. The early lines in the book that bears his name indicate as much: "Only be strong and very courageous, being careful to act in accordance with all the law that my servant Moses commanded you; do not turn from it to the right hand or to the left, so that you may be successful wherever you go. This book of the law shall not depart out of your mouth; you shall meditate on it day and night, so that you may be careful to act in accordance with all that is written in it. For then you shall make your way prosperous, and then you shall be successful" (Josh 1:7-8). Wisdom is not free floating but tied directly to the study of Torah. If Joshua is to conquer and partition correctly the promised land, he must possess intimate knowledge of the instruction for distributing the land in the book of Numbers. If, then, Deut 34:9 depicts a subsequent endowment of the spirit of wisdom, it is one that is accompanied by strict, and far more extensive, instructions about meditation upon and meticulous attention to written words of instruction. There can be no dichotomy between a full endowment of the spirit of wisdom and scrupulous attention to Torah. This is, after all, a spirit *of wisdom.*

The marvel of the word "spirit," as we have seen, is that it cannot be neatly diced into various domains. We cannot happily divvy up the texts and leave neat piles — breath, wind, human spirit, angel — on our interpretive cutting board. Deut 34:9 supplies a clear example of this. Is the *spirit* of wisdom imparted to Joshua at the end of Moses' life, or is a fresh infusion of *wisdom* imparted to a finely honed spirit? Ultimately, despite our penchant for tidiness, the narrators do not permit us a neat decision. The realm of the spirit is unbounded; the boundaries between human and divine vitality are porous. This realization is not a limit to our interpretation; it is an ambiguity that drives us to the mysterious world of energy and life.

No matter whether the accent rests upon *spirit,* imparted afresh, or upon *wisdom,* imparted in full, what lies behind this unexpected and intrusive mention of the spirit in Deut 34:9 leads to what we identified throughout Chapter 1: a vitality within that keeps death at bay. This fundamental dimension of the spirit can be spun from the thread of an unobtrusive yet quaintly profound detail in Deut 34:7: "Moses was one hundred twenty years old when he died; his sight was *not dimmed* [*lō'-kāhătâ*] and his *freshness* [*lēḥōh*] was not gone." The word "freshness" occurs typically with plants: fresh grapes in contrast to dried (Num 6:3); the green or fresh tree as opposed to the dry (Ezek 17:24); and Samson tied with fresh cords (Judg 16:7-8). This is a subtle but supreme tribute which details the sort of vitality — both in the form of spirit and wisdom — that Moses, after decades of discouragement and bouts with exhaustion, still possessed. Having given his life to a community of refugees, Moses was still fresh, still green, still alive, capable still of imparting, one last time, wisdom to his friend and faithful protégé.

Spirit to the nth Degree: Daniel

The novella of Joseph and his inscrutable ability to interpret dreams, to devise plans to save Egypt from famine, and to rescue Israel for its unique future left its mark on Israel. Already we have had pause to observe the impress of Joseph upon the succession of Israelite leadership from Moses to Joshua. In Num 27:18, Joshua, like Joseph, is a person "in whom is spirit." In Deut 34:9, Joshua is described as "full of spirit of wisdom." For what more was Joseph, a person "in whom is spirit of God," known than his remarkable wisdom, insight, and foresight? The whole drama of this hero encapsulates the heart of Israel's wisdom tradition.

Yet the story of Joseph exercised an even more impressive level of influence over the first six chapters of the book of Daniel, which consists mostly of a series of stories about this remarkable alien in the courts of

Nebuchadnezzar. Israel lay once again in grave danger, not now from famine and drought, but from exile in hostile empires. In Daniel, the simple query "Can we find anyone else like this — one in whom is (the) spirit of God?" (Gen 41:38) — which a startled Pharaoh raised of his prisoner-interpreter, is spun out successively in stories, not now about Joseph in the courts of Pharaoh, but about Daniel in the courts of other foreign rulers. In the first of these stories, King Nebuchadnezzar of Babylon claims three times that Daniel has "spirit of holy god(s) in him," so that no difficulty is beyond him (Dan 4:8, 9, 15[MT 5, 6, 16]).[32] This is impressive testimony, though it is not ungrounded, for Daniel has interpreted a dream that no one else could fathom.

In the next story, mysterious handwriting appears on a wall for King Belshazzar, Nebuchadnezzar's son. When the queen hears the discussion of the mysterious handwriting, she tells Belshazzar about Daniel, who had been Nebuchadnezzar's chief of magicians and diviners: "There is a man in your kingdom in whom is (a) spirit of holy god(s) [*dî rûaḥ ʾĕlāhîn qaddîšîn bēh*]. In the days of your father he was found to have enlightenment, understanding, and wisdom like the wisdom of the gods." The queen continues, "Your father, King Nebuchadnezzar, made him chief of the magicians, enchanters, Chaldeans, and diviners, because an 'excellent' spirit [*dî rûaḥ yattîrâ*], knowledge, and understanding to interpret dreams, explain riddles, and solve problems were found in this Daniel . . ." (Dan 5:11-12). The king summons Daniel with the words, "I have heard of you, that (a) spirit of god(s) [God] is in you, and that enlightenment, understanding, and excellent wisdom are found in you" (5:14).[33]

The third story about Daniel's remarkable abilities occurs neither in the courts of Nebuchadnezzar nor Belshazzar. Both have died, and Darius the Mede now appoints Daniel to one of the three highest positions in the empire. Daniel soon distinguishes himself — he is faithful and virtuous — above the other two leaders, who will become extremely jealous. And why? Because "an 'excellent' spirit is in him [*dî rûaḥ yattîrā' bēh*]" (6:3[MT 4]).

What is the source of Daniel's clairvoyant abilities, that he should be chief of the magicians in one era and one of a trio of leaders in a subsequent one? Sheer repetition suggests that it is a remarkable spirit within

32. The problems of translation are enormous. The Hebrew can be translated: "the spirit of the holy God in him"; "the spirit of a holy god in him"; "the spirit of holy gods in him"; "the spirit of the holy gods in him"; "a spirit of the holy God in him"; "a spirit of a holy god in him"; "a spirit of holy gods in him"; "a spirit of the holy gods in him."

33. Aramaic: *dî rûaḥ ʾĕlāhîn bāk wĕnahîrû wĕśokĕltānû wĕḥokmâ yattîrâ hištĕkaḥat bāk.*

Daniel which is variously identified as "spirit of holy god(s)," "spirit of god(s)," and "excellent spirit." And what is the nature of this much referred to spirit? Is it given as a fresh endowment to Daniel in order to interpret Nebuchadnezzar's dream, or is this the divine spirit that has filled him from birth?

It would be disingenuous to suggest that the recurrence of the phrase "spirit of god(s)" in Gen 41:38 and Dan 5:14 requires that the latter occurrence must be Daniel's God-given spirit because its description is spun from the former occurrence, which refers to the quality of Joseph's God-given spirit rather than a charismatic endowment. Later interpreters and spinners of tales were rarely bound by the parameters of earlier texts. More telling is the longevity implied by the phrases, "spirit of (holy) god(s)" and "excellent spirit," in successive tales of Daniel's mercurial rise to power. Throughout three generations of rulers — Nebuchadnezzar, Belshazzar, and Darius — Daniel proves to have understanding and wisdom, with the result that he can be appointed first as chief of all the clairvoyants and subsequently chief over the entire kingdom of Media. If he is the quintessence of wisdom, it is not because on occasion he receives a special endowment of the spirit of God but because the spirit within him is the perennial source of enlightenment, wisdom, and understanding, because he is an extraordinary human whose spirit-of-god, like Joseph's, exhibits distinguishing qualities of prescience and leadership.

It is this quality of life-giving spirit that is encapsulated in the tales of Daniel in a single word that is too tamely translated "excellent," as in the NRSV: "because an excellent spirit, knowledge, and understanding. . . ." This word does not typically connote a specific characteristic, such as intelligence or understanding. It tends rather to communicate degree or extraordinary measure. Thus the expression "an excellent spirit" does not characterize an intelligent or wise or understanding spirit. The word, rather, is an indication of measure, and full measure at that. This is a word that even has a dimension of quantity — and quantity to the nth degree — throughout the book of Daniel.

- Nebuchadnezzar's statue was huge, and its brilliance was "excessive" [*yattîr*] or, in this context, "blinding" (Dan 2:31).
- The fiery furnace was "excessively" or "so very" overheated [*yattîrā'*], with the result that "the raging flames killed the men who lifted Shadrach, Meshach, and Abednego" (3:22).
- Restored from an illness, Nebuchadnezzar proclaimed that his majesty

and splendor were restored to him for the glory of his kingdom. Re-established over his kingdom, "*even more* greatness was added [*ûrĕbû yattîrâ hûsĕpat*]" to him. The latter glory, splendor, and character of his rule *exceeded* the former. There were more of these qualities than before (4:36[MT 33]).

- In a vision, a fourth beast was "terrifying and dreadful and *exceedingly* [*yattîrā'*] strong. It had great iron teeth and was devouring, breaking in pieces, and stamping what was left with its feet. It was different from all the beasts that preceded it, and it had ten horns" (7:7).
- The fourth beast in this vision was also different from all the rest, more terrifying than the rest, that is, "*exceptionally* [*yattîrâ*] terrifying" (7:19).

The statue was *extremely* brilliant, the furnace *extraordinarily* hot, Nebuchadnezzar's reign *even more* full of greatness, the beast *exceedingly* strong and *exceptionally* terrifying. In all of these expressions, the word that is translated as "excellent" in Dan 5:12 and 14 indicates an extreme degree: brilliant to the nth degree, glorious to the nth degree, hot to the nth degree, strong and terrifying to the nth degree!

The choice of this word to describe Daniel's spirit indicates more than mere excellence. It communicates, on the one hand, lavishness, extraordinary measure, and fullness. There is so much brilliance, so much heat, so much glory, so much terror and strength — and so much spirit. This word communicates, on the other hand, quality. There is sheer brilliance, sheer heat, sheer glory, sheer terror and strength — and sheer, untainted spirit. This is spirit to the nth degree.

What rendered Daniel's spirit so distinctive was the wisdom that characterized it to no less a degree. In Daniel 5 there is a striking parallel between spirit and wisdom. Daniel has:

"*yattirah* spirit [*rûaḥ yattîrâ*] . . . in him" (5:12);
"*yattirah* wisdom [*ḥokmâ yattîrâ*] in him" (5:14).

This parallel does not, however, stand alone. It is linked to another important parallel, in which the queen tells Belshazzar that Daniel has:

"in him a spirit of (the) holy gods [God]" (5:11)
"wisdom like the wisdom of (the) gods [God]" (5:11).

If Daniel's spirit is *yattîrâ*, so is his wisdom; if Daniel's wisdom is divine, so is his spirit. With such lavish language, the story of Daniel is reminiscent of Joseph, though not exclusively so. Daniel's supersaturated spirit and wisdom recollect as well the grandeur of the desert, when extraordinary artisans brought exceptional spirits, full to the brim, to the task of constructing the tent of presence.

This spirit, further, is not given to Daniel in the flash of a moment. On the contrary, Daniel is among those exiled young, noble Israelite men who already are "young men without physical defect and handsome, versed in every branch of wisdom, endowed with knowledge and insight, and competent to serve in the king's palace; they were to be taught the literature and language of the Chaldeans" (Dan 1:4). The "endowment" which they bring consists of the acquired knowledge and insight they learned as Israelite nobility; they are learned — as in the parlance of scribal training — in all wisdom.[34]

It is, then, in the context of their refusal to accept the royal rations that Daniel and his three companions are given further wisdom: "To these four young men God gave knowledge and skill in every aspect of literature and wisdom" (1:17). This first story is the harbinger of what is to follow. It is here, in the crucible of resistance to the royal rations, that Daniel is first seen as one who has "insight," the ability to interpret "all visions and dreams." If, therefore, he is endowed with this ability, this endowment is not at first associated with an endowment of the spirit. He is not, in other words, filled with the spirit in order to interpret dreams.

This story, rather, offers a clear signal that wisdom, the wisdom that radiates from Daniel's spirit, is allied with the basic quality of faithfulness. These are, after all, the only four from among the Israelite exiles who distinguish themselves. When the days of their refusal to accept royal rations are past, the four are presented to Nebuchadnezzar, where, "in every matter of wisdom and understanding concerning which the king inquired of them, he found them ten times better than all the magicians and enchanters in his whole kingdom" (Dan 1:20). What is so telling here is that Daniel

---

34. They are identified by the Hebrew word *maśkîlîm*, which conjures the memory of Ezra the scribe and shares the landscape of Early Judaism with the Teacher of Righteousness, who claims this word and the status it confers. See also Dan 11:33: "The wise among the people [*ûmaśkîlê ʿām*] shall give understanding to many."

and his friends do not have wisdom because they have studied more than all the others or because they have been filled with an influx of the spirit, but simply because they have been faithful in what seems to be an unrelated matter: food laws. These food laws could easily have been forfeited in a world in which Babylon's gods appear to have soundly defeated Israel's God. There was no more temple, no more king, no more claim to a land of milk and honey. The other young men, therefore, expressed no reservations about eating fine food and drinking the king's wine. Only Daniel and his friends did.

There is no apparent relationship between food laws and wisdom, between keeping kosher and having spirit to the nth degree within. Nevertheless, there is in the book of Daniel an integral relationship, not because food and wisdom necessarily go together nor because clairvoyance is linked to diet. Yet underlying Daniel's commitment to a vegetarian diet, his wisdom, and his exceptional spirit is the practice of dogged faithfulness.

When later Nebuchadnezzar and the wife of Belshazzar recognize and recall the divine nature of Daniel's spirit, it is the quality of his hard-earned wisdom that lies in the foreground. The issue here is not one of an endowment that Daniel has received; he already had the ability to understand dreams and visions when he refused the royal rations. What these stories underline is that Daniel's spirit is the locus of divine wisdom, or, in other words, Daniel has within him a wisdom-imbued spirit.

This first story, therefore, offers a clear signal that the quintessence of wisdom is allied with unusual faithfulness rather than an influx of the spirit. The result of Daniel's commitment, again without recourse to the language of the spirit, reinforces the power of fidelity. When the days of their refusal to accept royal rations are past, Daniel and his friends are presented to Nebuchadnezzar, where, "in every matter of wisdom and understanding concerning which the king inquired of them, he found them ten times better than all the magicians and enchanters in his whole kingdom" (1:20).

In the final story of Daniel, the foundational role of fidelity continues to occupy center stage. Daniel's wisdom has been acquired in the context of pure fidelity to God, and it is his quite apart from the demands that Nebuchadnezzar, Belshazzar, and Darius place upon him. His wisdom-imbued spirit is due to a lifelong fidelity to God. This is the gist of the entire first story in the book, in which Daniel and his companions refuse the royal rations and manage nonetheless to emerge hale and hearty, and it is this integrity that punctuates the final reference to Daniel's spirit in Dan 6:3-4:

Soon Daniel distinguished himself above all the other presidents and satraps because *spirit to the nth degree was in him,* and the king planned to appoint him over the whole kingdom. So the presidents and the satraps tried to find grounds for complaint against Daniel in connection with the kingdom. But they could find no grounds for complaint or any corruption, *because he was faithful, and no negligence or corruption could be found in him.*

The stories of Daniel combine in rare form the elements of spirit, fidelity, and wisdom. Energizing Daniel is a recognizable vitality, the source of knowledge and understanding that is the locus of his ability to interpret dreams and to explain riddles and to solve problems which the sages cannot. Yet this is only part of the story. Such spirit also thrives within Daniel in far greater measure than all others, so that he is the natural choice for chief, the clear selection to become interpreter of the handwriting on the wall. This is an astonishing combination. Yet that is not even all. The divine spirit within Daniel which is the locus of extraordinary wisdom in exceptional measure is rooted in fidelity to God. There is no shortcut to spirituality in this book, no fleeting irruption of the spirit that transforms Daniel into a sage. In a quick succession of stories, rather, we learn a breathtaking amount about Daniel: the spirit within him is at once spirit "of the (holy) god(s)"; this spirit is a perennial source of wisdom; the spirit within him exists to the nth degree; and his abilities are rooted in wholehearted fidelity to the God of Israel.

Conclusion: Elihu's Rage and Daniel's Wisdom

These stories surrounding Daniel are perhaps the latest in the Jewish Bible, and they provide an apt resumption of earlier themes. They amplify earlier adumbrations by accentuating themes that appear in but do not dominate earlier narratives. In the book of Daniel, they are inescapable, as characteristics of the spirit that were apparent in earlier narratives now reverberate, in these stories, through the corridors of Babylonian and Median power.

The spirit given at birth was considered no less divine, no less the spirit of God, than the spirit understood as a subsequent, charismatic endowment. Elihu enters the colloquy on theodicy held on the ash heap with the observation that "it is the spirit in a mortal, the breath of the Almighty that makes for understanding" (Job 32:8). Not age. Not charismatic endowment. Spirit and breath. This is the source of wisdom. And Elihu can actually feel this breath, as it lays siegeworks against him, filling him with words that are about to burst the dam of his tongue: "And am I to wait, because they do not speak, because they stand there, and answer no more? I also will give my answer; I also will declare my opinion. For I am full of words; the spirit within me besieges me. My heart is indeed like wine that has no vent; like new wineskins, it is ready to burst. I must speak, so that I may find relief; I must open my lips and answer" (32:16-20). Of course, though he is correct in principle, his words belie his lack of wisdom, of sensitivity, of knowledge.

The figures of Elihu and Daniel, surprisingly, concur on this point: God-given spirit within, the source of vitality which Elihu identifies as breath, is also the font of wisdom. In the book of Daniel, this spirit was recognized by the rulers of three successive foreign kingdoms. Daniel, who made no boastful claim to the wisdom of spirit, was nonetheless identified as a person "in whom is spirit of (holy) god(s)" — or "[the] spirit of the (holy) God." Daniel, who made no self-serving identification between the vitality of youth and the custody of wisdom, was nonetheless identified as a person whose wisdom, knowledge, and insight could be traced to spirit within to the nth degree. There is no doubt that "spirit" is understood in the stories that coalesce around Daniel as the spirit which is the God-given spirit in him understood as a lifelong presence. For three generations, he is identified by this spirit; for three generations, this spirit is the source of wisdom, knowledge, and insight.

This God-given spirit within was believed, at least in some quarters, to be of no less value than brief charismatic bursts of the spirit. Joseph's knowledge, for instance, led to the preservation of Israel in a way that the ephemeral experience of the elders in Numbers 11 did not. Daniel's wisdom was no less remarkable — and far more beneficial to Israel's long-term survival — than Samson's temporary ability to kill a horde of Philistines with the jawbone of an ass. Those who were filled with the God-given spirit, with intelligence, knowledge, and wisdom, may have had an ineluctable, albeit less dramatic, impact upon Israel, even more so than its elders, its judges, and even its first king.

The qualities of this spirit — wisdom, knowledge, and insight — are to be cultivated. Perhaps better than all others, Elihu expresses the Israelite conviction that "truly it is the spirit in a mortal, the breath of the Almighty that makes for understanding" (Job 32:8). As we have come to expect of him, however, he has skewered the truth by failing abysmally to recognize that the breath of the Almighty does not automatically make for understanding, the spirit in a mortal does not inevitably yield wisdom. Because Elihu errantly assumes that an excess of energy and an abundance of vitality equal a surfeit of the spirit and surplus wisdom, he chides rather than instructs the defeated man on the ash heap.

The relationship between wisdom and spirit in Israelite literature is far more closely aligned with the cultivation of skill and knowledge than Elihu cares to recognize. The wisdom of the spirit within demands the painstaking mastery of crafts and the persistent pursuit of understanding. Micah, to begin with, derides his prophetic opponents, whose claim to transitory, even illusory, methods of inspiration — visions, revelations, and divinations — will leave them speechless and in the dark. His are of a different order altogether, an order marked by permanence, by qualities that must be continually embraced to the full despite drastic opposition: a way of life rich with justice; a lifelong vitality of the spirit of the Lord within; deep resources of power and fullness of might. His declaration is long-term, relentless, and vigorous, learned not through trumped up, self-serving revelations but through practice and an unremitting commitment to what Micah knows to be true.

Joseph has acquired knowledge through the pain of human experience. His interpretation of Pharaoh's dream is foreshadowed by a dream about himself and his ability to interpret the dreams of the imprisoned cupbearer and butler. His abilities are not latecomers to his repertoire of wisdom. No less intriguing is that Joseph does not stop with interpretation; he continues with a full-scale domestic policy intended to solve the dark clouds of famine that lie ahead. This is also an ability forged in the crucible of hard-fought experience: in the home of Potiphar and an Egyptian prison, where his expertise at leadership is so exceptional that Potiphar and the chief jailer leave everything in his hands. His spirit is finely tuned by the time he offers advice to Pharaoh. Therefore, in light of both his ability to interpret Pharaoh's dream and to offer wholesale advice on how to implement measures to hedge against the famine ahead, it is no surprise that Pharaoh discerns in this man an unsurpassed spirit and unparalleled wisdom.

We encounter as well in Israel's literary legacy a symphony of skilled laborers, the wise of heart, who contribute to the construction of the tent of presence. When Bezalel and Oholiab, leaders in this skilled labor, are introduced, they are described as being filled, not only with (the) divine spirit, but with ability, intelligence, and knowledge in every kind of craft. When they are reintroduced later, they are depicted as both "filled with spirit of wisdom" and "filled with wisdom of heart," that is, with wisdom and understanding of every craft (36:1-3a). They are, in other words, chosen because they are highly skilled artisans in Israel. God prompts them, not to learn new skills, but to teach the ones they know.

Joshua is selected to succeed Moses because he is *already* "a person in whom (the) spirit is." He has been Moses' apprentice and close companion during the depths of war and at the peak of revelation, both at Mount Sinai and at the tent of presence. The God whom Moses and Aaron identify as "the God of the spirits of all flesh" discerns in Joshua "one in whom is (the) spirit," on the basis of which he is selected to succeed Moses. He is not appointed so that he may receive spirit but because there is spirit already in him. Even the laconic and more ambiguous depiction in Deut 34:9, "Joshua son of Nun was full of spirit of wisdom, because Moses had laid his hands on him. . ." is set squarely in a context that points to the hard labor ahead if Joshua is to lead the Israelites aright. He must be studious and stridently diligent in meditation upon the book of Torah (Josh 1:7-8).

There is a symbiosis between spirit within and acquired learning in Israelite scripture. Whether we look to the prophet Micah, the Israelite ancestor Joseph, the artisans of the tabernacle, or Moses' successor, we discover this clear conviction, that those with the spirit (of God) within are identified because they have certain skills and knowledge that emerge from experience and learning. Micah's commitment to justice, Joseph's interpretative and administrative insights, Bezalel and Oholiab's skills in crafts and construction, Joshua's wisdom in leadership — all of these emerge out of a life of learning. Ultimately, they become so identified by this skill, knowledge, and wisdom that they are seen to have a rare and rich fullness of God-given spirit within them. These are figures whose character is galvanized, not by transitory moments of inspiration, such as we discover in the book of Judges and 1 Samuel 10, but by a reservoir of knowledge and wisdom, from which they are able to draw. These are figures who exhibit, unlike all others, the salient symbiosis between spirit within and wisdom.

While the association of spirit with the cultivation of skill is apparent in these narratives, it explodes in the stories surrounding Daniel. Daniel is portrayed first and foremost as someone with a consuming passion for understanding. It is in response to this passion that he receives revelation. He "tries to understand visions" (Dan 8:15), prays at length in an effort to understand (9:20-23), and is credited for persisting with such passion by an angel: "from the first day that you set your mind to gain understanding and to humble yourself before your God" (10:12). This passion for wisdom, moreover, takes practical shape in the life of Daniel. He undertakes a three-year education in the literature and language of the Chaldeans (1:4-6), is able to read Aramaic (5:17, 24-25), records dreams in writing (7:1), and incorporates written Torah in his prayers (9:11-14). No less important, he refuses to accept royal rations; he resists the seduction of good food and wine. He is, in brief, doggedly faithful to the straightforward Israelite traditions which he knows so well.

The language of the spirit is lavish. Elihu understands that the spirit does not trickle down to the wise. The spirit exists in such measure, with such force, that it holds a sage hostage, laying siegeworks against him. His heart is like a wineskin about to burst.

Elihu's claims, misguided though they be, uncover what may have been a presumption of Israelite belief in the spirit. Though we must tread lightly when we speak of this because of the paucity of data, we should not for that reason avoid the implication altogether that the spirit was understood as a physical presence. Filling with the spirit may not have been understood exclusively as spiritually lavish. Filling with the spirit was perhaps believed to be material. Elihu feels he must either speak or burst because the spirit-breath in him lays siegeworks against him. Micah has a slew of words that will roll over his tongue, while false prophets have no spirit-breath rolling over theirs because they have stopped their mouths with their hands. The artisans and their teachers, Bezalel and Oholiab, are believed to possess an excess of this spirit-breath because they are so knowledgeable, so conspicuously competent (Bezalel and Oholiab in all sorts of crafts). Joshua too can receive the vitality that is in Moses — physical, tangible vitality — when Moses' hand(s) rests upon him. Finally, Daniel's extraordinary wisdom is identified with a surfeit of spirit-breath in him.

Elihu and Micah, coupled with Daniel, provide bookends, of sorts, to this notion of the materiality of the spirit that fills individuals. The first two cannot help but speak because of the force of the spirit, as it rolls across their tongues. Of course, Elihu has it wrong because he mistakes irrepressible energy for inspiration; Micah alone speaks the truth because his words are rooted, not in a youthful and unfounded claim to wisdom, but in a studied knowledge of Israel's traditions. In short, Micah has lived faithfully and so can claim to be filled with spirit; Elihu has lived self-centeredly and so cannot. Daniel, like Micah, has lived faithfully and can, therefore, lay claim to the spirit, though it is indicative that he — unlike Elihu or Micah, for that matter — lays no claim for himself; others, outsiders to Israel from foreign empires, are the ones who identify the spirit to the nth degree within him — the quintessence of spirit and, perhaps, a surfeit of spirit.

Whether or not ultimately the spirit was understood as a material presence that filled particularly gifted individuals, Elihu's sensation of compulsion goes a very long way toward explaining why select Israelites are depicted as full of or filled with (the) spirit. This is lavish language because these are not individuals who follow God half-heartedly.

Micah, for example, contrasts the mouths of his opponents with his own. These prophets, from Micah's perspective, live in a world of emptiness, a world without vision, without sun, without an answer from God, without a word on their lips. Micah's, in contrast, is a world full of power, spirit of the Lord, justice, and might. Divine spirit within does roll over Micah's tongue, and in lavish measure, as he declares Israel's sin and Jacob's transgression. Even Micah's parataxis is lavish — power, spirit of the Lord, justice, and might — especially when we consider that he is comparing the words of his mouth with those of the empty-mouthed prophets over whose tongue no breath will flow, as their lips will be covered by their hands.

Pharaoh's question implies the presence of a lavish draft that rises from within Joseph: "Can we find anyone else like this — one in whom is (the) spirit of God [gods]?" The sages and magicians of Egypt are captive to their ignorance. Joseph alone solves the conundrum of Pharaoh's dream and then, without external prompting, takes the initiative to devise a strategy for survival that would serve the common good. Joseph alone, of all the leaders in Egypt, mirrors the divine world with a full measure of discernment and wisdom.

This lavishness of spirit continues in the midst of Israel's recalcitrance and Sinai's desolation, where Israelites *en masse* offer much more than is needed until Moses is compelled to tell them to stop, where hearts are prompted, spirits lifted to offer with unmatched munificence. There are others as well — artisans, the wise of heart — who are filled with (the) spirit of wisdom. The materials from which they spin and hammer are depicted with bright colors, vivid hues, and rife detail. This is all part of the lavish tapestry that contributes to the tent of presence — a lavish scene that contrasts with the void of Sinai, the impatience of Israel, and the debacle of the golden calf.

The language of filling once again is part of a lavish tapestry, describing people whose skills are extraordinary and expansive in a narrative that is preoccupied with a singularly unrepeatable moment in Israel's history. Small wonder that their leaders, Bezalel and Oholiab, are described as being *filled* with (the) spirit of God and wisdom of heart — and with an additional cumbersome parataxis that drips with lavish praise: Bezalel was filled with spirit of God, wisdom, intelligence, and knowledge. Here in the unyielding wilderness of Sinai is an inexplicable excess, an imposing generosity, a stunning collection of skills, a fullness marked by adept artisans who exhibit extraordinary craftsmanship and, no less salient, hearts at the ready to teach.

Even one bare-boned depiction of Joshua characterizes him in a way that is reminiscent of the grandeur of Joseph as "one in whom is (the) spirit." The other brief depiction suggests perhaps that Joshua first was filled with spirit of wisdom when Moses laid his hands upon him. This too is a clear indication of vitality, for he is selected as the only one who carries the life-breath of God in such fullness that he is prepared to take over for Moses, of whom it can be said that, even at one hundred and twenty years of age, "his sight was not dimmed and his vigor had not abated." At the core of his existence lies what is required of him in order to receive from Moses' own majesty; he is *full* of (the) spirit of wisdom.

The stories of Daniel in foreign courts galvanize these strands. There may be no parataxis, as in Micah's claim to power and justice or the description of Bezalel, but three successive narratives about three successive reigns call attention to his extraordinary wisdom and knowledge. Throughout these stories he garners enormous praise, for he, like Joseph, is both an unparalleled interpreter of the inscrutable and an administrator par excellence. And why? Because in him is God-given spirit to the nth degree — an extraordinary measure of the divine vitality that is the source of knowledge and wisdom.[35]

---

35. On degrees of filling with various amounts of spirit, see H. Gunkel, *The Influence of the Holy Spirit*, 42; esp. excursus 4 in C. Bennema, *The Power of Saving Wisdom: An Investigation of Spirit and Wisdom in Relation to the Soteriology of the Fourth Gospel*. WUNT, 2nd ser. 148 (Tübingen: Mohr, 2002) 253-55.

CHAPTER 3

CHAPTER 3

Spirit and New Creation in the Shadow of Death

Notwithstanding the lavish world of Micah, Joseph, Bezalel, Joshua, and Daniel, the vitality of spirit within was too frequently choked by death, which would cover the land of Israel. In the course of time, the shadow of death swathed the valley of Israel's parched faith with darkness and doubt. Esarhaddon of Assyria would decimate the northern tribes, while less than a century and a half later the remaining two tribes of Judah and Benjamin would fall. A decade and a half of Babylonian pressure and partial exile would leave Israel without land, king, and temple. In the wake of this destruction, in a dust-ridden valley, Ezekiel would climb on thousands and thousands of dry bones left in the distant aftermath of slaughter. In such a valley the people's faith would crumble: "Our bones are dried up, and our hope is lost; we are cut off completely" (Ezek 37:11). In such a desolate valley Ezekiel would outlandishly gather more references to the spirit within than in other texts of Israel's Bible — eight in the brief compass of a few lines — to propel a despondent and despairing nation into a freshness of faith and a future rich with fidelity.[1]

‑Lavish. Ezekiel's vision is lavish in detail. Lavish in location. Lavish in

---

1. The formula in Ezek 37:1 is an indication that this is a vision rather than an actual visit to this valley.

The substance of this chapter was published, though in a different version, as "The Promise of the Spirit of Life," in *Israel's God and Rebecca's Children: Christology and Community in Early Judaism and Christianity. Essays in Honor of Larry W. Hurtado and Alan F. Segal*, ed. David B. Capes, April D. DeConick, Helen K. Bond, and Troy A. Miller (Waco: Baylor University Press, 2007) 247-59, 432-33.

hope. Ezekiel predicts in the most unlikely of locations — a valley of very many, very dry bones — that Israel will again be inbreathed, re-created again, once more filled with the spirit. There will be a grand rattle of re-creation, an astounding inbreathing of the spirit, and the formation of Israel anew.

Yet this hope was not borne afresh in the valley of dry bones. Ezekiel's conviction that Israel would have a new spirit was forged earlier, when Israel had not yet been finally exiled, massacred by its oppressors. There had been a time, in fact, when Ezekiel had believed that God would respond to Israelite repentance by giving them a new spirit. There had even been a time when Ezekiel had believed that Israel could make a new spirit for themselves. By the time he roamed in the shadow of the valley of death, these hopes were long past, dashed by Babylonian brutality.

Still, these three iterations of the belief that Israel will have a new spirit coexist within Ezekiel's prophetic corpus. (1) In response to the proverb in which Israelites lay the blame at their parents' feet, Ezekiel lays singular responsibility for re-creation squarely at his hearers' feet when he tells them to make for themselves a new heart and a new spirit (Ezekiel 18). (2) In the context of a vision in which the glory departs in stages from the tainted temple, he links divine initiative to human. God will give a new heart and a new spirit within when Israel takes care of itself, when the nation puts pollutants aside (Ezekiel 11). (3) When there is, in the wake of 587 B.C.E., not a trace of hope left, Ezekiel lays responsibility wholly at the feet of God. God will cleanse Israel. God will bring Israel back to life in a series of remarkable acts that entail bones clanking, sinews growing, flesh overlaying, and inbreathing by a convergence of the winds — the spirits — at the four corners of the earth (Ezekiel 37).

As the situation in Jerusalem deteriorated with successive deportations during that first and fateful decade of the sixth century B.C.E., Ezekiel adapted his view of renewal by the spirit. His earliest oracles of restoration are less trenchant and more optimistic; later, however, Ezekiel receives an oracle to preach to a disheartened Israel, and it is here that his conceptions of the spirit begin their metamorphosis. Only in these subsequent oracles does Ezekiel grapple with the protracted process that is required to lead Israel from its old ways, its familiar, faulty worship, to a new way of life in the land of Israel. Yet this is still not the end of the road; the truest end is a valley of very many, very dry bones. Here, in the valley of the shadow of death, Ezekiel reckons with the discontinuity that surely must divide the ghastly present from a splendid future.

A New Heart and Spirit

Hope in Human Initiative

As the Babylonian noose tightened around Israel's neck, some Israelites naturally, and probably justifiably, raised the question of responsibility. This probing was encapsulated in a proverb, "The parents have eaten sour grapes, and the children's teeth are set on edge" (Ezek 18:2). Ezekiel's older contemporary, Jeremiah, quotes this maxim in order to dispel the shadow of death. God has broken down and destroyed; God will build and plant. In those days, no one will any longer quote this maxim, and people will die for their own sins. The shadow of death, therefore, will be dispelled by a new covenant that God will initiate: God will write Torah on Israel's hearts, and Israel will no longer even need teachers (Jer 31:27-34). In short, the dawn of a new day will eclipse the days of destruction; it will be a day that occurs at God's initiative, with God's provision, through the inscription of God's Torah on human hearts.

Ezekiel attends to this maxim far more elaborately than Jeremiah. He demonstrates at length, with many case studies, what Jeremiah dispenses in a few words, that each individual's sin or obedience determines his or her destiny. This lengthy response to the maxim concludes climactically with a divine challenge:

> Therefore I will judge you, O house of Israel, all of you according to your ways, says the Lord God. Repent and turn from all your transgressions; otherwise iniquity will be your ruin. Cast away from you all the transgressions that you have committed against me, *and make yourselves a new heart and a new spirit!*[2] Why will you die, O house of Israel? For I have no pleasure in the death of anyone, says the Lord God. Turn, then, and live. (Ezek 18:30-32)

The perspective of this oracle is riveting: Ezekiel commands the people to *make for themselves* a new heart and spirit. These are realities that the Israelites can bring about themselves, a condition they can ensure. This is a remarkable claim, prompted by the maxim about sour grapes, that individuals have it under their own control, not only to repent, but even to develop in themselves a new heart and a new spirit. It is similar to the Deuteronomic command to circumcise the foreskin of the heart, but Ezekiel's ora-

---

2. Hebrew: *wa'ăśû lākem lēb ḥādāš wĕrûaḥ ḥădāšâ.*

cle goes far beyond this. He expects Israelite individuals to do more than snip the foreskin; they are able to create for themselves a new heart and a new spirit.

Jeremiah's and Ezekiel's responses to the maxim about sour grapes form a striking contrast. Though each Israelite is said to die for his or her sins in Jeremiah, God exercises the initiative entirely in Jeremiah's vision of the future. *God* will establish a new covenant. *God* will put Torah within Israel. *God* will write Torah on human hearts. Ezekiel grasps the other end of the stick. It is left to individual Israelites to repent, to throw away their sins, and to make *for themselves* a new heart and a new spirit. Ezekiel expects Israel to manufacture their own liberation through repentance by making a new heart and a new spirit.[3]

Hope in the Symbiosis of Divine and Human Initiative

This vision of human initiative contrasts as well with Ezekiel's oracles at the eastern gate, in which he presumes that *God* will place the new heart and new spirit within. These oracles are prompted by an ever-growing consciousness of the horrendous state of the temple and its worship. In a series of visions, Ezekiel sees successively the sins that are committed in the temple's inner chambers, and he watches as the cherubim, symbols of the glory of God, withdraw from the temple's inner sanctum, finally to fly away altogether (Ezek 8:1–11:25). During this period of growing awareness, just prior to the final departure of the cherubim from the temple's east gate, Ezekiel, in a further vision, observes twenty-five leaders of Israel gathered together. The spirit explains that these elders mislead the people, so Ezekiel prophesies against them, during which time his friend, Pelatiah, dies. Ezekiel reacts to Pelatiah's death by falling on his face and crying out, "Ah, Lord God! Will you make a full end of the remnant of Israel?" (11:13).

---

3. The compilation of the book of Ezekiel is complicated. Although the community which survived the devastation of 587 B.C.E. would have been capable of understanding the implication that Israel failed to repent, the command itself suits the period prior to 587, when repentance was still a possibility. While K.-F. Pohlmann (*Das Buch des Prophet Hesekiel [Ezechiel] Kapitel 1–19.* ATD 22/1 [Göttingen: Vandenhoeck & Ruprecht, 1996] 274), for example, regards Ezek 18:1-13 as the kernel of this chapter, which is then developed after 587, he still recognizes that the opportunity of repentance "vor der Katastrophe bis zuletzt die Möglichkeit der Umkehr für jeden einzelnen mit entsprechend positiven Folgen gegeben war" ("before the catastrophe to the end, the possibility of repentance for each individual, with appropriately positive results, was given").

In response, Ezekiel receives a divine word in which he learns that the leaders are unfaithful because they presume that the land is theirs alone, that those in exile have forfeited their right to the land. Consequently, Ezekiel receives the command to offer two oracles. In the first, God explains that God is a sanctuary to those who are scattered (11:16). The second oracle, which is longer, promises a fresh gathering of Israelite exiles and a new heart and spirit within:

> Therefore say: Thus says the Lord God: I will gather you from the peoples, and assemble you out of the countries where you have been scattered, and I will give you the land of Israel. When they come there, they will remove from it all its detestable things and all its abominations. *I will give them one heart, and put a new spirit within them;*[4] I will remove the heart of stone from their flesh and give them a heart of flesh, so that they may follow my statutes and keep my ordinances and obey them. Then they shall be my people, and I will be their God. But as for those whose heart goes after their detestable things and their abominations, I will bring their deeds upon their own heads, says the Lord God. (Ezek 11:17-21)

Despite what he has observed in his vision of temple irregularities, Ezekiel's optimism is not yet extinguished, perhaps because he is giving hope in this particular oracle, not to the inhabitants of Jerusalem, but to those in exile who now have nothing to do with the temple. Ezekiel promises that God, who is now a temporary sanctuary for those in captivity, will gather these faithful and falsely accused exiles in their homeland. This will prompt them to put away idols and other stumbling blocks. Once they have taken this step of removing the causes of sin, God will give to the restored exiles a fleshy heart and a new spirit to enable them to be fully God's people. If there is a pessimistic tone in Ezekiel's prophecy, this has only to do with those who refuse to receive such a heart and who allow their hearts to continue to embrace idolatry.

The Indispensable Core of Divine Initiative

Despite the difference about the roles of divine and human initiative, Ezekiel's oracles at the eastern gate (Ezek 11:14-21) and his response to the

---

4. Hebrew: *wĕnātattî lāhem lēb 'eḥād wĕrûaḥ ḥădāšâ 'ettēn bĕqirbĕkem.*

maxim about sour grapes (18:30-32) share a perspective in common that is absent during the period following the catastrophe of 587 B.C.E.[5] According to each of the earlier oracles, Israelites are capable of putting away their sins and setting aside their idols. In the oracle from the eastern gate, the gift of a new heart and spirit is contingent upon repentance. Human responsibility lies even more at the center of the oracle delivered in response to the maxim about sour grapes. In this oracle, Israelites must do more than set aside their sins; they must also cultivate for themselves a new heart and a new spirit.

It is absolutely essential to grasp the role of initiative in those oracles that precede the devastation of Jerusalem in order to appreciate the contrast of these oracles with Ezekiel's later oracles and his vision of the valley of dry bones. Neither of the earlier oracles of a new spirit reflects the concomitant experiences of divine anger and human desolation that come in the wake of the annihilation of Jerusalem in 587. Thus far the deportations have been partial, leaving many still in Jerusalem — those who are sufficiently well-situated so as to denigrate their brothers and sisters who are exiled in Babylon (11:1-4). During this period prior to the devastation of Jerusalem, Ezekiel's oracles assume that individual Israelites can repent, can cast away their transgressions, and, as a consequence, obtain a new heart and spirit, either as a gift of God or entirely of their own doing. The situation in which Ezekiel introduces a new heart and spirit a third time is altogether different. Now the Israelites are in the throes of grief, which they utter in the triadic threnody, "Our bones are dried up, and our hope is lost; we are cut off completely" (37:11). Now Ezekiel, too, reckons with the harsh reality that Israel is unable to catalyze its own liberation from exile. In its third iteration, therefore, lying under the surface of this promise for Israel's future is the darker side of Israel's past, the irredeemable aspect of Israel's character that rules out human initiative:

> Thus says the Lord God: It is not for your sake, O house of Israel, that I am about to act, but for the sake of my holy name, which you have profaned among the nations to which you came. I will sanctify my great name, which has been profaned among the nations, and which you have profaned among them; and the nations shall know that I am the Lord, says the Lord God, when through you I display my holiness before their

---

5. Secure dating of Ezekiel's oracles is rarely certain. These oracles do appear to reflect a period before the final destruction of the temple.

eyes. I will take you from the nations, and gather you from all the countries, and bring you into your own land. I will sprinkle clean water upon you, and you shall be clean from all your uncleannesses, and from all your idols I will cleanse you. *A new heart I will give you, and a new spirit I will put within you;*[6] and I will remove from your body the heart of stone and give you a heart of flesh. *I will put my spirit within you,*[7] and make you follow my statutes and be careful to observe my ordinances. Then you shall live in the land that I gave to your ancestors; and you shall be my people, and I will be your God. (Ezek 36:22-28)

This promise has not emerged from thin air but out of Ezekiel's fidelity to the Deuteronomic tradition:

When all these things have happened to you, the blessings and the curses that I have set before you, if you call them to mind among all the nations where the Lord your God has driven you, and return to the Lord your God, and you and your children obey him with all your heart and with all your soul, just as I am commanding you today, then the Lord your God will restore your fortunes and have compassion on you, gathering you again from all the peoples among whom the Lord your God has scattered you. Even if you are exiled to the ends of the world, from there the Lord your God will gather you, and from there he will bring you back. The Lord your God will bring you into the land that your ancestors possessed, and you will possess it; he will make you more prosperous and numerous than your ancestors. (Deut 30:1-5)

Although Ezekiel is faithful to this tradition, the dire situation brought about by the fall of Jerusalem propels him to transpose this tradition into a higher key. While Deuteronomy 30 promises restoration without cleansing, the dire situation of Israel in protracted exile evokes from Ezekiel a more radical solution of purification: "I will sprinkle *clean* water upon you, and you shall be *clean* from all your uncleannesses, and from all your idols I will *make you clean*" (Ezek 36:25).

It is not possible, from Ezekiel's point of view in the aftermath of the events of 587, to gather Israel in the land, for this will be a collection of Israelites with the same tendency toward idolatry, the same sort of people whose actions led to the fall of Jerusalem. Gathering them without cleans-

---

6. Hebrew: *wĕnātattî lākem lēb ḥādāš wĕrûaḥ ḥădāšâ 'ettēn bĕqirbĕkem.*
7. Hebrew: *wĕ'et-rûḥî 'ettēn bĕqirbĕkem.*

ing, as in Deut 30:1-5, would simply not be enough to remove the kernel of disloyalty that lay at the heart of exiled Israel. Nor is circumcision of the heart, as in Deut 30:6, adequate; an entirely new heart and spirit are required by the extent of Israel's fall.[8] Nor can Israel be asked to repent, as in Ezek 11:14-21, for they failed to do so even as the Babylonian armies deported and decimated them for more than a decade. Nor is it possible any longer to expect that Israel can make for themselves a new heart and a new spirit, as in his earlier oracle in 18:30-32; Israel no longer has any life in them to enable them to cultivate a new heart and a new spirit. Israel has been eclipsed by the shadow of death.

Spirit in a Valley of Very Many, Very Dry Bones

Spirit and the Valley of the Shadow of Death

Ezekiel can hardly be characterized as reticent about his alleged experiences of the spirit. He claims frequently to have been transported by the spirit — though whether in vision or body is never entirely clear — to meet the exiles in Babylon (Ezek 3:14-15), back to Jerusalem to the temple's inner court (8:3), then to its east gate (11:1) to watch the disheartening departure of the cherubim, and back again to the exiles (11:24). Following the catastrophe, he returns once more in a vision to a meticulously restored and glory-laden temple whose reality is still in the offing (43:5). The spirit leads Ezekiel's imagination full circle from the departure of God's glory from a temple scarred by idolatrous graffiti and vile priests to the return of God's glory to an ideal temple. This is both transportation, physical or otherwise, between exiles and the temple, and the transport, the sheer delight, of hope. It is a hope measured not in vague visions of the future but in the measurements of cubits and handbreadths. These measurements press the possibility of restoration into the collective moribund psyche of exiled Israel. They are repeated for each wall — precise, exact, repetitive, deliriously mundane except to those whose deadened imaginations begin to track with the vision. The exact restatement of the measure of each of

---

8. The promise of a new heart and spirit is more radical than circumcision of the heart in Deuteronomy 30, which continues with the promise that "the Lord your God will circumcise your heart and the heart of your descendants, so that you will love the Lord your God with all your heart and with all your soul, in order that you may live" (Deut 30:6). In Ezekiel's promise, circumcision of the heart is supplanted by a new heart and spirit altogether.

the four walls exhibits the precision of an exiled priest whom an angel, holding a linen cord and measuring reed in his hand, has ordered, "Son of *adam*, look closely and listen attentively, and set your mind upon all that I shall show you . . ." (40:3-4). The spirit leads ultimately to the transport of imagination, fueling the dreams of a nation.

Yet between the departure of glory and its reappearance lies a vast wasteland that is emblematized by a vision which encapsulates the protracted nature of restoring a dead nation to life. Fundamental to this vision is the overpowering reality of death that must be overcome, a horrible reality which Ezekiel captures as he describes the unthinkable. The spirit transports him, of priestly stock, to the land of the dead, to a valley where the bones lie brittle and bleached by the sun and sands of time: "The hand of the Lord came upon me, and he brought me out by the spirit of the Lord and set me down in the middle of a valley; it was full of bones. He led me all around them; there were very many lying in the valley, and they were very dry[9]" (37:1-2). It is in the echo of this valley of death that Ezekiel gives ear to Israel's triadic and tragic lament: "Our bones are dried up, and our hope is lost; we are cut off completely." Immediately Ezekiel measures the death around him: *very* many bones and *very* dry bones. This is death to the core, to the extent that even Ezekiel — with his fertile imagination, which had depicted in detail the siege of Jerusalem on a brick, which had led him to climb through a wall in exile, which had conjured parables and allegories and erotic depictions of Israel's sordid dalliances with other nations — cannot answer "Yes" to God's question, "Son of *adam*, can these bones live?" (37:3). Life in such a valley of death is inconceivable even to the boundless imagination of Ezekiel.

And yet, it is in this valley of death that the spirit has deposited him, and it is in this valley, among these very many, very dry bones, that the spirit will accomplish its most astounding act of vivification. In this valley, Ezekiel discovers hope, hope that resides in the presence and the power of the spirit:

> Then he said to me, "Prophesy to these bones, and say to them: O dry bones, hear the word of the Lord. Thus says the Lord God to these bones: *I will cause spirit to enter you, and you shall live.*[10] I will lay sinews

---

9. Hebrew: *wĕhinnēh rabbôt mĕʾōd ʿal-pĕnî habbiqʿâ wĕhinnēh yĕbēšôt mĕʾōd.*

10. Hebrew: *hinnēh ʾănî mēbîʾ bākem rûaḥ wiḥyîtem.* I have translated *rûaḥ* with "spirit" rather than, with NRSV, "breath" to preserve the relationship to Ezek 36:25-27 and other such texts.

on you, and will cause flesh to come upon you, and cover you with skin, *and put spirit in you,* and you shall live; and you shall know that I am the Lord." (37:4-6)

With these words, Ezekiel peers beyond the cusp of death to a world with bones clattering, fresh sinews laid on the bones like a linen tablecloth, flesh layered on the sinews, skin covering the flesh. Notwithstanding the vividness of this vision and the promise of the spirit, there is still "no spirit in them" (37:8). These are not just the bones of those who died naturally, but the bones of those who were "slain," those who died under the Deuteronomic curse: "You shall become an object of horror to all the kingdoms of the earth. Your corpses shall be food for every bird of the air and animal of the earth, and there shall be no one to frighten them away" (Deut 28:25-26). These bones cannot, therefore, easily return to life. They cannot be raised as they had been, in the throes of sin and the pangs of disloyalty to God. Their dismemberment is due to disloyalty, and they cannot be brought back simply by being layered with sinews, flesh, and skin.

This bringing-back, re-creation, will take place only in stages. Ezekiel's ponderous repetition underscores the theme of this vision, that the spirit brings life to a dead nation in stages, each of which is punctuated by the promise or the presence of life brought about by the spirit within.

I will cause *spirit* to enter you, and *you shall live.*" (Ezek 37:5)

I will lay sinews on you, and will cause flesh to come upon you, and cover you with skin, and put *spirit* in you, and *you shall live.*" (37:6)

So I prophesied as I had been commanded; and as I prophesied, suddenly there was a noise, a rattling, and the bones came together, bone to its bone. I looked, and there were sinews on them, and flesh had come upon them, and skin had covered them; but there was no *spirit* in them. (37:7-8)

Then he said to me, "Prophesy to the breath, prophesy, mortal, and say to the *spirit:* Thus says the Lord God: Come from the four winds, O *spirit,* and breathe into these slain, that *they may live.*" I prophesied as he commanded me, and the *spirit* came into them, *and they lived,* and stood on their feet, a vast multitude. (37:9-10)

This sequence, with its prediction of the spirit within followed by reconnection of bones and restoration of bodies followed by the perception that there is still no life, no spirit, followed by the inbreathing of spirit, amply expresses the realization of how difficult the transition to a new national existence can be. Life-giving takes place in phases, from prediction to partial reality to complete fulfillment.

The Spirit and Vitality

While repetition in Ezekiel's vision underscores the process of re-creation, there exists in this vision also a dynamic quality of reinvigoration which is apparent in the odd charge that Ezekiel should prophesy *to the spirit* that it should come from the four *wind-spirits* and become the *breath-spirit* within Israel. Ezekiel fills the imagery of the spirit to the brim. By exploiting its semantic potential in this way, Ezekiel effectively stirs up a flurry of activity and movement rather than a static experience of God's presence. As the exiles will be gathered from earth's ends as one nation in the land of Israel, so is the spirit commanded to gather itself from the four winds to revivify Israel.

The dynamic dimension is, throughout the book of Ezekiel, integral to Ezekiel's conception of the spirit. The very first vision Ezekiel receives as he sits by the river Chebar in 593 begins with the movement of a "spirit-wind of storm" coming[11] out of the north (1:4), accompanied by a cloud and fire — images not unlike the images of accompaniment that represented God's presence to Israel in their wilderness trek on the way to the land: angel, cloud, and fiery pillar (Exod 14:19-20, 24). Movement is evidently once again afoot, and, despite all appearances, God is beginning to take note and to move a disconsolate chosen people once again toward the promised land.

This rather linear movement from the north is suddenly supplanted in Ezekiel's imagination by a flurry of movement in the eye of the storm, living creatures with four faces and four wings, and wheels that move impossibly and simultaneously in every direction. And the explanation for this unimaginable phenomenon? The spirit of life within the wheels causes them to move in such remarkable ways: "When the living creatures moved, the wheels moved beside them; and when the living creatures rose from the earth, the wheels rose. Wherever the spirit would go, they went, and the wheels rose along with them; *for the spirit of life was in the wheels*[12]" (Ezek

11. Hebrew: *rûaḥ sĕʿārâ bāʾâ.*
12. Hebrew: *kî rûaḥ haḥayyâ bāʾôpannîm.*

97

1:19-20). In retrospect, Ezekiel identifies the living creatures with the same cherubim who now depart from the temple. They are, once again, accompanied by the impossibly active wheels — impossible were it not for the spirit of life within them:

> The cherubim rose up. These were the living creatures that I saw by the river Chebar. When the cherubim moved, the wheels moved beside them; and when the cherubim lifted up their wings to rise up from the earth, the wheels at their side did not veer. When they stopped, the others stopped, and when they rose up, the others rose up with them; *for the spirit of life was in them.*[13] (10:15-17)

This stunning image of the spirit of life as that which bustles within the wheels that accompany the cherubim multi-directionally throughout the world marks a turning point in Israelite interpretations of the spirit within. No longer does the spirit merely give life, as it had to *adam* and as it does to the animals and all of humankind; now the spirit gives *movement* to life. Further, though Ezekiel's vision pulses with motion inspired by the spirit of life, he gazes upon the spirit of life as he sits disconsolately by the river Chebar, or as he watches with chagrin the cherubim's departure from the temple, or as he is led around a valley of death, filled with very many, very dry bones. Ezekiel peers into a world that is teeming with the spirit of life from a perspective that is permeated by disappointment and grief, from static locales in which he is surrounded by the remnants of death. He discerns the spirit of life, in short, in the shadow of death.

Ultimately, however, this bustling world of the spirit of life will come to rest. At long last all of this commotion will settle in a single location. The placement of the spirit within Israel will bring about a homeward journey: "'*I will put my spirit within you, and you shall live,*[14] and I will place you on your own soil; then you shall know that I, the Lord, have spoken and will act,' says the Lord" (37:14).

The truth of this promise does not lie exclusively on the historical level; the whole of the vision is not about the placement of Israel on its own soil. The vision is also metaphorical. The threnody, "Our bones are dried up, and our hope is lost; we are cut off completely," is about the lifeless nation that still exists, the living remnant that deems itself dead. Consequently, this living valley of dried-up bones is told, "Thus says the Lord

---

13. Hebrew: *kî rûaḥ haḥayyâ bāhem.*
14. Hebrew: *wĕnātattî rûaḥ bākem wiḥyîtem.*

God: I am going to open your graves . . . O my people. . . . And you shall know that I am the Lord, when I open your graves, and bring you up from your graves, O my people. I will put my spirit within you, and you shall live . . ." (37:12-13). It is not the physically dead — though they number many — who will be raised up, but the living dead, people who walk through the valley of the shadow of death. These will be the ones whose graves will open, who will return to their land, who will live, who will know God.

As in the first narratives of Torah, the Psalms, and the musings of the sages, it is not possible to explore the spirit of life without facing squarely the reality of death. This association is of such fundamental importance to Israel's conception of the life-giving spirit that it plays out time and again in Israel's scriptures. Ezekiel provides the most radical and unequivocal association of the life-giving spirit with death when he places the re-creation of Israel in a valley of very many, very dry bones. Yet others affirm the association as well. Israel's sages and poets know full well that the spirit within provides the razor-thin boundary between life and death, that whatever is left of the spirit should flow in truth-telling (Job), that princes and the poor alike, humans and animals face death when the spirit is taken away. It is the spirit alone that gives life, whether to a human fresh from the earth, to animals engulfed by floodwaters, to a prince or a pauper, to a man who sits dying on an ash heap, or to a nation in the throes of grief.

The Spirit and Ezekiel's Experience

The vision of the very many, very dry bones may have several points of origin. It provides a concrete fulfillment of Ezekiel's promise of a new spirit (Ezek 11:19-20; 18:30-32; 36:26-27). It may also be a radical revisioning of the Deuteronomic promise that God will circumcise Israel's heart (Deut 30:6). It may be related in some way to the promise of his contemporary, Jeremiah, that God will write Torah on Israel's hearts (Jer 31:31-34). It may, as we have just seen, be a reflection of Ezekiel's initial call, in which the spirit of life provides a bustle of activity and movement.

The impetus for this vision may lie as well in Ezekiel's own experience of being filled with the spirit. In the course of this vision, he prophesies to the spirit, and "the spirit came into them, and they lived, and stood on their feet, a vast multitude" (Ezek 37:10). Though it may be coincidence, the detail that the reintegrated bodies "stood on their feet" when the spirit went into them is not dissimilar to Ezekiel's experience of the spirit within. After seeing "the appearance of the likeness of the glory of the Lord," Ezekiel fell on his face, only to be commanded, "Son of *adam*, stand up on your feet, and I will speak with you." When he heard the voice, Ezekiel recalls, "spirit entered into me [*wattābō' bî rûaḥ*] and set me on my feet . . ." (1:28–2:2). Later, Ezekiel had another vision of the glory of the Lord. This vision was "like the glory that I had seen by the river Chebar," that is, like the first time the spirit entered into him. His response this second time is the same as the first: Ezekiel fell on his face, he recalls, and "spirit entered into me, and set me on my feet . . ." (3:23-24). In both instances, the voice of the Lord sets Ezekiel upon his feet and speaks a word of commissioning to him.

It may be, then, that Ezekiel's vision of the revitalization of the nation by the spirit which enters them and sets them on their feet is modeled upon his own experience of having the spirit enter him and set him on his feet. Prophets, of course, were known to have used their own experiences as a lens for understanding God's message for Israel. Micah's rural roots result not surprisingly in a good deal of anti-urban, particularly anti-Jerusalem, polemic. Isaiah's own children become prophetic, political symbols (Isa 8:1-4). Hosea's family experiences, particularly his ill-fated marital and familial relationships, become the lens by which he construes God as a father and Israel as a recalcitrant son, or God as a husband and Israel as an adulterous wife (Hos 1–3; 11:1-7). Jeremiah discerns in a pot boiling over the outpouring of God's anger for Israel (Jer 1:13-19). It is possible that the profound and unique vision of Israel's being filled by the spirit is due in part to the coalescence of a variety of Ezekiel's own experiences: the dynamic role of the spirit in his initial vision of the four living creatures; the entrance of the spirit into him and setting him on his feet; and the conviction that God will fulfill the promise of a new spirit within. Despite the potency of his experiences, however, Ezekiel was not wholly shaped by those experiences. He remained as well a student — if a somewhat imaginative and idiosyncratic one — of Torah.[15]

The Spirit and a New Eden

Israel's story-telling begins in Eden. Ezekiel's vision for re-creation returns to Eden. In a renewed promise of the spirit after the final deportation of Is-

15. Not least in the three so-called histories of Israel in Ezekiel 16, 20, and 23.

rael's leaders to Babylon (Ezek 36:26-27), Ezekiel includes, quite understandably, the promise that the land will be restored:[16]

> Thus says the Lord God: On the day that I cleanse you from all your iniquities, I will cause the towns to be inhabited, and the waste places shall be rebuilt. The land that was desolate shall be tilled, instead of being the desolation that it was in the sight of all who passed by. And they will say, "*This land that was desolate has become like the garden of Eden;*[17] and the waste and desolate and ruined towns are now inhabited and fortified." (36:33-35)

This promise is rich with the imagery of Eden. The land will be tilled, as in Gen 2:15. Those who pass by will take note of how the former wasteland is now like a garden of Eden. Even the ensuing vision of dry bones may contain a reminiscence of creation in Gen 2:23. Ezek 37:7 describes the initial connection of the bones with the words "bone to its bone"[18] — words that are familiar from the creation of woman, whom Adam recognizes as "bone of my bones."[19] Though the resemblance is not exact, it is nonetheless evocative, for this expression appears now in a context that is rife with reminiscence: a new spirit enters Israel, which has been reconnected, bone to its bone, and brings them to life so that eventually they may again till their homeland and transform it into a region like the garden of Eden.

To this magnificent vision of the transformation of Israel's homeland into a pristine state akin to Eden Ezekiel still clings, despite three deportations to Babylon, devastation of temple, forfeiture of land, and capture of king. Such imagery, of course, is at home in the book of Ezekiel. Ezekiel makes rich play of the story of Adam and Eve in his mock lamentation for the king of Tyre, whom Ezekiel describes as if he were Adam in the garden of Eden prior to a plummet into arrogance and violence: "You were in Eden, the garden of God; every precious stone was your covering. . . . You were blameless in your ways from the day that you were created. . . . I cast you as a profane thing from the mountain of God, and the guardian cherub drove you out . . ." (28:13-16).

---

16. The theme of cleansing, a theme absent from the first two promises of a new spirit (Ezek 11:14-21; 18:30-32), provides both a new dimension to the promise of a forgiven and spirit-filled people and a transition to the related topic of the restoration of the land.

17. Hebrew: *hā'āreṣ hallēzû hannĕšammâ hāyĕtâ kĕqan-'ēden.*

18. Hebrew: *'eṣem 'el-'aṣĕmô.*

19. Hebrew: *'eṣem mē'ăṣāmay.*

Ezekiel is himself addressed by the divine being as "son of *adam*" (2:1), a phrase that, even if it means merely "mortal," conjures up memories of the first *adam*, especially in its earliest occurrences. When he is first addressed in this way, Ezekiel, like the first *adam*, receives a spirit that sets him on his feet (2:1-2; Gen 2:7). As a son of *adam*, moreover, Ezekiel accepts the divine charge to act as a sentinel or watchman for Israel: "Son of *adam*, I have made you a sentinel for the house of Israel. . . . If I say to the wicked, 'You shall surely die,' and you give them no warning . . ." (Ezek 3:17-18). It is incumbent upon Ezekiel to repeat the words, "You shall surely die"; this is the warning that occurs first and famously in Gen 2:17, where God makes clear the consequences for eating the tree of the knowledge of good and evil.[20]

Ezekiel is never, ever prosaic. As a consequence, his perspective on Israel's re-creation is no mere reiteration of the creation story. Salient among his innovations is the entrance of the spirit into a reconnected community; there is no single inbreathing into Adam's nostrils, but the spirit speeds its way from around the world, even as the exiles will be gathered from around the world to receive the spirit and to be restored to a land which they will till until it resembles Eden. This is a breathtaking vision that begins at the beginning of time and concludes in the certain future, when life comes full circle, when Israel receives the spirit within, when bone connects to bone, when the homeland is tilled and Eden restored. Yet Eden comes around, re-creation occurs, only in the throes of grief. It is the grieving exiles who hear the promise of a new heart and a new spirit. It is the survivors of catastrophe, the living dead in the valley of the shadow of death, who will receive the spirit and begin, haltingly perhaps, life afresh.

Arguably the most lavish vision in an altogether dramatic book is Ezekiel's trampling the valley of very many, very dry bones. When hope was alive, in the wake of partial deportations but not yet in the face of a final flourish of national collapse, the thrust of the new spirit retained the notes of promise to beleaguered exiles and rebuke to the arrogant inhabitants of Jerusalem; the promise of a new spirit was bound to the responsibility the returned exiles would have to remove anything detestable in their homeland (11:17-

---

20. Ezekiel is also commanded to eat what God offers to him (Ezek 2:8); this may provide an intriguing counterpoint to the illicit eating of the tree of the knowledge of good and evil.

21). For those who complained that God's ways were unfair, for those who claimed that their teeth were set on edge by the sour grapes their parents had eaten, Ezekiel had another message. Individual Israelites must turn from evil and make for themselves a new heart and a new spirit. They must not wait passively for a promise to be fulfilled. They must not pine away, longing for a pristine future. They must not remain docile because they expect to receive a gift of life. On the contrary, they have a responsibility, right here and right now, to produce a new heart and a new spirit. "Why will you die?" asks Ezekiel. "Turn, then, and live" (18:31-32). To the plaintiffs who put God in the dock over the issue of fairness, then, the so-called promise of the eschatological spirit had the character of command. Following the final crushing blow, however, there was so little left to the Israelites that hope lay only in divine initiative, in the promise of divine cleansing, in the expectation of revitalization by the rushing of the spirit afresh into a vast gathering of reconnected bones, in the dream of tilling the land once again until it would become nothing less than a new garden of Eden. Yet even this renewal would be, from Ezekiel's perspective, a process that transpires in stages. Fulfillment begins with rattling bones that come together, covered with sinews and flesh and skin, though without the spirit within. Israel is still void of life. The spirit must be called, commanded, to the reconstituted body; there can, in other words, be the form of the body without spirit pulsing and moving within. At that stage of re-creation, there is still no life. The protracted process of re-creation will require still more: the rush and return of the spirit-winds to a new Eden, which a newly clean Israel, a second Adam of sorts, will till once again.

From the tragic quaintness of a tale of two lovers, we have been led down the garden path. The intimacy of a potter-God's lips pressed against a freshly formed human figure, poised to blow breath within, brings the promise of unending love, at which we are privileged to peek. This is wildly exciting, if somewhat awkward. Yet even before that first kiss of life, we are alerted to the underside of creation: Adam, like the animals who are also made from the ground, is dust from the ground. The new life, full and rich and pulsing with potential, is blown into someone who, in short measure, will be condemned to return to the earth, ashes to ashes, dust to dust.

Like the rivers that extend from Eden to cover the earth's expanse, the understanding that just beyond the world of the spirit is the aching presence of death would spread through Israel's scriptures. We have glimpsed some of the more transparent instances in which death is believed to be the inevitable underside of life. The psalmists recognize that death skirts the edge of the spirit, that the spirit is like a dike that holds death at bay. Princes and animals alike receive the life-giving spirit from God and give up their life, forfeit their plans, leave God's presence, when that spirit — the holy spirit in the Fifty-first Psalm — is taken away.

Nor does such an understanding of the spirit escape the keen awareness of Israel's sages. God's hand holds, they know, "the life of every living thing and the spirit of every human being" (Job 12:10). Only the arrogant, such as Job's hostile companion Elihu, fail to reckon with their mortality and allow their arrogance to be transformed into a triumphalistic claim to superior knowledge. Elihu is too young to realize that each and every breath is, or ought to be, a warning against hubris and haughtiness.

Another fist is raised in the face of death — a gentler one but defiant nonetheless. Embedded in Israelite literature is a string of stories and sayings that recognize the vitality of the spirit understood along the lines that Elihu understands accurately but implements clumsily. Micah, Joseph, Bezalel (and his co-worker Oholiab), Joshua, and Daniel are distinguished because they have God-given spirit within to a lavish degree. This spirit is imbued with acquired qualities — justice, power, wisdom, skill, and knowledge — that distinguish these Israelites from false prophets and foreign diviners alike, from others of Israel's artisans and potential leaders. In the latest of these stories, a Maccabean composition that recapitulates these themes, Daniel's spirit is so divine, so imbued with the quintessence of wisdom, that he can be said to have spirit in the fullest measure. And how does he come to have such a spirit within? Daniel, who came to Babylon already learned and wise, proves himself unstoppably faithful. The keen relationship between his wisdom and spirit, between his wisdom and his integrity, is hardly incidental. Here is a person full of the vitality of wisdom, with the backbone of integrity, with spirit to the nth degree.

The firmest fist is raised in the face of death by Israel's most extraordinary visionary, yet it is a fist that grows firmer with the passing of time, tighter with the looming presence of Babylon. Ezekiel's conviction crescendos with the increasingly catastrophic condition of Israel. While in his earlier years he appears at first to believe that individual Israelites can transform themselves, making for themselves a new heart and a new spirit, in the wake of the disaster in Jerusalem in 587 B.C.E., he abandons this hope and finds himself, not just in the valley of the shadow of death, but in the valley of death itself, of very many dried and bleached bones heaped together. It is here that hope rises against hopelessness and that the visionary envisages the regathering and reforming of bones, sinews, and flesh, and the infusion of the spirit into them that brings new life to Israel. This is the new spirit and new heart that God promised. This is the new creation, the rescuing of life from death, the raising of the dead from their graves in order once again to cultivate the promised land. A new national body. A new spirit. A new Eden. A new creation altogether. And all of this in a valley of very many, very dry bones. The spirit accomplishes its most lavish task of re-creation, it would seem, in a grotesque valley of death.

PART II

Jewish Literature

Hermann Gunkel, the Spirit, and the Impoverishment of Judaism

As a student at Göttingen in the mid 1880s, Hermann Gunkel joined with a small circle of friends in silent opposition to the methods of their teacher, Albrecht Ritschl. Writing nearly forty years later, Gunkel would muse, "Admittedly, it was a peculiar 'School' that arose. A School without teacher and chiefly without students! It was a tightly bound circle of young scholars bound by mutual friendship."[1] Following the lead of Albert Eichhorn, this small circle comprised the heart and soul of what would become the history of religions school, which included William Wrede and Wilhelm Bousset. Ernst Troeltsch and Wilhelm Heitmüller would later join the ranks, and Johannes Weiss would associate with the group.[2] These young academics — the oldest was Eichhorn, born in 1856, and the youngest Heitmüller, born in 1869 — stood in vociferous opposition to a form of "biblical theology" that sought to identify central biblical teachings in support of dogmatic theology. Dogmatic theology, they contended, could not be independent of history. Gunkel would write in 1906, "Revelation is not contrary to history or outside of history but comes to pass within the history of the Spirit."[3] This vision of biblical scholarship contained more than an antidogmatic or antiecclesial agenda. It entailed a complete redirection; periods of biblical history would need to be examined in intimate association with other cultures of the respective periods. As late as 1922, when he

---

1. Cited by W. Klatt, *Hermann Gunkel: Zu seiner Theologie der Religionsgeschichte und zur Entstehung der formgeschichtlichen Methode*. FRLANT 100 (Göttingen: Vandenhoeck & Ruprecht, 1969) 20, n. 13.

2. Klatt, *Hermann Gunkel*, 20-21.

3. Cited by Klatt, *Hermann Gunkel*, 27.

was sixty years old, Gunkel occupied himself with clarifying the fundamental commitments of this movement:

> It [the movement] struggled out of the narrowness of the barriers of scholarly activity at that time into expanse and freedom, out of the barriers of the canon and church dogma about the Bible, out of the narrow-mindedness of dogmatic "biblical theology" and an all-too-philological form of literary criticism, out of an all-too-hair-splitting or modernizing exposition of scripture . . . also out of the isolation of Old and New Testaments from their historical connections with other religions. . . . Because this was our most essential and ultimate aspiration: to grasp *religion itself* in its depth and breadth.[4]

The history of religions school would lead some of its exponents, Hans Leisegang for instance, deep into the recesses of Hellenistic culture. It led Gunkel to the heart of Judaism.

This appreciation for the crucible of Judaism, which formed Christianity, compelled Gunkel to chide H. H. Wendt, who had a few years earlier written a book on spirit and flesh in Paul's writings, for attempting to explain Paul's writings on the basis of Israel's scriptures alone.[5] While the gospel spread in part, at least, due to the influence of Jewish scripture, Gunkel insisted that "the assumption of Jewish influence always carried much greater probability than does the assumption of the influence of the Old Testament." Though the gospel expanded under the influence of the scriptures, then, "We must therefore view Judaism as the real matrix of the gospel . . . but without denying the influence of a reading of the Old Testament."[6]

Palestinian Judaism informed the early apostolic community: "the apostles emerged from Jewish ideas, and with Jewish ideas they had to come to terms with one another."[7] Paul too was Jewish through and through, and it is erroneous to interpret his writings from any other context.

---

4. Cited by Klatt, *Hermann Gunkel,* 27.

5. *Die Wirkungen des heiligen Geistes nach der populären Anschauung der apostolischen Zeit und der Lehre des Apostels Paulus* (Göttingen: Vandenhoeck & Ruprecht, 1888) 3; English translation: *The Influence of the Holy Spirit: The Popular View of the Apostolic Age and the Teaching of the Apostle Paul,* trans. R. A. Harrisville and P. A. Quanbeck II (Philadelphia: Fortress, 1979) 12. He also criticizes Wendt for his rejection of Hellenistic ideas.

6. *The Influence of the Holy Spirit,* 12-13. He observes also that the apostles emerged from Judaism.

7. *The Influence of the Holy Spirit,* 13.

It is a grave error in method, which must result in a mass of misconceptions, to attempt to derive Paul's sphere of ideas or even his usage directly from the Old Testament and consequently to ignore the apostle's origin in Judaism. The question can only be, Is Paul dependent on Palestinian or Hellenistic Judaism or is he not?[8]

With such a commitment, Gunkel made a dramatic departure from earlier students of the spirit who had looked for the origins of early Christian pneumatology in the pages of Israel's literary legacy.[9] His was an independent — one might say idiosyncratic — departure. Hugo Gressmann would subsequently note the emergence of this independent perspective. Even as a student, Gressman recalled, Gunkel had begun to search for a fresh interpretation of the New Testament rooted in the conviction that it ought not to be interpreted exclusively on the basis of Israelite literature. This explains why Gunkel began to study the Apocrypha and, at least for a time, why Gunkel identified Jewish apocalyptic as the first stage of understanding the New Testament.[10]

There are noteworthy facets of this approach. First is what we have noted, that the path Gunkel traced was fresh and independent; he looked for the origins of early Christian pneumatology in the living world of Judaism rather than in Israel's literature. Second, this approach to pneumatology was informed by a wider community that was concerned with the history of biblical religion. Or, to put it another way, a company of friends, among whom Gunkel was counted, forged the parameters and emphases of the history of religions school; the emphasis upon Judaism in Gunkel's study of the spirit anticipated the appreciation for the cultures that surrounded Christianity which characterized studies such as Wilhelm Bousset's *Kyrios Christos* or his own *Schöpfung und Chaos*. And third, Gunkel's ability to navigate the waters of Second Temple Judaism was difficult — this is relatively easy in our era — because nothing existed like E. Kautzsch's or R. H. Charles's editions of the Apocrypha and Pseudepigrapha, or H. F. D. Sparks's and James H. Charlesworth's respective English editions of the Pseudepigrapha. He had to frame ancient points of view

8. *The Influence of the Holy Spirit*, 76. He continues by noting that the question is hard to answer because Paul was a Diaspora Jew who was educated in Jerusalem. The neat division between Palestinian and Diaspora Judaism dissipates, observes Gunkel with prescience, because there were Hellenistic Jews in Jerusalem.

9. Klatt, *Hermann Gunkel*, 29.

10. Cited by Klatt, *Hermann Gunkel*, 29.

through the painstaking process of reading untranslated manuscripts. Gunkel himself contributed the entry on 4 Ezra to Kautzsch's pioneering edition. Bringing Second Temple Judaism to the study of early Christianity was a feat that required firm methodological and linguistic grounding and an ability to grasp the essence of ancient texts, such as 4 Ezra, without the convenience of consulting a standard edition.

Gunkel's ability to make the case, over against the regnant scholarly consensus of his day, that an understanding of early Judaism is integral to an understanding of early Christian pneumatology must be acknowledged and applauded. Yet he failed in his characterization of Judaism. Dependent upon Emil Schürer's view of Judaism as a legalistic religion that had lost Israel's prophetic fervor, Gunkel contended that what distinguished Judaism from Israelite religion and early Christianity was "the fact that it produced no or, stated more cautiously, only very few pneumatic phenomena."[11]

In the context of this form of Judaism, John the Baptist was the first prophet since the Persian era and, concomitantly, the first person of the Greco-Roman era to be in possession of the spirit.[12] The preaching and miracles of Jesus constituted a fresh experience. The scribes and Pharisees of Jesus' day would preach very differently from the preaching of a *Pneumatiker* such as Jesus, and miracles *(Geisteswunder)* could never "originate out of sober study of the Law."[13] Jesus must have made, therefore, an impression upon the Jews of his day, though the near absence of Jewish conversions confirms how far behind they had left prophetic Israelite religion. Gunkel joins these unrelated pieces of the puzzle — scribal interpretation of scripture with resistance toward Jesus — to create a spurious indictment of Judaism at the time of Jesus: "But what a powerful impression the *pneuma* must have made when its fullness appeared to a Judaism bereft of the Spirit. Despite that fact, the number of converted Jews must be reckoned as few, which proves how strong the antiprophetic and thus antievangelical tendency in Jesus' time was, a tendency later culminating in the Talmud."[14] Such a dismal characterization of Judaism had practical consequences, for it meant that

---

11. *The Influence of the Holy Spirit,* 21.

12. *The Influence of the Holy Spirit,* 69.

13. *The Influence of the Holy Spirit,* 70.

14. *The Influence of the Holy Spirit,* 70-71. He admits (70) of a few scattered experiences of the spirit: "So far as we know, during Jesus' time and in the first two decades of the apostolic age, activities of the Spirit in Judaism could only be identified in highly scattered instances." He cites references in the writings of Josephus that describe Jewish figures, such as the Essenes and John Hyrcanus, as prophets (69-70).

Gunkel felt compelled to return to Israelite literature to explain the rise of Christianity — although he criticized Wendt for doing precisely this, for discovering points of contact between the Hebrew scriptures and New Testament literature. Jesus' preaching reached back past his own Jewish era, which had lost the prophetic and spiritual dimension, and appeared as "a fresh sprout from the old, all-but-withered root of Old Testament prophecy."[15] In fact, Jesus could not have been a child of this time. That era "appears so spiritually impoverished . . . that a man such as Jesus cannot come from it. He is not a child of his time. He must belong to Israel's antiquity, long past and mighty of spirit."[16] In short, if there are analogies to early Christianity to be unearthed, they must be found, not in the arid soil of Judaism, but in the fertile soil of Israelite religion.[17] What Gunkel gave with one hand, then, he took with the other. As a founder of the history of religions school, he traced early Christian pneumatology to the world of Judaism, though his characterization of Judaism as "spirit-impoverished" (*geistesverlassene*) renders this crucible of Christianity useful only as a negative foil for the spiritual vitality of early Christianity.[18] He was compelled, therefore, to return, with the

---

15. *The Influence of the Holy Spirit*, 12.

16. *The Influence of the Holy Spirit*, 68. He generalizes the rather isolated and puzzling story of John the Baptist's disciples in Ephesus, in which they confess that they have never heard of the holy spirit, in such a way that it characterizes all of Judaism (51).

17. *The Influence of the Holy Spirit*, 21.

18. In the preface to his third edition, written twenty years later, a more mature Gunkel attempted to explain — we might better say excuse — this characterization of Judaism (*The Influence of the Holy Spirit*, 3-5). He noted that, at that time, New Testament scholars looked exclusively for points of contact in the Old Testament, and that the use of Judaism was a novelty. He explained that this scenario changed between 1888 and 1909, though he cautioned that "there is still much to do until we gain an intimate knowledge of the religious life of Judaism" (3-4). He also readily admitted that he had spent too little time on history of religions data but then went on to say how unavailable they had been, though he did confess how little he had known at that time about Israel's prophets. Finally, he wrote, "What depressed me then with regard to Judaism was the still-universal prejudice that there were no pneumatic experiences at all in that period" (4).

He then proceeded to say that he was prevented in some measure from exploring the meaning of *pneuma* by the chronic scholarly disease of "biblical theological concepts," in which the meaning of the phenomena related to *pneuma* was constricted by a preoccupation with the word itself. Though he had resisted this disease, he was not entirely free of it. It is particularly Gunkel's statements about Judaism that seem disingenuous. The quotations I have included in this chapter do not indicate a reluctant purveyor of the absence of spirituality in Judaism but an ardent proponent of the view that the spirit had virtually no life in early Judaism.

predecessors whom he chided, to Israelite literature in an effort to explain that very vitality.

Notwithstanding his negative portrayal of Judaism, Gunkel left a substantial legacy during his own lifetime. In the early 1900s, scholars would follow his history of religions instincts and become engaged in serious debate about the appropriate locus in which to situate early Christian pneumatology. Paul Volz, like Gunkel, contributed pioneering studies of both eschatology and pneumatology to the annals of scholarship. Slightly more than twenty years after the appearance of Gunkel's *Wirkungen,* Paul Volz included Judaism in his study. He even included Judaism in the title of an impressive book: *Der Geist Gottes und die verwandten Erscheinungen im Alten Testament und im anschliessenden Judentum.* Of signal importance is that Volz adopted Gunkel's emphasis upon Judaism without inheriting his negative assessment. Gunkel, we may recall, had contended that Jesus was not a child of his own time, of a Judaism abandoned by the spirit, because the era was so spiritually impoverished. Volz ran in the opposite direction and argued that the vitality of Judaism gave rise to the vitality of Christianity: "The habit of comparing a form of Judaism that is coming to an end with a youthful form of Christianity has led regularly to a misunderstanding of the former. This is historically unsuitable and, moreover, it is far more probable that the new religion arose out of a period of religious stirring and deep feeling rather than out of a torpid and dying one."[19]

Unfortunately, many twentieth-century studies have followed in the steps of Gunkel rather than Volz and caricatured the vitality of early Judaism. This defective perspective was based in part upon the faulty assumption that Jews during the Greco-Roman era believed in the loss of the spirit, a loss that allegedly occurred when the last of Israel's prophets died. Accordingly we find a formidable array of twentieth-century scholars who hold to this position. Erik Sjöberg, in the *Theological Dictionary of the New Testament,* refers to "a widespread theological conviction"[20] about the withdrawal of the holy spirit and Johannes Vos to "the widespread tradition."[21] C. K. Barrett cites George Foot Moore with approval: "The Holy

19. Volz, *Der Geist Gottes* (Tübingen: Mohr, 1910) 144.

20. "πνεῦμα III: רוּחַ in Palestinian Judaism," *TDNT* 6:385.

21. *Traditionsgeschichtliche Untersuchungen zur Paulinische Pneumatologie* (Assen: Van Gorcum, 1973) 72.

Spirit is the Spirit of prophecy. . . . The Holy Spirit is so specifically prophetic inspiration that when Haggai, Zechariah, and Malachi, the last
prophets, died, the Holy Spirit departed from Israel."[22] W. D. Davies suggests, with characteristic caution, "we may now assume that Paul was
reared within a Judaism which, to use very moderate language, tended to
relegate the activity of the Holy Spirit to the past."[23] In the *Interpreter's
Dictionary of the Bible,* G. W. H. Lampe generalizes, "In the main, the
Spirit continues to be thought of as being, pre-eminently, the Spirit of
prophecy, manifested in the distant past in such great figures as Elijah
(Ecclus. 48:12) or Isaiah (vs. 24), but which was now no longer present in
Israel."[24] Joachim Jeremias subtitles section nine of his *New Testament
Theology* "The Return of the Quenched Spirit"; he summarizes: "With the
death of the last writing prophets, Haggai, Zechariah and Malachi, *the
spirit was quenched* because of the sin of Israel. After that time, it was believed, God still spoke only through the 'echo of his voice' . . . a poor substitute."[25] David Hill writes, "There can be no doubt that, long before the
turn of the eras, the Jews believed that prophecy as such had ceased in Israel and that the prophetic Spirit had withdrawn."[26] James D. G. Dunn
concurs: "with the rabbis the belief becomes very strong that Haggai,
Zechariah and Malachi were the last of the prophets and that thereafter the
Spirit had been withdrawn."[27] F. W. Horn discerns evidence "of a general
consciousness of the loss-of-prophecy or loss-of-Spirit."[28] Gordon Fee as-
serts, "Noticeably missing in the intertestamental literature . . . is the sense
that the Spirit speaks through any contemporary 'prophet.' This is almost
certainly the result of the growth of a tradition called 'the quenched Spirit,'

22. *The Holy Spirit and the Gospel Tradition* (London: SPCK, 1947) 108-9.

23. *Paul and Rabbinic Judaism: Some Rabbinic Elements in Pauline Theology,* 4th ed.
(Philadelphia: Fortress, 1980) 215. This statement follows a serious analysis (208-15) of other
data which indicate the continued working of the holy spirit. Professor Davies subsequently
communicated to me in private conversation that he no longer espoused this position.

24. "Holy Spirit," *IDB* 2:630.

25. *New Testament Theology* (New York: Scribner's, 1971) 81.

26. *New Testament Prophecy* (Atlanta: John Knox, 1979) 21.

27. *Christology in the Making: A New Testament Inquiry into the Origins of the Doctrine
of the Incarnation,* 2nd ed. (Grand Rapids: Wm. B. Eerdmans, 1996) 135. See also *Baptism in
the Holy Spirit: A Re-examination of the New Testament Teaching on the Gift of the Spirit in
Relation to Pentecostalism Today* (Philadelphia: Westminster, 1970) 27, where he states that at
the baptism of Jesus "the long drought of knowing the Spirit comes to an end."

28. *Das Angeld des Geistes: Studien zur paulinischen Pneumatologie.* FRLANT 154
(Göttingen: Vandenhoeck & Ruprecht, 1992) 31.

which begins in the later books of the Old Testament and is found variously during the Second Temple period."[29]

On the simplest of planes, Part II of our study debunks this false conception of Judaism during the Greco-Roman era.[30] Time after time we will encounter ancient claims, from Palestine to Egypt, that falsify the perception of Judaism as a religion void of the spirit. It will no longer be possible to dismiss Second Temple Judaism as a spiritually impoverished religion that functions as a negative foil for the birth of early Christianity.[31] Paul Volz had already argued for the vitality of early Judaism — persuasively, in my opinion — but his analysis obviously did not hold the day during the twentieth century. Ours, however, is a new century. We must contend with a fresh paradigm that embraces the vitality of early Judaism.

The vitality of early Judaism, in fact, led to an expansion, even an explosion, of the dimensions of Israelite literature which we explored in Part I of our study. Belief in the virtue of the spirit within would gain enormous momentum; Jewish writers would apply the moniker "holy spirit" to the spirit within and explore the significance of this spirit. They would reckon with the possibility that this holy spirit within, the life-breath — but more than mere life-breath — could be forfeited in the wake of duplicity, sold by the ambitious for cash. And so, stories were told and advice

29. *God's Empowering Presence: The Holy Spirit in the Letters of Paul* (Peabody: Hendrickson, 1994) 914.

30. Scholars have effectively chipped away at this position. See R. Meyer, "προφήτης C: Prophecy and Prophets in the Judaism of the Hellenistic-Roman Period," *TDNT* 6:812-16; R. Leivestad, "Das Dogma von der prophetenlosen Zeit," *NTS* 19 (1972-73) 288-99; D. E. Aune, *Prophecy in Early Christianity and the Ancient Mediterranean World* (Grand Rapids: Wm. B. Eerdmans, 1983) 103-6; F. E. Greenspahn, "Why Prophecy Ceased," *JBL* 108 (1989) 37-49; J. R. Levison, "Did the Spirit Withdraw from Israel? An Evaluation of the Earliest Jewish Data," *NTS* 43 (1997) 35-57. The impact of these studies is apparent in the response of New Testament scholars such as M. Turner; see his *The Holy Spirit and Spiritual Gifts in the New Testament Church and Today* (Peabody: Hendrickson, 1998) 193-95.

31. In this introduction I have adopted the word "Christianity" to refer to the movement that was responsible for the writings that have been collected in the New Testament. While I recognize that this is anachronistic — "Christianity" initially was at heart a Jewish movement — the scholars whom I review have used the terms "Christianity" and "Christian," so that it is awkward to use another term, such as "early church." Further, the adoption of this term for purely descriptive purposes allows me to distinguish early Christian literature from early Jewish literature. Otherwise, I would constantly be compelled to distinguish different corpora in early Jewish literature. For the same reasons, I adopt "New Testament" descriptively to denote a corpus of literature.

given to withstand the temptations that could lead to the loss of virtue, the soiling of the spirit, even physical death itself.

This belief about the spirit within was not an isolated explosion because Judaism was also a participant in the intellectually and religiously dizzying Greco-Roman world, which devoted significant attention, among both populace and intellectual elite, to the issue of inspiration. Under the inexorable compulsion of Greco-Roman culture, Judaism would outstrip its Israelite roots by incorporating all sorts of novel conceptions of inspiration. Vivid portraits of ecstasy, modelled after the Delphic Pythia or Bacchic worship, would dominate the skyline, while detailed descriptions of the inspired interpretation of Israel's scriptures would emerge from the shadows. Some of these descriptions would reflect the glory of Socrates, reshaping the spirit into the guise of Socrates's inspiring *daemonion.* Notwithstanding tenuous toeholds in Israelite literature, therefore, early Jewish authors would lay claim to fabulous forms of inspiration by the spirit.

One more brand of inspiration would emerge, this time from the chrysalis of Ezekiel's vision of a nation raised. At the shores of the Dead Sea, a miniscule, isolated, belligerent community would understand itself, against all odds, as a new Eden and a spirit-filled temple. Filling with the spirit, in other words, would transcend individuals and encompass the entire community. Purity would be communal, holiness corporate, sanctity complete.

The Greco-Roman era, then, would provide fertile soil for eclectic transformations of Israelite beliefs in the spirit, some of which would remain firmly rooted in Israelite literature and others of which would strain the ties that bound Jewish authors to their Israelite heritage. In this, the second part of our study of the spirit, I will be able to offer only a smattering of these experiences, a smidgen of those descriptions, though these will be adequate, I imagine, to show how the range and acuity of those metamorphoses attest to the thoughtfulness with which Jewish authors could attend to the vitality of the spirit.

CHAPTER 1

A Wise and Holy Spirit Within

Ben Sira and the Scribal Vocation

During a period of calm before the storm that erupted with the appointment of Antiochus IV Epiphanes in 175 B.C.E., Jesus Ben Sira directed a scribal academy in Jerusalem. The collection of his sayings, which his grandson translated from Hebrew to Greek in 132 B.C.E., is expansive, insightful, and occasionally offensive.[1] At its center is a memorable hymn in praise of Torah, in which universal wisdom comes to reside in Israel through the word of Torah (Sirach 24); at its end is a magnificent review of Israel's famed figures (Sirach 44–50). Of no less salience is Ben Sira's description of the successful scribe, which no doubt contains no small measure of autobiography:

> If the Lord Almighty desires,
>   he [the scribe] will be filled by spirit of understanding;[2]
> he will pour out his own words of wisdom
>   and by prayer he will give thanks to the Lord.
> He will direct his counsel and knowledge
>   and he will reflect upon hidden matters.
> He will make known the instruction of what he has learned
>   and boast in the law of the covenant of the Lord. (Sir 39:6-8)

---

1. His ruminations on evil daughters (Sir 26:10-12) and wives, both good and bad (26:5-9, 13-18), e.g., are nothing if not opinionated.

2. Greek is anarthrous: *pneumati syneseōs emplēsthēsetai autos.*

118

Naturally, most interpreters take the "spirit of understanding" to signal a charismatic endowment of the spirit.[3] This is the inspired scribe *par excellence.*

If we take the tenor of this collection and the context of this saying seriously, however, we are left to admit that Ben Sira would not have understood the scribal task in this way. There is every indication in Sirach, and none to the contrary, that the scribe will be filled with a spirit of understanding in the course of his study, travel, and prayer — and not through a moment of inspiration.

Ben Sira is utterly taken with the splendor of the scribal vocation, and he urges his students not to recoil at the exhausting labor this vocation will demand of them. Therefore, he tenders this clearheaded advice to his students: "If you are willing, child, you can be taught, and if you devote your soul (to it), you can be clever" (Sir 6:32).[4] His students must love to listen, pay attention, stand in the company of elders, seek mentors, listen to every godly discourse, let no wise proverb escape, rise early to meet an intelligent person, and — in what is a delightful image of tenacity — let their foot wear out their mentors' doorsteps. The student must "reflect on the statutes of the Lord, and meditate at all times on his commandments." Once all of this is done, and done tenaciously, the Lord "will give insight to your mind, and your desire for wisdom will be granted" (Sir 6:32-37). This promise situates the impartation of divine insight in the context of listening and studying and devoting oneself to a mentor rather than in the hope of a charismatic endowment. Such an experience would violate Ben Sira's

---

3. E.g., F. Büchsel, *Der Geist Gottes im Neuen Testament* (Gütersloh: Bertelsmann, 1926) 58-59; H. Stadelmann, *Ben Sira als Schriftgelehrter: Eine Untersuchung zum Berufsbild des vormakkabäischen Sôfēr unter Berücksichtigung seines Verhältnisses zu Priester-, Propheten- und Weisheitslehrertum.* WUNT, 2nd ser. 6 (Tübingen: Mohr, 1980) 216-46; D. E. Orton, *The Understanding Scribe: Matthew and the Apocalyptic Ideal.* JSNTSup 25 (Sheffield: Sheffield Academic, 1989) 70-71; C. Bennema, *The Power of Saving Wisdom: An Investigation of Spirit and Wisdom in Relation to the Soteriology of the Fourth Gospel.* WUNT, 2nd ser. 148 (Tübingen: Mohr, 2002) 55-60. I accepted this interpretation in Levison, *The Spirit in First Century Judaism.* AGJU 29 (Leiden: Brill, 1997) 198-99. J. Liesen demurs by suggesting that the understanding which the scribe of Sir 39:6 exhibits is not a miraculous superadditum that distinguishes him from inferior scribes and all other people but "the creational endowments [*sic*] come to full fruition. . . ."; *Full of Praise: An Exegetical Study of Sir 39,12-35.* JSJSup 64 (Leiden: Brill, 2000) 64.

4. Greek: *ean thelēs teknon, paideuthēsē kai ean epidōs tēn psychēn sou, panourgos esē.*

grasp of the scribal student's time-consuming, text-centered, and mentor-dependent task, which requires unparalleled diligence.

The scribe's vocation, which is depicted later in the collection of Ben Sira's sayings, is no less demanding than the student's.[5] In order to accentuate the worth and intensity of a scribal vocation, Ben Sira compares the task of the scribe with the task of the tradesman. He observes, for instance, that the scribe will rise early, not to labor, but to pray. There are, in fact, three distinguishing tasks of the accomplished scribe that are inaccessible to the tradesman: travel, study of Torah, and prayer. No one else — not the businessperson or the farmer or the painter or the blacksmith or the potter — is sought out for counsel or judgment. While they maintain the world, keep cities functioning, even provide food to the hungry, their concern ultimately must be for the exercise of their trade.

"How different," continues Ben Sira, "is the one who devotes himself to the study of the law of the Most High! He seeks out the wisdom of all the ancients, and is concerned with prophecies; he preserves the sayings of the famous and penetrates the subtleties of parables; he seeks out the hidden meanings of proverbs" (38:34b–39:3). The scribe "serves among the great and appears before rulers; he travels in foreign lands and learns what is good and evil in the human lot" (39:4). He is, as well, a person who rises early to pray and to ask pardon for his sins (39:5).

Torah study. Travel. Prayer. These provide the crucible in which the scribe receives insight. Through study of Torah, serving in foreign courts, and prayer he will be filled with a spirit of wisdom. If, in other words, Ben Sira can assure his students that God will "give insight to your mind, and your desire for wisdom will be granted" (6:37), here he assures scribes that, by means of study, travel, and prayer, "if the great Lord is willing, he [the scribe] will be filled with a spirit of understanding" (39:6).[6] Diligent labor will not go unrequited.

Throughout this collection of his sayings, Ben Sira, as a teacher of scribal students, lays inordinate emphasis upon the significance of study and the

---

5. See also the pursuit of wisdom in Sir 14:20-27.

6. It is not clear whether the pronoun "his" in 39:6b refers to God or the scribe. I am prone to think that the "words of wisdom" which pour forth are not God's but the scribe's: "he *himself* will pour forth words of *his* wisdom" *(autos anombrēsei rhēmata sophias autou)*. The repetition of the pronoun *autos* functions to lay the weight of insight upon the scribe *himself*. It is *his* counsel and knowledge that he will offer as he meditates. On the basis of his achievements, he will become famous.

essential qualities of experience. Nowhere apart from this alleged reference to a charismatic endowment does Ben Sira champion ways of acquiring wisdom other than study and experience. This resounding note of diligence for student and scribe alike explains in part another dimension of Ben Sira's convictions that undermines the interpretation of the words "filled with (a) spirit of understanding" in Sir 39:6 as an endowment of the spirit.

Ben Sira, quite simply, rejects with a vengeance knowledge that is allegedly acquired by means of both artificial and natural divination. Artificial divination entailed the quest for omens, whether through such methods as the examination of animals' internal organs or deciphering the formations in which birds would fly. Natural divination included forms of inspiration, such as being filled with *pneuma* at Delphi and prophesying, or seeing visions, or having dreams. Ben Sira is intolerant of fools who turn for knowledge either to the artificial divination of omens or to the natural divination of dreams: "The senseless have vain and false hopes, and dreams give wings to fools. As one who catches at a shadow and pursues the wind, so is anyone who believes in dreams. . . . Divinations and omens and dreams are unreal" (Sir 34:1-2, 5a). Ben Sira counts himself in no uncertain terms among the circle of those who are learned in Torah: "For dreams have deceived many, and those who put their hope in them have perished. Without such deceptions the law will be fulfilled, and wisdom comes to completion in the mouth of the faithful" (34:7-8).

There is a telling parallel between the final clause in this rejection of natural divination: "wisdom comes to completion in the mouth of the faithful." That is, in the mouths of those who are devoted to Torah, who resist the deceptions of dreams, wisdom will be complete. Similarly, the scribe who is filled with a spirit of wisdom through Torah study, travel, and prayer will have a mouth that "pours forth words of wisdom of his own" (39:6-7). Mouths are not filled with words of wisdom through quick revelations, and only through diligence will scribes be prepared to offer wise teaching.

We shall explore in detail later how quintessentially filling with *pneuma* fit the bill of natural divination.[7] Greek and Roman prophets, often female ones, would enter states of ecstasy when they would be filled with *pneuma,* whether that *pneuma* was construed as the breath of a god or a physical vapor that rose into the lungs of the prophet. For now it is enough to observe that Ben Sira would have avoided any sort of inspiration that smacked of dreams and visions, and that filling with *pneuma* was

7. See below, Part II, chapter 2.

121

just another sort, perhaps even the preeminent sort, of natural divination that stood over against learning and diligent study. The sine qua non of such infilling in the Greco-Roman world was prophecy spoken in an ecstatic state, with a loss of sense and often an inability even to remember what was spoken while in that state.

There is no room in Ben Sira's collection of sayings for this sort of inspired prophecy. Wisdom can be attained in all sorts of ways, including aging (Sir 25:3-6), but it is absolutely unattainable through the sort of prophecy that was believed by the Greeks to result from infilling with the spirit. Even when Ben Sira takes on the guise of wisdom and the garb of the prophet, he explains in the final line the source of his outpouring of words:

> As for me, I was like a canal from a river, like a water channel into a garden. I said, "I will water my garden and drench my flower-beds." And lo, my canal became a river, and my river a sea. I will again make instruction shine forth like the dawn, and I will make it clear from far away. I will again pour out teaching like prophecy, and leave it to all future generations. Observe that I have not labored for myself alone, but for all who seek wisdom. (24:30-34)

Like the scribe he depicts later in the collection (39:6), Ben Sira will pour out words of wisdom — here, "teaching like prophecy" — and leave it to future generations (24:33; 39:1).[8] The source of this prophetic teaching will not be the *pneuma* of the ecstatic prophet or the divination of the dreamer. The font of Ben Sira's wisdom lies elsewhere: Ben Sira has *labored* in the study of Torah on behalf of all who seek wisdom.

Ben Sira is first and foremost a teacher of Torah. He is passionate about Torah. In a lovely little play on Genesis 1–3, he claims that the book of the covenant, the Torah of Moses, "overflows, like the Pishon, with wisdom, and like the Tigris at the time of the first fruits. It runs over, like the Euphrates, with understanding, and like the Jordan at harvest time. It pours forth instruction like the Nile, like the Gihon at the time of vintage. The first man did not know wisdom fully, nor will the last one fathom her. For her thoughts are more abundant than the sea, and her counsel deeper than the great abyss" (Sir 24:25-29). The qualities of Torah, which he details here, render dreams superfluous, omens immaterial, visions irrelevant. The heart and soul of wisdom lie primarily in the diligent study of Torah.

---

8. The verb translated "will pour out" *(ekcheō)* in Sir 24:33 is different from the verb translated "will pour forth" *(anombrēsei)* in 39:6.

Students in his academy and accomplished scribes are not, therefore, to wait for an infilling of the spirit. They become filled rather, day by day, in study and prayer, with a spirit of understanding, for the focus of their study, the source of their meditation is itself overflowing with wisdom, running over with understanding, and pouring forth instruction.

There is still another indication of Ben Sira's understanding of the spirit in this description of the scribe, which can, for starters, be stated negatively: nowhere else in this compilation does the word "spirit" *(pneuma)* refer to other than the spirit of human beings understood in terms of the power or life of an individual.[9] Nowhere else does he use the term of some form of charismatic endowment. When he describes those who fear God, he states aphoristically that "the spirit of those who fear the Lord will live"[10] and, just a few lines later, "Blessed is the soul of the one who fears the Lord!" Spirit and soul are seemingly interchangeable here.[11] When Ben Sira advises concerning mourning the dead, he sets limits: "When the dead is at rest, let his remembrance rest, too, and be comforted in him in the departure of his spirit" (38:23).

There are, more significantly, instances in Ben Sira's praise of Israel's ancestors (chs. 44–50) in which mention of a charismatic endowment would have been especially suitable, though in these cases Ben Sira fails to take this interpretative route. The judges, whose feats are repeatedly attributed to the onrush or presence of the spirit of God in the book that bears their name, Ben Sira depicts without recourse to the spirit: "The judges also, with their respective names, whose hearts did not fall into idolatry and who did not turn away from the Lord — may their memory be blessed! May their bones send forth new life from where they lie, and may the names of those who have been honored live again in their children" (Sir 46:11-12).

Ben Sira begins his praise of Elisha by saying that he was filled with Elijah's spirit: "When Elijah was enveloped in the whirlwind, Elisha was filled with his spirit" (48:12).[12] Because this is an epitome of the dramatic

---

9. There is no need to discuss 39:28 and 43:17, where winds are in view.

10. Sir 34:13a(Eng. 14). Greek: *pneuma phoboumenōn kyrion zēsetai.*

11. Sir 34:15a(Eng. 17). Greek: *phoboumenou ton kyrion makaria hē psychē.* See 34:20, as well as 9:9, a more difficult verse to interpret.

12. Sir 48:12. Hebrew version adds, "He performed twice as many signs, and marvels with every utterance of his mouth." Particularly intriguing is Ben Sira's observation that Elisha never trembled before any ruler, nor could he be intimidated — like the well-educated scribe.

story of Elijah's ascension in the chariot and Elisha's request, "Please let me inherit a double share of your spirit," it is difficult to grasp precisely what Ben Sira means by the words, "filled with his — Elijah's — spirit."[13] Nevertheless, what is important for understanding the spirit in the scribe is that Ben Sira does not move at all in the direction of depicting Elisha's inspiration as a charismatic endowment of the spirit *of God.* It is Elijah's spirit that fills Elisha; the spirit of the mentor amply fills the protégé.

Most stunning of all, Ben Sira does not incorporate the language of inspiration in his description of Isaiah, who, "By his great spirit saw the future, and comforted the mourners in Zion" (48:24).[14] It was not the spirit of the Lord, understood as a charismatic endowment, that enabled Isaiah to see the future and to comfort mourners in Zion but the majesty of his own spirit. This is remarkable testimony to Ben Sira's belief that the source of prophecy lay in the strength of Isaiah's God-given spirit rather than in the spirit understood as a power that came upon him. What is more stunning is that Isaiah (and those in his prophetic school) had understood that the spirit rested upon Israel's leaders to anoint them with insight and able proclamation. Furthermore, authors of the postexilic era had already begun to look retrospectively at Israel's prophets and understood those prophets as the means by which the spirit — not their God-given spirits — spoke: "Many years you were patient with them, and warned them by your spirit by the hand of your prophets; yet they would not listen. Therefore you handed them over to the peoples of the lands" (Neh 9:30). Zechariah complains, "They made their hearts adamant in order not to hear the law and the words that the Lord of hosts had sent by his spirit through the hand of the former prophets. Therefore great wrath came from the Lord of hosts" (Zech 7:12). This is not the tack that Ben Sira takes; Isaiah's great spirit, not the spirit's speaking through him, caused Isaiah to see the future and to comfort the mourners in Zion.[15]

Ben Sira, then, offers several indications of the ways in which he understands the word *pneuma,* and none of them suggests the slightest whiff of a charismatic endowment. First, he uses spirit and soul interchangeably. Second, he uses the word of the lifelong spirit within a human being when he refers to the departure of the spirit at death. Third, he states that Elisha

13. 2 Kgs 2:9-12.

14. Greek: *pneumati megalō eiden ta eschata kai parekalesen tous penthountas en Ziōn.*

15. See also Sir 49:10: "May the bones of the Twelve Prophets send forth new life from where they lie, for they comforted the people of Jacob and delivered them with confident hope."

was filled with Elijah's spirit. Fourth, he includes no references to the spirit when he praises the judges and Samuel despite the preeminence of the charismatic spirit in the books that bear their names. Fifth, he attributes the prophet Isaiah's knowledge to his own great spirit.

If Ben Sira attributes scribal wisdom to a charismatic endowment in Sir 39:6-7, then he does so in isolation from his understanding of "spirit" in the entire book. Such an understanding runs against the grain of the compilation, in which scriptural references to "spirit" fail to appear where they might be expected and prophetic insight is, in contrast to the views of other postbiblical interpreters, ascribed to greatness of spirit rather than to the reception of the spirit.

Within two centuries of Ben Sira's death, a hymn writer in Palestine would thank God for spirit-inspired insight:

> And I, the Instructor, have known you, my God,
> through the spirit which you gave (in)to me,
> and I have listened loyally to your wonderful secret through
> your holy spirit.
> You have opened within me
> knowledge of the mystery of your wisdom,
> the source of your power. (1QH 20:11-13)

Philo Judaeus, in Alexandria, would make repeated claims to being filled with the spirit, or taken to the heights on the inspired winds of knowledge, or to have the spirit within speak peaceably to him like an old friend.[16] The author of the book of Acts would claim that the followers of Jesus could be filled with the spirit and speak God's marvelous acts in foreign languages, leaving rulers spellbound by their insight in the interpretation of scripture.

The rich legacy of these later writers, with their frequent references to filling with the spirit, may make it natural to interpret Ben Sira's words "filled with spirit of understanding" to mean that a divine spirit would, at one or more moments in a scribe's life, enter into that scribe and endow him with wisdom.

As natural as this interpretation may seem at first blush, it fails to pay due attention to the tenor of Ben Sira's sayings, which provide every indication that he puts no stock in a charismatic endowment with a spirit of

---

16. See, e.g., J. R. Levison, "Inspiration and the Divine Spirit in the Writings of Philo Judaeus," *JSJ* 26 (1995) 271-323.

understanding. He espouses instead a strenuous work ethic for his students, which includes study and shadowing a mentor; only in the context of this process will God give insight to students' minds. This tenacity does not end with an exit from Ben Sira's academy. Scribes combine study, lectures, travel, and prayer; only through this process will a scribe be filled with a spirit of understanding.

Nor should scribes await an endowment of the spirit. Ben Sira vehemently rejects forms of natural divination, with their underlying conviction that the divine world reveals itself through dreams and visions. The scribe will not receive the spirit, like Cassandra, the Delphic priestess, or sibyls, in order to teach. This ability comes through study, travel, and prayer — and all of this focused upon Torah, which itself overflows with wisdom and understanding.

Ben Sira never once, in his interpretation of scripture, attributes the actions of focal Israelite figures to the divine spirit, even when the scriptural texts do precisely that. Neither the judges nor Samuel is identified by the gift of the spirit. On one occasion, Ben Sira even attributes knowledge of the future, not to the gift of the prophetic spirit, but to the greatness of Isaiah's own spirit.

In brief, Ben Sira was not an inspired scribe, nor did he advise his students to aspire to this image of a scribe. When he paused to trace these contours, he described a scribe whose "understanding will never be blotted out" and who "will leave a name greater than a thousand" (Sir 39:9-11). To develop this auspicious reputation, contended Ben Sira, the scribe must devote endless hours to the study of scripture, to the company of others in the lecture hall, to travel and the observation of dignitaries and rulers, and to early mornings of prayer. Nothing else would do. And he, of course, as his compilation tells us, knew he was that successful scribe, whose memory would not disappear, whose name would live through all generations, for, at one moment in this collection, when the instruction of wisdom personified metamorphoses into the instruction of Ben Sira, he lays claim to eternity for himself: "I will again pour out teaching like prophecy, and leave it to all future generations" (24:33). And how did he cultivate this legacy? Through hard work — nothing more and nothing less — on others' behalf: "Observe that I have not labored for myself alone, but for all who seek wisdom" (24:34).

Ben Sira's convictions lead us back, yet again, to the self-serving claims of a hapless Elihu:

It is the spirit in a mortal, the breath of the Almighty, that makes for understanding. (Job 32:8)

For I am full of words;
    the spirit within me lays siegeworks against me.
My heart is indeed like wine that has no vent;
    like new wineskins, it is ready to burst.
I must speak, so that I may find relief;
    I must open my lips and answer. (32:18-20)

The figure of Elihu is young and impatient, defiant and overconfident. Yet his claim that God's spirit, or breath, within him is laying siegeworks against him and is ready to burst is quite like Ben Sira's scribe, who "will be filled by a spirit of understanding" and who "will pour out his own words of wisdom." For Elihu and Ben Sira alike, the font of wisdom is a God-given spirit within. For both, this spirit — God's breath within Elihu — bursts into words, as Elihu expresses it, or "pours out his own words of wisdom."

The point at which Elihu and Ben Sira part company concerns the long and arduous process of study. A youthful Elihu derides the mentors whom Ben Sira commends and offers little evidence of long hours of study and early mornings in prayer. In brief, Elihu fails to grasp what lies at the heart of Ben Sira's instruction: a spirit of understanding fills a scribe exclusively through a life filled with lecture halls, study of Torah, experiences such as travel, meditative prayer, even greying hair. Torah is inspired, not the scribe, whose principal vocation is "to glory in the Torah of the Lord's covenant" (Sir 39:8).

The Fragile Sanctity of the Holy Spirit

Stirring a Holy Spirit

Arguably the most picturesque acknowledgement of the gifted spirit within, its association with the cultivation of wisdom, knowledge, and various skills and a profusion of vitality, occurs in the tale of Susanna, a young woman of inordinate beauty and impeccable virtue. One day, having sent her servants to fetch what she needed, she bathed in a garden. Two elders, who had longed for her sexually, hid themselves in the garden. While

Susanna's servants were away, the elders approached her and demanded that she have sexual relations with them or else they would accuse her of adultery with a young man. She refused. When Susanna was put on trial the following day, the word of the two elders was naturally taken as truth, despite her protests. God, however, "raised up the holy spirit of a young man"[17] (Sus 45[Theodotion]), Daniel, who began to shout, "I am innocent of this woman's death!" He then devised a plan to discern the truth: he interrogated each separately and asked under which tree each saw her committing adultery. Each elder identified a different tree, and so they were put to death — the same penalty that they had sought for Susanna.

This quaint yet disturbing tale, composed sometime during the Greco-Roman era, is a lightning rod of sorts, around which several of the themes of biblical literature coalesce. Daniel's spirit exhibits the sort of wisdom that is typically characteristic of elders, and so the other elders follow his strategy for discerning the truth of the matter. This is one of the main points of the story, which is made with an exclamation point when the elders say to him, "Come, sit among us and inform us, for God has given you the standing of an elder" (Sus 50). Here, then, we see yet again in story form the point Elihu had made in fractious dialogue with Job:

> But truly it is the spirit in a mortal,
>> the breath of the Almighty that makes for understanding.
> It is not the old that are wise,
>> nor the aged that understand what is right. (Job 32:8-9)

Unfortunately, Elihu's words belie his ignorance; Daniel's do not.

This story also places the accent upon the raising up or prompting of Daniel's spirit. His spirit is already holy, and this propitious moment demands that it be prompted into action. God raises his holy spirit, therefore, to disrupt the situation and to devise a plan to exonerate Susanna. This is reminiscent of the magnificent outpouring of possessions and skills that accompanied the construction of the tent of meeting. Time and again the narrative accentuates the amazing generosity that came about when God prompted the spirits and lifted the hearts of the Israelites (Exod 35:5, 21; 36:2).

This simple tale, therefore, gathers emphases that have emerged throughout Israel's literary tapestry, including the attribution of virtue to

---

17. Greek: *exēgeiren ho theos to pneuma to hagion paidariou neōterou.*

the God-given spirit, the conviction that this spirit rather than age brings wisdom, and the belief that this spirit can be prompted to achieve extraordinary ends. All of this occurs in a single line: "God raised up the holy spirit of a young man." While this line functions as a theological précis of sorts, it also introduces in narrative form a new element: the spirit that Daniel has within him is the holy spirit. He is characterized as having a holy spirit within that decries injustice and exhibits wisdom well beyond his years. Rather than accepting a false verdict, he screams, "I want no part in shedding this woman's blood!" (Sus 46). This reaction is certainly dense with holiness.

This description of Daniel's spirit is not a bit surprising in a tale that was appended to the book of Daniel, a book which contains more than one reference to a man who was full to the brim of the spirit. In fact, the Septuagint translation contains references to the holy spirit within Daniel even where the original Aramaic version does not.[18] We may recall that twice the queen recognizes that Daniel has spirit to the nth degree *(rûaḥ yattîrâ/ yattîrā')* (Dan 5:12; 6:3[MT 4]). Theodotion's translation reads, "spirit to the nth degree" *(pneuma perisson)*, but the Septuagint contains references to the "holy spirit" *(pneuma hagion* in 5:12; 6:4).[19] Given the Septuagint's penchant for literal, even wooden, translation,[20] the shift from "excellent spirit" in Aramaic to "holy spirit" in the Septuagint may prove significant. It suggests either how readily a translator could have preferred the translation *pneuma hagion* to *pneuma perisson* as a description of the human spirit within, or, even more evocatively, that the original Aramaic underlying the Septuagint may actually have read "holy spirit."[21]

Whether it belongs to the Aramaic stratum or is the result of a translator's hand in the biblical book of Daniel, the unequivocal description of the spirit which Daniel has from birth — it is *his* in the tale of Susanna — as

18. On the Greek versions, see J. J. Collins, *Daniel*. Hermeneia (Minneapolis: Fortress, 1993) 3-11; T. J. Meadowcroft, *Aramaic Daniel and Greek Daniel: A Literary Comparison*. JSOTSup 198 (Sheffield: Sheffield Academic, 1995); English translations on 281-306.

19. The reference in Dan 5:14 to *rûaḥ 'ĕlāhîn* reads, in Theodotion's version, *pneuma theou.* Dan 5:14-15 is missing from the LXX version.

20. See Meadowcroft, *Aramaic Daniel and Greek Daniel,* 23-26.

21. Theodotion's version of Daniel 4–6 contains references to the holy spirit within Daniel where the Aramaic version does not. Three times in succession, Nebuchadnezzar recognizes that Daniel has within him *rûaḥ-'ĕlāhîn qaddîšîn* (4:5, 6, 15[Eng. 8, 9, 18]); Theodotion's version reads instead *pneuma theou hagion* (4:8, 9, 18; the LXX version lacks vv. 6-9). In Dan 5:11, the words *rûaḥ 'ĕlāhîn qaddîšîn bēh* are spoken by the queen; but here Theodotion's version reads *en hō pneuma theou.* The LXX version lacks this reference.

holy spirit opens a fresh vista. Storytellers and translators, both Theodotion and Septuagint translators, did not shy away from references to the holy spirit within. Daniel's spirit in this tale is very much like the sort of spirit that filled Micah with a declaration of justice, that enabled Joseph to interpret dreams, that equipped Bezalel to teach the artisans in his charge how to construct the tent of meeting, that Daniel possessed to the fullest degree, so that he could interpret, solve, plot and scheme. Yet this vitality within is now clearly conceived of as a *holy spirit* that can be prompted to decry deception and to scheme for the cause of justice. This clear identification of the spirit humans possess from birth as holy spirit opens a new chapter in reflections upon the holy spirit in the emerging world of Judaism.

Defiling a Holy Spirit

What the tale of Susanna offers in story form, the Dead Sea Scrolls offer in prescriptive language. In the Damascus Document, which prescribes a way of life for communities related to the community at Qumran but scattered throughout Palestine, the human spirit is referred to as a "holy spirit":[22]

> . . . to keep apart from every uncleanness according to their regulations, without anyone *defiling his holy spirit* [*rwḥ qdšyw*], according to what God kept apart for them. For all those who walk according to these matters in perfect holiness, in accordance with his teaching, God's covenant is a guarantee for them that they shall live a thousand generations. (CD VII 3-6)[23]

Although the precise nature of this spirit is not altogether clear in this particular admonition, it becomes clear when this statement from the seventh column is placed alongside the occurrence of similar language in the twelfth column: "No one should *defile his soul* with any living being or one which creeps, by eating them, from the larvae of bees to every living being

22. For an overview of the word *rwḥ* in the Dead Sea Scrolls, see the appendix in A. E. Sekki, *The Meaning of* Ruaḥ *at Qumran.* SBLDS 110 (Atlanta: Scholars, 1989) 225-39.

23. We cannot be completely sure that the possessive "his" in the words "his holy spirit" refers to a member of the community rather than to God, even though the antecedent of this possessive pronoun is a member of the community rather than God. Quotations of the Dead Sea Scrolls are taken, for the most part, from F. G. Martínez and E. J. C. Tigchelaar, *The Dead Sea Scrolls: Study Edition.* 2 vols. (Leiden: Brill and Grand Rapids: Eerdmans, 1997, 1998).

. . . which creeps in water" (CD XII 11-13). The formulations and vocabulary of VII 4 and XII 11 are forged on the same anvil; the Hebrew word "soul" *(npš)* in one reappears as "holy spirit" *(rwḥ)* in the other.

These similarities, including the reappearance of the verb "defile," suggest that the words "his holy spirit" in CD VII 4 are synonymous with "his soul" in CD XII 11-12. A further signal that soul and holy spirit are synonymous here is the incorporation of the language of Leviticus:

> You shall not make yourselves [*napšōtêkem*] detestable with any creature that swarms; you shall not defile yourselves with them, and so become unclean. (Lev 11:43)

> You shall not bring abomination on yourselves [*napšōtêkem*] by animal or by bird or by anything with which the ground teems, which I have set apart for you to hold unclean. (Lev 20:25)

The way in which CD VII 4 draws upon the phraseology of Lev 11:43 and 20:25 is an indication that the words "holy spirit" in the Damascus Document were considered an apt replacement for the word *nephesh* in Leviticus.[24] The intensity of the command not to defile one's *nephesh* in Leviticus, in other words, is transposed into an even higher key by the introduction of the words "holy spirit" in CD VII 4.

For the people of Qumran, the issue is not one of animals or birds, but unwavering commitment to the covenant, as they understand it. What is incumbent upon them is apparent by way of contrast with what the wicked priests in Jerusalem do. These priests have condemned themselves simply by opposing the statutes of the covenant people near the Dead Sea: "And also they defile their holy spirit, for with blasphemous tongue they have opened their mouth against the statutes of God's covenant, saying: 'they are unfounded.' They speak abomination against them" (CD V 11-13).

The terms holy spirit and *nephesh* are used synonymously elsewhere in the Dead Sea Scrolls in several early wisdom-oriented fragments that together have been entitled *4QInstruction*. In a portion that deals pragmatically with financial wherewithal, including the prompt repayment of debts, there occurs an admonition against dishonesty, possibly some sort of disingenuousness that is intended to allay or delay the problem of in-

---

24. For background and bibliography, see Sekki, *The Meaning of* Ruaḥ *at Qumran*, 112-14. For a more detailed layout of the relevant Hebrew, see Levison, *The Spirit in First Century Judaism*, 74-75.

debtedness.[25] This admonition cautions against exchanging a holy spirit for money:

> [Do not in your affairs demean] your spirit; do not for any money exchange your holy spirit [*rwḥ qdškh*], for no price is adequate. . . . (4Q416 fr. 2 II 6-7)

As is typical of wisdom literature, these instructions are reiterated slightly later.

> [Do not se]ll your soul [*npškh*] for money. It is better that you are a servant in the spirit, and that you serve your overseers for nothing. (4Q416 fr. 2 II 17)[26]

The clearest indication in these two texts that the holy spirit comprises the core substance of life and not a subsequent endowment is the interchangeability that exists between one's holy spirit and the soul or *nephesh,* as in CD VII 4 and CD XII 1: ". . . do not for any money exchange your holy spirit"; "[Do not se]ll your soul for money." Adherents of the covenant must not exchange their *holy spirits* for money; that is, they must not sell their *souls* for money. Holiness is more important than financial gain; integrity must always take priority over economic ambition.

Another indication that the holy spirit in this context is construed as the core of a human being whose integrity or holiness can be lost — exchanged or sold — is the further recurrence of the word "spirit" in the first directive: the command not to "exchange your holy spirit" comprises a slightly richer repetition of the command not to "demean your spirit":

> Do not in your affairs *demean your spirit* [*rwḥkh*];
> do not for any money exchange your holy spirit [*rwḥ qdškh*].[27]

These are but three brief snippets from the Dead Sea Scrolls, yet together they provide a lucid perspective on the beliefs of at least some inhabitants of Palestine during the Greco-Roman era prior to the mid-first

25. For a discussion of this text, including the key themes of spirituality and poverty, see M. J. Goff, *The Worldly and Heavenly Wisdom of 4QInstruction.* STDJ 50 (Leiden: Brill, 2003) 80-167, and on debt repayment and one's holy spirit, see 226.

26. See parallel fragments 4Q417 fr. 1 II 8, 21; 4Q418 fr. 8 3-4, 14.

27. In the second directive, the command not to sell one's soul is explained in this way: one should serve "with the spirit" for no pay at all if this is the way to preserve one's integrity. In this command, the words "soul" and "spirit" are synonymous.

century C.E. The authors of the foundational Damascus Document and the aphorisms and advice in *4QInstruction* readily refer to the human *nephesh* as the holy spirit in contexts pervaded by a concern for holiness and integrity. The human *spirit* is not neutral territory. The human soul, or *nephesh*, is not unaligned. Both are holy regions. The spirits of adherents to the new covenant in locations scattered throughout Palestine, therefore, are considered holy spirits that can be defiled, as the wicked priests in Jerusalem have defiled theirs. These holy spirits can be sold off, bartered for paltry money, and so the wisdom teacher of *4QInstruction* urges his readers not to demean the spirit in daily affairs, not to exchange their holy spirits or to sell their souls to the world of finance and property.

Forfeiting a Holy Spirit

If the holy spirit within can be defiled or exchanged, according to writings from the Judean Desert, it can also be so purloined that it brings premature death, as in the *Liber antiquitatum biblicarum* of Pseudo-Philo, a wonderful retelling of scripture from creation to the death of Saul. In the course of this fascinating reassessment of the ambiguous figure of Balaam, the story of Balaam and his trustworthy ass undergoes some significant metamorphoses, three of which have to do with the spirit of God.

The first modification (*LAB* 18:3) is an extrabiblical addition to Numbers 22 that is placed into Balaam's mouth as he addresses the messengers whom Balak, king of Moab, has sent in an effort to persuade Balaam to curse the Israelites: "Behold, this has given pleasure to Balak, but he does not know that the plan of God is not like the plan of humans. Now he does not realize that the spirit that is given to us is given for a time. But our ways are not straight unless God wishes."[28] This is a generalized expression of

---

28. Latin: *Ecce placuit Balac, et nescit quoniam non ita est consilium Dei sicut consilium hominis. Ipse autem non novit, quoniam spiritus qui nobis datus est in tempore datus est. Vie autem nostre non sunt directe nisi velit Deus.* Quotations from pseudepigraphical literature, including the *Liber antiquitatum biblicarum,* tend on the whole to be based upon J. H. Charlesworth, ed., *The Old Testament Pseudepigrapha.* 2 vols. (Garden City: Doubleday, 1983, 1985). Occasionally I have altered the translation, and frequently I have rendered translations in more gender-inclusive language. The best resources for the Latin text include H. Jacobson, *A Commentary on Pseudo-Philo's* Liber antiquitatum biblicarum *with Latin Text and English Translation,* 2 vols. AGJU 31 (Leiden: Brill, 1996); and D. J. Harrington, J. Cazeaux, C. Perrot, and P. Bogaert, ed., *Les antiquités bibliques: Pseudo-Philon.* 2 vols. SC 229-30 (Paris: du Cerf, 1976). The *Liber antiquitatum biblicarum* is probably not based upon the Septuagint

Gen 6:3, in which God limited human life to three generations: "My spirit shall not abide in mortals forever, for they are flesh; their days shall be one hundred twenty years." If the Genesis text provides any guidance for the reading of the *Liber antiquitatum biblicarum*, then Balaam has in mind here the spirit which God gives to all human beings to keep them alive rather than the spirit understood as an endowment that inspires some sort of utterance.

The second adaptation (*LAB* 18:10a-b) occurs in a highly truncated version of Num 22:36–23:6, in the depiction of Balaam's arrival in Moab: "And he came into the land of Moab and built an altar and offered sacrifices. And when he saw part of the people, the spirit of God did not abide in him."[29] This is a remarkably blatant contradiction of the biblical text. According to Num 24:2, Balaam uttered his first oracle when "the spirit of God came upon him." According to *LAB* 18:10, Balaam uttered his oracle when "the spirit of God did not abide in him." While in Israel's tale the oracle is produced by the *presence* of the spirit, in Pseudo-Philo's version the oracle is produced despite the *absence* of the spirit.

The particular shaping of these words, which dissolve the ambiguity of Balaam in the biblical book of Numbers by denying him the spirit altogether, suggests that Pseudo-Philo has deepened the impact of Gen 6:3, which he introduced in *LAB* 18:3. Initially Balaam acknowledged the essential thrust of Gen 6:3, that "the spirit that is given to us is given for a time." In this second reference to the spirit of God, the allusion to Gen 6:3 is unmistakable:

Liber antiquitatum biblicarum 18:10	Vulgate Gen 6:3
non	non
permansit	permanebit
in eo	in homine
spiritus	spiritus
Dei	meus (Deus)[30]

---

but, more likely, upon a Hebrew text on which the LXX depended. On that text, see D. H. Harrington, "The Biblical Text of Pseudo-Philo's *Liber Antiquitatum Biblicarum*," *CBQ* 22 (1971) 1-17; "The Original Language of Pseudo-Philo's *Liber Antiquitatum Biblicarum*," *HTR* 63 (1970) 503-14; L. H. Feldman, "Prolegomenon," to *The Biblical Antiquities of Philo*, ed. M. R. James (New York: Ktav, 1968) li-lii.

29. Latin: *Et venit in terram Moab, et edificavit sacrarium et obtulit oblationes. Et cum vidisset partem populi, non permansit in eo spiritus Dei.*

30. I have compared the text from *LAB* with the Vulgate because *Liber antiquitatum biblicarum* is extant only in Latin.

With the insertion of language from Gen 6:3, *Liber antiquitatum biblicarum* 18:10 becomes vastly different from Num 24:2, in which the spirit of God "came/was in" Balaam.[31] The startling exactness with which *Liber antiquitatum biblicarum* 18:10 mirrors Gen 6:3 serves to substantiate the initial allusion to Gen 6:3 in *Liber antiquitatum biblicarum* 18:3. The second allusion reinforces the first impression that the spirit which Balaam possessed but now loses is not a special prophetic endowment but the life-giving spirit which each human has for a limited time.

The third reference to the spirit brings the significance of these allusions to Gen 6:3 irrevocably to the fore. Balaam interrupts his oracle in the presence of Balak, in a moment of critical self-reflection, to draw an intimate association between loss of the holy spirit and the imminence of death:

> I am restrained in my speech and cannot say what I see with my eyes, because there is little left of the holy spirit that abides in me. For I know that, because I have been persuaded by Balak, I have lessened the time of my life. And behold my remaining hour. (*LAB* 18:11)

Each reference in *LAB* 18 has to do with a loss of the spirit: 18:3 states that the spirit is given for a time; 18:10 contradicts Num 24:2 by stating that the spirit of God did *not* continue to abide in Balaam; and in 18:11 Balaam himself laments the loss of the holy spirit.[32] It is not as if Balaam simply does not succumb to the powerful prophetic spirit. Much more is at stake: he loses the vital power of life in the face of impending death. Restraint in speech, loss of the holy spirit, and a shortened life span conspire to bring Balaam to his final hour.

Here, then, the holy spirit is situated securely in the shadow of death.

---

31. The Vulgate of Num 24:2 differs sharply from *LAB* 18:10, reading: *et inruente in se spiritu Dei* ("And the spirit of God rushed into him"). The Vulgate here appears to be influenced by the many instances in which the spirit comes forcefully upon people (e.g., Judg 14:6, 19; 15:14; 1 Sam 10:6-10). The additional reference in LXX, but not in Hebrew or Latin, Num 23:7 reads: *kai egenēthē pneuma theou ep' autō*.

32. This consistency suggests that H. Jacobson's complicated hypothesis is unnecessary (*A Commentary on Pseudo-Philo's* Liber antiquitatum biblicarum, 594). He proposes that Pseudo-Philo wrote what essentially occurs in Num 24:2 *(egenetō pneuma)*, and that this was misread as *emene to pneuma*, i.e., *permansit spiritus*. He conjectures further that "the negative may have been introduced by a scribe who thought he was improving the sense, or might simply have arisen through paleographical corruption, if e.g. the verb in question was compound rather than simplex (ἐνεγένετο, ἐπεγένετο, *vel sim.*)." Jacobson's reason for this suggestion is that he does "not see how such a sense [the loss of the spirit] could work in LAB's context." The loss of the spirit, we have seen, is integral to the context.

More accurately, perhaps, Balaam's lack of integrity actually precipitates the loss of this holy spirit, hastening the darkness of death. There is hardly any speech left in Balaam, hardly any holy spirit to prompt his words, hardly any holy spirit to keep him alive. This death is premature death, prompted by a lack of integrity. Balaam has done precisely what the author of 4QInstruction cautioned against: he has exchanged his holy spirit for money.

Summary

Though the tale of Daniel's heroism, these snippets of the Dead Sea Scrolls, and such a creative recasting of the story of Balaam represent divergent literary genres — a freely narrated tale, wisdom instruction, and rewritten scripture — and exist currently in three different languages — Greek, Hebrew, and Latin — they offer together an unmistakable indication of the readiness with which Jewish authors of the Greco-Roman era could identify the human spirit as a holy spirit. This is particularly evident when later Jewish authors adapt biblical references to the soul or spirit by referring instead to the holy spirit. In the Damascus Document, for example, the words "holy spirit" provide an apt surrogate for *nephesh* in the book of Leviticus. Similarly, the author of the tale of Daniel and Susanna begins with a familiar expression, *to stir up the spirit of someone*. God had "stirred up the spirit of King Cyrus of Persia" to issue an edict that returned Jews to their homeland (Ezra 1:1; 2 Chr 36:22). God had "stirred up the spirit of Zerubbabel son of Shealtiel, governor of Judah, and the spirit of Joshua son of Jehozadak, the high priest, and the spirit of all the remnant of the people; and they came and did work on the house of the Lord of hosts, their God" (Hag 1:14). These people, "everyone whose spirit God had stirred," set out to rebuild the temple (Ezra 1:5).[33] This expression is adapted, ever so slightly, in the tale of Susanna by the addition of a single word, "holy": "God stirred up the *holy* spirit of a young lad named Daniel" (Sus 45). And the author of *Liber antiquitatum biblicarum*, by means of the repeated importation of language from Gen 6:3, in which the spirit is regarded, not as a temporary prophetic endowment, but as that which keeps human beings alive for a limited time, transforms the temporary advent of the spirit of God into the permanent presence of the holy spirit that gives life. In the original version, the spirit of God comes upon Balaam and

---

33. Ezra is modeled after Exod 35:21, in which the spirits of the Israelites were stirred to contribute to the tent of presence.

prompts a prophetic vision, while in this later version the seer loses the holy spirit and faces death. This is not the spirit of God that has come upon him temporarily to prompt a vision, as in the book of Numbers, but the holy spirit that would have kept him alive longer had he not acted avariciously on behalf of Balak, king of Moab.

There exists as well in each of these texts a strong sense that the spirit within is not neutral. Daniel's spirit, which prompts him to act justly (over against the entirety of his community), is a holy spirit. The holy spirit, according to the Damascus Document, can be defiled; in *4QInstruction,* it can be exchanged for money. Balaam, in the *Liber antiquitatum biblicarum,* actually loses this holy spirit within and faces premature death because he has acted without integrity and served Balak rather than the Israelites. This observation, that the adjective "holy" is not superfluous, that it does convey a conviction in which the core of a human being can be characterized by integrity and purity and justice, flows from the font of Israel's own narratives, in which figures such as Joseph, Bezalel, Joshua, and Daniel have within them an extraordinary spirit that enables them to unravel the inscrutable. The apparently simple addition of the adjective "holy" is then much more than a matter of nomenclature. Rooted in scriptural precedent, it points in a profoundly fresh direction — toward a life of justice (Daniel and Susanna), of purity (Damascus Document), of contented poverty *(4QInstruction),* and of integrity *(Liber antiquitatum biblicarum).* Further, this ready identification of the spirit as holy was far more widespread than the author of the Damascus Document would probably have cared to admit, for the hegemony of Stoicism — the most influential philosophical tradition for at least five hundred years, and certainly the dominant cosmological and anthropological perspective of the first century — cast its spell upon many Jewish authors. The impact of Stoicism upon Judaism would lead inevitably to fascinating and frequent transformations in Jewish conceptions of the spirit.

The Spirit and the Stoa

Pneuma, Cosmos, Psyche

During the year 313 B.C.E., a philosopher by the name of Zeno, from the village of Citium, on the island of Cyprus, made his way, as philosophers tended to do, to Athens, where he studied with Crates the Cynic,

Antisthenes the Socratic, as well as Xenocrates and Polemon, two distinguished philosophers from among the Academics. Their efforts, particularly Polemon's, who emphasized the notion of nature, did not go unrewarded, as Zeno (335-263 B.C.E.) began to teach in the *Stoa Poecile* — the Painted Colonnade — which gave rise to the name of Stoicism. Zeno's successor, Cleanthes (331-232), would put his own distinctive mark upon Stoicism, as would his successor, Chrysippus (ca. 280-207). Within two centuries, Stoicism would claim its place as the preeminent frame of reference in philosophical and, to some extent, popular culture throughout the Roman era. It may be that our modern preoccupation with Plato and Aristotle is due in part to historical accident, as the writings of Zeno, Cleanthes, and Chrysippus exist in only fragmentary form, in contrast to the treatises of Aristotle, the dialogues of Plato, and Plutarch's *Lives*. While distinguished exponents of Stoicism, Cicero and Seneca, have bequeathed a good measure of significant literature, we have little of the actual words of its founding philosophers.[34]

There exists, nonetheless, much that we do know about Stoicism and, for the purposes of a book that encompasses formative Judaism and Christianity, much that is more important than founding philosophers, for our interest lies not in the origins of Stoic thought about the *pneuma* but the ways in which Stoics of the Greco-Roman era conceived of *pneuma*. The conception of *pneuma* underwent significant metamorphoses in the first two centuries of Stoic thought, due in no small measure to the growing stature of Alexandrian physicians, who accorded increasingly dominant roles to the *pneuma* in human physiology.

By the first century C.E., one of the foundational conceptions of Stoicism was that *pneuma* pervades a living and rational cosmos. According to Diogenes Laertius, who offered a summary of Stoicism, perhaps in the second century C.E., Stoics believed that "the world is a living being, rational, animate and intelligent . . . endowed with soul" (*Lives* 7.142). This soul consists of a mixture of fire and air that comprises *pneuma*, which maintains the tension or cohesion that is necessary to unify the cosmos. Alexander of Aphrodisias would later summarize the view of Chrysippus: "He assumes that the whole material world is unified by a pneuma which wholly pervades it and by which the universe is made coherent and kept together"

---

34. For extensive analysis of Zeno, Cleanthes, and Chrysippus, see G. Verbeke, *L'Évolution de la Doctrine du* Pneuma: *du Stoicisme a S. Augustin: Etude philosophique* (Paris: Desclée de Brouwer, 1945) 11-90.

(*De mixtione* 216, lines 14-17).[35] Diogenes Laertius attributed to the Stoic Antipater of Tyre the belief that "the whole world is a living being, endowed with soul and reason, and having aether for its ruling principle" (*Lives of the Philosophers* 7.139). Lucilius Balbus, a competent and careful summarizer of Stoicism in Cicero's *On the Nature of the Gods* (46-44 B.C.E.), claimed that the world order is "maintained in unison by a single divine and all-pervading spirit" (*On the Nature of the Gods* 2.19).

This distinctive view of the cosmos as pervaded by *pneuma* drew its inspiration, by way of analogy, from Stoic anthropology. The Stoics' view of the cosmos as a living, unified organism derived from their observation that human beings are living, unified organisms. For instance, because Cleanthes believed that the human soul consisted of heat, with the heart as its ruling part, by analogy he also believed that the world soul consisted of heat, with the sun as its ruling part. Chrysippus who, from 232 B.C.E. was head of the Stoa, modified this view slightly. Because he believed that the human soul consists of *pneuma*, with the mind as its ruling part, by analogy he also believed that the world soul consists of *pneuma*, with its ruling part, aether, at its farthest and purest periphery (Diogenes Laertius *Lives* 7.139).

Even the shift from Cleanthes' focus upon the centrality of heat to Chrysippus's upon *pneuma* is illuminating. Zeno, the founder of Stoicism, had regarded *pneuma* and heat as elements that lay in tension in a human being. However, at this later time, the four-element theory dominated in both cosmology and biology, in which all things were composed of heat and cold, dry and wet. *Pneuma* did not fit this scheme, so Cleanthes ascribed all activity of the soul to heat. Yet even as Cleanthes made this move, new currents were churning the waters of Alexandrian medical thought. Praxagoras, for instance, believed *pneuma* to be the main element of psychic (that is, nonphysical) movement: blood flows through the veins to produce nutrition and growth, while *pneuma* fills the arteries, transferring movement from the heart to the sinews that move the body.[36] As this emphasis upon *pneuma* among physicians increased, a concomitant decrease in interest in heat ensued, so that, by the third century B.C.E., two prominent Alexandrian physicians, Herophilos of Chalcedon (ca. 330-260) and Erasistratus of Ceos (ca. 315-240), attributed perception and move-

35. Citation is from A. A. Long and D. H. Sedley, *The Hellenistic Philosophers* (Cambridge: Cambridge University Press, 1987) 2:120-21.

36. For precise introductions to the topic and select bibliography, see H. von Staden's entries in *OCD*. More details on the medical schools, including Erasistratus, are available in Verbeke, *L'Évolution de la Doctrine du* Pneuma, 175-220.

ment to the *pneuma*. Chrysippus, as head of the Stoics, allowed this perspective to eclipse the once dominant role of heat that his predecessor, Cleanthes, had championed.

In this way, the view that *pneuma* unifies both cosmos and psyche would become regnant in Stoic thought — which itself dominated Greco-Roman culture. What is of signal importance, for the purpose of this study, is the realization that *pneuma* was believed to be the unifying element that permeates both cosmos and psyche — and that in Stoic thought there is a correspondence between these two elements, so much so that the human soul was considered to be a fragment of the cosmic soul: "the world . . . is a living thing in the sense of an animate substance. . . . And it is endowed with soul, as is clear from our several souls being each a fragment of it" (Diogenes Laertius *Lives* 7.143).[37] The human soul is, in brief, a fragment of the divine. *Pneuma* unifies both cosmos and the soul, which is a portion of it, by maintaining each in a living, unifying tension.

These cosmic and physiological conceptions of the *pneuma* do not exhaust Stoic thought. Stoicism did still more to catalyze a change of conceptions during the Greco-Roman era by acknowledging the porous borders that separate anthropology and ethics, that is, by identifying *pneuma* with the capacity for virtue. No one accomplished this with more panache and perspicuity than Seneca, a renowned Stoic statesman, who penned a letter on this topic to his friend, Lucilius, sometime during the years 63-65 C.E. — just before the Jewish War began in Palestine and perhaps while Paul was under house arrest in Rome. In this letter, Seneca describes the human *pneuma* as a holy spirit that requires careful tending.

---

37. As a fragment of the divine, the human soul was believed to carry divine characteristics. Like the purest *aether*, the ruling portion of the cosmos, the mind as *pneuma* is the ruling (hegemonic) part of the soul. Sextus Empiricus, in *Against the Mathematicians* 8.400, lucidly defines the Stoic position: "since therefore the soul and the ruling spirit is purer than any spirit. . . ." See also H. von Arnim, *Stoicorum Veterum Fragmenta*. 4 vols. (Leipzig: Teubner, 1903-24) 4:65. Diogenes Laertius gives expression to the Stoic conception of the human soul: "Nature in their view is an artistically working fire, going on its way to create; which is equivalent to a fiery, creative, or fashioning breath. And the soul is a nature capable of perception. And they regard it as the breath of life, congenital with us; from which they infer first that it is a body and secondly that it survives death. . . . Zeno of Citium and Antipater, in their treatises *De anima*, and Posidonius define the soul as a warm breath; for by this we become animate and this enables us to move" (*Lives* 7.156-57).

The Quintessence of the Holy Spirit: Seneca

There is no ancient author, Jew or Roman, male or female, who expresses the character of the spirit more poignantly than Seneca (ca. 4 B.C.E.–41 C.E.), who counsels Lucilius, the recipient of the forty-first of his moral letters, to aspire to sound understanding by looking to himself rather than to external gods and idols. Seneca focuses in this letter upon a "holy spirit" that indwells human beings:

> We do not need to uplift our hands towards heaven, or to beg the keeper of a temple to let us approach this idol's ear, as if in this way our prayers were more likely to be heard. God is near you, he is with you, he is within you. This is what I mean, Lucilius: a holy spirit dwells within us, one who marks our good and bad deeds, and is our guardian.[38] As we treat this spirit, so are we treated. (*Moral Epistles* 41.2)[39]

The person who fulfills the Stoic ideal of being unterrified in the face of dangers, untouched by desires, etc., does so by virtue of a spirit which, while abiding within, remains first of all allied with its heavenly origin:

> When a soul rises superior to other souls, when it passes through every experience as if it were of small account, when it smiles at our fears and at our prayers, it is stirred by a force from heaven. . . . Therefore, a great part of it abides in that place from whence it came down to earth . . . the great and hallowed soul, which has come down in order that we may have a nearer knowledge of divinity, does indeed associate with us, but still cleaves to its origin. (41.5)

The concept of the soul as that which "has come down in order that we may have a nearer knowledge of divinity" suggests quite clearly Seneca's adherence to the Stoic notion that the human soul is a fragment of the cosmic soul. What marks this perfect soul is not external accoutrements that can be passed on to someone else but a life lived according to reason, a life lived according to one's nature:

---

38. Latin: *sacer intra nos spiritus sedet, malorum bonorumque nostrorum observator et custos.*

39. Translations and texts for classical authors (e.g., Seneca; Plutarch; Diogenes Laertius; Dio Chrysostom), including Philo Judaeus and Flavius Josephus, are taken typically from the Loeb Classical Library.

Praise the quality in him which cannot be given or snatched away, that which is the peculiar property of the person. Do you ask what this is? It is soul, and reason brought to perfection in the soul. For a human is a reasoning animal. Therefore, a person's highest good is attained, if he has fulfilled the good for which nature designed him at birth. And what is it which this reason demands of him? The easiest thing in the world, — to live in accordance with his own nature. (41.8-9)

In this eloquent essay, the task and character of the holy spirit, understood in Stoic terms, are explained with exceptional clarity: living according to reason (the Stoic ideal) and living according to one's own nature are synonymous because one's own nature consists in part of a holy spirit, the god within, which has descended from the divine, rational world and continues, within humans, to seek association with the divine world.

It is no leap at all from Seneca's pen to the parchment of the Wisdom of Solomon, from the mind of Chrysippus to the musings of Philo Judaeus. The impact of Stoicism was immense, not least in the development of Jewish perceptions of the *pneuma,* particularly in the Egyptian city of Alexandria, a hotbed of Greco-Roman philosophical dialogue.

A Holy Spirit and the Path to Virtue:
The Alexandrian Jewish Tradition

The author of the Wisdom of Solomon transforms the biblical portrayal of inbreathing by pressing Gen 2:7 through the sieve of Stoic cosmology and Alexandrian physiology. The Septuagint translation of Gen 2:7 reads: "[God] implanted/breathed into his (the human's) face a breath of life, and the human became (into) a living soul." This translation is wooden, including even the preposition *eis* for the Hebrew *le,* which makes little sense in Greek.

In contrast, in the context of a lengthy and vitriolic indictment of those who construct idols, Gen 2:7 becomes in the Wisdom of Solomon so rich in nuance as to be untranslatable. This reconfiguration of Gen 2:7, which can be translated only provisionally as "the one who [God] breathed into him an energizing soul and implanted a living spirit" (Wis 15:11),[40] reveals traces

40. Greek: *ton empneusanta autō psychēn energousan kai emphysēsanta pneuma zōtikon.* The LXX translation of Ps 17:16(Eng. 15; MT 18:16) resembles this statement: *kai ōphthēsan*

of the Alexandrian medical tradition. The prolific medical historian Galen, for instance, could attribute to Erasistratus, the Alexandrian physician, the belief that the body contained not only "a living power" *(zōtikēn dynamin)*, but also a "psychic" one *(psychikēn);* these dimensions are reflected in the words "soul" *(psychēn)* and "living spirit" *(pneuma zōtikon).* Further, although the author of the Wisdom of Solomon has moved well beyond it, he apparently continues to bear in mind the creation of human beings from clay. The idolater is a potter or, better still, an anti-potter who provides a negative mirror of God's creativity; the verb "to form" *(plassein)*, lifted from Gen 2:7, densely populates Wis 15:7-13.[41] Like the author of Ecclesiastes, the author believes that the spirit is borrowed from God for a time and destined to return to God; because idol-crafters fail to recognize this spirit and the God who implanted it, "their heart is ashes, their hope is cheaper than dirt, and their lives are of less worth than clay" (Wis 15:10).[42]

The author of the Wisdom of Solomon anticipates this construal of creation in the opening lines of his instruction.

> For a holy spirit of discipline [*hagion gar pneuma paideias*] will flee from deceit, and will leave foolish thoughts behind, and will be ashamed at the approach of injustice. . . . For wisdom is a humane spirit [*philanthrōpon gar pneuma*], but will not free blasphemers from the guilt of their words; because God is witness of their inmost feelings, and a true observer of their hearts, and a hearer of their tongues. Because the spirit of the Lord has filled the world, and that which holds all things together knows what is said [*hoti pneuma kyriou peplērōken tēn oikoumenēn, kai to synechon ta panta gnōsin echei phōnēs*], therefore those who utter unjust things will not escape notice, and justice, when it punishes, will not pass them by. (Wis 1:5-8)

Among these earliest lines in the entire book occurs a reference to a "holy spirit" as one leg of the triangle of human existence, alongside the body and the soul: "wisdom will not enter a deceitful *soul*, or dwell in a *body* enslaved to sin. For a holy *spirit* of discipline will flee from deceit" (1:4-5a).[43]

---

hai pēgai tōn hydatōn, kai anekalyphthē ta themelia tēs oikoumenēs apo epitimēseōs sou, kyrie, apo empneuseōs pneumatos orgēs sou.

41. Its literary foreground, in part, is Isaiah 44, an earlier trenchant attack upon idolaters.

42. See further J. R. Levison, *Portraits of Adam in Early Judaism: From Sirach to 2 Baruch.* JSPSup 1 (Sheffield: JSOT, 1988) 53-54.

43. D. Winston, *The Wisdom of Solomon* (Garden City: Doubleday, 1979) 99. E. G.

This anthropological triad of body, soul, and spirit, like the later iteration of Gen 2:7 in Wisdom of Solomon 15, provides yet another instance in which the spirit, what characterizes human beings from birth, is identified as a *holy spirit*.

Yet there is much more in this claim that a holy spirit will avoid deceit and sin than a lesson in physiology. The author has drawn an implicit association, along Stoic lines, between the spirit within a human and the spirit which fills the world. The spirit within, "a disciplined holy spirit," avoids deceit, foolishness, and injustice. It corresponds to the spirit of the Lord, which is described in quintessential Stoic terms as that which "has filled the world" and which "holds all things together." This cosmic spirit, like a disciplined holy spirit, cannot tolerate injustice. The effect of these three references to the spirit in such rapid succession in relation to humanity, wisdom, and the cosmos is to give the distinct impression that all belong together, that all share in the same substance as *pneuma*, that all evince the same commitment to virtue and an abhorrence of vice.

No less significant is the addition of the adjective, "of discipline," or "of teaching," to the words "holy spirit." This holy spirit within can be taught, educated, corrected so as to flee deceit, leave foolish thoughts behind, and be ashamed at the onslaught of injustice. There is nothing particularly alien in this description of the spirit. Micah had cultivated the practice of justice. Bezalel and other skilled laborers who constructed Aaron's garments and the tent of meeting were filled with a spirit of wisdom, with skill that they had honed and were now prepared to offer in generous volunteer labor. Joshua was selected to be Moses' successor because he had spirit in him, because he had been perfectly mentored for the task. Daniel might well have been identified, in the book that bears his name, as a hero with a "holy spirit of discipline," for he had studied, prayed, and fasted along the hard-fought journey to wisdom.

Though there is nothing especially alien, from a scriptural point of view, in the Wisdom of Solomon, such an appraisal of the capacity of the holy spirit within to receive instruction in the ways of wisdom, so as to avoid evil and injustice, bears an uncanny resemblance to Seneca's descrip-

---

Clarke (*The Wisdom of Solomon* [Cambridge: Cambridge University Press, 1973] 17), for example, translates this sentence, "The holy spirit, that divine tutor, will fly from cunning stratagem." According to this interpretation, the holy spirit is to be identified in its context with wisdom that will not enter a deceitful soul (1:4), with wisdom understood as a philanthropic spirit (1:6), and with the spirit of the Lord that "has filled the world" and "holds all things together . . ." (1:7).

tion of the holy spirit as that which "indwells within us, one who marks our good and bad deeds, and is our guardian." The swift movement, further, from "a holy spirit of discipline" within a human being to "the spirit of the Lord" which "has filled the world" and which "holds all things together" is also intimately evocative of Stoicism, as Seneca gave expression to it, according to which "the great and hallowed soul, which has come down in order that we may have a nearer knowledge of divinity, does indeed associate with us, but still cleaves to its origin" (*Moral Epistles* 41.5).

The Stoic tone of the opening lines of the Wisdom of Solomon serves as well to underscore that a holy spirit of discipline can lead *all* people in the ways of wisdom; what permeates the cosmos resides within every single human being. Nowhere in these opening lines does the author of the Wisdom of Solomon offer safe haven to a single soul. *All people,* not only those with exclusive claims to inspiration, can be guided by a disciplined holy spirit; the idolaters, whom the author subsequently condemns, fail precisely because they refuse to recognize this aspect of God's creativity, and not because they lack this spirit. Theirs is not a failure of physiology but a failure of recognition. In these opening lines, therefore, scriptural conceptions of the cultivation of the spirit within, which we have traced from Micah to Daniel, are deftly interwoven with Stoic conceptions of the *pneuma.*

If the Wisdom of Solomon provides glimpses of the rapprochement that existed between scripture and Stoicism, these glimpses are relatively slender and fleeting. Philo's commentaries, by way of contrast, are so rife with Stoic conceptions that his indebtedness can be documented while barely having to stray from his interpretation of a single scriptural text, Gen 2:7. Here Philo does not in the least shy away from identifying the spirit within a human as a marvellous, divine component. This accentuation of the value of the spirit-breath within is due, in part, to Stoic influence, though his adoption of Stoic concepts is anything but uncritical.

With no apparent reticence, Philo interprets Gen 2:7 expansively to mean that God "breathed into him [humankind] from above of God's own Deity" (*The Worse Attacks the Better* 86).[44] This is no mere life-giving moment but the investiture of the human being with a dimension of the divine. The human being was "judged worthy to receive his soul not from

---

44. All texts and translations of Philo's works are taken from the Loeb Classical Library, though occasionally I have rendered translations in more gender-neutral terms. For commentary on *On the Creation of the Cosmos (De opificio mundi),* see D. T. Runia, *Philo of Alexandria, On the Creation of the Cosmos according to Moses* (Leiden: Brill, 2001).

any other thing already created, but through the breath of God imparting [empneusantos] of His own power in such measure as mortal nature could receive" (On the Virtues 203). The "essence of substance of that other soul is divine spirit" because, as Moses "in his story of the creation says . . . God breathed a breath of life into the first human, the founder of our race. . . . And clearly what was then thus breathed was aether-spirit, or something if such there be better than aether-spirit, even an effulgence of the blessed, thrice blessed nature of the God" (On the Special Laws 4.123).

The notion of the spirit as a fragment of the divine spirit comes to the fore time and again in Philo's commentaries on scripture. In his most literal interpretation of the "divine breath" of Gen 2:7, for instance, Philo falls headlong into Stoic thought when he writes, "for that which God breathed in was nothing else than a divine breath that migrated hither from that blissful and happy existence for the benefit of our race" (On the Creation 135). Similarly, he writes only slightly later of the human soul and body, "Every person, in respect of the mind, is allied to the divine Reason, having come into being as a copy or fragment or ray of that blessed nature, but in the structure of his body is allied to all the world" (On the Creation 146).[45] In his allegorical treatises, when he interprets the curse of Gen 3:14, "earth you shall eat all the days of your life," he presses the Stoic interpretation of Gen 2:7 even more vigorously: "The body, then, has been formed out of earth, but the soul is of the aether, a particle detached from the Deity: 'for God breathed into his face a breath of life, and the human became a living soul'" (Allegorical Interpretation 3.161).[46]

Philo, then, identifies the breath that humankind receives in Gen 2:7 with the mind, the ruling part of the soul, in contrast to the body, which is left out of this formula, as is also the lower part of the soul that is given either to passion or to virtue, for it is too closely aligned with the body to be considered pure aether. Only the purer soul, the mind, is divine breath: "he [Moses] did not make the substance of the mind depend on anything created, but represented it as breathed upon by God. For the Maker of all says, 'blew into his face the breath of life, and the human became a living soul'" (Who Is the Heir? 55–57).

Notwithstanding how frequently Philo adopts the Stoic perspective,

---

45. On the relationship between the effulgence of pneuma and fragments of it, see T. H. Tobin, The Creation of Man: Philo and the History of Interpretation. CBQMS 14 (Washington: Catholic Biblical Association of America, 1983) 78.

46. See also On Dreams 1.34 and Who Is the Heir? 283.

not least in his interpretation of the inbreathing of Gen 2:7, he does not ultimately accede to Stoic notions of *pneuma*.[47] In *On Planting* 18–19, where the polemical edge is sharper, Philo's own conception of the spirit functions neither as an affirmation of Stoicism, as in *On the Creation* 135, nor as a qualification of Stoicism, as in *On the Special Laws* 4.123, but as a frontal refutation of Stoicism:

> Now while others, by asserting that our human mind is a particle of the ethereal substance, have claimed for humans a kinship with the upper air; our great Moses likened the fashion of the reasonable soul to no created thing, but averred it to be a genuine coinage of that dread [unseen] Spirit, the Divine and invisible One, signed and impressed by the seal of God, the stamp of which is the Eternal Word. His words are "God in-breathed into his face a breath of life" [Gen 2:7]; so that it cannot but be that the one that receives is made in the likeness of Him Who sends forth the breath. Accordingly we also read that a human has been made after the image of God [Gen 1:27], not however after the image of anything created.

Philo, who is otherwise so prone to eclecticism, earmarks here with precision and clarity his own opinion, differentiating it from those whose influence in many cases has overwhelmed Philo's own points of view.[48]

47. Philo begins by unequivocally distinguishing himself from the Stoics: "Now while others, by asserting that our human mind is a particle of the ethereal substance, have claimed for man a kinship with the *aether* . . ." (*On Planting* 18). The "others" are the Stoics. Diogenes Laertius, in the context of a summary of Stoics (*Lives* 7.143), including Chrysippus, Zeno, Apollodorus, and Posidonius, attributes to Stoicism the view that the world is "a living being, rational, animate and intelligent," which is "endowed with soul, as is clear from our several souls being each a fragment of it." Cicero, quoting Chrysippus, describes the human being as "a small fragment of that which is perfect" (*On the Nature of the Gods* 2.38; see *On Old Age* [*De senectute*] 21.78). On this Stoic language, see the illuminating notes on *On Divination* 2.38 in A. S. Pease, *De Divinatione* (Darmstadt: Wissenschaftliche Buchgesellschaft, 1977) 2:631. Epictetus describes human souls as "parts and portions" of God's being (1.14.6)

48. Philo differentiates his own view from the Stoic conception by demonstrating the superiority of the biblical view of the human soul to the Stoic. To this end, Philo associates Gen 2:7 with a Platonic interpretation of Gen 1:27 by identifying the breath in 2:7 with the image of God in 1:27. The effectiveness of this identification for establishing the *uncreated* character of the spirit hinges upon this Platonic interpretation of Gen 1:27, according to which the image of God is not what characterizes human beings but an independent reality, the rational logos of God, an incorporeal idea, the blueprint according to which the world is created. This Platonic interpretation is part of *On the Creation* 13–35, in which Philo interprets "day one" of Genesis as the creation of the incorporeal ideas of the intelligible world. On Philo's incorporation of Stoic and Platonic interpretations in his accounts of creation, see Tobin, *The Cre-*

Philo's attitude toward Stoicism is, therefore, elastic, stretching from acceptance (*On the Creation* 135) to critical adaptation (*On the Special Laws* 4.123) to vociferous opposition (*On Planting* 18–26). His movement away from the Stoic position, in fact, is a key indicator of how highly he prizes God's inbreathing, how much he considers this fragment of the divine spirit to be superior to the purest aether, how committed he is to the conviction that the spirit within is uncreated and immaterial. This conception of the spirit is hardly foreign to Israelite sensibilities, in which the spirit occupies a fragile border between mortality and vitality. Philo's bifurcation of mind and soul, immortal and mortal, and his belief that the immortal spirit descends as the mind to inhabit a mortal body (*On the Creation* 134–35), sets the divine spirit very much in the shadow of death. Further, he provides a supreme example of the way in which Gen 2:7 came to be understood as the gift of the spirit at creation. He leaves no doubt that inspiration coincides with creation. An interpretation of Gen 2:7, such as the one he offers in *Who Is the Heir?* 55-57, pointedly associates inspiration with creation: "and the divine breath or spirit that of its most dominant part . . . he [Moses] did not make the substance of the mind depend on anything created, but represented it as breathed upon by God. For the Maker of all says, 'blew into his face the breath of life, and the human became a living soul.'" Further still, by identifying the *nephesh* with the purest soul, rather than the soul that is associated with the body and prone to vice, Philo demonstrates how readily a first-century author could understand the inspiration of Gen 2:7 as a *superior* form of inspiration by the divine spirit. This is no mere inbreathing of breath but a full infusion of deity. We discover, therefore, in Philo's interpretations of Gen 2:7, the elements of Part I of this study: the spirit is set in the shadow of death; inspiration is identified with creation rather than with a subsequent endowment;[49] and the breath is nothing inferior but, on the contrary, spirit that is superior even to the rarest form of aether.

---

ation of Man: Philo and the History of Interpretation. CBQMS 14 (Washington: Catholic Biblical Association of America, 1983). Given his Platonic agenda, Philo understands the phrase "according to the image" in Gen 1:27 to mean that the logos of God is the ideal image according to which the world is constructed. This identification of the breath of Gen 2:7 with the uncreated image or logos of Gen 1:27 affords Philo the opportunity to infer that the soul, because it is a portion of the uncreated breath or image, is itself uncreated. In this way, Philo distinguishes the divine spirit of Torah from the Stoic conception of the spirit as a created element, composed of fire and air, in which the rational part of the soul participates.

49. On subsequent endowments, see below, Part II, chapters 2 and 3.

Philo's interpretation of Gen 2:7 is also an extension of Israelite beliefs about those who were filled with spirit because all that Philo says of the spirit is prologue to his conception of human virtue. As in the Wisdom of Solomon, where a soul can be deceitful, a body enslaved to sin, and a holy spirit subject to teaching or discipline, so also for Philo can the spirit which God inbreathes provide the basis for virtue and vice. As in Seneca's letter to Lucilius, where the purpose of the holy spirit within is to attain the highest human good, so also for Philo does life lived in accordance with the mind lead to the highest good of being lifted in a rapturous vision of God. It is this spirit within, according to Philo, which exists principally to provide the foundation for virtue and the culpability for vice. It is this *pneuma* that can draw a human from his or her tether to the passions of the body and provide release to fly in the heavens toward the divine.

This association of the spirit with virtue is no more evident than in Philo's effort to solve some of the difficulties of the image of inbreathing in Gen 2:7. For example, Philo asks first of all why God breathed into "the earthly and body-loving mind" (*Allegorical Interpretation* 1.33) of Genesis 2 rather than the Platonic ideal of mind, whose creation, according to Philo, is recounted in Genesis 1. Philo responds that God loves to give, *even to the imperfect,* in order to encourage in them a "zeal for virtue." The inbreathing, then, is the means by which God "created no soul barren of virtue, even if the exercise of it be to some impossible" (*Allegorical Interpretation* 1.34).

Philo continues on the theme of virtue by pressing the point that those "into whom real life" had been breathed are now culpable. Had God not inbreathed this authentic life into those "without experience of virtue," they might have claimed injustice in God's punishment, as they failed through ignorance and inexperience. Thus, they have no right to blame God for having "failed to breathe into him [or her] any conception of" virtue (1.35).

Second, he asks simply what the verb "breathed into" means (1.33). In the context of a complex answer, Philo associates the inbreathing with the ability to conceive of God: "For how could the soul have conceived of God, had God not breathed into it and mightily laid hold of it?" (1.38).

In a third question — why God breathed into the *face* — virtue retains its prominent role. By incorporating Stoic physiology, Philo is prepared to contend that God breathes only into the mind, which in turn inspires that portion of the soul which is devoid of reason:

> As the face is the dominant element in the body, so is the mind the dominant element of the soul: into this only does God breathe. . . . For the

mind imparts to the portion of the soul that is devoid of reason a share of that which it has received from God. . . . For the mind is, so to speak, God of the unreasoning part.

The inbreathing of Gen 2:7, therefore, is much more than a mere making alive of a body. It is the impartation of the capacity for virtue, the possibility of knowing God, the vitalization of the mind, the purest portion of a human being, which shares its substance with the cosmos. Little wonder, according to Philo, that the first man lived in unalloyed bliss, in concert with the stars, "since the divine *pneuma* had flowed into him in full current." Because of this current, the first man "earnestly endeavored in all his words and actions to please the Father and King, following God step by step in the highways cut out by virtues" (*On the Creation* 144).[50]

50. Human existence, of course, has not remained one of unalloyed bliss, one of the uninterrupted pursuit of virtue. That is why Philo is compelled, at several points in his interpretative *tour-de-force*, to explain that there are "two men" or "two types of people." This formula functions on several levels. On the cosmic level, which entails the Platonic conception of the ideal and real worlds, the "two men" represent the ideal creation according to God's image of Genesis 1 and the real molding of the first man from dust in Genesis 2, who received the *pneuma* through inbreathing. On the level of Philo's anthropology, the "two men" represent the mind, the purest *pneuma*, which rules the soul, and the soul as a whole, which is encumbered by physical passions: "We use soul," writes Philo, "in two senses, both for the whole soul and also for its dominant part, which properly speaking is the soul's soul. . . . And therefore the lawgiver held that the substance of the soul is twofold, blood being that of the soul as a whole, and the divine *pneuma* that of its most dominant part" (*Who Is the Heir?* 55). Once again, Philo appeals to Genesis 1 and 2 to make this case:

> . . . he [Moses] did not make the substance of the mind depend on anything created, but represented it as breathed *into* by God. For the Maker of all, he says, "blew into his face the breath of life, and man became a living soul," just as we are also told that he was fashioned after the image of his Maker. (56)

Yet there is something even more in Philo's writings than the cosmic and anthropological dimensions of the two creations, more than the "two men" who are created. Not only are they the humans of Genesis 1 and 2 or the mind and soul of a human being; the "two men" represent as well those who choose to live either by the soul, in its alliance with the passions, or the mind, which is the divine *pneuma* within. One path leads to virtue, the other to vice. Philo, therefore, continues his discussion by inferring, "So we have two kinds of people, one that of those who live by reason, the divine *pneuma*, the other of those who live by blood and the pleasure of the flesh. This last is a molded clod of earth, the other is the faithful impress of the divine image" (*Who Is the Heir?* 57). In his *Questions and Answers on Genesis* 1.8 (on Gen 2:8), Philo makes very much the same point by blending the Platonic, anthropological, and ethical levels of interpretation. Paradise, says Philo, symbolizes wisdom, since "the earth-formed person is a mixture and consists of soul and body, and is in need of teaching and in-

Conclusion

We have so far in this study been ineluctably drawn to paradise, to pristine moments of inspiration. When the curtain rises on the human drama, revealing an unspoiled garden, the human being, who is merely dust from the earth, rises when the creator God meets him face-to-face in order to breathe life. This is a simple scene, a love scene of sorts, an intimate scene in which it is difficult to shake off the notion that what passes between God and the first human is a kiss of life.

Compare this simplicity with the complexity of Philo's take on this action. This is no kiss, no embarrassingly intimate contact between a creator and the creation. Philo understands this moment of inspiration in anything but such simple terms. This may be the descent of a ray of aether, which now indwells the first human, but it is no kiss of life. It may be the impartation of the human mind — something even better than aether — but it is no simple puff of enlivening breath. It may be the infusion of a capacity for virtue, but it is certainly no mere enlivening of the earth. Yet, although this simple and unvarnished first narrative in Torah has become a tool in Philo's cache, with which he tinkers with the comparative veracity of Stoicism and neo-Platonism, Philo never forfeits his fascination with the divine inbreathing. On the contrary, he is riveted by this first moment of inspiration to the extent that he cites it, word for word, dozens and dozens of times in his effort to explain the beneficence of God, the incomparable gift of "real life," the unparalleled capacity for virtue, the inestimable opportunity for an intimate knowledge of God that this first breath gives to human beings.

Although it may lead him bewilderingly far away from the simple story line of two lovers in paradise, Philo's enchantment with Gen 2:7 demonstrates how assuredly he grasps the importance of the divine spirit within. And in this he is certainly not alone. Other Jewish authors are no less able to capture this as well, though in quite different terms. The author of the Wisdom of Solomon, who understands Gen 2:7 as the temporary loan of a soul, opens his book of wisdom with a fleeting reference to the "holy spirit of discipline" that flees from deceit. Though the reference is terse, the author has packed into it a good deal that is Stoic, not least its relation to a cosmic spirit with an equal penchant for justice. More signifi-

---

struction." The human in God's image, in contrast, "is self-hearing and self-taught." For further discussion and bibliography, see Levison, *Portraits of Adam in Early Judaism*, 81-82, 84-85.

cantly, this nearly passing reference to a holy spirit that exists alongside body and soul provides the basis for his teaching on the pursuit of virtue and wisdom.

This appreciation for a holy spirit within was not the exclusive intellectual property of the Alexandrian Jewish philosophical tradition. It is hardly surprising that members of a sectarian (or what would later become sectarian) community believed themselves to be the possessors of holy spirits that could be defiled or exchanged for money. More startling are the profound metamorphoses that the figure of Balaam undergoes in the *Liber antiquitatum biblicarum*, in which Balaam, rather than receiving the spirit of God and prophesying, loses the holy spirit and finds death near at hand. The denial of the spirit to a figure who receives the spirit in scripture is noteworthy, though the change can readily be attributed to the ambiguous character of Balaam who, according to a brief note in Num 31:16 that is picked up by the author of the *Liber antiquitatum biblicarum* (*LAB* 18:13-14), plots to deceive and desecrate Israel through the actions of certain Midianite women. Balaam becomes consequently a tragic figure, a failed seer who faces premature death.

The quaint tale of the book of Susanna also contains as a matter of course a clear reference to the holy spirit of Daniel. There are no surprises here, as Daniel, in the book named for him, is characterized time and again by an extraordinary spirit within, by a robust degree of spirit, even by a holy spirit, according to various Greek translations. Nor is there any surprise in the metamorphosis of a scriptural expression, "God prompted the spirit," by the addition of the word "holy": "God prompted the holy spirit of a young man." The book of Daniel depicts a young man of extraordinary integrity who faithfully honed his skills through fasting and study. To introduce him now without the necessity of explanation, as the author of the tale of Susanna does, as a young man whose holy spirit compels him to decry injustice, is entirely in character with the stories that circulate around his rise to power in the courts of the Babylonians and Medes.

The earliest of these authors, and the most traditional, is Ben Sira, who brooks no shortcuts to wisdom, no place for artificial and natural forms of divination. Students wear out the doorsteps of their mentors. Scribes study Torah assiduously and pray early, attaining wisdom from a variety of sources — though not from an irruption of the divine spirit. Not even Isaiah prophesied because he was a recipient of the spirit; the source of his oracles lay in the greatness of his spirit. The greatest scribes whose teachings are like prophecies — and here Ben Sira is self-referential —

have acquired their knowledge through no other means than dogged and diligent labor. In this way, they come to be filled with a spirit of understanding and thus are able to pour out their own words of wisdom, words that will make them renowned in generation after generation.

All of these texts — and they span a world from the pre-Maccabean period early in the second century B.C.E. to an interpretation of scripture composed during the first century C.E. — share the conviction that the locus of virtue in human beings can be characterized as a spirit of understanding (Ben Sira), a holy spirit that God prompts (Daniel and Susanna), a holy spirit that can be defiled (Damascus Document) and exchanged for financial security *(4QInstruction)*, a holy spirit, a life-breath akin to Gen 6:3 that can be forfeited due to a lack of fidelity *(Liber antiquitatum biblicarum)*, and a "holy spirit of discipline" that flees deceit (Wisdom of Solomon). Philo alone does not adopt the words, "holy spirit." Yet it is Philo who, despite the complexity of his interpretative agenda and his preference for the words, "divine spirit" *(pneuma theion)*, offers us the richest glimpse of a world bursting with the divine spirit. In this world, other authors, though with less flamboyance than Philo, could refer readily, unequivocally, unambiguously to the locus of virtue and wisdom within as the holy spirit.[51]

51. The Septuagint translation of Ps 51:12-14(Eng. 10-12) is less ambiguous than the Hebrew original because it contains several translational pointers to an understanding of the holy spirit as the spirit-breath within human beings. (1) This identification of the holy spirit with the life-breath is supported by the translation of the Hebrew verb *tiqqaḥ*, by the Greek verb *antanelēs* (MT 51:13[Eng. 11]; LXX 50:13). Though this verb occurs only ten times in the Septuagint, eight of them in the Psalms, two of these are situated in contexts in which life and death are at issue. Of the animals it can be said that, when God takes away their spirit *(antaneleis to pneuma autōn)*, they are cut off and return to the ground (LXX Ps 103:29[MT 104]). (2) Further, the psalmist implores God not to take away his life or soul *(mē antanelēs tēn psychēn mou)* in LXX Ps 140:8(MT 141). In both instances, the verb is associated with the presence or loss of life. If the choice of this verb in LXX Psalms 103 and 140 provides any clue, then the psalmist in LXX Ps 50:13 is presumably begging God not to take away the holy spirit, understood as that which sustains life and prevents return to the earth. (3) The translation in LXX Ps 50:14 of the third reference, to the willing or generous spirit, could also be construed as a reference to the human spirit. The words *pneumati hēgemonikō stērison me* may refer to the human spirit, which steadies the psalmist by ruling over the human soul. This interpretation approximates the understanding of the holy spirit as the vivifying force of life, such as in Gen 6:3 or *Liber antiquitatum biblicarum* 18, although this conception of the spirit is interpreted along the lines of Stoicism as the rational component of a human being.

Spirit and the Allure of Ecstasy

Ben Sira's utter disdain for divination could not ultimately hold the day against the seductive and sheer force of Greco-Roman culture. Nor did the conviction that human beings could be characterized by their holy spirit, as were Daniel and the devotees at Qumran, impede Greco-Roman conceptions of inspiration from informing, or overwhelming, the distant eastern shores of the Mediterranean. If Rome constructed its surface roads, Greco-Roman culture made no less intractable inroads into the warp and woof of Jewish cultures that were scattered across the Mediterranean world, from Rome to Alexandria, and even as far removed as Palestine.

The inability of Jewish sages such as Ben Sira to withstand the flood of Greek and Roman preoccupation with inspiration was due less to weak spots in the sages' positions than to the alluring and long-standing seduction of ecstasy. As early as the fifth century B.C.E., according to Plato, Socrates believed that "the greatest of blessings come to us through madness, when it is sent as a gift of the gods. For the prophetess at Delphi and the priestesses at Dodona when they have been mad have conferred many splendid benefits upon Greece both in private and in public affairs, but few or none when they have been in their right minds" (*Phaedrus* 244A-B). This sort of inspiration would overtake the poet and prophet as well. The poet, claimed Socrates, "is unable ever to indite until he has been inspired and put out of his senses, and his mind is no longer in him" (*Ion* 534B). Composition of odes, dance songs, and verse are uttered "not by art . . . but by divine influence." Therefore, "God takes away the mind of these and uses them as his ministers, just as he does soothsayers and godly seers, in order that we who hear them may know that it is not they who utter these words of great price, but that it is God himself who speaks and addresses us through them" (534C-D).

The Legacy of Delphi

The most illustrious inspired figure, though neither a queen nor a member of the aristocracy, held Greece spellbound by her words. She fired the Greek imagination with her oracles. The Greek *poleis* were dependent upon her for guidance on topics as diverse as cult and urban pollution. She, the Pythia at Delphi, was an ordinary woman who remained a virgin while she served, and the nature of her service, the source of her inspiration, ignited an untold number of discussions throughout a millennium of Delphic dominance.

Enquirers at the temple of Delphi paid their consultation tax, offered their sacrifice, and, if the animal reacted as it should when sprinkled with water, entered the temple, offered another sacrifice, then entered, probably with the oracular interpreters, to the adytum, a space from which the Pythia was not visible. She, in turn, prepared herself by purification at the Castalian Spring and by burning laurel leaves and barley meal on the altar inside the temple. Crowned with laurel, she took her place on a tripod, was possessed by the god, shook a laurel branch, and prophesied. The interpreters, in some way that is still unclear, shaped her oracle for the enquirer.[1]

The experience of the Pythia at Delphi was shrouded in mystery, and there may have been little historical reality to this conception of Delphic inspiration. Nevertheless, the mysterious figure of the Delphic Pythia riveted the attention of other writers during the Greco-Roman era, who, in the shadow of Delphi, frequently associated filling with the spirit, whatever its precise nature, with uncontrolled but legitimate prophetic ecstasy. Strabo (born ca. 63 B.C.E.) refers to an enthusiastic spirit *(pneuma enthousiastikon)* that causes the Pythia to speak while she sits on her tripod

---

1. The Pythia at Delphi was not the only figure to be inspired in this sort of way. She served at the behest of Apollo, while three priestesses at Dodona served at the behest of Zeus in what may have been the oldest Greek oracular shrine. The Delphic Pythia employed the laurel; the priestesses at Dodona received oracular responses from a sacred oak — or from two doves that sat in it. The Delphic Pythia frequently served the needs of the state; the priestesses at Dodona typically responded to individuals, who scratched inquiries on a lead table and received a simple answer of yes or no. Yet, these differences notwithstanding, both were believed to be inspired in a trance induced by divine possession.

(9.3.5). Pliny the Elder (ca. 23-79 C.E.) attributes oracles to an intoxicating exhalation *(exhalatione temulenti)* from the earth in locations such as Delphi *(Natural History* 2.95.208). The treatise *De mundo,* falsely attributed to Aristotle, contains a reference to *pneumata* that arise from the earth at Delphi and Lebadeia and cause their recipients to become enthusiastic (395b). Pseudo-Longinus refers to an enthusing breath *(atmos entheos)* (13.2).[2] Iamblichus (ca. 245-325 C.E.) refers to a fiery *pneuma* that arises from the earth to envelop her *(On Mysteries* 3.11). John Chrysostom (ca. 347-407 C.E.) derides the Pythia by contending that it was actually an evil *pneuma,* which entered her genitalia when she sat upon the tripod *(Homily on 1 Corinthians* 29.1).[3]

The Pythia's fame became so well established that variations on the theme of becoming filled with an inspiring *pneuma* were entrenched by the end of the first century C.E. In a discourse devoted to philosophical attire and why philosophers should be followed rather than disdained, Dio Chrysostom refers to legendary philosophers from the Greek past, whom Plato had first designated the Seven Sages. He refers to them in order to demonstrate that their aphorisms, which were inscribed as dedications at the sacred shrine of Delphi, were actually more divine than the Pythian priestess's own inspired words. And why? Because their words were universal, while her oracles were given as responses to particular questions (72.12). In this context, in which Dio Chrysostom is concerned rather more with the Seven Sages than the priestess herself, he adopts what appears to be an altogether familiar image of her as a woman who sat upon the tripod and was filled with the spirit *(empimplamenē tou pneumatos).* This description is no invention, no thoughtful reflection upon the mechanics of inspiration, no well-conceived attempt to explain a mystical experience; it is rather a simple, straightforward summary, in the context of a discussion dedicated to the Seven Sages, of a common perception of two distinguishing marks of Delphic inspiration: the tripod and filling with the spirit.

2. Next to nothing is known about the life of Longinus, whose major work of literary criticism, *On the Sublime,* was ascribed to Dionysus Longinus when first printed in 1554. Owing to the subsequent authorship controversy, the author is now called Pseudo-Longinus. *On the Sublime,* which contains seventeen chapters on figures and styles of rhetoric, dates to ca. 200 C.E.

3. Even Lamprias, in Plutarch's *On the Obsolescence of Oracles* 438B, relates a negative mirror image of this filling, in which the Pythia was forced, against her will, to deliver an oracle. According to Plutarch, she was filled with an inarticulate, *evil* spirit, and she died days later. See also Origen's *Against Celsus* 3.25; 7.3.

Like Dio Chrysostom, Plutarch (ca. 46-120 C.E.) wrote during the late first or early second century C.E. Unlike Dio Chrysostom and other authors who describe the Pythia, Plutarch had actually visited Delphi, and his are the writings that offer the most detailed and descriptive discussion of Delphic inspiration.[4] They are rendered more valuable because Plutarch, in the spirit of the New Academy, was less concerned with definitive answers than with laying out alternative points of view. Consequently, he gathers several colorful characters around the conundrum of why, during his day, there occurred less oracular activity at Delphi than in prior eras. It is a sign of the entrenched association between loss of control and filling with *pneuma* that several competing explanations preserve this association.

Spirit-filling and Ventriloquism

One of the characters in Plutarch's dialogue *On the Obsolescence of the Oracles,* Cleombrotus, attributes the paucity of oracles at Delphi to the departure of guardian daemons. Another participant in the discussion, Lamprias, summarizes Cleombrotus's view: "When the demigods withdraw and forsake the oracles, these lie idle and inarticulate like the instruments of musicians." Cleombrotus leaves the precise mechanics of inspiration inchoate, though the simile of musical instruments expresses some notion of infilling, of breath blown into the instrument to produce sound.[5]

Ammonius, another figure in the dialogue, whose point of view Lamprias also summarizes, is less reluctant than Cleombrotus to detail the mechanics of inspiration. According to Lamprias, Ammonius holds a rep-

---

4. The treatises we shall cite are included in Plutarch's *Moralia.* They consist of dialogues and essays on ethical, literary, and historical subjects, such as *The Late Vengeance of the Deity, On Superstition,* and *Advice to Married Couples.*

5. Lamprias is dissatisfied by this explanation, for it fails to clarify the precise mechanics of inspiration. Cleombrotus's conviction about the guardian spirits, in Lamprias's opinion, "raises another question of greater import regarding the causative means and power which they employ to make the prophetic priests and priestesses possessed by inspiration and able to present their visions. For it is not possible to hold that the desertion by the demigods is the reason for the silence of the oracles unless we are convinced as to the manner in which the demigods, by having the oracles in their charge and by their presence there, make them active and articulate" (*On the Obsolescence of Oracles* 431B). The view propounded by Cleombrotus may represent Plutarch's own view. See R. Flacelière, ed., *Sur la Disparition des Oracles* (Paris: Belles Lettres, 1947) 48; E. de Faye, *Origène, sa vie, son oeuvre, sa pensée.* 2: *L'ambiance philosophique* (Paris: E. Leroux, 1927) 110.

rehensible view: the gods are thought to possess people directly, much like a ventriloquist manipulates a dummy. Ammonius imagines "that the god himself after the manner of ventriloquists (who used to be called 'Eurycleis,' but now 'Pythones') enters into the bodies of his prophets and prompts their utterances, employing their mouths and voices as instruments" (414E). The lessening of Delphic oracles during the first century, then, is due to a lessened tendency of the gods to possess prophets and priestesses.[6]

The association of filling with *pneuma* and the prophet's loss of control could hardly be more bluntly expressed than in Ammonius's explanation of why oracular activity at Delphi declined. This is the sort of inspiration that Philo applies to Israel's prophets. His interpretation of the word *ekstasis* in Gen 15:12 prompts him to describe the experience that "regularly befalls the fellowship of the prophets. The mind is evicted at the arrival of the divine Spirit [*tou theiou pneumatos*], but when that departs the mind returns to its tenancy. Mortal and immortal may not share the same home. And therefore the setting of reason and the darkness which surrounds it produce ecstasy and inspired frenzy [*ekstasin kai theophorēton manian*]" (*Who Is the Heir?* 264–65). When the prophet is inspired, "he is filled with inspiration [*enthousia*], as the reason withdraws and surrenders the citadel of the soul to a new visitor and tenant, the Divine Spirit which plays upon the vocal organism and dictates words which clearly express its prophetic message" (*On the Special Laws* 4.49).

It is a signal of the extensive influence of this point of view, in which infilling effects ecstasy, that both Josephus and Philo adopt it, independently yet in stunning consonance, to resolve the problem that is raised in Numbers 22–24, when Balaam, the quintessential false prophet, delivers instead an oracular blessing upon Israel.[7] According to Philo, Balaam delivered his first oracle when "he advanced outside, and straightway became possessed, and there fell upon him the truly prophetic spirit which banished utterly from his soul his art of wizardry" (*Life of Moses* 1.277). Later, "he was suddenly possessed, and, understanding nothing, his reason as it

---

6. This is, according to Lamprias, a ridiculous position, for it fails to draw sufficient space between the divine and human worlds: "For if he [a god] allows himself to become entangled in people's needs, he is prodigal with his majesty and he does not observe the dignity and greatness of his preeminence" (*On the Obsolescence of Oracles* 414E).

7. Detailed analyses are available in J. R. Levison, "The Debut of the Divine Spirit in Josephus' *Antiquities*," *HTR* 87 (1994) 123-38, and "The Prophetic Spirit as an Angel according to Philo," *HTR* 88 (1995) 189-207.

were roaming, uttered these prophetic words which were put into his mouth" (1.283). Josephus's narrative summary of Balaam's first oracle is uncommonly similar to Philo's: "Such was the inspired utterance of one who was no longer his own master but was overruled by the divine spirit to deliver it" (*Ant.* 4.118). Balaam himself confronts Balak: "Do you think that it rests with us at all to be silent or to speak on such themes as these, when we are possessed by the spirit of God? For that spirit gives utterance to such language and words as it will, whereof we are all unconscious" (4.119).

Perhaps with the exception of Ezekiel, Israelite prophets offer only the barest sketches of their experience. If there exists in this large literary corpus an inkling of ecstasy, it has been plunged beneath the surface of comprehensibility.[8] Yet Philo probes more deeply the mechanics of prophetic inspiration. He discovers in the rich veins of Greco-Roman discourse a conception of inspiration that permits a full disclosure of prophetic inspiration: the divine spirit takes hold of the prophet and produces, through his vocal chords, words and sounds of God's choosing. This explanation aptly serves as well to explain how a scoundrel such as Balaam could bless Israel: the spirit of God spoke through this unconscious seer.

Spirit-filling and Enthusiasm

Despite the impact this interpretation of Delphic inspiration had in Greco-Roman antiquity, neither Ammonius's view nor Cleombrotus's satisfied still another figure in Plutarch's treatise *On the Obsolescence of Oracles*. Lamprias, their ardent critic, considers Cleombrotus's position too vague and Ammonius's ludicrous because the gods become too intimately intertwined by it in human affairs. His solution is to adopt a very different explanation that preserves nonetheless the intimate association between filling with *pneuma* and prophetic ecstasy: the familiar Stoic theory of secondary causes. The inspiring vapor, which in the past rose from the ground to inspire the Delphic prophetess, has simply ceased due to changes in sun and earth. Physical changes, then, led to the lessening of Delphic inspiration.[9]

8. See J. R. Levison, *The Spirit in First Century Judaism.* AGJU 29 (Leiden: Brill, 1997) 34-42.

9. *On the Obsolescence of Oracles* 431E-434C. On the theory of the vapors, see J. Fontenrose, *The Delphic Oracle: Its Responses and Operations* (Berkeley: University of California Press, 1978); H. W. Parke and D. E. W. Wormell, *The Delphic Oracle, 1: The History* (Oxford: Blackwell, 1956) 19-26; Flacelière, *Sur la Disparition des Oracles,* 42-46.

This physical explanation of the Delphic vapor does not preclude the firm Stoic belief that the human soul is predisposed by its affinity with the world soul or *pneuma* to achieve an inspired state in "which the reasoning and thinking faculty of the soul is relaxed and released from their present state as they range amid the irrational and imaginative realms of the future" (*On the Obsolescence of Oracles* 432C). This state, in which the soul withdraws from the body, "is brought about by a temperament and disposition of the body as it is subjected to a change which we call inspiration [*enthousiasmon*]" (432D). Precisely what is the most suitable catalyst for this change in bodily temperament? It is the *pneuma*, a physical entity that enters the body and produces a condition free of mental restraint — enthusiasm.

> Often the body of itself alone attains this disposition. Moreover the earth sends forth for people streams of many other potencies, some of them producing derangements, diseases, or deaths; others helpful, benignant, and beneficial, as is plain from the experience of persons who have come upon them. But the prophetic current and breath is most divine and holy [*to de mantikon rheuma kai pneuma theiotaton esti kai hosiōtaton*], whether it issue by itself through the air or come in the company of running waters; for when it is instilled into the body, it creates in souls an unaccustomed and unusual temperament, the peculiarity of which it is hard to describe with exactness. (432D)[10]

This view differs from those held by Ammonius or Cleombrotus. What characterizes them all, notwithstanding the differences that separate them, however, is a firm belief that the Pythia at Delphi is filled with *pneuma*. All three manage to agree as well that the inspired state is characterized by a loss or relaxation of mental control. It is a measure of the influence this association between infilling and loss of control exercised that Philo, in Alexandria during the early first century, and Josephus, in Rome late in the first century, would both retrieve views strikingly similar to those held by Lamprias and Ammonius to explain how a despicable Mesopotamian seer could provide a magnificent blessing of Israel.

Though she provided the focal point for discussion, therefore, the Pythia did not claim exclusive rights to this form of inspiration. Israelite prophets were inspired in this way, according to Philo, as was Balaam, ac-

---

10. This occurs in a discussion that is indebted to Plato's enumeration of the four forms of *mania* (*Phaedrus* 265B).

cording to both Philo and Josephus. This view of inspiration, in fact, reigned so universally that it included all sorts of figures other than the Pythia, including, among others, the famed Cassandra, the sybils, and the priestesses of Dodona. When Plutarch delineates four kinds of inspiration in general — not just the inspiration of the Pythia — he writes, "There is a second kind, however, which does not exist without divine inspiration. It is not intrinsically generated but is, rather, an extrinsic afflatus that displaces the faculty of rational inference; it is created and set in motion by a higher power. This sort of madness bears the general name of 'enthusiasm' [*enthousiasmon*]" (*Amatorius* 758E).

Because early Jewish authors who wrote during the Greco-Roman era discovered no equivalent repository in their scriptures to explain with precision the mechanics of inspiration, it is small wonder that at least some of these Jewish authors, such as Philo and Josephus, opted to import fundamental dimensions of this sort of inspiration into their own perceptions of prophetic inspiration. More surprising is that this proclivity is evident in the *Liber antiquitatum biblicarum,* the Palestinian reinvention of biblical narratives from Adam and Eve to Samuel, to which we earlier referred.[11] If there is a corner of ancient literature where we might expect to discover resistance to Greco-Roman culture, its legacy would be apparent in a Palestinian rewriting of the Hebrew scriptures, which itself was probably originally composed in Hebrew. Yet even over this literary text the shadow of Delphi, and the discussions of inspiration more generally that whirled around it, was cast unmistakably.

The tenacity with which the association of infilling and ecstasy reached even into the Palestinian world is especially evident in the final vision of the obscure scriptural figure of Kenaz, the father of Othniel, the first Israelite judge. The centrality of Kenaz in *Liber antiquitatum biblicarum* is evident, not only in the disparity between the scant mention he receives in the biblical book of Judges and the immodest space he occupies in Pseudo-Philo's version, but in the attentive care Pseudo-Philo exercises as he spins the episode of Kenaz's prophesying nearly out of thin air: "And when they [Israelite prophets and elders of Israel] had sat down, [a][12] holy

11. See Part II, chapter 1.

12. D. J. Harrington (*OTP* 2:341) translates *spiritus* with the indefinite article "a." M. R. James (*The Biblical Antiquities of Philo* [New York: Ktav, 1971] 235) translates "the spirit"; and C. Dietzfelbinger (*Pseudo-Philo: Antiquitates Biblicae.* JSHRZ 2/2 [Gütersloh: Gerd Mohn, 1975] 257) translates "der heilige Geist." This translational and theological issue we encountered before; it is difficult to determine whether the anarthrous *spiritus* should be

spirit came upon Kenaz and dwelled in him and elevated his mind [put him in ecstasy], and he began to prophesy, saying . . ." (*LAB* 28:6).[13] This brief snippet offers, from an unexpected quarter, a quintessential expression of the association between infilling by *pneuma* and an ecstatic loss of control.

This depiction of Kenaz's final experience of the spirit is rooted in Israelite literature. First, the communal context of this vision is reminiscent of Ezekiel, whose vision of abominations in the temple took place among the elders: "as I sat in my house, with the elders of Judah sitting before me, the hand of the Lord God fell upon me there" (Ezek 8:1).[14] Similarly, Kenaz experienced his vision when the prophets and elders sat down. Second, the spirit is an integral component of the prophet's experience in both instances. Ezekiel recounts, "and the spirit lifted me up between earth and heaven, and brought me in visions of God to Jerusalem" (8:3). Pseudo-Philo writes that "[a] holy spirit came upon Kenaz." Third, the choice of the verb *insilire* echoes 1 Samuel 10–11; in the Vulgate of 1 Sam 10:6, 10, and 11:6, the verb *insilire* translates the Hebrew *ṣlḥ*, which depicts the powerful rush of the spirit when it overcame Saul, causing him to prophesy or to gather his people for war by cutting a yoke of oxen in several pieces.[15]

---

translated as "a spirit" or "the spirit." The latter interpretation is supported both by literary antecedents and by prior references in *Liber antiquitatum biblicarum* (hereafter *LAB*). First, references to the spirit in other instances of prophetic inspiration in *LAB* can be traced to biblical references to the spirit of God (*LAB* 18:10 to Num 24:2 or LXX 23:7; *LAB* 20:2 to Deut 34:9; *LAB* 27:9-10 to Judg 3:10 and 6:34; and *LAB* 28:6 to Ezek 8:1). Second, Pseudo-Philo has already established that the spirit which inspires is God's spirit: Kenaz was empowered for battle by the spirit (*LAB* 27:9); Barak attributed Deborah's prophetic ability to God's spirit, for upon discovering Sisera dead, he said, "Blessed be the Lord, who sent his spirit and said, 'Into the hand of a woman Sisera will be handed over'" (32:9); and Gideon put on "the spirit of the Lord" to defeat the Midianites (36:2). By this point in the narrative, therefore, the reader can probably assume that (the) spirit which inspired Saul was God's spirit.

13. Latin: *Et dum sederent, insiluit spiritus sanctus habitans in Cenez, et extulit sensum eius, et cepit prophetare dicens.* . . . The association between Kenaz's ability to prophesy and possession of the spirit is drawn from biblical roots, particularly 1 Sam 19:20-24. Five times the verb "to prophesy" occurs in 1 Sam 19:20-24, as well as another five times in the parallel account of Saul's experience of the spirit in 1 Sam 10:5-6, 10-13.

14. See also Ezek 20:1, according to which Ezekiel's vision began when "certain elders of Israel came to consult the Lord, and sat down before me."

15. The exportation of the verb *insilio* from the biblical story of Saul's prophetic experience to Pseudo-Philo's story of Kenaz is consistent with Pseudo-Philo's exegetical method: he transforms his descriptions of Joshua in Deut 34:9 and Kenaz in Judg 3:9-10 by importing the notion of transformation into another person from 1 Sam 10:6 and by the image of

Although Pseudo-Philo portrays the advent of the spirit with select biblical hues, the effects of the spirit cannot be traced to Israelite literature. They do, however, reveal the imprint of Greco-Roman conceptions of inspiration.[16] The spirit is said to spring upon Kenaz *and* to inhabit him *(insiluit spiritus sanctus habitans in Cenez)*. Neither conception — springing upon and indwelling — taken independently is unbiblical. The verb *insilire*, we have seen, recalls Saul's experience of the spirit. However, what distinguishes Kenaz's experience from its Israelite antecedents is the juxtaposition of these two very different conceptions of the spirit: the spirit both sprang upon Kenaz *and* indwelt him. The impact which the spirit had upon Kenaz was to oust his senses or, possibly, elevate his mind: *extulit sensum eius*.[17] Kenaz's vision concludes, no less graphically, when Kenaz "was awakened."[18] In other words, Kenaz's mind returned to him; he came back to his senses *(reversus est sensus eius in eum* in 28:10).[19]

---

clothing in Judg 6:34 (*LAB* 20:2 and 27:9-10); he transforms Num 24:2 by means of allusions to Gen 6:3 (*LAB* 18).

16. The impetus for Kenaz's vision is his impending death, which transpires shortly after the completion of his vision (*LAB* 28:10). This scenario, in which an extraordinary vision precedes death, is not characteristic of biblical portrayals of death. Perhaps the nearest antecedent, Jacob's blessing of his sons (Genesis 49), serves to underscore the difference between the *Liber antiquitatum biblicarum* and its biblical precedent: Jacob blesses his sons with modest predictions, while Kenaz ranges the cosmos to receive a vivid depiction of judgment. Moreover, never in the biblical literature does the spirit inspire such a vision in the face of impending death. See Levison, *The Spirit in First Century Judaism*, 109-30.

17. Although the verb in *LAB* 28:6, *effero*, differs from the verb *elevare* in Vulgate Ezek 8:3, both have the semantic range to suggest the action of lifting and ascent. The mode of this experience, which is expressed ambiguously in Latin, may be inferred from a biblical allusion to Ezek 8:1. This may suggest that the spirit's effect — the elevation of Kenaz's mind — was prompted by the elevation of Ezekiel by the spirit in Ezek 8:3 (see also 3:12, 14).

18. Although this verb usually denotes physical awakening from sleep (*LAB* 6:15; 27:14; 31:5, 6; 53:3), it can also be used metaphorically to describe springs awakened from their sleep (28:7; 32:8). Whether Kenaz awoke from physical sleep or from a trance is, therefore, unclear.

19. The verb *reverto* usually denotes a return from a variety of journeys (*LAB* 6:12; 10:3; 15:1; 18:14; 20:6, 12; 27:6, 7, 9; 31:6, 7, 9; 39:10; 40:1, 3, 8; 41:1; 47:10; 58:4; 61:1), return to one's tent after a burial (24:6), or return to the ground at death (39:5). This denotation of *reverto* elsewhere in *LAB* supports interpreting Kenaz's inspired experience in 27:9, 10 as the ascent and subsequent descent of his mind. According to this interpretation, Kenaz's mind travelled in its vision and returned to Kenaz upon completion of his vision. Other references are more ambiguous. The occurrence of the verb in *LAB* 10:6 could mean that the sea either began again to flow (so Kenaz's ecstasy and return to sense) or returned to its original course (so Kenaz's ascent and descent). The occurrence of the verb in Jephthah's query, "Does love so return after hatred" (39:4), may imply either that love has retreated in the face of hatred only to return when hatred

From the mere mention of a name in Judges 3, Pseudo-Philo has spun an astonishing episode of inspiration that is a mirror of the Greco-Roman world. Kenaz's vision begins when the spirit leaps upon him, indwells him, and causes his mind to ascend or to leave altogether (*extulit sensum eius* in *LAB* 28:6). This is the external afflatus, the inspiring *pneuma* that enters the Delphic Pythia or the priestesses of Dodona or the sybils. "It is not intrinsically generated but is, rather, an extrinsic afflatus that displaces the faculty of rational inference; it is created and set in motion by a higher power. This sort of madness bears the general name of 'enthusiasm'" (*Amatorius* 758E). It corresponds to what, in Philo's view, "regularly befalls the fellowship of the prophets. The mind is evicted at the arrival of the divine Spirit [*tou theiou pneumatos*], but when that departs the mind returns to its tenancy" (*Who Is the Heir?* 264–65).

As if this were not adequate to accentuate the Greco-Roman qualities of Kenaz's vision, Pseudo-Philo includes a final embellishment. If there is an exclamation point to the ecstatic state that is effected by the springing and indwelling of (a) holy spirit, it lies not only in the need for Kenaz to return to his senses but also in his inability to recollect what he had said or seen:

> And when Kenaz had spoken these words, he was awakened, and his senses came back to him. *But he did not know what he had said or what he had seen.*[20] But this alone he said to the people: "If the repose of the just after they have died is like this, we must die to the corruptible world so as not to see sins." And when he had said these words, Kenaz died and slept with his fathers. And the people mourned for him thirty days. (*LAB* 28:10)

---

disappears (so Kenaz's ascent and descent) or that love is extinguished by hatred and then restored (so Kenaz's ecstasy and return to sense). The use of this verb to describe iron in *LAB* 30:6 may support the view that Kenaz's mind, originally intact, was extinguished until it was once again restored: ". . . like iron cast into the fire, which when made molten by the flame becomes like water, but when it comes out of the fire it reverts to its original hardness." Here the emphasis lies rather more on loss-restoration than on return from a journey. Therefore, although the predominant occurrence of the verb *reverto* describes the return from a journey, the verb suggests in some contexts restoration to an original state. In my opinion, allusions to the experience of Ezekiel, as well as Kenaz's vision itself, which entails a visionary journey throughout cosmos and time, suggest that the verb in *LAB* 28:10 should be interpreted to mean that Kenaz's mind has returned following its ascent in a visionary journey.

20. Latin: *Ipse autem nesciebat que locutus fuerat, neque que viderat.*

The inability to recall what was experienced stands squarely against the biblical prophetic tradition. The Hebrew Bible contains numerous instances in which prophets were to remember the divine words communicated during revelation. The man of Judah in 1 Kings 13 refuses to go home with another "man of God" because he remembers God's warning: "thus I was commanded by the word of the Lord" (13:9). Isaiah recalls what he heard during what may have been an ecstatic experience: "For the Lord spoke thus to me while his hand was strong upon me, and warned me not to walk in the way of this people, saying . . ." (Isa 8:11). Ezekiel, following his extended visions of the temple in chs. 8–11, has perfect recollection: "The spirit lifted me up and brought me in a vision by the spirit of God into Chaldea, to the exiles. Then the vision that I had seen left me. And I told the exiles all the things that the Lord had shown me" (Ezek 11:24-25). The paradigmatic Israelite reference to prophetic recollection is Ezek 3:10-11: "Mortal, all my words that I shall speak to you receive in your heart and hear with your ears; then go to the exiles, to your people, and speak to them."[21]

This view, however, is traceable to Plato's *Apology* 22C and *Meno* 99C, in which Plato contends that inspired poets do not know what they are saying. This view spawned interpretations in which the inability to recall what was experienced during a period without mental control signalled the authenticity of the prophetic condition.

Already during the late first or early second century c.e., the pseudonymous Jewish author of *4 Ezra* reveals an awareness of this interpretation in a description of an inspired experience, in which Ezra allegedly dictated ninety-four books. During this period, Ezra's heart poured forth understanding, and wisdom increased in his breast *because (nam)* his own spirit retained its memory (*4 Ezra* 14:40). The need to explain that Ezra retained his memory suggests that the author is refuting a form of inspiration that entailed the loss of memory.[22]

The conviction that inspiration may bring a loss of recollection appears more explicitly in the writings of the second-century c.e. public speaker

---

21. According to Ezek 10:20-22, Ezekiel was able to identify elements of a prior vision that occurred in a subsequent one: "These were the living creatures that I saw underneath the God of Israel by the river Chebar; and I knew that they were cherubim." See also Ezekiel 40, in which Ezekiel was brought to Israel "in visions of God" (40:2) and told by God to "declare all that you see to the house of Israel" (40:4).

22. M. E. Stone (*Fourth Ezra*. Hermeneia [Minneapolis: Fortress, 1990] 120) contends correctly that this statement about the retention of memory constitutes a "deliberate" reversal of this *topos*, i.e., the loss of memory.

and man of letters Aelius Aristides. Following his defense of the Delphic priestesses of Apollo, Aelius Aristides discusses the inspiration of the priestesses of Zeus in Dodona, "who know as much as the god approves, and for as long as he approves." These inspired priestesses have no knowledge of Zeus's oracles prior to inspiration, "nor afterwards do they know anything which they have said, but all inquirers understand it better than they."[23]

The second- or third-century Christian author Pseudo-Justinus, in his *Cohortatio ad Graecos,* discusses Plato's admiration for the Sibyl because her prophecies came to pass. To support his case, Pseudo-Justin paraphrases Plato's *Meno,* in which prophetic persons are said to be divine. Twice in this paraphrase, Pseudo-Justin expresses the opinion that the Sibyl cannot recall what she said while inspired:

> For, unlike the poets who, after their poems are penned, have power to correct and polish . . . she was filled indeed with prophecy at the time of the inspiration, *but as soon as the inspiration ceased, there ceased also the remembrance of all she had said.* (37.2)

> . . . they said also that they who then took down her prophecies, being illiterate persons, often went quite astray from the accuracy of the metres; and this, they said, was the cause of the want of metre in some of the verses, *the prophetess having no remembrance of what she had said,* after the possession and inspiration ceased, and the reporters having, through their lack of education, failed to record the metres with accuracy. (37.3)[24]

This conviction concerning inspiration characterizes as well a passage in the *Collationes* or Institutes for monastic orders written by John Cassian, who lived during the late fourth and early fifth centuries. In the context of a discussion of demon possession, he contrasts two types of possessed people, those who "are affected by them [demons] in such a way as to have not the slightest conception of what they do and say, while others know and afterwards recollect it."[25]

---

23. *In Defense of Oratory* 43.

24. Trans. by M. Dods in *The Ante-Nicene Fathers,* ed. A. Roberts and J. Donaldson (repr. Grand Rapids: Wm. B. Eerdmans, 1975) 1:289. For the Greek text, see *Pseudo-Justinus: Cohortatio ad Graecos, de Monarchia, Oratorio ad Graecos,* ed. M. Marcovich. Patristische Texte und Studien 32 (Berlin: de Gruyter, 1990) 76.

25. *Collationes* 12. Trans. by E. C. S. Gibson in *Nicene and Post-Nicene Fathers,* ed. P. Schaff and H. Wace (repr. Grand Rapids: Wm. B. Eerdmans, 1973) 11:366. For the Latin text, see *Jean Cassien: Conférences I-VII,* ed. E. Pichery. SC 42 (Paris: du Cerf, 1955) 256.

The Christian prologue to the *Sibylline Oracles,* which was composed no earlier than the end of the fifth century, advances this same interpretation of Plato's view of prophetic inspiration in an effort to explain an occasional absence of metrical accuracy. The author does not claim to invent this explanation but appeals instead to the Christian apologist Lactantius,[26] who, claims the Sibylline author, "set forth in his own works what had been said by the Sibyls about the ineffable glory." The author of the prologue explains:

> When the Sibylline verses found with us can easily be despised by those who are knowledgeable in Greek culture, not only because they are easily available (for things which are rare are thought valuable) but also because not all the verses preserve metrical accuracy, he has a rather clear argument. This is the fault of the secretaries, who did not keep pace with the flow of speech or even were ignorant, not of the prophetess. *For the memory of what had been said ceased with the inspiration. With regard to this even Plato said that they describe many great things accurately while knowing nothing of what they say.* (*Sib. Or.* Prologue 82-91)[27]

Although Plato himself had not contended that authentic inspiration entails an inability to remember, these interpreters did. The persistence of this interpretation, spanning several centuries, is impressive, as is the variety of adherents to it: an affluent second-century Greco-Roman orator (Aelius Aristides); a second-century Christian apologist (Pseudo-Justinus); a fourth-century Christian monastic leader (John Cassian); and an anonymous Christian editor who "set forth the oracles called Sibylline, which are found scattered and confusedly read and recognized, in one continuous and connected book" (*Sib. Or.* Prologue 9-10) — as well as a Jewish author who contended that Ezra had *not* lost his memory. The diversity of these witnesses to a shared view of inspiration indicates how popular this viewpoint came to be during the Greco-Roman era. Moreover, the persistent attribution of this interpretation to Plato, as well as the adherence of Aelius Aristides to this view, indicates a clear awareness that this belief about prophetic inspiration lay along a Greco-Roman trajectory.

A rich collection of details, therefore, distinguishes the effects of the

---

26. Or Firmianus, ca. 240-320 C.E.

27. Trans. by J. J. Collins, *OTP* 1:328. For the Greek text, see *Die Oracula Sibyllina*, ed. J. Geffcken (Leipzig: Hinrichs, 1902) 4. Despite its attribution to Lactantius, this statement occurs nowhere in his extant writings.

spirit on Kenaz from biblical accounts of the spirit's effects. The spirit springs upon Kenaz, indwells him, and elevates or ousts his mind just prior to his death. A vision ensues in which Kenaz's mind traverses the cosmos to see the judgment that will transpire far in the future. Once he is awakened and his mind returns from its travels, Kenaz is unable to recollect what he saw. Compared with biblical accounts of "visions of God," Pseudo-Philo's description of Kenaz is remarkably lucid, detailed, and consistent. The contours of the holy spirit's effect upon Kenaz are clear and well conceived, but they are decidedly *not* the contours supplied readily by the biblical story he purports to retell. These elements are explicable rather within the early Jewish and Greco-Roman *milieux* in which the *Liber antiquitatum biblicarum* was composed.

Slivers of this rich collection punctuate as well Pseudo-Philo's reinterpretation of Saul's final and strange self-referential experience of prophesying.

> And [a] spirit abided in Saul, and he prophesied, saying, "Why are you led astray, Saul, and whom are you pursuing in vain? The time allotted to your kingdom has been completed. Go to your place. For you will die, and David will reign. Will not you and your son die together? And then the kingdom of David will appear." And Saul went away and did not know what he had prophesied. (*LAB* 62:2)[28]

Once again, the spirit prompts prophesying when it comes within, though without any recollection. In *Liber antiquitatum biblicarum*, then, even Israel's first king is baptized in the waters of the Greco-Roman world: he cannot recall a word that he said when the spirit was in him. Notwithstanding his foibles and flaws, he stands, at least in this regard, in the good company of the virgin priestess at Delphi.

Spirit-filling and Drunkenness

Perhaps it was inevitable that the ecstatic prophet was seen to be drunk with enthusiasm, that the ecstasy of the poet was deemed comparable to

---

28. Latin: *Et mansit spiritus in Saul et prophetavit dicens: Quid seduceris, Saul, aut quem persequeris in vanum? Completum est tempus regni tui. Perge in locum tuum. Tu enim morieris, et David regnabit. Nonne tu et filius tuus simul moriemini? Et tunc apparebit David regnum. Et abiit Saul et non scivit que prophetavit.*

the inebriation of Bacchic delight. Lamprias, once again in Plutarch's rich reservoir on the topic, *On the Obsolescence of Oracles*, draws an association between filling with *pneuma* and intoxication, in the course of which Bacchic ritual describes the process of inspiration:

> But the prophetic current and *pneuma* is most divine and holy, whether it issue by itself through the air or come in the company of running waters; for when it is instilled into the body, it creates in souls an unaccustomed and unusual temperament, the peculiarity of which it is hard to describe with exactness. It is likely that by warmth and diffusion it [*pneuma*] opens up certain passages through which impressions of the future are transmitted, just as wine, when its fumes rise to the head, reveals many unusual movements and also words stored away and unperceived. 'For Bacchic rout/And frenzied mind contain much prophecy,' according to Euripides, when the soul becomes hot and fiery, and throws aside the caution that human intelligence lays upon it, and thus often diverts and extinguishes the inspiration. (432E-F)

There are three dimensions of inspiration. First, external forces, the most potent of which is "the prophetic current and pneuma," provide the catalyst for inspiration. Second, this *pneuma* functions like wine, whose fumes rise to the head and reveal otherwise imperceptible movements and words. Lamprias's appeal to Bacchic or Dionysian rout and prophetic frenzy suggests, of course, that wine was not merely a simile for the spirit but a necessary component of Bacchic inspiration.[29] Third, the soul enters a "hot and fiery state," in which human intelligence, which has the capacity to squelch inspiration, becomes relaxed and incautious — like a person intoxicated.

This association of drunkenness with inspiration is put to frequent and good use by Philo, who periodically compares the sober intoxication that comes from God with intoxication by wine.[30] He composes a detailed, ide-

---

29. In *Roman Questions* (*Moralia* 291A), Plutarch asks why the Roman priest is not permitted to touch ivy. He wonders whether this prohibition is "a symbolic prohibition of Bacchic revels and orgies? For women possessed by Bacchic frenzies rush straightway for ivy and tear it to pieces, clutching it in their hands and biting it with their teeth; so that not altogether without plausibility are they who assert that ivy, possessing as it does an exciting and distracting breath of madness, deranges persons and agitates them, and in general brings on a wineless drunkenness and joyousness in those that are precariously disposed towards spiritual exaltation." On the related effect of plants, see *Convivial Questions* 3.1, 2.

30. See esp. H. Lewy, *Sobria Ebrietas: Untersuchungen zur Geschichte der antiken Mystik.* BZNW 9 (Giessen: Töpelmann, 1929) 3-41.

alized sketch of a mystical community, the Therapeutae, which he admires. The Therapeutae sing as a choir until dawn, "drunk with this drunkenness in which there is no shame" (*On the Contemplative Life* 89). On another occasion he describes those who yearn for wisdom as "drunken with the drunkenness which is soberness itself" (*Every Good Man Is Free* 13). In his commentary on the *imago dei*, Philo, in a picture of the ascent of the mind that is rooted in Plato's *Phaedrus*, describes the mind's glimpse of the intelligible world; that person is "seized by a sober intoxication, like those filled with Corybantic frenzy, and is inspired, possessed by a longing far other than theirs and a nobler desire" (*On the Creation* 71). This last example alone suggests a form of ecstasy that approaches the Pythia or inspired poets of Greece and Rome. The Therapeutae, in contrast, do not lose control but stand "more alert and wakeful than when they came to the banquet."

Not unnaturally, Philo is drawn to the Greco-Roman association of ecstasy and intoxication — accompanied as well by the image of fire — when, as the interpreter of Noah's story, he devotes an entire treatise, *On Drunkenness*, to the nature of intoxication. The topic at hand is Hannah, the mother of Samuel; the text is 1 Sam 1:11, in which it is said that Samuel will never drink wine. Pausing at the name of Hannah, which he translates succinctly as "grace," Philo begins to describe a form of inspiration that takes place when someone is filled with grace. Although he adopts the word "grace," which the context demands, his description is a clear account of being filled with the spirit, of Bacchic possession: "Now when grace fills the soul," writes Philo, "that soul thereby rejoices and smiles and dances, for it is possessed and inspired [*bebakcheutai*], so that to many of the unenlightened it may seem to be drunken [*methyein*], crazy [*parakinein*], and beside itself [*exestanai*]" (146).

Hannah's actions are erroneously thought to be the product of intoxication, but this is absolutely wrong. "For with the God-possessed [*theophorētois*] not only is the soul wont to be stirred and goaded as it were into ecstasy [*exoistran*] but the body also is flushed and fiery [*pepyrōmenon*], warmed by the overflowing joy within which passes on the sensation to the outer person, and thus many of the foolish are deceived and suppose that the sober are drunk [*methyein*]" (147). Philo admits that such possessed people are drunk, in a way, though not by wine; they are drunk from the cup of perfect virtue. Like those who are drunk, the God-possessed are "flushed and fiery, warmed. . . ."

Spirit-filling and Inflammation

Philo is hardly idiosyncratic in his description of people possessed by God as "flushed and fiery." The *pneuma* was reputed to effect in the Delphic Pythia, whose inspired rapture riveted those who reflected upon her, a condition of inflammation. Lucan, a Latin poet, whose brief life spanned the mid-first century (39–65 c.e.), offers an imaginative depiction of her possession by Apollo. Lucan (*On the Civil War* 5.118-20) explains the silence of oracles at Delphi by the Pythia's dread of Apollo, for possession by him would bring early death "because the human frame is broken up by the sting and surge of that frenzy, and the stroke from heaven shatters the brittle life." When Appius, for instance, wanted to consult Delphi, Phemonoe, who was at that time the Pythia, resisted. Forced by the priest into the temple, she feigned inspiration and frenzy. Yet her voice did not fill the cavern, her laurel wreath remained unmoved, her hair stayed unbristled. Cowed by Appius's fury at the apparent absence of inspiration, Phenomoe took her place on the tripod and drew near to the chasm, "and her bosom for the first time drew in the divine spirit [*spiritus*], which the inspiration of the rock, still active after so many centuries, forced upon her." Apollo forced himself into her body, drove out her former thoughts, and urged her to forfeit her nature so that he could have a place in her chest. As a result, the Pythia became uncontrolled — or controlled by the *pneuma* of another — and bounced about the cave, dislodged the garland with her wild, tossing, bristling hair, scattered the tripod, and "now she boils over with fierce fire [*igne iratum*], while enduring the wrath of Phoebus. Nor does he ply the whip and goad alone, and dart flame into her vitals [*stimulus flammasque in viscera mergis*]" (5.173-75), but she is also painfully constrained and cannot say all that she knows, though she sees beforehand in this possessed state the events of centuries.[31]

What could illustrate the pervasiveness of the association of fire and filling more vividly than this imaginatively cast mid-first-century projection of spirit-filled, flaming ecstasy? All of the elements are here — *pneuma*, fierce fire, and the driving out of the Pythia's own thoughts, in addition to physical signs of ecstasy, such as bristling hair — that characterize the inspired state.

While Lucan, in the mid-first century, casts the ecstasy of the Delphic Pythia in the brightest of imaginative poetic hues, decades later Plutarch

---

31. Lucan's narrative is probably based upon Vergil's *Aeneid* 6.77-78.

purveys her ecstasy in the sobriety of philosophical inspection. We may recall Lamprias, an informed proponent of Stoic thought in *On the Obsolescence of Oracles*. Because he cannot pinpoint exactly the condition that is
produced by the *pneuma*, Lamprias is compelled to fetch for analogies
which explain the physical condition of enthusiasm that is set in motion
by the physical reality of *pneuma*. We may recall that he associates Bacchic
rout with a soul that "becomes hot and fiery, and throws aside the caution
that human intelligence lays upon it, and thus often diverts and extinguishes the inspiration." Inspiration, in other words, likely takes place
when "by warmth and diffusion it [*pneuma*] opens up certain passages
through which impressions of the future are transmitted, just as wine,
when its fumes rise to the head, reveals many unusual movements and also
words stored away and unperceived."[32]

Though perhaps the most prominent, the Delphic Pythia was not the
sole claimant to the fire of ecstasy. There existed in Greek and Roman antiquity the conviction that many other inspired figures could lose control
of their own thoughts when they entered a fiery condition that was precipitated by filling with *pneuma*. Cassandra, who in mythology is reputed to
be the most beautiful daughter of Priam, exhibited extraordinary prophetic powers. Aeschylus, in the play *Agamemnon*, narrates that Apollo bequeathed these prophetic powers to Cassandra in exchange for promised
sexual favors, which she subsequently withheld. Apollo therefore transformed blessing into curse by ensuring that she would always be disbe-
lieved. Yet one person would believe — she herself, as she predicted her
own death (*Agamemnon* 1207–12).

Cassandra would become the prophetic centerpiece of Cicero's *On
Divination*, in which his Stoic brother, Quintus, says in thumbnail form
that Cassandra "prophesied . . . under a heaven-inspired excitement and
exaltation of soul" (1.89).[33] She provides for Quintus an exceptional illus-

32. He contends as well that inspiration can transpire because the prophetic spirit exhibits an affinity with the soul (*On the Obsolescence of Oracles* 433A-B, E). Just as a bean has a
peculiar suitability for the dyeing of purple and sodium carbonate, scarlet, so the Delphic
vapor has a peculiar ability to inspire: "It is not, therefore, anything to excite amazement if,
although the earth sends up many streams, it is only such as these that dispose souls to inspiration and impressions of the future. Certainly the voice of legend also is in accord with my
statement."

33. This thumbnail description belies a rich preoccupation with Cassandra, who aptly
illustrates the Stoic principle of how the human soul's ability to foreknow the future can be
abnormally developed: "Therefore the human soul has an inherent power of presaging or of

tration of the general principle "that true prophecies [*vaticinari*] are made during frenzy [*furor*]" (1.67).

When he attends to this phenomenon less with catchphrases than with thoughtful analysis, Quintus turns naturally to Plato's famed image of the soul's ability to sprout wings and to fly abroad, which exercised inexorable influence over Greco-Roman conceptions during the first century (*Phaedrus* 246A-47E). Plato's image of the soul's ascent undergoes a metamorphosis in Quintus's adaptation of it. In the first place, the journey does not begin with the power of recollection and a love of things divine but with the impact of an external impulse, such as Delphic vapors. In the second place, Quintus describes this ascent in terms that Plato did not: as the inflammation and arousal of the soul.

> Those then, whose souls, spurning their bodies, take wings and fly abroad — inflamed and aroused by a sort of passion — these people, I say, certainly see the things which they foretell in their prophecies. Such souls do not cling to the body and are kindled by many different influences. For example, some are aroused by certain vocal tones, as by Phrygian songs, many by groves and forests, and many others by rivers and seas. I believe, too, that there were certain subterranean vapors which had the effect of inspiring persons to utter oracles. (*On Divination* 1.114)[34]

The addition of inflammation is in no way Quintus's invention; elsewhere in *On Divination* he deftly cites one of the earlier tragic poets who depicted Cassandra with "those flaming eyes, that sudden rage [*oculis rabere visa est derepente ardentibus*]" (1.66).

How pervasive during the Greco-Roman era was this association between inflammation and possession by the spirit? So widespread that it ignored

---

foreknowing infused into it from without, and made a part of it by the will of God. If that power is abnormally developed, it is called 'frenzy' or 'inspiration' [*ea, si exarsit acrius, furor appellatur*], which occurs when the soul withdraws itself from the body and is violently stimulated by a divine impulse [*divino instinctu*]" (*On Divination* 1.66). For Cassandra, that divine impulse is unwanted possession by Apollo and Paris.

34. Latin: *Ergo et ei, quorum animi spretis corporibus evolant atque excurrunt foras, ardore aliquo inflammati atque incitati, cernunt illa profecto quae vaticinantes pronuntiant; multisque rebus inflammantur tales animi qui corporibus non inhaerent, ut ei qui sono quodam vocum et Phrygiis cantibus incitantur. Multos nemora silvaeque, multos amnes aut maria commovent. Credo etiam anhelitus quosdam fuisse terrarum quibus inflatae mentes oracla funderent.* The subterranean vapors are probably to be associated with Delphi.

all sorts of boundaries. Lucan wrote imaginative poetry, Cicero and Plutarch dialogues, and Philo scriptural commentaries. Cicero and Lucan composed in Latin, Plutarch and Philo in Greek. Cicero was born late in the second century B.C.E., Philo late in the first century B.C.E.; Lucan died after the mid-first century C.E., while Plutarch died a few decades into the second century C.E. Their lives, taken together, span two complete centuries. Notwithstanding what divides them, all four authors provide evidence of the tenacity of this association of fire with filling because each describes the inspired state, which is precipitated by an external impulse — typically this is *pneuma* — as a fiery one. Scattered throughout the Greco-Roman world, then, lay dramatic and entertaining images of such figures as the Delphic Pythia, who boiled over with fierce fire when Apollo darted flame into her vital organs, or the renowned and tragic Cassandra, who cowered before "that bloody torch" which would inflame her, causing her "hair to bristle and her eyes to flame" (*On Divination* 1.66-67).

The power of this association extended beyond the reaches of Cicero's Italian home, Arpinum, Philo's Egyptian home, Alexandria, Plutarch's Greek home, Chaeronea, permeating even the porous borders of the Roman East. Pseudo-Philo, the Palestinian author of the *Liber antiquitatum biblicarum*, assimilates precisely this association between fire and filling in his revision of Joshua's commissioning prior to Moses' death. The description of Joshua's authority among the people, we may recall, is stated prosaically: "Joshua son of Nun was full of (a) spirit of wisdom, because Moses had laid his hands on him; and the Israelites obeyed him, doing as the Lord had commanded Moses" (Deut 34:9). Pseudo-Philo's revision is more nuanced: the spirit is plunged under the surface, only to re-emerge subtly by means of direct speech, allusions, and metaphor. God speaks to Joshua bluntly: "Moses is dead. Take his garments of wisdom and clothe yourself, and with his belt of knowledge gird your loins, and you will be changed and become another person" (*LAB* 20:2). Although there is no simple reference to the spirit in this iteration, the prediction that Joshua will "become another person" when he puts on Moses' garments is lifted from the story of Saul: "Then the spirit of the Lord will possess you, and you will prophesy along with them and be turned into a different person" (1 Sam 10:6).[35] The origin of the metaphor of clothing or garments is no harder to

---

35. Pseudo-Philo takes up similar words to attribute the transformation of Kenaz to the spirit: "he [Kenaz] was clothed with the spirit of power and was changed into another man . . ." (*LAB* 27:10).

trace. It is taken from Israel's story of Gideon: "But the spirit of the Lord clothed Gideon" (Judg 6:34).[36]

Though on a relatively small scale, this is a breathtaking metamorphosis of a dreary description of a transition in Israelite leadership — yet this does not exhaust the extent of this transformation. Joshua's experience is depicted no less dramatically, not only by the importation of phrases from other Israelite stories, but through the incorporation of the widespread Greco-Roman understanding of inspiration as inflammation: "And Joshua took the garments of wisdom [*vestimenta sapientie*] and clothed himself and girded his loins with the belt of understanding. And when he clothed himself with it, his mind was afire and his spirit was moved [*ea incensa est mens eius et spiritus eius commotus est*], and he said to the people . . ." (*LAB* 20:3).

Nothing in Israel's scriptures can explain the inflammation of Joshua's mind and the agitation of his spirit.[37] And nothing need do. The understanding of prophetic inspiration as inflammation and agitation was so entrenched in the Greco-Roman world that it may have been little more than a reflex to include this dimension of inspiration in a narrative that is otherwise grounded in a reference to Joshua's spirit of wisdom, coupled with allusions to Saul's possession and Gideon's being clothed by the spirit. The combination of inflammation and agitation follows the familiar pattern in which prophecy is attributed to people "whose souls, spurning their bodies, take wings and fly abroad, *inflamed and aroused by a sort of passion*" (*On Divination* 1.114). This is a world in which Cassandra is distinguished by "those flaming eyes, that sudden rage" (1.66). Joshua is kin to the reluctant Pythia, who boils over with fierce fire and whose insides are full of divine flame.

These are, of course, not exact parallels, and they are not intended to suggest any sort of literary relationship between the literature of Cicero, Philo, Lucan, Pseudo-Philo, Josephus, and Plutarch. Nonetheless, because these are such different scenes and figures and genres — poetry, commentary, biblical paraphrase, and literary dialogue — and because the detail of inflammation in the *Liber antiquitatum biblicarum* is so patently an addition to the Israelite story of Joshua, the recurrence of the association of a

---

36. A similar image characterizes Gideon: "And as soon as Gideon heard these words, he put on the spirit of the Lord and was strengthened" (*LAB* 36:2).

37. The closest scriptural antecedent to a fiery mind is the heat of Ezekiel's spirit (Ezek 3:14), though this would be at best a distant allusion.

fiery experience with the presence of the divine spirit in this Palestinian revision of Israelite literature demonstrates how far-reaching this association was.

Conclusion

With the sole exception of Ezekiel, Israelite prophets left only shards of their experience; their fragile memoirs must be pieced together carefully and cautiously. It was, in fact, only in the postexilic era that authors began retrospectively to associate the spirit with Israel's prophets as a whole. Apart from Ezekiel, there are only faint hints of ecstasy, which may, in the end, prove to be only fool's gold anyway. There is no bristling hair, no ecstatic transport, no inflammation, no appearance of drunkenness apart from a solitary reference in Hos 9:7: "The prophet is a fool, the man of the spirit is mad!" — which can refer just as easily, and more likely, in my opinion, to the *content* of prophetic condemnation as to the demeanor, or means of communication, of the prophet.

The legacy of the Greeks, in contrast, was vibrant and open-mouthed about its prophets, among whom could be counted the Delphic Pythia, Cassandra, the priestesses of Dodona, and the sybils. Fiery-eyed, inflamed, drunk with the spirit, bounding and bouncing about, agitated by the onslaught of enthusiasm. These prophets were like sirens, from whom so many Greco-Roman writers could not look away.

Nor, would it seem, could Jewish Greco-Roman writers. Philo describes the entire race of Israelite prophets as ecstatics, whose minds are ousted when the divine spirit takes up its tenancy. He and Josephus even manage to solve a fundamental conundrum by importing the Greco-Roman view that God — in Balaam's instance, the divine spirit — enters into a prophet and takes hold of his or her vocal chords; this explains how Balaam, a false diviner, was able to bless Israel.

These Jewish writers evince no reluctance to import Greco-Roman conceptions of inspiration into Israelite literature, in which the mechanics of inspiration are expressed so laconically, or not at all. Drunkenness is nowhere in Israel's legacy associated with the spirit, yet Philo can transform the story of Hannah, whom Eli accuses of drunkenness, into a quintessential episode of ecstasy. The author of *Liber antiquitatum biblicarum* is no more reticent when he metamorphoses the terse Israelite observation that Joshua had a spirit of wisdom in him into a brilliant image of prophetic ecstasy, in which Joshua's mind is inflamed and his spirit agitated. Yet even this importation of Greco-Roman culture into a revision of Israelite literature pales in comparison with Pseudo-Philo's transformation of Kenaz. Though he is mentioned only by name in Judg 3:9, in *Liber antiquitatum biblicarum* the spirit leaps upon him and indwells him, ousting or elevating his mind. He exits this state when he is awakened and his sense returns to him, though he, like Saul, cannot recollect what he heard or saw. This collection of the elements of prophetic ecstasy is nearly magical; from the standpoint of Greco-Roman conceptions of *pneuma* — though not Israelite ones — it is unmistakably authentic, a panorama of Greco-Roman qualities of inspiration. Or, to express this thought in more pedestrian terms, Kenaz offers a clinic in the elements of spirit-induced ecstasy.

The shreds that Israel left behind, then, are supplanted by the pulsating interest that Greco-Roman authors felt for their own prophets. Enthusiasm would capture the minds of Josephus in Rome, Pseudo-Philo in Palestine, and Philo in Alexandria — three corners of the Mediterranean world — and would lead to extraordinary metamorphoses of their own Israelite prophets and kings, as well as lesser lights, such as Hannah and Kenaz, who would, in the new world of Rome, shine far more intensely than they had in their own traditions.

CHAPTER 3

Spirit and Inspired Knowledge

Despite its powerful allure, some Jewish authors were able to resist the headiness of inspired ecstasy. Perhaps it would be more accurate to say that some of the same Jewish authors of the Greco-Roman era who left a legacy of inspired ecstasy have, on other occasions, left a different legacy, in which the divine spirit was believed to impart extraordinary knowledge apart from the familiar experiences of ecstasy that authors such as Cicero, Lucan, and Plutarch so vividly documented. Though perhaps less dramatic than images of prophetesses who bounced around caves with hair bristling and eyes enraged, images of inspired knowledge are more rarified; an aversion to clichés and the familiar lends to these experiences an undeniable air of profundity.[1]

Escaping the Allure of Ecstasy

Although Philo is an aficionado of ecstasy, he does not inevitably allow the Israelite figures upon whom he comments to be backed into the corner of the Delphic cave, so to speak. Philo's avoidance of the ecstatic is never clearer than when he discusses Moses, whom he considers to be a prophet in the strictest sense of the term. Yet Moses is not like other prophets, whose minds are eclipsed by the presence of the divine spirit, whose vocal chords move with the influx and exhalation of the spirit. Though Moses is

---

1. For more detailed analysis, including significantly more citations of Greek, see J. R. Levison, *The Spirit in First Century Judaism*. AGJU 29 (Leiden: Brill, 1997) 167-214.

the prophet *par excellence,* his prophetic powers do not obviate his intellect. On the contrary, his mind is sharpened by the presence of the divine spirit.

Take, for example, the Sabbath, which Moses predicted under divine inspiration (*Life of Moses* 2.259). The whole of this context underscores Moses' prophetic abilities, his inspiration, his state of possession.[2] Yet when Philo explains more precisely how Moses came to discern in the sixth-day provision of manna the need for Sabbath, the tack of Philo's explanation turns leeward rather than in the more fashionable windward direction:

> Moses, when he heard of this [the manna] and also actually saw it, was awestruck and, guided by what was not so much surmise as God-sent inspiration, made announcement of the Sabbath. I need hardly say that conjectures of this kind are closely akin to prophecies. *For the mind*

---

2. Philo's explanation suggests, on the one hand, that Moses' oracles concerning the Sabbath were the product of an ecstatic form of prophecy. According to LXX Exod 16:15, Moses responded to the Israelites' question about the manna with a straightforward description of it as bread, prefaced by the simple words "Moses said [*eipen*] to them." Philo records that Moses commanded under inspiration that the Israelites should gather only enough for each day (*On the Life of Moses* 2.259). According to LXX Exod 16:23, Moses merely "said to them" that they should rest on the Sabbath. Philo writes instead that Moses, "under God-sent inspiration, made announcement of the Sabbath" (*On the Life of Moses* 2.264). According to LXX Exod 16:25-26, Moses said that the people should eat what was preserved from the prior day rather than searching in the field on the Sabbath. Philo transforms this statement in *On the Life of Moses* 2.268-69 into a prediction by emphasizing that it transpired, not on the Sabbath, but on the day prior to the Sabbath, by describing the oracle as "most portentous" and by replacing "said" with "prophesied." The result of these Sabbath predictions, Philo records, was Israel's acknowledgement of Moses, "the prophet as a true seer, an interpreter of God, and alone gifted with foreknowledge of the hidden future."

As if this recasting were not enough, Philo includes three narrative transitions in the Sabbath story that accentuate Moses' inspired state. He begins by characterizing Moses' prior utterance at the Red Sea as the beginning of Moses' prophetic work, implying by this that the subsequent oracles concerning the Sabbath would be its continuation: "It was thus that Moses began and opened his work as a prophet possessed by God's spirit" (*On the Life of Moses* 2.258). After the first Sabbath oracle about the manna, he then writes, "Not long after, Moses delivered a second inspired pronouncement concerning the sacred seventh day" (2.263). Before turning to the subsequent biblical episode, Philo recapitulates: Moses' explanation of manna was "his pronouncement under divine inspiration" (2.270). Thus Moses' utterances concerning the manna and the Sabbath, described consistently in LXX Exodus 16 with the simple verb, "said," are transformed by Philo into instances of prophetic inspiration. Moses was a prophet who spoke "when possessed by God and carried away out of himself" (2.188).

could not have made so straight an aim if there was not also the divine spirit guiding it to the truth itself.[3]

Three words — conjecture, mind, guide — signal that Moses remains *compos mentis* throughout his prophetic experience.

Philo consistently employs the word "conjecture" in contexts that have to do with thought, opinions, and guessing. In *Embassy to Gaius* 21, for example, he observes, "The human mind in its blindness does not perceive its real interest and all it can do is to take conjecture and guesswork for its guide instead of knowledge." He includes conjecture alongside human ideas, purposes, and aims (*On the Posterity of Cain* 80) and describes as "second to the true vision . . . conjecture and theorizing and all that can be brought into the category of reasonable probability" (*On the Special Laws* 1.38).[4]

The verb "guide" occurs without exception in Philo's writings in association with the path toward virtue. Guides in the ascent to virtue include love of wisdom (*On the Creation* 70) or divine reason (*On the Unchangeability of God* 182). When Philo describes wisdom itself as a guide, he presents the essential role of the conscious mind with exceptional clarity: "The mind is cleansed by wisdom and the truths of wisdom's teaching which guide its steps to the contemplation of the universe and all that is therein, and by the sacred company of the other virtues and by the practice of them shown in noble and highly praiseworthy actions" (*On the Special Laws* 1.269). The road to virtue is therefore concomitant with the purification of the mind. Philo's use of these two words, conjecture and guide, alongside the straightforward statement that the divine spirit guided Moses' *mind* to the truth, underscores the depth of Philo's effort to explain Moses' magnificent prophetic ability without recourse to the clichés of Greco-Roman ecstasy.

Yet there is something more here that transports us to a world beyond the confines of Philo's writings. This portrayal of the spirit resonates with Greek and Roman reflections on the nature of Socrates' inspiration. Of special interest was the nature of his inspiring *daimonion,* which Plato

---

3. Greek: *ho gar nous ouk an houtōs euskopōs euthybolēsen ei mē kai theion ēn pneuma to podēgetoun pros autēn tēn alētheian.*

4. E.g., *Allegorical Interpretation* 3.228; *On the Confusion of Tongues* 159; *On the Cherubim* 69; *On Dreams* 1.23; *On the Special Laws* 1.63; 4.50; *Who Is the Heir?* 98; and *On the Life of Moses* 1.68. For further analysis, see J. R. Levison, "The Prophetic Spirit as an Angel according to Philo," *HTR* 88 (1995) 197-98.

consistently designated *to daimonion* (*Euthyphro* 3B; *Apology* 40A), or "something divine and daemonic" (*Apology* 31D). Socrates associated it with a sign and reflected, "I thought I heard a voice from it" (*Phaedrus* 242C). Writers including Xenophon,[5] the author of the pseudo-Platonic dialogue *Theages*,[6] Cicero,[7] Maximus of Tyre,[8] and Diogenes Laertius[9] devoted serious attention to the nature of Socrates' *daimonion* for more than half a millennium. Josephus belongs to this current of thought when he attributes Socrates' death to his claim "that he received communications from a certain daemon [*daimonion*]" (*Against Apion* 2.263-64).

Plutarch devotes two substantive discussions in his *On the Sign of Socrates* to the nature and function of this daimonic sign (580B-82C and 588B-89F). These conversations begin with a question raised by Theocritus:

> . . . but what, my dear sir, do we call Socrates' daemon [*daimonion*]? For my part, nothing reported of Pythagoras's skill in divination has struck me as so great or so divine; for exactly as Homer has represented Athena as 'standing at' Odysseus's 'side in all his labors,' so heaven seems to have attached to Socrates from his earliest years as his guide [*propodēgon*] in life a vision of this kind, which alone 'Showed him the way, illumining his path,' in matters dark and inscrutable to human wisdom, about

5. Xenophon begins his *Memorabilia* with a refutation of the charge that Socrates rejected the gods of the state, defending Socrates by demonstrating his conformity to the state religion. Therefore, he refers to this *daimonion* in a way that assimilates it to the state religion rather than in ways that distinguish it from that religion. Xenophon goes so far as to include it alongside commonplace forms of divination, such as augury (1.1.4), and twice states in general terms that it pointed the way (*sēmainein*) for Socrates (*Memorabilia* 1.1.2-3). The process of assimilating Socrates' daemon to the state gods extends to the point of referring to it as a god (1.1.5).

6. This dialogue, written by an admirer of Plato, probably during the second century B.C.E., concludes with a lengthy discussion between Socrates and Theages on the nature of this daemonic sign. Taking his cue from *Phaedrus* 242C, the author of this dialogue gives no uncertain answer: what accompanied Socrates from his youth up was a voice that functioned as a sign to Socrates to prohibit an action (*Theages* 128D-29D).

7. Socrates supplies the precedent for the conviction in *On Divination* that "the power of divination exists" (1.124): "It is this purity of soul, no doubt, that explains that famous utterance which history attributes to Socrates and which his disciples in their books often represent him as repeating: 'There is some divine influence [*divinum*]' — daimonion, he called it — 'which I always obey, though it never urges me on, but often holds me back'" (1.122).

8. In his eighth exhortation.

9. In *Lives of the Philosophers* 2.32, he mentions that Socrates "used to say that his supernatural sign warned him beforehand of the future."

which the daemon [*daimonion*] often conversed with him, (and) inspired [*epitheiazon*] him in his own decisions. (580C-D)[10]

Several elements in this conception of inspiration are similar to Philo's description of communication from the spirit in *On the Life of Moses* 2.265.[11] First, while Theocritus designates the *daimonion* a guide *(propodēgon),* Philo uses the cognate verb *podēgetoun* to describe the guidance of the divine spirit in *On the Life of Moses* 2.265. Second, the primary function of Socrates' *daimonion* in this introduction corresponds to the primary function of inspiration in the introduction to Philo's treatment of Moses' prophetic gift in *On the Life of Moses* 2.187-292, of which Moses' ability to predict the Sabbath is an illustration. The *daimonion* illumined matters inscrutable to human wisdom; Moses as prophet was to "declare by inspiration what cannot be apprehended by reason" (2.187). Third, inspiration is described by the same verb. The *daimonion* inspired *(epitheiazon)* Socrates' decisions; the Sabbath prediction (2.263) was a product of Moses' inspiration *(epitheiasas).*

This correspondence between Socrates' and Moses' inspiration should not surprise us if we recollect that Philo frequently adopts Greco-Roman conceptions of inspiration to elucidate and expand Israelite literature, such as when he transforms Balaam's inspiration into a form of ventriloquism. It is consistent with his exegetical tendencies to explain Moses' inspiration via Greco-Roman conceptions of inspiration. Similarly, we are not left to guess in *On the Life of Moses* 2.265 whether Philo has assimilated Greco-Roman conceptions, for he does so in a narrative aside that is clearly intended to explain Moses' experience in a manner that is comprehensible to his first-century Greco-Roman readers: "I need hardly say that. . . ." Little wonder, then, that Moses and Socrates experience similar forms of inspiration:

. . . the intelligence of the higher power guides the gifted soul (*On the Sign of Socrates* 588E)

. . . the understanding may be guided by a higher understanding and a diviner soul (589B)

. . . the divine spirit guiding it [the mind] to the truth itself (*On the Life of Moses* 2.265)[12]

10. My translation.
11. See also *On Rewards and Punishments* 55.
12. Once again, *On the Cherubim* 27–29 is relevant here.

Abraham, too, is inspired — possessed, even — though the result is not a state of exquisite ecstasy but transformation into the ideal orator. Philo attends effusively to this model proselyte, who left idols behind to follow the God of Israel:

> Thus whenever he was possessed, everything in him changed to something better, eyes, complexion, stature, carriage, movements, voice. For the divine spirit which was breathed upon him from on high made its lodging in his soul, and invested his body with singular beauty, his voice with persuasiveness, and his hearers with understanding. Would you not say that this lone wanderer without relatives or friends was of the highest nobility, he who craved for kinship with God and strove by every means to live in familiarity with Him, he who while ranked among the prophets, a post of such high excellence, put his trust in nothing created rather than in the Uncreated and Father of all, he who as I have said was regarded as a king by those in whose midst he settled. (*On the Virtues* 217-18)[13]

The heart of inspiration is Abraham's power of persuasion. The transformation of his body — eyes, complexion, stature, carriage, movements, voice — resembles a catalogue of elements which comprise the orator's delivery. The author of the first-century rhetorical handbook *Rhetorica ad Herennium*, for instance, defines delivery as "the graceful regulation of voice, countenance, and gesture" (1.3).[14] Cicero lists the components of delivery: "bodily carriage, gesture, play of features and changing intonation of voice" (*On Oratory* 1.18).

Compare this description with the fiery eyes of the Delphic Pythia or Cassandra, or even the sybil, who is goaded to speak what she does not understand. Abraham's skill occupies the opposite position on the spectrum of speech. His is, to adopt the description in *Rhetorica ad Herennium*, a "graceful regulation of voice, countenance, and gesture."

Compare as well the beauty of Abraham with the Greco-Roman prophetesses' bristling hair and enervated bodies, wracked as they were by the whips of the gods and *pneuma* that entered them. Abraham, in contrast, gains better eyes, complexion, stature, movements, and voice. The spirit, in short, "invested his body with singular beauty."[15]

---

13. For further discussion, see Levison, *The Spirit in First Century Judaism*, 90-98.

14. See also 3.19-27.

15. Homer (*Iliad* 3.167-70) associates beauty, even more than physical size, with kingship in the words of the elderly Priam to his daughter-in-law, Helen, about Agamemnon:

What is so rich and subtle in Philo's description is not Abraham's royal rhetorical ability. What is so splendid, rather, is that Abraham, who was already a king "because of his greatness of soul" (*On the Virtues* 216) and a prophet, was transformed into the ideal orator when the divine spirit lodged in his soul. He found himself, not in a condition of ecstasy, but in a state of rhetorical finesse and force. He exhibited skills that, according to the handbooks on rhetoric, such as *Rhetorica ad Herennium*, and other treatments of the topic, such as Quintilian's *Institutio Oratoria* and Dio Chrysostom's discourse on training for public speaking — not to mention the inclusion of rhetoric in Roman curricula — were acquired through diligent training.[16] Even his hearers were given a heightened ability to comprehend. These are the forceful ways of the divine spirit, Philo tells us; circumventing ecstasy's seduction, it invested Abraham with royal beauty and rhetorical prowess.

Josephus, too, finds occasion to evade the allure of ecstasy in his revision of the story of Daniel. Rather than following Dan 5:14, in which spirit is within Daniel, Josephus records that the spirit accompanied Daniel; Beltasares took note of "his wisdom and of the divine spirit that attended him and how he alone was fully able to discover things which were not within the understanding of others" (*Ant.* 10.239). There is no possession of Daniel, no inspiring spirit within; the spirit, rather, accompanies Daniel.[17]

". . . this man of Achea so valiant and so tall. Verily there be others that are even taller by a head, but so comely a man have mine eyes never yet beheld, neither one so royal: he is like unto one that is a king." On the relationship between physical presence and rhetorical skill, Antenor's words to Helen about Odysseus in *Iliad* 3.221-24 are illuminating: "But whenso he uttered his great voice from his chest, and words like snowflakes on a winter's day, then could no mortal man beside vie with Odysseus; then did we not so marvel to behold Odysseus's aspect." Plato (*Republic* 2.402D) praises the combination of inner and external beauty: "when there is a coincidence of a beautiful disposition in the soul and corresponding harmonious beauties of the same type in bodily form — is not this the fairest spectacle for one who is capable of its contemplation?" Plato (*Republic* 7.535A) also contends that this combination characterizes the ideal ruler: "The most stable, the most brave and enterprising are to be preferred, and, so far as practicable, the most comely." Cicero, following this line of thought, praises both the spiritual and physical qualities of Romulus, the mythical founder of Rome: "And when he grew up, we are told, he was so far superior to his companions in bodily strength and boldness of spirit that all who then lived in the rural district where our city now stands were willing and glad to be ruled by him" (*On the Republic* 2.4).

16. See S. F. Bonner, *Education in Ancient Rome: From the Elder Cato to the Younger Pliny* (Berkeley: University of California, 1977) 65-89; and G. Kennedy, *The Art of Rhetoric in the Roman World: 300 B.C.–A.D. 300* (Princeton: Princeton University, 1972) 318-21.

17. The verb *sympareinai* is employed by Josephus in seven of twelve instances of God's

Josephus also revises Dan 6:4(Eng. 3), according to which "an 'excellent' spirit was in" Daniel. He avoids yet again the biblical portrait of a spirit within by adding the perfect participle *pepisteumenos* ("was believed"): "And so Daniel, being held in such great honor and such dazzling favor by Darius and being the only one associated with him in all matters because he was believed to have the divine [spirit] in him, became a prey to envy" (*Ant.* 10.250).[18] With the participle *pepisteumenos,* Josephus effectively evokes an air of ambiguity around the view that Daniel had extraordinary wisdom because he was full of extraordinary — and even an extraordinary amount of — *pneuma.*[19] This may have been, in Israel's literature, what Darius and his Median contemporaries believed, but this is not Josephus's own opinion. Daniel, for all his prophetic knowledge and skilled interpretation, was no ecstatic. The furnace may have flamed, but Daniel's eyes did not.

Spirit and the Interpretation of Scripture

The Qumran Hymns

While the Hasmonean Dynasty exercised its hegemony over Palestine, the splinter group of Jews that gathered along the shores of the Dead Sea would develop an alternative Israel, with its own rules of ritual order, its own priestly hierarchy, and its own idiosyncratic methods of interpretation that handsomely served its own political and social aims. Initiates at Qumran were obligated to take an oath to follow Torah *as it was interpreted by means*

---

presence, and in five of these seven, including *Ant.* 10.239, it explains the occurrence of a distinctive accompaniment: Abimelech was jealous of God's presence, which caused Isaac to be blessed (1.260); the voice from the burning bush predicted Moses' honor amongst the people because God was with him (2.268); the Israelites crossed the Red Sea because God accompanied them (2.340); Moses could not calm the angry Israelites himself, but God who accompanied him prepared them for his words (3.316).

18. Josephus omits the word *pneuma,* though *to theion* could arguably be interpreted as an elliptical reference to the spirit; still, its absence softens the basis for interpreting Daniel's experience as spirit possession.

19. L. H. Feldman observes that Josephus concludes the entire story of Daniel with similar caution: "Now I have written about these matters as I have found them in my reading; if, however, anyone wishes to judge otherwise of them, I shall not object to his holding a different opinion" (*Ant.* 10.281); "Josephus's Portrait of Daniel," *Hen* 14 (1992) 84. Josephus may reserve judgment because of the implications of Daniel's prophecies concerning Rome.

of revelation at Qumran, "in compliance with all that has been revealed concerning it to the sons of Zadok, the priests who keep the covenant and interpret his will" (1QS V 9).[20] More specifically, the central — even legendary — figure of Qumran was the Teacher of Righteousness, to whom, according to the Commentary on Habakkuk, "God has disclosed all the mysteries of the words of his servants, the prophets"(1QpHab VII 4).[21]

On the rarest of occasions, the Qumran hymn writer, who may have been the Teacher himself, mirrors this self-perception with an uncommon glimpse of optimism, a whiff of the possibility that individual human beings can recount God's wonders by virtue of the breath they possess, the spirit that is theirs from birth, and the intellect with which God has endowed human beings. There remains even the possibility that the spirit, the breath God has given to each at birth, because it was designed by God may speak and sing what God intends:

> You created breath [*rûaḥ*] on the tongue, you know its words, you instituted the fruits of the lips, before they came to be; you placed words to the rhythm, and the puff of breath [*rûaḥ*] from the lips to the beat; you make the rhythms emerge according to their mysteries and the puffs of breaths by their measures. (1QH IX 27-29)

20. On inspired interpretation in the Dead Sea Scrolls, see O. Betz, *Offenbarung und Schriftforschung in der Qumransekte.* WUNT 6 (Tübingen: Mohr, 1960); D. E. Aune, "Charismatic Exegesis in Early Judaism and Early Christianity," in *The Pseudepigrapha and Early Biblical Interpretation,* ed. J. H. Charlesworth and C. A. Evans. JSPSup 14 (Sheffield: JSOT, 1993) 126-50; D. E. Orton, *The Understanding Scribe: Matthew and the Apocalyptic Ideal.* JSNTSup 25 (Sheffield: Sheffield Academic, 1989) 121-33.

21. See also II 7-9. Unfortunately, a lacuna renders two reconstructions of 1QpHab 2.7-9 possible. F. García-Martínez translates, "the Priest whom God has placed wi[thin the Community,] to foretell the fulfilment of all the words of his servants, the prophets"; *The Dead Sea Scrolls Translated,* 2nd ed. (Grand Rapids: Wm. B. Eerdmans, 1990) 198. G. Vermes translates, "The priest [in whose heart] God set [understanding] that he might interpret all the words of His servants the Prophets"; *The Dead Sea Scrolls in English,* 3rd rev. ed. (London: Penguin, 1987) 284. Only the second translation, which fills the lacuna with the words "into whose heart," rather than "in the Community," suggests overtly the presence of revelation to the Priest. Other texts from the Judean Desert lay an implicit claim to authority in other ways. The Deuteronomic Paraphrase, for example, merges the text of Deuteronomy with subsequent interpretation without distinguishing them from one another. It is as if interpretation and text have the same authority. Still other texts that were apparently treasured at Qumran were considered authoritative for different reasons. Jubilees, which comprises a creative revision of Torah, from creation to the Passover, in its opening lines stakes its claim to having been revealed at Sinai.

Although this lovely account of the mechanism of praise is not, of course, directed at the mechanics of inspiration or the practice of interpretation, it provides a vivid glimpse of the view we have encountered time and again: the spirit within that issues in words, that follows the rhythm of praise, is God's breath. God has given spirit-breath and tongue and rhythm, and these are the dimensions of a human being, claims the hymn writer, that "show your glory and recount your wonders, in all the deeds of your truth and your just judg[ments], to praise your name through the mouth of all. And they will know you according to their intellect and they will bless you for [everlasting] centuries" (1QH IX 29, 31). This is an uncommon glimpse of optimism, a rare expression that the spirit-breath which God gives at birth, the intellect which is resident in all people, provide the resources of praise, the reservoir for singing God's wonders.

More typical in the Scrolls is a view adopted by the writer of the *Hymns*, whose reflections upon the stories of Eden break into shards of pessimism:

> And I, from dust [I] have been gathered, [and from clay] I have been [fo]rmed to be a source of impurity, and of vile filth, a pile of dust, mixed with [water, . . .] a lodging of darkness. . . . What is he (to do that), he who returns to his dust. I have kept silence, for what can I say about this matter? In accordance with my knowledge /I spoke/, spat saliva, one fashioned from clay. (1QH XX 24-26, 31-32)

Such darkness leads nowhere but to a chain of questions:

> What can I say unless you open my mouth?
> How can I understand unless you teach me?
> What can I pro[pose] if you do not open my heart?
> How can I keep a straight path unless you steady [my] ste[ps?
> (1QH XX 32-34)

It is perhaps puzzling that just a few lines earlier, the hymn writer has already answered these questions. Dust and a source of darkness though he may be, he does have something to say. God has opened his mouth, taught him understanding, given him matters to propose, and straightened his path — at least with respect to the interpretation of scripture:

> And I, the Instructor, have known you, my God
> through the spirit [*běrûaḥ*] which you gave in me,

and I have listened loyally to your wonderful secret through
    your holy spirit.
You have [op]ened within me
knowledge of the mystery of your wisdom,
the source of [your] power. . . . (1QH XX 11-12)

These brief lines contain more than they might appear to at first glance because they evoke powerful images of knowledge and wisdom.

The hymn writer cements the association of inspiration and interpretation by sandwiching "your holy spirit" between references to "your
wonderful secret" and "knowledge of the mystery of your wisdom." The
word "mystery" *(rāz)* refers in the Habakkuk Commentary to "the mysteries of the words of his servants, the prophets" — that is, to prophetic
texts which the Teacher of Righteousness interprets with divine aid (e.g.,
1QpHab VII 5). The Habakkuk Commentary holds myriad illustrations of
the Instructor's claim to inspiration, multiple examples of his *pesher*
method of interpretation.

The hymn's author, further, refers to himself as "instructor" *(maśkîl),* a
Hebrew word that is built from the same verbal root, *skl* ("to instruct"),
that occurs in Nehemiah's description of a day immemorial, following the
return from exile, on which Ezra and his cohort instructed the people
(Neh 8:8, 13). It is the same root, as well, that Nehemiah adopted subsequently in his prayer, where he associated the spirit with scribal teaching:
"You gave your good spirit to instruct them *[lĕhaśkîlām]*" (Neh 9:20). In
the hymn counted among the scrolls, the spirit, the holy spirit, is the
source of the "instructor's" insight, knowledge, and wisdom concerning
God's secrets.

The hymn writer's experience of inspiration is couched no less in language that evinces a level of reflection upon and interpretation of Ezekiel's
visions: God has "given" or put the spirit within him to give him insight
into the meaning of scripture. The texts upon which he has reflected, interestingly enough — Ezek 11:19; 36:26-27; and 37:14 — associate the gift of
the spirit with obedience to Torah: "a new spirit I will put within you . . .
and make you follow my statutes and be careful to observe my ordinances"
— a cornerstone Qumran conviction.

For a community so steeped in the biblical tradition that truth cannot be conceived of without recourse to biblical conceptions and phraseology — a community in which the holy spirit can be a means of knowing God, God's secrets, God's mysteries (1QH XX 11-12), a community

whose initiates are obligated to follow Torah as it is interpreted peculiarly by its priestly leaders (1QS V 9), a community whose central figure receives divine aid to interpret prophetic texts (1QpHab VII 4) — for this community, it is not difficult to envisage that inspired interpretation by authorized, learned leaders did not enter the realm of the ecstatic. The demeanor and acquired skills of the interpreter are indicated by a series of words that point to inspired interpretation that circumvents the allure of ecstasy: the interpreter is an *instructor,* like scribes before him; he simply *listens* to God; he gains *knowledge* and *understanding* of God's scriptural secrets. Nevertheless, the authority of the instructor is grounded not in status, nor in rank within the community, nor in his native abilities, but in his experience that God has placed God's holy spirit in him. If he holds the interpretative key to the divine secrets and mysteries, he does so exclusively because the spirit which Ezekiel had envisaged beforehand, the good spirit that had instructed Israel, is now to be found in him.

Philo Judaeus

This faint association of inspiration with interpretation, which evokes the distant memory of Ezekiel and Nehemiah, pales in the brilliant hues of Philo's self-portraits. There is no single hue in Philo's commentaries; Philo's palette rather is a studied concoction of ecstasy and inspired intellect.

Occasionally, ecstasy pierces the heart of Philo's self-understanding as an interpreter of Israel's scripture. In a moment of autobiographical reflection, he describes occasions of dryness when he is bereft of insight, presumably insight into the meaning of scripture, upon which he otherwise comments so prolifically. During these momentary lapses, he has definite plans but comes up empty.

> On other occasions, I have approached my work empty and suddenly become full, the ideas falling in a shower from above and being sown invisibly, so that under the influence of the Divine I have been filled with corybantic frenzy and been unconscious of anything, place, persons present, myself, words spoken, lines written. For I obtained language, ideas, an enjoyment of light, keenest vision, pellucid distinctiveness of objects, such as might be received through the eyes as the result of clearest shewing. (*On the Migration of Abraham* 35)

In a stunning moment of self-disclosure, Philo describes himself as filled with the movement of Corybants, nature spirits who dance about the new-born Zeus and function with the Curetes in Despoina's cult at Lycosura (Pausanias 8.37.6), who guard the infant Dionysus in Orphic myth and dance to the sound of flutes in the orgiastic cults of Dionysus (Strabo 10.3.11) and Cybele (Diodorus Siculus 5.49). Philo discovers nothing less than the most pagan of dances to describe what happens to him on those occasions when he is utterly stumped by the interpretation of Torah, those moments when God steps in — quite nearly literally — and offers him an ecstatic unawareness of anything but a vision of keenest light.

These moments of frenzied insight, however, are not entirely typical of Philo. There are other occasions when Philo believes that the divine spirit actually intensifies his interpretative powers. In one instance, while he is in the throes of a full-fledged allegorical interpretation, Philo pauses uncharacteristically to describe his experience:

> I hear once more the voice of the invisible spirit [*pneuma aoraton*], the *customary* [*eiōthos*] secret tenant, saying, 'Friend, it would seem that there is a matter great and precious of which thou knowest nothing, and this I will ungrudgingly shew thee, for many other well-timed lessons have I given thee. (*On Dreams* 2.252)

Philo's description of this experience occurs in a brief parenthetical digression that is prompted by his allegorical interpretation of Jerusalem as a "vision of peace." This identification leads him to reflect on the vision-seeking mind, which leads him in turn to the experience of his own (vision-seeking) mind. While it is necessarily brief, perhaps even truncated, it describes the spirit by the evocative word "customary" *(eiōthos)*, which could scarcely have been read without reminding Philo's readers of Socrates' daemon, whom Socrates himself referred to as "the customary prophetic inspiration of the daemon" (*Apology* 40A), "the daemonic and customary sign" (*Phaedrus* 242B), and "my customary daemonic sign" (*Euthydemus* 272E).[22]

This resonance with Socrates, which characterizes Moses' inspiration in Philo's *On the Life of Moses* 2.264-65 as well, has resounding implications for apprehending Philo's description of inspired interpretation. There occurs a conversation in *On the Sign of Socrates* about "the problem

---

22. See also *Euthyphro* 3B.

of the nature and mode of operation of the so-called sign of Socrates"
(588B), in which Simmias ventures: "Socrates . . . had an understanding
which, being pure and free from passion, and commingling with the body
but little, for necessary ends, was so sensitive and delicate as to respond at
once to what reached him. What reached him, one would conjecture, was
not spoken language, but the unuttered words of a daemon, making voiceless contact with his intelligence by their sense alone" (588D-E). Simmias
conjectures further "that Socrates' sign was perhaps no vision, but rather
the perception of a voice or else the mental apprehension of language, that
reached him in some strange way" (588D), and that "what reached him,
one would conjecture, was not spoken language, but the unuttered words
of a daemon, making voiceless contact with his intelligence by their sense
alone" (588E).

By adopting the word "customary" to signal that he, like Socrates,
hears the voice of a daemonic presence, Philo steers clear of the siren of ecstasy. Not with a mad spree of frenzy, but by listening to the voice of the invisible spirit, as it addresses his pure intellect, is Philo able to interpret Israel's scripture. Though oblique, this is a vaunted claim that would have
raised the price of Philo's stock, at least among those who took his claim to
inspiration seriously.

On a similar occasion, recalls Philo, while puzzling over the question
of why two cherubim were required to guard paradise, Philo had a comparable experience of inspiration, in which he received a "higher word," by
which he means his allegorical interpretation of the two cherubim:

> But there is a higher thought than these. It comes from a voice in my
> own soul, which oftentimes is god-possessed [*theolēpteisthai*] and di-
> vines [*manteuesthai*] where it does not know. This thought I will record
> in words if I can. The voice told me that while God is indeed one, his
> highest and chiefest powers are two, even goodness and sovereignty. . . .
> O then, my mind [*dianoia*], admit the image unalloyed of the two
> Cherubim, that having learnt its clear lesson of the sovereignty, and be-
> neficence of the Cause, thou mayest reap the fruits of a happy lot. (*On
> the Cherubim* 27–29)

Philo's ability to discover that there are two cherubim because they represent the sovereignty and beneficence of God is due to a voice within, a possession that does not obviate his intellectual powers, even though he is in an
inspired state. The voice tells Philo — better yet, Philo's mind — the mean-

ing of the mystery. In this way, both *On the Cherubim* and *On Dreams* are of a piece.[23] According to both texts, in the process of interpretation, Philo encounters difficulties which require explanation. He ponders them and is led to a solution when he listens to the voice of another within him, which he identifies in *On Dreams* as "the customary unseen spirit."[24]

Philo walks a very fine line in all of this talk of inspiration. His vocabulary leans toward the ecstatic, toward possession, even divination. This is the language used of inspired poets and prophets, of sibyls and diviners filled with the presence of an invasive god. Yet his vocabulary leans as well toward sobriety. The occurrence of the verb "teach" *(anadidaskō)* indicates that the voice, or spirit, in *On Dreams,* is a teacher.[25] Further, it is Philo's

23. Both accounts also exhibit similar formal features: an introduction which identifies the source (soul; spirit) and means (prompting; divining) of inspiration; a description of the content of teaching; and a concluding self-directed exhortation ("Receive the image unalloyed" and "Let it then be").

24. Philo recounts yet another encounter with an exegetical difficulty in *On Rewards and Punishments* 50. He marvels at the facility with which the mind solves the conundrum: "For good abilities and natural gifts are a matter of rejoicing. The mind exults in the facility of its apprehension and the felicity of the process by which it discovers what it seeks without labor, as though dictated by an inward prompter. For to find the solution of difficulties quickly must bring joy." The single word, "as though" *(kathaper)*, signals the ambiguity inherent in this form of experience. Philo knows that the mind's ability to solve a difficulty quickly is "as though" there were external aid at work from within; he does not pinpoint precisely how that aid affects the mind. The need for external aid is apparent in one of his prayers, which he records in *On Dreams* 1.164-65: "But even if we do close the eye of our soul and either will not take the trouble or have not the power to regain our sight, do thou thyself, O Sacred Guide, be our prompter and preside over our steps and never tire of anointing our eyes, until conducting us to the hidden light of hallowed words thou display to us the fast-locked lovelinesses invisible to the uninitiate. Thee it beseems to do this." This prayer is Philo's request that God lead people to the allegorical level of interpretation, for it is preceded by praise of "the sacred oracles" which gives "the gift of eyesight, enabling them to judge of the real nature of things, and not merely rely on the literal sense" (1.164). That concern and the request for prompting draw this prayer into the circle of texts on interpretation we have cited; God's prompting in this prayer, then, corresponds to the voice of the invisible spirit in *On Dreams* 2.252, the higher thought from within Philo's own soul in *On the Cherubim* 27–29, and the insight "as though by an inward prompter" in *On Rewards and Punishments* 50.

25. Philo's account of his experience with Consideration in *On Flight and Finding* 53–58 confirms the preeminence of a form of inspiration that involves teaching and learning in these experiences. Philo begins by observing an exegetical difficulty. This observation leads first to an internal debate and subsequently to the lectures of Consideration. She "taught" *(edidaxe)* him the exegetical solution, confirmed by appeal to other related biblical texts.

pure mind that the voice addresses — "O then, my mind . . ." — as in *On Dreams,* in which Philo's autobiographical aside is prompted by a reference to the "vision-seeking mind, the mind which is eager to see all things and never even in its dreams has a wish for faction or turmoil."[26] Further, the product of such possession is surprisingly sober; for instance, Philo understands that the two cherubim represent the sovereignty and benevolence of God. This is an interesting, inventive, and incontrovertibly sane allegorical interpretation of the two cherubim. Even the experience of possession in *On the Cherubim* leads directly to a concrete experience, in which Philo's mind appears to be alert and alive. And finally, the introduction of the word "customary," alongside the presence of a voice, resonates both with the renowned Socrates, whose daemon communicated to his pure mind through a voice, and Moses, whom the divine spirit guided to truth otherwise unknowable.

Philo is nothing if not enthusiastic about these moments of inspiration during which the higher allegorical meaning of scripture is revealed to him by this voice, this customary friend. This enthusiasm is not without reason, as he is led directly to fresh allegorical interpretations during moments when he simultaneously is possessed by God and possesses an alert and peace-loving mind, when, at one and the same time, his soul divines where he cannot possibly anticipate and his mind hears comprehensible and meaningful allegorical explanations of otherwise puzzling scriptural details.

Philo's untamed enthusiasm leads him to take his experiences as an inspired interpreter in still another direction in the third book of *On the Special Laws,* where, in an extensive autobiographical reflection, he once again walks a thin line between ecstasy and inspired intellect. Here he borrows the famed language of the ascent of the soul from Plato's *Phaedrus* 246A-253C to describe his uncanny ability to interpret scripture.[27] Philo recalls wistfully a time when he had "leisure for philosophy" and "seemed always to be borne aloft into the heights with a soul possessed by some God-sent inspiration [*epitheiasmon*], a fellow-traveller with the sun and moon and the whole heaven and universe. Ah then I gazed down from the upper air. . . ." He regrets that he is now sucked into civil affairs.[28] Yet he still manages unexpectedly to "obtain a spell of fine weather and a calm from

---

26. The prominence of the mind is evident also in *On Flight and Finding* 54–55, both in Philo's own internal debate and in the name Consideration.

27. More details are available in Levison, *The Spirit in First Century Judaism,* 151-58, 208-9.

28. This we know to be true; he was so active in civic life that he was selected to journey to Rome on an embassy to Emperor Gaius on behalf of Alexandrian Jews.

civil turmoils," on which occasions he is able to "open the soul's eyes," to be wafted on the winds of knowledge, and to become "irradiated by the light of wisdom." During these rare moments of respite, Philo finds himself "daring, not only to read the sacred pages of Moses, but also in my love of knowledge to peer into each of them and unfold and reveal what is not known to the multitude."

This autobiographical reflection contains a striking correspondence between the ascent of the philosopher's mind and the ascent of the interpreter's mind. Philo structures his experience as an interpreter in such a way that it mirrors the experience of the philosopher. The passage begins with philosophical ascent and possession (3.1-2), is interrupted by a plunge into the ocean of civil cares (3.3-4), and concludes with an ascent on the winds of knowledge to interpret Torah (3.5-6). Within this structure, the initial ascent to contemplate the upper air corresponds to the final ascent to interpret Torah. Philo reinforces this correlation, moreover, by employing the same verb, "to stoop" (diakyptein), to describe the experiences of ascent and interpretation. The words, "Ah then I gazed down [diakyptōn] from the upper air . . ." (3.2), correspond to "Behold me daring . . . to peer into [diakyptein] each of them [the sacred messages of Moses] and unfold . . ." (3.6).[29]

Fundamental to this reflection is the essential preparation of learning. Philo's ascent as interpreter is possible because of his yearning for education, because he is wafted on the winds of knowledge, because of his love of learning. Yet his inclusion of the catchword "possessed" (epitheiasmon),

29. On the relationship between *On the Special Laws* 3.5-6, *On Planting* 22–24, and *On the Giants* 53–54, see J. R. Levison, "Inspiration and the Divine Spirit in the Writings of Philo Judaeus," *JSJ* 26 (1995) 288-98. The correlation between Philo as inspired interpreter and Moses as inspired teacher is evident in *On the Cherubim* 48, which makes explicit what is implicit in *On the Special Laws* 3.6. Philo directly addresses the initiates, that is, those who have listened to Philo's allegorical interpretation of the writings of Moses (*On the Cherubim* 43–47), under whom Philo was initiated (49): "These thoughts, ye initiated, whose ears are purified, receive into your souls as holy mysteries indeed and babble not of them to any of the profane. Rather as stewards guard the treasure in your keeping. . . . But, if ye meet with anyone of the initiated, press him closely, cling to him, lest knowing of some still newer secret he hide it from you; stay not till you have learnt its full lesson" (48). The words *hiera . . . mystēria* correspond to *tois hierois Myōseūs* in *On the Special Laws* 3.6 and *tas hierōtatas teletas* in *On the Giants* 54. Reference to the initiates as those with "purified ears" is made in both *On the Giants* 54 and *On the Cherubim* 48. Consequently, the distinction, one — many — uninitiated/profane, which is implicit in *On the Special Laws* 3.6, is explicit in *On the Cherubim* 48 and *On the Giants* 54.

in relation to the ascent of his mind, is reminiscent of Philo's interpretation of the command for Abraham to leave his home in Gen 12:1: "Like persons possessed and corybants, be filled with inspired frenzy, even as the prophets are inspired [*prophētikon epitheiasmon*]. For it is the mind which is under the divine afflatus, and no longer in its own keeping, but is stirred to its depths and maddened by heavenward yearning . . . with truth to lead the way. . . . To that mind I say, 'Fear not to tell us the story of thy departure'" (*Who Is the Heir?* 69–71). There can be no doubt that this is a dramatic sort of simultaneous possession and ascent.[30]

What Philo describes in *On the Special Laws* is an ecstatic rapture, a form of possession, of infilling by the spirit that is very much like how he perceives prophetic inspiration — though not exactly. Prophets speak when they fall under the power of ecstasy and divine possession, "when the mind is evicted at the arrival of the Divine spirit." Yet this is only a partial disclosure of Philo's gift of interpretation. Philo is also fully prepared for his ascent by an avid yearning for knowledge, by the constant companionship of philosophy. Once wafted on the breezes of knowledge, the eye of his soul opens and he is able "not only to read the sacred pages of Moses, but also in my love of knowledge to peer into each of them and unfold and reveal what is not known to the multitude." His mind is more, not less, alert. His ability to read becomes stronger, not weaker. His capacity to understand the meaning of Torah that is hidden to the masses is heightened, not diminished. The prophets under ecstatic possession lose their wits; Philo, free momentarily of the tyranny of civil cares, regains his. He experiences, in brief, an exquisite brew of sober intoxication.

Philo's claim to both forms of inspiration — ecstasy and inspired intellect — is nothing short of remarkable, for with such claims he puts himself on a par with Moses, the prophet *par excellence*. Like Moses and the prophetic race, Philo experiences the suddenness of prophetic possession, "that divine possession in virtue of which he [Moses] is chiefly and in the strict sense considered a prophet" (*On the Life of Moses* 2.191). More important, as with Moses, the divine spirit guides Philo's mind to the truth in a form of inspiration that mirrors Moses' reception of oracles, such as the one in anticipation of the Sabbath, which "are spoken by Moses in his own

30. This account shares undeniable affinities with *On Planting* 24–26, in which he describes the moment at which the mind of the philosopher is "rendered buoyant and raised to the utmost height by the native force of the divine spirit, overcoming as it does in its boundless might all powers that are here below." On this, and the *Phaedrus* myth underlying it, see Levison, *The Spirit in First Century Judaism*, 151-58.

person." These forms of inspiration — a sudden loss of consciousness and the conscious reception of divine teaching — characterize both Moses and Philo. Or to put it another way, though Philo writes of the oracles of Moses, "a prophet of the highest quality" (*On the Life of Moses* 2.188), that they "are spoken by Moses in his own person, when possessed by God and carried away out of himself," he can just as well be describing his own experience of inspiration, which leads him to marvellous (in his opinion, of course) allegorical insight.

4 Ezra

In an apocalyptic text that grapples with the destruction of Jerusalem at the hands of the Romans and the more trenchant question of the grip of sin upon humankind, a legendary Ezra, who led in the reformation of Israel following their return from exile, is transformed into a scribal superhero. He drinks no less potent a draught than Philo, though there is no question in this case of ecstatic intoxication. Ezra begins with a bold request for the holy spirit:

> For the world lies in darkness, and its inhabitants are without light. For your Law has been burned, and so no one knows the things which have been done or will be done by you. If then I have found favor before you, send the holy spirit to me [*inmitte in me spiritum sanctum*], and I will write everything that has happened in the world from the beginning, the things which were written in your Law, that people may be able to find the path, and that those who wish to live in the last days may live. (*4 Ezra* 14:20-22)

God responds to Ezra's request with alacrity, commanding Ezra to isolate himself for forty days from the people:

> But prepare for yourself many writing tablets, and take with you Sarea, Dabria, Selemia, Ethanus, and Asiel — these five, because they are trained to write rapidly; and you shall come here, and I will light in your heart the lamp of understanding [*lucernam intellectus*], which shall not be put out until what you are about to write is finished. And when you have finished, some things you shall make public, and some you shall deliver in secret to the wise; tomorrow at this hour you shall begin to write. (14:24-26)

There is no equivocation here, no teetering between experiences of ecstasy and inspired intellect. The promise of a light of understanding in the heart until writing is done prepares Ezra for an experience of inspiration in which his mind will remain intact from beginning to end.

If the promise was brief but definite, its fulfillment is a magnificent achievement that embraces at once both the scribal and prophetic tasks, for it outstrips, not just Ezra's scribal skills, but Ezekiel's consumption of a scroll (Ezek 2:8–3:3).

> I took the five men, as he commanded me, and we proceeded to the field, and remained there. And on the next day, behold, a voice called me, saying, "Ezra, open your mouth and drink what I give you to drink." Then I opened my mouth, and behold, a full cup was offered to me; it was full of something like water, but its color was fire. And I took it and drank;[31] and when I had drunk it, my heart poured forth understanding, and wisdom increased in my breast, for my spirit retained its memory; and my mouth was opened, and was no longer closed. And the Most High gave understanding to the five men, and by turns they wrote what was dictated, in characters which they did not know. They sat forty days, and wrote during the daytime, and ate their bread at night. . . . So during the forty days ninety-four books were written. (*4 Ezra* 14:37-44)

Ezra's experience as the quintessential tradent of wisdom fulfills God's original promise that the lamp of understanding would burn without interruption. At the earliest moment of his experience, his heart bursts with understanding *(intellectum)*, while wisdom *(sapientia)* increases within him.

Ezra gushes with understanding and wisdom because in the last seventy-four books, which are preserved for the wise, are "the spring of understanding [*intellectus*], the fountain of wisdom [*sapientiae*], and the

---

31. M. E. Stone (*Fourth Ezra*. Hermeneia [Minneapolis: Fortress, 1990] 120) suggests three possible reminiscences in the correlation between the giving of the spirit and Ezra's drinking: (1) Ezekiel's consumption of a scroll (Ezek 2:8–3:3); (2) the Greco-Roman theme of divine drunkenness as a way of describing inspiration (e.g., Philo *On Drunkenness* 146–48); (3) various cups of poison mentioned in biblical prophecy (e.g., Isa 51:17, 22) or salvation (e.g., Ps 116:13). It is important to observe that Ezra drinks the cup but is not consequently described as intoxicated; therefore, this text ought not to be interpreted as an instance of the Greco-Roman topos of divine drunkenness. See further the discussion of H. Lewy, *Sobria Ebrietas: Untersuchungen zur Geschichte der antiken Mystik*. BZNW 9 (Giessen: Töpelmann, 1929) 94-98.

river of knowledge [*scientiae*]" (14:47). This profound trio is reminiscent of Ben Sira's praise of Torah, the book of the covenant, which overflows with wisdom, runs over with understanding, and pours forth instruction (Sir 24:23-27). From beginning to end, therefore, Ezra's scribal ability, and the content of what he dictates, are rife with wisdom: the lamp of understanding remains lit; the drink initiates a pouring forth of Ezra's understanding and an increase in his wisdom; the product of this inspired experience is ninety-four books, which are themselves springs, fountains, and rivers of understanding, wisdom, and knowledge.

The very simple request, "send the holy spirit into me," is met, therefore, with an extraordinary experience of inspiration. Ezra is filled with a cup of what is not water but, at least in color, fire — fire that catalyzes an overwhelming outpouring of wisdom, knowledge, and understanding.

We have noticed already that fire was frequently, during the Greco-Roman era, a sign of ecstasy. *4 Ezra*, however, projects a different sort of inspired experience. The emphasis the author of *4 Ezra* places upon knowledge, understanding, and wisdom throughout Ezra's scribal experience serves well to counter the association of fire and spirit with an ecstatic loss of control. The concluding indication — the least equivocal, in fact — that Ezra's achievement was due to the heightening rather than displacement of his intellectual powers by the holy spirit is evident in the detail that Ezra poured forth understanding and wisdom increased in his breast because *(nam)* his own spirit retained its memory *(nam spiritus meus conservabat memoriam)*. We paused earlier to catalogue the view that the loss of memory was a distinguishing mark of ecstasy. Authors as diverse as Pseudo-Philo, Aelius Aristides, Pseudo-Justinus, John Cassian, and the author of the late prologue to the *Sibylline Oracles* legitimated ecstatic states by claiming — in errant dependence upon Plato — that those possessed by the spirit could not recall what they had said (or seen).[32] Ezra's assertion that he retained his memory constitutes a straightforward rejection of this conception of inspiration.[33] When the spirit filled Ezra, when he drank a cup of liquid with the color of fire, he entered a state in which the light of wisdom remained lit, in which he poured forth understanding, in which wisdom increased in his breast because he retained his memory. In a flurry of scribal activity that kept five adept copyists busy for forty days, Ezra, the quintessentially inspired scribe, produced books, in which could be found

32. See above, Part II, chapter 2.
33. See Stone, *Fourth Ezra*, 120.

"the spring of understanding, the fountain of wisdom, and the river of knowledge."

Conclusion

A Palestinian Jewish author who composed hymns for an isolated, sectarian community that was voluntarily sequestered from most other Jews. An Alexandrian Jewish philosopher and civic leader who commented voluminously upon Torah during the early decades of the first century c.e. A Palestinian apocalyptic Jewish author who labored to offer hope to a disheartened Judaism following the destruction of Jerusalem at the hands of Rome. In innumerable respects these authors have very little in common. The date of their compositions spans as many as twenty-five decades. Their attitudes to Rome could hardly be more disparate: one detested the Romans; another catered to the Romans, incorporated Roman ideas in his writings, and made an official visit to the Roman emperor, Gaius; still another had little recourse but to accept the rubble that remained in the wake of Roman military prowess and to offer resistance by developing an alternative reality. Even the sorts of compositions they authored share very little: hymns; commentaries on Torah that drip with Greco-Roman culture but are void of hymnody or apocalyptic visions; and a classic apocalypse, rife both with dialogue between Ezra and a mediating angel and visions.[34]

These differences serve to underline what these authors hold in common: the conviction that God can inspire the interpretation (or in the case

34. Because of its ambiguity vis-à-vis the words *enthous genomenos,* and because I have dealt at length with it elsewhere, I have not included Josephus's claim to inspired interpretation: ". . . and Josephus overheard the threats of the hostile crowd, suddenly there came back into his mind those nightly dreams, in which God had foretold to him the impending fate of the Jews and the destinies of the Roman sovereigns. He was an interpreter of dreams and skilled in divining the meaning of ambiguous utterances of the Deity; a priest himself and of priestly descent, he was not ignorant of the prophecies in the sacred books. At that hour he was inspired to read [*enthous genomenos*] their meaning, and, recalling the dreadful images of his recent dreams, he offered up a silent prayer to God" (*J.W.* 3.351-53). Josephus's ability to interpret dreams recalls, of course, his namesake, Joseph, as well as Daniel, whom Josephus elsewhere designates "one of the greatest prophets," whose "memory lives on eternally" (*Ant.* 10.266). His ability to interpret prophetic texts to persuade the Jews to acquiesce to the Romans recalls as well Jeremiah's prophetic appeal to the Israelites to capitulate to Babylon. See L. H. Feldman, "Prophets and Prophecy in Josephus," *JTS* 41 (1990) 388, 404. See also Levison, *The Spirit in First Century Judaism,* 202-4.

of Ezra, the re-writing) of scripture. The Qumran hymn writer claims, "and I have listened loyally to your wonderful secret through your holy spirit." Philo hears an inner "voice," the "customary friend," and, in a condition of rapt possession, wafts on the breezes of knowledge and peers into every page of Moses' writings. Ezra, in the pseudonymous book that bears his name, drinks a fluid with the color of fire and begins to pour out understanding, as wisdom increases within him, to the end that he dictates, at record pace, ninety-four books that overflow with understanding, wisdom, and knowledge.

Under the umbrella of inspired interpretation, Philo and the author of *4 Ezra* hold together in tension two significant dimensions of this experience: the penchant for ecstasy and the firm belief that the inspired interpreter remains alert. Whether the instructor who claims to understand God's "wonderful secret through your holy spirit" and the "knowledge of the mystery of your wisdom" holds these in tension we cannot ultimately know, as his experience is too laconically expressed. Philo and the author of *4 Ezra*, in contrast, offer extended insight into this tension that underlies inspired interpretation.

Ezra is no stranger to this tension within inspiration. He appears to fall under the sway of possession when he is presumably filled with the spirit, in response to his request, and drinks a liquid that is colored like fire — a sure sign of ecstasy in the Greco-Roman world. Yet such inspiration, from start to finish, unexpectedly travels the road toward heightened understanding rather than ecstasy. The light of understanding stays lit. His heart pours forth understanding, and wisdom increases in his breast. His spirit retains its memory. Even the understanding of the scribes who wrote what Ezra dictated increased, for "the Most High gave understanding to the five men, and by turns they wrote what was dictated, in characters which they did not know" (*4 Ezra* 14:42). The author of *4 Ezra*, then, while edging the arena of ecstasy, clearly opts for a form of inspiration that leaves the mind intact. When the spirit fills Ezra, he is able to accomplish an amazing feat, as are his scribes, and it is a feat of which he is fully aware, a feat which he, unlike other Greco-Roman contemporaries who are possessed by *pneuma,* will not forget.

Philo Judaeus, as we have come to expect, offers in bold strokes a variety of images of inspiration. At times, he is overwhelmed by a state of possession, a rapturous condition that produces in him a sort of frenzy, as his soul divines in directions he does not control. At other times, he is prompted more genially by his customary companion, the divine spirit within, a higher voice that teaches him, instructing his mind concerning what he needs to know as he interprets scripture.

Neither of these suffices. Philo holds tenaciously to both sides of this tension. According to *On the Special Laws*, he becomes possessed, gripped by the divine spirit, and raised to the heights of philosophical rapture. Simultaneously, the ascent of his mind does not eradicate his native abilities. He remains alert throughout the experience and continues to read while he is inspired. He becomes "irradiated by the light of wisdom," so that he is able "not only to read the sacred pages of Moses, but also in my love of knowledge to peer into each of them and unfold and reveal what is not known to the multitude."

The border between these two forms of inspiration is permeable, and it seems more likely that Philo's highest claim is to a simultaneous experience of both forms of inspiration. No matter that they may seem to be incompatible. For Philo, they are two sides of the same denarius.

CHAPTER 4

Ezekiel's Vision and the Dawn of Purity

Spirit and Creation

The association of the spirit and the shadow of death would not dissipate during the Greco-Roman era, though it would take a more radical and less poetic form in scrolls that were discovered in the Judean wilderness. It is not over-reaching to suggest that no community during the Greco-Roman era was held more spellbound by the supremacy of sin than the devotees of the covenant who gathered by the Dead Sea.[1] Sequestered from their Jewish compatriots, whom they despised, and the Romans, whom they abhorred, these people took pains to establish a pure community that would last through the final judgment untainted by the vast array of impurities that could lead them down the wide paths of destruction.

Because of its preoccupation with purity, this community understood the shadow of death as more than the forfeit of spirit, the dissipation of breath. More often — nearly without exception, in fact — the author of many of the hymns that were preserved in Judean caves takes the language of creation in Gen 2:7 as more than a muted harbinger of physical death; inbreathing, dust, and earth become instead the ingredients of despair.[2]

1. Although I am aware that not all of the scrolls reflect the views of the residential community at Qumran, there is a scholarly consensus that the *Hymns* (1QH) and the *Community Rule* (1QS) probably do. The bulk of the analysis in this chapter — and the book as a whole — is grounded in these two documents.

2. There are occasional moments of optimism about the constituency of human beings, such as in the prayer prescribed for the first day of the week, according to which God fashioned Adam in the image of God's glory and blew "into his nostril, and intelligence and

202

The hymn writer asks, for instance, "But I, a creature of clay, what am I? Mixed with water, as whom shall I be considered? What is my strength? For I find myself at the boundary of wickedness and share the lot of the scoundrels" (1QH XI 23-25). The *Hymns* are peppered with this appraisal of human beings, with an altogether pessimistic take on Gen 2:7.

This is essential to the theological chiaroscuro that features so prominently in the *Hymns,* where nearly unsalvageable flaws are merely the backdrop for the sensational ability of God to purify human beings. In gratitude for just such a contrast, the hymn writer acknowledges,

> I thank you, Lord, because you saved my life from the pit, and from the Sheol of Abaddon have lifted me up to an everlasting height, so that I can walk on a boundless plain. And I know that there is hope for someone you fashioned out of dust for an everlasting community. The depraved spirit you have purified from great offence so that he can take a place with the host of the holy ones, and can enter communion with the congregation of the sons of heaven. (1QH II 19-24)

As he is so often in these hymns, the writer is drawn to the image of creation. He is, quite benignly, "fashioned out of dust," a limited, mortal being, but not with a penchant for evil. Yet the simple act of inbreathing, which is hopeful and invigorating in the tale of Eden, has become now ugly, transformed into "the depraved spirit." There is no quarter in this arena for a good spirit within, for a spirit of understanding, for a spirit and justice, power, and might. The hymn writer, fashioned out of dust, is in his totality a depraved spirit.

This pessimistic grasp of Gen 2:7 is no last gasp of the living, no final gulp of the cup of damnation. It is, rather, the stepping-off point for an unfathomable act of divine grace. The hymn writer has been transferred from the pit to the everlasting height, from the confines of Sheol to a boundless plain, from depravity to an everlasting community, from impurity to a place with the host of the holy ones, with the congregation of the sons of heaven. All have indeed sinned and fallen short of God's glory — to adopt the language of Paul the apostle — and all are saved by grace, transferred to the community of the faithful and the company of angels.

Acceptance into this little community, which claimed to share in wor-

---

knowledge" (4Q504 fr. 8 4-5 recto). This burst of confidence in knowledge, at least the intelligence the first human possessed prior to turning away, goes well beyond the simple inbreathing of Gen 2:7.

ship with the angels, culminated in more than a divine act of purification, the erasure of sin. Those who were received into this remnant of the faithful themselves received revealed knowledge. Yet this was not as a matter of course, not in their natural state, for they too were people whose nature is framed by the dust and breath of creation. The hymn writer, to reinforce this, begins one hymn by compounding the language of Ps 8:4 with allusions to Gen 2:7 and 3:19, as well as the sobriquet "dust and ashes," with which mere mortality becomes a clear signal of repentance.[3]

> What, then, is man? He is nothing but earth. *Blank.* [From clay] he is fashioned and to dust he will return. But you teach him about wonders like these and the foundations of [your] tru[th] you show to him. *Blank.* I am dust and ashes, what can I plan if you do not wish it? What can I devise without your will? How can I be strong if you do not make me stand? How can I be learned if you do not mould me? What can I say if you do not open my mouth? And how can I answer if you do not give me insight? (1QH XVIII 3-7)

Question after question tumbles from the pen of the hymn writer, with the implied answers, God makes plans, God makes strong, God imparts knowledge, God gives words, God grants insight. Humans cannot know, plan, speak; they are earth, dust, and ashes, destined to return to dust.

Elsewhere in the *Hymns,* Gen 2:7 is not neutral territory but, in more desperate terms, the source of a profoundly negative view of people: "These things I know through your knowledge, for you opened my ears to wondrous mysteries although I am a creature of clay, fashioned with water, a foundation of shame and a source of impurity, an oven of iniquity and a building of sin, a spirit of error and depravity without knowledge, terrified by your just judgments" (1QH IX 21-23). If question after question flows from the hymn writer's pen in the eighteenth column, here, in the ninth, image after image of depravity rises from the dust of Gen 2:7: creature of clay; foundation of shame; source of impurity; oven of iniquity; and building of sin.[4] Even inbreathing no longer offers a glimmer of life; the spirit of life, the source of vitality, has been metamorphosed into "a spirit of error and depravity without knowledge." Still, this sober judgment is merely the backdrop for the light of God's goodness, the impartation of God's knowl-

---

3. E.g., Gen 18:27; Job 30:19, 42:6; Ezek 27:30.
4. The expression "building of sin" may comprise an allusion to the creation — building — of woman in Gen 2:22.

edge: "These things I know through your knowledge, for you opened my ears to wondrous mysteries."

Throughout these hymns, then, above the din of human depravity and ignorance rises the melody of divine graciousness. Though human beings are creatures of clay, spirits that are nothing more than depravity and error, God gives to them — those who join the community — purity and knowledge. The dramatic contrast between creatures of mud and the wonderful works of God provides a toehold of hope: "I give you thanks, my God, because you have done wonders with dust; with the creature of mud you have acted in a very, /very/ powerful way. And I, what am I that you have [ta]ught me the basis of your truth, and have instructed me in your wonderful works?" (1QH XIX 3-4).

Spirit and the Valley of Dry Bones

This transition from depravity to purity is often fed from a different spring — not from Gen 2:7 but from Ezekiel 36–37, not from the story of creation but from the vision of a new creation. Protracted reflection on scripture, Gen 2:7 in particular, combined with a trenchant pessimism about human beings merge to anchor a conviction that the dust, clay, water, and spirit of creation yield an intractable penchant for sin. Yet this is not the end of salvation's story, for those who enter the community are purified, taught, and counted among a few faithful on earth and countless spirits in the heavenly entourage.

On more than one occasion, the hymn writer adopts the language of Ezekiel 36–37 to thank God for the knowledge that arises from the placement of the spirit within:

And I, your servant, have known thanks to the spirit you have placed (lit., "given") in me. (1QH V 24-25)

I have appeased your face by the spirit which you have placed [in me], to lavish your [kind]nesses on [your] serv[ant] for [ever,] to purify me with your holy spirit, to bring me near by your will according to the extent of your kindnesses. (1QH VIII 19-20)

And I, the Instructor, have known you, my God, through the spirit which you gave in me, and I have listened loyally to your wonderful secret through your holy spirit. (1QH XX 11-12)

[And I, cr]eature from dust, I have known by the spirit which you have given in me. . . . (1QH XXI 14)

This description of inspiration as putting the spirit in someone is reminiscent of Ezekiel's final oracle of the new spirit and vision of the valley of dry bones, in which the spirit within will yield the produce of obedience and fidelity to God: "I will give my spirit within you, and make you follow my statutes and be careful to observe my ordinances" (Ezek 36:27).[5] Further, three of these four hymns contain the refrain "I have known. . . ." The object of this knowledge, according to the twentieth hymn, is God: "And I, the Instructor, have known you, my God, through the spirit which you gave in me." With this shorthand expression, the hymn writer captures the single most important refrain perhaps in the entire book of Ezekiel and certainly in Ezekiel 36–37: "shall know that I am the Lord . . ." (Ezek 36:11, 23, 38; 37:6, 13; cf. 37:14). In 37:6, such knowledge is intimately related to the gift of the spirit within: "I will lay sinews on you, and will cause flesh to come upon you, and cover you with skin, and put spirit-breath in you, and you shall live; and you shall know that I am the Lord." With these expressions, then, the hymn writer takes us to a valley of very many, very dry bones, in the brutal and apparently hopeless terrain where God works an extraordinary act of re-creation and restoration through the gift of the spirit.

Although the eighth column lacks a direct reference to knowledge of God, it may tell us the most about the function of the phrase that is so reminiscent of Ezekiel, "I have given my spirit in you," for in this hymn, the spirit, claims the hymn writer, "brings me near." This is most likely an expression of gratitude for entrance into the community and the concomitant purification this incorporation offers, for the words "bring near" express elsewhere in these hymns the ability to join the community at Qumran.[6] The spirit, in this context, is a lavish gift of re-creation that brings purification and inclusion within the Qumran community.

The conception of the spirit in the *Hymns* has a clear symmetry, an obvious balance. The spirit within that is rooted in Gen 2:7 has been transformed into something depraved and errant. No hope for purification and

---

5. The language of the Qumran *Hymns* sounds very much like these texts, as well as the vivid depiction of new life in Ezek 37:6. See also LXX 4 Kgs 19:7; Isa 42:1, though here the spirit comes upon rather than into the prophetic figure.

6. H.-W. Kuhn, *Enderwartung und gegenwärtiges Heil: Untersuchungen zu den Gemeindeliedern von Qumran mit einem Anhang über Eschatologie und Gegenwart in der Verkündigung Jesu.* SUNT 4 (Göttingen: Vandenhoeck & Ruprecht, 1966) 120-39, esp. 124-26.

inclusion resides in the gift of this spirit. The spirit within that is rooted in Ezekiel 36–37, on the other hand, is the source of purity and communal embrace. The spirit of creation, of Gen 2:7, a spirit of error and depravity, has now been neatly supplanted, through the force of Ezekiel 36–37, by the spirit that purifies and grants entrée to the community of the covenant.

While they adopted the vision of Ezekiel and applied it exclusively to entrance into their particular community, the devotees at Qumran gave Ezekiel's oracles and visions a distinctive turn by individualizing it. We may recall that Ezekiel, prior to the fall of Jerusalem, believed that individuals could make *for themselves* a new heart and a new spirit. He understood that they could repent, throw away their idols, and recast themselves as obedient individuals. Yet this hope was soon obliterated by Israel's resistance to Ezekiel's message despite the relentless onslaught of Babylon. When, therefore, Ezekiel promised the new spirit as a *gift*, he addressed *groups* rather than individuals. Prior to the fall of Jerusalem, to those who had already been deported Ezekiel held out the promise of a new spirit *en masse*. Ezekiel's oracle concerns a group of people; this is why the promise of *one* heart among them is given, a new spirit in *your* (plural: *běqirběkem)* midst (Ezek 11:19). The point is that the exiles would reemerge intact, revivified, and that the inhabitants of Jerusalem would need to reckon with their renewed and righteous existence. The fall of Jerusalem would further solidify the corporate dimension of the promise of a new spirit. This gift would establish afresh the relationship between God and the people as a whole, who are consistently addressed in the second person plural: "A new heart I will give you (plural), and a new spirit I will put within your midst. . . . I will put my spirit within you (plural)." The result will be a communal renewal of the Sinaitic covenant between God and the people: "you shall be my people, and I will be your God" (Ezek 36:26, 28).

Ezekiel maintained this corporate tenor as he traipsed through the valley of dry bones. The gist of this vision is corporate: the winds come from the earth's corners to inspire the bones, sinews, and flesh of Israel. Individuals are subsumed under the image of a resurrected mass: when the breath came into them, *they* lived, *they* stood on their feet, a very, very large crowd (Ezek 37:10). Although the barest hint of the individual arises in the related oracle, according to which God will "open your graves, and bring you up from your graves" (37:13), this promise of resurrection, too, is not unlike the others, national in scope, with its goal being restoration to the land of Israel. The resurrection of individual bodies is submerged in the hope of a national resurgence.

The sublime national destiny that Ezekiel is trying desperately to conjure in the minds of his disconsolate hearers, both in the promise of a new heart and spirit in Ezekiel 36 and in his vision of death valley, eclipses the role of the individual. Yet when the hymn writer picks up the language of Ezekiel a half millennium later, his understanding of filling pertains to the individual. The spirit is placed within "your servant" (1QH V 25). The servant is thankful that God would "purify me with your holy spirit," which God had put within him (1QH VIII 19-20). The Instructor knows God "through the spirit which you gave in me, and I have listened loyally to your wonderful secret through your holy spirit" (1QH XX 11-12). The hymn writer, though a creature from dust, has "known by the spirit which you have given in me . . ." (1QH XXI 14 = 4Q427; 4Q428 11). In each of these hymns, the language is that of the promise made to Israel as a whole in Ezek 36:26-27, but its appropriation belongs to individual devotees of the covenant along the shores of the Dead Sea.

In these hymns, therefore, we discover an extraordinary pinprick, a very slight trace of the metamorphoses which the oracles and visions of Ezekiel would undergo during the Greco-Roman era. Although his was primarily a promise and vision for the nation as a whole, each Qumran hymn writer applied the language of the spirit to himself, embracing as an individual the fulfillment of that promise in his relationship to God, in his own peculiar experience of purification. Though the corporate dimension of filling with the spirit was not entirely effaced at Qumran, as we shall see in our study of temple imagery, Ezekiel's corporate language has become individual, and solidarity is supplanted by personal experience.

Spirit and New Creation

One of these hymns boldly imagines the transformation of individual believers by the spirit as transport to life in Eden.

> You embellish him with your splendour, you install [him over an abun]dance of pleasures, with everlasting peace and length of days. For [you are the truth, and] your word does not depart. *Blank.* And I, your servant, have known thanks to the spirit you have placed in me [. . .] and all your deeds are just. . . . (1QH V 23-25)

This is a description of Edenic restoration, of long days rather than premature death, of splendor rather than ashes and dust (Gen 3:17-19), with dominion over all edenic pleasures *('dnym)*. The devotees at Qumran possess the original life span of Adam, and they rule over the pleasures of Eden rather than over the thorns and thistles to its east.[7]

These images of purification and inclusion suit the corporate consciousness of the Qumran community. Notwithstanding the desolation and isolation of a locale alongside the Dead Sea, the devotees who relocated to Qumran envisaged themselves as the inhabitants of Eden. Never mind that the mineral-rich lake offered no fish, that the soft limestone desert surrounding them held no water, that their sole refuge from their enemies lay in caves that dotted the recesses of nearby cliffs. Despite an inescapable disparity between topographical reality and communal ideology, the devotees at Qumran managed to claim that they, and they alone, inhabited Eden, and that all the lost glory of Adam would be theirs. These are the holy ones, the sons of Adam whose root

> will sprout like a flo[wer of the field f]or ever, to make a shoot grow in branches of the everlasting plantation so that it covers all the wo[rld] with its shade, [and] its [crown] (reaches) up to the skie[s, and] its roots down to the abyss. All the streams of Eden [will water] its [bra]n[ch]es and they will be [seas without] limits; and its forest will be over the whole world, endless, and as deep as to Sheol [its roots.] (1QH XIV 15-17)

The author of one of the *Hymns* unreservedly thanks God:

> Because you have set me at the source of streams in a dry land, at the spring of water in a parched land, in a garden watered by channels [. . .] . . . a plantation of cypresses and elms, together with cedars, for your glory. Trees of life in the secret source, hidden among all the trees at the water, which shall make a shoot grow in the everlasting plantation. . . .

7. They are "those who have returned from the wilderness, who will live for a thousand generations, in salva[tio]n; for them there is all the inheritance of *adam,* and for their descendants for ever" (4Q171 III 1-2). Their little desert community is nothing less than Eden restored. C. H. T. Fletcher-Louis (*All the Glory of Adam: Liturgical Anthropology in the Dead Sea Scrolls.* STDJ 42 [Leiden: Brill, 2002] 108) argues, on the basis of *Jub* 3:4-16, that the people of the Scrolls believed that creation took place outside of Eden and that Adam and Eve were subsequently brought into Eden. Analogously, unbelievers are brought into the Eden of the community.

But the plantation of fruit [. . .] eternal, for the *Eden of glory* [*lĕʿēden kābôd*] will bear [fruit always]. (1QH XVI 4-6, 20; my translation in italics)

This hymn appears to have been inspired by Ezekiel 31, an indictment of Egypt, which Ezekiel compares with another great empire, probably Assyria. Egypt is depicted as a magnificent, mythical tree set at the source of a world river, home to birds of the air, and surrounded by other trees, including trees of life. God revels in this tree: "I made it beautiful with its mass of branches, the envy of all the trees of Eden that were in the garden of God" (Ezek 31:9). The tree, this empire, is too proud, and God consigns it, and the other trees with it, to Sheol, though "all the trees of Eden, the choice and best of Lebanon, all that were well watered, were consoled in the world below" (31:16). Ezekiel concludes with a question aimed at Pharaoh of Egypt, "Which among the trees of Eden was like you in glory and in greatness? Now you shall be brought down with the trees of Eden to the world below" (31:18).[8] What Pharaoh failed to embrace now belongs to the Qumran hymn writer and his community. Though in reality they live in an area of unimaginable desolation, he and his people are, to their own minds at least, trees of life set at the very source of water in an Eden of glory.

While some may be qualified for transport to Eden because God has placed the spirit within them — because they are, in other words, the resurrected of Ezekiel's vision — there is yet another point in time, the end of time, when the spirit will be active in transporting the faithful to Eden. At a literary transition between the Teaching on the Two Spirits and the surrounding portion of the *Community Rule* occurs a vivid description of final judgment:[9]

Then God will refine, with his truth, all human deeds, and will purify for himself the structure of a human, ripping out all spirit of injustice from the innermost part of his flesh, and cleansing him with the spirit of holiness from every wicked deed[s]. He will sprinkle over him the

---

8. For a detailed analysis, see T. Stordalen, *Echoes of Eden: Genesis 2–3 and Symbolism of the Eden Garden in Biblical Hebrew Literature*. CBET 25 (Leuven: Peeters, 2000) 431-33; Fletcher-Louis, *All the Glory of Adam*, 107.

9. I have not included an analysis of the Teaching on the Two Spirits (1QS III-IV), which is available in my article, "The Two Spirits in Qumran Theology," in *The Dead Sea Scrolls and the Qumran Community*, ed. J. H. Charlesworth, vol. 2 of *The Bible and the Dead Sea Scrolls* (Waco: Baylor University Press, 2006) 169-94.

spirit of truth like lustral water (in order to cleanse him) from all the ab-
horrences of deceit and (from) the defilement of the unclean spirit, in
order to instruct the upright ones with knowledge of the Most High,
and to make understand the wisdom of the sons of heaven to those of
perfect behaviour. For those God has chosen for an everlasting covenant
and to them shall belong all the glory of Adam. There will be no more
injustice and all the deeds of trickery will be a dishonour. (1QS IV 20-23)

This will be the "appointed end and the new creation" (1QS IV 25), a final
cleansing when the elect of the community will inherit all the glory of
Adam.[10]

There is book end symmetry between hymns that describe individuals' cleansing by the spirit — those texts listed at the opening of this section — and this text, which imagines a new creation in which the faithful
will possess all the glory of Adam. First, cleansing by the spirit (of holiness) is integral to both entry into the community and the new creation.
Second, both images of restoration, present and future, individual and
communal, are rooted in Ezekiel 36–37. Third, the purpose of purification
in both the hymns and the Community Rule is often the attainment of divine knowledge; this dimension of purification is also rooted in Ezekiel's
expectation that Israel will know God.

While the devotees by the Dead Sea regard themselves as the heirs of Adam's
glory and the inhabitants of Eden, there is no talk of actually tilling the garden as there is in Ezekiel's vision of Israel, in which Israel will till the land until it becomes like the garden of Eden (Ezek 36:34-35). Eden at Qumran is not
a reality to be effected by the sweat of the brow, by planting and harvesting;
Eden is rather a reality that God grants, an ideology that this small band embraces. If Eden lies at Qumran, it is a spiritual Eden, in which the spirit does
not so much impart life itself as it does knowledge. The glory they would inherit had nothing to do with real life-giving — clay inbreathed or bones clattering and sinews forming — or actual ground-tilling but with the impartation of knowledge, with the gift of spiritual cleansing from ignorance and
impurity, with life together in an ideal community.

Nonetheless, Ezekiel's vision of the restoration of Eden, the gift of the

10. Although the Hebrew, *kôl kĕbôd 'ādām*, could be translated "all human glory" (lit.,
"all the glory of man"), this seems unlikely in light of the profound and prominent place
that reflection upon Genesis 1–3 occupies in the Scrolls. See Fletcher-Louis, *All the Glory of
Adam*, 91-101.

spirit within, and intimate knowledge of God found new life in the unlikeliest of places — in an isolated desert community that subsisted at the edge of the Dead Sea, a community cut off from the rest of Judaism, from the temple and normal economic concourse, from the pulse of daily Jewish life. None of these incongruities kept the devotees at Qumran from seeing themselves as the inhabitants of a new Eden, the possessors of an intimate knowledge of God by virtue of the spirit which God had given within. Nor did their sense of sinfulness, which is evident, not only in the *Hymns,* but also in myriad rules that were necessary to regulate life together, restrain them from the hope that they would one day possess all the lost glory of Adam. This community — and this community alone, from their perspective — embodied Ezekiel's vision and, in the bluntest of terms, defined the parameters of paradise.

Spirit, Eden, and Temple

Following from Ezekiel's vision of Edenic restoration is a massive vision of a purified temple, rich with details aimed at firing the imaginations of those mired hopelessly in exile (Ezekiel 40–48). In truth, these spaces, Eden and temple, were not conceived of as disparate or distant. They were, rather, spaces that overlapped or even coincided with one another. The tale of creation itself is imbued with the hues of the temple. Standard features of the temple, the cherubim that guard the temple sanctuary, appear as well in the story of Adam and Eve as guardians of the sanctuary of paradise. Eden is portrayed in Gen 2:10-14 as a mountain from which flow downward the great rivers of the earth, including the Gihon, where, in the environs of Jerusalem, the coronation of Solomon took place (1 Kings 1). This contiguity of Eden and temple rises to the surface of several psalms, where the Temple Mount is described as a cosmic center, with the characteristics of paradise (e.g., Ps 46:4-5; 48:2), and especially in Psalm 36, which extols the Israelites, who feast from the abundance of God's "house" and who "drink from the river of your delights." God's "house," of course, is the temple, "delights" is the plural, "edens," and the description of God as the "fountain of life" evokes the image of the Gihon spring, which flows through Jerusalem from Eden. The renewed temple, in brief, has the architecture of Eden, while Eden shares its topography with the Temple Mount.[11]

11. See J. D. Levenson, *Sinai and Zion: An Entry into the Jewish Bible* (Minneapolis:

There are in addition those similes that compare the restoration of Jerusalem to an edenic existence. The exilic author who writes in the Isaianic strain claims that God "will comfort Zion; he will comfort all her waste places, and will make her wilderness like Eden [*kĕʾēden*], her desert like the garden of the Lord [*kĕgan-yhwh*]" (Isa 51:3). And Ezekiel, we saw, envisions a time when the nations will say, "This land that was desolate has become like the garden of Eden [*kĕgan-ʿēden*]; and the waste and desolate and ruined towns are now inhabited and fortified" (Ezek 36:35).[12] Ezekiel's oracles, such as his indictment of the king of Tyre, offer some of the most transparent identifications of Eden and temple. Even many of the stones worn by the king of Tyre match the priestly breastplate (Exod 28:15-20): "You were in Eden [*bĕʿēden gan-ʾĕlōhîm*], the garden of God; every precious stone was your covering, carnelian, chrysolite, and moonstone, beryl, onyx, and jasper, sapphire, turquoise, and emerald; and worked in gold were your settings and your engravings. On the day that you were created they were prepared. With an anointed cherub as guardian I placed you; you were on the holy mountain of God [*bĕhar qôdeš ʾĕlōhîm*]; you walked among the stones of fire" (Ezek 28:13-14).[13] Finally, in Ezekiel's vision of the restored temple, what appears to be the river Gihon begins in the temple sanctuary, circles the altar, and passes through the outer courtyard (Ezek 47:1-12).[14]

This mutual attraction of temple and Eden persisted over the centuries. In *Jubilees*, a text which the people of the covenant at Qumran cherished, temple and Eden are one: "And he knew that the garden of Eden was the holy of holies and the dwelling of the Lord" (*Jub.* 8:19).[15]

Winston, 1985) 131-33; Stordalen, *Echoes of Eden*, 307-10, for a superb analysis and *Forschungsbericht*.

12. See Stordalen, *Echoes of Eden*, 321-31. The prophet Joel envisages the opposite shift from Eden to wasteland: "Fire devours in front of them, and behind them a flame burns. Before them the land is like the garden of Eden [*kĕgan-ʿēden*], but after them a desolate wilderness, and nothing escapes them" (Joel 2:3).

13. See Levenson, *Sinai and Zion*, 128-29; for a characteristically excellent analysis, see Stordalen, *Echoes of Eden*, 332-56.

14. See Stordalen, *Echoes of Eden*, 357-72, on the river Gihon.

15. See also *Jub.* 4:25-26 and 4Q265 fr. 7 II 11-17, in which Adam and Eve are brought into Eden forty and eighty days after their creation; these are the days required after birth before the presentation of children in the temple. In a description of the temple altar, *Let. Aris.* 89 describes "an uninterrupted supply not only of water, just as if there were a plentiful spring rising naturally from within, but also of indescribably wonderful underground reservoirs, which within a radius of five stades from the foundation of the Temple revealed innumera-

The charter document of the Qumran community, the *Community Rule*, which expresses the conviction that these isolated Palestinian Jews of the Roman era consider themselves to be the inhabitants of Eden, also attests to the belief that they are a living temple, whose spiritual worship and holy life supplants the Jerusalem temple. The community is to "make atonement for all who freely volunteer for holiness in Aaron and for the house of truth in Israel." They are, then, a living temple, the "house of Israel," which exercises the priestly vocation of "atonement" (1QS V 5-6).

The community council, a circle of long-standing members and communal leaders, is characterized as "an everlasting plantation, a holy house for Israel and the foundation of the holy of holies for Aaron, true witnesses for the judgment and chosen by the will (of God) to atone for the land" (1QS VIII 5-6).[16] This community is a "precious cornerstone," "the most holy dwelling for Aaron . . . a house of perfection and truth in Israel" (VIII 8, 9).

The depth of their self-understanding is discernible in the breadth of detail which the community includes to depict itself as a living temple:

> When these exist in Israel in accordance with these rules in order to establish the spirit of holiness in truth eternal, in order to atone for the guilt of iniquity and for the unfaithfulness of sin, and for approval for the earth, without the flesh of burnt offerings and without the fats of sacrifice — the offering of the lips in compliance with the decree will be like the pleasant aroma of justice and the perfectness of behaviour will be acceptable like a freewill offering — at that moment the men of the Community shall set apart a holy house for Aaron, in order to form a most holy community, and a house of the Community for Israel, those who walk in perfection. (1QS IX 3-6)[17]

All of the familiar elements of Qumran temple imagery are here — the holy of holies or holy house for Aaron, atonement without actual sacrifices

---

ble channels for each of them, the streams joining together on each side." See also *1 En.* 26:1-2; *2 Bar.* 4:1-7; Adam's sacrifice in *Jub.* 3:27. Stordalen (*Echoes of Eden*, 410) refers as well to *1 En.* 24-25; *3 En.* 5:1-5; *Odes Sol.* 20:7. D. E. Aune (*Revelation*. WBC 52C [Waco: Word, 1998] 3:1175) points as well to *T. Dan* 5:12-13; *1 En.* 90:33-36; and *4 Ezra* 8:52.

16. On the likelihood that this passage characterizes the council at one and the same time as both paradise and temple, as both a planting and a building, see B. E. Gärtner, *The Temple and the Community in Qumran and the New Testament.* SNTSMS 1 (Cambridge: Cambridge University Press, 1965) 27-30.

17. On a similar combination of conceptions in *4QFlorilegium*, see Gärtner, *The Temple and the Community,* 30-42.

in the Jerusalem temple, and a holy community. Yet this passage also includes an evocative reference to the "spirit of holiness." It is evocative because it introduces something new to the cache of Qumran beliefs: the spirit exists in the *community* in a way that it does not quite exist within individual believers. It is the community, and not merely a collection of spirit-filled individuals, that establishes the spirit of holiness. Further, this spirit is related to distinctive qualities. It is, of course, holy, but it is also associated with *eternal truth*. There is content here, knowledge, comprehensibility. And finally, this spirit is actively at work in the process of purification. The spirit is a spirit of *holiness*, whose task is to bring holiness to bear upon the community and, in this text, to the whole earth. It is a spirit that by nature purifies and atones.

This forceful and unique communal emphasis reemerges in a pivotal description of the annual covenant renewal ceremony, in which new members were taken into the community at Qumran (1QS I 21–III 12). At one point in this description, the holy spirit comes to the fore:

> For it is by the spirit of the true counsel of God that are atoned the paths of man, all his iniquities, so that he can look at the light of life. And it is by the holy spirit of the community, in its truth, that he is cleansed of all his iniquities. And by the spirit of uprightness and of humility his sin is atoned. And by the compliance of his soul with all the laws of God his flesh is cleansed by being sprinkled with cleansing waters and being made holy with the waters of repentance. (1QS III 6-9)

It is not at all clear what is meant by "spirit of the true counsel of God" in this description. This notion may preserve shades of the messianic figure presaged in Isa 11:2: "The spirit of the Lord shall rest on him, the spirit of wisdom and understanding, the spirit of counsel and might, the spirit of knowledge and the fear of the Lord." Or perhaps its literary ancestor is the question, "Who has directed the spirit of the Lord, or as his counselor has instructed him?" (Isa 40:13). Whatever its forebear, this spirit is given a communal point of reference by its relation to the "holy spirit of the community," which cradles the initiate with purity.

Not everyone has access to life in this community of the holy spirit. Only those with a "spirit of uprightness and of humility" will be permitted entrée. An individual will be allowed to enter, in other words, because of "the compliance of his soul."

Those individuals who do enter, those with a "spirit of uprightness and of humility," those who are cleansed by the "holy spirit of the community," will be refreshed and purified, according to the familiar cleansing of Ezek 36:25, when they are "sprinkled with cleansing waters" and "made holy with the waters of repentance."

This instruction is of considerable importance because of how clearly it locates the spirit within the community as a whole rather than simply within individuals that make up the community.[18] These two conceptions are complementary. According to the perspective that dominates the *Hymns*, the spirit purifies individuals and incorporates them in the community. This is the language of initiation, of individuals drawn into, brought near to the community: ". . . to purify me with your holy spirit, to bring me near by your will according to the extent of your kindnesses" (1QH VIII 19-20). According to the other conception, which complements it, the spirit provides unity beyond what a collection of spirit-filled individuals can concoct. At Qumran, there is "the holy spirit of the community," into which individuals are absorbed, to whose instruction individuals must submit. This spirit exhibits clear qualities: true counsel or teaching and, above all, holiness.

In brief, *individuals* with a spirit of humility and uprightness are brought into the community when God places the spirit within them, as in Ezekiel 37, interpreted along an individualistic axis. The *community* they enter is itself a temple filled with a spirit of holiness, a spirit of the counsel of God.[19]

Conclusion

We have again taken our inevitable journey back to Eden, drawn to its rivers, its clay, the breath blown into the first human being. If we intended

18. In this respect, the sprinkling of waters may recall the communal purification of Ezek 36:25-27.

19. Alongside this communal understanding of the holy spirit as a reality that transcends individual spirit-filling, these instructions from Qumran address as well the relationship of inner and outer purification. It is clear from this text that moral or inner cleansing was thought to be an indispensable companion of cleansing with water. Anyone who refused to undergo this covenant renewal would "not be purified by the cleansing waters . . . nor shall he be purified by all the water of ablution" (1QS III 4-5). No amount of physical cleansing could make any difference if persons were stubborn and untaught by the community as a whole, if they were not cleansed by the holy spirit of the community. If they were to become part of this spiritual temple, a temple filled with God's holy spirit, they would, as individuals, have first to be cleansed spiritually by that spirit.

to discover a world of hope and vitality, we did not, at least not at first. We discovered instead a hymn writer obsessed with the clay, mud, and dust that limit the aspirations and expectations of human beings. We discovered no fresh breath or embarrassingly intimate kiss; instead we were made to reckon with a spirit of error and depravity.

Hope would spring, not from the divine inbreathing, but from Ezekiel's vision of a resurrected nation, sprinkled with cleansing water, full of spirit and life. This vision the people of the Scrolls would adopt enthusiastically, though they would understand the divine inbreathing as an individual experience.

This, however, is only part of the story, for the devotees of the covenant who occupied a small setting near the Dead Sea believed that they occupied Eden, that they worshiped with the angels, that they would, in the not so distant future, receive all the glory of Adam. Individuals cleansed by the spirit would enter Eden, a community of the faithful, only to anticipate the resplendence of a future Eden.

Like Israel's prophets, storytellers, and psalmists before them, the people of the Scrolls believed that the true temple was located at Eden, that the Gihon River flowed from paradise through Jerusalem. They could, therefore, unswervingly claim that they occupied as well the world of the temple, a living temple that offered spiritual sacrifices, a temple filled with the spirit of holiness in eternal truth. It is astonishing that such a small desert enclave, bordered by waterless limestone and a lifeless sea, could claim to inhabit Eden, that such a tiny band living a scant twenty miles or so from Jerusalem could claim to be the true, spirit-filled temple, that these very few looked to the day when they, and they alone, would be purified entirely by the spirit of holiness and inherit all the glory of Adam. As presumptuous as their claims may seem, they did not hesitate to wrest these claims from their Jewish brothers and sisters in order to lay exclusive claim to a belief that the spirit of holiness cleanses and incorporates individuals, fills the temple community, and will cleanse the faithful as a precursor to the inevitable new creation.

Just a decade before the Jews' tectonic plates shifted with the rise of a violent egomaniac, Antiochus IV Epiphanes, Ben Sira placidly retrieved the Israelite belief that some people have a spirit of understanding. In the grand desert drama of the tent of presence, fulsomely skilled artisans had possessed such spirits. Ben Sira diverged only slightly by reckoning that scribes, and not artisans, are filled with a spirit of understanding. Unlike even the loftiest of artisans, only scribes, through decades of study, travel, meditation, and prayer, come to be filled with a spirit of understanding. Only scribes are capable of pouring out their own prophetic teaching. Only scribes establish reputations that will resonate among future generations. There is nothing particularly novel in Ben Sira's perspective; he has dipped his toe into Israelite literature and simply tweaked it, applying to scribes what artisans before him had claimed. Ben Sira, in other words, represents the end of the beginning, a traditional point of view clearly consonant with scripture, with a strong dose of resistance to Greek culture. His view was unshaken, even as Israel was as yet unshaken by the tremors of Syrian politics.

The following decades would crack the façade of stability with dramatic geopolitical shifts, from the Maccabees' grand victory and the establishment of an independent Jewish state to grumblings that would grow thunderously into another rebellion, a full-fledged and ill-considered upheaval against Rome. No less potent, however, would be the hegemony of Greco-Roman culture, with its inevitable spillover into the Roman south and east. The allure of Greco-Roman culture would inexorably and subtly permeate the façade of resistance that is reflected in the wisdom of Ben

Sira. Jewish authors would happily fall prey to notions of inspiration that Ben Sira considered alien to Israelite faith.

During this new era, muted and muffled sparks within Israelite literature were detonated by their contact with Greek and Roman views of inspiration. There are but slivers of ecstasy, if any at all, embedded in Israel's corporate memory. Johannes Lindblom, in a classic study of prophecy, unearthed a few questionable hints of ecstasy.[1] Israel's Jewish heirs, in contrast, delighted in the possibilities of ecstatic forms of inspiration. Israel's prophets, said Philo, lost their minds altogether when the divine spirit ousted them. In the *Liber antiquitatum biblicarum*, a near nobody in Israelite tradition, Kenaz, the father of a merely mentioned judge, offers a clinic in the methods of ecstasy: the spirit leaps upon him, indwells him, elevates or extinguishes his mind, and leaves him with no memory whatsoever of his experience (though, oddly enough, he is able to recount some of it to the benefit of Israel). His experience is so finely honed that with it we could understand ecstasy in antiquity even without the rich resources of Plutarch's *On the Obsolescence of Oracles* or Cicero's *On Divination*.

These reimaginings of Israelite figures bear almost no resemblance to their scriptural forebears; they share a clear family resemblance, however, with popular Greco-Roman accounts of the Delphic Pythia or fiery-eyed Cassandra or other inspired prophets and poets, who seem to be drunk with the wine of ecstasy. Much the same can be said of early Jewish proponents of the inspired interpretation of scripture.

There is scarcely a trace of inspired interpretation in Israel's literature, except perhaps obliquely in the belief that God had given the Israelites in the wilderness the good spirit to instruct them (Neh 9:20). Yet during the Greco-Roman era, belief in the inspired interpretation of scripture flourished — and in distinct geographical contexts. Philo, in Alexandrian Egypt, believed that the spirit had guided Moses' mind to the truth, even as it imparted to Philo's own mind the allegorical meaning of Torah. He called this spirit a "customary friend" and, by doing so, recalled the swath that had been cut by Socrates, whose claim to a "customary" daemonic inspiration was of legendary proportions. Moses and Socrates become cousins of a sort, and Philo a second cousin once removed; all in the family have inspired minds. There was also the scribe Ezra, who, in an apocalypse that bears his name, drank of the holy spirit. Wisdom, knowledge, and understanding overwhelmed him and filled the books he dictated, and he, so unlike the po-

---

1. *Prophecy in Ancient Israel* (Philadelphia: Muhlenberg, 1962).

ets and prophets who succumbed to ecstasy, retained his memory from start to finish because the light of understanding was never once extinguished. We learn less from the Dead Sea Scrolls about the process of inspiration, though we do know they held feverishly to this claim and the belief that their interpretation of scripture, and theirs alone, held any stake in the truth. It was not through any dalliance with Greco-Roman culture that they developed this point of view; internal affairs and rivalries within Judaism, and the priesthood in particular, led their fabled hymn writer to believe that the holy spirit unlocks the mysteries of Israel's scriptures.

There were other ways in which the dim hues of Israelite literature burst onto the scene even without the combustible aid of Greco-Roman culture. Micah, Joseph, Bezalel and Oholiab, Joshua, and Elihu had been characterized by virtuous spirits that led to powerful justice-driven speech, knowledge beyond the ken of others, extraordinary skill, a unique capacity for leadership, and allegedly wise (in Elihu's own opinion) advice. This belief swelled during the second century B.C.E., beginning with Ben Sira's conviction that a scribe could painstakingly and gradually be filled with a spirit of understanding and the repetitive portrait of Daniel as a faithful, learned alien who was filled with spirit to the nth degree.

A singular sign of this burgeoning interest is the increasing application of the phrase "holy spirit" to depict the God-given spirit within. What in Psalm 51 had been merely an adumbration became explicit and widespread. Devotees at Qumran were urged not to defile or to trade their holy spirits. Balaam, in the *Liber antiquitatum biblicarum*, forfeited his soul and felt death loom because of his duplicity. Even the author of the Wisdom of Solomon, who was shaped by Stoic conceptions of *pneuma*, believed that a well-taught holy spirit could flee deceit. Philo, in his own way, which did not include a reference to the *holy* spirit, expressed no less a conviction about the spirit within when he transformed the inspiration of Gen 2:7 into the impartation of virtue. These are far from facile interpretations of the spirit; they comprise intense expressions of the conviction that God's spirit-breath within is the locus of virtue; the spirit is a fragile sanctuary of holiness in a world rife with deception and avarice.

Equally noteworthy about this era is that this swelling of reflection upon the worth of the spirit within could be combined with a flourishing interest in ecstasy and inspired interpretation. One did not exclude the other. The people of the Scrolls could believe fervently that their holy spirit could be defiled and traded for mere money *and* that the holy spirit could purify them for initiation into the community. Philo could interpret the inbreathing of Gen 2:7 as the infusion of the divine spirit to give each person a capacity for virtue *and* believe that the divine spirit had ousted the minds of Israel's prophets, had guided Moses' mind to the truth, and, like Socrates' daemon, spoke to his own mind as he meditated upon scripture. The author of the Wisdom of Solomon could refer to the well-taught holy spirit within individuals *and* to the holy spirit as an additional endowment that inspired the wisdom of Solomon (Wis 9:17).

Then, of course, there is the development of Ezekiel's vision by the devotees at Qumran, who believed that God had "given the spirit within" each member of the community. Yet this individualized interpretation did not necessarily win the day, for this community also understood itself at once to be the new Eden, a temple filled with the holy spirit, purified and purifying a relentlessly misguided world.

The era that gave birth to Judaism was, then, an era of spiritual dynamism, during which pinpricks in Israel's scriptures burst into life. It was an era when more, not less, attention was accorded the holy spirit within, when the fiery inebriation of ecstasy took hold, when authors legitimated their modes of scriptural interpretation by appealing to the presence of the spirit within, when an entire community could be filled with the spirit. These are phenomenal developments that simply cannot be overlooked without hamstringing our perception of early Judaism and early Christianity. So many central facets of life are represented here, each of which pivots around the presence of the spirit: the locus of virtue and learning; the rapture of religious experience; the appropriation of sacred texts for later generations; and life together, where the spirit transcends individual boundaries. This era witnesses to the presence of the spirit from the deepest recesses of individuals to the borders of community, from mind-numbing ecstasy to intellectual acuity.

PART III

Early Christian Literature

Hermann Gunkel, the Spirit, and Diversity in Early Christian Literature

It required of the twenty-six-year-old Privatdozent Hermann Gunkel but a few lines of the first page of *Die Wirkungen des heiligen Geistes* to stake his claim for a new approach to Paul's perspective on the holy spirit. Though his claim was not entirely novel — his predecessors included Bernhardt Weiss and Otto Pfleiderer — Gunkel took to his task with aplomb, as he excoriated the sort of biblical-theological scholarship that failed, in his opinion, to consider adequately Paul's relationship to the apostolic community: "For it cannot be disputed," he wrote, "that even Paul's position at this point in his teaching can be properly understood and evaluated only when we first consider the ideas that were available to the apostle within Christian circles."[1]

What Paul found in the apostolic church did not displease him entirely. The emphasis upon the mysterious and inexplicable Paul wholeheartedly affirmed. Paul too believed that "the sole mark of the gifts of the Spirit is the appearing of a supernatural power in the Christian."[2] It would be entirely misguided, therefore, to assume that the apostolic church iden-

---

1. *Die Wirkungen des heiligen Geistes nach der populären Anschauung der apostolischen Zeit und der Lehre des Apostels Paulus* (Göttingen: Vandenhoeck & Ruprecht, 1888); English translation: *The Influence of the Holy Spirit: The Popular View of the Apostolic Age and the Teaching of the Apostle Paul,* trans. R. A. Harrisville and P. A. Quanbeck II (Philadelphia: Fortress, 1979) 1. See B. Weiss, *Lehrbuch der Biblischen Theologie des Neuen Testaments,* 2nd ed. (Berlin: Hertz, 1873); O. Pfleiderer, *Paulinism: A Contribution to the History of Primitive Christian Theology* (London: Williams and Norgate, 1877; German original: Leipzig: Fues, 1873).

2. *The Influence of the Holy Spirit,* 88.

tified the spirit's presence through the mysterious and miraculous, while Paul identified that presence through the moral or ethical life of the Christian — a view of Paul that scholars such as F. C. Baur had contended. Paul valued glossolalia as a pneumatic experience,[3] and the prayer which addresses God as Abba, according to Paul, exhibits symptoms which point to a superhuman origin; it is a prayer uttered in ecstasy, in which not the individual but the spirit itself prays.[4]

Paul's original contribution to early Christian pneumatology, on the other hand, arose from his own experience as a pneumatic. He was seized by a higher hand as there dawned in him the realization that a new creation was taking place, in which God said, "Let light shine out of darkness."[5] With the dawning of this realization dawned as well the insight that the whole of the Christian life is a pneumatic experience, a mysterious and powerful miracle. While the apostolic church identified that supernatural power with extraordinary but intermittent experiences, Paul identified this supernatural power with the typical and ordinary and permanent. While the apostolic church understood the spirit in terms of the sporadic and miraculous, Paul understood the spirit in terms of the constant miracle of the Christian life. The symptoms are the same. The origins are the same. The reality, however, is not transitory but permanent. In brief, Paul made an original contribution to early Christian pneumatology, though it was not to interpret the spirit in moral and religious terms: "Our decision," claimed Gunkel over against Wendt and Pfleiderer, "is that Paul found ready-made the conception of the *pneuma* as a wonder-working power, but on the basis of his experience, by which the Christian himself appeared to be the greatest miracle, he described the Christian life as an activity of *pneuma* in a completely original way."[6] In brief, "the Christian life is absolutely inconceivable in earthly terms; it is a miracle of God. . . . Christian existence comes into being through a break, through the intervention of something supernatural, something new, that is, through the intervention of the Spirit of God."[7]

Paul, then, differed from the apostolic church, not in denying the relationship between the spirit and the supernatural, but in extending the

---

3. *The Influence of the Holy Spirit*, 88.

4. 1 Cor 14:14. *The Influence of the Holy Spirit*, 80.

5. 2 Cor 4:6.

6. *The Influence of the Holy Spirit*, 102. See H. H. Wendt, *Die Begriffe Fleisch und Geist im biblischen Sprachgebrauch* (Gotha: Perthes, 1878); Pfleiderer, *Paulinism*.

7. *The Influence of the Holy Spirit*, 94, 95.

sphere of the supernatural to encompass the entire Christian life: "With this idea Paul is farthest removed from the soil from which he sprang. There the Spirit was merely the power that works specific miracles and guarantees even greater ones; for Paul the present possession of the Spirit . . . is everything the Christian has for time and eternity."[8] The gifts of the spirit must be interpreted, as Gunkel understood Paul, within this long-term perspective. They remain miraculous and mysterious, but they must always be subject to the conditions of the Christian life; they must always promote the upbuilding of others because the pneumatic state and the moral life are one and the same new life.[9]

These assertions proved to be incendiary, and with them Gunkel ignited the question of the relationship between conceptions of the holy spirit in Acts, which he took to represent the early church, and the letters of Paul. Within a generation, Friedrich Büchsel offered a lengthy rebuttal of Gunkel when he contended that both the early church and Paul agreed with each other fundamentally because they shared the conviction that the spirit was primarily the source of sonship with God — what constitutes life as a *Pneumatiker*. Eduard Schweizer, in contrast, drove an even wider wedge than Gunkel between Paul and the early church. Luke, argued Schweizer, understood the spirit as a supplementary endowment which inspired proclamation; Paul, in contrast, understood the spirit as the source of salvation, as the power that binds people to God and transfers them to the sphere of salvation.[10] With varying degrees of intensity, other scholars would address this question, including David Hill, James D. G. Dunn, Johannes Vos, Gonzalo Haya-Prats, and Max Turner.[11]

Once again, Gunkel galvanized an issue that would inform discussion about the spirit well beyond his own lifetime, even though several details of his argument cannot bear the weight of close scrutiny. First, for the reconstruction of views held by the pre-Pauline Palestinian church, the usefulness of the book of Acts — a text that was written decades after the last of Paul's letters, a

---

8. *The Influence of the Holy Spirit*, 111.

9. On spiritual gifts, see *The Influence of the Holy Spirit*, 85-90; on the unity of the pneumatic and moral dimensions, see 108.

10. E. Schweizer, "The Spirit of Power: The Uniformity and Diversity of the Concept of the Holy Spirit in the New Testament," *Int* 6 (1952) 259-78; "πνεῦμα," *TDNT* 6:389-455.

11. There is no need to rehearse this further because R. P. Menzies offers an excellent *Forschungsbericht* in *The Development of Early Christian Pneumatology: with Special Reference to Luke-Acts*. JSNTSup 54 (Sheffield: JSOT, 1991) 18-47.

narrative that may even presuppose the existence of Paul's letters — is debatable, as even Gunkel was compelled to acknowledge.[12]

Second, Luke does not write univocally about the mysterious and inexplicable effects of the spirit. On the contrary, we will soon observe that the author of the book of Acts evinces a deep-rooted ambivalence toward the mysterious effects of the spirit; the book of Acts is, consequently, extremely thorny ground in which to isolate the flowering of ecstatic experience, particularly inexplicable experiences that predated Paul.

Third, though Paul's letters offer important autobiographical glimpses of his experience, traces of his autobiography are relatively rare and, when they do appear, are often embedded in portions of his letters that address other topics. In other words, Paul occasionally appeals to his experiences of the spirit, not to retell them, but to confront issues that have arisen in the churches to which he writes. Autobiography is not, as a consequence, straightforward and frequent, with the result that Paul's experiences must often be skimmed, by way of inference, from letters that are concerned with other issues. For example, Gunkel inferred that the words, "Let light shine out of darkness," are autobiographical; he attributed Paul's conviction that the entirety of the Christian life is a miraculous new creation of the spirit to this experience. Is this, however, so unequivocally autobiographical that it can function to provide a reliable breach with which to divide experiences in the apostolic church from the experience of Paul? Is this autobiographical at all?

Fourth, Gunkel incorrectly attributed to Paul's experience what was traditional language of the spirit that circulated in the apostolic church. The language of God's "giving" the spirit and believers' "receiving" the spirit, which Gunkel naturally attributed to Paul, since they occur in his letters, were already in use both in the Dead Sea Scrolls — which, of course, he could not have known — and in the apostolic church.[13] Paul's adoption of this vocabulary would, therefore, be a primary indication that his view of the spirit as a permanent gift which believers receive had its origin in the early church — and its Jewish environment.

On the heels of this fourth critique comes a fifth: many dimensions of the spirit were more widespread in early Judaism and the early church than Gunkel recognized. For example, Paul is not alone in portraying the church as a spirit-filled temple; the Dead Sea Scrolls, as we saw, understand

12. *The Influence of the Holy Spirit,* 11.
13. *The Influence of the Holy Spirit,* 93.

their community as a temple of the spirit. There are as well a good many other dimensions that permeated early Christian literature. Because I have adopted the prism of filling with the spirit to understand inspiration in Israelite, Greco-Roman, and Christian antiquity, we will not pause to explore in detail every one of these references. Still, in order to provide a backdrop for our more focused foray, it may be beneficial to sketch the more ubiquitous dimensions of the spirit in the early church: the spirit as teacher and guide; opposition to the spirit; the spirit and prayer; and the spirit and prophecy.

Spirit as Teacher and Guide

Some Israelite and early Jewish authors tended to attribute somewhat more personality to the spirit in this regard. Isaiah 63:7-14 remembers that "the spirit of the Lord gave them rest" (v. 14), and Haggai encourages, "my spirit stands in your midst. Do not fear" (Hag 2:5). Further, the psalmist prays, "Let your good spirit lead me on a level path" (Ps 143:10), while Nehemiah recalls, "You gave your good spirit to instruct them" (Neh 9:20). Josephus and Philo, in independent ways, identify the angel that stood before Balaam (Num 22:25) with the divine spirit that would come upon him (24:2); this is an angelic spirit (Philo *On the Life of Moses* 1.274-77; Josephus *Ant.* 4.108).[14] Philo's customary friend resembles Socrates' customary sign, the daemon (*On Dreams* 2.252).

Similar perceptions of the spirit as an individual figure characterize many early Christian references to the spirit. The spirit teaches (Luke 12:12; John 14:25-26; 16:13; 1 Cor 2:13), speaks (John 16:13; Acts 8:29; 10:19; 11:12; 13:2; Heb 3:7 [= Ps 95:7-11]), testifies (Acts 20:23 [through prophets]; John 15:26 [along with the disciples]; Heb 10:15 [through scripture]), leads (Gal 5:18; Rom 8:14), reveals (Luke 2:26; 1 Cor 2:6-16; Eph 3:5; Heb 9:8), forbids (Acts 16:6-7), predicts (1 Tim 4:1), searches God's depths (1 Cor 2:11), and participates in prayer by crying Abba (Gal 4:6) and interceding with wrenching sighs for those in a state of weakness (Rom 8:26-27). The spirit also functions as a leader by sending out apostles (Acts 13:2-4), appointing overseers (Acts 20:28), and distributing spiritual gifts (1 Cor 12:11).

---

14. See J. R. Levison, "The Debut of the Divine Spirit in Josephus' *Antiquities*," *HTR* 87 (1994) 123-38; and "The Prophetic Spirit as an Angel according to Philo," *HTR* 88 (1995) 189-207.

Spirit as the Object of Opposition

Not all of the realities that coalesce around the spirit are positive. The indictment, "But they rebelled and grieved his holy spirit" (Isa 63:10), roots opposition to the holy spirit in the exodus tradition, in which Israel is ordered not to "rebel" against the angel who leads and guards Israel following the exodus (Exod 23:20-21; cf. Num 20:16). The unfortunate reality of opposition to the holy spirit emerges as well in several early Christian texts. Ephesians 4:30 commands, "and do not grieve the holy spirit of God." The context, which urges the need for gracious words rather than bitterness, wrangling, and slander, provides a poignant counterpoint to the Israelites, who complained bitterly of their plight.

In the Synoptic gospels, Jesus exorcises a demon in a mute (and blind, in Matt 12:22) man. Some are amazed; others accuse him of alignment with Beelzebul, the ruler of demons. Jesus responds that a house divided cannot stand, that Satan cannot disarm himself, and that he exorcises by the spirit (Matt 12:28) or finger of God (Luke 11:20; see Exod 8:19). In Mark and Matthew's gospels, the puzzling statement that blasphemy against the holy spirit comprises the unpardonable sin occurs directly after this confrontation (Mark 3:28-30; Matt 12:31-32). The implication is that the Jewish leaders who accuse Jesus of being aligned with Satan are blaspheming the holy spirit. Luke places the word about blasphemy in a context that has to do with testimony under constraint rather than Jesus' ministry (Luke 12:8-12). It may be the Jewish leaders who blaspheme, as in the gospels of Mark and Matthew, or it may be that it is believers brought before the authorities who will be pressed to blaspheme the holy spirit (12:8-10). For those who do not give up, there is no need to worry: "for the holy spirit will teach you at that very hour what you ought to say" (12:11-12).

Opposition to the spirit occurs twice in Acts. Peter accuses Ananias of being filled with Satan and lying to the holy spirit because he and Sapphira held back some of the money they received from selling their property (Acts 5:1-3). The verb "hold back" *(nosphizein)* occurs in the septuagintal translation of Hebrew scripture only in the story of Achan, whose holding back of booty had a dreadful impact upon Israel's fortunes at war (Josh 7:1). This parallel points to the communal dimension of the spirit; to deceive the community is to lie against its driving force, the holy spirit.

Stephen, following the lead of Neh 9:29-30 and Zech 7:12, indicts his "stiff-necked" hearers for "forever opposing the holy spirit, just as your ancestors used to do" (Acts 7:51). Stephen, who is "filled with the holy spirit" (7:55), becomes another victim of Israel's recalcitrance. Because "they could not withstand the wisdom and the spirit with which he spoke" (6:10), they stoned him.

The possibility of grieving the holy spirit extends to the community addressed in Heb 10:28-29. Slightly earlier, the author expressed the view that those who had been enlightened, tasted the heavenly gift, "shared in the holy spirit," and tasted the word of God, but then lapsed would have enormous difficulty repenting (Heb 6:4-6). In a similar vein, he reproaches those who persist in sin "after having received the knowledge of the truth" (10:26). Such believers have nothing but judgment ahead, no sacrifice for sin, because they "have spurned the son of God, profaned the blood of the covenant by which they were sanctified, and outraged the spirit of grace." The inclusion of the spirit in both texts alongside enlightenment, Jesus, and his blood is an indication of how integral the spirit is to the process of initiation and the prospect of future salvation.

While the holy spirit, therefore, can be received by and fill believers, it can also be the object of resistance. For Matthew, Luke, and Stephen (Acts 6–7), the Jewish leaders oppose the spirit. Yet the gospel of Luke, Acts, Ephesians, and Hebrews together indicate that followers of Jesus also have the potential to oppose the spirit — to blaspheme, to lie to it, to grieve it, and to outrage it.

Spirit and Prayer

Another widespread dimension of the spirit in early Christianity is its pivotal role in prayer. Luke associates the holy spirit with prayer and praise. Elizabeth and Zechariah praise God when they are filled with the holy spirit (Luke 1:41-42, 67). Jesus receives the spirit at his baptism while he is praying (3:21-22). When the seventy return from their mission, he rejoices in the holy spirit and addresses God in prayer (10:21). In instructions about prayer, Jesus asks, "how much more will the heavenly father give the holy spirit to those who ask him?" (11:13).

This Lucan promise of the spirit is fulfilled, not during Jesus' own lifetime, but after his resurrection — and then in good measure — when believers are filled with the holy spirit and begin to recite God's powerful acts (Acts 2:1-13; see 10:44-48). Following prayer, the newly founded community prays for boldness and is immediately filled with the spirit (4:31).

Later, Peter receives the programmatic vision of Cornelius while he prays at lunchtime (10:9-16).

Prayer in the holy spirit is also a topic in early Christian letters. Paul explains that the holy spirit intercedes with groans beyond words in the process of agonizing prayer, in which a believer does not know how he or she ought to pray (Rom 8:26-27). The author of Ephesians urges readers to alertness and persistence as they pray on behalf of all the saints (Eph 6:18). The author of Jude recalls the predictions of the apostles, that those "devoid of the spirit" would be lustful and divisive, and he encourages his readers, in contrast, to build themselves up "on your most holy faith" and to "pray in the holy spirit" (Jude 20). It is not possible to determine conclusively whether prayer in the spirit refers to mindless prayer in tongues, as in 1 Cor 14:13-15, or to comprehensible prayer; prayer in Ephesians 6 seems comprehensible, for it concerns intercession for the saints.

Spirit and Prophecy

The association of prophecy and the spirit occurs in many early Christian texts, though prophecy has a variety of meanings. At times, inspired prophecy refers to Israelite literature. Paul says, in Acts 28:25, that the holy spirit spoke through the prophet Isaiah. The author of 1 Peter offers a telling description of the phenomenon of prophecy; prophets searched salvation beforehand, "inquiring about the person or time that the spirit of Christ within them indicated when it testified in advance to the sufferings destined for Christ and the subsequent glory" (1 Pet 1:11). How the spirit of Christ, before his appearance on earth, could speak through the prophets is unclear, though the author moves quickly to more traditional language in the following clauses (1 Pet 1:12) when he attributes such predictions to the holy spirit, as does 2 Pet 1:21.

Luke portrays John the Baptist as a figure who, filled with the spirit from before birth, comes in the spirit and power of Elijah (Luke 1:15, 17). Zechariah, his father, prophesies once he is filled with the spirit (Luke 1:67). Jesus himself, according to Luke 4:16-21, claims the endowment of Isa 61:1-2.

Prophecy is paradigmatic in Acts. In his explanation of the events of Pentecost, Peter amends the quotation of Joel that describes the outpouring of the spirit by adding "and they shall prophesy" (Acts 2:17-18). Various prophets show up in the ensuing narratives: an Agabus who predicts a famine (11:28); an Agabus who predicts Paul's imprisonment (21:10-11; cf. 20:23); and Philip's four daughters, all of whom have the gift of prophecy (21:9). It may be that prophets, in the context of prayer and fasting, are those through whom the spirit instructs Paul and Barnabas to begin their journeys (13:1-2).

Paul himself offers advice on spiritual gifts and urges the Corinthians to pursue the gift of prophecy because it is comprehensible, edifying for the church, rather than glossolalia, which is not (1 Corinthians 14). He recognizes that prophecies may be false and, consequently, instructs the Thessalonians not to quench the spirit, by which he means that the community should neither despise prophecy nor accept it uncritically, without discernment (1 Thess 5:19-21).

Other letters, some possibly post-Pauline, also value prophecy. Eph 3:5 regards latter-day apostles and prophets as recipients of a revelation that eluded past generations. A swirl of prophetic activity surrounds Timothy's call. The author charges him to wage the good fight "in accordance with the prophecies made earlier about you" (1 Tim 1:18). He is instructed not to neglect the gift "which was given you through prophecy with the laying on of hands by the council of elders" (1 Tim 4:14).

Such discernment remains the critical issue in other letters. While the problem of false prophets emerges in Matthew's gospel (Matt 7:21-23), in the community of 1 John it becomes pivotal in the battle for the truth because a real-life crisis is still fresh. To navigate this crisis, the author commends a principle of discernment: "Beloved, do not believe every spirit, but test the spirits to see whether they are from God; for many false prophets have gone out into the world. By this you know the spirit of God: every spirit that confesses that Jesus Christ has come in the flesh is from God, and every spirit that does not confess Jesus is not from God. And this is the spirit of the antichrist, of which you have heard that it is coming; and now it is already in the world" (1 John 4:1-3). Though minimal, this is an irrefutable, verifiable principle of discernment that is related to the confession that Jesus Christ came in the flesh. Its function is similar to the confession "Jesus is Lord," and Paul's contention that "no one can say, 'Jesus is Lord' except by the holy spirit" (1 Cor 12:3).[15] The author of 2 Peter faces a similar situation and responds by condemning the false prophets who "arose among the people" (2 Pet 2:1), though he offers no principle of discernment. Instead he argues that false prophets misinterpret prophecy (Israelite and

---

15. On prophecy in 1 John, see Part III, chapter 4.

perhaps early Christian). This is anathema "because no prophecy ever came by human will, but men and women moved by the holy spirit spoke from God" (2 Pet 1:19). If prophets were inspired, the interpreters must be as well — though the content of that interpretation is left inchoate.

The problem of distinguishing between true and false prophets came to dominate the skyline of the early church, so much so that the *Didache* offers practical markers for identifying false prophets, e.g., staying more than three days, asking for money, not living as they taught, ordering a meal and actually eating it (*Didache* 11).

The problem edges its way as well into the book of Revelation, which is itself designated a prophecy (Rev 22:7, 19; 1:3, based, perhaps by way of oral tradition, upon the blessing in Luke 11:28), and in which John is, like Ezekiel, commanded to eat a scroll and to prophesy to the nations (Rev 10:8-10). Even the introduction of the four visions by the same phrase, "in the spirit" (1:10; 4:2; 17:3; 21:10), is reminiscent of the book of Ezekiel (e.g., Ezek 3:12).

True prophets populate the pages of this self-proclaimed prophecy. Some are Israelite prophets (Rev 10:7; 11:18). Others are joined with saints and apostles (18:20; cf. 22:6-9). The essence of true prophecy is defined in Rev 19:10: "For the testimony of Jesus is the spirit of prophecy." Prophecy may entail visions — revelations — and prophetic insight, but at its core the spirit of prophecy inspires testimony on behalf of Jesus, witness in the face of persecution by all believers rather than by a specific group of prophets. This testimony concerns the resurrection of Jesus, if other texts from the early church provide a clue: 1 Cor 12:3; 1 John 4:2-3; John 15:26-27. The book of Revelation alleges to comprise, then, an inspired prophetic testimony to the risen Christ.

Though Gunkel wrenched the topic of the holy spirit from the grasp of biblical theologians, whom he criticized for creating too monolithic a portrait of the early church, he focused perhaps too narrowly on Paul and the book of Acts. By spreading our nets wider, we have seen that there was much more shared ground in the early church than Gunkel was able to admit. The pivotal role of the spirit in teaching, the place of the spirit in prayer, the relationship between the spirit and prophecy, even opposition to the holy spirit — each of these represents widespread phenomena in the early church that extend well beyond the perspective of single authors. Notwithstanding the undue focus Gunkel placed upon the uniqueness of Paul's understanding of the spirit, he can still be credited with impressive prescience. If he took missteps in his analysis, this may be due less to his limitations than to the nature of the sources with which he was compelled to deal and the sources, such as the Dead Sea Scrolls, that were as yet unavailable to him. The issue of the relationship of Paul and Acts, after all, continues to thrive, and Gunkel did recognize a substantial overlap between Paul's letters and the book of Acts. Moreover, the intractable issue of continuity and discontinuity, or unity and diversity, in early Christian literature remains, a century and a quarter later, vital to our perception of what early followers of Jesus understood when they claimed to be filled with the spirit. In this final portion of our study, I will follow in the steps of Gunkel by interpreting the letters of Paul and Luke-Acts in separate chapters, though I will include as well a detailed analysis of the fascinating array of Johannine literature, to which he devoted a single line in his final paragraph: "The theology of the Gospel of John clearly indicates its dependence on Paul on this subject."[16] In the course of this study, we will discover that early Christian authors held in common with one another more — and less — than Gunkel himself surmised.

---

16. *The Influence of the Holy Spirit,* 127.

CHAPTER 1

Vestiges of Earlier Eras

A few moments, an assortment of literary texts, a smattering of clues from a variety of literary genres — this is all that eight centuries of literature yield to help us to determine what ancient Israelite and Jewish authors believed filling with the spirit might entail. Though the remains are scattered and relatively few, they provide nonetheless a surprisingly substantial sketch of the association that existed between the spirit within and various dimensions of virtue and knowledge.

Israelite and Jewish literature offers a clear picture of those few — Micah, Joseph, Bezalel (and the makers of Aaron's garments), Joshua, Daniel, and Jesus ben Sira — who were distinguished by the spirits within them. Their experiences were *not* like those of Philo's prophets or Kenaz in the *Liber antiquitatum biblicarum,* for whom a decisive endowment took place at some point of time long after birth. Time and again we discovered clues which pointed to a belief that the spirit within, in contrast to the spirit that would rush upon or descend upon or be poured out upon select Israelites, was the product of God's initial gift of filling with the spirit. To say that they were full of or filled with the spirit is to lay claim for them to a remarkable spirit within that is characterized variously by power, justice, and might (Micah), by discernment and wisdom (Joseph), by skill, knowledge, and intelligence (Bezalel), by wisdom (Joshua), by understanding (Ben Sira), and by enlightenment, wisdom, and knowledge (Daniel).

The sort of wisdom and knowledge that may have occasionally characterized Israelite figures would come to much fuller flower in Jewish literature following the Maccabean rebellion. Without hesitation, for example, the author of the tale of Susanna transforms the formula "God prompted the spirit of . . ." into "God prompted the *holy* spirit of a young man. . . ." While this is a more explicit characterization of the spirit within as holy, it is certainly not an infelicitous characterization. Daniel had been identified several times by the abundance and quality of his spirit within, so that it was only natural, in later reflection upon this faithful Israelite, to attribute to him the sort of holy spirit that, when prompted, would decry injustice. Divergent authors who represented different corners of Judaism — from very early sectarians who would later settle along the western shore of the Dead Sea to an Alexandrian Jewish philosopher who would be selected by his people to travel to Rome to meet with the emperor — would agree that the spirit within could be either holy and a source of virtue or a commodity to be exchanged for ephemeral treasure. That the authors of the *Damascus Document* and *4QInstruction,* along with Philo Judaeus, could adhere so resolutely, and in such different forms, to such similar conceptions of the divine spirit within attests to the tenacity with which some Jews during the Greco-Roman era held to this belief.

The Jewish beneficiaries of Israelite faith inevitably reshaped their traditions. The subtlest of those developments is the very slight displacement of special knowledge by some authors. In Israelite literature, the God-given spirit within is the source of all sorts of knowledge — of oracular judgments, dreams, architectural skills, leadership, strange writing, or the meaning of Torah. In later Jewish literature, by contrast, the spirit within is associated primarily with virtue. The identification of the spirit within as *holy,* as in the tale of Daniel and Susanna, the Damascus Document, *4QInstruction,* and *Liber antiquitatum biblicarum,* signals the association of virtue with the spirit within. Philo goes so far in this regard as to identify the spirit-breath of Gen 2:7 with the capacity for virtue. The boundaries, of course, between virtue and knowledge are fluid. Micah, for example, claims to be filled with the spirit, with justice and knowledge and power; the practice of justice has a good deal to do with virtue. Further, the wisdom and knowledge which scriptural figures have is not unrelated to the virtuous lives they lead; Daniel is the quintessential illustration of this connection, for he has extraordinary insight in some measure because he has cultivated the divine spirit within through study and fasting.

The conviction that virtue resides in a holy spirit — whether it is expressed in the simple language of the tale of Susanna, in which Daniel's holy spirit is prompted, or the flamboyant language of Philo's commentaries, in which God inbreathes into every human being the capacity for virtue — offers a dramatic contrast to the convictions of early Christian authors. Their letters and gospels contain precious few vestiges of this conception of the holy spirit, a holy spirit given to all human beings by dint of creation, a spirit that is the energy and essence of life, a spirit that can be cultivated through study and discipline, a spirit that is the locus of virtue. This conception of the spirit within nearly evaporates in early Christian writings, where it is eclipsed almost entirely by the belief that the good gifts of God arrive only with a subsequent filling by the holy spirit. Barely a handful of vestiges of Israel's conception of the spirit within remain.

Vestiges in Early Christian Literature

Paul's Letters

Such remnants emerge occasionally in Paul's letters, as in 2 Cor 6:6-7, where the expression "holy spirit" is included in a list of virtues: "by purity, by knowledge, by patience, by kindness, by (a) holy spirit, by genuine love, by truthful speech, and by the power of God."[1] Although this may be a reference to *the* "holy spirit" rather than *a* holy spirit, it is more plausible, in light of the early Jewish identification of the spirit within as a holy spirit and this particular context, with its catalogue of virtues, to regard these words as vestiges of the Israelite and early Jewish conviction that the holy spirit with which God has endowed human beings is the locus of virtue.[2]

---

1. Greek: *en hagnotēti, en gnōsei, en makrothymia, en chrēstotēti, en pneumati hagiō, en agapē anypokritō, en logō alētheias, en dynamei theou.* It is noteworthy that the last four items in the list contain a noun and an adjective or a noun with a genitive noun; in other words, literary consistency demands that we acknowledge the adjectival character of the word "holy"; it is not, in other words, merely an identity marker which indicates that this is "the holy spirit." I am not convinced by G. Fee's attempt (*God's Empowering Presence: The Holy Spirit in the Letters of Paul* [Peabody: Hendrickson, 1994] 332-35) to demonstrate that this is "the Holy Spirit," understood, presumably, as a divine and subsequent endowment that "entails the powerful working of the Holy Spirit" (335).

2. Paul is aware of a distinction between the divine spirit and the human spirit, for he refers in Rom 8:16 to "that very spirit bearing witness with our spirit that we are children of God" *(auto to pneuma symmartyrei tō pneumati hēmōn hoti esmen tekna theou).* This distinction is especially evident in 1 Cor 2:11, where Paul attempts to explain the divine spirit through a comparison with the human spirit: "For what human being knows what is truly human except the human spirit that is within? So also no one comprehends what is truly God's except the spirit of God." It is this spirit within that can pray and sing without the mind or, as Paul prefers, in tandem with the mind (1 Cor 14:14-16). A similar conception applies to prophesying in 1 Cor 14:32, where the prophets have responsibility over their own spirits.

Paul also expresses his conviction that the human spirit, the locus of holiness and virtue, can be tainted, as in the *Damascus Document,* or even exchanged, in a loose sense, as in *4QInstruction,* when he advises the Corinthian church to exclude a man who is committing the egregious sin of living with his father's wife; Paul hopes with this decision that "his spirit may be saved in the day of the Lord" (1 Cor 5:5). When Paul turns his attention, slightly later in the letter, to sexual relations within marriage, he offers a rare moment of accord when he agrees with the Corinthian suggestion that an unmarried woman is not preoccupied with human affairs and pleasing a husband; she can instead "be holy in body and spirit" (1 Cor 7:34).[3] Then, in support of his view that believers should not be too intimately associated with unbelievers, Paul urges the Corinthians to cleanse themselves "from every defilement of body and of spirit, making holiness perfect in the fear of God" (2 Cor 7:1). Each of these brief bits of Paul's Corinthian correspondence provides a sliver of his conviction that the spirit in believers, though not to the exclusion of the body, can become holy by the practice of virtue, by single-minded devotion (1 Cor 7:34), by a process of self-cleansing (2 Cor 7:1).[4]

If Paul's letters offer a few unambiguous glimpses of a spirit that can

---

3. See also the more formulaic triad of spirit, soul, and body, which are to be kept sound and blameless, according to 1 Thess 5:23.

4. Even early interpreters of Paul's letters recognize the worth of the spirit which all human beings possess. The author of the letter to the Ephesians associates renewal with the virtues of the human spirit: "You were taught to put away your former way of life, your old self, corrupt and deluded by its lusts, and to be renewed in the spirit of your [plural] mind, and to clothe yourselves with the new self, created according to the likeness of God in true righteousness and holiness" (Eph 4:22-24). The "spirit of your mind" *(tō pneumati tou noos hymōn)* ought perhaps to be contrasted with the spirit of your body. Philo makes such a distinction in his discussion of the human soul, which can become united with the mind by the practice of virtue or with the body by the practice of vice. Vice, or the spirit that is tied to the body, would be reflected in Ephesians by the "old self" and "its lusts." Virtue, or the spirit of the mind, would be reflected by the "new self" and "true righteousness and holiness." This is a remarkable text. First, the view of the spirit is somewhat different from Israel's wisdom tradition; now the spirit is more an independent entity that can attach itself to body or mind than it is the vital breath within that rolls over the tongue. Yet, second, the essential role of virtue in the development of the spirit remains true to Israel's conception of the spirit within. Third, there is a fascinating transformation of Paul's point of view. Paul does not locate transformation or renewal in the human spirit; it can progressively become holy or unholy by the practice of virtue or vice, but it is not made holy by an act of transformation. The author of this letter conceives of the human spirit as the locus of transformation, the place of transition from the old to the new self.

be holy, the Pastoral Letters contain one of the most puzzling references to the spirit in early Christian literature.[5] Timothy is urged "to rekindle the gift of God that is within you through the laying on of my hands; for God did not give us a spirit of cowardice, but rather a spirit of power and of love and of self-discipline" (2 Tim 1:6-7).[6] Is this spirit what filled Timothy from birth or what filled him subsequently in tandem with the laying on of hands?[7] In other words, is this a vestige of the trajectory we traced in Israelite and early Jewish literature or something new and unrelated to it?

On the one hand, this spirit is described by means of a list of virtues — cowardice, power, love, and self-control. This, of course, fits neatly the conception of a holy spirit as the locus of virtue. The contrast of this spirit with cowardice, moreover, mirrors the Wisdom of Solomon, in which a spirit is portrayed as strong and courageous, "for a holy spirit of discipline will flee from deceit . . . and be ashamed at the approach of injustice" (Wis 1:5). Nor does the portrayal of Daniel's holy spirit, which is prompted courageously to decry injustice, lie far afield of the contrast that is drawn between Timothy's spirit and a spirit of cowardice. This piece of advice, against this background and in this context, would be a reminder to Timothy that the core God has given him — the essential strength, the vitality that he possesses by virtue of being human — must be continually kindled. Timothy is urged to dig deep into that resource, to delve into that reservoir of power, love, self-discipline, to rekindle the fire that is in his spirit because Paul laid his hands upon him.

On the other hand, this could be a simple reference to the gift of the spirit which Timothy received subsequently. We ought to recall in this regard that the verb "give" occurred frequently and formulaically in both the

5. For the sake of this study of the spirit, for which questions of authorship are relatively inconsequential, I will assume that Paul's undisputed letters include: Romans, 1-2 Corinthians, Galatians, Philippians, 1-2 Thessalonians, and Philemon. I will also adopt the more mainstream scholarly consensus that the disputed letters may include Ephesians, Colossians, 1-2 Timothy, and Titus. Again, the methodology of this study, which draws few trajectories, chronological or otherwise, is not dependent upon whether Paul wrote the letters of disputed authorship that are attributed to him.

6. Greek: *di' hēn aitian anamimnēskō se anazōpyrein to charisma tou theou, ho estin en soi dia tēs epitheseōs tōn cheirōn mou. ou gar edōken hēmin ho theos pneuma deilias alla dynameōs kai agapēs kai sōphronismou.*

7. The NRSV understands this spirit as the human spirit, presumably because it is used with genitive nouns: of cowardice, of power, of love, and of discipline. TNIV, in contrast, understands it as a subsequent gift: "For the Spirit God gave us does not make us timid, but gives us power, love and self-discipline."

Dead Sea Scrolls and the literature of the early church to describe a subsequent gift of the spirit. The gift of God within may be nothing other than the spirit that was given to Timothy when he became a believer. Ultimately, it may not be possible to determine whether the author of the Pastoral Letters understands the spirit as the vitality which all human beings possess — vitality which Timothy is urged to rekindle into a life of power, love, and discipline rather than cowardice — or as a gift that was given to Timothy subsequently by the laying on of hands.

Luke-Acts

There is a remnant exactly where we would expect it, in the opening of Luke's gospel, which is permeated by the language and style of the Septuagint. Luke writes of John the Baptist that "the child grew and became strong in spirit, and he was in the wilderness until the day he appeared publicly to Israel" (Luke 1:80). This statement precisely parallels the progressive maturing of the child, Jesus, who "grew and became strong, filled with wisdom" (2:40a):

> to de paidion nyxanen kai ekrataiouto pneumati (1:80)
> to die paidion nyxanen kai ekrataiouto plēroumenon sophia (2:40)

In these depictions of John and Jesus, the words "in spirit" and "filled with wisdom" are in parallel positions, following the verbs "grew" and "became strong." Luke's preservation of this traditional scriptural conception of the spirit as the force within that, from birth, can be strengthened, along with the implicit association of the spirit with wisdom, evokes images of Israel's illustrious leaders, such as Joseph, Bezalel, Joshua, and Daniel. Luke does not yet supplant the age-old conception with the picture of a subsequent infilling that will become familiar territory in the portrayal of Jesus' preaching and the successful sermons that pepper the book of Acts.[8]

---

8. A summary of the power of the spirit in Jesus' life occurs in Acts 10:38: ". . . how God anointed Jesus of Nazareth with the holy spirit and with power; how he went about doing good and healing all who were oppressed by the devil, for God was with him." This summary identifies three pivotal points in Jesus' public ministry: (1) anointing (his baptism, testing, and early preaching); (2) doing good; and (3) exorcisms.

Anointing. Despite several differences, the Synoptic gospels, and the Fourth Gospel, in several respects, identify the presence of the holy spirit with the initial experiences of Jesus:

This Israelite and early Jewish association of the spirit with wisdom reemerges in a dispute that takes place — again where we would expect such a reminiscence — in the early Jerusalem community. To resolve a dispute over the alleged neglect of Greek-speaking widows, "seven men of good standing, full of spirit and wisdom [*plēreis pneumatos kai sophias*]," are selected to wait upon tables rather than teaching the word of God (Acts 6:3). One of these, Stephen, is further distinguished as "a man full of faith and holy spirit [*plērē pisteōs kai pneumatos hagiou*]" (6:5). By pulling back the curtain of a dispute in the early church, we are able to glimpse again the lavishness of a wise spirit within, the supersaturated measure of a holy spirit, of wisdom, of faith. These men, in short, are the heirs of Bezalel, whom God filled with spirit, wisdom, intelligence, and knowledge (Exod

---

(1) John the Baptist predicts or recognizes that Jesus will baptize with the holy spirit (Mark 1:8/John 1:33); this prediction in Luke and Matthew has an added note of judgment through the addition of "and fire" — Jesus will baptize "with the holy spirit and fire" (Matt 3:11/Luke 3:16; see Isa 4:4). (2) The spirit descends upon Jesus like a dove (in bodily form, according to Luke) during or after his water baptism by John the Baptist (Mark 1:10-11/Matt 3:16-17/Luke 3:21-22/John 1:29-34). (3) The holy spirit accompanies Jesus in the wilderness during a time of testing (Mark 1:12-13/Matt 4:1-11/Luke 4:1-13). In Luke's gospel, Jesus enters this period of testing full of the spirit (4:1); he returns filled with the spirit, and he teaches in the synagogues of Galilee (4:14), where he claims the spirit in his work of preaching good news to the poor (4:18-19).

Doing Good. The words at Jesus' baptism, "my beloved," are reminiscent of the Isaianic servant (Isa 42:1). Luke continues this appeal to the later oracles of Isaiah with Jesus' first public sermon, in which Jesus lays explicit claim to such an anointing with a quotation of Isa 61:1-2: "The spirit of the Lord is upon me, because he has anointed me to bring good news to the poor." The text continues with release to prisoners, sight for the blind, freedom for the oppressed (see 58:6), and proclamation of God's favorable year.

Matthew too connects the baptism of Jesus with the public doing of good. After a summary statement about Jesus' curing all of the sick, Matthew concludes with the characteristic formula "This was to fulfill what had been spoken through the prophet Isaiah" and a quotation from Isa 42:1-4, 9, which begins, "Here is my servant, whom I have chosen, my beloved, with whom my soul is well pleased. I will put my spirit upon him. . . ." (Matt 12:17-21).

Exorcisms. Jesus' doing good extends beyond preaching and healing. In a context rife with polemic, Jesus exorcises a demon in a mute (and blind, according to Matt 12:22) man. Some are amazed; others accuse him of alignment with Beelzebul, the ruler of demons. Jesus responds that a house divided cannot stand, that Satan cannot disarm himself. Then, in Matt 12:28, he continues, "But if it is by the spirit of God that I cast out demons, then the kingdom of God has come to you." Luke's version reads: "But if it is by the finger of God that I cast out the demons . . ." (Luke 11:20). The word "finger" draws the reader directly to the confrontation brought about by the plagues in Exod 8:19(MT 15), "And the magicians said to Pharaoh, 'This is the finger of God!'"

31:3), of Joshua, who was full of spirit of wisdom (Deut 34:9), of Daniel, who had spirit to the nth degree and wisdom like the wisdom of God (Dan 5:11), and of Ben Sira's scribe, who is filled with a spirit of understanding through the arduous labor of study, prayer, and meditation (Sir 39:6). Here, then, in the Jerusalem church lies an authentic vestige of the scriptural perspective that a disciplined spirit within yields a harvest of wisdom.

Still, the depiction of the seven, who are full of spirit and wisdom, and Stephen, who is full of wisdom and holy spirit, is not free from ambiguity. On the one hand, this vestige suits the tapestry created by Daniel's holy spirit in the tale of Susanna, a holy spirit of discipline that flees deceit in the Wisdom of Solomon, Balaam's forfeit of his holy spirit in *Liber antiquitatum biblicarum,* and the commands in the *Damascus Document* and *4QInstruction* not to defile or trade one's holy spirit. On the other hand, wisdom was attributed to a later gift of the holy spirit in the Wisdom of Solomon, so that the association of faith and holy spirit might imply a subsequent endowment in a book in which the gift of the holy spirit is linked to repentance and faith (Acts 2:37-38).

What tips the scales in favor of seeing this spirit as a lifelong endowment of spirit is that, throughout Acts, the holy spirit, when it is understood as a subsequent endowment, inspires only those who speak and teach, those who interpret scripture. It inspires speech, prophecy and tongues, even occasional miracles, perhaps even scattered visions, but *never* practical acts, such as waiting on tables, or virtues such as wisdom and faith. In other words, the holy spirit throughout Acts inspires precisely what Stephen is appointed *not* to do: preaching the word of God. Were it the holy spirit understood as a supplemental endowment that he is said to possess, then we would expect him to be among those who teach the word of God rather than waiting upon tables.

No sooner, however, is the ambiguity resolved than it inveigles its way in when Stephen is portrayed, just prior to his death, as an eloquent and compelling speaker, to the extent that his opponents in debate "could not withstand the wisdom and the spirit with which he spoke [*kai ouk ischyon antistēnai tē sophia kai tō pneumati hō elalei*]" (6:10).[9] We are once again compelled by the ambiguity that inheres in this description to ask whether

---

9. Stephen's accusation in Acts 7:51, "you are always opposing the holy spirit [*hymeis aei tō pneumati tō hagiō antipiptete*]," is about Israel and reflects Isa 63:10; Neh 9:30; and Zech 7:12. It is unrelated to Stephen's holy spirit.

Luke has portrayed Stephen as a man whose spirit has been unusually cultivated or whether he is someone who has received the spirit to transform him into an eloquent speaker. On the one hand, this description of Stephen does fit beautifully within a tradition represented by Micah, Elihu, Job, Ben Sira, and Daniel in the tale of Susannah, in which the spirit, the powerful spirit-breath within, inspires cogent speech and stirs compelling debate. On the other hand, the transformation of a speaker by a fresh filling with the spirit is familiar territory in Acts; the holy spirit has just transformed an unlearned Peter into an impressive speaker (Acts 4:8-13). Once again, the association of wisdom and spirit leans in the direction of an intractable ambiguity.

As if this were not enough, Luke writes that Stephen, in his final moments, as his enraged hearers are about to stone him, "being full of holy spirit [*plērēs pneumatos hagiou*]. . . gazed into heaven and saw the glory of God and Jesus standing at the right hand of God" (Acts 7:55). This may be one final characterization of Stephen as inspired, a dramatic effort on Luke's part to describe the powerful work of the holy spirit as the source of visionary experiences. Stephen's experience of having a vision while full of the holy spirit mirrors, though in a truncated form, Kenaz's in the *Liber antiquitatum biblicarum*. Yet being full of holy spirit and gaining access to the divine world also provides a salient counterpoint to Balaam, an altogether different figure in the *Liber antiquitatum biblicarum*, who surrenders the opportunity for further visions because there is little left of holy spirit in him. The vitality and vision that Balaam forfeited due to deception and duplicity, Stephen possesses in full measure, to the moment of his death. Such an interpretation of *pneuma* in the narrative of Stephen would give a particular punch to his climactic prayer, "Lord Jesus, receive my spirit [*Kyrie Iēsou, dexai to pneuma mou*]" (7:59). His is a holy spirit, a spirit full of faith and wisdom, a spirit that is the source of his vitality. God will surely receive this holy spirit.

There is a residual tension within the narrative of Acts. Luke receives a scriptural tradition in which holy spirit lay within the wise, within Israel's leaders. He incorporates this conception in the birth narratives of his gospel and in narratives that circulate around the figure of Stephen. In each of these instances in Acts, Luke prefers language of fullness rather than filling; there is here no indication of an influx of the holy spirit, of inspiration at that particular moment. Each description, rather, is an indication of lavish wisdom, a full measure of holiness, that distinguishes Stephen and the seven:

plēreis pneumatos kai sophias (6:3)
plērēs pisteōs kai pneumatos hagiou (6:5)
plērēs pneumatos hagiou (7:55)

Although it is elsewhere more typical of Luke to portray the holy spirit as the singular power that fills believers in subsequent experiences, he has left in the story of Stephen a few remnants of Israel's tradition. We are left, therefore, holding the fragile remains of a rich tradition that is transported along the course of an alternative perspective.

The Fourth Gospel

If traces of this tradition remain in the Fourth Gospel, they are virtually undetectable, and no one other than Jesus is accorded the honor of being characterized in this way. Yet even the characterization of Jesus, unique as it may be, is barely recognizable from the standpoint of the belief that human beings receive at birth the gift of a holy or divine spirit. The most closely the Fourth Gospel brushes against this perspective lies in a possible oblique association between the laying down of his life *(psychē)* (John 10:17; 15:13)[10] and his handing over of spirit or breath *(pneuma)* on the cross (19:30). This is barely even a distant relation to the conception of the holy spirit of Daniel, or the holy spirit that can be forfeited and defiled in the Dead Sea Scrolls, or the divine *pneuma* that flowed into the first human "in full current," so that he "earnestly endeavored in all his words and actions to please the Father and King, following God step by step in the highways cut out by virtues" (Philo, *On the Creation* 144). John, in contrast, lays no emphasis upon the potential for virtue that resides in the inspired spirit within. If John is saying that, at his death, "Jesus possibly handed over the divine Spirit that had sustained his physical life as well as empowered his mission," he does so with stunning subtlety.[11]

Perhaps another brush with this tradition lies earlier in the gospel, toward the conclusion of Jesus' soliloquy about the life-giving bread: "It is the spirit that gives life; the flesh is useless. The words that I have spoken to

10. See also John 13:37.
11. C. Bennema, *The Power of Saving Wisdom: An Investigation of Spirit and Wisdom in Relation to the Soteriology of the Fourth Gospel*. WUNT, 2nd ser. 148 (Tübingen: Mohr, 2002) 253.

you are spirit and life" (John 6:63). The contrast of flesh and spirit, along-side the association of words and spirit, may suggest that the spirit about which Jesus is speaking in this context is "the life-giving spirit . . . Jesus' breath, the breath from his mouth on which his spoken words are carried."[12] While the association of word and spirit may follow the tradition of Micah and Elihu, whose claims to inspiration were rooted in the spirit-breath within, the clarity of this spirit-breath is muddied by Jesus' earlier reception of the spirit at his baptism (1:32-33). Jesus has *already*, in the Fourth Gospel, received a subsequent endowment of the spirit. Further, this baptismal endowment does not lie far afield of the servant figure in the middle chapters of Isaiah; the servant has "the spirit upon him" and teaches justice as far as the coastlands (Isa 42:1-4). If Jesus' vocation is reminiscent of the servant's, then his inspired words are due to a special endowment of the spirit rather than to the gift of the spirit that comes with birth. If, therefore, John preserves the traditional association of words and spirit-breath, he does not make it clear that this is the spirit that Jesus received at birth. In the narrative context of the Fourth Gospel, on the contrary, the inspiration of Jesus must be traced primarily, if not exclusively, to his reception of the spirit at his baptism.

Vestiges of the scriptural and early Jewish tradition, then, are barely discernible in the Fourth Gospel. In both of these instances — the association of the spirit with words in the teaching about the true bread and a questionable connection between the handing over of Jesus' spirit and the laying down of his life — it is especially difficult to trace the spirit to the inbreathing of God, to creation, to birth because Jesus received a special endowment of the spirit at his baptism.

Supplanting This Spirit

The paucity of texts and their inherent ambiguity is an indication of how little confidence early Christian authors placed in the capacity of the human spirit to cultivate virtue and holiness. The clues to this conviction which we discover are few and uncertain, and their ambiguous nature provides a startling contrast to a variety of early Jewish texts. There is in early Christian literature nothing as uncomplicated as the narrative detail that

12. D. R. Burkett, *The Son of the Man in the Gospel of John.* JSNTSup 56 (Sheffield: JSOT, 1991) 139-40.

God prompted the holy spirit of a young man, Daniel. There is no simple command not to defile or to exchange one's holy spirit. Nor is there anything as strongly worded as Philo's belief that the inbreathing of Gen 2:7 imparted a capacity for virtue. Paul's metamorphosis of Gen 2:7 into a scriptural citation which envisages a *second* Adam illustrates, in fact, the chasm that divides him from an author such as Philo Judaeus, who interprets Gen 2:7 in myriad contexts as the first instance of inspiration, as the singularly most significant inbreathing of the capacity for virtue into all human beings. While early Christian literature, then, may contain vestiges of the belief that the human spirit is the locus of life and virtue, these remnants are few and decidedly more ambiguous than comparable Israelite and early Jewish texts. They are subsidiary conceptions which have been supplanted by an overwhelming belief that the truest filling with the spirit is a later gift, a subsequent endowment of believers.

What, in fact, distinguishes Christianity from its early Jewish milieu is the absence of both dimensions of the spirit: the God-given spirit within *and* the spirit as a supplemental endowment. This coexistence, which is virtually nonexistent in early Christian literature, is a robust characteristic of early Jewish belief in the spirit.

What the author of the Wisdom of Solomon identifies sparingly as a holy spirit of discipline, which he sets alongside the body and soul, Philo describes with flourishes as "something if such there be better than *aether-spirit*, even an effulgence of the blessed, thrice blessed nature of the God" (*On the Special Laws* 4.123), as "a genuine coinage of that dread [unseen] Spirit, the Divine and invisible One, signed and impressed by the seal of God, the stamp of which is the Eternal Word" (*On the Planting of Noah* 18), and as the "divine breath that migrated hither from that blissful and happy existence for the benefit of our race a copy or fragment or ray of that blessed nature" (*On the Creation* 146). We might be led to expect by these fulsome descriptions of the spirit within that there would be no need for any further occasion of inspiration. Yet while positing an initial inspiration which fills all people with the divine and holy spirit, both authors believe as well that later moments of inspiration can be vital, even if only to a select few. Solomon requested wisdom and received the holy spirit and wisdom, according to the Wisdom of Solomon. Philo would lay claim to two forms of inspiration, one in which his empty mind was filled with divine spirit and frenzy and the other in which the spirit prompted and taught from within with his mind intact.

The ability of these authors to embrace the coexistence of an initial filling with the spirit alongside subsequent moments of infilling may appear at first blush to border on incompatibility. If human beings have within them a spirit as marvellous as both authors, Philo in particular, suggest, how could there be any need for further inspiration? For the Wisdom of Solomon, the answer lies in a dual commitment to Stoicism and to scripture. With his partisan commitment to Stoicism, the author can believe nothing other than that the cosmic spirit is resident as well within each human being — what Seneca calls a holy spirit or god within. Yet the Wisdom of Solomon is not merely a repository of Greco-Roman conceptions. The author is dependent as well upon the story of Solomon in 1 Kings 3, in which Solomon receives an endowment of wisdom in response to his prayer. Therefore, the author of the Wisdom of Solomon incorporates Solomon's reception of wisdom, though the author identifies this wisdom with the spirit, understood in Greco-Roman terms, that pervades the cosmos. In the portrayal of Solomon's reception of spirit-wisdom, the spirit is evidently Stoic in character: in wisdom is a spirit that is intelligent and holy, a spirit that pervades all things and holds all things in unison (Wis 7:21-28).

If inconsistency were at issue, it would surely rise to the surface in Philo's many discussions of inspiration, especially in light of how exquisitely he sculpts the contours of the divine spirit in these initial and subsequent acts of inspiration. Yet he, even more forcefully than the author of the Wisdom of Solomon, holds in tension his belief that God inbreathed the divine spirit in an act of creation and his conviction that the divine spirit comes as well in later moments of inspiration. Philo manages to embrace both by portraying them as inspirations of a different sort. The initial inbreathing he associates principally with the capacity for virtue, with a yearning for God, with the potential for a vision of God. In *Allegorical Interpretation* 1.34, we may recall, Philo explains that God breathes even into the imperfect to encourage in them a "zeal for virtue," for God "created no soul barren of virtue, even if the exercise of it be to some impossible." What distinguished the first human in this regard is that "the divine *pneuma* had flowed into him in full current," with the result that he "earnestly endeavored in all his words and actions to please the Father and King, following God step by step in the highways cut out by virtues. . . ."[13]

---

13. *On the Creation* 144. There is perhaps a polemical edge to this association of the first inspiration with virtue. Shortly following the reference to a holy and disciplined spirit and directly after a reference to the spirit which filled the world and holds everything together,

Later moments of inspiration, in contrast, are not principally about the life of virtue but about the revelation of a special sort of knowledge. Philo typically receives, through experiences of revelation, solutions to a scriptural conundrum, a higher word, such as why there must be two cherubim, rather than one, to guard paradise after the expulsion of Adam and Eve. He can describe these experiences in the most expansive of terms — "language, ideas, an enjoyment of light, keenest vision, pellucid distinctiveness of objects"[14] — though not as a moment on the path toward virtue. Nor do prophets surrender "the citadel of the soul to a new visitor and tenant, the Divine Spirit" in order to edge further toward the perfection of virtue.[15] The purpose of this experience rather is to transform them into a virtually mindless channel of God's message, the instrument of God's insistent words.

Philo distinguishes between initial and subsequent moments of inspiration without overtly discussing the distinction. The first inbreathing of the spirit imparts to *all people* the capacity for virtue so that they may have the ability to walk the path of virtue. Subsequent moments of inspiration impart to *select individuals* new ideas, fresh interpretations, God's words, and hidden truths by way of visions and auditory revelations. This distinction makes it possible for Philo to adhere to a belief that the divine and holy spirit imparts wisdom and new revelations to select people, such as Moses, the prophets, and Philo himself, without forfeiting the belief that an initial inspiration instilled in every human being the capacity for virtue.

This ability to hold together a conception of the holy spirit as the power of life that human beings have from birth with later moments of filling by the holy spirit characterizes as well the *Liber antiquitatum biblicarum*. We have seen already how the author adopts the language of Gen 6:3 to portray the holy spirit within Balaam as the spirit of life. When

---

the author of the Wisdom of Solomon continues, "therefore those who utter unrighteous things will not escape notice, and justice, when it punishes, will not pass them by" (Wis 1:8). This is consistent with a dominant theme of these early lines, that God is fully aware of, and will punish, the actions of evil people, particularly their persecution of the righteous. Philo continues on the theme of virtue by pressing the point home that those "into whom real life" has been breathed are now culpable. Had God not inbreathed this authentic life into those "without experience of virtue," they might have claimed injustice in God's punishment, as they failed through ignorance and inexperience. Thus, they have no right to blame God for having "failed to breathe into him [or her] any conception of" virtue (*On the Allegorical Laws* 1.35).

14. *On the Migration of Abraham* 34–35.
15. *On the Special Laws* 4.49.

he forfeits it due to a lack of integrity, Balaam's death becomes imminent. Slightly later in the *Liber antiquitatum biblicarum,* a figure who is merely mentioned in the biblical book of Judges grows into mammoth proportions. In this revision of scripture, Kenaz obtains an extraordinary military and prophetic status. Pseudo-Philo incorporates allusions to 1 Sam 10:6 — Saul's transformation into another person — and Judg 6:34 — the spirit clothes Gideon — to accentuate Kenaz's mercurial heroism: "he was clothed with the spirit of power and was changed into another man" (*LAB* 27:10). Equally significant for our study is a slightly later instance of prophetic inspiration, in which Kenaz, prior to his death, sees a vision far in advance: "And when they [the prophets and elders of Israel] had sat down, [a] holy spirit came upon Kenaz and dwelled in him and elevated his mind [put him in ecstasy], and he began to prophesy, saying . . ." (28:6). The impulse for this prophetic vision, or at least the prophetic recounting of that vision, is the indwelling of holy spirit within Kenaz. These two forms of inspiration — one in which the initial gift of the life-giving holy spirit is forfeited and another in which the holy spirit inspires an ecstatic vision — coexist peaceably in the *Liber antiquitatum biblicarum.*

The pattern that is discernible in the *Liber antiquitatum biblicarum* is surprisingly similar to the pattern that is evident in the Wisdom of Solomon and in Philo's commentaries and treatises. All three authors assume the presence of a divine or holy spirit within which is related in various ways to virtue. In the Wisdom of Solomon, it is a holy spirit of discipline or teaching that flees from deceit. In Philo's commentaries, filling with this spirit at creation is tantamount to the impartation of the capacity for virtue. And in the *Liber antiquitatum biblicarum,* Balaam loses this holy spirit and shortens the span of his life because he acted treacherously at the behest of the hostile king Balak. All three authors, in short, believe that the holy or divine spirit lives within a human being. All three also embrace the possibility of subsequent endowments of the holy spirit. While there is certainly an area of overlap between virtue and special knowledge, between what Philo calls real life and the reception of special revelation, subsequent receptions of the spirit tend to be limited to the revelation of otherwise inaccessible knowledge. Philo receives special knowledge, such as solutions to scriptural conundrums, and the prophets become the channels of divine utterances when they are filled with the spirit. Solomon receives a special gift of spirit in response to his request for wisdom. And Kenaz, in the *Liber antiquitatum biblicarum,* also receives a special vision of the future when the spirit leaps upon him and indwells him. The correspondence concerning subsequent experiences of being filled with the spirit is strongest between Philo and the *Liber antiquitatum biblicarum:* Kenaz and Philo's prophets, as well as Philo himself, lose their own consciousness when the spirit comes suddenly upon them and enters within them. Kenaz cannot remember what he saw, and the prophets become channels of God's insistent utterances.

Early Christianity could hardly accommodate this dual vision, with its forceful emphasis upon transformation and discontinuity. It is hard to ignore the all-encompassing character of an exclamation such as "if anyone is in Christ, there is a new creation: everything old has passed away; see, everything has become new!" (2 Cor 5:17). Even the act of faith is depicted by Paul as an act of creation: "For it is the God who said, 'Let light shine out of darkness,' who has shone in our hearts to give the light of the knowledge of the glory of God in the face of Jesus Christ" (4:6). In the letter to the Colossians, the language of Gen 1:26, of clothing oneself with "the new self, which is being renewed in knowledge according to the image of its creator," is integral to a bold vision of humankind free of distinctions between Greek and Jew, slave and free (Col 3:10-11).

Paul's radical bifurcation between old and new creations shares a family resemblance with the book of Acts, in which a tidy line between belief and unbelief shapes community and mission. The base line from which all variations emerge is a direct plea for repentance: "Peter said to them, 'Repent, and be baptized every one of you in the name of Jesus Christ so that your sins may be forgiven; and you will receive the gift of the holy spirit. For the promise is for you, for your children, and for all who are far away, everyone whom the Lord our God calls to him'" (Acts 2:38-39).[16]

The Fourth Gospel, in which the Paraclete is prepared to reveal marvellous knowledge, exhibits no less consanguinity with the letters of Paul and the book of Acts. What knowledge the Paraclete will reveal is strictly unavailable to a world that is shaped by the values of the old creation, by the darkness of this world. There is no spirit of God within, no sense of justice, power, and might, no one extraordinarily skilled, no uncanny knowledge of dreams or strange handwriting, no one among the Jews of the Fourth Gospel who is filled to the brim with a spirit that has been cul-

---

16. On the one occasion when Paul, in Athens, eschews such a bifurcation and claims instead that God "gives to all mortals life and breath and all things [*autos didous pasi zōēn kai pnoēn kai ta panta*]," his message is met with far less success than Peter's; there is no overwhelming response, no recounting of thousands upon thousands of baptisms (Acts 17:25-27).

tivated through prayer, study, meditation, or even travel. There is no holy spirit to be prompted among its young men and women, no holy spirit ready to be taught and to flee deceit, no holy spirit that has not already been exchanged for power or defiled in service to a misdirected temple cult. There is no divine spirit within that guides the characters who populate the Fourth Gospel along an uninterrupted path to virtue. In the Fourth Gospel — and even more so in the letter of 1 John — knowledge and virtue, love and friendship, belong to another world altogether, a world of the spirit, to be sure, but a *supplemental* world of the spirit.

CHAPTER 2

Filled with the Spirit and the Letters of Paul

Antiquity has bequeathed to us no writer more enamored of the spirit than the Apostle Paul, whose letters are awash in the spirit, so much so that isolating a single point of entrée is a monumental task. There is, nonetheless, a concrete point of entry that suggests itself because of its importance to both the community at Qumran and to Paul, and this is Ezekiel's vision of the resurrected nation that emerged from the valley of very many, very dry bones. Paul will take this vision in unexpected directions that may not have entirely pleased the visionary himself, though they reflect the apostle's restive mind and wrestling posture toward the people whom he pastored.

The Spirit *Given*

Ezekiel's Vision in a New Key

The phrase, "God gave the spirit," we noted, expresses incorporation into the community in the *Hymns* of the Dead Sea Scrolls.[1] In language reminiscent of Ezekiel 36–37, the poet recollects gratefully, "And I, the Instructor, have known you, my God, through the spirit which you gave in me, and I have listened loyally to your wonderful secret through your holy spirit" (1QH XX 11-12).[2] In the midst of trenchant self-criticism, the hymn

---

1. See above, Part II, chapter 4.
2. See also 1QH IV 17; V 25; XXI 14 = 4Q427, 4Q428 11.

writer grasps the transforming reality that "I have appeased your face by the spirit which you have given [in me,] to lavish your [kind]nesses on [your] ser[vant] for [ever,] to purify me with your holy spirit, to bring me near by your will according to the extent of your kindnesses" (1QH VIII 19-20). This vocabulary of initiation is also part and parcel of the literature of the early church, which made frequent use of the formula, "God gave [aorist tense] the spirit in us" (e.g., Acts 5:32; 15:8; Rom 11:8; 2 Cor 1:22; 5:5; 2 Tim 1:7; 1 John 3:24; 4:13). This language is drawn from the colorful draught of Ezekiel 36–37:

> A new heart I will give you, and a new spirit I will put within you; and I will remove from your body the heart of stone and give you a heart of flesh. I will put my spirit within you, and make you follow my statutes and be careful to observe my ordinances. (Ezek 36:26-27)

> I will lay sinews on you, and will cause flesh to come upon you, and cover you with skin, and give breath in you, and you shall live; and you shall know that I am the Lord. (37:6)

> I will give my spirit within you, and you shall live, and I will place you on your own soil; then you shall know that I, the Lord, have spoken and will act, says the Lord. (37:14)

The early church takes precisely the same tack as the community at Qumran by transforming this vision of corporate re-creation into an expression of individual re-creation; Paul, following the same vein, writes twice that the spirit is given "into our hearts," and once he depicts the spirit as a "seal" and "pledge":

> . . . and hope does not disappoint us, because God's love has been poured into our hearts through the holy spirit that has been given to us. (Rom 5:5)

> *hē de elpis ou kataischynei, hoti hē agapē tou theou ekkechytai en tais kardiais hēmōn dia pneumatos hagiou tou dothentos hēmin.*

> . . . by putting his seal on us and giving us his spirit in our hearts as a pledge. (2 Cor 1:22)

> *ho kai sphragisamenos hēmas kai dous ton arrabōna tou pneumatos en tais kardiais hēmōn.*

The one who has prepared us for this very thing is God, who has given us the pledge of the spirit. (2 Cor 5:5)

ho de katergasamenos hēmas eis auto touto theos, ho dous hēmin ton arrabōna tou pneumatos.

The thrust of each of these expressions suggests a grounding in Ezekiel's vision of the very dry bones, for in each of these three references to the (holy) spirit that is given to believers we discover a grappling hook of sorts that grips the rock as a believer, like the shattered exiles of Ezekiel's vision, makes the hard climb from the agony of the present to the glory of the future.

In the first of these texts, Rom 5:5, this could hardly be more in evidence: the very reason why hope will not disappoint, the very basis for knowing that believers will not be duped in the end by a deceptive false promise, is the reality of God's full measure of outpoured love that has accompanied the giving of the holy spirit within. God's giving of the holy spirit is the root from which the tree of life, both present (the love of God) and future (hope), grows. This is not, of course, national resurrection, a resurrection of an entire valley of very dry bones. It is, still, that same spirit which fills believers when it is given to them — not so much in smaller measure than in Ezekiel but in more personal terms, in terms which each believer can grasp. The drama, of course, is no less dramatic than in Ezekiel. There will indeed be a grand act of salvation that corresponds and outshines the fateful act of Adam, which brought death — a point Paul will make shortly in Rom 5:12-21. But it is experienced now, heart by human heart, in the context of personal rather than national suffering that requires perseverance and hope.

In his second letter to the Corinthians, Paul picks up two vivid metaphors for the spirit, both of which underline this certainty of resurrection in the future: "seal" and "guarantee." These may be commercial metaphors. The metaphor of the seal may be based upon an imprint set in wax which denoted ownership and, by extension, protection.[3] A seal such as this might also have been put alongside, or have replaced, a signature, serving as proof of identity. In legal documents, such as a will, a seal safeguarded against violation. In the Septuagint, a seal could validate a document (Jer

---

3. G. Fee, *God's Empowering Presence: The Holy Spirit in the Letters of Paul* (Peabody: Hendrickson, 1994) 292.

39:10-11, 25, 44[MT 32]). The metaphor of the seal, understood from the commercial perspective, presents the spirit as the irrefutable authentication of God's presence in the believer. The metaphor of a guarantee or down payment may also have arisen from commercial life, where it functioned as a deposit or first instalment paid for services or rent or wages or goods. Both the giver and the recipient were under a legal obligation to complete the contract.[4] The meaning of both commercial terms, understood in this commercial context, is that God has given a legal seal in the form of a down payment, which consists of the spirit, to guarantee the whole of salvation, including the resurrection, about which Paul had written extensively in his earlier letter to the Corinthians (1 Corinthians 15).

The idea of a seal may also be a religious metaphor that explains circumcision, baptism, or wearing a mark or seal of the god.[5] Yet the use of "seal" as a religious metaphor for relation to a god does not explain Paul's adoption of the notion of a pledge or down payment, which seems not to have functioned within a religious context. It is possible, of course, that Paul here adopts both a religious and a commercial metaphor in order to accentuate the importance of the spirit.

There is, however, still another foreground for both images, lying much closer at hand, that provides a single, credible locus from which to interpret the images of the pledge and seal. In Paul's scriptures, there occurs one text — and only one text — in which seal and pledge occur in tandem: the story of Judah and Tamar in Genesis 38. There Tamar is compelled to dress up like a prostitute and deceive her father-in-law, Judah, so that he will have sex with her and produce an heir; his sons, in order of age, have died after they married her, and Judah refuses Tamar the right of levirate marriage. During their sexual encounter, Judah has nothing to give Tamar in payment, so he asks: "What pledge shall I give you?" This is the word *arrabōn,* which occurs three times in this story and nowhere else in the Bible apart from Paul's two references and a related text, Eph 1:14. Judah leaves three items with Tamar in "pledge" until he will return and pay her properly. His messenger, when he returns, does not find a prostitute, but he does discover that Tamar is pregnant. Judah is, of course, indignant

4. On legal and commercial metaphors, see M. E. Thrall, *A Critical and Exegetical Commentary on the Second Epistle to the Corinthians.* ICC 34 (Edinburgh: T. & T. Clark, 1994) 1:156-58.

5. See Thrall, *Second Epistle to the Corinthians,* 1:156-57, on religious metaphors. Fee (*God's Empowering Presence,* 294-95) questions how Christian texts more than a century later than Paul's letters can yield the association of the metaphor of sealing with water baptism.

until Tamar brings out the items she took as a "pledge" of a gift that Judah had intended to pay for her sexual services.

The first item Judah leaves in pledge is his seal. The meaning of this word, "seal," is somewhat complicated. Although the Septuagint, with which Paul was no doubt familiar, translates the Hebrew word that occurs in Gen 38:18 as "ring" *(ton daktylion sou)*, Hebrew *ḥôtām* is more often translated in the Septuagint by the Greek word *sphragis*, "seal."[6] The septuagintal translation in Gen 38:18, in other words, is an anomaly. Had Paul read the Hebrew or a Greek version with a more typical translation of the Hebrew than the Septuagint of Gen 38:18, he would undoubtedly have been led to understand the Hebrew as a "seal" *(sphragis)* rather than a "ring" *(daktylios)*.

The gist of these observations is that Gen 38:18 is the only instance in the Hebrew Bible where the Hebrew words "seal" and "pledge" occur in intimate association with one another. This association is obscured in the Septuagint translation by the unusual use of the Greek word "ring" to translate a Hebrew word that is otherwise translated "seal." This means that the juxtaposition of the words "seal" and "pledge" in 2 Cor 1:21-22 mirror the Hebrew of Gen 38:18. These are not words that occur regularly together. Yet precisely in a literary text where we would normally look to understand Paul's letters — in his scriptures — we find both in juxtaposition: "He [Judah] said, 'What *pledge* shall I give you?' She [Tamar] replied, 'Your *signet* [seal] and your cord, and the staff that is in your hand.' So he gave them to her, and went in to her, and she conceived by him."[7]

Why does Paul describe the holy spirit so as to reflect the language of the story of Tamar and Judah? Perhaps the most obvious answer is that Perez, one of the twins who was conceived by this sexual union, was the ancestor of David, the messiah. Tamar herself is included among the ancestors of Jesus in Matthew's genealogy (Matt 1:3). In other words, Judah and Tamar occupy a pivotal point in a long lineage of promise. Judah was descended from Abraham, David from Judah and Tamar, and Jesus from David. The promise of God is forwarded in this most remarkable and unexpected of stories, in which a bereft widow is mistaken by her father-in-law for a prostitute, made pregnant by him, and made to become an ancestor of David, the messiah.

---

6. See Esth 3:10; 8:8, 10 (Old Greek).

7. Philo follows the LXX in *On Flight and Finding* 149–51 when he interprets this story allegorically. In *T. Jud.* 12:5, 7, Judah gives Tamar a belt or girdle rather than a ring.

This story of promise fits perfectly the context of the conclusion to 2 Corinthians 1. Paul is passionate in his affirmation that all of God's *promises* are fulfilled in Christ Jesus: "For the Son of God, Jesus Christ, whom we proclaimed among you, Silvanus and Timothy and I, was not 'Yes and No'; but in him it is always 'Yes.' For in him *every one of God's promises* is a 'Yes.' For this reason it is through him that we say the 'Amen,' to the glory of God" (2 Cor 1:19-20). The issue that leads directly to Paul's description of the spirit as a seal and pledge is the viability of God's promise, and it is the unexpected but unmistakable process of promise that permeates the story of Tamar and Judah.

There is little of novelty in this interpretation of 2 Cor 1:22. Either Paul, in a later letter, or one of his interpreters penned Ephesians, which begins with a prayer of extraordinary length. The climax and conclusion of this prayer preserves the tandem metaphors of sealing and pledge:

> In him you also, when you had heard the word of truth, the gospel of your salvation, and had believed in him, were *sealed* with the holy spirit of promise [*esphragisthēte tō pneumati tēs epangelias tō hagiō*]; this is the *pledge* [*arrabōn*] of our inheritance toward redemption as God's own people, to the praise of his glory. (Eph 1:13-14)

This conclusion crisply captures the essence of Paul's use of these metaphors to depict the spirit. In 2 Corinthians 1, the spirit's relationship to past promises is expressed in muted terms, by way of allusion to Genesis 38. In Ephesians 1, this relationship to the past is brought into the open: believers are sealed with "the holy spirit of promise . . . the pledge of our inheritance," with the spirit that incorporates believers into a grand drama extending as far back as Abraham and Sarah. Yet in both 2 Corinthians 1 and Ephesians 1, this same "spirit of promise" which unites believers with the extended past is also a pledge, a signal of certainty that God will effect salvation in the future.[8]

---

8. Another Pauline passage, Rom 15:7-13, shares a similar coalescence of concerns (though without reference to the images of seal and pledge) that brings it into the same theological orbit as 2 Corinthians 1. First, both texts find their focal point in ancestral promises. In Romans, Paul writes: "For I tell you that Christ has become a servant of the circumcised on behalf of the truth of God in order that he might confirm [*eis to bebaiōsai*] the promises given to the patriarchs" (15:8). Second, the word *"confirm"* in this sentence is similar to 2 Cor 1:21, where Paul writes that God *confirms* us [*ho de bebaiōn hēmas*] with you in Christ." Third is the key element of hope. Paul strings together several scriptural citations about the nations, ending with LXX Isa 11:10: "The root of Jesse shall come, the one who

Filling with the holy spirit, therefore, ties believers to the drama of God's promises, once anticipated and now fulfilled. The unique juxtaposition of the words "seal" and "pledge" point to one story, and one story alone: Tamar and Judah. Here, in the unlikeliest of circumstances, God furthered a promise made earlier to Abraham that would eventuate in the birth of David and his distant heir, Jesus.

The certainty with which that promise was fulfilled, despite forces to the contrary, gives impetus to certainty about a believer's future. God confirmed the promise to Israel's ancestors in this unlikely story, and God confirms believers' future with a seal and pledge. What a believer possesses, in Paul's opinion, pales in relation to that destiny; a believer's experience is but a seal and pledge of that destiny. Filling with the holy spirit is intended to provide certainty of the future and an orientation toward the future. If it does not — if this filling yields a preoccupation with the present, a spiritual narcissism — then the fullness of that pledge, the wholeness of that seal, the power of the holy spirit (Rom 15:13), is sadly diminished.

Filling with the spirit, in brief, sets believers in the context of a magnificent drama that stretches from Abraham and Sarah to an unknown future. The seal and pledge of the holy spirit confirm for believers that their future is secure, that the God who fulfilled ancestral promises will fulfill the promise made to believers. To put it in Pauline terms: "For in him every one of God's promises is a 'Yes'" (2 Cor 1:20).

All this talk of hope, in the end, can be reduced to one conviction, to the certainty which the love of God engenders for people of faith. Those who grasp God's love recognize that this love compels God, in the end, to keep the divine word, to lead those whom God loves to their destiny (Rom 8:28-30). This, of course, is the gist of Rom 5:5: ". . . and hope does not disappoint us, because the love of God has been poured into our hearts through the holy spirit that has been given to us."

Whether Paul intended the allusion or not, his mention of sealing in

---

rises to rule the Gentiles; in him the Gentiles shall *hope*." Fourth, the ingredient of hope is raised to new heights by the closing benediction, which associates that hope integrally with the holy spirit: "May the God of hope fill you with all joy and peace in believing, so that you may abound in hope *by the power of the holy spirit*" (Rom 15:13). Romans 15 and 2 Corinthians 1 share, then, several dimensions: the promises (to the ancestors), confirmation of believers, hope, and the holy spirit. From this it is hardly possible to overlook the past and future dimensions of the holy spirit, dimensions that look far into the past and long into the future, that give confirmation and grounding at the present moment and in the progression toward a believer's destiny.

relation to the heart evokes the passion of Song 8:6. The root Paul selects in 2 Cor 1:22 — God puts God's *seal* upon us — is a bold one. The metaphor of sealing evokes, not only the illicit and short-lived sexual dalliance between Judah and Tamar, but also the passionate love of the Song of Songs: "Set me as a *seal* [*sphragida*] upon your heart, as a seal [*sphragida*] upon your arm; for love is strong as death, passion fierce as the grave. Its flashes are flashes of fire, a raging flame." With this allusion we are reminded of how unsuitable dispassionate commercial and religious metaphors are for a context in which Paul is otherwise passionate about God's promises. God's love, fueled by the spirit in human hearts, is fiery and fierce, a passionate embrace that cannot be broken, even by the fierce enemy, death. To dissolve this passion, to ignore the drama of Tamar and the ferocious lover of the Song of Songs, is to violate the fabric of true love, to tear the oneness of lovers apart, and to bypass the passionate penetration of filling with the spirit.

We seem to have come a very long way from the valley of the shadow of death, in which the spirit thrived, from that razor sharp dividing-line between life and death that characterized so much reflection upon the spirit in Israelite literature. That distance is, however, more apparent than real. God's love is poured out through the holy spirit that has been *given* — as in Ezekiel 36–37 — in a life that is rife with suffering (Rom 5:3-5). Further, the affirmation that God's promises are "Yes," that God has given the spirit as seal and pledge, Paul delivers in a defensive stance, as he explains why he has delayed visiting Corinth (2 Cor 1:15-17). This delay, Paul explained slightly earlier in the letter, was due to enormous affliction, so much so that Paul and his colleagues despaired of life itself: "Indeed, we felt that we had received the sentence of death so that we would rely not on ourselves but on God who raises the dead. The one who rescued us from so deadly a peril will continue to rescue us; on him we have set our hope that he will rescue us again" (2 Cor 1:8-10). Paul's affirmation of God's promise, his description of the spirit as a seal and a pledge, is hardly a nonchalant, untested avowal of hope; it is rather a claim that was forged on the anvil of despair, a conviction that Paul would cherish once he emerged intact, though shaken, from the valley of the shadow of death.

When he next refers to the *giving* (Ezekiel 36–37) of the spirit as a *pledge* (Gen 38:18), the presence of death is palpable. Paul claims not to "lose heart" although the "outer nature is wasting away" (2 Cor 4:16). In this context, Paul picks up again the strands of Ezekiel's grand vision and Tamar's tale: "The one who has prepared us for this very thing is God, who has given us the pledge of the spirit" (2 Cor 5:5). This pledge leads to confidence: "So we are always confident; even though we know that while we are at home in the body we are away from the Lord — for we walk by faith, not by sight. Yes, we do have confidence . . ." (2 Cor 5:6-8a). If the spirit is the impetus for such confidence, the knowledge this confidence inspires is clearly a matter of hope: "For we know that if the earthly tent we live in is destroyed, we have a building from God, a house not made with hands, eternal in the heavens" (2 Cor 5:1).

Paul's discussion is turgid and obtuse. He claims, while he groans in his earthly tent, that he also yearns to be "further clothed" with a heavenly dwelling (2 Cor 5:2); he yearns not to be unclothed but to be "further clothed, so that what is mortal may be swallowed up by life" (5:4). This concern leads him to a confident statement that belies the groaning and yearning he actually feels: "The one who has prepared us for this very thing is God, who has given us the pledge of the spirit" (5:5). The verb *ependyein*, which can be translated "further clothed," contains two prefixes, and it is the first that is so troublesome. If the verb were merely *endyein*, then Paul would be expressing a clear-headed hope to be clothed by a resurrection body, as he does in 1 Cor 15:53: "For this perishable body must put on imperishability, and this mortal body must put on immortality." That is straightforward enough. Yet instead of this verb, he twice employs a verb with two prefixes, the first of which is *epi*, "upon." Is he thinking of the hiatus between death and the return of Jesus, when believers are naked, during which time they need to be clothed with something? The insurmountable problem with this conjecture is that Paul fails to give the slightest indication that he fears an intervening period — one in which naked bodies must have some form of clothing placed "upon" them — between his death and the return of Jesus. Nor can this verb be an accurate description of the resurrection of believers, for Paul expects a transformation from an earthly body to a heavenly one, not an overcoat of sorts, in which the earthly body is covered with a heavenly one.

The language of Ezekiel 36–37, which has undeniably influenced the way in which Paul expresses the giving of the spirit to believers, provides an essential piece to the puzzle of what Paul hopes for when he twice speaks of being "further (*epi*, "upon") clothed" rather than simply "clothed" with a resurrection body. Ezekiel's vision is rife with the preposition "upon":

Thus says the Lord God to these bones: I will cause breath to enter you, and you shall live. I will lay sinews *upon* you, and will cause flesh to *come up upon* you, and I shall stretch skin *upon* you, and put breath in you, and you shall live; and you shall know that I am the Lord. (Ezek 37:5-6)[9]

What Ezekiel sees subsequently evokes a description with an even more emphatic use of the preposition "upon": "there were sinews *upon* them, and flesh had *come up upon* them, and skin had *gone up upon* them; but there was no spirit-breath in them" (37:8).

The repetition of the preposition "upon" in this vivid description of resurrection cracks the conundrum of the "further clothing" of believers. Paul is not rendering a definitive doctrine of resurrection bodies. He is instead ruminating upon the vision of Ezekiel within his own context: believers who now groan in the context of present suffering (2 Cor 4:16-18) can confidently anticipate a time when Ezekiel's vision will become a reality, when new sinews, flesh, and skin will come *upon* dead, naked bones. Of this believers can be certain because God "has *given* the spirit," as in Ezekiel 36–37, as a pledge.

This reminiscence of Ezekiel 37 clarifies the otherwise puzzling verb *ependyein*. Ezekiel envisaged sinews, flesh, and skin coming upon the dead, followed by God's giving the spirit within. Believers have already been given the spirit, so they now anticipate the coming of new sinews, flesh, and skin upon their dead bones. Though the order is reversed, the end of this process for both Ezekiel and Paul is exactly the same — an overflowing of life. When the spirit-breath enters, says Ezekiel's God, "you shall live" (Ezek 37:5). When God will cause sinews, flesh, and skin to come upon the dead and put spirit-breath into them, "you shall live" (37:6). And so, recalls Ezekiel, "I prophesied as he commanded me, and the spirit-breath came into them, *and they lived,* and stood on their feet, a vast multitude" (37:10). The message this vision communicates to Israel is this: "I will put my spirit within you, and *you shall live,* and I will place you on your own soil; then you shall know that I, the Lord, have spoken and will act, says the Lord" (37:14). This vision is about lavish life. This vision is about life beyond measure, beyond hope, beyond suffering, beyond the shadow of death. The sum of Paul's reflections is simi-

---

9. Greek: *tade legei kyrios tois osteois toutois idou egō pherō eis hymas pneuma zōēs kai dōsō eph' hymas neura kai anaxō eph' hymas sarkas kai ektenō eph' hymas derma kai dōsō pneuma mou eis hymas kai zēsesthe kai gnōsesthe hoti egō eimi kyrios.* The Hebrew is more emphatic, for the verb "cause to be upon" is followed by the preposition "upon you," in reference to flesh: *wĕha'ălētî 'ălêkem bāśār.*

larly the lavish onslaught of life that transpires when believers are further clothed: "For while we are still in this tent, we groan under our burden, because we wish not to be unclothed but to be further clothed, so that what is mortal may be *swallowed up by life*" (2 Cor 5:4).

Though we may have travelled far from Ezekiel's valley of death, then, it is only to return home. At those poignant moments when Paul confronts death, the spirit is pivotal to that confrontation. The *giving* of the spirit — this expression comes ultimately from Ezekiel 36–37 — brings the certainty of glory to lives marred by suffering (Rom 5:5). The giving of the spirit as a *pledge and seal* confirms the improbable execution of God's promises even to those who, like Paul, have undergone death's crushing blows and survived (2 Cor 1:21-22). The spirit is given as a pledge that Ezekiel's magnificent vision of resurrection will flood the shadow of death, will replace outwardly decaying bodies with a jolt of spirit-filled life, with a lavish outpouring of vitality (2 Cor 5:5).

The Spirit and Sexual Sanctity

Another brief and creative twist on Ezekiel's vision occurs in 1 Thess 4:8, where Paul urges, "Therefore whoever rejects this rejects not human authority but God, who also gives his holy spirit *into* you [*didonta to pneuma autou to hagion eis hymas*]." The syntax of this reference to the spirit is slightly odd, for Paul employs the verb "give" rather than "send," and the preposition and pronoun "into you" rather than the plural dative case "to you" *(hymin)* or the prepositional phrase *en hymin* (as in Ezek 36:26). The reason for this slightly unexpected expression is, yet again, Paul's indebtedness to Ezekiel 37. Twice in this unified vision of the valley of very dry bones occurs the expression "give my spirit *into*. . . ." Four times the prepositional phrase "*into* you/them" occurs.

> *tade legei kyrios tois osteois toutois idou egō pherō eis hymas pneuma zōēs* (37:5)

> *kai dōsō pneuma mou eis hymas kai zēsesthe kai gnōsesthe hoti egō eimi kyrios* (37:6)

> *eisēlthen eis autous to pneuma kai ezēsan* (37:10)

> *kai dōsō to pneuma mou eis hymas* (37:14)

Here, in a letter to a Greek community, Paul preserves a nugget from Ezekiel's grand vision. Yet here, as in the literature of the Qumran sectarians, the language of Ezekiel is absorbed into the concerns of a particular literary moment. That preoccupation, what the Thessalonians would reject to their detriment, is sexual purity. The portion of the letter in which Paul urges the Thessalonians to maintain a life of sexual purity ends with an admonition that is grounded in Ezekiel 37; whoever rejects his advice rejects God who gave the holy spirit into them. In other words, according to the admonition in 1 Thess 4:8, Thessalonians who fail to maintain sexual purity are violating, not simply a Pauline prescription, but the spirit that God has given into them.

Lying in the foreground, then, of the concluding phrase of Paul's insistence upon sexual fidelity is an allusion to Ezekiel's vision of the renewal of Israel, which contains the highest concentration of references to the spirit in the entire Hebrew Bible. Two themes in particular are relevant for the interpretation of 1 Thess 4:3-8. One theme is sanctification and holiness: God's name will be sanctified when Israel lives in the presence of the nations in holiness (see also Ezek 36:28). The other is the knowledge of God.[10] These themes coalesce in Ezek 36:23:

> I will sanctify my great name, which has been profaned among the nations, and which you have profaned among them; and the nations shall know that I am the Lord, says the Lord God, when through you I display my holiness before their eyes.[11]

Both themes, sanctification and the knowledge of God, re-emerge in Paul's letter to the Thessalonians, in a discussion of sexuality that ends with an exclamation point rooted in Ezekiel 37: "I will give my spirit *into* you." Purity or sanctification lies at the heart of Paul's concerns in 1 Thess 4:1-8, to the extent that this theme opens and dominates the first subsection in the second half of the letter: "For this is the will of God, your sanctification [*touto gar estin thelēma tou theou, ho hagiasmos hymōn*] . . ." (1 Thess 4:3). The theme of the knowledge of God can be pinpointed to 1 Thess 4:5, where Paul urges the Thessalonians not to act "like the nations who do not

10. In the vision of the valley of very dry bones, Israel itself will "know that I am the Lord" (Ezek 37:6, 13).

11. Greek: *kai hagiasō to onoma mou to mega to bebēlōthen en tois ethnesin ho ebebēlōsate en mesō autōn kai gnōsontai ta ethnē hoti egō eimi kyrios en tō hagiasthēnai me en hymin kat' ophthalmous autōn.*

know God." The juxtaposition of these themes in a context that is punctuated by the unique grammar of Ezekiel — putting the spirit *into* Israel — mirrors Ezekiel's oracle of re-creation, in which the nations will know God *(gnōsontai ta ethnē)* because God will be sanctified *(en tō hagiasthēnai)* in their eyes through Israel.

Paul has picked up three facets of Ezekiel's vision — the spirit given into Israel, holiness, and knowledge of God — and adapted them to the situation of the Thessalonians.[12] No longer is the vision one of national resurrection, though on a much smaller scale the themes remain relevant. The Thessalonians are filled with the *holy* spirit, which God gives into them. They ought, therefore, to live accordingly. Equipped with the holy spirit and a knowledge of God that their pagan neighbors do not possess, they ought to live in holiness and purity *(hagiasmos;* 4:3). They must control their own vessel in holiness *(en hagiasmō;* 4:4), for God called them not in impurity but in holiness *(en hagiasmō;* 4:7). It is not now the nation but the local community whom Paul calls to embody the values of Ezekiel's vision. Filled with a holy spirit, they cannot, they *must* not live, like their neighbors, an unholy and impure life that is characterized by sexual lack of control (4:4, 7).

The struggle for sexual control appears to be alive and well in the Thessalonian community — hence the urgency and repetition of Paul's appeal. It is not merely a matter of the past, of their turn toward faith, when they "received the word with joy inspired by the holy spirit" (1 Thess 1:6) and "turned to God from idols" (1:9). Nor is it a matter alone for the future, when the dead in Christ will rise and the living be caught up in the clouds (4:16-17). It is in the present circumstances that the Thessalonians are in danger of falling asleep (5:6), of losing control over their sexual lives, of failing to grasp God's will: their holiness.

It is the urgency of the present, the ease with which marital fidelity could be forfeited in the Roman world, that impels Paul to localize Ezekiel's vision and to tweak his own use of tenses. Instead of writing that the Thessalonians ought to be holy because God *"gave* the holy spirit in them," Paul uses the present tense: God *is giving* the holy spirit into the Thessalonians (4:8). This is a salient departure from what Paul's use of the

12. M. V. Hubbard (*New Creation in Paul's Letters and Thought.* SNTSMS 119 [Cambridge: Cambridge University Press, 2002] 117) suggests that Paul may, with the word "taught by God" *(theodidaktoi;* 4:9), combine these allusions to Ezekiel with an allusion to Jer 31:34.

expression elsewhere would lead us to expect. In other occurrences of this expression, Paul refers to a point in time in the past, presumably baptism or an equivalent moment when his readers turned to God; in the Thessalonian case, of course, this would have been the moment when they received the message of the gospel and turned to God from idols (1:5-9). When he encourages the Thessalonians to maintain a life of sexual control, however, he adopts the present tense. God continues to give the holy spirit into the Thessalonians.

There is something salutary about this. The reminder Paul proffers when the issue at hand is sexual control and the exploitation of others for sexual gratification (4:6) is not "You have been filled with the holy spirit," as if a single moment in time could suffice for an ongoing life of struggle toward holiness. The reminder consists rather of this: "You are being filled with the holy spirit." There may have been a radical conversion in the past, and there may be the hope of resurrection in the future; but at the moment the struggle for sexual purity is grounded in the *ongoing* gift of God's holy spirit into the inner being of believers.

The biological element of the spirit is paramount if we are to understand what Paul is writing. The *pneuma* is what empowers the human being, according to ancient physiology; the *pneuma* energizes the limbs and organs of the human body, including, of course, the sexual "vessel" (4:4).[13] With every breath, a human being takes in *pneuma* and exhales *pneuma* that has already coursed through the veins. Every breath is new life. Breathing is inspiration and expiration. Paul reminds the Thessalonians that the spirit they receive in an ongoing way from God is *holy*, is what energizes the limbs and organs, even the genitalia, to function in a holy way. Holiness is not a by-product of one decision in the past, one transformation already undertaken, one moment of change. Holiness — sexual holiness in particular — is a product of God's continual inbreathing of the holy spirit; a life of sexual holiness demands of believers a continual reception of the holy spirit that is no less vital than breathing.

The importance of sexual purity for Paul cannot be overestimated. He begins his instruction by identifying nothing less than the will of God with holiness, which he immediately identifies with abstention from illicit sex (4:3). He tells the Thessalonians in the harshest of terms that "the Lord is

13. See G. Verbeke, *L'Évolution de la Doctrine du* Pneuma: *du Stoicisme a S. Augustin* (Paris: Desclée de Brouwer, 1945) 175-220. The word "vessel" *(skeuos),* may possibly refer to a spouse rather than to a bodily part.

an avenger in all these things" and that he had already warned them about this beforehand (4:6). Finally, he makes it clear that the rejection of this life of sexual purity is not a rejection of "human authority but [of] God, who also gives his holy spirit into you" (4:8). God's will, God's vengeance, and God's authority are at stake in the sexual habits of believers. Yet this is not too much to ask, for God continually breathes holy life into believers, energizing them toward a life of sexual control.

The Spirit *Received*

The *giving* of the spirit, then, is rich in reminiscence, rife with the urgency of purity, and ripe with hope. The Jewish scriptures, whether the tawdry tale of Tamar or the prolific visions of Ezekiel, are never far from view. Nor is the pressing need to maintain purity in the present. Equally taut is the relationship between the spirit and the certainty of God's work in the future. It is no wonder that the simple expression "God gives the spirit" was in wide use throughout the early church.

Another simple expression, "receive [*lambanein*] the spirit," also had wide currency in the early church. Three times the Fourth Gospel refers in shorthand to "receiving the spirit" (John 7:39; 14:17; 20:22). In the final occurrence, the familiar handprint of Gen 2:7 can be found. Jesus, now raised from the dead, entered a locked room filled with his disciples, commissioned them to be sent as he was sent, and then, just as God had done to *adam* in Gen 2:7, "breathed into them," and then said to them, "Receive (the) holy spirit." His sending is now theirs. His spirit is now theirs.[14] The disciples are created anew, so very like in Gal 6:15, in which the phrase "new creation" pithily gathers together the theological pieces of Galatians, particularly those claims to the spirit that link the paragraphs of the letter, from 3:1 to 6:15.

The tenor of Acts is shaped by this phrase even more frequently than the Fourth Gospel. At pivotal junctures — Pentecost (Acts 2:33, 38), the extension of the gospel to Samaria (8:15, 17, 19), the outpouring of the spirit to Gentiles in the wake of Cornelius's vision (10:47), and the reception of the spirit by John the Baptist's disciples, who have not yet heard of the holy spirit (19:2) — this phrase tersely conveys the experience of filling with the holy spirit. These are key moments in the early history of the church, ac-

---

14. See also 1 John 2:27, which refers to receiving the anointing or charism — presumably a reference to the holy spirit.

cording to Acts, and at each pivotal point people received the spirit: Jews gathered from the Diaspora, the Samaritans, the Gentiles, and John's band of disciples. These are the ripples in the waters of early expansion that were promised at the story's beginning: "But you will receive power when the holy spirit has come upon you; and you will be my witnesses in Jerusalem, in all Judea and Samaria, and to the ends of the earth" (Acts 1:8).

Paul himself employs this expression three times, in each of which an interesting pattern emerges.[15] In a section of his letter to the Romans that is chock full of references to the spirit, he writes: "For you did not receive a spirit of slavery to fall back into fear, but you have received a spirit of adoption. When we cry, 'Abba! Father! . . .'" (Rom 8:15). The expression in his letters to the Corinthians evinces a similar sort of *not-but* frame of reference. Early in his correspondence, Paul advises, "Now we have received not the spirit of the world, but the spirit that is from God, so that we may understand the gifts bestowed on us by God" (1 Cor 2:12). Toward the end of this correspondence, he adopts this *not-but* pattern in a polemically charged indictment of the Corinthians: "For if someone comes and proclaims another Jesus than the one we proclaimed, or if you receive a different spirit from the one you received, or a different gospel from the one you accepted, you submit to it readily enough" (2 Cor 11:4). Precisely this sort of edginess, this effort to clarify both what believers have *and have not* received characterizes Paul's introduction of the spirit in his letter to the Galatians: "The only thing I want to learn from you is this: Did you receive the spirit by doing the works of the law *or* by believing what you heard?" (Gal 3:2).[16]

The pattern that defines what it means to receive the spirit has now neatly emerged. Such filling is:

not of *slavery to fear*	but of *adoption*
not the spirit of *the world*	but the spirit that is *from God*
not from doing *works*	*but by believing the message*
of the law	that was heard

15. Caution is required in terms of chronology. Paul may have been the first to coin the phrase, and it may have subsequently spread to the communities in which the Fourth Gospel and the book of Acts were composed. Whatever we can, or cannot, say about chronological priority, we must still recognize that this expression was a standard way of referring to filling with the holy spirit in early Christian literature.

16. For a discussion of earlier and later stages in the development of this expression, see F. W. Horn, *Das Angeld des Geistes: Studien zur paulinischen Pneumatologie.* FRLANT 154 (Göttingen: Vandenhoeck & Ruprecht, 1992) 64-65.

There does indeed exist another spirit, another Jesus, another gospel with different origins (the world as opposed to God), other bases (works as opposed to faith), and discordant consequences (slavery as opposed to adoption). Being filled with the spirit — receiving the spirit — according to this pattern has a specific substance and significant consequences. It is not merely an experience of euphoria or anguish, an entrée to ecstasy, a sequence of actions or emotions void of content. On the contrary, filling with the spirit is the way in which the values of the gospel are concretized, the means by which the presence of Jesus is embodied in the world. In other words, filling with the spirit is no end in itself but a venue for God's presence in the vagaries and pressures of human community. This is why it is important, in order to apprehend the contrast between old and new, between the world as it is and a new creation, not only to unravel what filling with the spirit *is,* but also to pinpoint precisely what filling with the spirit, according to the apostle, *is not.*

Not Works of Torah but Faith

In a dramatic yet disciplined diatribe, Paul appears to have grabbed a community in Asia Minor by the scruff of the neck and dragged them back to their first experience of the faith, an experience defined wholly by the spirit, a remarkable collection of experiences which he apparently thinks they have no reason to deny. In trying to wrest them from an apparently superfluous adherence to Torah and the practice of circumcision without a thorough transformation of the heart, Paul asks pugnaciously,

> The only thing I want to learn from you is this: Did you receive the spirit by doing the works of the law or by believing what you heard? Are you so foolish? Having started with the spirit, are you now ending with the flesh? Did you experience so much for nothing? — if it really was for nothing. Well then, does God supply you with the spirit and work miracles among you by your doing the works of the law, or by your believing what you heard? (Gal 3:2-5)

The bedrock of Galatian experience, from Paul's perspective, is the spirit; there is not the slightest hint that their experiences of the spirit were inauthentic or that the miracles were spurious. Nothing is open to question with respect to the spirit. Not the conviction that the life of faith took root with the spirit — "Having started with the spirit. . . ." Not the recollection that the experience was generous rather than piddling — "Did you experience *so much?*" Not even the currency of miracles — "Does God supply you with the spirit and work miracles among you?" None of this is open to doubt. What is open to question, according to Paul, is the unexpected and ill-advised Galatian departure from these reliable, unassailable, spirit-charged beginnings. Paul is apoplectic! How could the Galatians abandon such an amazing experience of the spirit in order to chase after a life of uninspired obedience?

How, in other words, could the Galatians have forgotten that they are a new creation, where "neither circumcision nor uncircumcision is anything; but a new creation is everything" (Gal 6:15)? How can their memories be so short as to have forgotten that they have received the spirit (3:3, 14; 4:6), been made alive by the spirit (3:14, 21-22), been given birth by the spirit (4:29), lived by the spirit (5:16, 25), begun to walk by the spirit (5:18, 25), and received a divine inheritance through the spirit in their hearts (4:6-7)?[17] This is indeed a good deal to forget, claims Paul, and to return to Torah-adherence and its embodiment in the rite of circumcision is utterly incomprehensible to Paul. To forfeit this life inspired by the spirit would be tantamount to denying the entirety of God's history, the whole scope of salvation:

> Christ redeemed us from the curse of the law by becoming a curse for us — for it is written, "Cursed is everyone who hangs on a tree" — in order that in Christ Jesus the blessing of Abraham might come to the nations, *so that we might receive the promise of the spirit through faith.* (Gal 3:13-14)[18]

---

17. See Hubbard, *New Creation in Paul's Letters and Thought,* 229, for further discussion.

18. It is difficult to identify which promise Paul recalls here. The promise of outpouring upon sons and daughters, old and young, male and female slaves in Joel 3:1-4(Eng. 2:28-32), which is cited in Acts 2:17-21, could be construed as a promise to the nations, though its context in Joel is centered upon Israel, and even Peter, in the Pentecost sermon in Acts, appears to interpret its fulfillment exclusively in relation to Israel (Acts 2:38-39). The reference may be more general. We have seen that Paul understands the spirit as the seal and pledge of God's promises (2 Cor 1:15-22), and the author of the letter to the Ephesians brings a lengthy opening prayer with a reference to "the seal of the promised holy spirit; this is the pledge of our inheritance toward redemption as God's own people . . ." (Eph 1:13-14). He concludes a catena of Israelite scriptures that support his mission to the nations with the prayer, "May the God of hope fill you with all joy and peace in believing, so that you may abound in hope by the power of the holy spirit" (Rom 15:13).

Despite how compelling and cogent Paul's rhetorical questions may seem, his dramatic protest that Torah and spirit do not mix is, to some extent, disingenuous. While the Galatians, tucked somewhere in Asia Minor, may not have known of them, certainly Paul was at least acquainted with the community alongside the Dead Sea that avidly embraced the coexistence of life in the spirit and rigid adherence to Torah. The *Hymns* of the Dead Sea, we have seen, absorb the language of Ezekiel 36–37 — "I will give my spirit in you" — when they describe incorporation into the community. This spiritual inheritance, the privilege of knowledge, does not belong to the hymn writer or the Teacher of Righteousness alone. This revealed knowledge is shed upon the community as well: "[Fo]r you are the God of knowledge [and] every though[t . . .] [before you.] These things we know because you have favored [us] with a h[oly] spirit" (4Q504 fr. 4 4-5). Further, in a series of blessings occurs the benediction, "May he [God] be gracious to you with a spirit of holiness . . ." (1Q28b[1QSb] II 24).

Although the community at Qumran regarded itself as spirit-filled, covenant-fulfilling, favored and blessed, such claims did not lead away from Torah but toward it, to an ultrarigorous application of Torah in the to and fro of daily life. Theirs was the ultimate interpretation of Torah (4Q266 11) which demanded of the sectarians a scrupulous and inexorable adherence to Torah. According to their charter document, departure from this strict adherence was penalized severely: ten days' banishment from the community for interrupting a companion (1QS VII 9-10); thirty days for spitting or "giggling inanely" during a meeting (1QS VII 13-14); one year for lying about possessions (1QS VI 24-25); and two years for betraying the truth and walking in a manner that Jeremiah and Ezekiel had detested, in the stubbornness of the heart (1QS VII 18-19).

It is perhaps the existence of communities such as Qumran that led Paul to repudiate the mutual interdependence of spirit-filling and Torah observance. Perhaps Paul's vehemence can be traced to his inability to tolerate the possibility that life in the spirit would lead to an errant life of scrupulous devotion to Torah with the inevitable consequence that those who failed to live up to that standard, both Jews and Gentiles, male and female, were destined to live excluded from grace.[19]

Whatever Paul's motivations for his passionate, even pugnacious, attack upon the Galatians — and those motivations are ultimately inaccessible to us — this brief journey from Asia Minor to the shores of the Dead

---

19. See further J. D. G. Dunn, *Romans 1–8*. WBC 38A (Waco: Word, 1988) 253.

Sea provides an essential datum for understanding early Christian conceptions of filling with the spirit: Christians were not alone in laying claim to this experience. The Qumran community laid claim even earlier to that experience, and such a claim undoubtedly exercised some sort of influence on Paul as he developed his own perspectives on the holy spirit. In this instance, the Qumran community combined spirit-filling with observance of Torah in so stringent a way that they created a rigidly exclusive and isolated community. This, of course, was intolerable for Paul, and he fought tooth and nail to bifurcate Torah observance from spirit-filling, perhaps because he discerned what he considered to be deleterious, even deadly, consequences, for this coexistence of claims to the spirit and vigorous adherence to an extensive list of regulations led inevitably to a rejection of outsiders who failed to live up to these standards of holiness; the priests in Jerusalem are excoriated in the Scrolls alongside the Romans, and the Pharisees derided for their laxity with the moniker Seekers of Smooth Things.[20] Such an association between the spirit *and* Torah would have undermined entirely Paul's vision of a new creation, which abolishes artificial boundaries rooted in ethnicity (circumcision and uncircumcision), gender (male and female), and citizenship (slave and free).

Not Slavery but Sonship

The Roman province of Galatia, in Asia Minor, was a vast expanse of rural richness. Its few cities, including Ancyra and Pisidian Antioch, were settled amidst farmlands rich in grain, which supplied its basic needs. Galatia's wealth, according to Strabo, derived from wool, most of which came from vast sheep farms in its southern and central regions. And, alongside grain and wool, there were vineyards ripe with grapes for wine. Tombstones from Galatia are decorated with just such elements: a yoke of oxen with plow and sickle, to represent planting and harvesting grain; a distaff and bobbin, to represent the production of yarn from wool; and a vine or bunches of grapes.[21]

Those rural hearers of Paul's letter to the Galatians would have grasped the discordance in the metaphorical contrast between slaves and sons that

20. E.g., CD I 14-21; 1QH XII 9-11. See further J. VanderKam and P. Flint, *The Meaning of the Dead Sea Scrolls* (San Francisco: HarperSanFrancisco, 2002) 276-79.

21. G. W. Hansen, "Galatians, Letter to the," in *Dictionary of Paul and His Letters*, ed. G. F. Hawthorne, R. P. Martin, and D. G. Reid (Downers Grove: InterVarsity, 1993) 326.

Paul adopts in order to accentuate the qualitative disparity that existed between works of Torah and believing with faith, between life in the flesh and life in the spirit. Rural slaves, unlike their urban counterparts, were destined to a life in the fields without any hope of manumission, void of any expectation that they would be released for good behavior or at the death of the master. These slaves knew too well the disparity that existed between their harsh and interminable labor amidst the wheat and the vines and the privileged existence of sons, who were destined to inherit their slave-labor. When Paul draws a contrast between slaves and sons, therefore, his hearers understand the difference. Whatever baptism had done for male and female, for free and slave, it did not bring liberation from inexorable and arduous labor in the fields without the slightest hope of manumission.

And such a pointed contrast Paul does indeed draw. In the climax of the letter, in which he draws a bold and unsettling correspondence between enslavement to elemental spirits and Torah itself, Paul rips apart the possibility that one can be a slave to Torah and a son with Christ:

> But when the fullness of time had come, God sent his Son, born of a woman, born under the law, in order to redeem those who were under the law, so that we might receive adoption as children. And because you are children, God has sent the spirit of his son into our hearts, crying, "Abba! Father!" So you are no longer a slave but a child, and if a child then also an heir, through God. (Gal 4:4-7)

Sonship is altogether different from slavery. Slavery is hopeless labor and unrequited toil. There is no circle of security, no intimacy, no embrace, no spirit, no life — just relentless labor. Sonship, in contrast, comes from human embrace, from a desire to extend the circle of one's family to an adopted child. The life of faith takes place within that circle, where the spirit, from deep within, propels the familial cry, "Abba! Father!"

Although Paul adopts nearly the identical metaphor in his letter to the Romans, there are subtle but substantial differences that attended its public reading. Paul writes:

> So then, brothers and sisters, we are debtors, not to the flesh, to live according to the flesh — for if you live according to the flesh, you will die; but if by the spirit you put to death the deeds of the body, you will live. For all who are led by the spirit of God are children of God. For you did not receive a spirit of slavery to fall back into fear, but you have received a

spirit of adoption. When we cry, "Abba! Father!" it is that very spirit bearing witness with our spirit that we are children of God, and if children, then heirs, heirs of God and joint heirs with Christ — if, in fact, we suffer with him so that we may also be glorified with him. (Rom 8:12-17)

The emphases of Gal 4:4-7 are here: the contrast of slavery and sonship; adoption; the cry, "Abba! Father!"; and the inheritance believers receive as heirs. Other aspects of Galatians are also here, including the sharp contrast between flesh and spirit (Gal 5:21-22). There is so much the same that it would seem that Paul has preserved fragments of his letter to the Galatians and inserted them here — the ancient equivalent of our word-processing, our cutting and pasting.

These striking similarities notwithstanding, there are substantial differences, both unwritten and written, between Paul's recipients in Galatia and in Rome. First is that the metaphor of slavery may not have had the same punch in Rome as it did in Galatia. Galatia was rural, Rome urban. The Galatians, as we noted, would have felt deeply the harshness of the contrast with slaves who labored without hope of manumission. When the Galatians, therefore, heard the words of Gal 5:1, they would have understood precisely how absurd a return to slavery would have been, given that slavery was inexorable and permanent: "For freedom Christ has set us free. Stand firm, therefore, and do not submit again to a yoke of slavery." By comparing Torah obedience to slavery in a rural environment, Paul underlines the absurdity of returning to a life of involuntary adherence to ordinances. Even his rare use of the perfect periphrastic tense, which emphasizes the ongoing and continual nature of an act or state of being in Gal 4:3, is an exclamation point to this thought: "So with us; while we were minors, we were *being* enslaved [*ēmetha dedoulōmenoi*] to the elemental spirits of the world." Who could possibly choose this hopeless existence? Who could possibly choose a life of obedience to Torah? The Galatians must be positively bewitched if they intend to return to their permanent and relentless slave status.

In all likelihood, the metaphor of slavery in Romans 8 would have been powerful in a different way, particularly since Paul's readers in Rome may actually have seen the dramatic transference from slavery to social standing by means of manumission. There were still wide gaps between the rights of sonship and the property status of slaves. But it was in the city that Seneca urged masters to treat their slaves well, in the urban centers where ideas about the humanity of slaves were bandied about (*Moral Epistles* 47). Though never recommending complete manumission of all slaves, someone like Seneca could ridicule greedy slaveowners, praise skilled slaves (47.10), and acknowledge that one's slave "sprang from the same stock, is smiled upon by the same skies, and on equal terms with yourself breathes, lives, and dies." Although Seneca never goes so far as "offering the liberty-cap [of manumission] to slaves in general and toppling down lords from their high estate," he contemplates a world in which slaves are able to "respect their masters instead of fearing them" (47.17-18). Urban slaves could hold forth the hope of manumission, of being freed either during the life of the master, for long or meritorious service, or at the death of the master. Tombstones that portray the funeral procession of wealthy Romans occasionally contain the image of a grieving slave who is wearing what Seneca refers to as a liberty-cap, which symbolizes manumission.[22]

The second difference is that the master who enslaves human beings in Romans does not represent a misguided form of Torah-obedience but something to which Paul made no reference in Galatians: fear. Believers have not received a "spirit of slavery again to fear." This terse, verbless phrase is rich with both significance and puzzlement. What baffles is that fear is, in general, something quite positive for Paul. God is typically the object of fear or reverence (Rom 3:18; 11:20; 2 Cor 5:11; 7:1), and the empire too is the proper object of respect (Rom 13:3, 4, 7). Though Paul was unfortunately compelled to approach the Corinthians in this way, "fear and trembling" is also a suitable way to welcome auspicious guests (1 Cor 2:3; 2 Cor 7:15) and the right way to work out one's salvation (Phil 2:12). Paul includes fear in an odd list of virtues by which the Corinthians proved themselves guiltless: "eagerness to clear yourselves, indignation, alarm, longing, zeal, and punishment." It is only in 2 Cor 7:5 that the word "fear" is unequivocally undesirable: "For even when we came into Macedonia, our bodies had no rest, but we were afflicted in every way — disputes without and fears within."

Paul does not define the object of fear. Such imprecision would seem even to be deliberate, since the mastery of fear then functions as a magnet for the various objects of fear that raise their heads in this portion of his letter. What, in this context, is the fear to which a spirit of slavery, in contrast to a spirit of adoption, leads? Is it enslavement to a fear of condemnation (Rom 8:1, 34)? Slavery to a fear of death (8:11, 38)? A fear of suffering

---

22. See J. M. C. Toynbee, *Death and Burial in the Roman World* (Ithaca: Cornell University Press, 1971) 45; A. C. Rush, *Death and Burial in Christian Antiquity* (Washington: Catholic University of America Press, 1941) 192; T. Wiedemann, *Greek and Roman Slavery* (London: Routledge, 1981) 45-60; and J. R. Levison, "The Roman Character of Funerals in the Writings of Josephus," *JSJ* 33 (2002) 271.

(8:18, 35-36)? Or does Paul delay disclosure of the object of fear until the climax of this chapter, in which he raises many sources of fear:

> If God is for us, who is against us? . . . Who will bring any charge against God's elect? . . . Who is to condemn? Who will separate us from the love of Christ? Will hardship, or distress, or persecution, or famine, or nakedness, or peril, or sword? . . . For I am convinced that neither death, nor life, nor angels, nor rulers, nor things present, nor things to come, nor powers, nor height, nor depth, nor anything else in all creation, will be able to separate us from the love of God in Christ Jesus our Lord. (8:31b, 33a, 34a, 35, 38-39)

Anxieties and apprehensions — what Paul in 2 Cor 7:5 calls "fears within" — can capture and enslave people, encircling them within an inescapable fear of worry and want, of abandonment by God, of separation from the love of Christ.

The spirit of adoption which believers have received, in contrast, belongs to a different sphere, a sphere of familial security, a sphere in which a believer can cry out intimately and boldly, "Abba! Father!" These very words resonate with Jesus' experience of the Father, with the model prayer he taught the disciples, and with a heritage of hymnody in which God pledges covenant loyalty, steadfast love, to David:

> "My faithfulness and steadfast love shall be with him;
>   and in my name his horn shall be exalted.
> I will set his hand on the sea
>   and his right hand on the rivers.
> He shall cry to me, 'You are my Father,
>   my God, and the Rock of my salvation!'
> I will make him the firstborn,
>   the highest of the kings of the earth.
> Forever I will keep my steadfast love for him,
>   and my covenant with him will stand firm.
> I will establish his line forever,
>   and his throne as long as the heavens endure." (Ps 89:24-29)[23]

All of the sensations of being a slave, of subsisting as property without rights, consigned to a life without any assurances, are banished when the

---

23. See also 4Q372 I 16.

spirit of adoption brings manumission and transference to a world of privilege, kinship, and irrevocable love.

Though it may not be possible to demonstrate conclusively that Paul's experience influenced his description of the spirits of slavery and adoption, we can be certain that Paul himself grasped at first hand the dramatic difference between the property status of slavery and the status of sonship. His awareness comes to the fore in a personal letter to his dear friend Philemon, the owner of Onesimus, a slave who had come to faith while in the company of Paul. Paul makes his appeal for the manumission of Philemon, in part, by recasting the relationship between Philemon, himself, and Onesimus in familial rather than social terms. Paul twice addresses Philemon directly as brother (Phlm 7, 20).[24] More significantly, Paul claims to have become the father of the slave Onesimus: "I am appealing to you for my child, whom I have given birth to in my imprisonment, Onesimus" (v. 10). This is a stunning metaphor for conversion, one that Paul appears to have taken quite literally, as if he loves Onesimus so deeply that he has *adopted* him. Onesimus is no mere slave, no property to be calculated for worth, no symbol of social status. He is Paul's child; Paul is his father.

As if it were not intimate enough for Paul to refer to Onesimus as his child and to himself as the child's father, Paul muses that Onesimus left Philemon for a while in order to be returned in a familial relationship to him: "Perhaps this is the reason he was separated from you for a while, so that you might have him back forever, no longer as a slave but more than a slave, a beloved brother — especially to me but how much more to you, both in the flesh and in the Lord" (vv. 15-16). This is no weak suggestion. This is no mere metaphor. This is not just literary imagery. Such a redefinition of the relationship between Philemon and Onesimus is a clear indication that they can be brothers, actual brothers, not only through a shared faith but through a shared flesh.

In light of his letter to Philemon, in which the master-slave relationship can be transformed into a relationship of brothers "in the flesh," we ought to recognize that the "spirit of slavery into fear" is more than an image of estrangement. If the transformation from slave to brother or son occurs in

24. Paul develops key values that he introduces in his thanksgiving, which functions as a *captatio benevolentiae* in the letter: love (vv. 5, 7, 9); good (vv. 6, 14); fellowship (vv. 6, 17); and heart (vv. 7, 12, 20). This thanksgiving provides a crucible of sorts in which Paul appeals to Philemon on an intimate emotional level. The letter is, in fact, a masterpiece of persuasion — a successful one, given the reference to an active Onesimus in Col 4:9 — not by means of logic but through the appeal of intimacy.

the flesh, there is no reason to believe other than that Paul understands the spirit of slavery as a force which operates in the flesh, that is, as a real and relentless power which induces profound fear. Those who have received that spirit live edged about by fear, permeated by anxiety, filled with apprehension, as if they are breathing polluted air. The "spirit of adoption" is no less real. Paul knows at first hand that Philemon and Onesimus, Paul's child, can become brothers both in the flesh and the Lord. By the same token, a believer is no longer filled with a spirit of slavery when he or she receives a spirit of adoption. The transfer is real for Paul, as real as the air one breathes, as palpable as the fears that confine and the hope that liberates.

As he did in his letters to the Corinthians, Paul understands filling with the spirit in terms that are earthy, with vocabulary that is more at home in gross anatomy than spiritual handbooks. His evocative use of the word "seal" to describe the spirit in 2 Cor 1:22 is redolent of the tawdry tale of Tamar and Judah, as well as the love affair in the Song of Songs, of sexual awakening, of fierce passion that is stronger than death. His claim that God has sent the spirit of his son into human hearts in Gal 4:6 to make children and heirs out of believers, rather than slaves, consists of language that may not be far from the language of sexual intercourse, as it was understood in Roman antiquity, where sperm travelled through *pneuma* into a woman's body.[25] His comparison in Rom 8:12-17 between the spirit of slavery that leads to fear and the spirit of adoption that leads to the cry "Abba! Father!" is no convenient description of the ethereal process of conversion. Both spirits are real. The one fills a human being with anxiety and apprehension from which there is no self-liberation. The other fills a human being with security and family devotion. The one treats its subject like property, driving it to fear; the other grants its subject humanity and humaneness, leading it to prayer. In light of his letter to Philemon, it appears that Paul means this in literal terms; if slavery and adoption are metaphors, they are not mere metaphors.

Being filled with the spirit, therefore, from Paul's perspective, is not a spiritual transformation that takes place on a sphere other than the human and earthy. It is not an experience that transpires without a radical revision of reality. His language prohibits that sort of interpretation. Filling with the

---

25. Various background studies include A. Preus, "Galen's Criticism of Aristotle's Conception Theory," *Journal of the History of Biology* 10 (1977) 65-85; M. Boylan, "Galen's Conception Theory," *Journal of the History of Biology* 19 (1986) 47-77; and T. Laqueur, *Making Sex: Body and Gender from the Greeks to Freud* (Cambridge: Harvard University Press, 1990) 41-42.

spirit, on the contrary, renders the spirits of this world obsolete (Gal 4:3), restructures human relationships (Gal 4:4-7; Rom 8:12-17; and Philemon), and causes the hegemony of fear to disintegrate (Rom 8:15). The sealing, sending, and receiving of the spirit convey the transformation of a slave into a human subject, into a son or daughter. This is a jarring experience that turns a property owner and his or her property into brothers and sisters, that supplants a spirit of lifelong anxiety with a fresh influx of familial embrace, and that produces a passionate love affair stronger than death.

Not the Spirit of the World but the Spirit from God

When Paul affirms that believers have "received" the spirit, we have noticed, he does so typically by way of contrast. Believers have received the spirit by faith rather than by scrupulous obedience to the ordinances of Torah. This is so because they have received a spirit of adoption, which leads to the cry "Abba! Father!" rather than a spirit of slavery that leads to fear. In his earliest extant letter to the Corinthians, he draws a similar contrast: believers have received the spirit from God rather than the spirit of the world. This contrast, more than the others, occurs in a context that is propelled by defensiveness, dripping with sarcasm, and resplendent with irony, to the extent that it is difficult to determine whether Paul is writing straightforwardly, whether he is adopting his Corinthian opponents' language to undermine their position, or whether he is adopting his Corinthian allies' language to affirm it. Are the "spiritual ones," the *pneumatikoi,* a group to be emulated, or are they Corinthian elitists whom Paul derides because they unjustifiably claim the finest spiritual gifts and insight for themselves? While his letter is undoubtedly comprehensible to the Corinthians, barbed though it is, its razor sharp tone makes it extremely difficult for us to interpret.

Paul launches this section of his letter by recalling that he came to Corinth without rhetorical polish and pedantry, that he approached the Corinthians with weakness, fear, and trembling. This self-deprecation, which by implication should be the attitude of the Corinthians, few of whom were educated and socially privileged (1 Cor 1:18-31), leads Paul to a contrast: "My speech and my proclamation were not with plausible words of wisdom, but with a demonstration of the spirit and of power, so that your faith might rest not on human wisdom but on the power of God" (2:4-5). What does Paul suggest about the spirit by associating it with the power of God in this context? Elsewhere in his letters, this power produces hope (Rom 5:5; 15:19; 2 Cor 1:21-22), and it is the source of signs and wonders, as in Rom 15:19, where Paul describes the obedience of the nations that has been won by word and deed, "by the power of signs and wonders, by the power of the spirit of God" (see Gal 3:5). This power is full of conviction in hearers, as in the case of the Thessalonians, to whom he writes, "our message of the gospel came to you not in word only, but also in power and in the holy spirit and with full conviction" (1 Thess 1:5).

While Paul believes that the spirit brought hope, effected signs and wonders, and produced conviction in hearers, the primary lesson of 1 Corinthians 2 is that the content of his message — and not just the demeanor of the messenger or the response of the hearers or attendant miraculous activities — consists of weakness: "For I decided to know nothing among you except Jesus Christ, and him crucified" (1 Cor 2:2). The spirit is what provides the *content* of the message; it is the *message* of the cross that "God has revealed to us through the spirit" (2:10). It is the cross that the rulers of this age cannot grasp. It is the cross that lies at the heart of God, where the spirit searches, from which the truest wisdom arises (2:11). It is this cross that the spirit, which "comprehends what is truly God's," transforms into a powerful message.

For this reason, Paul portrays the spirit in this discussion of wisdom and weakness as a revealer (1 Cor 2:10-11) and teacher (2:12-13) who has intimate access to God's deepest concerns.[26] It is not merely the demeanor of the messenger or the miracles accompanying Paul's speeches that the rulers and rhetoricians of this age cannot apprehend. They simply cannot grasp that God's power can be demonstrated in the weakness of the cross. That is, unbelievers simply cannot accept the *central content* of the gospel. This is the content that the spirit reveals; this is the lesson that the spirit teaches. This revelation dawns slowly even upon Paul, spirit-filled and tongues-speaking and miracle-working Paul, who three times prayed for relief from a messenger in the flesh, and who heard God say, "My grace is sufficient for you, for power is made perfect in weakness" (2 Cor 12:9). It was not as an initiate that Paul learned this lesson, it would seem, but as an experienced believer, who learned to say, through God's denial of his request, "So, I will boast all the more gladly of my weaknesses, so that the power of Christ may dwell in me" (12:9).

With this contrast between the spirit of the world and the spirit that comes from God, Paul addresses something other than what he has ad-

26. See further Fee, *God's Empowering Presence*, 98-99.

dressed elsewhere by way of contrast. He questioned the Galatians about their reception of the spirit and whether obedience to Torah or the spirit produced miracles. In other words, he challenged them about their *experience* of the spirit. In his letter to the Romans he drew a contrast between a spirit of slavery that leads to fear and a spirit of adoption that leads to intimate prayer. This too has specifically to do with *experience*. Yet the contrast between the spirit of the world and the spirit of God leads away from the arena of experience and toward the cross-centered *content* of Paul's preaching. Paul appears to recognize how easy it may be to lose sight of the content of preaching in the presence of powerful experiences of miracles. However, to allow an overpowering *experience* of the spirit, however wholesome it may appear to be, to eclipse the importance of *content* is to truncate the work of the spirit that is from God, for this spirit is no less a revealer and a teacher than it is the inspirer of miracles and the source of an experience of adoption.

The sort of dichotomy between these two spirits with which Paul frames reality has a parallel — an inexact one, admittedly — in the Teaching on the Two Spirits in the *Community Rule*.[27] The teaching contrasts, not unlike 1 Corinthians, a spirit of truth with a spirit of deceit. The discordant arenas over which they exercise control are marked by darkness and light, deceit and truth. The faithful who live in the sphere of the truth have:

> a spirit of meekness, of patience, generous compassion, eternal goodness, intelligence, understanding, potent wisdom which trusts in all the deeds of God and depends on his abundant mercy; a spirit of knowledge in all the plans of action, of enthusiasm for the decrees of justice, of holy plans with firm purpose. . . . These are the foundations of the spirit of the sons of truth (in) the world. (1QS IV 3-6)

In contrast,

> to the spirit of deceit belong greed, sluggishness in the service of justice, wickedness, falsehood, pride, haughtiness of heart, dishonesty, trickery,

---

27. From the start, however, there is a difference. Although the Teaching on the Two Spirits in 1QS III–IV envisages two opposing groups of people, it also assumes the presence of a good and an evil spirit that wrestle against one another *within* a human being from the moment of creation. Paul instead conceives of two groups of people: some humans who receive the spirit of the world, whether at birth or sometime later, and others who receive the spirit from God sometime later than birth. There is no apparent battle from birth in the human heart, at least according to 1 Corinthians 2.

cruelty, much insincerity, impatience, much foolishness, impudent enthusiasm for appalling acts performed in a lustful passion, filthy paths
in the service of impurity, blasphemous tongue, blindness of eyes, hardness of hearing, stiffness of neck, hardness of heart in order to walk in
all the paths of darkness and evil cunning. (1QS IV 9-11)

Though the comparison between 1 Corinthians 2 and the Teaching on the
Two Spirits begs all sorts of questions about the complicated nature of the
two spirits in 1QS III–IV, it is nonetheless instructive, particularly when it
is set against a text such as Gal 5:19-23:

> Now the works of the *flesh* are obvious: fornication, impurity, licen-
> tiousness, idolatry, sorcery, enmities, strife, jealousy, anger, quarrels, dis-
> sensions, factions, envy, drunkenness, carousing, and things like these. I
> am warning you, as I warned you before: those who do such things will
> not inherit the kingdom of God. By contrast, the fruit of the *spirit* is
> love, joy, peace, patience, kindness, generosity, faithfulness, gentleness,
> and self-control. There is no law against such things.[28]

The contrast between "fleshly people" *(sarkinos)* and "spiritual people"
(pneumatikos) in 1 Corinthians 2–3 is hardly less stark.

The correspondence between the Teaching on the Two Spirits and
Paul's letter to the Corinthians serves powerfully to illuminate the either-
or character of Paul's formulation, in which there is no neutral sphere between the old and new creations, no area of overlap between the spirit of
the world and the spirit that is from God. There is no safe-zone in which
people can find refuge. Consequently, the neutral territory the Corinthians
attempt to occupy does not exist. If the Corinthians attempt to hold on to
penultimate values while claiming to belong in a community of ultimate
truths, they forfeit the latter and retain only the former: "Now we have received not the spirit of the world, but the spirit that is from God, so that we
may understand the gifts bestowed on us by God" (1 Cor 2:12).

---

28. The difference in vocabulary — Paul's use of "the flesh" as opposed to a spirit of deceit — is negligible, for, in the Qumran *Hymns,* descriptions of the "spirit of flesh" (1QH IV
25; V 4) unmistakably resemble 1 Corinthians 2: "In the mysteries of your insight [you] have
apportioned all these things, to make your glory known. [However, what is] the spirit of
flesh to understand all these matters and to have insight in [your wondrous] and great counsel? What is someone born of a woman among all your awesome works? He is a structure of
dust fashioned with water, his counsel is the [iniquity] of sin, shame of dishonor and
so[urce of] impurity, and a depraved spirit rules over him" (V 19-22).

Yet there is a considerable distance separating Paul's conception of two spirits from the two spirits in the Teaching on the Two Spirits. The dark and demonic nature of the spirit of deceit is out of all proportion to Paul's construal of the spirit of the world. The "spirit from the world" seems to be precisely that, a spirit that gives the world its values, values that reject the weakness of the cross. Paul does not characterize the spirit of the world as particularly deceitful and vile; it is simply what it means to be merely a human rather than a spirit-from-God-filled human. The word "world," which Paul adopts to describe the "spirit of the world," is not even a particularly negative term for Paul.[29] The "wisdom of the world," which God has made to look foolish, is the best the world has to offer; Paul does not characterize it as especially evil or enslaved to a spirit of darkness (1 Cor 1:20). It is, in fact, from this world that the low and despised believers at Corinth have come (1 Cor 1:27-28). Those who are filled with the spirit of the world have not succumbed to a dark and demonic influence. They simply cannot understand the mysteries of God's insight, God's counsel.

The tragedy for Paul has less to do with those who have received the spirit of the world than with the Corinthians who, although they have received God's spirit, still act is if they have received the spirit of the world. They are a people that look as if they are still — to use the Qumran hymn writer's terms — ruled by a spirit of deceit. Because of their rivalries and quarreling, the Corinthians revel in their unfortunate status as fleshly people, although they should be spiritual people: "And so, brothers and sisters, I could not speak to you as spiritual people, but rather as people of the flesh, as infants in Christ" (1 Cor 3:1). Preoccupied by penultimate rivalries, they simply fail to grasp what only the spirit can teach, that the truest revelation of God finds its focus nowhere else than in the cross of Jesus Christ.

A New Temple[30]

When Paul raises the specter that the Corinthians ought to be more than a discordant band of converts, when he urges them to become more than a frayed knot of believers, when he pummels them for the penultimate rival-

---

29. E.g., Rom 11:12, 15.

30. Some of this study of the new temple appeared in J. R. Levison, "The Spirit and the Temple in Paul's Letters to the Corinthians," in *Paul and His Theology,* ed. S. E. Porter (Leiden: Brill, 2006) 189-215.

ries that preoccupy them, he does so by way of reminder: "Do you not know that you are God's temple and that God's spirit dwells in you? If anyone destroys God's temple, God will destroy that person. For God's temple is holy, and you are that temple" (1 Cor 3:16-17). In Paul's letters, the introductory phrase "Do you not know?" consistently reminds his readers of something that they presumably *ought* to know but apparently *fail* to remember.[31] What this means is that the image of the church as a holy temple does not arise from Paul's imagination or the urgency of the situation; he apparently already adopted this metaphor, which may have circulated in the early church, in his preaching, or in a prior letter.[32] The importance of this metaphor is apparent further when he puts it to good use a second time as he deals with the matter of illicit sexual behavior that arises from the faulty assumption, which some of the Corinthians apparently hold, that all things are lawful for them (6:12). In this context, he reminds his recalcitrant community yet again: "Or do you not know that your body is a temple of the holy spirit within you, which you have from God, and that you are not your own? For you were bought with a price; therefore glorify God in your body" (6:19). This metaphor features once more in still another letter that Paul writes to the Corinthians. Set in a series of rhetorical questions that are baffling because of their combative tenor, Paul asks, "For what partnership is there between righteousness and lawlessness? Or what fellowship is there between light and darkness? What agreement does Christ have with Beliar? Or what does a believer share with an unbeliever? What agreement has the temple of God with idols?" (2 Cor 6:14b-16a).[33]

These texts are rich, not only with the resonance of metaphor, but with the residue of communal misunderstanding. From each of the three occurrences in the Corinthian correspondence will emerge, in differing degrees, two distinctive characteristics of this metaphor: its power to communicate the need for unity as well as the indispensability of holiness. Both play piv-

---

31. E.g., 1 Cor 5:6; 6:2, 3, 9, 15, 16, 19; 9:13, 24.

32. W. Schrage (*1 Kor 1,1–6,11.* vol. 1 of *Der erste Brief an die Korinther.* EKK 7/1 [Neukirchen: Neukirchener, 1991] 288) supposes that the conception of the indwelling God Paul may have inherited from the early church, in part because it became relatively widespread in early Christianity (e.g., Eph 2:21-22; 1 Pet 2:5; *Barn* 6:15; 16:6-10; Ignatius, *Letter to the Ephesians* 9.1). Paul adopts such language in a different context in Rom 8:9, 11. If Paul referred to the Corinthians in this way earlier, it may have been in the prior letter he mentions in 1 Cor 5:9. On a pre-Pauline origin of the indwelling motif in hellenistic Judaism and early hellenistic-Jewish Christianity, see Horn, *Das Angeld des Geistes,* 62-76.

33. It appears again in Eph 2:21-22.

otal roles in Paul's adoption of the metaphor twice in 1 Corinthians. The scenario becomes more complicated, however, in 2 Corinthians, where Paul dispenses with his plea for unity and presses instead for holiness. Although the metaphor communicates unity and holiness, in each of these occurrences it is possessed of its own peculiar stamp, and so we shall, in this study, identify both what these three texts have in common and what gives the metaphor of the temple in each of them its distinctive hues.

A Foundation Well Laid, a Spirit-Filled Temple (1 Cor 3:16-17)

In the first portion of his first letter to the Corinthians, Paul's appeal to the holiness of the temple, filled as it is with God's spirit, is nothing less than a frontal critique of the splintering tendencies of those who shatter the church by their failure to appreciate and to appropriate the unifying presence of Christ in their midst.[34] The issue to which Paul has devoted the bulk of his letter to this point is the divisiveness of the church, the problem of divided and misguided allegiances to figures such as Apollos, Peter, even Paul himself. The way Paul structures his statements about the temple suggests that these divisions, casual membership with cliques, or informal alliances based upon alleged claims to wisdom, are anything but tolerable, casual, and informal modes of living in community. On the contrary, the disruption of unity is a direct attack upon the church:

Do you not know

A: that you are God's temple[35] and
   that God's spirit dwells in you?
B: If anyone destroys [damages][36] God's temple, God will

---

34. Paul introduces the principal issue of schisms early in the letter, directly following one of his typical benedictions: "Now I appeal to you, brothers and sisters, by the name of our Lord Jesus Christ, that all of you be in agreement and that there be no divisions among you, but that you be united in the same mind and the same purpose. For it has been reported to me by Chloe's people that there are quarrels among you" (1 Cor 1:10-11).

35. Paul refers to the temple as *naos* rather than *hieros*. Though *naos* often refers to the inner sanctuary rather than the temple as a whole, word usage is by no means consistent, and so it is unwise to extrapolate from Paul's use of *naos* rather than *hieros*. See J. R. Lanci, *A New Temple for Corinth: Rhetorical and Archaeological Approaches to Pauline Imagery* (New York: Peter Lang, 1997) 91-93.

36. On the plausible interpretation of *phtheirein* in reference to the damage rather than complete destruction of a building, see Lanci, *A New Temple for Corinth*, 67-68. The issue

destroy that person.

A¹: For God's temple is holy, and you are that temple.

Sandwiched between two two-part affirmations of the church as "God's temple" (A and A¹) is a judgment made in legal, or casuistic, form. This legal form is also familiar from Torah. "If someone leaves a pit open . . . and an ox or a donkey falls into it, the owner of the pit shall make restitution" (Exod 21:33-34a).[37] This casuistic form of legal discourse indicates that clear consequences follow from concrete crimes, *even inadvertent ones,* such as neglecting to cover a pit. Paul's adoption of the casuistic form of legal discourse underwrites the gravity of the situation at Corinth. The Corinthians' lack of awareness of consequences does not exonerate them; they have dug a pit of dissension, so to speak, into which they have fallen, and they will pay the penalty. The cliques at Corinth, in other words, are not casual but criminal.

And the penalty is extraordinary. While a man who has sexual intercourse with his father's wife — immorality that outstrips the most vulgar of pagan sexual practice — receives the penalty only of temporary ostracism (1 Cor 5:1-8), the dividers of the church are subject to destruction or severe damage, torn apart as they have torn apart the church.[38] Paul has unequivocally laid down the gauntlet. The Corinthians must stop destroying God's unified temple through cliques and quarrels or else they will be destroyed. It is inconceivable that the spirit of God should dwell in a portion of the holy of holies without filling the whole of it. God's spirit does not dwell in the midst of pockets of the church; its presence is not sequestered among those cliques with a peculiar claim to superior wisdom. Those who attempt to

---

raised by this interpretation concerns the so-called destruction of those who damage God's temple. Are they destroyed or just damaged? One could argue, I suppose, that this fits well the odd notion that the builder will be saved (i.e., only damaged), as through fire, though his or her work will be destroyed.

37. E. Käsemann ("Sätze heiligen Rechts im Neuen Testament," in *Exegetische Versuche und Besinnungen* [Göttingen: Vandenhoeck & Ruprecht, 1964] 2:69-71) has suggested that this was a sentence of holy law delivered by an early Christian prophet. Against Käsemann, see K. Berger, "Zu den sogenannten Sätzen Heiligen Rechts," *NTS* 17 (1970-71) 10-40.

38. It may be that Paul has here resorted to language and ideas that are familiar from Qumran documents. The cognate noun "destroy" *(šḥt)* occurs in the Dead Sea Scrolls of "men of destruction" who, because they are bent on ruining the community, are liable to eternal destruction (e.g., 1QS IX 16). See B. E. Gärtner, *The Temple and the Community in Qumran and the New Testament.* SNTSMS 1 (Cambridge: Cambridge University Press, 1965) 59-60. The verb *phtheirein* is used elsewhere by Paul in 2 Cor 11:3; see also Eph 4:22.

create a spiritual provincialism, sanctified subdivisions, are doing dire damage to the fabric of the church, according to Paul, for whom a parcelling of the spirit is an utterly unacceptable state of affairs.

Paul's ability to *remind* the Corinthians that they are a living temple, the readiness with which he is able to recall rather than to introduce the metaphor, suggests that it was embedded in the tradition he conveyed to them.[39] Certainly there was no lack of temples, and incense filling them, at Corinth, and we know from 2 Corinthians 8–9, taken in tandem with Rom 15:25-26, that Paul held the impoverished believers in Jerusalem close to his heart, so much so that he wanted to bring an offering to them. It is hard to imagine that Paul spoke or wrote about Jerusalem without reference to the temple. In Romans 9, for instance, where he lists the qualities of the Jews, he includes temple worship (9:4).

How early the metaphor of the church as a living temple emerged is impossible to pinpoint, though we discovered in the charter document of the Qumran community, the *Community Rule,* that a community of isolated Palestinian Jews of the Roman era considered themselves to be a living temple whose spiritual worship and holy life had supplanted the Jerusalem temple. The community, we may recall, is to "make atonement for all who freely volunteer for holiness in Aaron and for the house of truth in Israel." They are, then, a living temple, the "house of Israel," which exercises the priestly vocation of "atonement" (1QS V 5-6).[40] Their leaders, the community council, are characterized as precisely what Paul wants the Co-

---

39. This metaphor is not unrelated to the metaphors of planting and building that precede it in 1 Cor 3:5-15. As a background to this combination of planting and building, see possibly Jer 1:10; 12:16. It has also been suggested that the various elements which are destroyed may be influenced by descriptions of the construction of the temple of Solomon in 1 Chr 29:2; also 22:14-16. If this is so, then the transition to the temple metaphor would have been effortless. See A. C. Thiselton, *The First Epistle to the Corinthians.* NIGTC (Grand Rapids: Wm. B. Eerdmans, 2000) 311.

40. Fee (*God's Empowering Presence,* 114-15), while offering a concise survey of the foreground of 1 Cor 3:16-17, surprisingly makes no reference to the Dead Sea Scrolls. Whether Paul was influenced by such a community we, of course, cannot say with certainty, though the correspondences are striking. Since this conception of the church may have been pre-Pauline, it may be that the early Palestinian community was familiar with these conceptions or, in some way, shared these convictions with the devotees at Qumran. I do not intend to suggest with this comparison that Paul sought to replace the Jerusalem temple with a living temple. On the question of whether a replacement of the temple was meant or whether there is more simply a transfer of language in the Dead Sea Scrolls and 1 Corinthians, see J. R. Lanci, *A New Temple for Corinth,* 7-19.

rinthian church to become. They are "an everlasting plantation, a holy house for Israel and the foundation of the holy of holies for Aaron, true witnesses for the judgment and chosen by the will (of God) to atone for the land . . ." (1QS VIII 5-6).[41] This community is a "precious cornerstone," "the most holy dwelling of Aaron . . . a house of perfection and truth in Israel" (VIII 7, 9). The inhabitants of this desert enclave claim to exist "in order to establish the spirit of holiness in truth eternal, in order to atone for the guilt of iniquity and for the unfaithfulness of sin, and for approval for the earth, without the flesh of burnt offerings and without the fats of sacrifice," for they are "a holy house for Aaron, in order to form a most holy community, and a house of the Community for Israel, those who walk in perfection" (1QS IX 3-6).[42]

The profundity of the spirit in these passages lies in its communal character. The spirit exists in the *community* in a way that transcends individual believers. It is the community, not merely a collection of spirit-filled individuals, that establishes the spirit of holiness. The Corinthians, in contrast, are a fragmented community of cliques and individuals whose place in the communal hierarchy is determined by the alleged worth of the spiritual gifts each exercises (1 Corinthians 12–14). Further, this spirit is associated with concrete content, with *eternal truth*. The Corinthians, with their penchant for speaking in tongues, their prepossession toward an experience that entails an "unproductive mind" (1 Cor 14:14), are unlike a community that associates the spirit with truth. And finally, this spirit is actively at work in the process of purification. The spirit is a spirit of *holiness*, whose task is to bring holiness to bear upon the community and, in this text, to the whole earth. It is a spirit that by nature purifies and atones. The shameless episodes in their communal life that Paul is compelled to address suggest that the Corinthians have little conception of the ways in which holiness takes shape in day-to-day existence.

These elements reappear, we observed already, in a pivotal description of the annual covenant renewal ceremony, in which new members were taken into the community at Qumran (1QS I 21–III 12):

41. On the likelihood that this passage characterizes the council at one and the same time as paradise and temple, as both a planting and a building — two metaphors for the church that lead up to the language of spirit-filled temple — see Gärtner, *The Temple and the Community,* 27-30.

42. On a similar combination of conceptions in *4QFlorilegium,* see Gärtner, *The Temple and the Community,* 30-42.

For it is by the spirit of the true counsel of God that are atoned the paths of man, all his iniquities, so that he can look at the light of life. And it is by the holy spirit of the community, in its truth, that he is cleansed of all his iniquities. And by the spirit of uprightness and of humility his sin is atoned. And by the compliance of his soul with all the laws of God his flesh is cleansed by being sprinkled with cleansing waters and being made holy with the waters of repentance. (1QS III 6-9)

Again, the reality of the spirit's existence in the community as a whole rather than simply within individuals is lost to the Corinthians, among whom rampant rivalries and cliques thrive. They are not the locus of a spirit of holiness that provides unity beyond what a collection of spirit-filled individuals can concoct. Paul expends enormous energy to counteract this perspective and to communicate that they are an organic whole — a temple, a body, a new covenant community. They are not just a collection of individuals who can benignly coexist in cliques.

Alongside this communal dimension is, as earlier in the *Community Rule,* the matter of content. At Qumran, there is "the holy spirit of the community" into which individuals are absorbed, to whose instruction individuals must submit. This spirit exhibits clear qualities: true counsel or teaching, uprightness, humility, and, above all, holiness. The Corinthians have failed to appropriate such qualities as these. There is resistance to Paul's instruction, hubris rather than humility, and a moral laxity that puts pagans to shame in its rejection of holiness. The Corinthian church, in other words, is no temple at all; it is a splintered collection of individuals and cliques who regard individual spirit-filling as a basis for establishing a spiritual hierarchy.

In these instructions from Qumran, there is also the matter of the relationship between inner and outer purification. It is clear from this text that moral or inner cleansing was an indispensable companion of cleansing with water. Anyone who refused to undergo this covenant renewal would not "be purified by the cleansing waters . . . nor shall he be purified by all the water of ablution" (1QS III 4-5). No amount of physical cleansing could make any difference if a person was stubborn and untaught by the community as a whole, if they were not cleansed by the holy spirit of the community. This emphasis upon holiness and purity is fundamental as well to Paul's vision of the living temple. After identifying the church as a plant, a building, and finally, a temple, and after setting forth the punishment that fits the crime of damaging or destroying the church with schisms and quarreling, Paul then describes the sanctity of that temple: "for God's temple is holy, and you are that temple" (1 Cor 3:17). This is no new element in the letter, the twenty-first word (1 Cor 1:2) of which is "sanctified" *(hēgiasmenois)*. The further emphasis in the *Community Rule* upon both inner and outer purification resonates with the words with which Paul concludes another discussion of the church as a spirit-filled temple in 2 Cor 6:14–7:1: "Since we have these promises, beloved, let us cleanse ourselves from *every defilement of body and of spirit,* making *holiness* perfect in the fear of God" (7:1). Paul offers here a perfect précis of the teaching on the spirit that is encapsulated by the *Community Rule* — whether or not he is familiar with the text itself. This is the quintessential expression of the need for purification, both moral and physical, that issues in a life of holiness.[43]

It is as if Paul, or other followers of Jesus before him, has dipped into the self-perception of the Qumran community in order to straighten out his stubborn, unholy, impure, fractious, and fragmented community. Their Qumran covenant renewal ceremony, as we have just seen, contains precisely what the Corinthians give no signs of having understood: there is a *communal spirit* that transcends individuals yet *purifies* and *instructs* individuals who submit to the corporate will of that community; this spirit exhibits indispensable qualities, such as *humility, uprightness,* and *holiness,* which ought to be evident in community life.

The Qumran community had its faults, to be sure. The community was ingrown and exclusive; hateful — at least in the scrolls it has left behind — toward outsiders, both Jewish and Roman; preoccupied with the sort of minutiae that were demanded of a residential desert community; and perhaps overly confident in its perception of truth and its interpretation of scripture. Nonetheless, in many respects the Corinthian community must be compared unfavorably with this Palestinian community. The Corinthians were splintered, fractured by rival claims to leadership and competitive hierarchies that arose from misperceptions of the relative worth of spiritual gifts. They lacked a hunger for holiness and, instead, seem to have allowed reprehensible moral lapses to fester before their very eyes.

It is these faults that the metaphor of the temple so pointedly addresses. The metaphor of a spirit-filled temple presses the need for a spirit of holiness and a spirit of unity and, by doing so, provides a direct critique

---

43. See also 1QS IV 20-21.

of the Corinthian penchant for discordant cliques. It also introduces another powerful dimension of communal life that the Corinthians, in their self-absorbed existence, seem to have overlooked: the universal nature of that unity.

In order to apprehend how much the Corinthians failed to grasp, we must reckon with the hopes that were riveted to the temple and its glorious future restoration. Ezekiel, of course, provided the architectural plans of this temple in an exilic vision that exemplified purity and exclusion (chs. 40–48). Yet later prophets departed from this exclusive vision, and it was to these other prophets that Jesus and Paul were deeply indebted. An exilic or postexilic prophet in the tradition of Isaiah proffered a vision of an open temple:

> And the foreigners who join themselves to the Lord, to minister to him, to love the name of the Lord, and to be his servants, all who keep the sabbath, and do not profane it, and hold fast my covenant — these I will bring to my holy mountain, and make them joyful in my house of prayer; their burnt offerings and their sacrifices will be accepted on my altar; for my house shall be called a house of prayer for all peoples. Thus says the Lord God, who gathers the outcasts of Israel, I will gather others to them besides those already gathered. (Isa 56:6-8)[44]

The postexilic prophet Zechariah would share a similar vision in which the nations would be welcomed into the temple at Jerusalem:

> Thus says the Lord of hosts: Peoples shall yet come, the inhabitants of many cities; the inhabitants of one city shall go to another, saying, "Come, let us go to entreat the favor of the Lord, and to seek the Lord of hosts; I myself am going." Many peoples and strong nations shall come to seek the Lord of hosts in Jerusalem, and to entreat the favor of the Lord. Thus says the Lord of hosts: In those days ten men from nations of every language shall take hold of a Jew, grasping his garment and saying, "Let us go with you, for we have heard that God is with you." (Zech 8:20-23)[45]

---

44. See also Isa 60:4-5, 7. For further discussion, see R. J. McKelvey, *The New Temple: The Church in the New Testament* (Oxford: Oxford University Press, 1969) 9-15.

45. In another oracle, Zechariah envisions, somewhat less felicitously, a period of time when nations who had fought against Israel and been punished with a plague would "go up year after year to worship the King, the Lord of hosts, and to keep the festival of booths. If any of the families of the earth do not go up to Jerusalem to worship the King, the Lord of hosts, there will be no rain upon them" (Zech 14:16-17).

What these representative oracles suggest is that the postexilic prophetic tradition could envisage a future for the temple that was universal, attended to not just by Israel but by the entire world community. According to the gospel writers, Jesus was influenced by this strand in the prophetic tradition, as his citations of Isaiah 61 in Luke 4:16-21 and Isa 56:7 in his attack upon temple customs demonstrate.[46] Key moments in Paul's letter to the Romans give further purchase to the influence these prophets had upon his vision of a mission to the nations. At a climactic moment, Paul cites LXX Isa 65:1-2: "Then Isaiah is so bold as to say, 'I have been found by those who did not seek me; I have shown myself to those who did not ask for me.' But of Israel he says, 'All day long I have held out my hands to a disobedient and contrary people'" (Rom 10:20-21).

Later in the letter, following a catena of scriptural texts in which Paul anchors his hope "that the nations might glorify God for [God's] mercy" (Rom 15:9-12), Paul explains that God's grace was given to him "to be a minister of Christ Jesus to the Gentiles in the priestly service of the gospel of God, so that the *offering* of the Gentiles may be acceptable, sanctified by the holy spirit" (15:16).[47] He develops this self-perception as a priest who brings the offering of the nations to God in part from an allusion to Isa 66:20, which reads, "They shall bring all your kindred from all the nations as an *offering* to the Lord, on horses, and in chariots, and in litters, and on mules, and on dromedaries, to my holy mountain Jerusalem, says the Lord, just as the Israelites bring a grain offering in a clean vessel to the house of the Lord." This allusion is essential for understanding Paul's metaphor of the temple in his letters to the Corinthians. Isaiah envisages international pilgrimages to the temple, the holy mountain, with real camels and mules carrying grain in a pure vessel. Paul envisages a different sort of cosmopolitan pilgrimage; the offering of the nations will be made pure by the holy spirit.

Nor was Paul alone during the first century in following a tradition that perceived the temple as a point of unity rather than exclusivity. In his defense of the Jewish faith, *Contra Apionem*, Josephus writes aphoristi-

---

46. Matt 21:13; Mark 11:17; Luke 19:46.

47. What Paul describes sounds much like the Qumran self-presentation we noted earlier, in which they exist "to establish the spirit of holiness in truth eternal, in order to atone. . . . the offering of the lips in compliance with the decree will be like the pleasant aroma of justice and the perfectness of behavior will be acceptable like a freewill offering" (1QS IX 3-5). Qumran and Paul, of course, are separated by a wide rift. The community at Qumran functions as a priest in isolation from the world, while Paul's vocation is to travel to the far ends of the earth to present the nations as an offering.

cally: "We have but one temple for the one God . . . common to all as God is common to all" (2.193). More to the point, in his *Antiquities,* Josephus interprets the detail in 2 Chr 7:1, that "fire came down from heaven," as a combination of fire and air which composed the divine spirit. At the dedication of the temple Solomon had prayed, "Beside these things I entreat Thee also to send some portion of Thy *spirit* to dwell in the temple," in response to which "a *fire* darted out of the *air* and, in the sight of all the people, leaped upon the altar and, seizing on the sacrifice, consumed it all" (*Ant.* 8.114).[48] Solomon prayed for a portion of the spirit, and now a mixture of fire and air consumes the sacrifice. While the entirety of Josephus's paraphrase is permeated by Stoic vocabulary and concepts, his association of the spirit with fire and air encapsulates the quintessence of Stoicism, for according to Stoic cosmology, fire and air are the components of *pneuma.*[49] Further, the single defining function of *pneuma,* as a Stoic conception, is to unify the universe.[50] For example, as we saw (see above, pp. 138-39), Balbus, in Cicero's *On the Nature of the Gods* 2.19, claims that the world order is "maintained in unison by a single divine and all-pervading spirit," while Alexander of Aphrodisias recalls that the founder of Stoicism, Chrysippus, "assumes that the whole material world is unified by a

48. On the ways in which Josephus recasts the dedication of the temple (1 Kings 8) with a good deal of Stoic language, see Levison, *The Spirit in First Century Judaism.* AGJU 29 (Leiden: Brill, 1997) 133-37.

49. *De mixtione* 224, 15-16 (quotation from A. A. Long and D. N. Sedley, *The Hellenistic Philosophers* [Cambridge: Cambridge University Press, 1987] 1:282); *De anima* 26.6. See also Plutarch who, in a complex attempt to discredit the Stoics, says that, according to their view of mixture, earth and water maintain their unity "by virtue of their participation in a pneumatic and fiery power, whereas air and fire because of their intensity are self-sustaining" (*De communibus notitiis adversus Stoicos* 1085D). Alexander of Aphrodisias (*De mixtione* 225, 14-16) asks, in his argument against the Stoics, "Moreover, if breath composed of fire and air passes through all bodies. . . ." Galen (*De placitis Hippocrates et Platonis* 5.3.8), while objecting to Chrysippus, describes the two parts of *pneuma* which constitute the soul's commanding faculty as air and fire.

50. In order to underscore the universal accessibility of the temple, Josephus removes exclusivistic statements from 1 Kings 8 and adds touches that underscore the philanthropic center which the temple offers the world. Josephus also exercises creative exegesis by removing all traces of exclusivism from Solomon's prayer, particularly references to war and enemies in 1 Kgs 8:44-51, and by fanning the spark of the positive reference to foreigners in 1 Kgs 8:43 into a flame, at the prayer's conclusion: "For so would all know that Thou Thyself didst desire that this house should be built for Thee in our land, and also that we are not inhumane by nature nor unfriendly to those who are not of our country, but wish that all equally should receive aid from Thee and enjoy Thy blessings" (*Ant.* 8.117).

pneuma which wholly pervades it and by which the universe is made coherent and kept together and is made intercommunicating."[51]

There is, therefore, an extraordinary unifying dimension to temple imagery, particularly as it was envisioned by prophets following the return from Babylonian exile. Even Josephus, during the late first century, recognizes that the divine spirit which filled Solomon's temple was nothing less than the cohesive force of the entire universe. The Corinthians, though they are God's temple, fail to grasp that the spirit which fills them is intended to bring an uncommon unity into their midst; instead they shrink their capacities and minimize their potential by attempting to subdivide this living temple into cliques. The spirit which fills the temple cannot, of course, be subdivided; it has an existence that transcends merely individual experiences. Therefore, those who persist in privileging one group or individual over another, who hanker after quarrels and foster factions in the church, cut across the grain of God's inclusive vision.

Such recalcitrance Paul is unable to tolerate. He reminds the Corinthians, therefore, of what they should already understand themselves to be: "Do you not know that you are God's temple and that God's spirit dwells in you?" He then accuses divisive people of destroying or damaging this temple of God. This is a harsh image that summons miserable memories and marks those who divide the church as the heirs of the Babylonians, who dragged Israel into exile in the early sixth century B.C.E., and as the descendants of the infamous Antiochus IV Epiphanes, whose desecration of the temple by the sacrifice of a pig in the holy of holies precipitated one of the darkest periods in the tragic history of Israel's temples.[52]

The Body as a Temple (1 Cor 6:19)

Paul's reminder that the church is a living temple, coupled with the legal, or casuistic, condemnation of those who destroy it, comprises a more effective appeal than prosaic exhortations to unity. No wonder, then, that Paul picks this metaphor up once more, at a point in the letter when his attentions have shifted from the schisms that so rankle him to sexual mat-

---

51. *De mixtione* 216, 14-17. On related Stoic conceptions, see H. Wenschkewitz, *Die Spiritualisierung der Kultusbegriffe: Tempel, Priester und Opfer im NT.* Angelos 4 (Leipzig: Pfeiffer, 1932) 70-230.

52. E.g., 1 Maccabees 1–6; Daniel 7–8, 10–12.

ters, both the flagrant flaunting of self-evident morality by a man who sleeps with his father's wife (1 Cor 5:1-8) and, at the other end of the spectrum, by the eschewing of all things sexual even within marriage (7:1-16). Other issues rise momentarily to the surface — lawsuits among believers and lawful or unlawful food — but the predominant issues that Paul confronts in this portion of the letter are sexual. In this context Paul reintroduces the metaphor of the temple: "Or do you not know that your body is a temple of the holy spirit within you, which you have from God, and that you are not your own? For you were bought with a price; therefore glorify God in your body" (6:19). The introductory words, "do you not know?" are precisely the words that occurred earlier in 1 Cor 3:16-17 to signal that Paul was reminding the Corinthians of something they ought to have known, something he had preached or written about in his prior communication with the Corinthians.

This reminder occurs toward the end of an extremely obtuse discussion of sexual relations that begins with what seems to be a quotation of a position held by some of the Corinthians: "All things are lawful for me" (6:12). Interpreters of the temple metaphor, in this context, typically suggest that Paul has taken the more common *communal* metaphor of 1 Cor 3:16-17 and 2 Cor 6:14–7:1 and applied it here to *individuals*.[53] There are good grounds for this assessment. Sexual activity with a prostitute is an individual matter, a dangerous matter, because, when a believer has sexual relations with a prostitute, he "becomes one body with her" and "the two shall become one flesh" (6:16, citing Gen 2:24). Two individuals, in other words, become one during sexual intercourse.

Many elements of Paul's discussion, on the other hand, give the impression that this is not merely an individual metaphor. Not least, of course, is that Paul chooses to introduce the temple metaphor with the same words he had adopted to introduce the metaphor on the first occasion in 1 Corinthians 3. Presumably both reminders are intended to recall the same metaphor. Since the first occurrence of the temple image was decidedly communal, it would naturally have a similar communal dimension in the second occurrence. It need not be here exclusively communal, but it would be strange were Paul to recall a metaphor that clearly was communal — it is communal in every other instance in the New Testament —

---

53. E.g., Fee (*God's Empowering Presence*, 135-36) writes, "In referring to the body as the temple of the Spirit, of course, Paul adopted the imagery that first of all belongs to the church as a whole (cf. 3:16; 2 Cor 6:16; Eph 2:21-22) and applied it to the individual believer."

without at least signalling clearly that he intends now to interpret that metaphor in an individualistic way.[54] He gives no such clear signal.

Further, the word "body" *(sōma)*, which Paul uses several times in this discussion of sex with prostitutes, refers to the individual human body from 1 Cor 5:3 until 1 Cor 11:29. However, the word also becomes a dominant metaphor for the church in 1 Corinthians 12–14 and in Paul's letter to the Romans, particularly when it occurs, as it frequently does, in relation to the church-as-body's members *(melē)*.[55] Apart from 1 Corinthians 6, every instance in 1 Corinthians of the word "members" — six occurrences in all — occurs in a discussion of the communal metaphor of the body.[56] For example: "For just as the body is one and has many members, and all the members of the body, though many, are one body, so it is with Christ" (1 Cor 12:12); "Indeed, the body does not consist of one member but of many" (12:14); "If one member suffers, all suffer together with it; if one member is honored, all rejoice together with it. Now you are the body of Christ and individually members of it" (12:26-27). The communal dimension of the word "members" cannot be far from view, then, when Paul reminds his readers, "Do you not know that your bodies are members of Christ? Should I therefore take the members of Christ and make them members of a prostitute? Never!" (6:15).

The presence of these elements in Paul's discussion suggests that the communal dimension has, at the least, not been eclipsed by the individual. The metaphor of the temple, which he recalls, is elsewhere communal, and Paul does not here signal a shift from that perspective in this discussion. The words "body" and "members," particularly when they appear together, evoke another communal metaphor: the body of Christ. According to R. Kempthorne, in fact, Paul "is now writing unequivocally of the corporate Body." This discussion is not, according to Kempthorne, about illicit sexual activity in general. Rather, Paul here picks up the discussion of the man who is living with his father's wife and urges the community once again to guard against what he is doing, for he, as a member of the body, the church, is sinning, not only against his own body, but also against the body that is the church.[57]

54. The metaphor is communal in 1 Cor 3:16-17; 2 Cor 6:16; and Eph 2:21.

55. E.g., 1 Cor 10:16-17; 12:12-27; and Rom 12:4-5, where it occurs in relation to the "members" *(melē)* of the body. 1 Cor 11:29 is ambiguous.

56. 1 Cor 12:12 (twice); 12:14, 18, 19, 20.

57. R. Kempthorne, "Incest and the Body of Christ: A Study of I Corinthians VI.12-20," *NTS* 14 (1968) 568-74, esp. 572-73.

Whether or not Paul is introducing a new topic or returning to the case of this man, the permeable border between the individual and the community is particularly transparent in Paul's treatment of the man who was sexually involved with his father's wife, with whom Paul dealt just a few paragraphs earlier. Paul consigns the man to Satan "for the destruction of the flesh, so that the spirit may be saved in the day of the Lord" (5:5). The absence of pronouns in this directive is jarring. While we would expect to read "his" (i.e., the man's) flesh, Paul includes no personal pronoun. This permits an interpretation in which the community's flesh may also be included in this condemnation. Similarly, we would expect Paul to write that "his" (i.e., the man's) spirit will be saved, but once again Paul omits the personal pronoun. This permits an interpretation in which the community's spirit will be saved. Paul could readily have eliminated ambiguity by the addition of personal pronouns. Instead, his ambiguous syntax permits, perhaps even invites, a construal of the body and spirit as both individual and communal. What is at stake is not just the salvation of the man, but of the whole church, not just the arrogance of the individual, but also of the church (5:2). This sexual perversion has to do, not just with the individual man, but with the individual-in-community. Their thorough integration is, in fact, evident when Paul adopts, in the concluding paragraph of this discussion, the metaphor of the yeast. A little yeast leavens the whole batch of dough. A little impurity can infect the entire community.[58]

In light of the permeable border between individual and community that is reflected in this metaphor of yeast, which Paul adopts in relation to sexual scandal, it becomes difficult to ignore the communal dimension of the metaphor of the temple in 1 Cor 3:16-17 (and 6:19; Eph 2:21), as well as the corporate residue of words, such as "your bodies are *members* of Christ" and "sins against the *body*" in 1 Corinthians 6. There is inherent ambiguity in a statement such as "The body is meant not for fornication but for the Lord, and the Lord for the body" (6:13). Which body is meant here? The body of the individual? Yes. Of the community? Of course. This is not exclusively a private matter between the Lord and the physical body of an individual; this is a matter as well between the Lord and the body of the church. In other words, illicit sexual intercourse is an act that pene-

---

58. On this conception of porous borders in 1 Corinthians, see D. B. Martin, *The Corinthian Body* (New Haven: Yale University Press, 1999) 168-79; see also A. Y. Collins, "The Function of 'Excommunication' in Paul," *HTR* 73 (1980) 251-63.

trates the permeable boundary between the body of the individual and the body that is the community.

By crossing the border between individual and community, the metaphor of the spirit-filled temple returns us to the fundamental Corinthian failure, which Paul addressed when he first adopted the metaphor in 3:16-17. The Corinthians carry on with cliques and quarrels because they fail to understand that the church is more than a collection of spirit-filled individuals. They fail to grasp that the church as a whole, as a living temple, is filled communally in a way that transcends or, more emphatically, relativizes individual experience, that draws an indispensable relationship between the individual and the community. By the same token, the Corinthians do not excise the man who lives with his father's wife because they fail to understand that the yeast of his sin will infect the church as a whole. And now, they fail to understand that sex with prostitutes is also a communal affair. The individual is not an isolated body but a *member* of Christ's body, someone who is organically related to the church. When he has sex with a prostitute, the whole body is involved in this deleterious act.[59]

Paul is able to make this point vividly by using the word "members," which has a serious and unavoidable *double entendre*, as Paul's discussion of the "less respectable" and "less honorable" members that are to be covered with honor and respect in 1 Cor 12:23 indicates. Members are body parts and community members alike. The member that joins with a prostitute — that actually becomes one with a prostitute, according to Paul's citation of Gen 2:24 — can be easily inferred. It is, of course, the penis. Yet it is more than this, for the penis is a part, a member, of the person as a whole, and the person is a part, a member, of Christ. Therefore, Paul asks, "Should I therefore take the members of Christ and make them members of a prostitute?" (6:15).

In a labored argument, then, Paul drives home the point that individual believers do not live in isolation from Christ's body. When individuals

59. On this interpretation, see Martin, *The Corinthian Body,* 175-79. To penetrate a prostitute sexually is like compelling Christ's own member to penetrate her (1 Cor 6:15). In light of Gen 2:24, according to which "the two shall become one flesh," sex with a prostitute is uniting with her rather than with the Lord (1 Cor 6:16-17). In fact, while it may appear that the believing male is penetrating the prostitute, he is actually sinning "into his body," i.e., he is, morally speaking, being penetrated by the prostitute. The Greek preposition *eis* no doubt has the sense of sinning "against his body," but not without preserving the more typical sense of *into.* The irony, of course, is that the believing member, who is united to Christ, by penetrating a prostitute with his own "member," is himself penetrated morally by the prostitute.

from this community release *pneuma* through sex with prostitutes, they do not do so in isolation, but as members of Christ, as a part of a temple that is filled with holy *pneuma*. Paul does all he can — reminds, cites Torah, explains, commands, and tenders a familiar temple metaphor — to convince the Corinthians that they have no right to buy the services of prostitutes when they and the community of which they are members have been bought with an immeasurable price (6:20).[60]

Once again, what is at stake is the holiness of the community and not just the holiness of individuals. The metaphor of "a temple of the holy spirit" evokes images of a community at worship, a universal and unified community, a community permeated by holiness and awe, a community comprised of members who devote themselves to God — a community that is distinctly unlike the community at Corinth. Yet this is a community that Paul identified as "sanctified" (1:2), as God's "holy" temple (3:17). Paul knows — and he will tell the Corinthians so shortly — that relationships both within the community and with those outside are intended to make others holy. He even urges believing spouses to remain with unbelieving spouses in order to sanctify the unbelieving partner. Though this is difficult to understand, he recommends this because "the unbelieving husband is made holy through his wife, and the unbelieving wife is made holy through her husband. Otherwise, your children would be unclean, but as it is, they are holy" (1 Cor 7:14).[61] Yet precisely the opposite interchange is taking place, according to this discussion of sexual behavior, because members, or a specific member, of this community are being polluted by means of illicit sexual habits that are fueled by the utterly foolish assumption that "all things are lawful for me" (6:12). Rather than sanctifying unbelievers, members of the body are being polluted by uniting their members through illicit sexual activity, sometimes with the bodies of prostitutes, and thereby spreading that pollution throughout the body, the church.

The Corinthians have obviously gotten into a mess to be assiduously avoided: "Never!" Paul responds to his own question about whether Christ's members should be united to prostitutes, and then later he commands

60. The final command is also possessed of a sublime ambiguity: "Glorify, then, God in your (plural) body" (6:20). Is an individual to glorify God in his or her body? Yes. Is a church to glorify God in their body? Yes. The individual glorifies God as a member of Christ, and the church is a body composed of members.

61. On this notoriously difficult verse, see the excellent discussion of Thiselton, *The First Epistle to the Corinthians*, 525-33.

nearly as tersely, "Shun illicit sex!" (6:18).[62] Those Corinthians who embrace a reality in which all things are permissible live in moral and physical chaos; they fail to reckon with a communal reality in which their unholy behavior as individual members pollutes the entire body with unholiness, just as the use of a sexual member, or body part, in a relationship with a prostitute renders the entire body unholy. The spirit-filled sanctuary, in contrast, is a metaphor of stability, abundance, and holiness. It subordinates individual liberties to the communal spirit-breath as a whole. Paul offers a sharp contrast between such a disordered existence and a living temple that is filled with the holy spirit. There are, after all, two spheres represented here, one filled with the spirit of the world and the other with the spirit from God.

Christ, Beliar, and the Temple (2 Cor 6:14–7:1)

Despite his best efforts, something has apparently gone awry since the Corinthians received the letter in which Paul reminded them that they are a temple in which God dwells. Paul is driven, consequently, to ask a series of five rhetorical questions that follow from the mandate: "Do not be mismatched with unbelievers."[63] What is jarring about these questions is that their tone is harsh, their temperament belligerent, with each driving an uncharacteristic wedge between believers and unbelievers:

> For what partnership is there between righteousness and lawlessness?
> Or what fellowship is there between light and darkness?
> What agreement does Christ have with Beliar?
> Or what does a believer share with an unbeliever?
> What agreement has the temple of God with idols? (2 Cor 6:14b-16a)

The either-or nature of these questions, the contrasts Paul creates, are untypical:

Righteousness and lawlessness
Light and darkness

---

62. Paul employs a pun with the word "prostitute" *(tē pornē)* in 6:16 and "fornication" *(tēn porneian)* in 6:18.

63. While this may include marriage, Paul expresses himself in more general terms of other dimensions of relationships with unbelievers, including business ones. See, e.g., Thrall, *Second Epistle to the Corinthians,* 1:472-74.

Christ and Beliar
Believer and unbeliever
The temple of God and idols

Once again, Paul's temple imagery occurs in a context that is edgy and abrupt. In his first letter he had been edgy too. He promised destruction, and not just ostracism, to the subdividers of God's sanctuary. He answered, "Never!" to the question of whether Christ should be united to prostitutes (1 Cor 6:15) and urged curtly, "Shun illicit sex!" (6:18). Yet in this later letter that edginess has exploded into an irrepressible excoriation of both unbelievers and Corinthian dalliances with them.

The Corinthians appear *not* to have continued egregiously off course with respect to either of the issues related to the temple metaphor in 1 Corinthians. Paul's later letter, 2 Corinthians, has little to do with schisms or sexual immorality. There is no mention of the illicit relationship between a man and his father's wife, nor does Paul bring up again the issue of sexual intercourse with either a spouse or a prostitute. His sole mention of the two harassing Corinthians flaws, schisms and sexual immorality, with which he dealt passionately and at length in his earlier letter, occurs in a tendentious, formulaic, and tentative conclusion to his own self-defense:

> For I fear that when I come, I may find you not as I wish, and that you may find me not as you wish; I fear that there may perhaps be quarreling, jealousy, anger, selfishness, slander, gossip, conceit, and disorder. I fear that when I come again, my God may humble me before you, and that I may have to mourn over many who previously sinned and have not repented of the impurity, sexual immorality, and licentiousness that they have practiced. (2 Cor 12:20-21)

Paul is not entirely certain that he will find the community torn by schism and tattered by sexual immorality. Still, the blunt dichotomies of 2 Cor 6:14–7:1 suggest that something else has developed in the community or, at least, that Paul suspects that something else has grown like a blister on the Corinthian body. He confronts it with a series of rhetorical questions that end with the temple metaphor, a catena of scriptural texts, and an exhortation to purity.

The recurrence of the temple metaphor exemplifies Paul's ability to contrast deftly current Corinthian behavior with what he has already taught them. He signalled this in 1 Corinthians by twice introducing the metaphor with the words "Do you not know?" They should, but fail to, remember what they were taught through the temple metaphor. In this third occurrence of this metaphor, the bald dichotomies Paul develops suggest that the Corinthians have failed to incorporate Paul's insistence upon holiness, upon the maintenance of purity. He turns his attention, therefore, away from relationships between those *within* the church to relationships with those who are *outside* the church, that is, with the very nations to which he is called.

What possibly lies behind this insistence, behind this sharpening of tone, behind this unexpected shift in emphasis, is a Corinthian misappropriation of the familiar temple metaphor. The temple metaphor, we noted, had to do both with unity and *universality*, and it would seem from Paul's dichotomies that the Corinthians have not drawn adequate boundaries between themselves and unbelievers, between the particular and the universal. In other words, they have incorporated the unifying and universal dimensions of the temple metaphor — "Do you not know that you are God's temple and that God's spirit dwells in you?" (1 Cor 3:16) — without incorporating the second aspect: "For God's temple is *holy*, and you are that temple" (3:17b).

The Corinthians can hardly be blamed for taking Paul's teaching about unity and universality as encouragement to establish and strengthen their relationships with unbelievers. Certainly Paul did little to disabuse them of this in his directives about marriage to unbelievers, when he urged them to remain in such marriages (1 Cor 7:10-16). Nor did he, in his instructions about idols, respond in a way that would require an end to concourse with unbelievers, for he encouraged believers not only to eat with unbelievers but to eat the meat they had sacrificed to idols (1 Cor 10:23–11:1). Paul himself was accused of compromise because he extended an apparently indiscriminate invitation to the nations. Such an application of Paul's teaching would seem to be entirely consistent with Paul's own vision of his mission, as he expresses it in Rom 15:16: "to be a minister of Christ Jesus to the Gentiles in the priestly service of the gospel of God, so that the offering of the Gentiles [nations] may be acceptable, sanctified by the holy spirit." The implication of the temple metaphor, understood in this light, is clear: if the living temple is the sacred community into which the nations will be brought, believers ought to welcome new believers from among the nations without even a wisp of restraint or reprimand.

What is baffling about Paul's return to this temple metaphor is that he casts those outside, whom he otherwise works relentlessly to save, in the dreariest and most dangerous of hues. They are aligned with lawlessness, darkness, Beliar, unbelief, and idols. What is equally baffling is how terribly uncharacteristic this language is for Paul. Six of the key words in this paragraph are not found in the rest of the New Testament, and the harsh approach to unbelievers suggests that Paul has reversed course and, in so doing, seems to have adopted language that is more at home in the Dead Sea Scrolls than in others of his letters. It has even been suggested more than once that he has taken up a composition from Qumran and adapted it to the Corinthian situation.[64]

Whether or not that is the case, the surprising dichotomies Paul draws do suit perspectives that permeate the Dead Sea Scrolls. The contrast of light and darkness recalls in shorthand the frequent Qumran contrast between the "sons of light" and the "sons of darkness," or the "prince of light" and the "angel of darkness" (1QS I 9-11; III 9-22). Paul's dual contrast between righteousness and lawlessness, on the one hand, and light and darkness, on the other, corresponds to a Qumran fragment which reads, "And this will be for you the sign that this is going to happen. When those born of sin are locked up, *evil* will disappear before *justice* as *[da]rkness* disappears before *light*" (1Q27 fr. 1 I 5-6). Equally noteworthy is the contrast between Christ and Belial; while Belial is never in the Hebrew Bible or New Testament an evil figure, the Dead Sea Scrolls frequently mention a figure named Beliar. The War Scroll, for example, contains three elements that characterize Paul's letter as well: the presence of Belial (or Beliar) and the contrasts of darkness and wickedness with light and justice. According to the War Scroll, at the end of the final war, the priests, levites, and the elders of the community (the community at Qumran is divided according to cultic roles to fight this final war) will

> bless the God of Israel and all the deeds of his truth and they shall damn there Beliar and all the spirits of his lot. They shall begin speaking and say: Blessed be the God of Israel . . . and blessed be all who serve him in

---

64. The quintessential expression of this position is that of J. A. Fitzmyer, "Qumran and the Interpolated Paragraph in 2 Cor 6:14–7:1," in *The Semitic Background of the New Testament.* BRS (Grand Rapids: Wm. B. Eerdmans, 1997) 205-17 (originally published in *CBQ* 23 [1961] 271-80). Fitzmyer (217) regards this section as "a Christian reworking of an Essene paragraph which has been introduced into the Pauline letter." There are several balanced discussions of whether 2 Cor 6:14–7:1 is an interpolation. See, e.g., V. P. Furnish, *II Corinthians.* AB 32A (Garden City: Doubleday, 1984) 375-83; R. P. Martin, *2 Corinthians.* WBC 40 (Waco: Word, 1986) 190-95; and Thrall, *Second Epistle to the Corinthians,* 1:25-36.

justice. . . . Accursed be *Belial* for his inimical plan. . . . Accursed be all the spirits of his lot for their *wicked . . .* plan. . . . For they are the lot of *darkness* but the lot of God is for [ever]lasting *light.* (1QM XIII 1-6)

Something extraordinary has occurred during the time that separates 1 and 2 Corinthians. In 1 Cor 3:16-17, Paul adopted the metaphor of a spirit-filled temple to communicate a vision of unity and universality. In 1 Cor 6:19-20, he adopted this metaphor to communicate that there is an organic relationship between believing individuals and Christ's body. Both occurrences of this metaphor convey the reality that the border between individuals and community is porous, that schisms destroy the church as a whole, that one illicit sexual encounter is the yeast that infects the whole. The spirit does more than fill individuals; it also unites the whole, rendering perceived boundaries superfluous. In 2 Cor 6:16-17, Paul makes a dramatic about-face by situating the temple metaphor in a context rife with exclusive vocabulary that is more at home in the *Community Rule* than in a Pauline letter. His language is wildly uncharacteristic, less like his own and more like the Dead Sea Scrolls, the literary remains of an isolated and exclusive community. Even the scriptural citations he proffers provide the grounds for an exclusive, and not at all inclusive, interpretation of God's presence in the temple. The great vision of Ezekiel 37, which supplies Paul elsewhere with the building blocks of universal resurrection, is interpreted narrowly by a subsequent citation of Isa 52:11, which, in its original context, is not a command to separate from darkness but a portion of new exodus imagery that portends departure from exile. Paul, however, applies it to the universal separation of clean from unclean:

> I will live in them and walk among them (Lev 26:11, 12), and I will be their God, and they shall be my people (Ezek 37:27). Therefore come out from them, and be separate from them, says the Lord, and touch nothing unclean; then I will welcome you. . . . (Isa 52:11)[65]

The dramatic shift in Paul's application of the temple metaphor suggests that, from his perspective at least, the Corinthians have grasped the point that the temple is universal, but they appear to have done so with no true eye for holiness, for the chasm that separates light from darkness, Christ

---

65. On this catena of quotations and the interpretation of scripture at Qumran, see Gärtner, *The Temple and the Community,* 52-55, who sees resemblances between this catena and *4QFlorilegium* and *Jub.* 1:17.

from Beliar, the temple from idols. This sort of Corinthian misapprehension would explain why Paul shifts so precipitously from the universal vision of postexilic prophets, from a conception of the spirit as the universal, unifying presence of God, to an exclusive vision of the temple akin to the conception of the living, spirit-filled temple, which devotees at Qumran express in the *Community Rule.*

The clue to Paul's frustration may lie, then, in the inability of the Corinthians to grasp the complementarity of this metaphor, which combines universality with holiness. This is not the first time he has pressed the point about holiness. Paul began by calling the temple holy (1 Cor 3:17). He then adopted the temple metaphor in order to urge sanctity upon a portion of the community which apparently believed that extramarital sexual activity was not only permissible but even perhaps desirable (6:19). In 1 Corinthians 6, these boundaries have to do principally with sexual limits. In the later letter, he speaks even more emphatically about the border that separates what is holy from what is unholy (2 Cor 6:14–7:1). Though no clear, concrete issue rises to the surface, he urges the Corinthians, as he had earlier, to make holiness perfect both in body and spirit. His assumption appears to be that they have forfeited their penchant for holiness while embracing a passion for the unholy.

What Paul confronts in 2 Corinthians, however, is not merely Corinthian shortcomings. He may well encounter the tension that lies latent within the metaphor of the temple. This temple communicates a vision which eliminates divisions within, such as the quarrels that threatened to damage or destroy the Corinthian community, and dividing lines without, such as those that separated Jew from Greek, slave from free, and male from female (Gal 3:27-28). The spirit is the unifying force of the universe, in Stoic terms. It is, at its most fundamental level, akin to breath, which all breathe in common. The spirit-filled temple suggests powerfully that the Corinthians must live in the context of their community without schisms; they must also refuse to raise artificial borders against those outside the community, those they are called to make holy. Perhaps Paul's unexpected about-face in 2 Corinthians is an indication of the irresolvable tension between unity and holiness that is inherent in the conception of the community as a living temple in whom God, or God's holy spirit, is believed to dwell. How would it have been possible for the Corinthians to remain border-free with respect to their unbelieving neighbors while maintaining their holiness? Whether they ultimately did manage to become a community that balanced universality and holiness during Paul's lifetime we cannot finally know, as we have no continuing record of Paul's troubled relationship with the Corinthians from which to infer his later points of view or their communal character. What we do know is that Paul has bequeathed to succeeding generations an image of the church as a spirit-filled temple that lives within a tension: it is unifying and universal in scope, open to the nations, and, at its best, devoted, at one and the same time, to purity and holiness.

Summary

In these three brief passages, Paul has undertaken an enormous task. He employs all sorts of methods — reminders, rhetorical questions, scriptural citations, and metaphors — to address the significant points that the spirit has an existence which transcends individual experiences, that the spirit eradicates the alleged border between individual and community, and that the spirit is the source of holiness. Schisms are not benign; they violate the character of the holy spirit, which provides unifying and universal dimensions to the living temple that transcend personal proclivities. Nor is errant sexual behavior a matter of private interest only; the spirit lives in the individual body and the communal body alike, so that an individual's unholy sexual intercourse pollutes the body of Christ. Having established this, that the spirit is communal, holy, and universal, however, Paul then, in a subsequent letter, appears to turn tail and run from part of the vision he has labored so aggressively to inculcate. He apparently feels the need to teach wholeheartedly about holiness, perhaps because the Corinthians have become too intertwined with unbelievers with too little eye for holiness. This would certainly be an understandable misconstrual of Paul's instructions, delivered in 1 Corinthians, to eat idol meat and to remain married to unbelievers. It would have emerged as well from popular Stoic construals of the spirit as the unifying principle of the universe and idealized characterizations of the temple as the unifying point in the universe. The Corinthians may even have earnestly believed that they were carrying out Paul's mission to the nations. Whatever the reason, which we cannot finally know, Paul draws a line in the sand with respect to universality: believers share nothing with unbelievers. Holiness demands separation, cleansing of body and spirit — the ambiguity of Paul's syntax once again allows for the possibility of both an individual and a communal body — and necessitates a clear border between light and darkness, between Christ and Beliar.

This is not an entirely satisfactory moment in Paul's letters at which to end. Too much is left unsaid, and too many strands are left untwined. It was left to a later writer, or a more mature apostle, to restore the harmony of this metaphor. In the letter to the Ephesians, the tension between holiness and universality is left behind in favor of a vision of the church in which Jew and Gentile are unified by the cross, in which they have no dividing walls between them, in which those near and far are brought to God in one spirit. Strangers are now citizens, aliens are saints, and all are members of God's household, with Christ Jesus as the chief cornerstone. "In him the whole structure is joined together and grows into a holy temple in the Lord; in whom you also are built together spiritually into a dwelling place for God" (Eph 2:21-22). This is a splendid vision indeed, but its beauty must not be allowed to eclipse the faulty Corinthian assumptions that prompted Paul, despite what he had learned about their schisms and sexual proclivities, to remind a fractured and frayed community in Corinth that they remain a temple filled with the holy spirit.

A New Creation

Despite dramatically different ways of framing the priorities of daily life, Paul and devotees of the new covenant who lived near the Dead Sea understood the powerful role of the spirit as the means of entrée into the life and community of faith, and they grounded that vision, in part at least, in the language of Ezekiel 36–37. While Ezekiel's vision is conspicuously communal, the gift of the spirit a national treasure, Paul, along with the authors of the *Community Rule* and the Qumran *Hymns,* transformed this corporate gift into a deeply personal one. According to the Dead Sea Scrolls, God gives the spirit in an individual, drawing him near, purifying him, and revealing knowledge to him. Paul seems no less preoccupied with the individual when he adopts Ezekiel's vocabulary. In the clearest allusion to Ezekiel 37, Paul applies Ezekiel's words — to the point of adopting the odd expression, *into you* — to the sphere of sexual purity. Key themes in Ezekiel's vision — spirit, sanctification, and knowledge of God — are clearly here, though they are metamorphosed into directives for a life of sexual purity. Even when Paul powerfully and passionately depicts the *giving* of the spirit — perhaps another reminiscence of Ezekiel 36–37 — as a seal and a pledge, the orientation is toward the individual. The church is not given a new heart, as Israel is promised a new heart in

Ezek 36:26-27; the spirit is given "in our hearts," in the hearts of individual believers.

Although Paul and those who inhabit the enclave near the Dead Sea apply Ezekiel's communal vocabulary in striking concordance to the individual, Paul alone retains the association of the spirit with the shadow of death. Particularly in 2 Corinthians, where he writes that God "has given us the pledge of the spirit" (5:5), the obtuse expression of hope that mortal bodies will be "*further* clothed" (5:4) consists of a verb with two prefixes, including the apparently superfluous preposition "upon." With this whisper of Ezekiel's vision, in which the word "upon" occurs many times to describe the reconstitution of Israel's bodies, Paul effectively situates the impact of the spirit in the shadow of death.

Paul preserves this scriptural alliance between the spirit and the shadow of death when, late in his first letter to the Corinthians, he discusses the relationship between two Adamic beings. Paul presents the inbreathing of the first Adam as an antitype of the inbreathing by which the second Adam fills the faithful with resurrection life:

> So it is with the resurrection of the dead. What is sown is perishable, what is raised is imperishable. It is sown in dishonor, it is raised in glory. It is sown in weakness, it is raised in power. It is sown a physical body, it is raised a spiritual body. If there is a physical body, there is also a spiritual body. Thus it is written, "The first man, Adam, became a living being"; the last Adam became a life-giving spirit. But it is not the spiritual that is first, but the physical, and then the spiritual. The first man was from the earth, a man of dust; the second man is from heaven. As was the man of dust, so are those who are of the dust; and as is the man of heaven, so are those who are of heaven. Just as we have borne the image of the man of dust, we will also bear the image of the man of heaven. (1 Cor 15:42-49)

With this understanding of both Adam and Christ, Paul returns his readers' attention to Eden, not the Eden of future restoration alone, but Eden at the dawn of creation. Earlier we saw that Paul understood filling with the spirit as a nexus or nodal point for a promise that reaches back to the patriarchs and matriarchs and extends to God's final act of salvation. His comparison of the first and second Adams does much the same by reaching back to Adam made from dust while simultaneously lunging into the future toward the second Adam from heaven.

No sooner, however, do we plunge into the waters of Paul's argument than we find ourselves submerged in the complicated currents of having to discern the assumptions of Paul's readers and *their* convictions. Clearly, in 1 Corinthians 15 Paul bears in mind their argument or, at least, anticipates their response. The distinction between the two men, two adamic beings, he takes for granted, so much so that Paul uses Gen 2:7, in an adapted form, without further explanation as the basis for his argument that the perishable seed is raised imperishable, that dishonor is raised in glory, that weakness becomes power, that a physical body is raised a spiritual body (1 Cor 15:42-44). Without hesitation, he conjures the contrast, "'The first man, Adam, became a living being'; the last Adam became a life-giving spirit" (15:45). Yet the elusive presence of Corinthian assumptions is apparent in Paul's need to follow this citation with a more argumentative corrective: "But it is not the spiritual that is first, but the physical, and then the spiritual" (15:46). It looks as if Paul happily adopts the contrast of two Adams but then cautiously, even defensively, addresses a point of view that understands the sequence of the two in the reverse order: first the spiritual Adam, then the mortal Adam. Paul is determined to demonstrate that the opposite order is correct: first the mortal, then the spiritual Adam.

Fortunately, we are not left to fend for this point of view, which Paul dismantles, in an historical vacuum, for Paul was not alone in his ability to discern a first and second Adam in the earliest lines of Torah. Philo Judaeus, his prolific Alexandrian contemporary, also discerned two creations in Genesis, and his commentaries on the creation of Adam provide a sort of chiaroscuro, a palpable contrast that is amplified by how much the two first-century authors held in common. While it is not possible to determine whether Paul or the Corinthians or an antagonistic clique among them was influenced by Philo or whether they were heirs to a shared tradition, the similarities between their constructions of the two Adamic beings is nonetheless noteworthy, and scholars have been well advised to explain Paul's conception of the two Adams in light of Philo's more well-developed and much longer discussion of two creations in Genesis 1–2.[66]

In *On the Creation* 134, Philo cites the septuagintal translation of Gen 2:7 nearly verbatim: "God formed man by taking clay from the earth, and

---

66. See esp. B. A. Stegmann, *Christ, the 'Man from Heaven': A Study of 1 Cor. 15,45-47 in the Light of the Anthropology of Philo Judaeus.* Catholic University of America New Testament Studies 6 (Washington: Catholic University of America, 1927).

breathed into his face the breath of life [*enephysēsen eis to prosōpon autou pnoēn zōēs*]."[67] It is virtually axiomatic, according to Philo, "that there is a vast difference between the man thus formed and the man that came into existence earlier after the image of God." The first man, the one made according to God's image, is the Platonic "idea or type or seal," consisting neither of male nor female and "by nature incorruptible." The man of Genesis 2 is a copy of this ideal, a mortal made of body and soul, man or woman (134). In another treatise, he interprets Gen 2:7 even more tersely: "There are two types of men; the one a heavenly man, the other an earthly. The heavenly man, being made after the image of God, is altogether without part or lot in corruptible and terrestrial substance; but the earthly one was compacted out of the matter scattered here and there, which Moses calls 'clay'" (*On the Allegorical Laws* 1.31).

A fundamental correspondence to Paul's interpretation of the two Adams jumps from the pages of these brief interpretations of Gen 2:7: there are two Adams, the one immortal and the other mortal, whose existence can be traced to the creation narratives in the opening paragraphs of Torah.[68] The difference between Paul and Philo is no less apparent: for Philo the immortal comes first and the mortal second, while Paul sets them in the reverse order, with the mortal appearing first and the immortal second: not immortal-glorious-powerful-spiritual first but mortal-dishonorable-weak-physical-"image of dust" first. There is another difference as well. Philo's interpretation is somewhat more complicated than Paul's. The second man

---

67. He adds the participle "by taking" *(labōn)*.

68. Philo spins this interpretation of the two men out in other contexts as well. In his interpretation of the "helper" of Gen 2:18, Philo writes, "For there are *two* races of men, the one made after the (Divine) Image, and the one moulded out of the earth" (*Allegorical Interpretation* 2.4). The first man yearns after the image and, consequently, is not alone. The second man, which Philo identifies as the soul, attains two helpers: the senses and passions — which will ultimately lead the mind to sin when the serpent, which Philo interprets allegorically as pleasure, ensnares the woman, whom Philo interprets allegorically as sense-perception. In his *Questions and Answers on Genesis*, they are liable to no less than three levels of interpretation. The two men, understood Platonically, are the ideal man of Genesis 1 and its mortal copy, as in Genesis 2 (1.4a; 2.56). They are also, when interpreted anthropologically, the immortal human mind within the mortal body (1.4b). Yet Philo presses this anthropological level of interpretation to an ethical level; the two men represent two types of people: those who live in accordance with their minds as opposed to those who succumb to their senses and bodies and therefore allow their soul, which could tend in either direction — to mind or body — to become ensnared in the body (1.8). See further J. R. Levison, *Portraits of Adam in Early Judaism: From Sirach to 2 Baruch.* JSPSup 1 (Sheffield: JSOT, 1988) 84-85.

was not merely physical, or *psychikos,* as in the contrast Paul tenders. He was, rather, a composite being "made up of earthly substance and of divine spirit" (*On the Creation* 135). Philo believes that the divine breath Adam received was better even than Gen 2:7 suggests, which reads "breath of life"; Philo supposes that the first man received the "spirit of life."[69] In *On the Special Laws* 4.123, he describes the exceptional quality of this spirit, which outstrips even the finest of Stoic aether: "For the essence of substance of that other soul is divine spirit [*pneuma theion*], a truth vouched for by Moses especially, who in his story of the creation says that God breathed a breath of life [*pnoēn zōēs*] upon the first human, the founder of our race, into the lordliest part of his body, the face. . . . And clearly what was then thus breathed was ethereal spirit [*aitherion . . . pneuma*], or something if such there be better than ethereal spirit, even an effulgence of the blessed, thrice blessed nature of the Godhead."

Paul traverses a good bit of terrain alongside an interpretation such as Philo's, though he ultimately parts company. He too admits to the reality of two Adams. He too believes there is a sequence to their relationship. He too derives filling with the divine spirit from Gen 2:7. Yet over against a position such as Philo's, Paul contends that this filling has occurred only in the person of the second Adam, in the wake of his resurrection, in the shadow of the dust of death from which he has arisen. There are indeed two Adams but, as Paul writes so emphatically, the spiritual does *not* come first but second, and the mortal does *not* come last but first (1 Cor 15:45). Paul's contention is not dissimilar to the traditional formula that he embeds in the opening of his letter to the Romans. Though we may never know the full implications of the formulaic language of Rom 1:3-4 — whether it was an early confession of the church upon which Paul draws early in this letter — it is difficult to shake off the sense of how integrally related the resurrection and the holy spirit are for someone such as Paul, who writes that "Jesus Christ our Lord" was "declared to be Son of God with power according to the spirit of holiness by resurrection from the dead" (Rom 1:4).

There is a fundamental difference between Paul and Philo at this point, and it is Philo, rather than Paul, who comes out looking fundamentally more biblical. Philo recognizes, in a way that Paul does not, that the man of clay received the divine breath in full measure. In this, he is aligned with notions of filling with the spirit that dominate the Jewish scriptures,

---

69. In *Allegorical Interpretation* 1.42, Philo indicates an awareness of the distinction between breath and spirit.

EARLY CHRISTIAN LITERATURE

according to which mortal human beings receive the divine spirit from the start. Paul's commitment to the resurrection of Jesus, in contrast, leads him to drive a wedge within Gen 2:7 between the body of clay and the in-filling of divine breath. The first Adam is not an immortal being but an utterly mortal one, and the second Adam, though he gives the spirit, is not, as in Philo's interpretation, a composite being of spirit and dust but a purely spiritual being who gives the spirit. By driving this wedge so deeply, Paul divides the composite character of the human being in Gen 2:7 in a way that Philo, despite his belief that body and soul cannot happily commingle, does not.

Paul's effort to associate the divine spirit with the resurrected Christ rather than the Adam of Gen 2:7 also comprises a departure from his scriptures. True, Israelite literature had predicted a national outpouring of the spirit. True, Israelite literature had envisioned the revivification of a valley of dry bones. True, the resting of the spirit had come in part to be associated with the anointed one of God. Yet the belief that a second Adam would arise who would become a life-giving spirit lay far from the imagination of the authors of Israelite literature. Even Philo's importation of the divine spirit into Gen 2:7 pales in comparison, as does Philo's invention of two Adams from the dual perspectives of creation in Genesis 1 and Genesis 2. Consequently, despite Philo's relentless, and at times far-fetched, tendency to allegorize the creation story, despite the maze of Stoicism he navigates in his interpretation of the divine spirit, despite the way in which he holds inspiration captive to neo-Platonic conceptions of the ascent of the mind — despite all of this, Philo's firm belief that mortal human beings possess the divine spirit from birth, by dint of creation, is better grounded in the Jewish scriptures than is Paul's firm belief that mortals cannot be filled with the divine spirit until they have reckoned with the resurrection of Jesus Christ, the second Adam.

While Paul, therefore, may agree with his antagonists that there are two Adams, and not just one, he threshes the same grain into a very different sort of wheat. There may indeed be a spiritual and mortal Adam in Genesis 1–2, or even in the composite nature of Adam in Gen 2:7. Yet in light of Christ's resurrection, priority cannot be granted to the spiritual or *pneumatic* Adam. The *first* Adam is mortal, the *second* immortal — *not* vice versa. The immortal Adam has passed first through the dust of death, the inevitability of Gen 3:19, the mortality of the first Adam. There is no immortal existence, in other words, without a mortal existence, which emerges on the other side of resurrection as a life-giving spirit.

The sharp contrast that Paul devises between the uninspired mortal being and the inspiring immortal being is a shadow image perhaps of the beliefs that we discovered in the Qumran *Hymns*. Paul writes:

> The first man was from the earth, a man of dust; the second man is from heaven. As was the man of dust, so are those who are of the dust; and as is the man of heaven, so are those who are of heaven. Just as we have borne the image of the man of dust, we will also bear the image of the man of heaven. (1 Cor 15:47-49)

Although the hymn writer hardly discovers two Adams in Israel's creation literature, he does convey the sense that there is a sharp contrast between a mere mortal, who is "a creature of clay" (1QH IX 21-22; XI 23-24), a "creature of mud" (XIX 3-4), and those devotees of the new covenant into whom God has given the spirit, whom God has embellished with splendor and length of days (V 23-25), who inhabit an Eden of glory (XVI 20). There is this implicit contrast in the Qumran *Hymns* between the mortal creation and the immortal, between creation from dust and the restoration of Eden — and all of this pivots upon the presence of the spirit in the Edenic community and in the individuals who inhabit it.

While the seeds of Paul's contrast of the two Adams may lie in the arid soil of Qumran, theirs is nuanced and subtle, while his is bold, even brash. The resurrection of Jesus, and not entrée to the community, is the dividing line for Paul between mortal and immortal, between a life void of divine spirit and one rife with it.

It would, of course, be easier — and more consistent with Torah — for Paul to take up Philo's bold contrast of the two Adams or to retreat to the veiled contrast between creatures of clay and the inheritors of Edenic splendor in the Qumran *Hymns*. He might not sacrifice much by admitting that the first man was composed of clay and spirit or that the second man broke the bounds of clay and became a life-giving spirit. He shows his intimate knowledge of Gen 2:7 with the citation, "The first man, Adam, became a living being," and the tandem references to earth and dust (1 Cor 15:45, 47). Why does Paul then take a tack that leads away from a more credible interpretation of Genesis 2?

He no doubt takes this tack because the contrast of a first and second Adam, of a physical Adam from the earth, from dust, and a spiritual Adam from heaven, suits the contours of his argument about the resurrection, which is peppered with contrasts: sown perishable, in dishonor, in weakness, a physical body, but raised imperishable, in glory, in power, a spiritual body (1 Cor 15:42-44).[70] Paul is writing of a single, unrepeatable transformation that occurs with resurrection, and it may serve his purpose to keep the contrast pristine rather than muddying the waters with the notion of a composite being, even if that notion is derived more straightforwardly from Gen 2:7.

There is also a symmetry between this contrast of two Adams — one physical and the other spiritual — and the way in which Paul has already divided the *sarkinoi* from the *pneumatikoi* in the Corinthian community (1 Cor 3:1-3). He is determined to admit no neutral territory where the Corinthians can cower from the truth. Believers cannot be about the business of jealousies and quarreling (3:3) while claiming at the same time to be spiritual. Regardless of how spiritual a believer may *feel* he or she is, the primary indication of mature spirituality lies elsewhere, in consistency with the *content* of the gospel, the teaching which the spirit reveals about the cross, for "we have received not the spirit of the world, but the Spirit that is from God, so that we may understand the gifts bestowed on us by God" (2:12). The *content* of this revelation includes, furthermore, the resurrection of Jesus. This much is apparent from the outset of his discussion, when Paul refers to the tradition that was handed to him, which he now hands down: "For I handed on to you as of first importance what I in turn had received: that Christ died for our sins in accordance with the scriptures, and that he was buried, and that he was raised on the third day in accordance with the scriptures" (15:3-4). The gift of the spirit turns like a top upon the message of the cross and resurrection, so there is no retreating for Paul behind the gossamer of a more subtle contrast of mortality and immortality. No: the first Adam was mortal, the second a life-giving spirit.

Paul, then, may prefer the neat contrast between a physical Adam and a spiritual Adam to the notion of a composite being because the neat contrast fits so flawlessly the immediate exigencies of his argument about the transformation that is occasioned by resurrection and the larger context of the letter as a whole, in which Paul gives no ground to those in the Corinthian church who claim to be spiritual while engendering cliques based

---

70. Greek: *houtōs kai hē anastasis tōn nekrōn. speiretai en phthora, egeiretai en aphtharsia. speiretai en atimia, egeiretai en doxē. speiretai en astheneia, egeiretai en dynamei. speiretai sōma psychikon, egeiretai sōma pneumatikon. ei estin sōma psychikon, estin kai pneumatikon.*

upon jealousy and quarreling. Though less scripturally grounded than Philo's view, therefore, it is rhetorically compelling, relevant for the thorny state of the Corinthian church, and rooted in the tradition he has received.

There is nonetheless a thoughtful and richly scriptural dimension to Paul's contrast of the two Adams, for with it he puts death squarely in its place — in the shadow of life. In so much of Israelite scripture the spirit subsists and survives, though without thriving, in the shadow of death. We learn that God breathes, in intimate embrace, into the first human, whose origin and character, nonetheless, are dust and earth and whose destiny lies in the dust. Only at the moment before the waters rise above their heads do we learn that all living beings, animal and human, are full of the breath of the spirit of life. We learn that Elihu misunderstands the spirit, and the wisdom it gives, because he leaves it unmoored from the realm of suffering, from Job's ash heap, and because he disparages the hard-won wisdom of those who seem to have little spirit left in them. We learn that princes forfeit their plans and return to their earth when God takes away their spirit. We learn that animals feel dismay and return to the earth as well when God takes away God's spirit, and that they are re-created when God gives it again. We learn that there can be the hope of a new and pure and generous spirit and that God's holy spirit can remain within despite the threat that God may take it away and the fear that sin propels one away from God's presence. We learn that the darkest valley of death can succumb to the brightest hope, that bones and sinews and flesh can rekindle, and that the spirit can come from the four corners of the earth to fill the moribund nation, to re-create Israel into a new people who will till the land until it becomes a garden of Eden.

The resurrection is rooted in this scriptural realization that the spirit cannot linger any longer in the shadow of death. Mortality has been supplanted by immortality. The physical Adam has been succeeded by the spiritual. The image of the man of dust is effaced by the image of the man of heaven. The perishable will not inherit the imperishable. Ultimately death, which has overshadowed the spirit, will be "swallowed up in victory. Where, O death, is your victory? Where, O death, is your sting?" (1 Cor 15:54-55). Even still, these questions, as triumphalistic as they may appear at first blush, leave death in the shadows. It is not altogether gone; it has not completely disappeared. It has lost its sting, but it still lingers in the shadows of light. And this realization, that death continues to hold sway, albeit in the shadow of the spirit, returns us to the scriptural conviction that it is the spirit, and the spirit alone, that keeps death at bay.

It is no surprise that Paul should choose to root his discussion in Gen 2:7, even if it costs him the ability to interpret it straightforwardly as the gift of breath or spirit to a body of dust from the ground. The curtain rises on a world of dust and dirt and death, on a drama that, before a word, divine or human, is uttered, sets the unspoken parameters of the stage: life begins and ends in the shadow of death. The mortality that enshrouds the creation of the first Adam provides the perfect foil for Paul's conviction that the second Adam became a life-giving spirit at the resurrection. God had intimately imparted to the first Adam, in a face-to-face embrace, the life-giving breath. Now Christ, who is himself life-giving spirit, will thrive within believers. The resurrection of Jesus brings about this radical revision of Gen 2:7 and a reordering of the relationship between the spirit and death. And so, by means of a truncated citation and a mass of theological reflection that stretches the bounds of credulity, Paul leads us once again through a valley of very many, very dry bones back up the garden path to Eden.

CHAPTER 3

Filled with the Spirit and the Book of Acts

The Salience of a Slave-Girl

Two dramatic stories of conversion in the book of Acts crown Paul's achievements. Of Lydia, who exercised the respectable livelihood in Thyatira of dying purple, Luke writes, "The Lord opened her heart to listen eagerly to what was said by Paul." The result? She and her household were baptized, and Paul stayed in Lydia's home (Acts 16:11-15). To a jailer at Philippi who was so honorable as to plan suicide because Paul and Silas had apparently been freed by an earthquake that opened the prison, Luke attributes the great missiological setup question, "Sirs, what must I do to be saved?" to which Paul and Silas responded, "Believe on the Lord Jesus, and you will be saved, you and your household" (16:30-31). The result? He and his entire family were baptized immediately, and Paul ate in the jailer's home (16:34).

Two dramatic stories that emblematize a successful mission. Two honorable people. Two receptive listeners who were eager to know more about Jesus from Paul and Silas. Two accounts of household baptisms. Two stories of hospitality shown Silas and Paul — of lodging and a meal. Tucked away between these monumental narratives is a tale that is told in passing, a transitional little scene that appears to serve little more function than to explain how Paul and Silas found themselves in prison.

Before entering the heavily traveled territory of spirit-filling in the book of Acts, we will visit the less-traveled setting of this tale. By lingering over this short episode, we may become more susceptible to incongruities and unexpected dimensions of the book of Acts. This tale numbers a mere ninety-eight words in Greek:

One day, as we were going to the place of prayer, we met a slave-girl who had a spirit of divination and brought her owners a great deal of money by fortune-telling. While she followed Paul and us, she would cry out, "These men are slaves of the Most High God, who proclaim to you a way of salvation." She kept doing this for many days. But Paul, very much annoyed, turned and said to the spirit, "I order you in the name of Jesus Christ to come out of her." And it came out that very hour. But when her owners saw that their hope of making money was gone, they seized Paul and Silas and dragged them into the marketplace before the authorities. (Acts 16:16-19)

The central character of this brief episode could hardly strike a clearer contrast to Lydia and the Philippian jailer. She is a young slave-girl who, possessed of a spirit, engages in the disreputable profession of fortune-telling so that her owners can make fistfuls of money. Paul and Silas appear to be inattentive to her status, unaware of the oppression she suffers, even as she follows them around for several days, affirming their personae and their message. In fact, she seems hardly to catch Paul's attention until, finally, as an afterthought, he is so annoyed by her incessant screaming that he turns and orders the spirit out of her. Her owners, enraged by their potential loss of fortune, instigate hearings that lead to the imprisonment of Paul and Silas.

This short transitional tale offers a surprising and indispensable prism through which we can begin to distinguish the hues of Luke's conception of being filled by the holy spirit. It is surprising indeed, as it contains no conversion, no reference to the holy spirit, and no flattering portrait of a Paul moved by the vulnerability of a slave-girl who is compelled by avaricious owners to fortune-tell in order to pad their fortunes. Yet precisely because it lacks the accoutrements of a pivotal narrative that issues in extraordinary success — such as the outpouring of the holy spirit at Pentecost (Acts 2) or the descent of the holy spirit upon the Gentiles (Acts 10–11) or the reception of the holy spirit in Ephesus by John the Baptist's disciples, who speak in tongues and prophesy (Acts 19) — and precisely because potentially propagandistic elements are stripped bare in this episode of a mantic slave-girl, we are able, through a sideways glance, to garner an unvarnished glimpse of inspiration, as much through what Luke does not divulge as through what he does.

The most important dimension of this is Luke's description of this spirit as a "pythonic spirit" (*pneuma pythōna*) rather than an evil spirit or demon (16:16). The python was, according to legend, the snake that guarded Delphi, which Apollo killed. By the Roman era, however, the term python, in relation to prophecy, had attached itself to ventriloquists, belly-talkers, through whom gods were reputed to deliver oracles. The Hippocratic treatise *Epidemics* identifies belly-talkers, or ventriloquists, with "pythons" (5.63.7). The playwright Aristophanes admits that he first published his pieces pseudonymously in imitation of Eurycles; by this Aristophanes means that he entered the bellies of others and poured through them what is comical (*Wasps* 1019). We encountered these belly-talkers in our discussion of Greco-Roman prophecy. Allegedly the first was Eurycles who, during the fifth-century b.c.e., was said to have carried within him a source of speech.[1] In Plutarch's *On the Obsolescence of Oracles,* Lamprias derides a view of inspiration according to which it could be imagined "that the god himself after the manner of ventriloquists (who used to be called 'Eurycleis,' but now 'Pythones') enters into the bodies of his prophets and prompts their utterances, employing their mouths and voices as instruments" (414E).

This sort of ventriloquism was soundly rejected by Jews. In the Septuagint, ventriloquism is associated with proscribed practices such as idolatry, witchcraft, and necromancy (e.g., Deut 18:9-14; Isa 8:19; 29:4). The evil king Manasseh permitted this practice (2 Chr 33:6) and, according to a portion of the Septuagint that does not exist in the Hebrew, the noble king Josiah rid Judah of ventriloquists (2 Chr 35:19). In the Hebrew Bible (1 Sam 28:6-25), and Josephus's version following it (*Ant.* 6.327-30), the witch of Endor, whom Saul consulted in order to communicate with Samuel after his death, was both necromancer and ventriloquist; her body was a medium for the voice of the dead. Other Jewish authors continued this tirade against ventriloquists. Philo includes them among Egyptian augurs, soothsayers, charmers, bewitchers, and all of the devotees of artificial divination whom Philo so vehemently excoriates (*On Dreams* 1.220). The Jewish sibyl praises the Jews for worrying neither about "portents of sneezes, nor birds of augurers, nor seers, nor sorcerers, nor soothsayers, nor the deceits of foolish words of ventriloquists" (*Sib. Or.* 3.224-26), and, in his alleged testament, Judah groups ventriloquists with omen dispensers and demons of deceit (*T. Jud.* 23.1).

There are very few exceptions to this tendency. Philo and Josephus, we may recall, attribute this form of inspiration to Balaam, who said, accord-

---

1. E.g., Plato, *Sophist* 252C.

ing to Josephus, that the "spirit gives utterance to such language and words as it will" (*Ant.* 4.120) and to whom, according to Philo, the angel promised that it would "guide the reins of speech, and . . . employ your tongue for each prophetic utterance" (*On the Life of Moses* 1.274). Of course, the attribution of ventriloquism to such an ambiguous character as Balaam is understandable. More baffling is that this form of inspiration, despite Philo's rejection of it in *On Dreams* 1.220, shares family traits with Philo's description of prophecy in *On the Special Laws* 4.49, according to which, "no pronouncement of a prophet is ever his own" because "the divine spirit . . . plays upon the vocal organism and dictates words which clearly express its prophetic message."[2]

In Luke's story of the slave-girl, there is none of the excoriation we might be led to expect by Jewish and Roman rejections of pythonic spiritism. This is strange, as this episode appears at first blush to be a straightforward exorcism, with its reference to Jesus' name, as in Peter's healings (Acts 3:6, 16; 4:12), and, in particular, its mirroring of Jesus' own exorcisms. In Luke 4:31-37, for example, the evil spirit alone knows the truth about Jesus, and Jesus rebukes the demon, telling it to be quiet and to come out of the man, whom it has thrown to the ground. With this exorcism, Jesus establishes his authority, as the people continually utter, "For with authority and power he commands the unclean spirits, and out they come!"[3]

If Paul's alleged exorcism in Acts 16 is intended to mirror Jesus', however, it does so incongruously. While Jesus' exorcism is a clear confrontation between good and evil, staged at the synagogue, Paul's takes place on the way to prayer and, what is most remarkable, only because of Paul's annoyance. Paul and his coterie, in fact, accommodate themselves to her accompaniment. Luke underscores this with his use of the imperfect tense: "while following Paul and us . . . she continually cried out [*ekrazen*]. . . . While she continued to do [*epoiei*] this for many days, Paul, having become annoyed. . . ." Had Paul recognized in this slave-girl an evil demon intent upon his demise, it would have been expedient, from the start, to exorcise the demon. The very clear implication is that this slave-girl was *not* a

2. According to *On the Special Laws* 1.65, "nothing of what he [a prophet] says will be his own, for he that is truly under the control of divine inspiration has no power of apprehension when he speaks but serves as the channel for the insistent words of Another's prompting. For prophets are the interpreters of God, Who makes full use of their organs of speech to set forth what He wills."

3. See also Mark 1:21-26; Luke 4:41.

threat, that her divining because she had a pythonic spirit did *not* lie in opposition to his mission, that her inspiration was *not* illicit. Paul could hardly have been expected to permit her to accompany him and to cry out her message for many days if he had sensed in the occasion a confrontation between good and evil.

Nor does Luke's account censure the woman. There is certainly no rebuke, as in typical exorcisms in Luke's Gospel.[4] Annoyed, Paul simply turned and "spoke to the spirit" *(tō pneumati eipen)*. This lack of censure contrasts markedly with the exorcisms of Jesus, in which the evil dimension of the spirits comes to the forefront: a single story in Luke 4:31-37, for example, contains the designations "spirit of an unclean demon," a "demon," and "unclean spirits." Luke leaves the reader in no doubt that these are "demons," pure and simple; he renders no equivalent verdict in Acts 16.

There is even a difference in the messages, suggesting once again that the slave-girl's spirit lies not in opposition to but in alliance with the work of God. In the Gospel, the demon's first words to Jesus are a clear challenge, "Let us alone! What have you to do with us, Jesus of Nazareth? Have you come to destroy us? I know who you are, the Holy One of God" (Luke 4:34). In the Gospel, there is a turf battle between Jesus and the demons, waged from the start, in which demons must acknowledge that they have lost. By contrast, the slave-girl's words are irenic and supportive: "These people are servants of the Most High God; they are preaching to you the way of salvation." This is arguably, and surprisingly, the most concise encapsulation of the message of salvation in Acts; it is an accurate précis of key themes from Luke-Acts: servant, Most High, preaching, the way, and salvation. The slave-girl expresses the message of salvation better than anyone else in the book of Acts. The slave-girl is more uniquely Lucan than the Lucan Peter!

Another contrast between the demons and the pythonic spirit concerns the demeanor of the person possessed. In the Gospels, demons tend to drop a possessed person to the ground, to cause writhing and rolling, to effect diseases or conditions such as blindness (Matt 12:22) and the inability to speak (Luke 11:14). The slave-girl, in contrast, is physically able to accompany Paul and the others, and she is obviously not mute, for she speaks vociferously the whole while.

And finally, while exorcisms in the Gospels tend to conclude with an

4. E.g., Luke 4:35, 41.

acclamation of praise for the authority of Jesus (e.g., Luke 4:36-37),[5] the alleged exorcism of the pythonic spirit from the slave-girl ends anticlimactically with the expression, "And it went at that moment." Elsewhere, Luke repeatedly demonstrates his flair for the dramatic. Peter's healing of the crippled beggar is punctuated by Peter's claim to have no silver or gold; the healing is evidenced in the man's walking and leaping and praising God, and the story ends with the crowd's astonishment (Acts 3:1-10). In a narrative summary, Luke describes the "many signs and wonders" that took place: the laying of cots and mats on the street so that Peter's shadow would fall on them, the gathering of large crowds with the sick "and those tormented by unclean spirits," all of whom were cured (5:12-16). Certainly the story of Pentecost, the episode of Ananias's and Sapphira's conspiracy and death, the narrative of Stephen's death, the encounter of Saul with the risen Jesus, the threefold visionary experience of Peter followed by the stunning outpouring of the spirit on the Gentiles — all of these episodes demonstrate Luke's ability to develop narrative drama. The story of the slave-girl contains none of this drama. Her story does not so much rise to a conclusion as drift away.

In what may appear, then, to be an incidental and traditional exorcism, which ostensibly functions to explain why Paul and Silas were jailed in anticipation of an earthquake and conversion scene, we have discerned important dimensions of Luke's perception of inspiration. In a scene that mirrors the exorcisms of Jesus, Luke describes a spirit, without censure, as a pythonic spirit. There are no physical or mental ill effects of this spirit, apart from those precipitated by the greed of her owners, to match the ill effects that plague the possessed in the Gospels. On the contrary, in a demonstrably ironic way, the pythonic spirit inspires the slave-girl to accompany Paul and his coterie and to deliver the most concise collection of key Lucan terms in Acts — a summary that exceeds the concision even of the apostles' summaries. Small wonder, then, that Paul resorts to commanding this spirit to leave the girl, not because he is engaged in a cosmic battle between good and evil, but because he is annoyed by her yelling, which he and his colleagues endured for many days. There is accompaniment here that is cut short only by annoyance. The slave-girl's prophesying is permissible until, oddly enough, it grates on Paul's nerves.

5. On the heightened authority of Jesus in exorcisms in Luke's Gospel, see G. H. Twelftree, "Demon, Devil, Satan," in *Dictionary of Jesus and the Gospels*, ed. J. Green, S. McKnight, and I. H. Marshall (Downers Grove: InterVarsity, 1992) 170-71.

The episode of the slave-girl will remind us, as we proceed, of how little we know about inspiration, of how much we are compelled to piece together. It will remind us as well of how unexpectedly Luke can astonish us: the slave-girl gets the message straight. It will remind us, finally, that early Christian authors, for all of their commitment to Jesus, did not always scrupulously draw a line in the sand beyond which God was perceived not to labor. In the ninety-eight words of Acts 16:16-18, the work of God is found strangely and surprisingly in the belly and on the lips of a slave-girl. And finally, the story of the slave-girl offers a segue to consideration of another, very different story, for there is an enticing analogy between the slave-girl of Acts 16 and the believers at Pentecost; in Acts 2, two disparate conceptions of inspiration coexist which correspond to the unbridled inspiration of the slave-girl and Paul's calling an end to the pythonic spirit's ventriloquism. Neither conception obliterates the other.

Luke narrates, of the believers gathered on the Feast of Pentecost, that "all of them were filled with (the) holy spirit and began to speak in other languages, as the spirit gave them ability" (Acts 2:4).[6] It may well be that Luke has intertwined two traditions in Acts 2. Luke inherited a tradition that told of the early disciples' "speaking in tongues" in such a way that they appeared to be drunk. To blunt the edge of ecstasy, he included the single word "other" — they "spoke in *other* tongues" — and underscored the comprehensibility of their speech to those gathered in Jerusalem. Thus he reshaped an experience of inexplicable tongues-speaking into an ability to speak miraculously in comprehensible foreign languages.

Whether or not Luke's transformation took place on the level of literary sources we cannot finally determine.[7] He may have inherited a source about ecstasy and transformed it into a story about foreign languages, while retaining elements of ecstasy, though we cannot ultimately know this for sure. We can, nonetheless, discern in this passage points at which the uncontrollable or manic still presses up against the comprehensible, at which a seemingly unseemly mode of inspiration backs up against the proclamation of the good news of Jesus Christ — as in the story of the slave-girl.

6. Greek: *kai eplēsthēsan pantes pneumatos hagiou kai ērxanto lalein heterais glōssais kathōs to pneuma edidou apophthengesthai autois.*

7. E.g., J. A. Fitzmyer writes, "Luke is not using different sources here; he rather modifies the tradition he inherits, transforming 'tongues' into 'other tongues,' i.e., speaking in foreign languages, a miracle suited to the theological thrust of the episode, which is interested in the universality of salvation to which testimony is being made"; *The Acts of the Apostles.* AB 31 (New York: Doubleday, 1998) 239.

Both stories contain details that do not quite fit a consistent interpretation of inspiration. The permission the slave-girl has to accompany Paul for days on end, her ability to discern the salvific import of Paul's message, her capacity to do so, not by the holy spirit but by a pythonic spirit — each of these does not neatly fit one of the mainstays of Acts, that the *holy* spirit is the force and energy which inspires the mission of the nascent church. How can it be that a mere slave-girl filled by a pythonic spirit divines the truth so accurately? In the same way, the reference to filling by the spirit, coupled with the impression that the early believers were drunk, hardly fits a related dominant theme of Acts, that the holy spirit impels the early believers to preach inspired sermons.

In both stories something incomprehensible presses up against the narrative as it stands or as we would expect it to stand. In light of the view of demons and unclean spirits in Luke-Acts, and the literature of the early church as a whole, we would expect the pythonic spirit to enfeeble the slave-girl, to challenge Paul, and immediately to succumb to Paul's censure. Yet it does not. It leads the slave-girl instead to grasp the essence of the early church's message. Analogously, in light of the dominant role of the holy spirit as the inspiration for inspired speech in Luke-Acts, from the aged Elizabeth's song at the beginning of the Gospel (Luke 1:41-42) to Paul's defense at the end of the second volume (Acts 26), we would expect the holy spirit to do precisely what Luke says it does — to inspire the believers to communicate, in a compelling sermonic form, the mighty acts of God. Yet it does more than this. It leads the believers as well to appear to a large group of onlookers as if they are drunk, to the extent that Peter is compelled to begin his speech by addressing this charge: "Men of Judea and all who live in Jerusalem, let this be known to you, and listen to what I say. Indeed, these are not drunk, as you suppose, for it is only nine o'clock in the morning. No, this is what was spoken through the prophet Joel . . ." (Acts 2:14-16).

Both stories lie at the heart of the nature of inspiration. Both leave questions trailing after them. The story of the slave-girl raises the question of inspiration *outside of* the church's borders. Even if finally Paul impelled the pythonic spirit to leave, in the substantial meantime it grasped his message *in nuce* better than anyone else in the entire book of Acts. The pythonic spirit, which spoke through the lips of the slave-girl, with her mind disengaged, got it exactly right. The story of Pentecost raises the related question of inspiration *within* the borders of the early church. Even if Luke finally presents the Pentecost experience as one of comprehensible and convincing speech, he has left, in the meantime, the narrative door cracked open for the impression that there was an ecstatic dimension to the Pentecost experience. This question of the relationship between the ecstatic impulse and the imposition of restraint, between the incomprehensible and comprehensible, between the centripetal pull toward mania and the centrifugal push toward order in the early church, will occupy us for the rest of this chapter, as we explore spirit-filling in the book of Acts.

The Allure of Ecstasy at Pentecost

The story of Pentecost offers a clinic in the accoutrements of ecstasy, no less so than Kenaz did in the *Liber antiquitatum biblicarum* (see above, Part II, chapter 2). There is, first of all, filling with (the) spirit, which is accompanied by the presence of fire. The action which this inspiration produces is speaking in tongues — other tongues — which gives the impression that the earliest followers of Jesus were drunk. It is not impossible to discern in this Pentecost narrative a reminiscence of the fiery presence of God on Mount Sinai (Exod 19:18), especially as it was refracted through the interpretative lens of Philo:

> It was natural that the place should be the scene of all that was wonderful, claps of thunder louder than the ears could hold, flashes of lightning of surpassing brightness, the sound of an invisible trumpet reaching to the greatest distance, the descent of a cloud which like a pillar stood with its foot planted on the earth, while the rest of its body extended to the height of the upper air, the rush of heaven-sent fire which shrouded all around in dense smoke. (*On the Decalogue* 44)

Even if Luke cradled the story of Pentecost in the revelation at Sinai, he has not, with this background, effaced the ecstatic dimension in this story. Sinai comes with no account of filling with the spirit, nor does the fire of Sinai descend upon each individual who is filled with the holy spirit. The Israelites neither speak, in tongues or otherwise, nor do they act as if they are drunk, though they are elsewhere entirely capable of doing so, as in the revelry that surrounded the creation of the golden calves (Exod 32:25).

If the story of Sinai lies in the background of Pentecost, it does so quiescently, by way of subtle allusion rather than the shout of clear correspondence. Far more in the foreground of this narrative are those elements that lured Greco-Roman eyes to the presence of ecstasy: filling with the spirit, fire, and intoxication. Their prominence in this story suggests that Luke, though he ultimately opts for the preeminence of the comprehensible, is no less concerned to preserve the ecstatic. In this way, the inspiration of the earliest followers of Jesus is a distinctive miracle that incorporates both the allure of ecstasy and the appeal of inspired intellect — two principal emphases that we traced in our study of early Judaism.

Filled with the Spirit

We began our study of the allure of ecstasy with the dominant presence of the Delphic priestess who, for more than half a millennium, fired imaginations of Greeks and Romans, including Jews and Christians, with her oracles and the mysterious processes that led to them. The most basic component of that process consisted apparently of filling with (the) spirit. In Plutarch's *On the Obsolescence of Oracles*, Cleombrotus assumes that the lack of oracles in his day took place because, "when the demigods withdraw and forsake the oracles, these lie idle and inarticulate like the instruments of musicians. . . ." Ammonius, whose viewpoint is dismissed, thinks her inspiration is a sort of ventriloquism: "the god himself after the manner of ventriloquists (who used to be called 'Eurycleis,' but now 'Pythones') enters into the bodies of his prophets and prompts their utterances, employing their mouths and voices as instruments" (*On the Obsolescence of Oracles* 414E). Lamprias, we may recall, believes that *pneuma* enters the body and produces a condition of enthusiasm.

> But the prophetic current and breath is most divine and holy [*to de mantikon rheuma kai pneuma theiotaton esti kai hosiōtaton*], whether it issue by itself through the air or come in the company of running waters; for when it is instilled into the body, it creates in souls an unaccustomed and unusual temperament, the peculiarity of which it is hard to describe with exactness. (432D-E)

A litany of writers would refer to the spirit that filled the Pythia. Strabo's reference to an enthusiastic spirit (*pneuma enthousiastikon;* 9.3.5), Pliny the Elder's to an intoxicating exhalation (*exhalatione temulenti; Natural History* 2.95.208), Dio Chrysostom's to the spirit that filled her (*empimplamenē tou pneumatos;* 72.12), Pseudo-Longinus's to an enthusing breath (*atmos entheos;* 13.2), Iamblichus's to a fiery *pneuma* that surrounds her (*On Mysteries* 3.11), John Chrysostom's to an evil *pneuma* that entered her genitalia (*Homily on 1 Corinthians* 29) together attest to the long-standing Greco-Roman belief that an inspiring *pneuma* entered the Pythia, filled her, and caused her to prophesy.

In his list of four kinds of inspiration, Plutarch writes, "There is a second kind, however, which does not exist without divine inspiration. It is not intrinsically generated but is, rather, an extrinsic afflatus that displaces the faculty of rational inference; it is created and set in motion by a higher power. This sort of madness bears the general name of 'enthusiasm'" (*Amatorius* 758E). This is precisely the form of inspiration whose allure many Jewish authors of the Greco-Roman era were unable to resist. Philo, as we noted (see above, p. 158), discovered in the word *ekstasis* in Gen 15:12 a springboard for what is now to us a familiar description of what "regularly befalls the fellowship of the prophets. The mind is evicted at the arrival of the divine spirit [*tou theiou pneumatos*], but when that departs the mind returns to its tenancy. Mortal and immortal may not share the same home. And therefore the setting of reason and the darkness which surrounds it produce ecstasy and inspired frenzy [*ekstasin kai theophorēton manian*]" (*Who Is the Heir?* 2.264-65). When the prophet is inspired, "he is filled with inspiration [*enthousia*], as the reason withdraws and surrenders the citadel of the soul to a new visitor and tenant, the Divine spirit which plays upon the vocal organism and dictates words which clearly express its prophetic message" (*On the Special Laws* 4.49).

Kenaz in the *Liber antiquitatum biblicarum* (see above, pp. 161-68) is no less an exemplar of ecstasy than Philo's race of prophets, for "holy spirit came upon Kenaz and dwelled in him and elevated his mind [put him in ecstasy], and he began to prophesy, saying . . ." (*LAB* 28:6). The spirit leapt, filled, and put Kenaz's mind in ecstasy, enabling him to see far into the future. "And when Kenaz had spoken these words, he was awakened, and his senses came back to him." The state into which filling with the spirit propelled Kenaz required a reawakening and a return to his senses. Finally, "he did not know what he had said or what he had seen." His inability to remember what took place in the condition of ecstasy is the surest sign of his spirit-filled enthusiasm. This narrative depiction of inspiration is profoundly significant both because of its clarity — the infilling of the spirit effects a pure ecstatic state — and because this sort of clarity appears in a literary text that was not composed in Greek in Rome, Athens, Delphi, or Alexandria, but in the provinces, in Palestine, and quite possibly in Hebrew. Such a clearly conceived grasp of inspiration in Palestine during the first century is a powerful sign of the wide swath which the association of filling by the spirit and ecstatic loss of control occupied in the Greco-Roman world.

When Luke begins the founding narrative of the church, the singularly most significant event that will define and catalyze a burgeoning movement, the language he adopts echoes unmistakably the language which authors spanning the first century B.C.E. through the fourth century C.E., including both its champions and its detractors, employed to describe the quintessential experience of inspiration. The followers of Jesus "were filled with holy spirit." Luke's adoption of a conception of inspiration that mirrors such a long and impressive train of interpreters of inspiration, Delphic and otherwise, could hardly have been dissociated from the most renowned, the most ubiquitous, the most influential phenomenon of inspiration in Greco-Roman antiquity, in which this filling with divine or prophetic or holy *pneuma* effected an inspired, ecstatic state in which the Pythia or prophet forfeited self-control to the control of the spirit, however variously it may have been conceived. When, therefore, he adopts the language of filling with the spirit, Luke situates the experience of Pentecost in a robust cultural setting that saw filling with a *pneuma* as the precipitating factor in enthusiasm. When he adopts this conception alongside the image of tongues as of fire, he tightens even further the literary screws that associate filling with the spirit and ecstatic possession.

Aflame with the Spirit

The experiences of the followers of Jesus as they clustered together on the day of Pentecost were anything but controlled and orderly. They were met first by a sudden sound from heaven that was carried by a violent wind *(pnoē)* which filled *(eplērōsan)* the whole house. This detail alone draws the curtain back on the chaos that confronted the coterie that would shortly constitute the church in Jerusalem. This is followed or accompanied — the conjunction *kai* is merely that, vaguely conjunctive rather than decidedly sequential — by the appearance of divided tongues as of fire which sat upon each one of them. There occurs, then, a sudden sound carried on a violent wind and fiery tongues upon everyone present. This is followed or accompanied — again the conjunction is just that, conjunctive rather than sequential — by another filling *(eplēsthēsan)*, this time of Jesus' followers, and not by wind but by holy spirit *(pneumatos hagiou)*.

Luke has painted Pentecost with a dramatic palette by piling up uncontrollable element upon uncontrollable element. By the time the reader learns that Jesus' followers actually say something, pandemonium has erupted. There is noise, wind, fire, and spirit-filling. In this narrative context, the element of fire contributes to the impression of chaos — and this is vital to grasp — both within the house as a whole and within the followers of Jesus as individuals. The house lies suddenly in a state of uncontrollability, full as it is with sound, wind, and fire. This situation mirrors the experience of Jesus' followers, who are full of holy spirit, recipients of divided tongues as of fire, and whose voices resound as the spirit gives them utterance. When Luke continues the narrative by saying that the inhabitants of Jerusalem from every nation under heaven gathered "when this sound [*phōnēs*] took place," it is not altogether clear whether the sound that drew them was the sound that filled the house or the united voices of the disciples — or perhaps the cacophonous combination of both.

What is clear is that Luke adopts the image of fire only in relation to filling by the spirit. The two are tandem experiences. Fire is not a free-floating element of Pentecost that in some general way evokes God's presence, for the tongues as of fire that rest upon the believers are associated directly with filling: "Divided tongues, as of fire, appeared among them, and a tongue rested on each of them. All of them were filled with the holy spirit" (Acts 2:3-4a). It is this association of filling and fire that contributes to a distinct impression of entry into an ecstatic state over which Jesus' followers had no control; for with this association Luke situates the experience of Pentecost in a Greco-Roman literary context in which inspiration was depicted as a fiery experience, a context in which filling with *pneuma* was understood as an experience that ignited and inflamed a person possessed.

We have just lingered over the Delphic Pythia, whose inspired rapture riveted those who reflected upon her, though we did not recollect Lucan's description of the Pythia, who "now she boils over with fierce fire [*igne iratum*], while enduring the wrath of Phoebus. Nor does he [Apollos] ply the whip and goad alone, and dart flame into her vitals [*stimulus flammasque in viscera mergis*]," but she is cursed to be unable to say all that she knows (*On the Civil War* 5.118-20).

Lucan's vivid poetry is not altogether different from Quintus's discussion of inspiration in Cicero's *On Divination.* Quintus, who described Cassandra's "flaming eyes, that sudden rage" (*On Divination* 1.66), depicts the soul's ascent as the inflammation and arousal of the soul:

> Those then, whose souls, spurning their bodies, take wings and fly abroad — inflamed and aroused by a sort of passion — these men, I say, certainly see the things which they foretell in their prophecies. Such souls do not cling to the body and are kindled by many different influences. For example, some are aroused by certain vocal tones, as by Phrygian songs, many by groves and forests, and many others by rivers and seas. I believe, too, that there were certain subterranean vapors which had the effect of inspiring persons to utter oracles. (1.114)

Plutarch's reflections later in the first century convey a similar association of infilling with inflammation: "It is likely that by warmth and diffusion it [*pneuma*] opens up certain passages through which impressions of the future are transmitted, just as wine, when its fumes rise to the head, reveals many unusual movements and also words stored away and unperceived. 'For Bacchic rout/And frenzied mind contain much prophecy,' according to Euripides, when the soul becomes hot and fiery, and throws aside the caution that human intelligence lays upon it, and thus often diverts and extinguishes the inspiration."

We saw as well that this powerful association breached the borders of the Roman East and infected the *Liber antiquitatum biblicarum*, in which a prosaic Israelite description of Joshua's fullness of spirit is transposed into a dramatic and exemplary instance of inspiration: "And Joshua took the garments of wisdom and clothed himself and girded his loins with the belt of understanding. And when he clothed himself with it, his mind was afire and his spirit was moved, and he said to the people . . ." (*LAB* 20:3). Joshua, in this revision of Israelite literature, looks less like his forebear and much more like Cassandra, with her "flaming eyes, that sudden rage," or those inspired Greek and Roman figures, "whose souls, spurning their bodies, take wings and fly abroad — inflamed and aroused by a sort of passion" (*On Divination* 1.114).

Filling and fire. These are the tandem partners that effect and accent the inspired state. This is the fundamental association that characterizes the inspired condition. And how pervasive in the first century was this association? It ignored all sorts of boundaries of geography and genre as it pervaded the Greco-Roman world in which Luke lived and breathed. Within this extensive cultural matrix, it is difficult to avoid the conclusion that the paradigmatic description of inspiration in the book of Acts — "Divided tongues, as of fire, appeared among them. . . . All of them were filled with the holy spirit" — evoked images of the Delphic Pythia, who boiled over with fierce fire when Apollo darted flame into her vital organs, or the tragic and fiery Cassandra, who cowered before "that bloody torch" (*On Divination* 1.67).

These are, of course, not exact parallels, and they are not intended to suggest a literary relationship among Lucan, Cicero, Plutarch, Pseudo-Philo, and Luke. Nonetheless, given how far-reaching this association between fire and infilling was, its recurrence in the story of Pentecost is doubtless part and parcel of a widespread and commonplace Greco-Roman conception about inspiration. While Luke will impress upon the narrative of Pentecost his own stamp of comprehensibility, as we shall see shortly, he has left undeniable, overt elements in it which alert the reader to the realization that the sort of inspiration the believers experienced did not lie far from the experiences that were claimed by the most renowned prophets, priestesses, and Pythia, by famed seers and sibyls, all of whom were esteemed by some of the leading literary lights of the Greco-Roman world.

Drunk with the Spirit

If readers of Acts, Jewish and pagan, would have construed the chaos in the house and the inspiration of Jesus' followers in terms that lay within the great stream of Greco-Roman conceptions of inspired, fiery ecstasy, they would have found confirmation of this in the accusation that the followers of Jesus, who had fire resting upon them and (the) holy spirit filling them within, were considered by some of the spectators to be participants in a drunken spectacle. This accusation was sufficiently credible to prompt Peter to begin his speech by debunking its plausibility. Further, Peter addresses the entire crowd, as if all of them shared the perception that Jesus' followers were drunk (Acts 2:14). Peter dispels its credibility by addressing not some small segment of his hearers, a misguided minority. The so-called "others" who "sneered" must be understood as a sizeable mass of observers. The fire and the filling and the speaking in (other) tongues led the men of Israel to suppose that Jesus' followers were drunk.

At the most superficial level of Luke's narrative, the charge that Jesus' followers "are filled with new wine" sets out a clear alternative: either Jesus' followers are filled with spirit or drunk with wine. They are either inspired or intoxicated, speaking either with the loss of control that arose from inspired ecstasy or the loss of control that accompanied actual drunkenness. Although the sneering crowd, from Luke's perspective, is misguided, their charge tells the reader that they have heard or seen something which can be attributed by a sizeable number of people to intoxication.

Notwithstanding Peter's denial, therefore, Luke allows the residue of ecstasy to linger, the resonance of enthusiasm to permeate the events of Pentecost. Although Luke ultimately presents Jesus' earliest followers as preachers, as proclaimers of the powerful acts of God in foreign languages, he goes to no great length to dispel the impression that the filling and fire of inspiration led the first followers of Jesus into a state of ecstasy akin to drunkenness. Nor would the association of infilling, fire, and drunkenness have been lost on the readers of the book of Acts, for in many quarters of the Greco-Roman world, as we saw earlier, wine was believed to be integral to inspiration.

The accusation that the believers drank new wine may even offer a point of connection to Bacchic ritual. Drinking new wine in honor of Bacchus was integral to the festival of Anthesteria, which took place in late February and early March and became extremely popular in Greece, especially in Athens. The charge that was levelled against Jesus' followers, that they were drunk in the morning on new wine, may in this light comprise only a thinly veiled accusation that they were acting like the devotees of Bacchus, who entered an ecstatic state through inordinate drinking.[8] Understood from this perspective, the charge at Pentecost may have been less a denial of their inspiration than the accusation that they were indeed inspired, but through new wine drunk in honor of another, very popular god, who would have been unacceptable to the Jews gathered at Pentecost.[9]

Plutarch's *On the Obsolescence of Oracles* (432E-F), we saw, refers to Bacchic ritual to describe the process of inspiration (see above, pp. 168-69). The dimensions of inspiration in Acts are neatly detailed here: spirit, fire, and wine.

Then, of course, there is Philo's notion of sober intoxication. The Therapeutae become "drunk with this drunkenness in which there is no

8. P. W. van der Horst, "Hellenistic Parallels to the Acts of the Apostles (2.1-47)," *JSNT* 25 (1985) 54-55.

9. See further H. Lewy, *Sobria Ebrietas: Untersuchungen zur Geschichte der antiken Mystik.* BZNW 9 (Giessen: Töpelmann, 1929) 42-72.

shame" and arrive "more alert and wakeful than when they came to the banquet." The one who yearns for wisdom he considers "to be drunken with the drunkenness which is soberness itself" (*Every Good Man Is Free* 13). The one whose mind ascends is "seized by a sober intoxication, like those filled with Corybantic frenzy, and is inspired, possessed by a longing far other than theirs and a nobler desire" (*On the Creation* 71). The story of Hannah, whose name means "grace," provides him with a point of departure: "Now when grace fills the soul," he writes, "that soul thereby rejoices and smiles and dances, for it is possessed and inspired, so that to many of the unenlightened it may seem to be drunken, crazy, and beside itself" (*On Drunkenness* 146).

If we bear this description in mind, then we can discern in Luke's narrative of Pentecost no less than three legitimate levels of interpretation. On the most superficial level, Jesus' followers are *either* inspired *or* intoxicated. They are clearly not drunk, in Peter's estimation, so they must be inspired. A second level of reading arises from the context of Bacchic ritual, including Plutarch's serious depiction of the inspired state: the onlookers believe that the followers of Jesus are inspired because they have actually drunk wine. They are both drunk and inspired; Peter flatly disavows this association. Yet there is another reading of Pentecost in light of the integral relationship that Philo draws between apparent drunkenness and inspiration. At this level, Jesus' followers are falsely indicted for being inspired because they *appear to be* intoxicated by those whom Philo identifies as the unenlightened: the inspired soul is "possessed and inspired, so that to many of the unenlightened it may seem to be drunken, crazy, and beside itself." In this, Peter and Philo are one, for together they recognize that the sort of behavior and speech which the misguided attribute to too much wine are in fact the product of inspiration, of possession by a divine and holy spirit.

Yet Philo continues, shedding still more light on the drama of Pentecost: "For with the God-possessed not only is the soul wont to be stirred and goaded as it were into ecstasy but the body also is flushed and fiery, warmed by the overflowing joy within which passes on the sensation to the outer person, and thus many of the foolish are deceived and suppose that the sober are drunk" (*On Drunkenness* 147). Key ingredients emerge, with remarkable correspondence, in both texts. First, grace — the word, rather than "spirit," which is required by the scriptural text Philo interprets — fills Hannah's soul, as (the) holy spirit fills Jesus' followers. She is stirred into ecstasy and becomes God-possessed. Second, Hannah's body, like the bodies of ecstatic people, becomes flushed and fiery, warmed by joy;

tongues as of fire rest upon Jesus' followers. Third, "many of the foolish are deceived and suppose that the sober are drunk"; many in the crowd at Pentecost sneer, "They are filled with new wine," to which Peter replies, "Indeed, these are not drunk, as you suppose . . ." (Acts 2:13, 15).

Fire, Filling, Intoxication

How ought we to understand the evocative association of fire, filling, and intoxication that coalesces in Acts 2? These three dimensions of the Pentecost experience find only the most slender foothold in Luke's scriptures. Filling was not understood in Israelite literature as a subsequent endowment that onlookers would attribute to too much wine. Joseph and Daniel calmly interpreted dreams and scripts. Bezalel taught other artisans how to construct the tent of presence. Elihu, the ignominious youth who derided his elders, attributed his allegedly sagacious speech to spirit — spirit understood as the breath that God gives to human beings at birth. Ben Sira's scribe would pour forth his own teaching, presumably in the rarified confines of an academy. Nor is there the slightest hint of ecstasy in Micah's claim to be filled with spirit. He maintained rather, against his prophetic opponents, that he was filled with enduring qualities — power, might, knowledge, and spirit — that made him the prophetic voice that he was. Unlike his opponents, he needed no visions; he eschewed their so-called revelations.

Never in Israelite literature, then, is filling with the spirit associated with a fiery frenzy that could be mistaken for drunkenness. There is simply no scriptural reservoir that can explain this coalescence of fire, filling, and apparent intoxication in Luke's story of Pentecost. The corresponding Jewish resources for this coalescence are fiercely in the debt of Greco-Roman conceptions of inspiration, in which filling and a fiery demeanor — boiling up, flaming eyes, inflammation — combine to confirm the authenticity of prophetic possession. The fiery, drunken demeanor that can be mistaken for intoxication when one is filled with *pneuma* finds no home other than in Greco-Roman conceptions of inspiration, such as they are espoused by Cicero, as he depicts Cassandra, by Plutarch, as he discusses Delphi, and by Philo, as he interprets Hannah's prayer, which was mistaken by the unenlightened and foolish for drunkenness.

This coalescence of filling with the holy spirit, fiery tongues, and the appearance of intoxication clearly calls to a world of inspiration that arises from far beyond the bounds of Israel's scriptures; it is at home rather in the Greco-Roman world, where the sign of true prophetic possession is filling by an overpowering *pneuma* and by a fiery demeanor and activity that, to the ignorant onlooker, looks like a drunken spectacle. It is a form of inspiration that rivals Delphi and ranks Jesus' followers with inspired sibyls. Luke does not, it would seem, want to forfeit this dimension of inspiration. The modern scholarly suggestion that the holy spirit in Luke-Acts principally inspires divine speech, like the prophets of the Hebrew scriptures, is slightly misleading.[10] The product of divine speech is not the whole of the story. Lurking under the surface of Pentecost — arguably the most important surface in the book of Acts — is the suspicion that the work of the holy spirit is not altogether tidy, that it occurs in a house that is filled with wind and noise, that there is a fiery dimension to inspiration akin to prophetic possession in the world outside of Judaism, that there is an inflaming disorder that not unjustifiably can be mistaken for drunkenness.

And so we return to the puzzle of the slave-girl, whose pythonic spirit Paul tolerated until, out of sheer annoyance, he told it to leave. Was there a latent appreciation for mildly illicit Greco-Roman conceptions of inspiration? Perhaps there was. At Pentecost, that appreciation lies embedded in the texture of the narrative. Beneath Luke's penchant for order — apostolic hegemony, the authority of the Jerusalem church, clear proclamation that convinces and convicts — lies an appreciation for the less tidy and more passionate experience of possession, with its fiery face and chaotic qualities, which could raise the status of the early believers because such ecstasy was understood as the direct gift of the divine world. What has Pentecost to do with Anthesteria? What has Jerusalem to do with Delphi? What have tongues as of fire to do with the fiery visage of Cassandra and the possessed? Directly? Absolutely nothing. But by way of association, by means of suggestion, a great deal, for Pentecost is put on a par with the popular Anthesteria, Jerusalem is now the locus of oracles that have vanished from Delphi, and the earliest believers are the heirs of Cassandra, the Pythia, Philo's prophets, and the Therapeutae, who are tinged by the *Schadenfreude* that the shadowy mystery of their inspiration evokes.

---

10. For the nuances of this position, see M. Turner, "The Spirit of Prophecy and the Power of Authoritative Preaching in Luke-Acts: A Question of Origins," *NTS* 38 (1992) 66-88.

Speaking in Tongues

Luke's narration of the first inspired speech in the history of the early church is subtler and less straightforward than it appears at first. The image of a sizeable band of fiery-headed believers filled with holy spirit, followed in short measure by the charge of intoxication, gives the distinct impression that their experience was ecstatic. The amazing ability of the onlookers to hear the powerful acts of God in their respective, and varied, dialects, gives the distinct impression that their speech was utterly comprehensible. Peter's explanation that they are inspired by the spirit about which Joel spoke rather than drunk with new wine (Acts 2:15-21), and his compelling sermon, which illustrates that inspiration leads to the singularly accurate interpretation of scripture, contributes to the impression that comprehensibility ruled this day of Pentecost.

This incongruous compatibility of ecstasy and comprehensibility, this sober intoxication, raises its head in still another way in the inspired speech of Jesus' earliest followers, who "spoke in other tongues." Luke's concern ultimately to underline comprehensibility may be the impetus for the inclusion of the single word "other" in Acts 2:4, which changes the tenor of the entire narrative.[11] Rather than narrating that the believers "spoke in tongues," Luke narrates instead that they "spoke in *other* tongues." Had Luke written that Jesus' followers spoke in tongues, had he written that they experienced glossolalia, which certainly would have entailed linguistic incomprehensibility, then we would have no difficulty understanding why many in the crowd thought them drunk. Incomprehensible speech akin to babble would serve well to explain the charge of drunkenness that Peter is compelled to dispel at the outset of his sermon.

The experience of speaking in incomprehensible tongues, in addition to explaining the charge of intoxication, would also fit the pattern of Acts as a whole. Luke is fond of triads: Peter's threefold dream of unclean food, three versions of the Cornelius story, and three versions of Saul's call. Speaking in tongues, if it occurred at Pentecost, would present us with another triad at pivotal points in the narrative. During his visit to Cornelius, while Peter is speaking, the holy spirit descends upon Gentiles, who speak in tongues: "The circumcised believers who had come with Peter were astounded that the gift of the holy spirit had been poured out even on the

11. See A. J. M. Wedderburn, "Traditions and Redaction in Acts 2.1-13," *JSNT* 55 (1994) 48-52.

Gentiles, for they heard them speaking in tongues and praising God. Then Peter said, 'Can anyone withhold the water for baptizing these people who have received the holy spirit just as we have?'" (Acts 10:45-47). Later in the narrative, Paul comes across a wayward band of John the Baptist's followers, who also speak in tongues: "Paul said, 'John baptized with the baptism of repentance, telling the people to believe in the one who was to come after him, that is, in Jesus.' On hearing this, they were baptized in the name of the Lord Jesus. When Paul had laid his hands on them, the holy spirit came upon them, and they spoke in tongues and prophesied — altogether there were about twelve of them" (19:4-7), thus marking the end of the era of John the Baptist, the greatest, according to Jesus, of those born of woman.

At three epochal junctures, therefore — the beginning of the church's mission with power from on high (Luke 24:49; Acts 1:8), the breaking of a potential Jewish stranglehold on the church with the inclusion of Gentiles, and the completion of John's promise of baptism with the holy spirit — the phenomenon of speaking in tongues would have taken place, but only if Acts 2:4 had read they "spoke in tongues" rather than "spoke in other tongues [i.e. dialects]." The triadic symmetry is fractured by the occurrence of the word "other" in that passage. Yet the inclusion of this single word may have been a small price for Luke to pay to avoid making ecstatic tongues-speaking the *sine qua non* of the early church, for the introduction of speaking in tongues at Pentecost rather than speaking in other dialects would have drawn exclusive attention to the ecstatic dimension of inspiration, and it may have allowed Luke's readers to draw a conceptual bee-line from Pentecost to the practice of tongues-speaking at Corinth. Though the Corinthians may have regarded such tongues-speech as the language of angels, they certainly employed this practice to generate a communal hell in which a gift that, according to Paul, was intended to lift the whole church became the hinge pin of spiritual hierarchies. In his effort to bring the Corinthians back into line, Paul gives a fairly full picture of speaking in tongues.

Speaking in tongues, according to Paul's first extant letter to the Corinthians, excludes the activity of the mind. It is a form of prayer in which, observes Paul, "my spirit prays but my mind is unproductive" (1 Cor 14:14). It is the quintessence of ecstasy, of being outside oneself. Even the analogy of musical instruments Paul draws — flutes and harps and bugles are intended to give distinct notes (14:7-8) — bears a family resemblance to the analogy adopted by Plutarch's Cleombrotus, in *On the Obsolescence of Ora-*

cles 431B, to explain the demise of Delphi — "when the demigods withdraw and forsake the oracles, these lie idle and inarticulate like the instruments of musicians." Similarly, Philo describes the prophetic phenomenon: "he is filled with inspiration, as the reason withdraws and surrenders the citadel of the soul to a new visitor and tenant, the divine spirit which plays upon the vocal organism and dictates words which clearly express its prophetic message" (*On the Special Laws* 4.49).

Speaking in tongues also, at its worst, consists of mindless chatter that benefits no one but the person who speaks: "nobody understands them, since they are speaking mysteries in the spirit" (1 Cor 14:2). Like a military bugle that bungles the battle cry with an indistinct sound, tongues is "speech that is not intelligible," "speaking into the air" (14:8-9), an act in which the speaker is a foreigner to the hearer and the hearer is a foreigner to the speaker (14:11). It cannot even evoke the response of "amen" because no one understands the words (14:16). In fact, unbelievers who participate in a church in which tongues are spoken by all will be driven away from faith and conclude, "you are out of your mind" (14:23).

Paul is compelled by the Corinthian overvaluation of incomprehensibility to offer several correctives.

1. In a list of spiritual gifts, Paul refers first to wisdom and knowledge and last to glossolalia and their interpretation (1 Cor 12:4-11). This placement of glossolalia corrects the assumption that the communication of inspired wisdom or knowledge arises out of an experience in which the mind is dormant. Glossolalia, this order implies, is not the principal source of inspired wisdom and knowledge. In another list, Paul again sets glossolalia and their interpretation in secondary positions, perhaps to imply that no worship experience, not even glossolalia, is powerful enough to reverse the proper order of the church: first apostles, second prophets, third teachers, then powers, then gifts of healing, assistance, and leadership, and then various kinds of glossolalia (12:27-28). Apostles, prophets, and teachers are the anchors of the "greater gifts" (12:31). In Rom 12:3-8 Paul does not even mention glossolalia.[12]

2. Set dramatically within this discussion of spiritual gifts is a poetically conceived paean on love which relativizes the value of all spiritual gifts (13:1-13). Without love, the inspired ability to speak "in the tongues of

---

12. See also Eph 4:11-12.

mortals or angels" is mere clanging and crashing noise. Similarly, "prophetic powers" — the ability to "understand all mysteries and all knowledge," the gift of extraordinary faith, to the point of moving mountains, the exercise of inspired generosity, even self-sacrifice — are of no value without love. None of the gifts which appear to mesmerize the Corinthians is of any worth without an extraordinary exercise of love.

3. Paul topples the Corinthians' priorities by advising them to pursue prophecy rather than tongues in order to build up the community: "For those who speak in a tongue do not speak to other people but to God; for nobody understands them, since they are speaking mysteries in the spirit. On the other hand, those who prophesy speak to other people for their upbuilding and encouragement and consolation. Those who speak in a tongue build up themselves, but those who prophesy build up the church" (14:2-4).

4. The clarity of the discussion from this moment in 1 Corinthians 14 dissipates, as Paul shifts from glossolalia to the interpretation of glossolalia. He is now less troubled by glossolalia than by glossolalia left uninterpreted. Still, Paul unequivocally admits, "I would like all of you to speak in tongues, but even more to prophesy," though, he concedes, prophesying is greater than tongues "unless someone interprets, so that the church may be built up" (14:5). This caveat suggests that, despite Paul's preference for prophesying, interpreted glossolalia can be as edifying as prophecy. The tongues-speaker, advises Paul, should pray for the power to interpret, so that those around may say "amen" in agreement, may be built up, and may be instructed (14:13-19).

5. Among his corrections Paul cites (14:21) a solitary Israelite text to reinforce his preference for prophesying over uninterpreted tongues, though LXX Isa 28:11-12 is notoriously difficult to interpret. Although it has the catchwords "other tongues," this text is about the judgment of Israel at the hands of foreign nations. With a strained application of Isaiah 28, Paul suggests that uninterpreted glossolalia brings some form of judgment or sign to unbelievers. When the interpretative dust settles, what may be said is this: if in 1 Corinthians 12 Paul demonstrated that uninterpreted glossolalia did not edify believers, this solitary citation shows somehow that uninterpreted glossolalia also have a devastating effect upon unbelievers, who will charge that the church is mad (14:22-23). Prophesying, in contrast, will open their hearts and lead them to faith (14:24-25).

6. In order to draw the Corinthians to the clear priority that everything should be done "for building up" the community (14:26), Paul turns in conclusion to extremely practical advice: every gift in worship should be exercised one at a time, that is, in an orderly fashion. He even implies that interpretation and glossolalia are not uncontrollable acts when he advises tongues-speakers to keep it to themselves and to God if there is no interpreter present (14:27-28). Whether glossolalia or prophesying or hymns or revelations, these must take place in order, while all others remain silent (14:26-33).

7. Based upon his own experience, Paul suggests that the clearest arena for the exercise of glossolalia is private, personal prayer. In a thinly veiled boast, Paul thanks God that he speaks in tongues more than all of the Corinthians. Despite the vitality of his personal prayer life, Paul would prefer to speak five words in public with his mind intact "in order to instruct others also" (14:18-20).

The lack of benefit to others, the apparently idle and incomprehensible chatter, the indistinctness of tongues-speech — all of these suggest why Luke is reluctant to base the experience at Pentecost upon a filling with the holy spirit that produces the sort of unintelligible, indistinct, and mindless language which, at Corinth at least, could so handily be taken captive to the spiritual disarray and dissension of a church. Yet Luke has not effaced this element altogether. He has preserved the words "speaking in tongues" along with the word "other" and in this way ensures that an ecstatic experience does not lie terribly far under the surface of Pentecost. He could have, after all, found other ways of expressing that the first believers were able to speak languages they did not know. He has as well preserved the troubling words "they are drunk with new wine," which, though in a slightly different key, is not altogether different from what Paul presumes unbelievers will say upon observing a group in which each is simultaneously speaking in tongues: "you are out of your mind." The parallels between Pentecost and Corinth are eerily close — whether or not Luke was aware of the situation at Corinth in Paul's day — as is both Paul and Luke's keen effort to dam the flood of ecstasy without finally causing the experience to evaporate altogether.

Although the inclusion of the word "other" between "speaking" and "tongues" in Acts 2:4 fractures the triadic symmetry that would have existed between three instances of speaking in tongues in Acts (2:4; 10:46;

and 19:6), this word may also generate a triadic symmetry of its own, for in each of these three instances Luke is not satisfied to present speaking in tongues as an isolated experience of ecstasy. In Acts 2, of course, the believers spoke in "other" tongues, proclaiming the powerful acts of God in a variety of comprehensible foreign dialects.[13]

When, in the second instance, the holy spirit came upon Cornelius and his Gentile friends, Peter and his coterie heard them "speaking in tongues and praising God" (Acts 10:46). There must be a comprehensible dimension to this sort of speaking in tongues, for Peter and his Jewish companions were able to recognize that the ability to speak in tongues was associated with the comprehensible act of praise. This brief reference to praise, in fact, is not unlike the recitation of "God's powerful acts" at Pentecost; the verb "praise" *(megalynein)* in 10:46 is even related to the word "powerful acts" — perhaps "praiseworthy" would be a better translation — *(ta megaleia)* in 2:11.[14] Several points of correspondence, then, draw the stories of Pentecost and the Gentiles together: the inspiration of the holy spirit, the recitation of God's praiseworthy acts, and the phrase "speaking in (other) tongues." These striking correspondences may even lead to the inference that the *content* of the Gentiles' speech consisted of a recitation of God's praiseworthy acts, as at Pentecost, while the *mode* of praise was once again speech in comprehensible tongues — languages or dialects — which Peter and his Jerusalem colleagues, who themselves had spoken in other dialects at Pentecost, were surprised to be able to recognize.

This scenario characterizes as well the third instance of speaking in (other) tongues, in which Luke's readers meet a band of the Baptist's "disciples," about a dozen in all, whom Paul encountered in Ephesus. This group had not received the holy spirit when they were baptized; in fact, they claimed not to have heard of the holy spirit. They had therefore been baptized solely in the name of the Lord Jesus. When Paul laid his hands upon them, "the holy spirit came upon them, and they spoke in tongues and prophesied" (Acts 19:6). This association between speaking in tongues and prophesying, like the association between speaking in tongues and praise, provides another signal of Luke's willingness to preserve an ecstatic

13. Ben Sira's grandson, in the preface of his translation of Sirach from Hebrew into Greek, uses the words *eis heteran glōssan* in the context of describing the difficulties of translation. Luke's vocabulary is almost identical; filled by the spirit, the believers began to speak *heterais glōssais.*

14. Acts 10:46. Greek: *ēkouon gar autōn lalountōn glōssais kai megalynontōn ton theon;* Acts 2:11: *akouomen lalountōn autōn tais hēmeterais glōssais ta megaleia tou theou.*

element — speaking in tongues — while ultimately setting it alongside narrative elements which are suggestive of an experience that heightens human comprehension.

Prophesying in Acts is altogether comprehensible. Luke makes countless references to the very clear message of the Israelite prophets — a message that, resisted by the Jews in Acts, led to their demise.[15] The clarity and consequences of that prophetic message are incontrovertible. In continuity with Israelite prophets, the prophets who are alive and active in Acts punctuate the history of the early church with occasional but certain clarity about the future. Agabus correctly predicts a famine (11:27-29). At Antioch, prophets and teachers are active in worship, in the context of which the holy spirit says, presumably through them, "Set apart for me Barnabas and Saul for the work to which I have called them" (13:1-3). Once again, the divine revelation is marked by precision and clarity. Following the Jerusalem Council, Judas and Silas, themselves prophets, are sent to Antioch with a letter saying that they will communicate the Council's decision, supposedly what is in the letter, "by word of mouth." When they arrive in Antioch, they encourage and strengthen the believers — again, comprehensible speech with practical consequences (15:27-28, 32). Finally, Agabus, a prophet from Judea (who may be the same as the Agabus who predicted the famine), appears in Caesarea and dramatically takes Paul's belt, binds his feet and hands with it, and says, "Thus says the holy spirit, 'This is the way the Jews in Jerusalem will bind the man who owns this belt and will hand him over to the Gentiles.'" Those gathered around Paul take this prediction, which is once again precise and practical, so seriously that they urge him to stay away from Judea, to avoid Jerusalem altogether (21:10-12).

Prophets punctuate pivotal points in the life of the early church with precision, prediction, and practicality: ahead of a famine, at the headwaters of the church's mission, after the Jerusalem Council, and at the dramatic moment when Paul chooses to seal his fate by returning to Jerusalem. Prophets propel the church, and key persons in it, toward its destiny. When Luke associates speaking in tongues with prophesying, he simultaneously preserves and subordinates the ecstatic dimension of speaking in tongues; he mutes the ecstatic resonance of speaking in tongues, which is by definition incomprehensible, by tying the experience inextricably to an act of speech that is quintessentially comprehensible.

---

15. This is the focal point of Stephen's speech in Acts 7:2-53.

Each element in the triad of Pentecost, Cornelius and his coterie, and the bewildered disciples in Ephesus features the holy spirit and speaking in (other) tongues. Furthermore, the second and third episodes are related to the first. The Gentiles who come to believe in the wake of Cornelius's invitation to Peter, like the hearers at Pentecost, receive the "gift of the holy spirit" (2:38-39; 10:45). The dozen or so disciples at Ephesus are counted among the few in Acts who, in direct fulfillment of Joel's prophecy, actually prophesy. This triad becomes even tighter if we recognize that praise and prophesying, according to Peter's Pentecost sermon, are deeply intertwined. The earliest believers offer praise when they recite God's praiseworthy acts, while Peter identifies this activity of praise with prophesying by interpreting this speech as the fulfillment of Joel's prediction — though this is actually an addition to the quotation — that in the last days "they will prophesy."

Luke has, then, composed a remarkable triad to replace the ecstatic triad of a threefold speaking in tongues. When the first believers are filled with the holy spirit, they speak the praiseworthy acts of God in comprehensible other tongues — other languages or dialects — and Peter sees this as a fulfillment of Joel's prophecy that those upon whom the spirit would be poured out in the last days would prophesy. When Gentiles speak in tongues, they participate actively in praise, as had the followers of Jesus during Pentecost. When John's disciples speak in tongues, they participate actively in prophesying. In this way, the association of speaking in other tongues with praise-as-prophesying at Pentecost is extended when the Gentiles speak in tongues and praise, and then again when John's disciples speak in tongues and prophesy.

What, in the end, are we to make of speaking in tongues at key moments in the early church? The way scholars typically line up on one side of the debate or the other, according to whether they understand speaking in tongues *either* as speech in comprehensible foreign dialects *or* as incomprehensible speech, is unfortunate.[16] What Luke does is more subtle than to opt for *either* ecstatic tongues speech *or* comprehensible foreign languages. We reckoned with this subtlety in Luke's narrative of Pentecost, which preserves the ecstatic dimension by retaining the elements of filling

16. See Fitzmyer, *The Acts of the Apostles,* 239, for an extensive list of scholars who understand this phenomenon *either* as an ecstatic experience, speaking in tongues, *or* as xenolalia, speaking in foreign tongues.

with the holy spirit, fire, the phrase "speaking in (other) tongues," and the impression of intoxication. Luke is prepared not only to tolerate but even to appreciate the ecstatic dimension of Pentecost. Yet he recognizes that this is not the whole of the story, for he refers not to speaking in tongues, which would eclipse and obfuscate other dimensions of the narrative, but to speaking in other tongues, other dialects that the hearers are amazed to be able to understand. Luke appears happily to embrace the worth of both ecstasy and restraint. The power of Pentecost may lie, in Luke's estimation, not in either incomprehensibility or apprehension, but in the early believers' ability to straddle both worlds. Luke provokes his readers to recognize both forms of inspiration somehow melded into neither one nor the other but into some inscrutable amalgamation of both.

In a shorthand way, this is precisely what Luke accomplishes in Acts 10 and 19 as well. In both narratives he preserves the element of speaking in tongues — an element that can hardly do less than evoke the Corinthian experience of speaking in tongues to which Paul himself lays claim. This would seem to be an unequivocal claim to uncomprehending ecstasy, the *sine qua non* of which is the inability to understand — and perhaps to remember afterwards — what one is saying under the powerful influence of holy *pneuma*. But no sooner than Luke takes up the language of pristine ecstasy does he modify the force of that ecstasy by associating such tongues-speech with praise and prophesying. Luke, with an exquisite ability to maintain this tension at key moments that defined the early church, preserves the impression of ecstasy while simultaneously hemming such ecstasy into a realm of comprehensibility, into a numinous world of ecstasy that also communicates clearly by way of other dialects, praise, and prophesying.

And in this ability, Luke was not alone in the first century. Philo claimed both forms of inspiration for himself: the ecstasy of corybantic dance and the heightened alertness that imparts to him the ability to peer into Torah and to discern what others fail to see: inspired allegorical interpretations that solve and salvage otherwise inscrutable dimensions of scripture.[17] Yet the greatest honor is Moses', because he, at one and the same time, succumbed to the frequent and forceful power of ecstatic inspiration and was, in an unprecedented way, attuned to the divine spirit which guided his mind to the truth. It is with this strategy of attributing to

17. See *On the Migration of Abraham* 34–35; *On the Special Laws* 3.1-6; and *On the Cherubim* 27–29.

Moses simultaneous experiences of ecstasy and sharpened intellect that Philo intends to portray Moses as the greatest of all prophets, the most divine revealer of divine truths.[18] Though in a less overt way, the author of *4 Ezra* adopts a similar apologetic strategy when he presents the experience of the famed scribe Ezra. In response to his request that God send the holy spirit into him, Ezra drinks a cup of liquid that has the color of fire — the hues of ecstasy — yet finds his heart able to pour out understanding, his breast increasing in wisdom, and his spirit capable of memory, in contrast to inspired prophets for whom the loss of memory is the surest sign of ecstasy (*4 Ezra* 14:40).

Luke adopts a similar strategy when he preserves a combination of ecstatic elements — spirit-filling, fire, apparent intoxication, and speaking in tongues — with elements that entail heightened knowledge, such as speaking God's praiseworthy acts in *other* tongues, praise, and prophesying. All three authors adopt a similar strategy in which the most spendidly inspired human beings combine ecstasy and heightened intellectual acuity under the influence of the spirit. For Philo this is Moses, whose combined experience as the most sublime prophet and the giver of Torah eclipses even Philo's own notable experiences of ecstasy and intellectual acuity. In *4 Ezra,* this is the most renowned scribe, Ezra. For Luke, these are Jesus' prayerful followers, whom the spirit fills at Pentecost. To opt for either ecstatic tongues or comprehensible foreign languages in the interpretation of the Pentecost experience, not to mention subsequent moments of inspiration in Acts, is to diminish the fullness of the spirit and to deplete the levels of resonance that Luke, like Philo and the author of *4 Ezra,* preserves. Pentecost encapsulates not merely the ecstatic or the intellectual but a rare, inspired blend of both.

To appreciate the marvel of these magnificent moments in Acts, we should perhaps recall the closing events of a traditional Ionian festival in honor of Apollo held at Delos during the sixth and fifth centuries B.C.E., the so-called Homeric Hymn to Delian Apollo, in which these events comprise a "great wonder," consisting of praise to the gods, praise of notable figures from the past, and speaking in foreign languages. The girls of Delos, following the praise of Apollo, Leto, and Artemis, "sang a strain telling of men and women of past days, and charm the tribes of humanity." These two elements, of course, are not unlike the proclamation of God's praise-

18. See *On the Life of Moses* 2.264-65; 2.188-91.

worthy acts at Pentecost. So too is the great marvel that follows: "they can imitate the tongues of all people and their clattering speech: each would say that he himself were singing, so close to truth is their sweet song." Whether this ability to speak in the languages of all people is a miracle, the product of inspiration, or a practiced art of imitation is not entirely clear. The words *mega thauma* ("great wonder") can suggest both a great miracle or an amazing spectacle, though the verb "imitate" *(mimeomai)* suggests that the girls have memorized foreign languages — not unlike many modern college choirs which sing in Latin — in which they are now speaking, to the amazement of the gathered crowds. This awesome theatrical spectacle, in which the girls of Delos amazed with the sheer ability to represent all human languages in a single sacred festival, provides a salient backdrop for the drama of the inspired ability of Jesus' earliest followers to speak in foreign languages at Pentecost. While there is no genetic or historical or literary connection between the Hymn to Delian Apollo and the narrative of Pentecost, and while inspiration was probably not associated with the great spectacle during the Ionian festival, as a literary backdrop to Pentecost, the description of this festival underscores the awe and delight which attended even a theatrical imitation of the world's languages. And this is not all, for the content of both hymn and narrative is the marvels of "past days," the "powerful acts of God."

Luke, as we have seen repeatedly, preserves important Greco-Roman elements that would serve to heighten a Roman reader's appreciation for the events which he narrates. A dramatic infilling by the holy spirit, tongues as of fire, the impression of intoxication, speaking in tongues — even other languages — all of these are elements that set the Pentecost narrative against the background of the grand oracular history of Greece and Rome. Acts is not merely a history of the holy spirit in the early church; the early church is a magnet that draws together the very best and the most popular modes of inspiration, Greco-Roman modes of inspiration that had wide currency as well among authors of early Judaism. Such modes of inspiration extend from an apostle who has an ecstatic rooftop vision during lunchtime to a slave-girl whose pythonic spirit captures the essence of the early church's proclamation.[19] The reminiscence of the Ionian festival in the narrative of Pentecost may be still another instance of Luke's attempt to expand the canvas of his portrait, to stretch the allusive bound-

---

19. For further details, see C. Forbes, *Prophecy and Inspired Speech in Early Christianity and Its Hellenistic Environment* (Peabody: Hendrickson, 1997) 116-17, 119-23, and *passim*.

aries of his story. If even a rehearsed ability to speak in other tongues was considered a spectacle of noteworthy proportions, how much more so would the spontaneous inspiration of the holy spirit be noteworthy if it produced in unlettered Galileans the ability to communicate God's powerful acts in the foreign language of every single soul gathered from the Jewish Diaspora in Jerusalem?

Spirit and the Inspired Interpretation of Scripture

The turn of the first century, just about the time when Luke may have composed his history of the early church, was a period rife with strangeness and superstition. This was a time when scribes were believed to be able feverishly to copy ninety-four dictated books, and to do so in characters they did not understand (*4 Ezra* 14). Inspiration was so afoot during these decades that a Jewish general who had turned traitor did not expect to stretch the credibility of his readers when he had the gall to construe this treachery as piety and to attribute it to a diet of "nightly dreams, in which God had foretold to him the impending fate of the Jews and the destinies of the Roman sovereigns. He was an interpreter of dreams and skilled in divining the meaning of ambiguous utterances of the Deity; a priest himself and of priestly descent, he was not ignorant of the prophecies in the sacred books. At that hour he was inspired to read their meaning, and, recalling the dreadful images of his recent dreams, he offered up a silent prayer to God" (Josephus, *Jewish War* 3.351-53). And, as much as Plutarch's Simmias may have detested the popular appeal of unbounded enthusiasm, he was forced to admit that, "in popular belief . . . it is only in sleep that people receive inspiration from on high; and the notion that they are so influenced when awake and in full possession of their faculties is accounted strange and incredible" (*On the Sign of Socrates* 589D).

The atmosphere Luke establishes in his narrative of the early church is little different from this milieu, with its heavy dose of *Schadenfreude*. The story is populated by people who lay the sick on cots and mats in the street in the hopes that Peter's shadow might fall on them (Acts 5:15), by a magician who ingenuously believes that he can buy the power of healing (8:9-24), by trances and visions and divine voices on rooftops (10:9-23), by an angel who pokes a prisoner in the side (12:7),[20] by people who are eager to

20. On angels, see Acts 12:6-17; 27:21-26.

believe that Zeus and Hermes have taken human form (14:8-18),[21] by four sisters with the gift of prophecy (21:9), and, of course, by a slave-girl who grasps the nub of the early church's message because she is possessed by a pythonic spirit (16:16-18). This is a world full of magic and superstition, though it is nonetheless a world that Luke spends less time repudiating than he does taking it capture to the missionary impulse of the church. These are the extraordinary ways — at least some of the amazing ways — that establish the authority of the apostolic band, that lead people into the world of faith, into the lordship of Jesus and the community of the church. Luke does not altogether reject these bizarre — to our sensibilities, perhaps — occurrences.

Luke does not close the door on this atmosphere of the extraordinary, even when he describes the spoken word. Marvellous speech occurs during the Feast of Pentecost, when the house is full of a violent wind, when Jesus' followers have fiery tongues rest upon them, when they are filled with the holy spirit, and when they are charged with making a drunken spectacle of themselves. What this band of believers appears to do, at least in the eyes of a good many of the spectators, is to participate in the sort of fiery frenzy that characterized the Delphic priestess or the ribald devotees of Bacchus — enough so that Peter must disabuse the crowd of their impression that the band is drunk.

Without eradicating the ecstatic dimension of this story, Luke points the way toward a form of inspiration that prizes and raises native abilities, the sort of inspiration that Philo marks with the moniker "Sober Intoxication." Luke includes the word "other" in the phrase "spoke in tongues"; Jesus' inspired followers were able to proclaim the powerful acts of God in comprehensible foreign dialects. He presents Peter's disavowal of the charge that Jesus' followers are drunk with new wine; they are not drunk but filled with the holy spirit. And he includes a verb, "to declare" *(apophthengesthai)*, which, we shall soon see, signals the onset of a well-argued, rhetorically compelling speech: filled with (the) holy spirit, the followers of Jesus stun their hearers with their perspicuous ability to recount God's powerful acts in other dialects than their native Galilean. While set in a context that portends a rich experience of ecstasy, then, the Pentecost experience entails a heightening of the native abilities of Jesus' followers, and a heightening that is aimed at a uniquely viable interpretation of scripture.

21. Acts 14:8-18 includes a priest of Zeus who brings animals to sacrifice.

The Inspired Interpretation of Scripture

Filling with the spirit in the book of Acts is the sort of inspiration that amazes, that startles, because it catalyzes impressive and entirely unexpected abilities of scriptural interpreters. This inspiration is the primary effect, the principal consequence, of filling by the holy spirit in the book of Acts. Peter's speech at Pentecost (Acts 2:14-36), of course, features a catena of scripture references, each of which is interpreted to demonstrate that the experience of Pentecost fulfills Israelite scripture. In addition to citations of LXX Joel 3:1-5; Ps 15:8-11; and 109:1, this sermon is replete with numerous allusions, such as to 1 Kgs 2:10; Ps 132:11; Isa 32:15; 57:19; and Deut 32:5.

Yet it is in a subsequent speech that Luke ties Peter's speech explicitly and irreversibly to the holy spirit. Notwithstanding the brevity of his portrayal, the narrative contains essential ingredients. The day before this speech, Peter has healed a crippled beggar and delivered another characteristic speech from which peals the theme that Jesus was the wrongfully murdered Messiah, the prophet whom Moses had predicted, the servant whom God had raised, a messenger of the people of Israel. This talk of resurrection, which led five thousand to faith in Jesus at Pentecost, had the effect of provoking the Sadducees, who late in the day arrested him. On the following day, a grand congress gathered, consisting of elders, scribes, the high priest, and the high priestly families. The question? "By what power or by what name did you do this?" (Acts 4:7). The simple answer, of course, is that the name, the authority, of Jesus effected the healing. But Peter's response is not so simple, for it answers with something more than a direct response; Peter answers by appealing to the contemporaneity of Ps 118:22: "This Jesus is 'the stone that was rejected by you, the builders; it has become the cornerstone'" (Acts 4:11). Although this is the only text that Peter quotes in this context, it is doubtless an epitome of a lengthier speech, for we know that Psalm 118 was a cherished and popular scriptural text which had an integral role in the confession and preaching of the early church; 1 Pet 2:1-10 even provides an instance in which it is listed alongside other scriptural texts.

The centerpiece of the sermon, then, consists precisely of what Peter's sermon at Pentecost would lead a careful reader to expect: the inspired application of scripture to Jesus or, to put it the other way around, an explanation of the fate of Jesus through inspired scriptural interpretation. The introduction and conclusion to this abbreviated speech fit this centerpiece like masterful literary bookends. Peter's interpretation of scripture arises from his being "filled with the holy spirit." This filling enables Peter to deliver a speech that consists of more than mere assertion, more than his own conviction, more than a personal experience of Jesus. His sermon consists rather of interpretation, of credible ground for his conviction, of a scriptural foundation for his assertion. This is the sermon that catches the eye of Peter's elite hearers and looks to them like the fruits of education. "Now when they saw the boldness of Peter and John and realized that they were uneducated and ordinary men, they were amazed and recognized them as companions of Jesus" (Acts 4:13). Peter is able, once he is filled by the holy spirit, to interpret scripture as if he were educated, although he is not.

What lingers in the wake of Peter's application of scripture in the presence of the auspicious congress is, not surprisingly, the same sort of amazement *(ethaumazon)* that had accompanied the events of Pentecost, when the followers of Jesus were first filled with the holy spirit: "Amazed and astonished [*existanto de kai ethaumazon*], they asked, 'Are not all these who are speaking Galileans? And how is it that we hear, each of us, in our own native language?'" (Acts 2:7-8). This notion of amazement is not one that Luke bandies about lightly. Apart from these occurrences, a reference to Moses' amazement at the burning bush (7:31), and the occurrence of this word within a quotation of Hab 1:5 (13:41), it occurs elsewhere only when Peter asks those who have witnessed a healing, "You Israelites, why are you amazed at this? . . ." (3:12). This amazement, then, along with infilling by the holy spirit, provides still another literary bridge from Pentecost to Peter's speech before the Jewish leaders.

Peter, therefore, has taken up the gauntlet of Pentecost in the presence of the Jewish elite. He is, like the early believers — himself included — filled with the holy spirit. His inspired speech, like theirs, amazes the listeners. And his speech, like his earlier speech at Pentecost, hinges upon the interpretation of scripture in direct relation to Jesus the Messiah.

These correspondences with Pentecost persist into the next narrative scene, which follows the release of Peter and John from prison. Their report that the chief priests and elders have forbidden them to preach leads to a communal prayer which, in a pattern that has become increasingly predictable, contains a citation of Israelite literature, of Ps 2:1-2 applied directly to their situation. The nations and kings who rage "against the Lord and against his Messiah" are identified without hesitation as "Herod and Pontius Pilate, with the Gentiles and the peoples of Israel, gathered together against your holy servant Jesus." The community therefore prays for boldness — as in Peter's boldness before the elite in Acts 4:13 — and for signs and wonders to accompany their speech — as in Peter's citation of Joel in 2:19. The answer to this prayer comes quickly and in hues unmistakably reminiscent of Pentecost: "When they had prayed, the place in which they were gathered together was shaken; and they were all filled with the holy spirit and spoke the word of God with boldness" (4:31). Although the phrase "word of God" is not an overt indication of scriptural interpretation, when Luke furnishes the content of these sermons, which he identifies as the word of God, it is typically rife with scriptural allusions and citations.[22] Here again, therefore, are the elements that earlier characterized Pentecost: the community gathered in prayer, this time praying a prayer which applies Psalm 2 directly to their own situation; the shaking of a place not unlike the rush of a violent wind as it filled the entire house; filling with the holy spirit; and a bold proclamation of the word of God. This is Pentecost afresh, renewed boldness, continued inspiration.

This sort of inspiration would not belong solely to the Jerusalem community for long. Following his encounter with the risen Jesus while he is en route to Damascus in pursuit of Jesus' followers, Saul is transformed. He cannot see, and he neither eats nor drinks. Although he is blind physically, he and Ananias, like Peter and Cornelius in the next scene, have visions about one another, and Ananias, like Peter after him, resists his, for he claims to have heard how cruelly Saul has treated the followers of Jesus. Still, like Peter, Ananias relents and, having entered Saul's house, lays his hands upon him and says, "Brother Saul, the Lord Jesus, who appeared to you on your way here, has sent me so that you may regain your sight and be filled with the holy spirit" (Acts 9:17). As soon as Saul can see, he is baptized, eats some food, and regains his strength.

The impact of this filling by the holy spirit upon Saul is apparent immediately: "For several days he was with the disciples in Damascus, and immediately he began to proclaim Jesus in the synagogues, saying, 'He is the Son of God'" (9:19-20). The nature of this proclamation is more than

22. The expression *logos tou theou* occurs in Acts 4:31; 6:2, 7; 8:14; 11:1; 12:24; 13:5, 7, 46; 17:13; 18:11. In some of these instances, the phrase is a clear indication of preaching from the Jewish scriptures. E.g., the preaching of the word of God in Beroea is preceded by the narrative note, "These Jews were more receptive than those in Thessalonica, for they welcomed the message very eagerly and *examined the scriptures* every day to see whether these things were so" (17:11).

inspired preaching of a general sort. It is more than free-floating assertions about Jesus and unmoored but enthusiastically expressed convictions. It is not principally a recitation of what took place on the road to Damascus. Luke writes rather that "Saul became increasingly more powerful and confounded the Jews who lived in Damascus *by proving* that Jesus was the Messiah" (9:22). Saul's preaching entails arguments that demonstrate, to the amazement of his hostile Jewish hearers, the messiahship of Jesus. And how does he do this? By appeal to the scriptures, of course, which is how such preaching is always accomplished in the book of Acts. Even the participle "proving" *(symbibazōn)* connotes gathering up or bringing together — in this case, marshalling arguments from the Jewish scriptures to establish his contention.[23] Saul's compelling and confounding proclamation consists principally of scriptural interpretation inspired by the holy spirit.[24]

The final instance in Acts of filling by the holy spirit, which has to do with Saul's condemnation of the magician Bar-Jesus, adds an exclamation point to the association of inspiration with interpretation. In this episode, the magician and false prophet Bar-Jesus accompanies Sergius Paulus, a proconsul who appears to be particularly responsive to the teaching of Barnabas and Saul. When Bar-Jesus attempts to interrupt the process by turning the proconsul away from the faith, Saul, who is now also known by this point as Paul, "filled with the holy spirit, looked intently at him and said,

23. So Fitzmyer, *The Acts of the Apostles,* 436; F. F. Bruce, *The Acts of the Apostles,* 3rd ed. (Grand Rapids: Wm. B. Eerdmans, 1952) 241; R. W. Wall, "The Acts of the Apostles: Introduction, Commentary, and Reflections," in *NIB* 10 (Nashville: Abingdon, 2002) 153.

24. There is, in fact, a subtle association between the three verbs Luke selects to characterize Saul: become more powerful, confound, and prove. The association of the appeal to scripture and filling with the spirit we see repeatedly in Acts. The notion of becoming more powerful can be related to the spirit given from birth. John the Baptist, according to the gospel of Luke, "grew and became strong in spirit" (1:80). However, the immense rush in this increasing strength in Paul's case would have led Greco-Roman readers to attribute this to a new endowment of the holy spirit; Saul became a person who, filled to the brim with a new energy, was inspired to muster Israel's scriptures in a way that would demonstrate the messianic character of Jesus. The effect of such inspired interpretation upon the hearers, as has been so often the case, is consternation at the way in which Saul interprets the scriptures. This had been so at Pentecost, when Jesus' followers could speak God's powerful acts in foreign dialects. It was so when Peter preached to the Jewish elite, who were stunned by how such an unlettered person could speak. And, following the pattern, it is so now, where the Jews who hear Saul's arguments from scripture in support of the sonship of Jesus are confounded.

'You son of the devil, you enemy of all righteousness, full of all deceit and villainy, will you not stop making crooked the straight paths of the Lord? And now listen — the hand of the Lord is against you, and you will be blind for a while, unable to see the sun'" (Acts 13:10-11). This is a colorful indictment, and it looks as if Paul's speech is a specimen of rage rather than the inspired interpretation of scripture. It appears to be an *ad hoc* diatribe, a string of free-flowing invectives pouring from the mouth of a man who has lost his temper.

Nothing could be farther from the truth. Although some of Paul's phrases are more incidental than others (e.g., "now listen"), and while some may have been drawn more directly from the early church (e.g., "son of the devil" and 1 John 3:10), nearly every phrase — actually all words but one, *rhadiourgias* — have their counterpart in the Septuagint:

you enemy of all righteousness	*echthre pasēs dikaiosynēs*	Gen 32:11 *(apo pasēs dikaiosynēs)*; 1 Sam 12:7 *(tēn pasan dikaiosynēn)*
You son of the devil	*huie diabolou*	E.g., 1 Chr 21:1; Job 1:6 *(diabolos)*
full of all deceit and villainy	*ō plērēs pantos dolou kai pasēs rhadiourgias*	Sir 1:30 *(hē kardia sou plērēs dolou)*; see also 19:26; Jer 5:27
will you not stop making crooked the straight paths of the Lord?	*ou pausē diastrephōn tas hodous [tou] kyriou tas eutheias*	Prov 10:9 *(ho de diastrephōn tas hodous autou)*; Hos 14:10 *(eutheiai hai hodoi tou kyriou)*; see Isa 40:3
now listen	*kai nyn idou*	e.g., Gen 12:19 *(kai nyn idou)*
the hand of the Lord is against you	*cheir kyriou epi se*	1 Sam 7:13 *(cheir kyriou epi)*

Even if some phrases or words are drawn from elsewhere, the gauntlet Saul lays down, when he is filled with the holy spirit, is deeply imbued by the hues of scripture. Most important is that the climax of this indictment is the portion of Saul's speech that is indisputably indebted to Israelite literature; the direct question posed to Bar-Jesus, "will you not stop making crooked the straight paths of the Lord?" is an amalgamation of LXX Prov 10:9 and Hos 14:10.

What appears at first to be an extemporaneous string of invectives, then, is actually yet another instance of the inspired application of scripture to the situation of the early church. The question Saul puts to Bar-Jesus is a direct application of two otherwise separate scriptures that Saul, under the inspiration of the holy spirit, has combined into a forceful and extremely effective indictment of this false prophet. The prophet goes blind, after all, and the proconsul believes. And, of course, the proconsul, as we would expect, was "astonished" as well "at the teaching about the Lord" (*ekplēssomenos epi tē didachē kyriou;* Acts 13:12).[25]

In the heady world of inspiration evoked by the book of Acts, the holy spirit inspires more than short outbursts of inspired proclamation or prophetic speech.[26] The focus of the holy spirit's inspiration is the interpretation of Israel's scriptures. Peter's speech at Pentecost is little more than a string of scriptural pearls, a catena of quotations, intended to explain the marvels of latter-day events — the death, resurrection, and exaltation of Jesus, as well as the gift of the holy spirit. Even when Luke grants only a snippet of a speech that is prompted by filling with the spirit, in each case he is careful to convey the essence of that speech: Peter defends himself before the Jewish elite with a sermon that turns on Ps 118:22; the gathered believers are filled with the holy spirit immediately after they have prayed a prayer that is shaped on the anvil of Ps 2:1-2; Paul stays on in Damascus and musters arguments from the scriptures on Jesus' behalf; and, when he indicts the false prophet and magician Bar-Jesus, Paul unleashes a string of invectives that are composed of unambiguous allusions to Israel's scriptures, particularly a climax that is rooted in Prov 10:9 and Hos 14:10. In short, every instance of filling with the holy spirit in the book of Acts consists of the interpretation of scripture.

There is, therefore, in the book of Acts an intimate relationship between the interpretation of scripture and filling with the holy spirit. Further, if Paul's first experience of the holy spirit in Damascus provides a clue to the process of such inspired interpretation, then such inspiration is not, in Luke's opinion, the extemporaneous calling up of scriptures that were unknown prior to each sermon, speech, or prayer. Rather, it is the organizing and culling of scriptures — marshalling disparate texts — that have long been studied so as to become particularly persuasive in a concrete con-

25. This is my understanding, although this may also be understood as a reference to the teaching of the Lord through Saul.

26. See M. Turner, *Power from on High: The Spirit in Israel's Restoration and Witness in Acts.* JPTSup 9 (Sheffield: Sheffield Academic, 1996) 168.

text, whether in front of Pentecost pilgrims, before the Jewish elite, in the synagogues of Damascus, or in the presence of a proconsul. This is especially plain in Peter's citation of Ps 118:22. This psalm, this verse in particular, had circulated widely in the early church. It was not a discrete text that came off the top of Peter's head in a flash of inspiration or one that was spoken through him with his mind void of thought, propelled by the sort of inspiration that Philo attributes to Israel's prophets. This text was clearly part and parcel of early testimonia to Jesus rather than an inspired afterthought.

Luke's consistent association of filling with the holy spirit and the interpretation of scripture has decided implications for understanding the content of inspired speech at Pentecost. The hearers who gathered together that day, like so many others who would hear inspired scriptural interpretation throughout Acts, were amazed at what they heard, the content of which they described, in shorthand, as "God's praiseworthy acts" (Acts 2:11).[27] Jesus' followers were doing what everyone else did when they were filled with the holy spirit: interpreting the scriptures in light of the deeds of Jesus. God's praiseworthy acts, which had so often before been recited in song and study, were now presented afresh in what Jesus' followers, and perhaps those spectators who did not think his followers were drunk, would understand to be an indisputable instance of inspired speech.

Why Luke should draw together the presence of the holy spirit within and an impressive interpretation of scripture is scarcely a mystery, for other Jewish authors of the Greco-Roman era took precisely this tack to buttress their claim to a peculiar window into the truth of Israel's literature. I will touch only briefly now upon a few examples, since we explored them thoroughly earlier in this study.[28]

Though he was part of a long-standing and established literary tradition of Alexandrian exegesis, Philo still believed that his allegorical interpretation of Israelite literature arose from the presence of the divine spirit within. On some occasions, the spirit led him to corybantic frenzy, to unconsciousness of anything but the keenest light (*On the Migration of Abraham* 35). On other occasions, the invisible spirit, the "customary secret tenant," played the role of tutor to Philo's mind, aiding him in his relentless

---

27. On the phrase "praiseworthy acts of God," see Ps 71:19; 105:1 (which is followed by a litany of God's wonders, from the exodus onward, which the Israelites are said to ignore); 1QS I 21; 1QM X 8. See also Fitzmyer, *The Acts of the Apostles,* 243.

28. See above, Part II, chapter 3.

pursuit of the meaning of Torah, helping him to unlock its conundrums (*On Dreams* 2.252; *On the Cherubim* 27–29). Philo does not, it is essential to note, claim inspiration when he interprets ancient texts on a literal level; the spirit rather provides the groundwork for a higher level of meaning, for allegorical interpretation. The spirit is not, therefore, the inner presence that directs Philo as interpreter on all occasions, but only on those occasions when he needs particular help, when the literal meaning must be displaced by another, less obvious meaning, when he peers into the writings of Moses and sees what others miss (*On the Special Laws* 3.1-6). The spirit functions, in other words, to authenticate what is unique to his interpretation.

Philo lived in the pulsating urban center of Alexandria, and the Teacher of Righteousness inhabited a remote desert. Their postures toward Greco-Roman culture occupy opposing ends of the spectrum of assimilation; their methods of interpretation, allegory and pesher, differ fundamentally; and Philo was a civic leader, part of an entourage that visited the Emperor Gaius, while the Teacher of Righteousness excoriated the Romans. Despite this insurmountable divide, both Philo and the Teacher of Righteousness (or whoever authored the *Hymns* and various specimens of interpretation, such as the *Habakkuk Pesher*) shared the conviction that the root of authentic and accurate interpretation of Israel's literature emerges from the spirit within. Even more than Philo, the Dead Sea Scrolls, as we saw earlier (pp. 185-89), offer the clearest analogy to the interpretation of scripture in the book of Acts. Knowledge of God's mystery arises exclusively from God's spirit, according to the self-styled successor to Ezra and the esteemed scribal tradition:

> And I, the Instructor, have known you, my God
> through the spirit which you gave (in)to me,
> and I have listened loyally to your wonderful secret through
> your holy spirit.
> You have opened within me
> knowledge of the mystery of your wisdom,
> the source of your power. . . . (1QH XX 11-12)

We called attention already to the way in which the reference to "your holy spirit" is bordered by references to "your wonderful secret" and "knowledge of the mystery of your wisdom." The word "mystery," furthermore, is a catchword in the *Habakkuk Commentary* for those hidden dimensions of the text that the Teacher of Righteousness interprets with divine aid.

Equally conspicuous is that both the Teacher and Luke adopt a similar approach to scripture by applying ancient texts directly to their own contexts. The Babylonians in Habakkuk's day are interpreted as the Romans (1QpHab II 11-14); an evildoer is identified with the Wicked Priest who ousted the Teacher of Righteousness, who is himself the righteous of Habakkuk's oracles (1QpHab I 13). The sermons in Acts contain no less direct an application of Israel's literature to the situation of the early church. For example, Peter cites Ps 16:10 to prove that David spoke beforehand of the resurrection of the Messiah: "He was not abandoned to Hades, nor did his flesh experience corruption" (Acts 2:31). This is no less of an interpretative stretch than the identification of the wicked of Habakkuk's prophecy with a particular figure, the Wicked Priest. Both are shaped by a mode of interpretation that allows ancient texts to be brought directly into the contexts of their interpreters in order to demonstrate the veracity and validity of the events that lie close to their hearts. Both are attributed directly to the holy spirit within the interpreter.

Inspired Proclamation

Though rich with the atmosphere of ecstasy and comprehensibility, Luke's report is succinct: "all were filled with (the) holy spirit and began to speak in other tongues. . . ." Still, he adds to this report: "just as the spirit gave them to proclaim." These final words of the first paragraph in Luke's story of Pentecost, before he turns from Jesus' followers to focus upon the crowd, seem to be redundant: "as the spirit gave them to proclaim." This is odd. The readers know already that the origin of inspiration was the holy spirit. They know that those who were filled with the holy spirit spoke. The final six Greek words appear to add nothing at all to the narrative, at least nothing that we do not yet know; they do not even hint at the content of speech.

Notwithstanding their apparent redundancy, these words, an appendix of sorts, have an integral role in Luke's narrative, for they serve subtly but unmistakably to underscore the comprehensibility of inspired speech. The pivotal verb "to proclaim" *(apophthengesthai)*, which occurs but three times in Acts, introduces in two occurrences the interpretation of scripture and, in its last occurrence, the sanity of the speaker.[29]

---

29. No other New Testament author employs this verb. The only septuagintal occurrences that might shed light on Luke's choice are Zech 10:2 and Ezek 13:19.

Peter, in an effort to explain to the crowd what has just occurred, and to disabuse the crowd of their impression that the disciples are drunk, "raised his voice and proclaimed [*apephthenxato*] to them . . ." (Acts 2:14). He begins with a lengthy quotation of a prophecy from Joel that predicts the outpouring of the spirit which, claims Peter, the crowd has just observed. As we noted earlier, he continues with citations of LXX Ps 15:8-11 and 109:1, as well as several clear allusions to 1 Kgs 2:10; Ps 132:11; Isa 32:15; 57:19; and Deut 32:5.

All of these texts, according to Peter, with the sole exception of Joel 2:28-32(LXX 3:1-5), which explains the believers' behavior and speech, relate directly to the events surrounding the death and resurrection of Jesus. All of them provide certainty "that God has made him both Lord and Messiah, this Jesus whom you crucified" (Acts 2:36). Such interpretation of scripture is more than clever; it is the stuff of inspiration, according to Luke, kin to a similar phenomenon that took place at Qumran, where interpreters of Israelite literature applied Israel's ancient texts to the events of their own day. When Peter, then, lifts up his voice, his "proclamation" *(apephthenxato)* has a very specific message: scripture confirms the validity of recent events. The sermon is, quite simply, proclamation that consists of scriptural interpretation intended to demonstrate with certainty that the crucified Jesus is Lord and Messiah.

The brevity of the interval that separates the believers' proclamation from Peter's — the verb "to proclaim" *(apophthengesthai)* occurs twice in close succession, in Acts 2:4 and 2:14 — is illuminating. On the one hand, the association of the verb "to proclaim" with the holy spirit in 2:4 implies that Peter too is inspired by the holy spirit when he delivers his proclamation in 2:14. On the other hand, the taut association of the same verb in Peter's speech, with its interpretation of scripture in direct application to Jesus and the contemporary events of that particular Pentecost, implies that the other believers too were engaged in a similar interpretation of scripture. Such an understanding of the verb in 2:4 is cemented, of course, by Luke's insistence that the hearers could understand "the praiseworthy acts of God," that is, the acts of God from the time of Israel to that very day. They too were the inspired interpreters of scripture. By taking up this verb twice in close succession, therefore, Luke is able both to underscore the inspired nature of Peter's speech (2:14) and to give teeth to the content of the earliest believers' inspired speech (2:4).

Although the book of Acts is punctuated by inspired speeches, Luke does not take this verb up again until he depicts Paul in dire straits, left to languish in prison and itching for an appearance before the Roman governor. This Paul is granted and, at a turning point in Paul's defense before Herod Agrippa II and the Roman governor Porcius Festus, Festus interrupts Paul with the accusation, more emotional than forensic, "You are out of your mind, Paul! Too much learning is driving you insane." Twice in the brief compass of this reaction, Festus charges Paul with insanity: "You are *mad*, Paul. All of your education is driving you *mad!* [*Mainē, Paule. Ta polla se grammata eis manian peritrepei*]" (Acts 26:24). The verb "to be mad" occurs elsewhere in Acts in a comic and more benign context in the quaint story of the maid Rhoda, who answers the door of a house where the community is worshipping. Standing there is Peter, fresh out of prison through the intervention of an angel; Rhoda reacts by leaving him to stand there so that she can return to the group and tell them it is Peter. They respond, "You are mad [*Mainē*]," because they suppose it is not Peter but his angel.[30] Two people, then, are charged with being insane in the book of Acts: Paul and Rhoda. Both charges are informal, though the charge against Paul is deadly serious and against Rhoda, humorous and personal. The repetition in Paul's charge, further, is more emphatic and less offhanded: Paul is mad, driven by his learning to madness.[31]

Paul takes this accusation seriously and unequivocally denies it with a verb that provides the polar opposite of the sort of madness with which he is charged. He retorts, "I am not out of my mind, most excellent Festus, but I am *proclaiming* words of truth and sobriety" (26:25). Of all the words Luke might have chosen to express Paul's sanity, of all the ways in which Luke might have contrasted madness with mental composure, he chooses to contrast, in the clearest of terms, two expressions: "I am not mad" *(Ou mainomai)* and "I utter true and sober words" *(alla alētheias kai sōphrosynēs rhēmata apophthengomai).*

This is, furthermore, not sober proclamation of a generic sort but a clear instance of the inspired interpretation of scripture. If the early believ-

---

30. Acts 12:12-17. On the connotations of sober speech, see *TDNT* 1:447.

31. Elsewhere in the New Testament, some of the Jews in the Fourth Gospel draw a connection between demon possession and insanity with the accusation lodged against Jesus, "He has a demon and is out of his mind [*daimonion echei kai mainetai*]. Why listen to him?" (John 10:20). The only other use of this verb or noun in New Testament literature occurs in Paul's discussion of speaking in tongues: "If, therefore, the whole church comes together and all speak in tongues, and outsiders or unbelievers enter, will they not say that you are out of your mind [*mainesthe*]?" (1 Cor 14:23). It looks to outsiders as if those Corinthians who are speaking in tongues in a group have lost their senses.

ers' proclamation consisted of God's powerful acts and Peter's proclamation consisted of the interpretation of scripture, Paul's defense rises and falls as well upon the citation of scripture. Throughout the first part of Paul's defense, Festus and Agrippa listen without the slightest objection to Paul's autobiography (26:2-21). The interruption comes only when Paul adduces scripture to explain what he believes happened in the recent death and resurrection of Jesus, the Messiah: "To this day I have had help from God, and so I stand here, testifying to both small and great, saying nothing but what the prophets and Moses said would take place: that the Messiah must suffer, and that, by being the first to rise from the dead, he would proclaim light both to our people and to the Gentiles." At this point in Paul's defense, Festus interrupts, "You are out of your mind, Paul! Too much learning is driving you insane!" (26:22-24). The accusation that Paul is mad has to do with Paul's application of the scriptures — the prophets and Moses — to the messianic death and resurrection of Jesus.[32]

It is not, then, Paul's own story that upsets Festus but Paul's studied mode of interpreting the scriptures in light of Jesus. At stake is hermeneutics, interpretation that looks to Festus like insanity brought on by study; to Paul, of course, this use of scripture is the quintessence of sobriety and truth. For this reason, Paul subsequently puts a question to Agrippa that has to do squarely, not with teaching in general or Paul's personal experience, but with how the scriptures ought to be interpreted: "King Agrippa, do you believe the prophets? I know that you believe" (26:27).

The scenario at Pentecost offers a mirror image of this interchange. The early believers are engaged in the inspired expression of the praiseworthy acts of God. To some in the audience, this looks like intoxication — the narrative equivalent of Festus's charge of insanity. This indictment prompts Peter to quote prophets and psalms to demonstrate "that God has made him both Lord and Messiah, this Jesus whom you crucified"; Paul appeals to the prophets and Moses to demonstrate, in precisely the same terms, though with the characteristic addition of the inclusion of Jew and Gentile, that the Messiah must suffer and rise from the dead.

If there is a verb, therefore, in Acts that expresses intellectual acuity, it is this verb, *apophthengesthai*. Luke's adoption of this word in a seemingly

---

32. As B. Witherington (*The Acts of the Apostles: A Socio-Rhetorical Commentary* [Grand Rapids: Wm. B. Eerdmans, 1998] 749) puts it, "What is not meant is that Paul is incoherent or has taken total leave of his senses, but rather that he is given to outlandish ideas because of his 'much learning.'"

superfluous narrative gloss in Acts 2:4 is possessed of extraordinary significance. On the most rudimentary level its repetition in the Pentecost narrative ensures that Peter's "proclamation" will be seen as inspired by the
holy spirit and that the early believers' ability to "speak God's praiseworthy
acts" will be understood, like Peter's, as a form of "proclamation" in which
the scriptures are interpreted to demonstrate that Jesus is the crucified and
risen Messiah. This sort of proclamation is, of course, paradigmatic in
Acts, where the primary purpose of inspired speech is to provide a compelling interpretation of scripture in which Moses, the prophets, and the
psalms conspire to demonstrate that Jesus is the crucified and risen Messiah. On still another level of Luke's strategy, the adoption of this verb in
the context of the Pentecost narrative blunts the hard edge of ecstasy while
maintaining the rhetorical clout which that ecstatic dimension conveyed
within the confines of the Greco-Roman world. In a dazzling world of disarray overflowing with violent winds, filling with *pneuma,* tongues as of
fire, and the appearance of drunkenness, there occurs a trustworthy proclamation of scripture. These believers, like Paul before Agrippa and Festus
much later in the story, are not mad or drunk; their proclamation, like Peter's in quick succession and Paul's later, contains a fresh — Luke would
say inspired — interpretation of scripture that is, through and through,
the essence of sobriety and truth.[33]

33. Although Luke anticipates the experience of Pentecost with the promise that Jesus'
followers will be "clothed with power from on high" (Luke 24:49), "baptized with the holy
spirit" (Acts 1:5), and powerful "when the holy spirit has come upon you" (1:8), the image he
adopts at the moment of the event is filling: "all of them were filled with the holy spirit"
(2:4). This is not, of course, the first instance in Luke-Acts in which someone is filled with
the holy spirit. The aged Zechariah, on a tour of duty in the temple, was promised that his
son John would be filled by the holy spirit even before his birth (Luke 1:15). His elderly wife
too was filled with the holy spirit, as John leapt in her womb, and began to recite a blessing
for Mary (1:41-45), and Zechariah himself later added his own lengthier blessing of God
when he was filled with the holy spirit (1:67). These are rich with scriptural allusions and rife
with septuagintal style. Jesus, years later, would return to Galilee (4:14) "full of the power of
the holy spirit" (4:14), from the desert, where he had fasted for forty days while being
tempted by the devil. Not surprisingly, in light of the verbal blessings that flowed from Zechariah and Elizabeth's mouth when they were filled with the holy spirit, Jesus began to teach
in the synagogues of Galilee (4:15), and his first so-called sermon consists of claiming that
Isaiah 61 was now fulfilled in their midst.

Dreaming Dreams and Seeing Visions

This blend of an ecstatic atmosphere and mental acuity is encapsulated at Pentecost when Peter captures the moment with a citation of Joel 3:1-5(Eng. 2:28-32), which identifies the experience of speaking in other tongues as an instance of prophesying — an act which, as we have seen, entails a keen and clear perception of the future. Joel 3:1-5 (MT) reads:

> Then afterward I will pour out my spirit on all flesh; your sons and your daughters shall prophesy, your old men shall dream dreams, and your young men shall see visions. Even on the male and female slaves, in those days, I will pour out my spirit. I will show portents in the heavens and on the earth, blood and fire and columns of smoke. The sun shall be turned to darkness, and the moon to blood, before the great and terrible day of the Lord comes. Then everyone who calls on the name of the Lord shall be saved; for in Mount Zion and in Jerusalem there shall be those who escape, as the Lord has said, and among the survivors shall be those whom the Lord calls.

Peter's addition of the words "they shall prophesy" to this citation must not be played out so as to obfuscate other modes of natural divination: dreams and visions. Inspired prophesying was, of course, the *sine qua non* of natural divination, of inspired insight that arises without artificial means of divination, without having to consult omens, such as the organs of sacrificial animals or the formation of birds.

Yet the citation is more expansive than a single, prophetic focus can contain. This citation actually provides the consummate scriptural impetus for a blend of inspired ecstasy and intellectual perspicacity, for it includes as well dreams and visions, which were, alongside prophecy, considered forms of natural divination because they were believed to transpire when the soul had become freer than normal from the body. Cicero explains that when "the soul has been withdrawn by sleep from contact with sensual ties, then does it recall the past, comprehend the present, and foresee the future. For though the sleeping body then lies as if it were dead, yet the soul is alive and strong" (*On Divination* 1.63). Plutarch would contend that souls exercise their innate capacity "in dreams, and some in the hour of death, when the body becomes cleansed of all impurities and attains a temperament adapted to this end, a temperament through which the reasoning and thinking faculty of the souls is relaxed and released from their present state as they range amid the irrational and imaginative realms of the future" (*On the Obsolescence of Oracles* 432C). According to Simmias, in Plutarch's *On the Sign of Socrates,* this was a wildly popular point of view: "In popular belief, on the other hand, it is only in sleep that people receive inspiration from on high; and the notion that they are so influenced when awake and in full possession of their faculties is accounted strange and incredible" (589D).

When Peter, then, succumbed to an ecstatic trance (*egeneto ep' auton ekstasis;* Acts 10:10) while he prayed upon the roof prior to lunch, he fulfilled the expectation of Joel, interpreted along the lines of Acts 2:17-21, and embodied what was considered by the Greco-Roman populace to be a form of natural divination. While he was puzzling over the meaning of this vision *(to horama),* delegates who represented Cornelius arrived at his door. Still later, as he reflected upon his visionary experience before his colleagues in Jerusalem, Peter identified his visionary experience as ecstasy: "I saw by means of ecstasy a vision" *(eidon en ekstasei horama;* 11:5). This vision — arguably one of the most pivotal junctures in Acts — combines ecstasy with a plain and practical message. Both in the narrative of the vision and Peter's re-telling of it, this is a vision that takes place only when ecstasy overcomes him. Yet the outcome is precise and comprehensible, so much so that Peter does not hesitate to identify the food in the dream with the Gentiles at the door.

Conclusion

On its well-groomed surface, the story of Pentecost is a narrative about the ability of hearers from far-flung regions of the Roman Empire to comprehend the praiseworthy acts of God in their native languages. Peter's explanation of this event consists of a rich measure of scripture interpreted to explain this event as the final outpouring of God's spirit among a select community of Jesus' followers.[34] The holy spirit in Acts is the foundation

---

34. M. Welker (*God the Spirit* [Minneapolis: Fortress, 1994] 233) is correct when he emphasizes that what is decisive at Pentecost is not the apparently inexplicable and ecstatic dimensions — the sound from heaven, divided tongues as of fire, and speaking in tongues — but the more deeply miraculous ability of hearers from around the globe to comprehend what is said. Jews who could not understand one another comprehend in unison the powerful acts of God: "this *difference between the experience of plural inaccessibility to each other* and of *enduring* foreignness, and unfamiliarity, on the one hand, and of *utter commonality of*

for the authoritative interpretation of scripture; inspired interpreters employ Israel's literature to defend the authenticity of the death, resurrection, exaltation, and spirit-giving reality of Jesus the Lord and Messiah.

Although this emphasis upon the inspired interpretation of scripture comprises an impressive façade for the story of this unique Pentecost, bubbling under the surface are the accoutrements of ecstasy. Any one of these elements — filling, fire, intoxication, and tongues — is enough to suggest that something of the ecstatic or uncontrollable, something of the manic, may be at play here. Taken together, however, these ingredients combine to force the inevitable conclusion that filling with the holy spirit inspires more than eloquent and persuasive speech that is couched in poignant comprehensibility. Infilling evokes a host of associations that press the inexplicable, if not to the forefront of this narrative, at least to the edges and crevices of the story of Pentecost.

This comes as no surprise because the world Luke has narrated is an extraordinary one, full of signs above and wonders below (Acts 2:19).[35] It is a world in which Peter, while standing at the door, is mistaken for an angel. It is a world in which even evil spirits do the divine bidding by chasing evil men away naked, a world in which belly-talking spirits in slave-girls grasp the essence of God's design for humankind. This is a magical world indeed, a heady world, a breeze of ecstasy. It is also a world in which the breath of ecstasy is tempered by understanding, where ecstasy is the catalyst for comprehensibility, where speaking in tongues takes concrete form in the inspired and spontaneous mastery of all the languages of the gathered Jewish Diaspora or in praise or prophesying. This is a world where that inspired speech is not haphazard or harried or hurried but a proclamation of the praiseworthy acts of God, which provides the fundamental starting-point for the sort of covenant renewal that was suitable for Pentecost in Jerusalem. This is a world where unlettered believers are able to marshal the scriptures they have learned in an inspired demonstration of their belief that Jesus is the Messiah. This is also a world where the most profound miracle perhaps is that those who show a mastery of foreign languages and a grasp of God's praiseworthy acts are not a single community leader who decides on behalf of the whole, not just the priestly mediators of a community, not only Peter or James, not exclusively the apostolic few,

---

the capacity to understand, on the other hand — this is what is truly spectacular and shocking about the Pentecost event."

35. Peter inserts here the words "above," "signs," and "below."

not even just the men. In this world men and women, slaves and slave-girls, old and young alike can be filled with the holy spirit and astound on-lookers with words that at one and the same time resound with heightened comprehension and intoxication. Although this vision hardly materializes in the book of Acts, where Luke's attention tends to be riveted instead upon an authoritative group of male leaders, such a vision of an ecstatic and inexplicably intelligent band of slaves, women, and aged, lies nonetheless at the heart of what it meant to be filled with the holy spirit.

CHAPTER 4

Filled with the Spirit, the Fourth Gospel, and 1 John

In a gospel that is indebted to a vision of listening and learning, one that is rooted in the wisdom tradition, one in which Jesus as the *logos* speaks words that are "spirit and life" (John 6:63), the surprisingly firm claim that "as yet there was no spirit because Jesus was not yet glorified" (7:39) creates a substantial breach between the wisdom tradition, in which the spirit within is the locus of learning, and John's view of the spirit within as a subsequent endowment that could not possibly enter believers prior to the death of Jesus. Yet the Fourth Gospel still revels in knowledge, in wisdom, in learning. What occurs in the Fourth Gospel, however, is that an evidently unassailable continuity with Israelite literature takes a dramatic twist: no more is it thought possible that a spirit within can become holy or unholy, can be disciplined or careless, can be cultivated with wisdom or deteriorate due to ignorance. In the Fourth Gospel, the spirit may be the locus of wisdom, but not from birth. The spirit brings knowledge, but not until re-creation. The spirit gives richness of life, but only in a new temple of believers. The spirit brings truth, but only *after* Jesus is left to die on the cross. It brings instruction, but only *after* his resurrection.

This unassailable conviction that the presence of the spirit awaits the resurrection of Jesus sets the Fourth Gospel in the company of Paul's letters and the book of Acts. Yet the puzzle of the relationship of the Fourth Gospel to other literature in the early church, which has proved such an intractable nut to crack, infiltrates the world of the spirit as well. While John walks many of the same paths as Paul, for example, such as the certainty that the spirit inspires a new creation and a new temple, he does so with his own peculiar gait.

Spirit, a New Creation, and a New Temple

A New Creation

The image of a new creation that splashes across the pages of Paul's letters is a mere drop in the Fourth Gospel — but a drop that is rich with innuendo. This drop falls into a postresurrection scene, John 20:19-23, that is typical of the strange world of postresurrection appearances in the Synoptic gospels.[1] The scene could just as well be at home in the gospels of Matthew and Luke.

The disciples are huddled together fearfully; in this scene, they are behind closed doors.[2] Jesus makes an appearance[3] and greets them, almost casually, in the usual way, "Peace be with you."[4] The disciples recognize him.[5] Perhaps most important, and certainly the most persistent trait in this sort of scene, Jesus commissions the band of disciples. Each gospel lends its own hues to this element, but the thrust of each is the same. In the gospel of Matthew, Jesus sends the eleven to "make disciples of all nations" and to teach them all that he had commanded them; he promises his authority and his presence to the end of the age (Matt 28:16-20). The elements of teaching and Jesus' authority are, of course, key ingredients in Matthew's portrayal of Jesus, and it comes as no surprise when they reappear following his resurrection in the final commission of the gospel. In the commissioning story in the gospel of Luke, the disciples are urged to remain in Jerusalem to wait for power from on high because they are witnesses who will proclaim "repentance and forgiveness of sins" through a mission that begins in Jerusalem and extends "to all nations" (Luke 24:45-49). These elements of witness, proclamation of repentance and forgiveness, and the move from Jerusalem to all nations will comprise the thematic center of the book of Acts. Jesus authorizes a final commission in the Fourth Gospel as well, and this too is imbued with a distinctive element that characterizes this particular gospel: "As the Father has sent me, so I send you" (John 20:21b).[6]

---

1. On the form of this scene, see C. H. Dodd, *Historical Tradition in the Fourth Gospel* (Cambridge: Cambridge University Press, 1963) 142-51.

2. See Matt 28:1-10; Luke 24:33.

3. See Luke 24:36a.

4. See Luke 24:36b.

5. See Matt 28:17; Luke 24:31-32.

6. John 3:34; 5:23-24, 30, 36-38; 6:29, 38-39, 44, 57; 7:16, 18, 28-29, 33; 8:16-18, 26, 29, 42; 10:36; 12:44-45, 49; 13:20; 14:24; 15:21; 16:5; 17:3, 8, 18, 21, 23-25.

The dominant trait of this scene, however, could have been lifted from the pages of Matthew's gospel. Jesus authorizes his disciples to forgive sins: "If you forgive the sins of any, they are forgiven them; if you retain the sins of any, they are retained" (John 20:23). This commission looks very much like Jesus' words to Peter in Matthew's gospel, which are spoken just after Peter has identified him as the Messiah: "I will give you the keys of the kingdom of heaven, and whatever you bind on earth will be bound in heaven, and whatever you loose on earth will be loosed in heaven" (Matt 16:19). It mirrors as well Jesus' words to the church, which appear exclusively in Matthew's gospel: "Truly I tell you, whatever you bind on earth will be bound in heaven, and whatever you loose on earth will be loosed in heaven" (Matt 18:18).[7]

When John introduces the holy spirit into this traditional scene, therefore, he does so quite naturally in the traditional language of the early church: "Receive the spirit . . ." (20:22). We saw that the verb "receive" occurs several times in Acts and Paul's letters to describe the experience of being filled with the spirit.[8] The entire scene, therefore, is traditional, very much like the gospels of Matthew and Luke, with the elements of the fear of the disciples, the unexpected entry of Jesus into their circle, the typical greeting, the recognition of Jesus, the commissioning, and the promise of power or authority.

A fresh element inveigles its way into this familiar scene. The traditional words "Receive the holy spirit" are preceded by an isolated and distinctive act: "he breathed in them." The gospel tradition remembers that Jesus could spit on the eyes of the blind, lay his hands on the sick, have his feet caressed with hair and washed with tears, even wash his disciples' feet, but nowhere in the gospels does Jesus breathe into someone. Never does this level of physical intimacy characterize his physical relationship with those for whom he cares so deeply. The depth of that intimacy is reinforced by the traditional phrase "receive the holy spirit," without which it might conceivably be possible to infer that Jesus stood at a distance from his disciples or that his breath may have surrounded the disciples or settled upon them. This cannot be so, since Jesus' inbreathing and their receiving is the same occurrence, occupying the same narrative space, the same brief moment in time. Jesus "breathes *into*" the disciples, not *upon* them. Jesus'

---

7. See Mark 16:14-18.

8. Acts 2:33, 38; 8:15, 17, 19; 10:47; 19:2; Rom 8:15; 1 Cor 2:12; 2 Cor 11:4; Gal 3:2, 14; also 1 John 2:27.

inbreathing, in other words, is tied in this scene to *their* inhalation, not only by the word "inbreathe," but also by its association with their *receiving* the spirit-breath. His is not an exhalation, a breathing out, but an inhalation — an action that requires an object, someone into whom the breath enters.

The effect of this use of the verbs "inbreathe" and "receive" is to heighten the intimacy of this scene. This is a stunningly private scene to begin with, to which the reader of the gospel is privy. It occurs behind locked doors. It begins with a household greeting among friends. And it entails what looks very much like a kiss — not a kiss upon the cheek, like the betrayer's kiss, but a kiss upon the mouth by which the spirit of one is passed on to another. This is the only means by which the disciples' *receiving* of the spirit can coincide so closely with Jesus' *inbreathing* of the spirit.

Perhaps the closest ancient literary analogue is the romantic tale *Joseph and Aseneth,* which expands the brief biblical detail that the Egyptian pharaoh gave to Joseph a woman by the name of Aseneth, the daughter of Potiphera, priest of On, as a wife (Gen 41:45). This tale traces the love that develops between Joseph and Aseneth, a love that culminates in her conversion to Israelite faith. Prior to their marriage, Joseph puts his hands around Aseneth, and she around him, and "they kissed each other for a long time. . . . And Joseph kissed Aseneth and gave her spirit of life, and he kissed her the second time and gave her spirit of wisdom, and he kissed her the third time and gave her spirit of truth" (*Jos. Asen.* 19:10-11).

Jesus' breathing of the holy spirit into his disciples is not, of course, this sort of kiss. The verb John selects to present us with this reality is *enephysēsen,* precisely the verb that is used in the Greek version of Gen 2:7: "then the Lord God formed *adam* from the dust of the ground, and breathed into [*enephysēsen*] his nostrils the breath of life; and *adam* became a living being." While not a romantic one, this is indeed a kiss of life. As God had breathed into the face of the first man, Jesus breathes now into the face of his disciples, and they, in turn, receive — are filled with — this holy spirit. He imparts this spirit-breath, not at a distance, but mouth to mouth, face to face, in the shared intimacy of friends reunited in a locked room.

This is the dimension that must be preserved both from the perspective of the narrative, which opens a locked room, confidential words, and intimate touches to the reader, and in light of a verb that recollects the intimacy of Eden. It would be a violation of this narrative to move too precipitously to other levels of meaning, to more theological dimensions of this postresurrection scene, to an interpretation of this scene — for example, as John's version of Pentecost — without first coming to grips with the dimension of physical movement, the smack of intimacy, the sheer physicality of the holy spirit, the pulsing breath of the resurrected Jesus that energizes his followers.[9]

While the verb "inbreathe" returns us for a moment to Eden, to the first pulse of life within humankind, it also recollects two other scriptural images of new life. In the first, Elijah revived the son of the destitute widow with whom he lived (1 Kgs 17:17-24 [LXX 3 Kings]). Although Elijah had miraculously expanded her store of grain and oil, her son grew gravely ill, so much so that "there was no breath [pneuma] left in him." Elijah took him to his own room and set the boy on Elijah's own bed — intimate details indeed of another closed room — and accused God of bringing this horror upon the woman and her son. According to the Hebrew, Elijah lay upon the boy three times, and the boy returned to life. The Greek translation is less awkward, sparing Elijah from climbing three times on and off a human corpse. Yet the Greek translation, while less awkward, is no less intimate: three times Elijah breathed into (enephysēsen) the boy and asked God to restore his life (hē psychē). Immediately, the boy sprang to life, and Elijah returned him to his mother, with the simple words, "Your son lives [zē ho huios sou]."

The intimate and physical dimensions of the story that takes place behind closed doors in the Fourth Gospel rise to the surface in light of this story, in which Elijah raises the widow's dead son to life through inbreathing three times, with its association between the dead brought to life and the act of inbreathing. There exists in both stories the passing of breath, the giving of life by means of the intimate physical contact that is suggested by inbreathing. In the Fourth Gospel, Jesus breathes into the disciples and tells them to receive the spirit. In the story of the widow and her son, three times Elijah places mouth upon mouth and breathes into the

---

9. An example of the tendency to ignore the visceral dimensions of this scene in an otherwise reliable study is offered by M. M. Thompson, "The Breath of Life: John 20:22-23 Once More," in *The Holy Spirit and Christian Origins,* ed. G. Stanton, B. Longenecker, and S. Barton (Grand Rapids: Wm. B. Eerdmans, 2004) 69-78. Although he does not reckon with the visceral quality of the spirit-breath, C. H. Dodd comments, "the gift of the Spirit to the Church is represented, not as if it were a separate outpouring of divine power under the forms of wind and fire (as in the Acts), but as the ultimate climax of the personal relations between Jesus and His disciples"; *The Interpretation of the Fourth Gospel* (Cambridge: Cambridge University Press, 1953) 227.

corpse of a boy until he returns to life. What is also particularly poignant, from the standpoint of the Fourth Gospel, is the response of the widow to Elijah: "Now I know that you are a man of God, and that the word of the Lord in your mouth is truth [*kai rhēma kyriou en stomati sou alēthinon*]" (1 Kgs 17:24). These words resonate with the claims of the Fourth Gospel, such as those which punctuate the discourse on the "true bread from heaven," when Jesus claims that his words are spirit and life, and the remaining disciples respond, "You have the words of eternal life [*rhēmata zōēs aiōniou echeis*]" (John 6:68).

In the second example, Ezekiel too envisaged the sort of inbreathing that could bring the dead to life, although in his vision the intimacy that characterized creation in Eden is set aside to accommodate the resurrection of a nation: "Then he said to me, 'Prophesy to the breath, prophesy, mortal, and say to the breath: Thus says the Lord God: Come from the four winds, O breath, and breathe upon these slain, that they may live [*emphysēson eis tous nekrous toutous kai zēsatōsan*].' I prophesied as he commanded me, and the breath [*to pneuma*] came into them, and they lived, and stood on their feet, a vast multitude" (Ezek 37:9-10). Ezekiel's vision is global in scope: the nations will acknowledge the Lord.[10] Consequently, the convergence of the spirit of God is less a mouth-to-mouth infusion of breath than the rapid movement of God's chariot-winds as they hustle from the four corners of the earth to resurrect a valley of very many, very dry bones.[11]

Whether the author of the Fourth Gospel had any — or all — of these texts in mind is ultimately unknowable. Yet his selection of the unique verb "inbreathe," which occurs in the New Testament only here, certainly suggests that one, if not all, of these texts informed his construal of Jesus' commissioning of the disciples. This is a creation, even a re-creation, a resurrection of the disciples. Though formerly without breath, like a freshly formed *adam* in the dirt, the moribund widow's son on Elijah's bed and a despondent Israelite nation reduced to very many, very dry bones, the disciples into whom Jesus breathes his holy spirit become a new community, charged with a new task, and given new authority. The realization that this may be a re-creation of Jesus' followers should not, however, overshadow

---

10. On allusions to Ezekiel 37 in John 5, see G. T. Manning, *Echoes of a Prophet: The Use of Ezekiel in the Gospel of John and in Literature of the Second Temple Period.* JSNTSup 270 (London: T. & T. Clark, 2004).

11. See also Wis 15:11; and Philo, *On the Creation* 134–35.

the primary narrative dimension of this story. This is also a private story which offers a rare glimpse of an intimate act between Jesus and his disciples. The holy spirit does not "come upon" the disciples, as Jesus promises in Luke-Acts. It does not rush or overpower them, as in the tales of the Judges and Saul.[12] It does not accompany them, as it once did a fledgling nation.[13] It does not rest upon them, as it does upon the Messiah.[14] It is not poured out upon the land or the people of Israel.[15] In this story, rather, Jesus comes physically close enough to the disciples to fill them with his own holy spirit-breath. Eight days later, Jesus offers Thomas the chance to put his fingers in the wounds of his hands and to place his hand into Jesus' side; these too are rich and vivid images of the physicality and approachability of the risen Jesus. The story of Thomas, however, is not the only one to underscore the palpable presence of Jesus' resurrected physical body and his intimate relationship with his followers; this story of commissioning does that as well, though perhaps even more dramatically, for in this glimpse of the relationship between Jesus and his friends, their being filled by his spirit-breath is, we might say tongue-in-cheek, sealed with a kiss.

A New Temple

Much earlier in the Fourth Gospel, Jesus tells a Samaritan woman that the water he gives is "a spring of water gushing up to eternal life" (John 4:14). Slightly later in the conversation, the woman refers to a disagreement between Jews and Samaritans about where to worship: the Samaritans worship on Mount Gerizim, while the Jews worship in Jerusalem (4:20). These aspects of the conversation concerning running water and the temple are closely related. The Gihon spring bubbled up south of the temple, and in temple mythology, such as Ezekiel's vision of the restored temple, the Gihon would provide lavish flows of water from the temple.[16]

This association between water and worship foreshadows the more explicit association which Jesus draws between water and the temple during the celebration of the Feast of Tabernacles:

12. Judg 3:9-11; 6:34; 11:29; 14:6, 19; 15:14; 1 Sam 10:6, 10; 11:6.
13. Isa 63:7-14.
14. Isa 11:2; 42:1; 61:1.
15. Isa 32:15; Ezek 39:29; Joel 2:28-29(MT 3:1-2); Zech 12:10.
16. See Part II, chapter 4.

On the last day of the festival, the great day, while Jesus was standing there, he cried out, "Let anyone who is thirsty come to me, and let the one who believes in me drink. As the scripture has said, 'Out of *his belly* shall flow rivers of living water.'"[17] Now he said this about the spirit, which believers in him were to receive; for as yet there was no spirit, because Jesus was not yet glorified. (John 7:37-39)

The importance of this citation for our study is enormous. First, John identifies this water as the spirit which believers are to "receive." The traditional word "receive" once again comprises an implicit reference to the experience of being filled with the spirit which is promised to believers. No less important is the second aspect of this narrative aside: there was as yet no spirit. This is the principal dividing line in the Fourth Gospel with respect to the experience of being filled with the spirit. Even those who believe during the lifetime of Jesus cannot receive the spirit because the experience of being filled with the spirit cannot occur prior to the death of Jesus.

Despite what it does tell us about the spirit, a great many difficulties accompany the interpretation of this text, the thorniest of which is whether rivers of living water will flow from the believer's belly or Jesus' belly. The alleged scriptural text, for which there is actually no identifiable source, reads cryptically, "Out of *his* [*autou*] belly shall flow rivers of living water." Many early Christian writers, such as Justin, Hippolytus, Cyprian, and Tertullian, favored the interpretation that Jesus is the source of living water. They identified Jesus with the rock that produced water in the Sinai wilderness when Moses struck it (Exod 17:1-7),[18] and they discerned the fulfillment of this prediction in John 19:34, when water and blood flow from Jesus' side after he has died as the result of crucifixion. Other Christian writers, however, understood the source of these waters to be the interior, the bellies of believers: Origen, Athanasius, and Cyril of Alexandria, all from Alexandria; Eusebius of Caesarea and Cyril of Jerusalem, from Palestine; Basil, Gregory of Nyssa, and Gregory of Nazianzen, from Cappadocia; Chrysostom from Antioch; and Ambrose, Jerome, and Augustine, from the Roman West. These authors were able to tie this cryptic

---

17. The genitive pronoun *autou* can refer either to the believer or to Jesus. I cannot translate this inclusively because, were it inclusive, then the problem would be improperly solved, as the pronoun would then refer to the believer — he or she.

18. See also Ps 78:16; 105:41. The statement, in which God "made streams come out of the rock, and caused waters to flow down like rivers," has been interpreted christologically.

saying to Jesus' conversation with the Samaritan woman, when Jesus promised, "Everyone who drinks of this water will be thirsty again, but those who drink of the water that I will give them will never be thirsty. The water that I will give will become in them a spring of water gushing up to eternal life" (John 4:13-14). The tandem images of water or spirit flowing, springing from within, is expressed in shorthand by Jesus' claim to come to give abundant life (10:10).[19]

It is barely possible to regain a sense of equilibrium after entering the fray of opinions that attends the interpretation of this prediction, particularly the question of whether it is Jesus or a believer's belly from which the water-spirit will flow. The alleged fulfillment of this prediction when water and blood flow from Jesus' side after his death on the cross is a case in point. On the one hand, John 19:34 supports the view that it is Jesus' belly, for the prediction that water-spirit will flow out of a cavity in "his body" seems to find a suitable fulfillment — and the only possible narrative fulfilment in the Fourth Gospel — in this detail about Jesus' death. On the other hand, John 19:34 undermines the possible relationship of prediction-fulfillment, for the prediction of a *flow* of water is reduced to little more than a *trickle*. The passage states — understates, really — that the water and blood simply "went out"; there is not the slightest sense in this description of a flowing of water-spirit. Further, the Feast of Tabernacles was a *harvest* festival, and water was integral to the promise of a rich harvest. This promise of a rich harvest would seem to apply less to Jesus than to believers, who would have a full harvest to anticipate, made possible by the great outflow of the spirit. And finally, the notion of spirit that flows out fits the notion of an abundant filling with the spirit, which is an experience promised to those believers who will *receive* the spirit.

The intractable question of whether the source of living water is Jesus or the believer may never be satisfactorily answered. This is not altogether unfortunate, for the significance of the saying may lie less in the particular source of the water — certainly John is content to leave the pronoun ambiguous — than in the imagery of the Feast of Tabernacles, when Jesus is reputed to have delivered this brief speech. Tabernacles, or Sukkoth, was the third of the great harvest festivals, and Josephus referred to it as the

19. For an excellent discussion of the issues, see R. Schnackenburg, *The Gospel according to St. John* (New York: Crossroad, 1982) 2:152-57; R. E. Brown, *The Gospel according to John I-XII*, 2nd ed. AB 29 (Garden City: Doubleday, 1977) 319-24, 327-29; Manning, *Echoes of a Prophet*, 172-75. All three opt for the christological interpretation.

feast "especially sacred and important to the Hebrews" (*Ant.* 8.100). According to rabbinic tradition, during each of the seven mornings of the feast there was a procession to the Gihon spring, which supplied the pool of Siloam. Upon arrival, a priest filled a golden pitcher with water, while a choir repeated Isa 12:3: "With joy you will draw water from the wells of salvation." The procession then headed to the temple via the Water Gate, singing the Hallel psalms (Psalms 113–118) and holding signs of the harvest, including a *lulab* in one hand — willow twigs and myrtle tied with a palm, which were used to construct booths — and a lemon or citron, which symbolized the harvest. Upon reaching the sacrificial altar in front of the temple, they circled it, waving their *lulabs* and singing Ps 18:25: "With the loyal you show yourself loyal; with the blameless you show yourself blameless." On the last day, they circled the altar seven times. These magnificent processions, songs, and symbolic activities culminated in the priest's ascent to the altar, where he poured water into a silver funnel, through which it flowed onto the ground.[20]

The centrality of the temple during the Feast of Tabernacles is apparent in a reading from Zechariah 14 that accompanied it, in which it was predicted that "on that day living waters shall flow out from Jerusalem, half of them to the eastern sea and half of them to the western sea; it shall continue in summer as in winter" (Zech 14:8).[21] The impetus for this vision may in turn have been the final vision of restoration in the book of Ezekiel. This vision begins, as we would expect from Ezekiel, dramatically: "Then he brought me back to the entrance of the temple; there, water was flowing from below the threshold of the temple toward the east (for the temple faced east); and the water was flowing down from below the south end of the threshold of the temple, south of the altar" (Ezek 47:1). The defining characteristic of this river is life: "Wherever the river goes, every living creature that swarms will live, and there will be very many fish, once these waters reach there. It will become fresh; and everything will live where the river goes" (47:9). There will be verdant life as well along the river's banks: "On the banks, on both sides of the river, there will grow all kinds of trees for food. Their leaves will not wither nor their fruit fail, but they will bear fresh fruit every month, because the water for them flows

20. Based upon R. E. Brown, *The Gospel according to John I-XII*, 326-27. For rabbinic sources, see Manning, *Echoes of a Prophet*, 176.

21. Greek: *kai en tē hēmera ekeinē exeleusetai hydōr zōn ex Ierousalēm to hēmisu autou eis tēn thalassan tēn prōtēn kai to hēmisu autou eis tēn thalassan tēn eschatēn kai en therei kai en eari estai houtōs.* See also 13:1.

from the sanctuary. Their fruit will be for food, and their leaves for healing" (47:12).[22]

The impact of Jesus' words in the context of this feast is difficult to overlook. The water that flows from the Gihon spring — the water that the priest pours out — will now flow instead from a new temple. If the source is Jesus, then living water will flow from Jesus' temple, the body which his opponents will destroy (John 2:19-21). If the source is the believer, then living water will flow from a living temple, a temple perhaps analogous to the temple at Qumran or the temple of believers that Paul depicts in his letters to the Corinthians, a temple comprised by devotees of Jesus — though in the Fourth Gospel the water of the new temple is related particularly to the individual believer. In either case, in its wake this magnificent river from within will bring life: life to the fullest, life without measure. The flowing of living water from within is a fabulous symbol of life. It is the symbol of growth, the promise of a rich and full harvest. It will no longer flow from the Temple Mount, which is built of stone and is vulnerable to Roman ramparts. It will flow from within believers or Jesus himself.

If these words are intended to describe the future experiences of believers when they are filled with the spirit, then it becomes possible to trace their meaning a bit further. The image of water flowing from a cavity deep within a human body is anything but tidy. This prediction poses a reality that is visceral and, in this respect, not at all unlike the physical inbreathing of Jesus' holy spirit following his resurrection. The visceral quality of this saying is underscored by the location of the headwaters of this water-spirit: it is not the heart, as we might be led to imagine from Paul's letters, in which the spirit is sent into believers' hearts, but the belly, human viscera (7:38). The *koilia* or belly could be any cavity in the body, including the heart or womb or lungs. The word may have been selected because, unlike the heart, it provides a precise counterpart to the Gihon spring, which comes from a *cavity* in the earth. Not from the *cave* of Gihon, says Jesus, but from a *cavity* in the human body will flow living water, the spirit which is not yet given.

This is a jarring image of water flowing from a cavity within the human body, which evokes perhaps the experience of childbirth, with its excruciating pangs of labor followed by a flow of water mixed with blood

---

22. For an excellent, detailed discussion of the use of Ezekiel in relation to John 7:37-39, see Manning, *Echoes of a Prophet*, 172-86. The image of a river flowing out of Jerusalem reemerges in Rev 22:1-2; see D. E. Aune, *Revelation*. WBC 52C [Waco: Word, 1998] 3:1174-77.

and the emergence of a child from the womb's cavity.[23] This is uncontrollable and inevitable, relentless, inexorable. Equally plausible is the possibility that these words evoke an experience akin to the claim of Elihu, to whom we have so often returned in this study:

> And am I to wait, because they do not speak,
>> because they stand there, and answer no more?
> I also will give my answer;
>> I also will declare my opinion.
> For I am full of words;
>> the spirit within me besieges me.
> My belly is indeed like wine that has no vent;
>> like new wineskins, it is ready to burst.
> I must speak, so that I may find relief;
>> I must open my lips and answer. (Job 32:16-20)

The intensity which Elihu feels, the inexorable flow of words that will follow, the inevitable explosion of teaching that will ensue, are the product of the spirit within Elihu.[24] The association of the spirit-water's flow with words involuntarily spoken is a suitable precursor, not only to the inspiration of the paraclete, but to Jesus' prediction in the Synoptic gospels that the spirit will provide words, that the spirit will teach, in the context of persecution and synagogue trials.[25] Whether or not this is the most appropriate interpretation of Jesus' prediction, it highlights nonetheless a key dimension of the spirit in the Fourth Gospel: the inspiration that is associated elsewhere with an initial inbreathing, such as the words that flow when the spirit-breath within besieges, are postponed in the Fourth Gospel until a moment after the death and resurrection of Jesus.

Though there may be much that is inaccessible about this prediction, it is still possible to grasp essential dimensions of being filled with the spirit, of receiving the spirit, according to John 7:38. First, the spirit's flow from within is believed to supplant the flow of water from the Gihon spring. This temple will be a living temple, whether a temple of believers or Jesus' own crucified body. Second, living means more than being alive. Jesus' promise is rooted in Ezekiel's vision of a river in which fish swarm and

---

23. For the image of birth in relation to the spirit, see the story of Nicodemus (John 3:1-8).

24. The location of the headwaters is not specifically the heart but the belly, or the womb, the *gastēr*.

25. See Mark 13:11. Luke 12:11-12 underscores the teaching element with the verb *didaxei*.

alongside which trees flourish. The spirit creates life, life without measure, life from the ruined heap of the temple that Ezekiel experienced. Following from the imagery of the Feast of Tabernacles, the spirit is the water that promises survival during drought and a sure harvest. And third, this is a visceral experience. It would be short-sighted to overlook the visceral force of a saying such as "Out of *his belly* shall flow rivers of living water." Living or running water flowing from the recesses of a human being suggests a convulsive and involuntary experience, particularly if this prediction is fulfilled on the cross, at the moment of Jesus' death.

Summary

The two compass points of Paul's characterization of the spirit have reappeared in the Fourth Gospel, where filling with the spirit is associated with the creation of a renewed community and the inspiration of a new temple. While Paul expends far more energy than John to develop these images, we would be hard-pressed to characterize these in the Fourth Gospel as facile. On the contrary, with a single word, "inbreathe," John 20:22 recollects the face-to-face creation of the first human being, Elijah's mouth-to-mouth resuscitation of a widow's dead son, and Ezekiel's lavish vision of dead bones now covered with sinew and flesh, inbreathed and alive. John 7:38 incorporates the images of Tabernacles, especially the new temple with a river flowing from within, which Ezekiel and Zechariah had envisaged. In this climactic festal moment, Jesus claims that the spirit's flow from within will supplant the flow of water from the Gihon spring, even the promised flow in a future, restored temple. That temple, Jesus knows, will be a living temple.

The lightning rod for the new creation and new temple is *the sheer thrust of life*. Jesus promises a river of living water that flows from a cavity within. This flow is hardly a trickle or a drop, and it calls to mind the lavish imagery of life, the bounty of life in the restored temple which Ezekiel imagined. The spirit creates life, life without measure, life from the ruined heap of the temple that Ezekiel experienced. Nor are the images of life that are called to mind by the simple word "inbreathe" anything but extravagant. In the first scriptural occurrence of this word, a molded lump of dust from the earth is blown into life. In the second scriptural occurrence, in a dramatic moment, the narrator opens the window to Elijah's own upper room, where the prophet breathes life three times into a boy's corpse and cries out for life. In the third scriptural occurrence, the four winds rush to a valley of very many, very dry bones, which are now covered with sinews and flesh and breathe life into a disconsolate nation. When the narrator of the Fourth Gospel opens the window to a locked room, there is no less drama, as the risen Jesus breathes new life into the disciples.

These moments in the life and afterlife of Jesus point vividly to the future orientation of the Fourth Gospel. When John interprets Jesus' prediction of living water, which Jesus delivers during the last day of the Feast of Tabernacles, he does more than identify water with spirit. John offers as well a significant gloss, in which it becomes absolutely clear that the reception of the spirit lies at a moment in the near future. There is in this narrative explanation an explicit and irreversible breach between the present and the future, between the world the disciples now inhabit, which is void of the spirit, and a world shortly to come, in which the promise of being filled with the spirit will burst into reality. Jesus alone crosses that breach when he enters into a locked room and breathes life into his disciples. In this moment of commissioning, when the disciples are sent and authorized to forgive sins, Jesus also commands them to receive the spirit. Promise has been transformed into command, prediction into reality, as the disciples, who once were void of the spirit, are now filled with the life-giving spirit-breath of Jesus himself.[26]

It is absolutely essential, notwithstanding the invitation the Fourth Gospel offers to the world of theology, to bear in mind that this reception of life is a visceral and intimate process. The image of a river of running water

---

26. C. Bennema argues against this interpretation in *The Power of Saving Wisdom: An Investigation of Spirit and Wisdom in Relation to the Soteriology of the Fourth Gospel*. WUNT, 2nd ser. 148 (Tübingen: Mohr, 2002). In my opinion, however, there is a singular exception to this pattern of delaying inspiration, and that is the figure of Jesus; no one else in the Fourth Gospel can lay claim to the spirit prior to the resurrection of Jesus. In John 3:34, God seems to be doing the giving of the spirit without measure and Jesus the receiving, for Jesus is the one whom God sent, the one who "speaks the words of God, for he [God] gives the spirit without measure." In this text, Jesus has received the spirit from God without measure. If the water that is said to well up is the spirit in 4:11-15, then it may be implied that the spirit could be given to the woman during Jesus' lifetime. However, it is not clear in this narrative that she receives the spirit, and the emphasis, as the dialogue unfolds, is upon the *imminent* worship of God in spirit and in truth (4:23-24). In neither ch. 3 nor 4, then, does the person actually receive the holy spirit. The woman responds enthusiastically by telling her neighbors about Jesus, but there is no clear indication of a lifelong change in her that would signal the fresh presence of the spirit within. Moreover, both narratives are framed in such a way that they reflect the life of the community of the Fourth Gospel. The "we" saying in 3:11 suggested the muted presence of the community, and the success of the woman in John 4 suggests the success of a Samaritan mission in the early church.

from deep within a human body brings to mind wombs and lungs and stomachs, as well as wrenching processes that flush this water or breath out of those recesses — perhaps birth, perhaps an explosion of speech not unlike the coaxing of Elihu or even the oracles of the *engastrimythoi*, the enigmatic belly-talkers. The process of inbreathing, which inspires the disciples after Jesus' resurrection, by way of contrast, is not in the least bit violent or convulsive, though it is not for this reason any less visceral. It is an act that is not mere exhalation, not just out-breathing. It is not mere breathing upon. It is not in the least indirect or oblique. It is a moment of breathing into, a moment when people are so close to one another that the breath which exits one mouth is received into the lungs of another. The disciples' future — a spirit-filled future that is rife with the authority of Jesus — looks very much, in this private act, like it is being sealed with a life-giving kiss.

Spirit as a Promised Paraclete

The conviction of the Fourth Gospel, that "as yet there was no spirit because Jesus was not yet glorified," though by no means novel, is the summit of a long journey of transformation that emerged from reflection upon the relationship between spirit and virtue. It may even be possible to trace a tenuous development of views from Israelite literature to the Fourth Gospel. In Israelite memory, some heroes — Joseph, Bezalel, Daniel — were filled with spirits that were considered to be wise, knowledgeable, even divine; Elihu, at Job's expense, believed his spirit to be full of wisdom when it was decidedly not. Spurs of this point of view extended into the early Jewish world in various ways. One spur developed in which some authors unreservedly referred to holy spirits within: Daniel's was a holy spirit; devotees at Qumran were urged not to defile or forfeit their holy spirits; and Balaam in the *Liber antiquitatum biblicarum* forfeited his holy spirit because he served the king of Moab rather than Israel. Another spur developed especially under the influence of Stoicism in Alexandrian Egypt. The opening lines of the Wisdom of Solomon contain a relatively oblique reference to "a holy spirit of teaching," a spirit that can be taught the way of virtue, while Philo more flamboyantly and frequently interpreted the divine inbreathing as the implanting of a capacity for virtue.

The next stage consisted of a development of this second spur. Philo and the author of the Wisdom of Solomon, both of whom held fast to the belief that the spirit within could be holy and virtuous, would embrace the possibility as well of a further gift of the spirit within. In the Wisdom of Solomon, this was necessitated by the scriptural story of Solomon, whose prayer for wisdom marked a climactic moment in his development into a king whose wisdom expanded into legendary proportions. Much more complexity attended the development of Philo's conceptions of subsequent experiences of inspiration. Philo would claim for the prophets an experience of inspiration in which the spirit ousted their mental faculties and spoke through their vocal chords; not dissimilarly, he would claim for himself moments in which he lost control due to divine possession. Philo also portrayed Moses as unique among the prophets, for the spirit, which could put him into an ecstatic state at any moment, also guided his mind intact to truth; this experience Philo claimed as well for himself during those moments when the divine spirit, the customary friend, would teach him, mind intact, truths about the meaning of scripture. Philo was no less conversant in discussing the ascent of the philosopher's mind under the forceful uppersweep of the divine spirit; once again, he claimed this experience of being wafted on the winds of knowledge when, in an inspired state, while on break from the demands of urban leadership, he would offer an inspired allegorical interpretation of Moses' writings. What gives Philo's writings such a unique impress is his ability to describe these moments of subsequent inspiration so vividly without denigrating the force of the spirit that lies within from birth. He manages, in his own peculiarly profound way, to elevate both experiences.

A further stage of development is detectable in the Fourth Gospel, in which the inspiration of believers becomes possible *only* after the death and resurrection of Jesus. The function of the spirit as an accompanying and indwelling presence looks very much like the inspiration of Moses in Philo's treatises, but there is no corresponding conviction that the spirit given at birth also imparted the capacity for virtue or knowledge of God. The language of creation, whether the inbreathing of *adam* in Genesis 2 or the inbreathing of Israel in Ezekiel 36–37, comes into the picture behind locked doors only after the risen Jesus appears to the disciples. This is not at all an unforeseen development, for Paul and Luke, no less than John, associate filling with the spirit with a postresurrection world. Paul, like John, even understands the community of believers as a new temple and a new creation, neither of which existed prior to the resurrection of Jesus. What is new is the certainty with which John locates the presence of the spirit at a point beyond the crucifixion: the spirit was not yet given because Jesus was not yet glorified. This point is imminent — those who believed in him were about to receive the spirit — yet lodged decidedly in the future.

While Paul, Luke, and John hang the presence of the spirit on the hook of the resurrection of Jesus, and while John and Paul share the conviction that, in the wake of Jesus' resurrection the community will become a new temple and new creation, John puts his distinctive stamp upon the conception of filling with the spirit. The conception of filling with the spirit is very nearly obfuscated by other concerns of the Farewell Discourses. Nonetheless, the spirit is promised to be *in* the disciples, and so it is necessary in this study to explore what precisely John understands by the spirit within.

Much of what the spirit will be to believers is neatly summed up in the first of Jesus' sayings about the paraclete:[27] "If you love me, you will keep my commandments. And I will ask the Father, and he will give you another paraclete, to be with you forever. This is *the spirit of truth,* whom the world cannot receive, because it neither sees him nor knows it. You know it, because he remains with you, and he will be in you" (John 14:16-17).[28] This statement is pivotal for several reasons. It is, to begin, the *first* promise of the spirit in the Farewell Discourses; as such it provides the perspective from which the following three promises must inevitably, by dint of se-

27. The background of the word "paraclete" *(ho paraklētos)* is not absolutely germane to this study, so I will not take up the topic directly in this study. There are, moreover, excellent studies of the term. See O. Betz, *Der Paraklet.* AGSU 2 (Leiden: Brill, 1963); Dodd, *The Interpretation of the Fourth Gospel,* 213-27; R. E. Brown, *The Gospel according to John XIII-XXI.* AB 29A (Garden City: Doubleday, 1970) 1135-44; M. Turner, *The Holy Spirit and Spiritual Gifts in the New Testament Church and Today* (Peabody: Hendrickson, 1998) 77-79; M. M. Thompson, *The God of the Gospel of John* (Grand Rapids: Wm. B. Eerdmans, 2001) 145-88; Bennema, *The Power of Saving Wisdom,* 216-21; T. G. Brown, *Spirit in the Writings of John: Johannine Pneumatology in Social-scientific Perspective.* JSNTSup 253 (London: T. & T. Clark, 2003) 170-86. For parallels between the paraclete and Jesus, see T. G. Brown, *Spirit in the Writings of John,* 190; Turner, *The Holy Spirit and Spiritual Gifts,* 79-81; R. E. Brown, *The Gospel according to John XIII-XXI,* 1140-41.

28. Until this moment in the narrative, the actions and dialogue have been rather fast paced, as in the Synoptic Gospels. Jesus has gathered the disciples, as in the Synoptic Gospels, for a final meal together. He has washed their feet, claimed them as friends, eaten bread together with them, predicted his betrayal, issued the commandment to love, predicted Peter's denial, and talked with both Thomas and Philip (13:1–14:14). A brief catena occurs in 14:8-14; vv. 8-11 are a dialogue with Philip. Verse 12, on the topic of greater works than Jesus performs, provides a transition from the theme of belief to that of works; v. 13 is on prayer, with v. 14 repeating the theme. (See the parallel in Matt 21:21; on such petition statements in the farewell discourses and their resemblance to Synoptic sayings, see T. G. Brown, *Spirit in the Writings of John,* 634-35). Jesus' soliloquy begins in earnest moments later with another statement about love, followed instantly by the first reference to the spirit in the farewell discourses.

quence alone, be viewed. Second, this saying, from a literary point of view, comprises the only original promise in the gospel. John 14:1-31, in which this saying is situated, concludes, "Rise, let us be on our way" (v. 31). Originally this was probably followed by their departure in 18:1: "After Jesus had spoken these words, he went out with his disciples across the Kidron valley to a place where there was a garden, which he and his disciples entered." Chapters 15–17 interrupt this simple sequence by creating an awkward lengthy pause between Jesus' command to be on the way, in 14:31, and their actual departure in 18:1; chs. 15–17 ought, therefore, to be seen as a later insertion.[29] What this means is that the only *original* promise of the spirit is situated in the original Farewell Discourse in ch. 14. The others, which are situated in chs. 15–16, are either parallel promises that were inserted later or expansions of the original promise in 14:15-17. The third reason this promise is of such importance is that it is a salutary indication that the spirit will be within the disciples. And fourth, the importance of this saying stems from its introduction of key themes associated with the spirit in the Fourth Gospel: (1) the spirit is described by the term "spirit of truth," in a context rife with rejection of the world; and (2) the mode of the spirit's presence is described simultaneously in two ways, as accompaniment and indwelling, as a presence that exists within believers and alongside them. These dimensions of this brief promise provide a deep vein of insight into John's unique take on what it means to be filled with the spirit.

The Spirit of Truth

The expression "spirit of truth" introduces a note of edginess to the promise of the spirit, for with it an alien world intrudes into the private discourse between a teacher and his friends: "the spirit of truth, whom the world cannot receive, because it neither sees it nor knows it" (John 14:17). The disciples are not now led to expect halcyon days ahead; there will be no cease-fire between them and the world around them. This world cannot receive the spirit of truth. Jesus precipitated conflict between dark and light, religious leaders and himself, superficial followers and true disciples, the hostile world and the faithful. This scenario will not dissipate in Jesus'

29. R. E. Brown (*The Gospel according to John I-XII,* xxxvii) is by no means alone in proposing that chs. 13–14 were original, with chs. 15–17 added. John 16:4-33 looks like a variant duplicate of the discourse in ch. 14.

absence, when the paraclete, the spirit of truth, will reside exclusively in the portion of the human race that will receive Jesus (1:13-14; 14:17).

This is an essential insight that renders the spirit in the Fourth Gospel distinctive. The war between light and darkness, ignorance and wisdom, does not draw to a peaceful close with the advent of the spirit. No amount of peace, patience, kindness — the sorts of virtues Paul considers to be the fruit of the spirit — come in the wake of the presence of the spirit within. The Fourth Gospel leans much more in the direction of the contrasts Paul draws with respect to the spirit: not slavish obedience to Torah but faith; not slavery but sonship; not the spirit of the world but the spirit from God. This last contrast lies very close at hand to the Fourth Gospel, particularly since both Paul and John portray the spirit in this regard as revealer and teacher (1 Cor 2:10-13). Yet the spirit of the world in the letters of Paul, as we saw, is a more benign presence; it is simply a definition of the world's values. In the Fourth Gospel, in contrast, the world is a hostile presence that cannot receive or see the spirit, and the ruler of this world already stands under condemnation (John 16:11). In this context, the spirit is no peaceful and gentle presence that aids the war-weary, but a fierce and loyal companion, not unlike Jesus in the Fourth Gospel, who holds back neither his loyalty toward friends nor his excoriation of opponents. The spirit of truth is no less fractious and no more conciliatory than the first paraclete whose place it takes.

Therefore, the irenic function of guiding the community into truth, of interpreting the past afresh, is directed internally only to the community. The spirit of truth, the paraclete, will have an altogether different impact upon the world by bringing it to trial because it cannot receive, see, or know the spirit of truth (14:17): "When the paraclete comes, whom I will send to you from the Father, the spirit of truth who comes from the Father, he will testify on my behalf" (15:26).[30] Alongside this testimony on Jesus' behalf, the paraclete "will convince the world about sin and righteousness and judgment: about sin, because they do not believe in me; about righteousness, because I am going to the Father and you will see me no longer; and about judgment, because the ruler of this world has been condemned" (16:8-11).[31] As God testified on Jesus' behalf while Jesus was alive, the spirit

---

30. Greek: *hotan elthē ho paraklētos hon egō pempsō hymin para tou patros, to pneuma tēs alētheias ho para tou patros ekporeuetai, ekeinos martyrēsei peri emou.*

31. Greek: *kai elthōn ekeinos elenxei ton kosmon peri hamartias kai peri dikaiosynēs kai peri kriseōs. peri hamartias men, hoti ou pisteuousin eis eme. peri dikaiosynēs de, hoti pros ton*

of truth who comes from the Father will testify on Jesus' behalf (5:37; 15:26).[32] The spirit will not set aside the hostility that became evident in a particularly vitriolic exchange in which Jesus identified "the Jews" as the children of the devil, accused them of exercising their murderous inheritance as the devil's children, and set his own penchant for truth over against the devil's love of lies. Having thoroughly unmasked what he considered to be their murderous love of deceit, Jesus challenged the Jews with the question "Which of you convicts me concerning sin?" (8:46). The work of the paraclete mirrors this exquisitely; the paraclete will "convict the world concerning sin" (16:8). In the grand law court of truth, Jesus knew that the religious leaders could not convict him of sin; in that same grand law court, the paraclete puts the world on the defensive by convicting it of sin.

The drama of a cosmic contest between truth and deceit, between the children of the devil and the children of God, between darkness and light, that underlies the entire span of Jesus' life in the Fourth Gospel, may explain the edgy introduction of seemingly superfluous clauses that describe

---

patera hypagō kai ouketi theōreite me. peri de kriseōs, hoti ho archōn tou kosmou toutou kekritai. On the meanings of the word "convict" *(elenchein),* see Bennema (*The Power of Saving Wisdom,* 236-39), who thinks that the paraclete exposes the guilt of the world, as opposed to T. G. Brown (*Spirit in the Writings of John,* 226), who thinks that the paraclete "proves to the disciples the world's wrongness regarding sin, righteousness and judgment" (see 220-28).

32. There are, then, two principal functions of the paraclete: to teach by recollecting *and* to play advocate on behalf of Jesus (15:26) but against the world (16:8-11). The first function will occur because the spirit of truth exists within the disciples (14:17). They will be taught, prompted like Philo perhaps, to apprehend the teaching and actions of Jesus in light of Israel's scriptures. Yet making sense of the paraclete's forensic function in relation to its presence *within* the disciples holds much thornier prospects. Evidently the spirit of truth will testify, acting as advocate over against the world, on Jesus' behalf (15:26). Where does this leave the disciples? They too will testify, though the reason Jesus gives is not that the spirit is within but that they were with him from the beginning (15:27). Perhaps a clue lies in the Synoptic promise of the spirit in the context of persecution. Luke even associates this inspiration with teaching: "When they bring you before the synagogues, the rulers, and the authorities, do not worry about how you are to defend yourselves or what you are to say; for the holy spirit will teach you at that very hour what you ought to say" (Luke 12:11-12). Is a similar future envisaged in the Fourth Gospel, where the disciples are instructed to anticipate moments when the paraclete will supply them with testimony? This would certainly explain the sequence of the first promise, which leads directly to a subsequent promise: "I will not leave you orphaned" (John 14:18). Though without legal rights, the disciples will themselves have an advocate to stand by them and be within them.

the spirit of truth in its first appearance in the gospel: *whom the world cannot receive, because it neither sees nor knows him.* This is no mere fumarole in a dormant volcano but a fresh eruption that promises long-standing consequences. It is a redrawing of the battle lines — battle lines that are not unfamiliar. This expression, spirit of truth, occurs as well in the Dead Sea Scrolls, which antedate the Fourth Gospel. The Teaching on the Two Spirits, to which we referred in our discussion of Paul's letters, contains a vivid and detailed description of the spirits of truth and deceit. This teaching may have circulated independently and been more readily available to those outside the community at Qumran than its placement in the *Community Rule* would indicate. Consequently, though it may be incautious to try to establish direct influence of the Dead Sea Scrolls upon the Fourth Gospel, it would be no less irresponsible to neglect similar elements in the Fourth Gospel and *Community Rule.* Whether or not it was known to the author or the readers of the Fourth Gospel, the Teaching on the Two Spirits shares a keen resemblance to the teachings about the spirit of truth in the Fourth Gospel, and we would be negligent if we failed to attempt at least to fill out the laconic references in the Fourth Gospel by comparing them with the expansive discussion of the spirit of truth in the third and fourth columns of the *Community Rule.*[33]

According to the Teaching on the Two Spirits, the master of the community is to instruct the Qumran devotees, the "sons of light," about "the nature of all the sons of *adam.*" The instruction turns out, at least from our perspective two millennia later, to be tricky, ambiguous, and multilayered. Yet at the base of it lies an interpretation of the divine inbreathing of Gen 2:7, in which God

created *humanity* to rule the world and placed within him two spirits so that he would walk with them until the moment of his visitation: they are the spirits of truth and of deceit. From the spring of light stem the generations of truth, and from the source of darkness the generations of

---

33. When Jesus introduces this expression out of the blue toward the end of the Fourth Gospel, he does so as if the disciples are already familiar with it, for he elucidates who the paraclete is with the first of three references to the spirit of truth, followed by the words "whom the world cannot receive, because it neither sees it nor knows it. *You know it. . . .*" The claim "You know it" implies, and not very subtly, that the disciples, and presumably the readers of this gospel, already recognize this entity called the spirit of truth. What the disciples in this narrative are presumed to know, we can best ascertain from the Teaching on the Two Spirits. The references in *T. Jud.* 20 are perhaps too late, possibly even of Christian origin.

deceit. And in the hand of the Prince of Lights is dominion over all the sons of justice; they walk on paths of light. And in the hand of the Angel of Darkness is total dominion over the sons of deceit; they walk on paths of darkness. (1QS III 17-21)

In this introduction to the Teaching on the Two Spirits, the inbreathing of Gen 2:7 is construed uniquely: God "created humanity to rule the world and placed within him *two spirits*."[34] The amazing innovation, of course, is the impartation of *two* spirits rather than one. Even in comparison with the Alexandrian Philo, who diverges wildly from the biblical text, this interpretation, on Palestinian soil no less, is wilder still. Philo did not trace the tension of the virtuous life to two opposing spirits; he took the more natural interpretative step of explaining the presence of virtue and vice in terms of mind and flesh; the soul can tend toward virtue or to vice, depending upon whether it yields to the mind or to the body.[35] The master of the community, in contrast, is told explicitly to instruct his people concerning two spirits, one of light and the other of darkness, two diametrically opposed spirits within each human being that are the source of generations of truth and deceit.[36]

---

34. See also 4Q381 fr. 1 7 (4QNon-canonical Psalms B) for a combination of dominion (Gen 1:26-28) and inbreathing (Gen 2:7).

35. See, e.g., *On the Creation* 151–69; *Allegorical Interpretation* 1.31-42; 2.4; *Questions and Answers on Genesis* 1.51. See further J. R. Levison, *Portraits of Adam in Early Judaism: From Sirach to 2 Baruch.* JSPSup 1 (Sheffield: JSOT, 1988) 75-88.

36. It is small wonder, of course, that scholars have turned to Zoroastrian texts to explain this innovative interpretation of Gen 2:7. The salient aspect of Persian religion is its dualism. The main source of this belief lies in the *Gāthās* of Zarathustra — in Greek, Zoroaster — teachings that are a later literary product which undoubtedly preserve fundamental beliefs that preceded the Hellenistic and Roman eras. Herodotus, Plato, and Plutarch (in particular) show a clear awareness of Zoroastrian teaching, and Plutarch, in *De Iside et Osiride,* offers a fairly lucid précis of Zoroastrian belief. Zoroastrian dualism is embodied in a teaching about two spirits. In the *Gāthās,* two texts are among many that express this belief. According to *Yasna* 30.3-5 of the *Gāthās:* "There are two fundamental spirits, twins which are renowned to be in conflict. In thought and in word, in action, they are two: the good and the bad. And between these two, the beneficent have correctly chosen, not the maleficent. Furthermore when these two spirits first came together, they created life and death, and how, at the end, the worst existence shall be for the deceitful but the best thinking for the truthful person. Of these two spirits, the deceitful one chose to bring to realization the worst things. (But) the very virtuous spirit . . . chose the truth and (so shall those) who shall satisfy the Wise Lord continuously with true actions." This single statement contains key oppositions: good and bad; beneficent and maleficent; life and death; and deceitful and

These two spirits represent, we may recall, two spheres that are in conflict with one another. The spirit of truth is one of unmitigated virtue, including "intelligence, understanding, potent wisdom . . . a spirit of knowledge in all the plans of action . . . careful behavior in wisdom concerning everything . . ." (1QS IV 2-6). This spirit lies in conflict with the spirit of deceit, which is one of unmitigated vice, including "greed, sluggishness in the service of justice, wickedness, falsehood, pride" (IV 9-11). Second, in 1QS III–IV there is a distinction between the "generations of truth and . . . deceit," between "sons of light" and those "of darkness," be-

---

truthful people. Singularly important is that these oppositions reflect what we might loosely call an ethical dualism — two ways are envisaged, of good, life, and truth over against evil, death, and deceit. The chasm that separates good from evil is expressed as well in *Yasna* 45.2: "Yes, I shall speak of the two fundamental spirits of existence, of which the virtuous one would have thus spoken to the evil one: 'Neither our thoughts nor teachings nor intentions, neither our preferences nor words, neither our actions nor conceptions nor our souls are in accord.'" Singularly important in both of these representative texts is the embodiment of Zoroastrian dualism in two spirits, two "fundamental spirits of existence" which divide the virtuous from the wicked, deceitful people from people of the truth.

The influx of Persian influence upon conceptions of the two spirits at Qumran is not a given. It may be that the teaching in 1QS III–IV was an independent development of Gen 2:7 which focused, not so much upon two spirits in conflict, but upon a variety of spiritual stages in human beings that arose through the struggle between truth and perversity *within* the human heart. Thus, the language of "two spirits" does not reflect a cosmic conflict between the sons of light and darkness, the spirits of truth and deceit, but a conflict *within* each human heart that produces a variety of spiritual states. Quotations are from S. Insler, *The Gāthās of Zarathustra. Texts et mémoires 1;* Acta Iranica 8 (Leiden: Brill, 1975). These many spiritual states become apparent immediately at the opening of the teaching, in 1QS III 14, which refers to "all the ranks of their spirits." It is not here two spirits, but the ranking of spirits that is central. It is this ranking that explains why, in 1QS IV 2-12, the "sons of truth" are referred to twice in the list that catalogues at length the vices and virtues of the spirits of truth and falsehood (quoted above), while the "sons of deceit" are not mentioned at all. The perspective is not of two distinct groups but, rather, "sons of light," who participate nonetheless in a larger sphere of deceit and darkness. Their ranking in the community depends upon how successfully they have torn themselves from this deceit and injustice, etc., *within their own hearts*. It is this fierce struggle within the human heart that will be finished once and for all in a final moment of divine visitation, when there will be "an end to the existence of injustice" (1QS IV 18). And so the master is to teach that "until now the spirits of truth and injustice feud in the heart of *humankind:* they walk in wisdom or in folly" (1QS IV 23-24).

For a discussion of the Teaching on the Two Spirits, including alleged Persian influence and internal considerations, see J. R. Levison, "The Two Spirits in Qumran Theology," in *The Dead Sea Scrolls and the Qumran Community,* ed. J. H. Charlesworth, vol. 2 of *The Bible and the Dead Sea Scrolls* (Waco: Baylor University Press, 2006) 169-94.

tween the "sons of deceit" and the "sons of justice." There is a clear distinction between "those who walk" in the spirit of truth and "those who walk" in the spirit of deceit. There are two different generations, two different groups, whose ways of life depend upon the spirits of truth and deceit. Third, in 1QS III–IV those who follow these spirits do so "until the moment of his [God's] visitation." The sons of truth will be rewarded with "healing, plentiful peace in a long life, fruitful offspring with all everlasting blessings, eternal enjoyment with endless life, and a crown of glory with majestic raiment in eternal light" (IV 6-8). The fate of the sons of deceit will be very different, for God's "visitation" will bring to them "an abundance of afflictions at the hands of all the angels of destruction, for eternal damnation by the scorching wrath of the God of revenges, for permanent terror and shame without end with the humiliation of destruction by the fire of the dark regions . . . bitter weeping and harsh evils in the abysses of darkness until their destruction, without there being a remnant or a survivor for them" (1QS IV 12-14).

There are, then, two spirits, two ways of life, two sorts of people, two different judgments at the hands of God. The edgy introduction of the spirit of truth in the Fourth Gospel, with the wedge that is drawn between the disciples and the world, may belie a similar perspective. The clear distinction in the gospel between light and darkness, between truth and deceit, between the children who trace their origins to the devil and the children of God elsewhere in the Fourth Gospel, underscores the importance of these similarities.[37] These are stunning correspondences, salient points of continuity between the Fourth Gospel and the Teaching on the Two Spirits.

Yet there are also important, though not unexpected, moments of mismatch as well. As we expect from the Fourth Gospel, judgment is located at the cross rather than in the future. The ruler of the world has already been condemned by Jesus; the darkness has already been dispelled by the light (John 1:5-10). Nor is it surprising, in light of John's firm belief that the spirit had not yet been given, that the spirit of truth is only *promised* to the disciples while Jesus is alive. The spirit of truth will enter the disciples only when its presence is made necessary by the absence of Jesus. In the Teaching on the Two Spirits, by way of contrast, the inbreathing or placement of the spirits of truth and deceit within is situated naturally at the initial creation. In the Fourth Gospel, the insistent delay of the spirit's

37. E.g., John 8:44.

presence until after Jesus' death is silhouetted against the background of the two spirits, which are placed within human beings from the start.

Nonetheless, the neat and tidy dualistic symmetry of the Teaching on the Two Spirits in the *Community Rule* (1QS III–IV), which extends from a battle within a human being to distinctive ways of life to the respective angelic leaders of the sons of light and darkness, finds no exact match in the Fourth Gospel. There is no battle within the human heart that is occasioned by the presence of two spirits within from birth. Nor is there in the Fourth Gospel a division of humankind into the children of light and the children of darkness. The children of darkness, who have existed, like their satanic leader, from the beginning, do exist, and Jesus excoriates them: "You are from your father the devil, and you choose to do your father's desires. He was a murderer from the beginning and does not stand in the truth, because there is no truth in him. When he lies, he speaks according to his own nature, for he is a liar and the father of lies. But because I tell the truth, you do not believe me" (John 8:44-45). Yet the children of light do not yet exist. Jesus refers only once to the children of light, in his final words addressed to the crowd, following their persistent misunderstanding. In such a context, this word comes both as a promise and a thinly veiled indictment: "The light is with you for a little longer. Walk while you have the light, so that the darkness may not overtake you. If you walk in the darkness, you do not know where you are going. While you have the light, believe in the light, so that you may become [*genēsthe*] children of light" (12:35-36).

Human existence is divided, therefore, in the Fourth Gospel, as in the Teaching on the Two Spirits, but not symmetrically so. In the Teaching on the Two Spirits, although the spirit of truth within is tempered by the spirit of deceit, with which it battles, it is nonetheless present within as the source of a life of virtue. In the Fourth Gospel, in contrast, Jesus enters a world that is darkened by deceit, a world in which Jesus' enemies are children of the devil and the crowds are not yet children of light. There is no corresponding group of people who bask in the light. There is no group — not yet, anyway — with the spirit of truth in it.

Two Modes of Divine Presence

The Fourth Gospel is unique, in comparison with other literature in the early church, in its affirmation that the spirit simultaneously resides in and accompanies believers. This comes as no surprise in a gospel that is replete with intriguing *double entendre,* with poignant resonances of Israel's scriptures, and with a profound reinterpretation of traditions about Jesus, such as the metamorphosis of his crucifixion into a moment of glorification. The conception of filling with the spirit in the Fourth Gospel undergoes no less a profound and perplexing transformation. There is no facile adoption of the early church's traditional language of the spirit; the Fourth Gospel contains rather a startling metamorphosis in the mode of the spirit's presence. Rather than promising straightforwardly that the spirit of truth will fill the disciples, Jesus promises *two* modes of the spirit's presence: the spirit will be both within and alongside believers. The spirit of truth, in other words, "remains with you and will be in you" (John 14:17).[38] The first image of divine presence, marked by the preposition *para,* evokes accompaniment; the second preposition, *en,* evokes indwelling. How can this be? How can the spirit simultaneously accompany and indwell believers?

We cannot finally answer these questions with perfect certainty because of how sparingly the Fourth Gospel depicts the spirit's presence. To understand the meaning of the spirit's presence within in the Fourth Gospel, then, it will be necessary again to turn to other writings, in this instance the treatises of Philo Judaeus, which, as we have seen time and again, contain myriad discussions of the ways in which the divine spirit inspires human beings. The portal at which we may gain entry to Philo's contribution to our understanding of the Fourth Gospel is provided by the figure of Moses, to whose life Philo devotes two entire treatises. The rationale for this point of entry, of course, is that the Israelite stories associated with Moses provide the substratum of much that features in the Fourth Gospel. John refers overtly to Moses (e.g., John 1:17; 5:46), includes imagery that is taken from the life of Moses, such as the tabernacle (1:14) and the bronze serpent that Moses lifted in the wilderness (3:14), and probably even characterizes Jesus' miracles as "signs" in order to provide a distinctive resonance with Moses' miraculous signs in Egypt.[39] The Mosaic tenor of the gospel coalesces in John's version of the miraculous feeding of the crowd. Jesus contrasts the manna which the Israelites ate, after

---

38. Greek: *par' hymin menei kai en hymin estai.*

39. See R. E. Brown, *The Gospel according to John I-XII,* lx; T. F. Glasson, *Moses in the Fourth Gospel.* SBT 40 (Naperville: SCM, 1963); P. Borgen, *Bread from Heaven: An Exegetical Study of the Concept of Manna in the Gospel of John and the Writings of Philo.* NovTSup 10 (Leiden: Brill, 1965); W. A. Meeks, *The Prophet-king: Moses Traditions and the Johannine Christology.* NovTSup 14 (Leiden: Brill, 1967).

which they died, with the bread from heaven that he gives, which nourishes eternal life (6:48-50).

If we enter Philo's treatises at precisely this point, with the giving of the manna, we will encounter two forms of inspiration which illuminate Jesus' terse promise that the spirit of truth will be both *with* and *in* the disciples. Moses' oracles concerning the sabbath, explains Philo, were the product of prophetic possession — the result of a form of inspiration in which the spirit enters forcibly within. According to LXX Exod 16:15, Moses responded to the Israelites' question about the manna with a straightforward description of it as bread, prefaced by the simple words, "Moses said [*eipen*] to them." Philo records instead that Moses commanded *under inspiration (epitheiasas)* that the Israelites should gather only enough for each day (*On the Life of Moses* 2.259). According to LXX Exod 16:23, Moses merely "said [*eipen*] to them" that they should rest on the Sabbath. Philo writes instead that Moses, "under God-sent inspiration, made announcement [*theophorētheis ethespise*] of the sabbath" (*On the Life of Moses* 2.264). According to LXX Exod 16:25-26, Moses said *(eipen)* that the people should eat what was preserved from the prior day rather than searching in the field on the Sabbath. Philo transforms this statement into a prediction by emphasizing that it transpired, not on the Sabbath, but on the day prior to the Sabbath, by describing the oracle as "most portentous," and by replacing "said" with "prophesied" (*thespizei; On the Life of Moses* 2.268-69). The result of these Sabbath predictions, Philo records, was Israel's acknowledgement of Moses "the prophet as a true seer, an interpreter of God, and alone gifted with foreknowledge of the hidden future" (2.269).

In such a context, Philo consistently replaces the biblical word "said" with words that describe inspired possession in order to offer an apt illustration of "that divine possession in virtue of which he is chiefly and in the strict sense considered a prophet" (2.191). In fact, the entire section of *On the Life of Moses* which Philo devotes to Moses' prophetic vocation is introduced with a statement that could hardly have prepared Philo's readers for anything but a description of Moses' prophetic ecstasy: "I will proceed next to describe those delivered by the prophet himself under divine inspiration. . . . The examples of his possession . . ." (2.246). As prophet *par excellence,* Moses is repeatedly inspired, possessed, caught in the experience of enthusiasm. The spirit comes into him, affording him the capacity to speak God's words to the people of Israel.

When, however, Philo describes the process by which Moses actually brought about the inception of the Sabbath, he conceives of the prophetic inspiration of Moses in a manner that is jarringly different from the sort of prophetic possession that leaves a prophet temporarily out of his or her mind, filled with ecstatic possession, invaded by the divine spirit. In *On the Life of Moses* 2.264-65, a discussion of Moses that is rife with the vocabulary of prophetic possession, as we just noted, Philo explains Moses' ability to predict the Sabbath:

> Moses, when he heard of this [the manna] and also actually saw it, was awestruck and, guided by what was not so much surmise as God-sent inspiration, made announcement of the sabbath. I need hardly say that conjectures of this kind are closely akin to prophecies. For the mind could not have made so straight an aim if there was not also the divine spirit guiding it to the truth itself.[40]

In this explanation of Moses' insight, his mind remains intact, his mental faculties conscious, his intellect alert — all the while the divine spirit guides his mind to the truth itself. Moses does not, like other prophets, lose his mind when the divine spirit enters him; his mind, rather, is made more alert, not less.

Philo communicates the centrality of the inspiration of the mind alert, not only by using the words "mind" and "truth" without the slightest indication of Moses' loss of control, but also by his adoption of two other words, "conjecture" *(eikosia)* and "to guide" *(podēgetein)*. The noun "conjecture" occurs consistently in contexts that have to do with thought, opinions, and guessing. Philo includes conjecture alongside human ideas, purposes, and aims (*On the Posterity of Cain* 80), and he describes it as "second to the true vision . . . conjecture and theorizing and all that can be brought into the category of reasonable probability" (*On the Special Laws* 1.38).[41] The verb "guide" occurs without exception in Philo's writings in association with the path toward virtue, including love of wisdom (*On the Creation* 70) and divine reason (*On the Immutability of God* 182). When Philo describes wisdom itself as a guide, he presents the essential role of the conscious mind with exceptional clarity: "The mind is cleansed by wis-

---

40. Greek of the last sentence: *ho gar nous ouk an houtōs euskoptōs euthylobēsen ei mē kai theion ēn pneuma to podēgetoun pros autēn tēn alētheian.*

41. In *Embassy to Gaius* 21, e.g., Philo observes, "The human mind in its blindness does not perceive its real interest and all it can do is to take conjecture and guesswork for its guide instead of knowledge." See, e.g., *On the Confusion of Tongues* 159; *On the Cherubim* 69; *On Dreams* 1.23; *On the Special Laws* 1.63; 4.50; *Who Is the Heir?* 98; *On the Life of Moses* 1.68.

dom and the truths of wisdom's teaching which *guide* its steps to the contemplation of the universe and all that is therein, and by the sacred company of the other virtues and by the practice of them shown in noble and highly praiseworthy actions" (*On the Special Laws* 1.269). The road to virtue is therefore paved by the purification of the mind. Philo's adoption of these two words, "conjecture" and "guide," to explain Moses' ability to predict the future when he is under the control of the divine spirit indicates the presence of a view of inspiration in which the highest achievement of human thought is effected by the spirit.[42]

42. This explanation of Moses' ability to predict the Sabbath is part of a lengthy apologetic analysis of the various roles in which Moses functioned. Philo dedicates the first three quarters of his *On the Life of Moses* to demonstrating that "Moses was the best of kings, of lawgivers and of high priests" (2.187). In 2.188, he shifts his efforts to demonstrating that Moses was also "a prophet of the highest quality." To accomplish this, Philo, in what proves to be an extremely confusing discussion, distinguishes three types of oracles in the production of which Moses the prophet participates. The first two sorts of Moses' oracles Philo presents with relative clarity. The first group of oracles are given by God through Moses as an interpreter. These comprise the laws which expand the Decalogue. The second sort of oracles Moses receives through question and answer with God: "The prophet asks questions of God about matters on which he has been seeking knowledge, and God replies and instructs him" (2.190).

Consummately confusing, however, is Philo's description of the third sort of oracles, which "are spoken by Moses in his own person, when possessed by God and carried away out of himself" (2.188). This description of Moses contains two seemingly incompatible parts. One is Moses' speaking *in his own person,* and the other is Moses' being carried *out of himself* by inspired possession. What exactly these parts mean is explained in the following two descriptions of Moses as prophet *par excellence.* On the one hand, explains Philo, Moses received God's own knowledge: "God has given to him of his own power of foreknowledge and by this he will reveal future events" (2.190). What Philo means by this statement can be comprehended by Philo's earlier contention that Moses spoke "in his own person." When Philo introduces the first sort of oracles, he employs the words "in His [God's] own person" to describe God's condition while delivering the Decalogue. In the same context, while introducing the third sort of oracles, Philo reproduces exactly the same words to describe Moses' condition while he delivered other oracles to Israel: "Of the divine utterances, some are spoken by God in His own Person . . . and others are spoken by Moses in his own person . . ." (2.188). This parallel between God and Moses suggests that Moses, like God, possesses the capacity to produce oracles out of his own self. With respect to God, Philo need not explain how this is possible. With respect to Moses, Philo explains laconically that Moses can speak out of himself because "God has given to him of his own power of foreknowledge" (2.190). On the other hand — here Philo perfects his ability to confuse — these oracles, spoken out of Moses himself, are the sort "in which the speaker appears under that divine possession in virtue of which he is chiefly and in the strict sense considered a prophet" (2.191). This statement concurs with what Philo earlier said after he contended that Moses spoke out of him-

Like the Fourth Gospel, Philo offers a juxtaposition of two modes of inspiration. Moses was, at one and the same time, beside himself due to prophetic possession, due to the spirit's presence within, and capable of prophesying because the divine spirit guided his mind to the truth. Along the lines of the first understanding of inspiration, the spirit enters Moses, as it enters other prophets who succumb to the overwhelming force of the divine spirit. Along the lines of the second mode of inspiration, the spirit guides Moses' mind in a manner that is reminiscent of Socrates's *daimonion,* a unique presence that communicated directly to his mind, as it accompanied him throughout his profound and profoundly influential life.[43] What is stunning about Philo's unique portrayal of Moses is how deftly he intertwines both modes of the spirit's presence; as prophet par excellence, Moses both receives the spirit within and is guided by the spirit, which leads his mind to the truth.

There may be something more to be said about the presence of the spirit in the Fourth Gospel and the writings of Philo. In what amounts to a dis-

---

self: "others are spoken by Moses [in his own person], when possessed by God and carried away out of himself." This is the language of prophetic ecstasy of the most extraordinary sort. Moses, who is of course always a prophet, or better, *the* prophet, experiences a form of possession that is akin to the experience of the entire race of prophets, as Philo understands their experience.

The confluence of these streams is the product of Philo's apologetic strategy. He wants to demonstrate that Moses simultaneously embodies both the highest level of human insight ("in his own person") and the most intense form of prophetic ecstasy ("carried away out of himself"). Because the biblical texts are put to such unabashedly apologetic use, these two streams vie for prominence and converge wildly in the course of Philo's subsequent discussion of Moses. In 2.264-65, we are able to discern that the introduction of the spirit as the mind's guide into a context rife with expressions for enthusiastic inspiration expresses the convergence of the two apologetic currents in 2.188-91 that we have identified. The spirit both induces ecstasy and guides the mind intact to truth otherwise unknown. Despite the preponderance of words for inspiration and inspired possession which permeate Philo's portrait of Moses, therefore, the impression that Moses' mind was displaced, that his prophecies were the product of mantic frenzy, reflects only one of the currents that whirl through *On the Life of Moses.* The other complementary current entails the guidance of Moses' mind to the truth by the divine spirit. Moses speaks both while possessed (stream two in 2.188-91) *and* with his mind in possession of God's foreknowledge (stream one in 2.188-91).

See further *On Rewards and Punishments* 53-55 and the analyses in J. R. Levison, "Inspiration and the Divine Spirit in the Writings of Philo Judaeus," *JSJ* 26 (1995) 310-12; "The Prophetic Spirit as an Angel according to Philo," *HTR* 88 (1995) 195-206; and "Two Types of Ecstatic Prophecy according to Philo," *SPhilo* 6 (1994) 83-89.

43. See Part II, chapter 3 of this study.

tressingly complex and lengthy interpretation of the evil angels in Gen 6:1-4, Philo of Alexandria interprets the limitation of God's spirit within to 120 years by means of a threefold typology of souls. The evil angels represent one classification of souls, irredeemably incorrigible people, among whom "it is impossible that the spirit of God should dwell and make for ever its habitation" (*On the Giants* 19–20).

The second class of souls consists of the vast bulk of human beings, who are compelled to go about their lives variously preoccupied. With respect to this class of souls, Philo interprets the spirit, not as the spirit-breath which all possess, as in Gen 6:3, but as the spirit which infrequently grants a vision of God: "The spirit does sometimes stay a while, but it does not abide for ever among most of us. . . . Even over the reprobate hovers often a sudden vision of the excellent, but to grasp it and keep it for their own they have not the strength. In a moment it is gone and passed to some other place" (20–21). Philo is compelled to conclude that "in the many, those, that is, who have set before them many ends in life, the divine spirit does not abide, even though it sojourn there for a while" (53).[44]

There is only one class of souls, the third sort, with which the divine spirit abides forever. Only those who come to God naked, completely free of the flesh, can learn the holy and secret mysteries of God. This class of souls is represented quintessentially by Moses, the sage and prophet, who pitched his tent — his fleshly concerns — outside the camp and worshiped God in inner darkness, where he became teacher of the divine rites and holy mysteries to those whose ears were purified. Philo concludes his explanation of the classes of souls with a reference to Moses: "He then has ever the divine spirit at his side, taking the lead in every journey of righteousness, but from those others, as I have said, it quickly separates itself, from these to whose span of life he has also set a term of a hundred and twenty years, for he says, 'their days shall be a hundred and twenty years'" (55). The divine spirit accompanies Moses in a constant way, a way in which it does not accompany the mass of humanity and in a way that it cannot ever inspire those who devote themselves entirely to the flesh and its pleasures. Jesus' promise that the spirit will remain with the disciples, understood from this perspective, is an indication of how richly and permanently the spirit within will affect them.

It may be that the words "remain alongside you" provide a corrective to the sorts of enthusiasm that could be conjured by the words "in you" —

---

44. On these various preoccupations, see *On the Giants* 28–31.

from Cassandra's being thrown about by Apollo to Kenaz's final vision to Philo's prophets, who temporarily lose all control of their minds and whose vocal chords function like musical instruments as the vessels of God's words. Jesus' promise of the "spirit within" is first a promise of the "spirit alongside," which points in a very different direction: it promises constancy and companionship rather than temporary experiences of inspiration, occasional visions, transitory moments of prophetic rapture. While all of these can be desirable, they are not what Jesus promises. The spirit will instead remain with the disciples, constantly at their side. When Jesus explains further that the spirit will be in the disciples, it becomes obvious that the spirit's presence within will not be distinct from its constant accompaniment. The spirit will remain within the disciples even as God remained in Jesus (John 14:10) and as the disciples are expected to remain in Jesus (15:7) and remain in Jesus' love (15:10). This is no evanescent experience of inspiration. This is the constant accompaniment of the divine spirit that leads eventually to the deepest divine mysteries.

The significance of this lengthy departure from the Fourth Gospel should now have begun to emerge. In *On the Life of Moses* 2.264-65, we are able to discern two simultaneous modes of the spirit's presence. Because Philo puts biblical texts to an unabashedly apologetic use in his attempt to demonstrate the preeminence of Moses, these two streams vie for prominence and converge wildly in the course of Philo's discussion of Moses' grand abilities. The spirit at once accompanies Moses and fills him. In short, the spirit exhibits simultaneously in Moses' unusual, unsurpassed abilities all of the qualities of ecstasy and inspired knowledge.[45]

Jesus' prediction portends a similar simultaneity of experiences for the disciples: the spirit of truth remains with them and will be in them. Whether or not John intends to portray the spirit within as the impulse of an ecstatic experience we cannot know; John simply says too little about the presence of the spirit within or, in other contexts, about the prophetic experience.[46] Far more certain — and certainly more distinctive than the notion of the spirit within — is what Jesus says first: the spirit of truth will remain alongside *(para)* the disciples. It will be, for this reason, a *para*-clete.

45. Part II, chapters 2 and 3, respectively, of this study.

46. For a good discussion of altered states of consciousness in relation to the Fourth Gospel, particularly the contributions of B. Malina and R. Rohrbaugh, who regard the experience of "seeing" Jesus in John 20 as an instance of altered states of consciousness, see T. G. Brown, *Spirit in the Writings of John*, 205-8.

There is an inescapable correspondence between the promise of the spirit in the Fourth Gospel and the spirit in Philo's portrayal of Moses. In both, the spirit is an accompanying presence that guides the mind toward the truth. Philo writes of Moses: "For the mind could not have made so straight an aim if there was not also the divine spirit guiding it to the truth itself." Jesus promises that the spirit, the paraclete who remains with them, "will guide you in all the truth" *(hodēgēsei hymas en tē alētheia pasē).*

Were it certain that John was familiar with this discussion in Philo's treatises, then it would be possible to detect the strains of a Moses typology in the Fourth Gospel, not exclusively with respect to Jesus but equally with respect to the spirit. What Moses alone was believed to experience — the spirit alongside and the spirit within — now would be made available to the disciples *en masse.* Such certainty about John's knowledge of Philo's treatises, however, lies beyond our ken.[47] Therefore, it is enough to observe that, in both Philo's expanded description of Moses and Jesus' promise in the Fourth Gospel, the spirit will remain *with* them, *teach* them, and *guide* them to the *truth.* Their minds will be sharpened rather than eclipsed, as they are led to discern the meaning of the life of Jesus in light of Israel's scriptures. Whatever, therefore, Jesus may mean by promising that the spirit will be *in* the disciples, the spirit's capacity to prompt potentially ecstatic or uncontrolled behavior will be tempered by the accompanying presence of the spirit, which will guide the disciples — or, in light of Moses' experience, the disciples' *minds* — in the truth.

---

47. Dodd (*The Interpretation of the Fourth Gospel,* 54-73) is positive, as am I, about the suggestiveness of the correspondences between Philo and the Fourth Gospel, despite different iterations of common topics. He writes (73), "It seems clear, therefore, that whatever other elements of thought may enter into the background of the Fourth Gospel, it certainly presupposes a range of ideas having a remarkable resemblance to those of Hellenistic Judaism as represented by Philo. The treatment of those ideas is indeed strikingly different." Schnackenburg (*The Gospel according to St. John,* 1:124-25) thinks that "John stands very close to Hellenistic Judaism, whose reading and interpretation of the sacred Scriptures can be studied above all in Philo of Alexandria, though here much must be laid to the charge of his personal attitude, his philosophical formation and his training in allegorical exegesis." R. E. Brown (*The Gospel according to John I-XII,* lvii-lviii) tends to postulate dependence upon a common background rather than any sort of direct relationship. All three authors note, as they should, both similarities and differences.

Spirit and Revealed Knowledge

The pervasiveness of knowledge, the potency of divine guidance of the mind, is apparent in the depths to which the Fourth Gospel is indebted to Israel's wisdom tradition.[48] There is a rich web of shared imagery between Wisdom and Jesus that permeates the Fourth Gospel. The opening lines, in which the *logos* is with God in the beginning, sets the tone by evoking the rich imagery of Wisdom personified, who existed with God from the beginning, even prior to the creation of the earth.[49] Wisdom and Jesus alike descended from heaven to live among human beings.[50] Among the many resonances that Jesus and Wisdom share, the most salient is perhaps the penchant both exhibit for teaching. Both busy themselves with teaching.[51] Wisdom raises her voice in the heights, at the crossroads, and at the city gates, while Jesus cries out at the climax of the Feast of Tabernacles, and his final public teaching is tendered with a raised voice.[52] In both Wisdom literature and the Fourth Gospel, this teaching is depicted vividly as life-giving food. Among those who accept this teaching are disciples, who are referred to as the little children on whom Wisdom and Jesus lavish particularly focused attention.

The reach of Wisdom extends beyond what a list of parallels between Wisdom literature and the Fourth Gospel could conceivably communicate. There is something here greater than the parts; there is an atmosphere of learning in both the wisdom tradition and the Fourth Gospel, an ethos of study, a penchant for arriving at the truth. This dedication is a constant component of ancient proverbs: "Come, eat of my bread and drink of the wine I have mixed. Lay aside immaturity, and live, and walk in the way of insight" (Prov 9:5-6). Ben Sira's scribe, who represents the quintessence of the wisdom tradition, "seeks out the wisdom of the ancients and is concerned with prophecies" (Sir 39:1), meditates on God's mysteries (39:7), and "shows the wisdom of what he has learned" (39:8). A glimmer of this passion is apparent in just one of Philo's many autobio-

48. See R. E. Brown, *The Gospel according to John I-XII*, cxxii-cxxv.

49. John 1:1; 17:5; see Prov 8:22-23; Sir 24:9; Wis 6:22.

50. John 1:14; 3:31; 6:38; 16:28; see Prov 8:31; Sir 24:8; Bar 3:37; Wis 9:10. Compare John 3:13 with Bar 3:29 and Wis 9:16-17.

51. Bennema (*The Power of Saving Wisdom*, 228-34) provides a good discussion of the teaching vocation of the paraclete, including studies of key verbs. See also Turner, *The Holy Spirit and Spiritual Gifts*, 82-85.

52. John 7:37; 12:44.

graphical revelations. He longs nostalgically for the time in his life before he was involved in civic affairs, "a time when I had leisure for philosophy . . . when my constant companions were divine themes and verities. . . . I had no base or abject thoughts nor grovelled in search of reputation or of wealth or bodily comforts, but seemed always to be borne aloft." Now, he laments, these short-lived experiences permit but fleeting moments of respite in the presence of knowledge: "And if unexpectedly I obtain a spell of fine weather and a calm from civil turmoils, I get me wings and ride the waves and almost tread the lower air, wafted by the breezes of knowledge which often urges me to come to spend my days with her" (*On the Special Laws* 3.1, 5).

A similar tenor of learning is threaded through the Fourth Gospel. From the start, Jesus' first disciples call him rabbi, which, John explains, means *"teacher"* (John 1:38). Nicodemus's acknowledgement, "Rabbi, we know that you are a teacher who has come from God" (3:2), sets the scene for several conversations in which Jesus engages people firsthand in the to-and-fro of teaching and learning. There are as well the characteristic speeches that Jesus delivers in which he teaches at length: I am the bread from heaven, the light of the world, the good shepherd. The last of these autobiographical teachings contains a clear claim about the veracity of Jesus' words: "I am the way, *the truth,* and the life" (14:6).

It is in this atmosphere of teaching and learning that Jesus begins his final, most intimate hours with the disciples. Having washed their feet, he remarks briefly, "You call me Teacher and Lord — and you are right, for that is what I am. So if I, your Lord and Teacher, have washed your feet, you also ought to wash one another's feet. For I have set you an example" (13:13-14). It is in this atmosphere of learning and teaching that Jesus first promises the presence of the spirit of truth, another paraclete, whose vocation will be what Jesus' own vocation has been throughout the Fourth Gospel — to teach: "But the paraclete, the holy spirit, whom the Father will send in my name, will teach you everything" (14:26). This provides an apposite match for the final saying about the spirit, in which Jesus promises that, "when the spirit of truth comes, it will guide you into/in all the truth" (16:13).[53] Such promises are redolent of the psalmists' prayers, "Lead me in your truth, and teach me, for you are the God of my salvation" (Ps

---

53. There is a good deal of textual uncertainty about whether the spirit leads in or into truth. Of the major codices, Alexandrinus and Vaticanus read "into," while Sinaiticus and Bezae read "in."

25:5), and "Teach me to do your will, for you are my God. Let your good spirit lead me on a level path" (143:10).

Yet more is being promised than a vague sensation of guidance and teaching. Jesus promises that the spirit will teach the disciples all things, will guide them into all the truth. At first blush, this appears to be a fantastic promise, a voyage into the unknown realms of the future. Greco-Roman Antiquity could supply ample instances of this, of minds sent off in voyeuristic paths toward a vision of the future. Plutarch, we may recall, in an interpretation of Plato's *Timaeus*, described a condition, often in dreams or with the advent of death, when "the reasoning and thinking faculty of the souls is relaxed and released from their present state as they range amid the irrational and imaginative realms of the future."[54] Apocalyptic authors inherited this proclivity. Daniel was believed to be privy, centuries in advance, to horrific visions of the Greek and Roman worlds. John in the book of Revelation and Ezra in *4 Ezra* were the recipients of serious and sensational visions of the future. Further still, in a Jewish revision of scripture, the *Liber antiquitatum biblicarum*, Kenaz had a vision that reached thousands of years into the future when the spirit rushed upon and filled him. In such a context, where visions are rife with sensationalism, Jesus' promise that the paraclete will guide the disciples into all the truth appears to be spectacular as well.

Notwithstanding the blank check that Jesus is evidently bequeathing to the disciples, there is a more pedestrian but also a more essential strain to the promise, the scope of which is seriously constrained by the rationale that Jesus gives for the promise. This rationale precedes the promise that the paraclete will guide into all truth: "I still have many things to say to you, but you cannot bear them now. When the spirit of truth comes, he will guide you into [in] all the truth" (16:12-13). The many things that Jesus has yet to say consist of what he did not say when he was with the disciples: "I did not say these things to you from the beginning, because I was with you" (16:4). Now that he has begun to say them, his disciples have become despondent: "But because I have said these things to you, sorrow has filled your hearts" (16:6). In short, the disciples "cannot bear them now" (16:12). What are these many things which the disciples cannot bear because they fill the disciples with sorrow? These are sayings that have to do exclusively with Jesus' imminent departure. And this is where the spirit of truth enters the picture: what Jesus cannot now say about his impending death because

---

54. Plutarch, *On the Obsolescence of Oracles* 432C, based upon Plato, *Timaeus* 71E.

of the disciples' heavyheartedness, the spirit of truth will say on his behalf. Because the disciples cannot, at this moment prior to Jesus' death, accept any more of his teaching, the spirit of truth, the paraclete, will lead the disciples in retrospect into all the truth about his departure.

Within the perspective of the Farewell Discourses, then, "the things to come" are not events that lie in the *disciples'* future after they receive the spirit; it is not these teachings that the disciples cannot bear to hear because of the sorrow they generate. The "things to come" are those events that lay in *Jesus'* future, events that, from Jesus' perspective at this moment in the narrative of the Fourth Gospel, were still to come — his death, his departure, his glorification. These are the events for which Jesus cannot prepare his disciples beforehand because the disciples are too overcome by sorrow to bear hearing them. Because they cannot any longer endure such teaching, the paraclete, when it is given, will teach the disciples about Jesus' glorification — what Jesus would have taught — in precisely the way that Jesus would have done because "he will take what is mine and declare it to you" (16:14).[55] He will be, in brief, an *ersatz* paraclete who will teach in retrospect what the disciples were unable to understand beforehand.

To construe the paraclete's vocation principally as unrestrained prophetic prediction, therefore, is to misconstrue Jesus' promise by neglecting the constraints that the context places upon Jesus' promise. The focus of the paraclete's vocation is not to predict but to recollect. The spirit within will faithfully draw the disciples back to Jesus, particularly to those events that were soon to take place following their last night together. The nature of this peculiar vocation of recollection is clarified precisely by what Jesus says in the second paraclete promise of the Farewell Discourses. The holy spirit "will teach you all and remind you of all that I have said to you" (14:26). The "all" that the holy spirit will teach is the "all" that Jesus himself has said. The holy spirit, in brief, will teach by reminding.

The curtain is occasionally drawn back in the Fourth Gospel on the content of remembrance. After Jesus raises his protest against the temple, he barks, "Destroy this temple, and in three days I will raise it up." The Jews, of course, misunderstand and are, as a consequence, baffled, since the Herodian temple took forty-six years to build. But John ventures, by way

---

55. Prediction is not at all the gist of the word "will declare" *(anangelei)*, which John uses elsewhere of reporting or clarifying. The man healed at the pool reported to the Jews that Jesus had healed him (John 5:15). The Samaritan woman believed that the coming Messiah would "declare all things to us," i.e., make known all things that ought to be known (4:25).

of aside, "But he was speaking of the temple of his body. After he was raised from the dead, his disciples remembered that he had said this; and they believed the scripture and the word that Jesus had spoken" (2:19-22). This aside illuminates the process of teaching by recollection; we do not see here mere memory work, but the sort of recollection that entails deeper understanding. Much later, Jesus enters Jerusalem on a young donkey, to the resounding praise of the crowd. As in the Synoptic gospels, John sees this triumphal entrance as the fulfillment of Zechariah's words (12:15; Zech 9:9). However, unlike the authors of the Synoptic gospels, in a unique and fascinating aside he explains how the disciples came to see this event in relation to Zechariah: "His disciples *did not understand* these things at first; but when Jesus was glorified, then *they remembered* that these things had been written of him and had been done to him" (John 12:16). The fingerprints of the paraclete are evident in this aside, both in the pivotal place which remembrance occupies and in the association between understanding and remembrance that is so like the connection drawn between teaching and reminding in the Farewell Discourses (14:26).[56]

An integral dimension of the spirit's vocation, therefore, is to lead the disciples, in the aftermath of the glorification of Jesus in death and resurrection, into the truth of what they have already heard and already experienced. Though it may not be explicit, at least in the two examples of the process of recollection, this entails the recollection as well of Israel's scriptures. An understanding of the temple saying leads the disciples to believe both *the scripture* and *the word* that Jesus spoke. Their comprehension of Jesus' entry on a colt hinges upon their remembrance that these things had been *written of him* and had been *done to him*. Both narrative asides draw a taut correlation between particular scriptures and a particular word or event in Jesus' life.

In a narrative that begins with an overture, in which Jesus is identified evocatively as the *logos,* in a gospel that is rife with an appreciation for knowledge, in a portrait of Jesus that is tinged with the hues of Wisdom personified, it comes as no surprise that the paraclete, the holy spirit, the spirit of truth, should be involved in a process that entails teaching or believing or understanding in tandem with the ability to discern the significance of Israelite scripture (14:26; 2:22; 12:16). Ben Sira had praised, at least partially autobiographically, the scribe for his ability to unlock the mean-

---

56. See also John 13:7: Jesus answered, "You do not know now what I am doing, but later you will understand."

ing of Israel's scriptures and thus to pour forth wisdom. Philo claimed on more than one occasion to be able to solve scriptural conundrums. Although the language of the Fourth Gospel is slightly more oblique than the reflections of Ben Sira and Philo, its author also exhibits a keen interest in reflection upon the past, including Israel's scriptures.

Yet the source of that inspiration among these representative authors is slightly different. Ben Sira's wisdom arises from his own study, meditation, travel, experiences, and prayer. He is a breed apart, a member of an elite scribal guild, in which undivided devotion to the study of Torah causes the scribe to increase in wisdom until ultimately he is filled with a spirit that is characterized exclusively by understanding. For Philo, the scenario is different. Although he too is filled with the divine spirit from birth, he receives insight through further moments of inspired prompting and teaching.[57] During these moments he is possessed of a particularly perceptive ability to understand puzzling aspects of scripture — what Ben Sira refers to as the subtleties and obscurities of parables and the hidden meanings of proverbs (Sir 39:2-3). For the disciples who are promised the spirit of truth within, by way of contrast, there is no true understanding prior to the teaching they receive from the paraclete. It is only after they receive the paraclete that the disciples are able to recall with understanding the life and teachings of Jesus, in part by interpreting these events and sayings in light of Israel's scripture. Only after the death and resurrection of Jesus does the paraclete teach them all things and remind them of all things (14:26). Only after the painful events about which they can, in Jesus' final hours with them, no longer tolerate hearing will the spirit remain with them and be in them.

Summary

There is a hefty strain of defensiveness in the Fourth Gospel, a strong measure of maligning. The "Jews," whoever they may be exactly, have drawn the battle lines with Jesus, whom they regard as a bastard son of a spurious sexual relationship. Jesus is no less virulent about the "Jews," whom he regards as sons of the devil. The battle lines are drawn between Jesus and his opponents in the Fourth Gospel.

In many respects, this drawing up of battle lines is not unlike the

---

57. E.g., *On the Cherubim* 27–29.

Teaching on the Two Spirits, which circulated among the Dead Sea Scrolls, though the tenor of the Fourth Gospel is even more pessimistic. In the Teaching on the Two Spirits, there are clear insiders and outsiders, sons of light and sons of darkness, children of truth and children of deceit. There may be a battle that rages between two spirits within each human being, but the children of light have found a way to let the good spirit hold sway at the expense of the evil spirit by living in a community that embodies the most stringent interpretation of Torah and by following a daily regimen intended to resist the supremacy of the prince of darkness. In the Fourth Gospel, one person alone stands in the light; only one offers considerable resistance to those whose father is the devil. The crowd waffles, undecided, though Jesus offers one final appeal that they should believe in him and become children of light. The disciples remain fretful, so grief-stricken that Jesus cannot, even in his final moments alone with them, prepare them adequately for the appalling events that lie inevitably ahead. They remain anxious in the days following his death, gathered in a house with the doors locked "for fear of the Jews," where Jesus finally meets them and breathes into them the holy spirit.

Jesus, in the Fourth Gospel, promises that the spirit, when it commences its vocation as another paraclete, will hold this line as well. The most original promise of the spirit in the Fourth Gospel has an edgy, even pugnacious, tenor: the world cannot receive the spirit of truth, but the spirit of truth will be in and with the disciples (John 14:16-17). The tasks of the spirit of truth will be determined by this rigid distinction.

For those outside, for the world, there awaits a cosmic court drama in which the spirit of truth will take sides. Whatever the foreground of the word "paraclete" may suggest, its focus is forensic in this judicial context. The spirit of truth will testify on Jesus' behalf (15:26) and against the world with respect to sin, justice, and judgment. There is no benevolent judge in this scene — only a paraclete, who will play the role of defense on behalf of Jesus' disciples and prosecutor against the world for two reasons: the world does not believe in Jesus; and the ruler of this world has been condemned (16:8-11). For the disciples, on the one hand, though they are heartbroken by what Jesus has to say, there awaits the accompaniment and inner presence of the spirit (14:17). They will soon be graced with the privilege of friendship (15:12-17), and even now they may bask in the prospect of adoption (14:18-24). The spirit, when it arrives, will teach the disciples all and remind them of all (14:26) and guide them into all the truth of Jesus' death and resurrection (16:13). There is closeness, intimacy in these promises that offers adumbrations of the unexpected meeting behind locked doors when Jesus will be so close to his friends as to breathe into them the re-creative spirit of life. There is also more than the hope of emotional reconnection; there is the anticipation of memories, of minds alert and awakened, drawn back to the meaning of what their cherished teacher had taught them.

With this observation, we are drawn back to the tradition of teaching and learning in Israelite and early Jewish life. We are alerted to the belief that the study of sacred texts has a long-standing impact upon keenly virtuous individuals, filling them with a spirit of wisdom, with knowledge, with skill. This is the well from which Jesus draws so deeply in the Fourth Gospel, not least when he promises that the spirit of truth will be a teacher who reminds disciples, a coterie of select students, of the meaning of what his predecessor already taught. The Fourth Gospel is the beneficiary of a grand tradition of learning that includes Jesus ben Sira, Ezra, the authors of Proverbs, Isaiah,[58] and Moses. Jesus' invitation is Wisdom's invitation (Proverbs 8). Jesus' embodiment of Wisdom follows in the train of Ben Sira's belief that Torah is the concretization of wisdom (Sirach 24).

With one caveat. The consummation of learning arrives only with the spirit of truth. There is no provision in the crowd or the Jews or the disciples that enables them to understand the truth of Jesus' teaching. Such insight will come to bloom only in retrospect, when the spirit of truth leads the disciples in all the truth, when it teaches and reminds them of all that Jesus said, when it prompts the recollection of scriptural texts that illumine his otherwise inscrutable actions and sayings. For all its embrace of learning and knowledge and wisdom, then, the perspective of the Fourth Gospel is that understanding was unavailable, insight inaccessible, wisdom unattainable, because the spirit was not yet given.

In a related letter, the epistle traditionally called 1 John, the language and life of the spirit surface in no less vigorous a context, with no fewer implications for the claim to revealed knowledge than in the Fourth Gospel. In this brief but explosive letter, the impulses of the Fourth Gospel appear in the extreme, nearly to the point of caricature. Whether it is in the drawing of battle lines, which materialize vehemently in this letter, or in the role of teaching, which virtually disappears in this letter, the tenor of 1 John is more virulent than the tone even of the Fourth Gospel.

58. Isa 8:16.

Spirit and Self-Authentication in 1 John

Two Spirits and Two Communities

Lines have been clearly drawn between the community of the Letter and those who have left, those "who went out from us," those who "did not belong to us" (1 John 2:19). These are liars, deceivers, even the antichrist (2:22; 4:1-6; 2 John 7). In the drawing of these communal battle lines, the spirit plays an invaluable role, a role that reflects the tenor of the Letter, a letter which espouses a contrast between the spirits of truth and error: "We are from God. Whoever knows God listens to us, and whoever is not from God does not listen to us. From this we know the spirit of truth and the spirit of error" (1 John 4:6).[59] Here there are two spirits, two realms, two communities. This is a tidily divided world; to the one side belongs a community of the spirit of truth; to the other belongs those who do not listen to the teachers of this community and therefore situate themselves in the world of the spirit of error.

There is no such divide in the Fourth Gospel, in which there is only a promised spirit of truth and no corresponding spirit of deceit. In the Letter of 1 John, this spirit of truth now meets its match; the two spirits in this letter look like they are cut from the same ideological cloth as the Teaching on the Two Spirits (1QS III–IV), in which the world, as in 1 John, is divided neatly into two. Those who live by the spirit of truth are the sons of light, people of virtue (1QS IV 2-6); those who succumb to the spirit of deceit are the sons of darkness, evil people (1QS IV 9-11). In this division lies "the history of all people; in their (two) divisions all their armies have a share for their generations . . . every deed they do (falls) into their divisions. . . . For God has sorted them into equal parts until the last time, and has put an everlasting loathing between /their/ divisions. Deeds of injustice are an abhorrence to truth and all the paths of truth are an abhorrence to injustice. (There exists) a violent conflict in respect of all their decrees since they cannot walk together" (1QS IV 15-18a).

Whether the author of 1 John has been influenced by this teaching, or whether both inhabit the same ideological universe, the Teaching on the Two Spirits offers at length what appears only as catchphrases in 1 John 4:6.

---

59. Greek: *hēmeis ek tou theou esmen, ho ginōskōn ton theon akouei hēmōn, hos ouk estin ek tou theou ouk akouei hēmōn. ek toutou ginōskomen to pneuma tēs alētheias kai to pneuma tēs planēs.*

Between those who have left and the faithful believers in the author's charge, there is utter incompatibility, even conflict — what the Teaching calls "everlasting loathing" — so that these two groups "cannot walk together." Although the author does not frame this in the potentially violent terms of the *Community Rule,* there exists nevertheless a harsh disjuncture between these two groups, the beloved community and those who have left, whom the author identifies as liars, deceivers, and the antichrist.[60]

What the author of the Letter does not appear to consider is that there are different sorts of believers within each community. In the Teaching on the Two Spirits, the rigid allotment of humankind into two groups is not the sole partition that directs community life. The Teaching on the Two Spirits, in fact, is not introduced as a teaching about *two* spirits but about "the nature of all human beings [the sons of man], concerning all the ranks of their spirits" (1QS III 13-14). Final judgment may ultimately divide the just from the unjust, but for the present "the spirits of truth and injustice feud in the heart of a human" (1QS IV 23), and the level to which these respective spirits rise may determine, in part at least, the ranking which one's spirit obtains in the community. Those who have more of the spirit of error in them rank lower in community life than those who allow the spirit of truth to win the inner battle between the two spirits.[61]

In a similar way, name-calling and stone-throwing in the Fourth Gospel do not wholly obfuscate the tensions that exist *among* the followers of Jesus. Arguably the most poignant question in early Christian literature

60. The similarity is not surprising. Although 1QS III–IV may predate the founding of the Qumran community, that community did emerge with the expulsion of its leader, the Teacher of Righteousness, from the temple, perhaps at the behest of someone whom they would come to call the Wicked Priest. The Fourth Gospel, and particularly the story of the healing of the man born blind from birth, who was excluded from the synagogue (John 9), may have been written in response to the Jewish expulsion of Jesus' followers from the synagogue. Both communities, in other words, understood the pivotal moment in their history as an expulsion from central institutions in Jewish life, either temple or synagogue. Whether or not either was precipitated by a historical moment of exclusion, both corpora conceive of two distinct communities with a recognition that they are on the inside and others on the outside.

61. This is the thrust of the Teaching on the Two Spirits, which begins: "The Instructor should instruct and teach all the sons of light about the nature of all the sons of man, concerning all the ranks of their spirits, in accordance with their signs, concerning their deeds in their generations, and concerning the visitation of their punishments and the times of their reward" (1QS III 13-15). In 4Q186 *(4QHoroscope),* among physical descriptions of a stumpy and hairy human, presumably an evil one, is the line that "His spirit has [ei]ght (parts) in the house [of darkness] and one in the house of light" (4Q186 fr. 1 III 5-6).

arises in the disquieting moments following Jesus' dramatic discourse on the living bread. Many of his own disciples react dismissively, "This teaching is difficult; who can accept it?" After they turn back and no longer follow him, Jesus asks, "Do you also wish to go away?" (John 6:60, 66-67). Notwithstanding the fresh wound that opens with this rift, Jesus responds without excoriation, without censure.

Other instances of unevenness in the community of Jesus' followers appear in the Fourth Gospel. There are the Twelve, apart from Judas, chosen personally by Jesus (John 6:70), whose feet he washes and whom he calls friends. Yet there are others. There are those who remain quiet and closeted, for fear of the Jews — possibly Nicodemus (3:2), certainly Joseph of Arimathea (19:38). There are the women, one of whom, his own mother, he entrusts as a mother to a new son (19:26). There is Thomas, whose doubts Jesus takes seriously and without disapprobation (20:24-29). There is only one whom Jesus condemns: Judas, who will betray him, is the son of a devil (6:70-71).

The Fourth Gospel, like the Teaching on the Two Spirits, comes to grips with differing levels of faith within a disparate band of followers. The battle lines between Jesus and the Jews, between light and darkness, flesh and spirit, do not obfuscate the varieties of faith that characterize believers within the community of Jesus' followers. In contrast, the author of the Letter of 1 John draws no corresponding distinctions or rankings within the community. He acknowledges no struggle for justice within a human being, no internal feud between the spirits of truth and error. The shades or rankings that play a role in the Teaching on the Two Spirits and the Fourth Gospel have no quarter in this letter, where the truest division is between those who left and those who remain. There is nothing here even of the Pauline weaker brothers and sisters or the *pneumatikoi* and *psychikoi* to whom Paul is compelled so carefully to respond. There is left only a division of humankind into those who live by the spirit of truth and those who live by the spirit of error. What in the Fourth Gospel is an apt description of the holy spirit, the spirit *of truth,* is directed in the Letter to one side of a contrast, truth as opposed to error, deceit, lies, the antichrist.

The Spirit and Prophetic Authority

This preoccupation with self-definition leaves little room in the Letter for the sorts of distinctions of faith within the community that are discernible, however thinly, in the Fourth Gospel and in the Teaching on the Two Spirits. The spirits of truth and error function in 1 John principally as key markers in the identity of competing communities. When reality is bifurcated in this way, the demand for a principle of discernment arises; the author of the Letter meets this demand by providing a precise principle of discrimination.

> Beloved, do not believe every spirit, but test the spirits to see whether they are from God; for many false prophets have gone out into the world. By this you know the spirit of God: every spirit that confesses that Jesus Christ has come in the flesh is from God, and every spirit that does not confess Jesus is not from God. And this is the spirit of the antichrist, of which you have heard that it is coming; and now it is already in the world. (1 John 4:1-3)[62]

Though minimal, this is an irrefutable, verifiable principle of discernment that is related to the confession that Jesus Christ came in the flesh. Its function is similar to the confession "Jesus is Lord" and Paul's contention that "no one can say 'Jesus is Lord' except by the holy spirit" (1 Cor 12:3). Amidst a variety of itinerant prophets and prophetic messages, and the spirits that inspire them, it is difficult to discern the truth, and so this is the dividing line, the test of truth: Jesus is from God and in the flesh.

Yet this allegedly straightforward principle of discernment appears to be faintly disingenuous when it is set in the context of statements about the spirit that precede and follow it. Just prior to the establishment of this principle of discernment, the author advises: "And this is his commandment, that we should believe in the name of his son Jesus Christ and love one another just as he has commanded us. All who obey his commandments abide in him, and he abides in them. And by this we know that he abides in us, by the spirit that he has given us" (1 John 3:23-24).[63] There is self-authentication in this claim, for there is nothing here to be verified, no rule of faith, no credal content, no confession of faith — merely a general

---

62. Greek: *Agapētoi, mē panti pneumati pisteuete alla dokimazete ta pneumata ei ek tou theou estin, hoti polloi pseudoprophētai exelēlythasin eis ton kosmon. en toutō ginōskete to pneuma tou theou. pan pneuma ho homologei Iēsoun Christon en sarki elēlythota ek tou theou estin, kai pan pneuma ho mē homologei ton Iēsoun ek tou theou ouk estin. kai touto estin to tou antichristou, ho akēkoate hoti erchetai, kai nyn en tō kosmō estin ēdē.*

63. Greek: *kai ho tērōn tas entolas autou en autō menei kai autos en autō. kai en toutō ginōskomen hoti menei en hēmin, ek tou pneumatos hou hēmin edōken.*

description of keeping the commandments and loving. The real criterion is this: believers know that God abides within them because they have the spirit. Further, the command to love does not extend to "the world" (2:15-17; 2:28–3:3); it encompasses only those who are brothers and sisters (3:11-17), particularly sisters and brothers in need. Those who have left the community, those outside the family circle, are not in the purview of this command. This command to love does not include those who left this community, who are instead subject to vitriol (e.g., 2:18-25).

The advice, therefore, that precedes the principle of discernment about Jesus Christ's having come in the flesh tends to focus more stringently upon the presence of the spirit within. Similarly, the instructions that follow this principle of discernment tend to skirt the principle of verifiability and slide again into the sphere of self-authentication: "We are from God. Whoever knows God listens to us, and whoever is not from God does not listen to us. From this we know the spirit of truth and the spirit of error" (1 John 4:6).[64] It is not what a believer knows, what he or she professes, but the possession of the spirit, plain and simple, that matters, and the key element in discerning the spirit of truth from the spirit of deceit is whether someone "listens to us" or "does not listen to us." Such a collapsing of spirit and communal authority into one another is reminiscent of the covenant renewal ceremony that took place annually at Qumran, during which time new members began the long process of initiation and submitted to the spirit of the community. The stubborn person who refuses fully to submit to the teaching of the community is cursed: "Defiled, defiled shall he be all the days he spurns the decrees of God, without allowing himself to be taught by the Community of his counsel" (1QS III 5-6). Both here, in the charter document of the Qumran community, and in 1 John, the rejection of communal teaching comprises a rejection of God. In the *Community Rule*, not to be taught by the community is to spurn the decree of God and the holy spirit of the community. The annual covenant renewal ceremony at Qumran continues: "For it is by the spirit of the true counsel of God that are atoned the paths of humankind, all his iniquities, so that he can look at the light of life. And it is by the holy spirit of the community, in its truth, that he is cleansed of all his iniquities" (1QS III 6-8). Similarly, in 1 John 4:6, to listen to the community is to listen to God

---

64. Greek: *hēmeis ek tou theou esmen, ho ginōskōn ton theon akouei hēmōn, hos ouk estin ek tou theou ouk akouei hēmōn. ek toutou ginōskomen to pneuma tēs alētheias kai to pneuma tēs planēs.*

and to possess the spirit of truth; to remain within the community — those who left are excoriated — is to remain in the realm of the spirit of truth. The sign of the spirit in both contexts is whether one submits to the teaching of the community. This is, in effect, a circular way of viewing matters. Those who adhere to the spirit of truth are identifiable because they belong to the community that lays claim to the spirit of truth.

Therefore, although the author of this letter offers a principle of discernment, the confession that Jesus Christ has come in the flesh from God, the spirit functions predominantly in this letter in a self-authenticating way:

> And by this we know that he abides in us, by the spirit that he has given us. (1 John 3:24)

> We are from God. Whoever knows God listens to us, and whoever is not from God does not listen to us. From this we know the spirit of truth and the spirit of error. (4:6)

> By this we know that we abide in him and he in us, because he has given us from his spirit. (4:13)

There is in these claims no distinguishable content, no clear criterion of truth. Even the provision made in the Fourth Gospel, that the spirit's teaching would be entirely in line with Jesus' teaching, has evaporated. Further, the moniker "spirit of truth" in the Fourth Gospel is related to Jesus' truth claims, to his promise that the spirit of truth will illuminate what he taught, to the conviction that the spirit of truth will teach in perfect consonance with Jesus' own teaching; in the Letter of 1 John, the thrust of the spirit of truth is that it is most decidedly *not* the spirit of error. Its force lies in its opposition to the spirit of error rather than in its relation to the truth of Jesus. There is, in brief, only one criterion to which claims to the spirit are anchored in 1 John, and the strength of the criterion that Jesus Christ came in the flesh is seriously relativized, if not eroded, by the self-authenticating claims that precede and follow it.

This assessment, however, may be slightly unkind, for these self-authenticating claims are not merely unreflective, reactionary responses to a schism that has wracked this community. First of all, the author does associate the presence of the spirit with the criteria of faith and love — even if these criteria be vague in application and rather narrowly construed with respect to the community that has remained.

Second, the author also tethers faith to what has been taught:

> I write to you, not because you do not know the truth, but because you know it, and you know that no lie comes from the truth. Who is the liar but the one who denies that Jesus is the Christ? This is the antichrist, the one who denies the Father and the Son. No one who denies the Son has the Father; everyone who confesses the Son has the Father also. Let what you heard from the beginning abide in you. If what you heard from the beginning abides in you, then you will abide in the Son and in the Father. (1 John 2:21-24)

The author urges continuity with what the community was taught from the start; presumably those who have left have left behind this teaching, which focuses upon the confession that Jesus came in the flesh.

Third, the expression *"has given to us,"* which the author adopts (3:24), forms a part of the fabric of early Christian belief.[65] It may be a familiar catchphrase that does not require explanation, a reminder that connects the author's community to the larger church, notwithstanding the communal devastation they have experienced and the sense of isolation they now experience in its wake. The phrase also has content associated with it which may be self-evident to the readers of this letter. For instance, we learn from the occurrence of this phrase elsewhere that the giving of the spirit takes place in relation to an act of faith. This observation is not insignificant, for it suggests that the Letter of 1 John differs substantively from the *Community Rule* despite shared conceptions of the spirits of truth and deceit. It is safe to say that, in 1 John, as in the Fourth Gospel, the spirit of truth is not conceived, as in the Teaching on the Two Spirits, in relation to creation and birth. The spirit of truth is conceived of as a special endowment, an anointing, which in this letter is the nucleus of the claim to prophetic inspiration.

Fourth, the prepositional phrase *"from the spirit"* in 1 John 4:13 is unique in early Jewish and Christian literature.[66] Other writings of the early church and the Qumran *Hymns*, for example, lead us to expect "God has given us the spirit" rather than "God has given us *from* the spirit." This peculiar expression cannot easily be explained unless we recognize that the

---

65. See Part III, chapter 2.

66. This is different from 1 John 3:24, where the word *ek* provides the ground of belief. The additional word *hoti* in 1 John 4:13 is causal: "By this we know that we abide in him and he in us, because he has given us from his spirit."

author of 1 John has drawn from the language of Num 11:16-30, in which Moses, overwhelmed by his responsibilities in resolving cases for the Israelites, is told to gather seventy elders to help him. God promises to "take *from* the spirit" that is upon Moses and to place it on the elders, who will share Moses' burden (Num 11:17).[67] Moses gathers the elders, at which point "the Lord came down in the cloud and spoke to him, and took *from* the spirit that was on him and put it on the seventy elders" (11:25a). The impact of this distribution was ready and recognizable: "when the spirit rested upon them, they prophesied. But they did not do so again" (11:25b). The elders prophesied when they received *from* the spirit that was upon Moses.[68] Consequently, this prophesying endowed the elders with the distinction of Mosaic authority.

This foreground provides a remarkably apposite scriptural toehold for the sort of authority that the author of 1 John claims for himself and for those whom he considers to be true prophets in a world into which "many false prophets have gone out" (1 John 4:1). It provides, first, a lesson in authority. When God took "from the spirit" that was upon Moses and placed it upon the elders, God endowed them with the authority to handle the cases that Moses could not. Contested authority lies at the heart of 1 John; there is a tug-of-war that takes place between those who have left and those who remain. By claiming to have received "from the spirit," the author is able to characterize himself and his community as heirs of the elders who received authority to lead Israel when they received "from the spirit" that was upon Moses.

This scriptural story is also about prophesying. When the spirit rested upon the elders, they prophesied. By framing their reception of the spirit with the words "from the spirit," the author of 1 John summons a unique moment in Israel's history when a large group of elders prophesied. In 1 John, the community's authority rests principally in a self-authenticating endowment, and the phrase "*from* the spirit" suggests that they understand this authority, in light of Numbers 11, as prophetic authority, for Numbers 11 is the lone scriptural text where this odd phrase occurs. From them arise true prophets, whose words can be distinguished from false prophets, prophets who do not confess that Jesus came in the flesh, prophets of the

---

67. LXX translates: *aphelō tou pneumatos.*

68 Although prophesying in Numbers 11 is typically construed as ecstatic prophecy, I have contended instead that prophesying comprises the authorization to lead Israel on Moses' behalf; "Prophecy in Ancient Israel: The Case of the Ecstatic Elders," *CBQ* 65 (2003) 503-21.

antichrist — though the actual dividing line between true and false prophets may have lain less in the errant content of their message than in their simple failure to belong to the true community, the community of the spirit of truth. There are two spirits and two communities, with truth represented only by the author and his community and error represented by those who do not listen to the author and his community. If the author has received, as he claims for himself and his community, "*from* the spirit," just as the elders received from the spirit upon Moses, then their authority, like the elders' long before them, is prophetic as well.

The story of Moses and the inspired elders also evinces — and this is very possibly inadvertent though not irrelevant — an absolutely stunning resonance with the self-authentication that characterizes the spirit in 1 John, for this is one of a very few Israelite stories in which prophesying has no content. The narrative offers no glimpse of the content of their prophesying, no vivid depiction of the actions that accompanied this prophesying, no hint of the impact this prophesying had upon Israel. In this very puzzling narrative, what does the narrator offer? A clear association of spirit, authority, and prophesying — and Moses' tone of approval, when he expresses his desire that all Israel would prophesy. What this story communicates, and what it does not, is a mirror of the concerns that are expressed in the Letter of 1 John, where the author claims authority with a minimum of content, as well as true prophecy, again with a minimal criterion of truth.

The issue of the Letter, in the end, is authority: "Whoever knows God listens to us" (4:6). This communal claim does not mean that alleged principles of discernment — Jesus came from God in the flesh (4:2) or the Father sent the son as the savior of the world (4:14) — are entirely disingenuous. It means rather that these simple principles are just a part, perhaps a relatively small part, of the story of the community's authority. The real issue, it would seem, is that people show themselves to have the spirit of truth within by listening to the author's claims, the author's prophetic claims, claims to a portion of the spirit that had once been drawn from Moses and given to Israel's elders. This spirit, in short, is the resource for true prophecy, true community, true authority.

The Spirit and the Demise of Teaching

Such self-authenticating authority is nowhere more in evidence than in a pointed and vitriolic critique of those who have abandoned the community:

Children, it is the last hour! As you have heard that antichrist is coming, so now many antichrists have come. From this we know that it is
the last hour. They went out from us, but they did not belong to us; for
if they had belonged to us, they would have remained with us. But by
going out they made it plain that none of them belongs to us. But you
have been anointed by the Holy One, and all of you have knowledge.
(1 John 2:18-20)

I write these things to you concerning those who would deceive you. As
for you, the anointing that you received from him abides in you, and so
you do not need anyone to teach you. But as his anointing teaches you
about all things, and is true and is not a lie, and just as it has taught you,
abide in him. (2:26-27)

Within the scope of a few brief paragraphs, the author claims no less than
three times that his community has received an anointing. This is a disconcerting claim for more than one reason.

This claim to an anointing takes the work of the holy spirit beyond the
more cautious claims of the Fourth Gospel, in which Jesus alone receives
the anointing of the spirit. In one of the traditions that the Fourth Gospel
may have in common with the Synoptic Gospels, John the Baptist testifies
to the descent of the spirit upon Jesus at his baptism: "I saw the spirit de-
scending from heaven like a dove, and it remained on him. I myself did not
know him, but the one who sent me to baptize with water said to me, 'He
on whom you see the spirit descend and remain is the one who baptizes
with the holy spirit'" (John 1:32-33). The similarities that exist between the
Fourth Gospel and the Synoptic Gospels are not negligible. In all four versions, the spirit is said to come "upon" Jesus (Matt 3:16; Mark 1:10; Luke
3:22; John 1:32-33), perhaps as a reflection of the resting of the spirit upon
the messianic figure of Isa 11:2: "The spirit of the Lord shall rest on him,
the spirit of wisdom and understanding, the spirit of counsel and might,
the spirit of knowledge and the fear of the Lord." This is the Messiah's
anointing, just as the messianic figure in *11QMelchizedek* (11Q13) II 18, from
the Dead Sea Scrolls, is depicted as "the anointed of the spir[it]." The followers of Jesus are never depicted in the Fourth Gospel with the spirit
upon them; they are not even promised that the spirit will rest upon them.
This anointing belongs to Jesus alone.

The reason for this distinction is obvious: anointing had messianic associations and was reserved for Jesus, who alone would baptize with the

holy spirit, who alone could make claims that his followers could not. The followers of Jesus were promised something different, that the spirit would be with and within them. Yet they, unlike Jesus, would never experience the spirit's descent upon them like a dove; they were not promised any sort of anointing. In the Letter, in contrast to the Fourth Gospel, believers are the recipients of an anointing, and a remarkable anointing at that. Like the anointing Jesus received at his baptism, the anointing of the community "remains" (John 1:33; 1 John 2:26). This claim goes well beyond the promise to the disciples that the spirit of truth will be within believers (John 14:17; 1 John 2:27). It creates a disquieting continuity between Jesus' experience of the spirit and theirs.

This anointing is disconcerting as well because it renders teachers superfluous. The anointing means that "all of you have knowledge" (1 John 2:20), that is, "you do not need anyone to teach you" (2:27). The anointing itself "has taught you." Such expressions virtually unravel Israel's appreciation of learning and discipline. In Israel, especially among the literature that is preserved in the wisdom tradition, wisdom was learned from study and experience, and the human spirit could be cultivated into a locus of wisdom. In the Fourth Gospel, the hues of wisdom would inevitably shade the portrait of Jesus, and the holy spirit would also share a family resemblance to Wisdom. Central dimensions of that tradition remain intact in the various activities of the spirit: guiding in truth, teaching, reminding believers of Jesus, defending and testifying.

Yet in the Fourth Gospel, the presence of the spirit does not render study superfluous. Examples of this sort of reminding by the spirit, such as the saying about the temple and the entry into Jerusalem upon a colt, contain lucid scriptural citations and allusions that are the product of reflection and study — what the author of the Fourth Gospel might attribute to the inspired study of Israel's scriptures. The author of 1 John appears to wander from this path of study. In this letter, the giving of the spirit apparently gives birth to a community that needs no more teachers, that requires no further quest for knowledge. Learned wisdom is superfluous, education redundant.

This constitutes an eccentric, if not outlandish, claim to the spirit in 1 John — outlandish at least in relation to the more cautious claims elsewhere in early Judaism and Christianity. Even Philo Judaeus, who lays claim to as many experiences of inspiration as any Christian or Jewish writer of the first or early second century c.e., sets inspiration into a context of study, through which he is transported into the upper realms of knowledge, when the customary friend prompts him, when he hears a voice within that teaches him the solution to a scriptural conundrum.[69]

The community of the truth in 1 John, in contrast, needs no teaching, no probing for new knowledge; all of this is rendered superfluous by the anointing of the spirit. This claim, of course, is not void of irony, for underlying this rejection of teachers is an Israelite text that envisages a new covenant, a new day when there would no longer exist the need to teach one another:

> The days are surely coming, says the Lord, when I will make a new covenant with the house of Israel and the house of Judah. . . . But this is the covenant that I will make with the house of Israel after those days, says the Lord: I will put my law within them, and I will write it on their hearts; and I will be their God, and they shall be my people. No longer shall they teach one another, or say to each other, "Know the Lord," for they shall all know me, from the least of them to the greatest, says the Lord; for I will forgive their iniquity, and remember their sin no more. (Jer 31[LXX 38]:31, 33-34)

In contrast to Paul's letters, which pick up on many of the details of this prophetic text without ever eschewing the need for teaching, the Letter of 1 John lacks most of the details of this text, such as the writing of Torah upon human hearts, while isolating and adopting only the prediction that people of the new covenant would no longer teach one another.[70] Although it is not even apparent whether the author of 1 John sees the community as the constituency of a new covenant — certainly an indispensable theme in Jeremiah's vision — it is singularly inescapable that this prophetic community has no need of teachers.

This repudiation of education distinguishes the Letter from the Fourth Gospel in another way. Although the promise in the Fourth Gospel that the spirit of truth will "teach all things" may at first blush sound universal, its scope is immediately qualified by the words "remind (of) all" that Jesus said: "But the paraclete, the holy spirit, whom the Father will send in my name, will teach you all and remind you of all that I have said to you" (John 14:26). This promise, then, has to do less with new revelation than with clarifying the teaching that Jesus had already given while he was alive.

69. See Part II, chapter 3.
70. See M. V. Hubbard, *New Creation in Paul's Letters and Thought.* SNTSMS 119 (Cambridge: Cambridge University Press, 2002) 150-53.

The claims in the Letter of 1 John that "all of you have knowledge" and "you do not need anyone to teach you. But as his anointing teaches you about all things . . ." are both more ambitious and less moored to the person of Jesus. These claims are not about recollecting and clarifying the teachings of Jesus or grasping the full significance of Jesus' death, as in the Fourth Gospel. The Letter offers no such limitations on knowledge, no such backward glance at the person of Jesus, at his sayings, at the teaching in the upper room that he cannot give because the disciples are overwhelmed by grief. The Letter claims that this community has knowledge, plain and simple, and that this community, as a consequence, has no need for teachers. These are very different conceptions of the activity of the holy spirit within believers. The gospel limits the spirit's guidance to the elucidation of Jesus' life and death, typically through the study of Israel's scriptures. The Letter dispenses with the need for acquired knowledge altogether, for the spirit teaches all things, not merely all things about Jesus' life and death, without the aid of human teachers.

There is a sharp edge to this claim in the Letter, as if the embers of John 14:17 — the spirit of truth, whom the world cannot receive because it neither sees it nor knows it — have been fanned into furious flame. In the Letter, the knowledge which the anointing gives, the "all things" which the anointing imparts, functions to set the community apart from those enemies from within who chose to leave (1 John 2:18-25). This becomes evident if we recognize that both references to the anointing occur in a highly charged context. The author begins with the warning that it is the last hour, that the antichrist is coming, and that many antichrists have come already. He then recalls a communal rift that took place when a group left the community; the impact of the schism is accented four times with the prepositional phrase "from us" *(ex hēmōn)*. This historic break prompts the claim to the anointing: "But by going out they made it plain that none of them belongs to us. And you have been anointed. . . ." Following from this is a thinly veiled identification of those who left as the antichrist, presumably because they deny that Jesus came in the flesh.

Having then urged his readers to remain faithful to the original teaching about Jesus, the author writes bluntly "concerning those who would deceive you. As for you, the anointing that you received from him abides in you, and so you do not need anyone to teach you. But as his anointing teaches you about all things, and is true and is not a lie, and just as it has taught you, abide in it" (2:26-27). With this conclusion to a portion of the Letter that has already begun alarmingly with "Children, this is the last hour!" the author has shaken off the constraints of the Fourth Gospel. In this letter, something personal has happened. Supposed believers who have left the community now deny the truth. And the dividing line, while allegedly grounded in brief confessions about Jesus, in "what you heard from the beginning" (2:24), hangs upon the claim to anointing. The battle line between truth and falsehood, antichrist and Christ, false prophets and true prophets, materializes with the claim that the spirit taught the community and teaches the community. The author urges his recipients, therefore, not to be deceived by the false believers who went out from the community, those who as the antichrist deny that Jesus came in the flesh. The author's community should not be deceived because they should not be listening in the first place to this misplaced teaching, for *this* community — and not *that* community — has an anointing by the spirit that taught them and now teaches them all things. Not merely all things that Jesus said, as in John 14:26. Not simply the significance of Jesus' death, as in John 16:12-13. But all things, all truth. The spirit will teach in such a way, in fact, that all human teachers, whether false or true, anointed or not, become altogether superfluous.

Conclusion

With this claim to an anointing that teaches all things, with this conviction that the spirit of truth resides exclusively within this community, the Letter of 1 John breaks new ground, leaving behind Israel's belief that education plays a pivotal role in the passing on and application of earlier scriptures. The author of this epistolary sliver also leaves behind the Fourth Gospel, in which the promised spirit of truth teaches by reminding believers about Jesus' sayings and by guiding the community into the full significance of Jesus' death and resurrection. The gift of the spirit within is not construed, if the Fourth Gospel provides a clue, as a substitute for study or a surrogate for human teachers; the spirit, rather, submerges believers in the study of the life, death, and resurrection of Jesus. Notwithstanding the promise of the spirit as teacher and guide, then, there is no indication that faith obliterates education or that the revelation of the spirit renders study obsolete.

In the world of 1 John, however, this tradition of study appears to be set aside dramatically because something dramatic has shaken the community. People have left and set up camp in a competing theological arena. Rather than responding to this crisis by urging the community to undertake an assiduous study of scripture, instead of pressing his people to pore over the teachings of Jesus, in lieu of commanding them to meditate upon the meaning of Jesus' death and resurrection, the author of the Letter cites a few fragmentary confessions of faith, urges fidelity to what was taught from the beginning, then takes a different tack; he writes to tell them in the most unequivocal way that they possess an anointing which makes teachers superfluous. This is a prophetic community, the legitimate heirs of the elders who received from the spirit that was upon Moses. Prophets, therefore, remain, and they are the pivotal means of revelation. Teachers, he communicates with consummate clarity, are banished to oblivion.

This is an unprecedented claim, a radical surgical procedure for a festering communal wound. It is a conviction that disconnects the spirit from Israel's tradition of teaching and learning, of passing the faith from one generation to the next.[71] It is a position that distinguishes this letter from the surrounding world of early Judaism, where the spirit that is given at birth can be cultivated into a life of holiness and understanding, and where the spirit is understood as well to be an additional endowment that brings wisdom and insight to the virtuous and wise. The author of this letter espouses an ideology that distinguishes it even from early Christianity, where sustained study continues to be prized, despite a deep conviction among many that the spirit fills believers as they respond to God in faith. This is a disquieting belief that leaves the life of the spirit potentially unmoored, secured less to ancient literature and the life of Jesus than to the authority of contemporary leaders and unqualified communal values. It is a conception of the world as a hostile arena, in which prophets rather than teachers lead the way to truth and eternal life.

71. This is exemplified by the *Shema* in Deut 6:4-9.

If the authors of early Judaism were able to pinpoint the locus of virtue as the spirit that God inbreathed into each individual at birth, the small sub-set of Judaism which we somewhat inaccurately refer to as early Christians did not. They placed little stock in the worth of that spirit, in its capacity to hold true to virtue and wisdom. Scant vestiges of this perspective, which is rooted in Israel's conviction that the spirit within could be holy or flush with wisdom, can be cited in the literary legacy of the early church, though the pitch is lower, barely audible, in its literature. John the Baptist could grow and become strong in spirit, as Jesus could grow and be filled with wisdom. Yet both of these descriptions flower in the soil of the earliest nar-ratives of Luke's gospel, which emit the Israelite aura of the Septuagint. It is precisely here that we would expect to glimpse these traces, where Luke draws his readers back to a world that no longer exists.

There is, in other words, no Daniel in the early church, a person who is full to the nth degree with spirit, a strapping youthful figure who would shape the destiny of empires, whose holy spirit God would prompt to rise in outcry against the injustice perpetrated against a wholly innocent Susanna. The figure who comes closest to this heroic surplus of *pneuma* is Stephen, whose audience is not imperial leaders but his recalcitrant Jewish comrades, who does not rise in the courts of the Medes but falls prey to the vitriol and stones of his own countrymen and women. Still, Stephen is full of spirit and wisdom, full of faith, full of holy spirit; his freshly minted op-ponents, because they cannot resist him, transform him into the first named martyr of the early church.

These vestiges are slender indeed, anemic slivers of an ancient tradition that remain in small measure, as in Paul's reference to a "holy spirit" in a catena of virtues (2 Cor 6:6-7), possibly in a reference to a "spirit of power and love and self-discipline" that is given to believers (2 Tim 1:6-7), perhaps in Jesus' claim to words that are not flesh but "spirit-breath and life" (John 6:63). Precious little remains of the confidence that a God-given spirit can become the locus of virtue, a reservoir of wisdom, the head-waters of knowledge.

And how could this perspective remain for communities that believed they were a new creation, with the old having passed away? What could this new community, which was comprised of spirit-filled Jews and Gentiles who together proclaimed God's praiseworthy works and prophe-sied, have to do with other Jews who, they claimed, inherited Israel's pen-chant for resisting God's prophets? What else could be meant by the un-equivocal claim that, during Jesus' life, the spirit had not yet been given? Although pockets of the early church would understand the presence of the spirit differently, they sang in unison the conviction that the spirit came on the heels of faith in Jesus Christ. This fundamental and forceful conviction leaves only the slightest wiggle-room for the otherwise wide-spread belief that God breathes into every individual a spirit that can be-come filled with understanding, a spirit that rolls over the tongue in a flood of peculiar eloquence, a spirit that can be the locus of holiness or, under the care of the careless, a commodity to be traded for lucre.

Despite the profound departure from this dimension of their tradi-tion, early Christians clutched at other aspects of the legacy that was avail-able to them. Like the devotees of the new covenant at Qumran, Paul adopted the language of Ezekiel 36–37, with its promise of cleansing and of national resurrection, though he, like the keepers of the Scrolls, transposed a vision of national import into the belief that the spirit comes into indi-viduals. In the Fourth Gospel, the intimacy of inbreathing is enriched with a verb that is reminiscent of Eden, or perhaps Elijah as he spread himself, lips to lips, over the corpse of a widow's son, or possibly Ezekiel's vision of the re-creation of Israel in death's desert valley. Peter, in the book of Acts, recognizes that the spirit's presence at Pentecost is a fulfillment of Joel's prediction that the spirit would be poured out, though he too tweaks the ancient vision, not least by adding that the spirit would prompt prophecy.

There is, therefore, a distinctive unity in early Christian literature. There is a shared conviction that the spirit must be received as an addi-tional endowment that is other, or more, than the God-given spirit of birth. The roots of this conviction lie in various portions of Israelite literature. There is the common confession that the spirit could be "received"; Paul, Luke, John, and the author of 1 John adopt this expression to describe in shorthand the experience of being filled with the spirit. Yet there are other points in common as well. Both Paul and John understand the presence of the spirit as a new creation; they understand the new community of Jesus' followers, with its renewed mission to the nations, as a new temple. And both John and Luke connect the presence of the spirit to the inspired interpretation of Israel's scriptures, to the unearthing of texts that illuminate the life, death, and resurrection of Jesus.

Notwithstanding what they value in common, authors in the early church also exhibit a certain flamboyance, a resplendence of thought, in their effort to describe the marvels that attend filling with the spirit. Although he adopts the traditional language of receiving the spirit, for example, Paul uses this common conception as a springboard for pivotal contrasts: not slavish obedience to Torah but the life of faith; not the spirit of the world but the spirit that is from God; not slavery to fear but the experience of adoption. Yet this is only the edge of Paul's creativity. In a fascinating turn, in which he depicts the spirit as a pledge and *arrabōn*, Paul turns to the tawdry story of Tamar in his effort to grab the Corinthians by the scruff of the neck and compel them to believe that all of God's promises are fulfilled in Christ — and that his promise to visit, by association, will be fulfilled as well; the spirit glides adroitly from ancestral promise to become the anchor of hope. In another context, while writing to a far less recalcitrant community in Thessalonica, Paul goes so far as to incorporate an allusion to the giving of the spirit in Ezekiel 37 in his practical advice about stemming the tide of sexual license; yet he is not bound to the letter of the citation, for he changes the aorist tense — "God gave" — to the present, for the ongoing life of sanctity demands the ongoing gift of God's spirit. Paul's creativity is apparent in still another allusion to Ezekiel 37; his perplexing hope to have a resurrection body "clothed upon" his mortal body grows out of, albeit in an odd way, Ezekiel's vision, in which the word "upon" occurs again and again in a description of the freshly resurrected body, with sinews upon bones and flesh upon sinews. Still, these permutations fail to exhaust the resources of Paul's creativity, the apex of which occurs perhaps when he plays free and easy with Gen 2:7; the first Adam is a living being, but the last Adam is a life-giving spirit. With such a toppling of Gen 2:7, Paul's ingenuity outstrips even Philo's, who, in a more conventional move, roots the virtues of the first human in the pristine image of Gen 1:26-28 and the inevitable vices of the second human in the clay of Gen 2:7.

Paul's sense of the spirit cannot be captured by any single characteristic. His view of the spirit is not exclusively eschatological, nor is he preoccupied with the relationship of Torah and spirit; even spiritual gifts enter his purview when the troublesome Corinthians distort them with their inexorable plunge into rivalry and hierarchy. Paul, rather, darts here and there, expressing hope in God's promises in one instance, the demands of sexual purity in another; the baffling hope for a new body put upon a decaying body here, the overwhelming power of life-giving resurrection there; even the indispensability of communal unity, though without the rigorous exclusion of another spiritual temple, the isolated band of believers at Qumran. Paul's sense of the spirit, in other words, is more impulsive than systematic and single-lensed, even if it is unified in part by Ezekiel's vision, framed by the vocabulary and beliefs of the early church, and fired by the foundational belief, expressed in his letters to the Galatians and Corinthians, that the spirit is the force of a new creation.

Luke is easier to pin down than Paul. With predictable regularity, he attributes inspired speech to filling with the spirit. From the beginning of Luke's gospel, where the angel predicts that John before birth will be filled with the holy spirit, so that he will turn many Israelites to the Lord their God (Luke 1:15-16), and where Elizabeth exclaims her benediction for Mary, as the child leaps in her womb and she is filled with the spirit (1:41), to the paradigmatic experience of Pentecost (Acts 2:4), filling with the spirit is the source of inspired speech. Yet this inspired speech is not merely a species of eloquent rhetoric or impressive oratory; it consists fundamentally of the inspired interpretation of scripture. The earliest believers at Pentecost, along with Peter and Paul — each, when filled with the holy spirit, engages in speeches in which Israel's scriptures illumine, and are illuminated by, the life, death, and resurrection of Jesus. The early church in Acts is busy with God's praiseworthy acts, with the citation of texts from prophet and psalm, with marshalling them to demonstrate that Jesus is the Messiah.

This is a sober task, and Luke signals this sobriety with the verb "proclaim" *(apophthengesthai)*. Notwithstanding the claim that Paul is out of his mind, contorted by his learning and distorting scripture, Paul joins Peter and the Pentecostal crew before him with a firm denial. He is not crazed; he proclaims the sober truth. Yet for all of this emphasis upon sobriety, Luke does not slam the door on the ecstatic. On the contrary, he paints Pentecost with those hues of ecstasy that would not have been lost on Roman readers: there was fire upon the believers' heads, filling with the holy spirit, and the distinct impression that they were drunk. He even allows the phrase "speaking in tongues" to stand, though he is compelled to insert the word "other."

There is a remarkable combination, therefore, of ecstasy and inspired intellect in the book of Acts — precisely those dimensions of inspiration that we discerned in chapters 2 and 3 of Part II of our study. If we skim the surface of Acts, we see only sober truth, inspired but entirely comprehensible inspiration, the sort of experience that makes the earliest followers of Jesus look more intellectually sound rather than less. Yet underneath this neat emphasis upon the inspired intellect lies an underworld of ecstasy, an arena that is exemplified by the slave-girl. Paul, who functions as Luke's narrative alter ego in this episode, permits this pythonic seer, this belly-talking slave-girl, to hang around much longer than we might expect; after all, she captures the gist of the message more succinctly and accurately than anyone else in the book of Acts. By preserving a permeable border between ecstasy and inspired intellect, Luke is able to claim for the early church two grand forms of inspiration: the sort of ecstasy that attended the Delphic priestess or Cassandra or Kenaz or Israel's prophets, according to Philo, and the utter sobriety of scriptural interpretation that lends a peculiar gravitas to inspired speakers.

If, according to Acts, the spirit first fills believers by means of potent but impersonal signs, in the Fourth Gospel the disciples of Jesus are first filled with the spirit when Jesus enters a locked room and breathes into them. The intimacy of this scene is astounding, almost appalling, as Jesus stands so close, face-to-face, to his frightened friends that the breath which leaves his mouth enters theirs. In the narrative as it now stands, this is the gift of the paraclete, the spirit of truth, which will lead the disciples into all truth. The setting of this scene, with the disciples huddled behind locked doors, encapsulates the essence of Jesus' teaching about the spirit: it belongs to the disciples rather than the hostile world that surrounds them. An antagonistic world cannot receive it, as that world fails to know it. There is an edginess to this gift, an agitation that is inherent even in the moniker "spirit of truth," which makes the spirit look uncannily like the spirit of truth in the Dead Sea Scrolls. In the Fourth Gospel, however, this spirit will eventually convict the world of its sin, educate that otherwise hostile realm in the ways of justice, and confirm the inevitability of judgment.

The authority of this spirit of truth is constrained in the Fourth Gospel by its role as another paraclete, a successor to Jesus. All of the truth in which the spirit will guide the disciples is hardly unbounded; the spirit will remind his disciples of what Jesus said and did. As in the book of Acts, this calling to remembrance consists of understanding Jesus in the light of scripture; his early statement about destroying and rebuilding the temple, as well as his entry into Jerusalem on a colt, combine to illustrate how the spirit illuminates incomprehensible dimensions of Jesus' life by situating them in the context of Israel's fulsome literature.

In the little letter of 1 John, the emphases of the Fourth Gospel are taken to an extreme. According to 1 John, the spirit of truth, which is mentioned in the Fourth Gospel, is matched by the spirit of error, Christ by the antichrist, true prophets by false ones. The anointing, which in the Fourth Gospel is associated solely with Jesus, now belongs to all believers in the remnant community. The guidance of the spirit is now less tethered to the entirety of Jesus' life and the scriptures that undergird it. This is a community led by prophets, a church in which teachers have no place. There are, of course, criteria of truth, such as the coming of Jesus in the flesh and adherence to what was experienced from the beginning, but ultimately the orientation of the group lies in the grasp of prophets, who, like the seventy inspired elders of Moses' day, have received *from* God's spirit. With this conviction, the community discards parameters that are evident in the Fourth Gospel and the book of Acts, as it enters a disquieting world untrammeled by education and unimpeded by the pedestrian ardor of study.

Epilogue

When he was sixty-three years old, on September 8, 1925, Hermann Gunkel penned a letter to the illustrious New Testament scholar Adolf Jülicher. In this letter, Gunkel confided that he might have been responsible for the sense of isolation he felt in his earliest years as a scholar — presumably the years that encompassed his research on his *Wirkungen des heiligen Geistes:* "Long, long years have I waited in vain for understanding and collegiality," he wrote. "What a prize I would have had at that time if I had found an older friend to whom I could pose my one thousand questions and who might have advised me! So I have had to take the difficult way for such a long time thoroughly alone. Perhaps I myself bear the guilt for this loneliness because I, in youthful exuberance, was probably too blunt in opposition to older opinions, although I always took care not to drag the dispute into the personal realm."[1]

Hermann Gunkel was nothing if not blunt; his *Büchlein* does much to confront his opponents, leaving little space for compromise and negotiation. Yet in this letter, which is rife with regret, Gunkel is altogether too self-critical. There was no way for him to capture the early Christian preoccupation with the mysterious and miraculous effects of the spirit without undermining the assumptions of his colleagues and mentors. Nor could his appeal to Judaism as an indispensable key for understanding early Christian pneumatology win the affection and admiration of German biblical theologians, who leapt from the Old Testament to the New. Gunkel's loneliness was due at least in part, therefore, to his own pre-

---

1. Gunkel had hoped that his meeting with Jülicher might be a sign "that my life, which began with such a storm, will end in peace and calm" (H. Rollmann, "Zwei Briefe Hermann Gunkels an Adolf Jülicher zur religionsgeschichtlichen und formgeschichtlichen Methode," *ZTK* 78 (1981) 281-82 (my translations). Within four years of his meeting with Adolf Jülicher, Hermann Gunkel would be ill with gastrointestinal pain and arteriosclerosis, and within seven he would be memorialized in the Bartholomäus Kirche in Halle.

science. Hans Schmidt, on that wintry day in the Bartholomäus Kirche, understood all too well that here was a scholar whose work was new and surprising.[2]

For this reason, exactly one hundred years after the publication of the third edition of his first book, Gunkel's contributions play a significant role in my study of the spirit. This is not by necessity but by design. I might easily have left his little book out altogether, as it plays no essential role in the main arguments of the present book, or I might have dealt with his contributions, in a typical scholarly manner, in a five-page section of an introductory chapter. I have done neither. Instead, I have allowed the legacy of Gunkel to surface throughout this study because his life and thought have richly inspired the tenor and the spirit of this book, even, or perhaps especially, where I have found myself at odds with his findings and at loggerheads with his conclusions.

2. *TBl* 11/4 (1932) 97-98.

Index of Modern Authors

Index of Subjects and Ancient Names

84-85, 98; literature, xxii-xxvi, 9, 12, 32-33, 43-44, 55, 82, 105, 111, 113-14, 116-17, 163, 176-77, 182, 218-20, 229, 232, 236-37, 247, 260, 312, 330, 334, 339, 350, 353, 355, 358, 366, 380; prophets and prophecy, xic, 159-61, 165, 176, 233-34, 342; and repentance, 88, 90, 92, 103, 105; scripture, 15, 270n.18, 315, 349, 403, 418, 423; tradition/religion/beliefs, 41, 84, 112-13, 117, 148-49, 175, 218-19, 238, 380, 391, 415; worshippers, 24

Jacob, 42-43, 45, 47, 49n.16, 56, 124n.15, 163n.16

Jeremiah, 31, 35, 56, 89-90, 100, 199n.34, 271, 418

Jerome, 373

Jerusalem, 35, 41, 45, 88, 91-95, 100, 102, 105, 111n.8, 118, 131, 133, 162, 190, 196, 199, 207, 212, 214-15, 217, 242-43, 268, 272, 287, 291-92, 323-24, 328-29, 335, 341-42, 347, 351, 362-64, 367, 372-75, 376n.22, 403, 417, 427

Jesus Christ: in the Fourth Gospel, 245-46, 267, 366-86, 389-92, 396-409, 420, 423-24, 426-27; in 1 John, 233, 410-21, 427; in Luke-Acts, 125, 241-44, 317-37, 341, 343, 345-46, 348-64, 425-27; in Matthew, 257; in Paul, 233, 251, 258, 261, 265, 268-70, 273-74, 276, 280, 282-85, 290-92, 296-304, 424; person and life of, xxiii, xxivn.33, 7-8, 112-15, 259, 422-23; in 1 Peter, 252; in Revelation, book of, 234; in Synoptics, 230-36

Jew(s)/Jewish: Alexandrian, 193n.28; Alexandrian philosophy, 152, 199, 237; apocalyptic, 111; conceptions of the spirit, 67, 115, 137, 142, 238, 242, 247, 319-20, 334; culture, 154, 168, 212, 406, 408n.60; Dead Sea, 185, 202, 217, 290; Diaspora, 111n.8, 268, 347, 364; elite, 350, 352n.24, 354-55; eschatology, xvi, 114; in the Fourth Gospel, 251, 359n.31, 380; faith, 292; Greco-Roman, 114, 237, 326, 347; Hellenistic,

111n.8, 112, 284n.32; imagination, 16n.4; leaders, 230-31, 350; literature/authors, xxii, xxivnn.32-33, xxv-xxvi, 116-17, 136-37, 141, 151, 161, 165, 167, 176, 178, 199, 219, 229, 236-37, 240, 246-47, 319, 327, 354, 401, 413, 417; Maccabean, 218; mysticism, Hellenistic-Jewish, xxin.21; Palestinian, 214, 287; relationship to Christianity, 110, 228, 246-47, 271, 284n.32, 287, 337, 342, 352, 360, 363, 372, 385, 402, 404-6, 408n.60, 409, 422-23; Scripture, xxiiin.29, 47n.14, 52, 80, 110, 267, 311-12, 351-52; War, 140. *See also* Judaism

Job, 17-27, 32-33, 34-36, 41-42, 66, 99, 104, 128, 244, 315, 380

Joel, 213n.12, 232, 270n.18, 324, 336, 343, 358, 363, 423

John: author of 1 John, 424; the Baptist, xxiiin.32, 112, 113n.16, 232, 241, 242n.8, 267-68, 318, 337, 343, 352n.24, 416, 422; disciple of Jesus, 350; Fourth Gospel, xxi, xxv-xxvi, 234-35, 241n.8, 245-46, 251-52, 267-68, 359n.31, 366-420, 423-27. *See also* Life: of Jesus

John Cassian, 166-67, 198

John Hyrcanus, 112n.14

Jordan River, 57, 70, 122

Joseph, xxv, 36, 38-41, 48-51, 69, 74-76, 78, 81-87, 105, 130, 137, 220, 236, 241, 334, 380

Joseph of Arimathea, 409

Joseph and Aseneth, 369

Josephus, xxiiin.32, 112n.14, 158-61, 175-77, 181, 184-85, 199n.34, 229, 275n.22, 292-94, 319-20, 347, 374

Joshua, 36-38, 40-41, 67-74, 83-84, 86-87, 105, 136-37, 144, 162n.15, 174-77, 220, 236, 241, 243, 330

Judah (person), 256-60, 278

Judah (tribe), 36, 41-42, 57, 59-60, 87, 136, 162, 165, 319, 418

Judaism: xv-xviii, xxi-xxii, xxvi, 5, 30, 78, 110-17, 130, 137-38, 199, 212, 220-21, 228, 237, 326, 335, 346, 417, 421-22, 428; Hellenistic, xxin.21, xxiiin.32, 111,

Index of Ancient Sources

A. Hebrew Scriptures (MT)
B. Greek Versions of Hebrew Scriptures
C. Apocrypha
D. Pseudepigrapha
E. Josephus
F. Dead Sea Scrolls

G. Vulgate
H. Philo
I. Greek and Roman Authors
J. New Testament
K. Early Christian Literature
L. Zoroastrian

A. HEBREW SCRIPTURES (MT)

Genesis

1–3	122, 211	2:19	14, 26	29:21	56
1–2	309, 312	2:22	204	29:27-28	57
1	xvi, 149-50, 312	2:23	101	32:11	353
1:1	29	2:24	295, 298	37:5-11	50
1:1–2:4	26	3:8	26	38	256-58
1:26	251	3:14	146	38:18	257, 260
1:26-28	387, 424	3:17-19	209	39:3	50
1:27	147-48	3:19	15, 19-23, 26, 28,	39:6	50
2–3	15		204, 312	39:21	50
2	149-50, 310-13	6:1-4	396	39:23	50
2:7	15, 17-18, 22-23,	6:3	16, 48, 50, 134-36,	40:1-23	50
	26, 28, 59, 102,		153, 163, 249, 396	40:8	50
	142-51, 202-7,	6:17	8, 16-17, 49	41:1-36	50
	220-21, 237, 247,	7:15	8, 16-17, 49	41:8	49
	267, 309-16, 369,	7:22	8, 16-17, 49	41:16	48, 50
	386-88, 424	12:1	195	41:36	39
2:17	28, 102	12:19	353	41:38	36-40, 48-51, 60,
2:18	310	15:12	158, 327		69, 75-76
		18:27	204	41:39	48, 51
		21:19	55	41:45	369
		25:24	56	42:9	50
		26:34-35	49	42:25	55

447

Index of Ancient Sources

11:1	94	36:38	206	4:15 [MT 12]	75
11:1-4	92	37	29, 88, 216, 262-	4:18 [MT 15]	36-37
11:13	90		64, 304, 307, 424	4:19 [MT 16]	129
11:14-21	91, 94, 101	37:1	87	4:36 [MT 33]	77
11:16	91	37:1-2	95	5	77
11:17-21	91, 102	37:3	95	5:11	36-37, 77, 129,
11:19	188, 207	37:4-6	96		243
11:19-20	99	37:5	8, 96, 262-63	5:11-12	75
11:24	94	37:5-6	262	5:12	36, 77, 129
11:24-25	165	37:6	8, 96, 206, 254,	5:14	36-40, 75-77, 129,
13:19	357		262-64		184
16	100	37:7	101	5:14-15	129
17:24	74	37:7-8	96	5:17	84
18	88	37:8	96, 262	5:24-25	84
18:1-13	90	37:9	8	6:3	36, 39-40
18:2	89	37:9-10	96	6:3 [MT 4]	38, 75, 129,
18:30-32	89, 92, 94, 99,	37:10	99, 207, 262-63		185
	101	37:11	87, 92	6:3-4	79
18:31-32	103	37:12-13	99	7–8	294
20	100	37:13	206-7, 264	7:1	84
20:1	162	37:14	98, 188, 206, 254,	7:7	77
23	100		262-63	7:19	77
27:30	204	37:27	304	8:15	83
28:13-14	213	39:29	372	9:11-14	84
28:13-16	101	40–48	212, 291	9:20-23	84
31	210	40	165	10–12	294
31:9	210	40:2	165	10:12	84
31:16	210	40:3-4	95	11:33	78
31:18	210	40:4	165		
36–37	205-7, 211, 253-	43:5	56, 94	**Hosea**	
	54, 260, 261-63,	44:4	57	1–3	100
	271, 305, 381, 423	47:1	375	9:7	44, 176
36	208	47:1-12	213	11:1-7	100
36:11	206	47:9	375	14:10	353-54
36:22-28	93	47:12	376		
36:23	206, 264			**Joel**	
36:25	93, 216	**Daniel**		2:3	213
36:25-27	95, 216	1:4	78	2:28-29 [MT 3:1-2]	372
36:26	207, 263	1:4-6	84	2:28-32 [MT 3:1-4]	270,
36:26-27	99, 101, 188,	1:17	78		358, 362
	208, 254, 308	1:20	78-79	3:1-5 [MT]	362
36:27	5, 206	2:31	76		
36:28	207, 264	3:22	76	**Micah**	
36:33-35	101	4:5	39-40	2:6-7	42-43
36:34-35	211	4:8 [MT 5]	36-37, 75, 129	2:7	42, 47
36:35	213	4:9 [MT 6]	36-37, 75, 129	2:11	42

451